Energy Justice and Energy Law

Energy Justice and Energy Law

Edited by

ÍÑIGO DEL GUAYO, LEE GODDEN,
DONALD N. ZILLMAN, MILTON F. MONTOYA,
AND JOSÉ JUAN GONZÁLEZ

OXFORD
UNIVERSITY PRESS

OXFORD
UNIVERSITY PRESS

Great Clarendon Street, Oxford, OX2 6DP,
United Kingdom

Oxford University Press is a department of the University of Oxford.
It furthers the University's objective of excellence in research, scholarship,
and education by publishing worldwide. Oxford is a registered trade mark of
Oxford University Press in the UK and in certain other countries

First Edition published in 2020
Impression: 1

Published in the United States of America by Oxford University Press
198 Madison Avenue, New York, NY 10016, United States of America

British Library Cataloguing in Publication Data
Data available

Library of Congress Control Number: 2019953118

ISBN 978-0-19-886075-4

Printed and bound by
CPI Group (UK) Ltd, Croydon, CR0 4YY

Preface

In Memoriam Anita Rønne

This is the tenth book within a fruitful and long-standing collaboration among the International Bar Association's Section on Energy, Environment, Natural Resources, and Infrastructure Law (IBA SEERIL), the Oxford University Press (OUP), and the Academic Advisory Group (AAG) of the IBA SEERIL. This is a new outcome of the cooperation between the world's largest international organization of lawyers, the IBA, and a group of academic lawyers, the AAG. This network of academics is engaged in research and teaching activities in the areas pertinent to SEERIL and the six committees coordinated by the Section: Environment, Health and Safety Law; International Construction Projects; Mining Law; Oil and Gas Law; Power Law; and Water Law. The research and publications of the AAG traverse these areas where SEERIL members have demonstrated a strong leadership in these fields over many years.

For more than thirty years now, the IBA, SEERIL, and the AAG have been involved in a productive circle of ideas, practices, joint publications, and public events. From a traditional energy law perspective at the beginning, the exchange between academics and practitioners has now extended to the environment and to a modern understanding of energy law as a key source of legal instruments to fight climate change, and to promote robust legal values related to justice. The range of nations represented by the AAG has also expanded as evident from the fact that the current book has representatives from all continents among its authors.

As an international research network, the AAG reports to SEERIL on legal matters of interest of the Section. The longevity of the AAG is rooted in the support it gets from the practitioners of the Section. Among other benefits of this association, the AAG is able to test its academic work on the heterogeneous and countless problems, which day-to-day energy activities raise, and which are also addressed by members of SEERIL. The editors and authors gratefully acknowledge the assistance of the SEERIL Council and its officers that is provided to the AAG. In particular, we acknowledge the support of Jean-André Diaz, the Chairperson of SEERIL, members of the SEERIL executive, and committee chairs. We welcome the initiative to appoint a publications officer for SEERIL and we have worked productively with Matthias Lang, the current office holder. The Section particularly assisted the AAG with its biannual meeting in 2019. Ms Susan Burkert and later Ms Cheveon Badi, together with other IBA staff have provided much valuable administrative assistance to the AAG in regard to the workshop and in the general coordination of the group.

The content of this book is the result of the merger of two proposals from AAG members. The proposals were circulated before the SEERIL conference and meeting at Lisbon, which took place from the 8th to 11th April 2018. Anita Rønne and Hanri

Mostert led one of the proposals. Both participated actively in the meeting. While at Lisbon, the AAG had the opportunity to thoroughly discuss both proposals and arrive at a common project, which is reflected today in this book about 'Energy Justice and Energy Law'.

From 24th to 26th April 2019, the AAG members met for an intense three-day workshop to present new or refined ideas, discuss draft chapters, focus the topic, and to allow the editors to begin writing the Introduction and Conclusion. The mid-term workshop was tremendously useful to address the comments we had already received from the OUP reviewers, in order to reach a common understanding of the meaning of Energy Justice and its dimensions, and to mark a distinction from other perspectives on energy transition issues, such as those of the environment lawyers. A big thank you is due to Professor Hanri Mostert who served as a marvellous host for the AAG mid-term meeting at the Montfleur Conference Venue at Stellenbosch (Western Cape, South Africa). We thank also Chege Kennedy (PhD student at the SARChI: Mineral Law in Africa at UCT) for his efficient help in the arrangements for the meeting. Our thanks must go also to Dr Louie van Schalwyk (Postdoctoral Fellow at the SARChI: Mineral Law in Africa at UCT) and Ms Andrea Thornton (administrative assistant). In addition to organizing the AAG meeting, Hanri and Catherine Banet (from the University of Oslo) arranged an 'Electricity Markets Design Workshop', on 2nd May 2019, at the University of Cape Town, in which several AAG members participated as speakers. Some AAG members were involved in May 2019, in teaching tasks in the Oil and Gas course, which Hanri coordinates and teaches at that university.

The current transition towards a decarbonized energy system is being driven by environmental and climate concerns, and it raises countless issues related to energy justice, in all its dimensions, particularly in distributive and participation matters. We wanted to analyse the challenges of the transition in justice terms, but, simultaneously, we wanted to build a distinct body of thinking concentrated upon the field of energy itself. Anita proposed to write a chapter for this book about the need to empower energy consumers. She could not write it due to her illness and death, but to honour her we decided to keep such a chapter and were lucky enough to identify a prestigious colleague of Anita's from the University of Stirling, Annalisa Savaresi, who addresses in her chapter, among other interesting issues, how to reinforce 'community energy', something which Anita would have strongly appreciated.

We are thankful for the thoughtful and constructive input from the OUP book reviewers for their time and expertise, which helped to give the final shape to the project. We extend great appreciation to the editorial staff at Oxford University Press. Merel Alstein, senior commissioning editor for international law titles, encouraged our initial scoping book proposal, supported us through the review and revision stages and in many other ways she kindly assisted the AAG to bring this work to fruition. A particular gratitude must also be expressed to Jack McNichol, assistant commissioning editor to Merel, who patiently helped both the editors and authors of the book in bringing the project to completion. He was always available for our inquiries and questions and provided the group with valuable guidance on how to give a final structure to the entire project. We thank Oliver Sellers, also at OUP, for his invaluable assistance as a contact for the AAG in the procedure of drafting the final manuscript. We thank the other OUP staff who 'make it happen' in such a professional manner.

We would like to acknowledge the collegiality of editors in drawing together the many threads of the book proposal, overseeing the proposal review process and in generally coordinating the many and diverse tasks in assembling and submitting a manuscript of twenty plus chapters from authors across the world. The cooperation of authors with their editors was pivotal to the process as the book moved from inception to completion.

A particular and sad circumstance has dominated the work of the AAG over this 2018–2020 period in which we have been working on this book. On the 13th December 2018, Anita Rønne passed away. Anita was Associate Professor in Law at the University of Copenhagen, and she served for many years as a member of the AAG, including as Chair for a long period. An expert in Energy Law and Regulation, Professor Rønne gained a remarkable prestige worldwide in those fields. She was our friend, our beloved colleague, our partner. We shall never forget her enthusiasm for her family and work, her keen ability to know the right path to follow, her many kindnesses to all of us. These attributes made her such a wonderful, kind, and accomplished person. Her spirit will burn brightly, but we have all lost one of the finest persons ever to have walked the world. She was always an example to follow. We all reflect on the many good memories we have of her from over the years, whether in Denmark, or in many other parts of the world. She was open, caring, engaging, and thoughtful.

Anita was astute and industrious, as a lawyer, writer, academic, organizer, and leader. She always brought good sense and a good spirit to our dealings. Anita was one of the warmest and kindest people we have ever met, and with such zest for life. She was such an important part of the group, both in its intellectual endeavours and in making it feel like a genuine academic family. We learned a lot from her, enjoyed many good times with her, and benefitted from her personal support and friendship. We have lost a kind and generous person who was the guiding light and the unifying force for the AAG. She was a lovely and beautiful soul, cheerful, warm, and so friendly. Anita was a great academic, who maintained an excellent standard as an author and editor and brought a great depth of scholarship and passion to energy and environmental law. Anita gave us the strong leadership, which the AAG projects need. We will miss her so much.

We dedicate this book to her with all our affection.

The Editors

Table of Contents

PART IV. CONSUMERS AT THE FRONTLINE OF A NEW ENERGY JUSTICE

PART V. ACCESS TO ENERGY, POVERTY, AND DISTRIBUTIVE JUSTICE

PART VI. ENERGY AT THE CENTRE OF SOCIAL (OR RECOGNITION) JUSTICE

PART VII. CONCLUSION

List of Contributors

Daniela Aguilar Abaunza Academic Researcher, Universidad Externado de Colombia, Bogotá, Colombia.

Ignacio Herrera Anchustegui Researcher, Faculty of Law of the University of Bergen, Norway, and member of the Bergen Center for Competition Law and Economics.

Alberto Cairampoma Arroyo Associate Professor of Administrative Law, Pontifical Catholic University of Peru PUCP, and member of the Peruvian Association of Administrative Law.

Catherine Banet Associate Professor, Scandinavian Institute for Maritime Law, Petroleum and Energy Law Department, University of Oslo, Norway. The author is affiliated to CREE—Oslo Centre for Research on Environmentally friendly Energy.

Barry Barton Professor of Law and Director of the Centre for Environmental, Resources and Energy Law, University of Waikato, Hamilton, New Zealand.

Juan Justo Bautista Professor of Administrative Law, School of Law and Social Sciences, Universidad Nacional del Comahue, Neuquen, Argentina.

Anatole Boute Professor, Faculty of Law, Chinese University of Hong Kong, Hong Kong.

Jennifer Campion Lecturer and Member of the Centre for Environmental, Resources and Energy Law, University of Waikato, Hamilton, New Zealand.

Lea Diestelmeier Post-doctoral researcher, Groningen Centre of Energy Law and Sustainability, Faculty of Law, University of Groningen, Netherlands.

Marina Motta Benevides Gadelha President of the National Commission of Environmental Law of the Brazilian Bar Association. Federal Councillor of the Brazilian Bar Association. University Professor.

Lee Godden Professor of Law and Director, Centre of Resources, Energy and Environmental Law, Melbourne Law School, The University of Melbourne, Australia.

José Juan González Professor of Law, Metropolitan Autonomous University, Azcapotzalco, Mexico and Director of the Mexican Institute for Environmental Law Research, Mexico.

Íñigo del Guayo Professor of Administrative Law, University of Almería, Spain.

Alastair R. Lucas Professor Emeritus, and Senior Research Fellow, Canadian Institute of Resources Law, Faculty of Law, University of Calgary, Alberta, Canada.

Liber Martín Professor, Universidad Nacional de Cuyo, Argentina; CONICET Researcher.

Aileen McHarg Professor of Public Law and Human Rights, University of Durham, United Kingdom.

Wang Mingyuan Professor of Law, School of Law, Tsinghua University, Beijing, China.

Milton F. Montoya Research Director of the Mining and Energy Law Institute, Externado de Colombia University, Bogotá, Colombia.

Hanri Mostert DST/NRF SARChI Research Chair: Mineral Law in Africa and Professor of Law, University of Cape Town, South Africa.

Tjakie Naude Professor of Private Law, University of Cape Town, South Africa.

Damilola S. Olawuyi Associate Professor of Law, HBKU Law School, Hamad Bin Khalifa University, Qatar and Chancellor's Fellow and Director of the Institute for Oil, Gas, Energy, Environment and Sustainable Development, Afe Babalola University, Nigeria.

Yinka Omorogbe Attorney General and Commissioner for Justice, Edo State, Nigeria, and Research Professor of Law, Nigerian Institute of Advanced Legal Studies, Abuja.

LeRoy C. Paddock Associate Dean of Environmental Law Studies, George Washington University Law School, Washington D.C., United States.

Lavanya Rajamani Professor of International Environmental Law, Faculty of Law, University of Oxford and Yamani Fellow in Public International Law, St Peter's College, Oxford.

Catherine Redgwell Chichele Professor of Public International Law and Fellow of All Souls College, University of Oxford, United Kingdom.

Daniel Gutierrez Rivera Attorney at Law, Expert in Energy Law, Founder Director at BGS Energy Law, Chile.

Martha Roggenkamp Professor of Energy Law and Director of the Groningen Centre of Energy Law and Sustainability, Faculty of Law, University of Groningen, the Netherlands.

Annalisa Savaresi Senior Lecturer in Environmental Law, University of Stirling, United Kingdom, and Associate Editor of the Review of European, Comparative and International Law.

Don C. Smith Associate Professor of the Practice of Law, Sturm College of Law, University of Denver, Colorado, United States.

Paul Villegas Vega Professor of Administrative Law, Pontifical Catholic University of Peru.

Achinthi Vithanage Visiting Associate Professor of Law & Environmental and Energy Law Fellow, The George Washington University Law School, Washington D.C., United States.

Yang Xue PhD Candidate, School of Law, Tsinghua University, Beijing, China.

Donald N. Zillman Godfrey Professor of Law, University of Maine Law School.

List of Abbreviations

AAG	Academic Advisory Group
ACCC	Australian Competition and Consumer Commission
ACE	Affordable Clean Energy
ACER	Agency for the Cooperation of Energy Regulators
AEMC	Australian Energy Market Commission
AEMO	Australian Energy Market Operator
AER	Australian Energy Regulator
ARENA	Australian Renewable Energy Agency
BPE	Bureau of Public Enterprise
CAREA	Central Alberta Rural Electrification Association
CBDR	common but differentiated responsibilities
CBDRRC	common but differentiated responsibilities and respective capabilities
CBDRRC-NC	common but differentiated responsibilities and respective capabilities – national circumstances
CBN	Central Bank of Nigeria
CC	Constitutional Court
CEC	citizen energy community
CEER	Council of European Energy Regulators
CEPAL	Economic Commission for Latin America and the Caribbean (CEPAL in Spanish and Portuguese)
CJEU	Court of Justice of the EU
CNOOC	China National Offshore Oil Corporation
COAG	Council of Australian Governments
COP	Conference of the Parties
CPA	Consumer Protection Act
CPC	Communist Party of China
CPP	Clean Power Plan
CRE	Energy Regulatory Commission (Commission de régulation de l'énergie)
DECC	Department of Energy and Climate Change
DOE	Department of Energy
DSO	distribution system operator
EC	Energy Commission
ECJ	European Court of Justice
ECtHR	European Court of Human Rights
ECN	Electricity Commission of Nigeria
EEZ	Exclusive Economic Zone
EIA	environmental impact assessment
EPA	Environmental Protection Agency
EPOV	Energy Poverty Observatory
EPSRA	Electricity Power Sector Reform Act
ERA	Electricity Regulation Act

ESC	Essential Services Commission
ETS	Emissions Trading System
EU	European Union
EV	electric vehicle
FAO	Food and Agriculture Organization
FEJA	Future Energy Jobs Act
FISE	Energy Social Inclusion Fund
FMEdu	Federal Ministry of Education
FMF	Federal Ministry of Finance
FOSE	Electrical Social Compensation Fund
GCC	Gulf Cooperation Council
GCCIA	GCC Interconnection Authority
GDP	gross domestic product
GECF	Gas Exporting Countries Forum
GHG	greenhouse gas
HEPC	Hydro-electric Power Commission
IBA SEERIL	International Bar Association's Section on Energy, Environment, Natural Resources, and Infrastructure Law
IBGE	Brazilian Institute of Geography and Statistics
ICJ	International Court of Justice
ICREEE	Inter-Ministerial Committee on Renewable Energy and Energy Efficiency
IDA	International Development Association
IEA	International Energy Agency
IEM	internal energy market
ILA	International Law Association
ILO	International Labour Organization
IPCC	Intergovernmental Panel on Climate Change
IPP	independent power producer
ISMO	Independent System and Market Operator
LFC	compact fluorescent lamp
LIHC	low-income high cost
LNG	liquefied natural gas
LPG	liquefied petroleum gas
MENA	Middle East and North Africa
MNE	Multinational Enterprise
MIGA	Multilateral Investment Guarantee Agency
MOFEP	Ministry of Finance and Economic Planning
MS	Member State(s)
MuD	Multi-unit Dwelling
NAACP	National Association for the Advancement of Colored People
NBET	Nigerian Bulk Electricity Trading
NCC	National Consumer Commission
NCT	National Consumer Tribunal
NDA	Niger Dam Authority
NDC	Nationally Determined Contribution
NECF	National Energy Customer Framework
NEL	National Electricity Law
NEM	National Electricity Market

NEPA	National Electric Power Authority
NERC	Nigerian Electricity Regulatory Commission
NERL	National Energy Retail Law
NERR	National Energy Retail Rules
NERSA	National Energy Regulator of South Africa
NGO	Non-governmental organization
NorREG	Nordic Energy Regulators
NRA	National Regulatory Authority
NSA	non-state actor
NSR	New Source Review
NVE	Norwegian Water Resources and Energy Directorate
OECD	Organisation for Economic Cooperation and Development
OPEC	Organization of Petroleum Exporting Countries
OPEX	operating expenses
OPG	Ontario Power Generation
P3	public–private partnership
PAJA	Promotion of Administration Justice Act
PSNR	permanent sovereignty over natural resources
PSO	public service obligation
PURC	Public Utilities Regulatory Commission
PV	photovoltaic
RE	rural electrification
REA	Rural Electricity Association/Rural Electrification Agency
REG	Rwanda Energy Group
RES	renewable energy source
RET	Renewable Energy Target
SDG	Sustainable Development Goal
SEforALL	Sustainable Energy for All
SE4ALL-AA	Sustainable Energy for All Action Agenda
SIS	Synthesis of Social Indicators
SME	Small and Medium Enterprise
SOE	State-owned Enterprise
SoLR	supplier of last resort
SSA	Sub-Saharan Africa
TFEU	Treaty on the Functioning of the European Union
TOU	time of use
TSO	Transmission System Operator
TSSE	Social Electricity Tariff (Brazil)
TURPE	tarifs d'utilisation des réseaux publics d'électricité
UAE	United Arab Emirates
UCS	Union of Concerned Scientists
UFA	United Farmers of Alberta
UPME	Unit of Mining Energy Planning
UN	United Nations
UNDP	United Nations Development Programme
UNEP	United Nations Environment Programme
UNFCCC	United Nations Framework Convention on Climate Change
USA	United States of America

VAT	Value Added Tax
VCWG	Vulnerable Consumer Working Group
VRA	Volta River Authority
WAPCo	West African Pipeline Company
WEC	World Energy Council
WHO	World Health Organization
YEC	Yukon Energy Corporation
ZRT	Technical Responsibility Areas (Peru)

PART I
INTRODUCTION

1

Introduction

Íñigo del Guayo, Lee Godden, Donald N. Zillman, Milton F. Montoya, and José Juan González

I. Introduction—Energy Justice: Defining the Scope

Energy law and energy justice are the central themes explored in this book. The Sustainable Development Goal (SDG) that recognizes the need of 'clean energy for all' is one example of energy justice.[1] Yet clearly there are many ways in which we can understand 'energy justice'. This collection canvasses thematic explorations of energy law and justice, as well as studies which draw upon international, national, and regional experience to articulate the diverse parameters of energy justice and energy law, as part of a growing body of research that is defining this rapidly developing field. Some insights into the significance of this scholarship for contemporary society and legal systems can be gained from the following example drawn from the work of Yinka Omorogbe, a long time Academic Advisory Group (AAG) author who has championed the cause of energy justice in Africa for many years. She takes us into the world of those who experience energy poverty and who do not have fair access to energy. Her portrayal is framed by reference to Amartya Sen's renowned theory of justice as freedom, and as the means to build the capacity of individuals and societies.[2]

Energy justice issues are of great relevance for Africa and, in general, for developing countries:

> In words that are reminiscent of Amartya Sen's concept of development as freedom, energy poverty can be seen as the deprivation of the many freedoms that accrue when persons are released from the grind of daily lives devoid of engine power and electricity. Energy lies at the heart of life and impacts on practically every sector. It is critical to development, particularly for the poor and vulnerable, and its absence can cause severe deprivations that amount to a denial of basic human rights, including the right to life. Examples that could lead to such final outcomes easily come to mind. For instance, if a pregnant woman in an impoverished rural area falls into labour in the middle of the night and she has to walk to the nearest dispensary in the dark; or if she is delivered at night,

[1] United Nations, 'Transforming our World: The 2030 Agenda for Sustainable Development', Resolution Adopted by the General Assembly on 25 September 2015 A/Res/70/1, http://www.un.org/ga/search/view_doc.asp?symbol=A/RES/70/1&Lang=E, accessed 14 July 2019 (hereafter SDG).

[2] A.K. Sen, *The Idea of Justice* (Harvard University Press, 2009)

Íñigo del Guayo, Lee Godden, Donald N. Zillman, Milton F. Montoya, and José Juan González, Introduction In: *Energy Justice and Energy Law*. Edited by Íñigo Del Guayo, Lee Godden, Donald N. Zillman, Milton F. Montoya, and José Juan González, Oxford University Press (2020). © The Several Contributors. DOI: 10.1093/oso/9780198860754.003.0001

> using light from an oil or kerosene lamp, in a clinic that is necessarily devoid of modern implements because of the absence of electricity, her child may not survive, and in such an instance that child will be suffering deprivations that have occurred as the result of lack of access to modern electricity services. If she does survive, the presence or absence of electricity will often impact on whether she goes to school, as her presence may be necessary for the energy and basic needs of her family to be met (she may have to scavenge for biomass and fetch water for the family). Ultimately, the type and amount of energy she has at her disposal will decide whether she will ever be able to arise from the drudgery of life as a rural female in an energy-poor community. Therefore, energy access is about giving power to the people, so that they can make choices, and live life sustainably.[3]

Similar concerns to those revealed in Yinka's narrative about energy access and its function in capacity-building can be found today in many countries and contexts around the world which stimulate the need for 'energy justice'. In this volume there are acute analyses of similar issues in parts of the world, such as Central and South America.[4] In countries located in these two regions there has been a remarkable increase of electricity provision, close to full coverage, but there are relevant energy justice issues of relative energy poverty and difficulties of access which still remain. Similarly, a combination of public and private initiatives, stimulated by law is needed to achieve energy justice goals for the one billion citizens of the planet who presently lack one or more of reliable and affordable electric service, clean fuel for home cooking and heating, and adequate transportation to allow for the economic and personal development of rural residents.[5] The lack of these modern energy services harms human health (e.g., breathing heavily polluting fuels while cooking or heating the home), limits night-time activity (that could be used for education or employment), and precludes economically productive activity.

This volume shows also that energy justice issues emerge not only in rural areas or developing countries, but also in countries classified as developed countries, and in both urban and rural areas.[6] The fight of institutions such as the European Union (EU) against energy poverty illustrates this idea. The long and deep economic crisis (2007–2018) has deprived thousands of European citizens of their ordinary means to live, including the affordability to pay their electricity and/or natural gas bills.[7] On the other hand, the lack of proper investment in energy networks worsens the quality of service. In this region of the world there is another kind of energy poverty; that occurring through the use of pollutant fuels with too many existing coal-fired electricity power

[3] Quotation extracted from Chapter 19 by Yinka Omoroge in this book.

[4] See, e.g., Chapter 13 by Milton Fernando Montoya and others, and Chapter 17 by José Juan González in this book.

[5] Laura Cozzi, Olivia Chen, Hannah Daly, and Aaron Koh, 'Population without access to electricity falls below 1 billion' International Energy Agency 2018 https://www.iea.org/newsroom/news/2018/october/ accessed 20 September 2019.

[6] See, e.g., Chapter 14 by Alistair Lucas, and Chapter 12 by Barry Barton and Jennifer Campion in this book.

[7] For an analysis of EU responses see, e.g., Chapter 5 by Annalisa Savaresi, and Chapter 10 by Martha Roggenkamp and Lea Diestelmeier in this book.

stations. The challenges of undertaking an energy transition to less polluting sources, whilst redressing significant disparities in energy affordability will require concerted legal and political efforts.

Thus, energy justice has emerged over the last decade as a matter of vital significance in energy law. Concerns with energy justice find resonances in energy poverty, the United Nations' (UN) SDGs, and in areas of law as diverse as human rights, consumer protection, international law and trade, and in many forms of regional and national energy law and regulation. Energy justice issues arise in nations and regional economies with well-established energy generation profiles and liberal, market-based distribution systems, as well as in nations and regions where the access to energy is less comprehensive and forms of energy generation and distribution are more limited. These legal issues are given specific momentum by thinking through how we might achieve a 'just' energy transition as the world faces the challenges of climate change, and of ensuring that energy is fairly and effectively made available—a position which we might term 'distributional' energy justice.

Previous AAG collections engaged with energy transition from several perspectives. This book builds on that foundation, but addresses the new challenges by analysing the relationship between energy law and energy justice. Examination of that relationship comprises studies that probe how law contributes to energy justice or injustice internationally, and in specific countries and regions; and also by reference to the energy laws that pertain in those areas. The examination of energy justice marks a continuing maturing of energy law as a recognizable field of law where the complexities of legal issues can be examined while drawing on legal developments in related fields, such as consumer protection laws. Currently, while issues of energy justice are growing in importance, as Salter (et al.) noted in 2018, research and scholarship in the area remains undertheorized, and 'few have considered how theories of energy justice might be applied practically'.[8] Accordingly, the book contributes to research in offering a blending of theoretically-informed scholarship and grounded case studies that identify legal frameworks (institutional, regulatory, contractual, commercial, and financial) that can assist or hinder more just energy outcomes.

II. Defining Energy Justice

Law and justice are typically seen as having shared objectives, but, the objectives of law can exist in tension with justice. How we better align law and justice outcomes in energy law is part of the normative analysis of justice that is integral to this research collection. According to classical philosophers, together with the need for justice between individuals, there is a distributive justice defined as 'justice in the distribution of economicgoods between members of a society' or 'in the distribution between persons,

[8] R. Salter, C.G. Gonzalez and E.A.K. Warner (eds), *Energy Justice: US and International Perspectives—New Horizons in Environmental and Energy Law Series* (Edward Elgar, 2018), 2.

of goods that are scarce and transferable'[9]. Energy is an economic and social good that is both scarce and transferable.

In contemporary times given diverse perspectives on justice, the authors of this book have sought to reach consensus about the different dimensions of justice in its application to energy law. The authors have adopted a common understanding that, 'Law is an instrument to achieve Justice Goals'. For example, SDGs recognize the need for clean energy for all, and energy law will be an important component in establishing the just manner in which to achieve this goal. Yet we also acknowledge that there are several kinds of energy justice. Chapter 2, by Aileen McHarg, identifies three main dimensions: (a) distributive justice; (b) procedural justice; and (c) recognition justice. McHarg however, realizes that there are other possible perspectives, such as restorative justice, corrective justice, inter-generational justice, and intra-generational justice. Some authors tend to identify social justice with distributive justice, whereas other authors use the term, social justice to identify what other authors conceptualize within the idea of recognition justice.

A. Four Modes of Energy Justice

To circumvent unending terminological discussions, while being alive to the qualifications and overlaps in any categorization of 'Justice', in this book, we articulate 'Energy Justice' as comprising four broad themes:

1. Distributive justice: the equitable distribution of the benefits and burdens of energy activities, which is challenged mainly by the existence of people suffering from energy poverty. Energy justice is the conceptual lens through which energy poverty issues are addressed. The concept is also associated with substantive energy equity through such measures as the realization of 'energy' rights;
2. Procedural (or participation) justice: the right of all individuals and communities to participate in decision-making regarding energy projects and policies that affect them (this dimension of energy justice often includes procedural rights to information and access to courts);
3. Restorative (or reparation) justice: even-handed enforcement of energy statutes and regulations, as well as access to remedies when legal rights are violated; and
4. Recognition justice: the recognition that energy injustice cannot be separated from other social ills, such as poverty and subordination based on caste, race, gender, or indigeneity. This conception acknowledges the need to take into account the various needs, rights, and experiences of those affected by energy decisions, and which parts of the society become privileged or ignored in this process (this will be called 'social justice' by some authors).

[9] H. Bojer, *Distributional Justice: Theory and Measurement* (Routledge, 2003).

Addressing the legal matters that arise in the context of these four themes represent pressing challenges that confront energy law and the energy sector today. Each chapter of the book addresses the legal dimensions of one or several of the energy justice themes above.

In addressing these themes, it is recognized that energy justice issues are of a heterogeneous, complex nature. They are universal in the sense that they should be routine considerations in energy policy choices and energy law frameworks everywhere. Energy justice issues, however, have disparate manifestations. For example, in Qatar, electricity is free of charge to consumers, but in that country, there are still issues related to distributive justice and energy poverty, as ageing infrastructure is not replaced and some citizens face looming power shortages, despite energy being 'free'.[10] This example highlights the pertinence of contextually informed analyses that can finely calibrate questions of relative energy access and distributive justice. Moreover, claims about distributive justice typically involve addressing: who are the people and entities to whom distributive justice is due? What are the energy benefits and burdens to be distributed? And what are the principles or criteria of distribution to be applied?

Importantly, we ask what is the legal response to the energy justice issues? Thus a major part of each chapter is devoted to exploring specific legal issues (how law addresses or should/could address the energy justice problems that are identified). The chapters probe what law emerges from the analysis? For example, assuming there is a need to address distributive concerns when drafting energy policies, what are the best legal structures to address them? How can law help to facilitate the outcome of just results? Do we need better contracts, institutions, or regulations to achieve justice energy policy goals?

In this light, this book also examines a range of legal and policy measures which impinge on energy justice. These include: legal rights of access to energy services (whether conceived as consumer rights or fundamental constitutional or human rights); price caps and other interventions in energy markets; questions of energy organization; energy facility ownership and industry structure, such as community energy or public energy supply; and measures to improve energy efficiency.

Several recurring themes of analysis can be identified across the chapters which include: (i) the fight against energy poverty; (ii) the national and international efforts to ensure the right of access to affordable, reliable, sustainable, and modern energy; (iii) the protection of consumers; (iv) the participation of communities in energy decisions; and (v) the restoration of justice in the energy sector. In turn the ways in which energy injustice manifests can tell us something about how energy justice may be enhanced. Among the factors that indicate energy injustice, there are issues concerning *access to* energy services, or fuel poverty.[11] Unaffordability of energy is a significant

[10] For discussion see Chapter 15 by Damilola Olawuyi in this book.

[11] G. Walker and R. Day, 'Fuel Poverty as Injustice: Integrating Distribution, Recognition and Procedure in the Struggle for Affordable Warmth' (2012) 49 *Energy Policy*, 70. Fuel poverty is traditionally defined as households that spend more than 10 per cent of their income on heating services. See Jenkins, et al., *Energy Justice: A Whole Systems Approach* 81 (n 13).

consideration. If energy-efficient appliances and vehicles are not available or affordable, the problem is exacerbated. Social justice concerns—including concerns of the public about corrupt energy governance and utility regulation practices—also join the chorus.

Various chapters offer an examination of energy law and justice across a specific legal field or within a jurisdiction field, such as international law or consumer protection; or provide 'case studies' illustrating how energy justice plays out in specific energy law contexts. Combining approaches allows for a conceptual 'top down' and grounded 'bottom up' approach to the multi-scalar problem of energy justice.

B. Energy Justice and Environmental Justice

While there has been significant scholarship in environmental justice that considers environmental protection and sustainability from the perspective of the justice themes analysed in this book, this collection is not primarily concerned with environmental justice. Instead, it offers a parallel process for energy justice to that which has occurred for environmental justice, where scholarship has mapped out the research and its application to law. Energy justice and energy law scholarship is newer, and its pathways less clearly defined, but we are aware of the strong links between these two kinds of justice and law inquiry. Even so, many energy justice matters are not encountered in environmental justice, especially since energy is a matter of household and commercial necessity and a key economic input which must be balanced against environmental impacts. Clearly though , the two strands of legal scholarship have a point of intersection in the SDGs.

C. The Sustainable Development Goals

The United Nations' 2030 Agenda for Sustainable Development was adopted by 193 of its members and the Agenda provides seventeen goals to 'transform our world'.[12] Sustainable Development Goal number 1 ('No poverty': SDG1), and, in particular number 7 ('Affordable and Clean Energy': SDG7) deal with many of the justice issues analysed in this book. The SDG7 specifically refers to the need of ensuring access to affordable, reliable, sustainable, and modern energy. Sustainability concepts impose the exigencies of fairness and equity, when sharing among states the burdens and benefits of achieving the SDGs. Two umbrella ideas which cover issues mentioned by the SDG7 are human rights (insofar as access to energy might be conceived as a human right) and

[12] United Nations, 'Transforming our World: The 2030 Agenda for Sustainable Development', Resolution Adopted by the General Assembly on 25 September 2015 A/Res/70/1, http://www.un.org/ga/search/view_doc.asp?symbol=A/RES/70/1&Lang=E, accessed 29 July 2019.

consumer protection (insofar as contemporary law tends to include access to clean or sustainable energy within consumers' rights).

Energy justice also can be framed in the light of the sustainability goal of affordable, reliable, clean energy for all, expressed in SDG7.The convergence of energy justice and sustainability is rooted in the challenges facing the energy sector, including global climate change and the policy dilemmas that this situation poses for governments and regulators worldwide. We urgently need an energy transition, but we need one that is just, fair, and equitable. The demanding exigencies of the transition are illustrated by the increasing number of articles on energy justice,[13] and recent publications exploring related topics to those included in this book.[14]

III. Content and Structure

The twenty chapters are structured thematically as follows: (i) conceptual and international law context; (ii) procedural justice, community participation, and restorative justice; (iii) consumers at the frontline of a new energy justice; (iv) access to energy, poverty, and distributive justice; and (v) energy at the centre of recognition or social justice.

The first chapter of part II is written by McHarg, whose main conceptualizations of energy justice are referenced above. In her chapter, Aileen outlines recent attempts by energy law scholars to provide a coherent normative framework for energy law, by building centrally on the idea of energy justice. She explores the origins and multiple dimensions of energy justice and discusses its potential as an organizing framework for energy law, and underlines the need for an 'ethical turnout'. The close relationship between energy justice and access to energy (including affordability) is analysed by del Guayo in Chapter 3, who provides clarifying terminology and explains the remarkable, multi-faceted ideas intertwined when dealing with energy poverty, and who examines the legal techniques to fight it. The core part of the chapter is devoted to the links of energy poverty with the three pillars of the so-called 'energy trilemma': security, efficiency, and sustainability. From an international law perspective in Chapter 4, Redgwell and Rajamani analyse the extent to which (and what) notions of energy justice permeate attempts internationally to achieve the SDGs. The focus of the chapter is on locating energy justice in international law by reference to core principles of energy justice which

[13] See, e.g., R.J. Heffron, A. Rønne, J.P. Tomain, A. Bradbrook, and K. Talus, 'A Treatise for Energy Law' (2018) 11 *Journal of World Energy Law and Business*, 1, 34–48; R.J. Heffron and D. McCauley, 'What is the "Just Transition"?',(2018) *Geoforum*, 88, 74–7; K. Jenkins, D. McCauley, R. Heffron, H. Stephan, and R. Rehner, 'Energy Justice: A Whole Systems Approach' (2016) *Energy Research & Social Science*, 11 174–82; and D. McCauley, V. Ramasar, R.J. Heffron, B.K. Sovacool, D. Mebratu, and L. Mundaca (eds), 'Energy Justice in the Transition to Low Carbon Energy Systems: Exploring Key Themes in Interdisciplinary Research' (2018) 233/234 *Applied Energy*, 916–21 (a special issue devoted to 'Low Carbon Energy Systems and Energy Justice').

[14] Besides the book referred to in (n 2), there are these other two volumes: B.K. Sovacool and M.H. Dworkin, *Global Energy Justice. Problems, Principles, and Practices* (Cambridge University Press, 2014); A. Halff, B.K. Sovacool, and J. Rozhon (eds), *Energy Poverty: Global Challenges and Local Solutions* (Oxford University Press, 2014).

reflect strong distributional justice elements, namely: sustainability, the intersection with human rights, intra-generational and inter-generational equity, and the related concept of common but differentiated responsibilities, with particular reference to the climate change regime. The chapter concludes, '[w]hether it is the "sustainability constrained" exercise of permanent sovereignty over natural resources, transparency and accountability of IOs, or the equitable distribution of the benefits and burdens of tackling climate change within and between generations, there is increasing evidence of the core principles of energy justice emerging in international law and policy'.

The following four chapters are grouped under the heading 'Procedural Justice, Community Participation, and Restorative Justice' (part III). Savaresi notes that the involvement of local and rural communities in renewable energies projects has been promoted strongly in recent years. The chapter scrutinizes whether these policies have been successful in achieving energy justice aims and seeks to identify regulatory challenges and gaps, with the purpose of providing suggestions on how community energy ought to be regulated, in order to deliver greater energy justice. Banet links network regulation with energy justice. The transition towards a new electricity model implies an increase in network costs, which will be passed on to final customers. There is the need therefore to update existing models of remuneration for operators and for cost allocation for consumers, if a fair share of costs between network operators and consumers is to be established. The chapter also reviews the theory and practice of grid tariff regulatory reforms in the context of current energy transition with a primary focus on European initiatives. Paddock and Vithanage explore a number of distributive injustices which underserved communities are suffering in the USA, such as exposure to pollutants from fossil-fuelled power plants and from petroleum-fuelled vehicles, since many of those communities are located near coal-fired power plants. These underserved communities have limited opportunities to participate in decisions affecting energy use in their communities. The chapter examines several legal developments that hold promise for addressing those distributive energy injustices. Boute offers an analysis on how to balance investors' and consumers' rights in Central Asia. Since most energy companies of the region are on the verge of bankruptcy, and given the sensitivity of energy price increases and tight budgetary constraints in the region, Boute examines what legal options are available to restore utilities' financial viability without jeopardizing the affordability of energy supply.

Part IV includes chapters recognizing the relevance of consumers in the forthcoming energy paradigm, where laws are drafted from the perspective of the demand, rather than from the supply, side. They are grouped under the heading 'Consumers at the Frontline of a New Energy Justice'. Mostert and Naude engage with the question of what the role of the state should be in ensuring supply to, and protection of, end-consumers of energy within different energy market models. The analysis relies on a comparison between jurisdictions. On the one end of the spectrum, there are markets dominated by virtual state monopolies, for example, where one state-owned enterprise is responsible for the supply (including production, transport, and distribution) of electricity to end-consumers. On the other end of the spectrum, where supply of energy to end-consumers is privatized, consumer protection takes on a different shape. Issues of procedural and participatory justice are considered. Roggenkamp and Diestelmeir deal with a different focus on energy poverty and energy justice in the context of recent market reforms in the EU. In particular, the chapter deals with the amended internal electricity market directive (2019), re-emphasizing the aim to 'activate' customers. This chapter contains a combination of perspectives of energy justice, in particular between distributive and social justice. Godden notes the complexity of the Australian energy sector when she looks at the energy transition occurring in Australia through the lens of energy justice with a focus on distributive and social justice. The chapter explores those issues in relation to two case studies: access to energy for remote communities (especially Aboriginal people), and energy affordability and consumer protection in the energy market in the south-eastern part of the continent.

Under the heading 'Access to Energy, Poverty, and Distributive Justice', part V groups contributions whose particular focus is the distributive component of energy justice. Barton and Campion apply the concept of energy justice to the specific legal problem of making climate change policies and laws, asking how these laws can be designed so as to reduce adverse consequences for low-income households. It examines in particular the distributional effects of those policies. Montoya leads a group of experts in the legal analysis of the meaning of energy poverty in the South American context. Energy poverty is so multi-faceted that each of the countries reviewed adopts a different form; and the fight against energy poverty requires different legal instruments. Lucas, by reference to Canada, provides three case studies that illustrate the challenges faced by developed countries and the lessons learned for those nations still engaged in network extension for rural electrification. He examines the role of public and private institutions in that process. The focus is on distributive justice and the historical measures that Canadian jurisdictions sought to use to protect vulnerable energy consumers. Jurisdictions addressed are the provinces of Alberta and Ontario, and Yukon, one of Canada's Northern Territories. Lucas notes that the Roosevelt 'New Deal' which was of great importance for redressing rural energy poverty in the USA, had parallel policy programmes in Canada. In respect of the USA programme of rural electrification, historian Robert Caro's masterful biography of President Lyndon Johnson relates what the lack of electricity meant for working and living in rural Texas hill country in the early 1930s.[15] Much of the work in homes of this era included hauling water and wood, canning fruits and vegetables that could not be refrigerated without electricity, doing the washing by hand in multiple tubs, and ironing the cleaned laundry with six or seven pound wedges of iron heated over a wood stove. Doctors found that several illnesses were linked to these activities and, ultimately, to the lack of electricity. Some of Lyndon Johnson's earliest political work involved leading successful efforts as part of President Franklin Roosevelt's New Deal that sought to bring electricity to rural America. By contrast, the 'free market' had not been receptive to rural electrification due to the limited economic return on investment in extensive and expensive power lines needed to serve

[15] R. Caro, *The Years of Lyndon Johnson* (four volumes) (Alfred A. Knopf, 1982, 1990, 2002, and 2012).

small numbers of rural customers. The last chapter of this part has been written by Olawuyi. It deals with the divergent dimensions of energy poverty in the Middle East and North African region. It discusses law and governance innovations for promoting the availability, affordability, and accessibility of sustainable energy, especially electricity and modern fuels, across the region.

Part VI groups chapters under the heading 'Energy at the Centre of Social (or Recognition) Justice'. Zillman and Smith examine the challenge the USA is currently facing to address energy justice issues since the election of President Donald Trump in 2016. Special attention is given to the range of areas in which law can be used to advance energy justice goals consistent with popular electoral sentiment. From a Mesoamerican perspective, González evaluates the connections between law and energy justice with a focus on the social justice dimension of distributional justice. This chapter surveys the way legislation addresses the main drivers of energy poverty and how the law deals with them. Wang and Yang address the specific manifestations of energy justice, in particular distributive justice and inter-generational justice in China's energy policies and laws, and their implementation. The chapter reviews the objectives, principles, regime, and mechanism of energy justice in China. The last chapter, by Omorogbe, examines the extent to which the existing legal and regulatory regimes have encouraged or impeded energy access in rural and urban areas in Ghana, Rwanda, and Nigeria; measured by the UNs' goal of universal access to energy services.

PART II
CONCEPTUAL AND INTERNATIONAL LAW CONTEXT

2

Energy Justice

Understanding the 'Ethical Turn' in Energy Law and Policy

Aileen McHarg

I. Introduction

Over the past decade, there has been an explosion of scholarly interest in the concept of energy justice. Barely mentioned prior to 2010,[1] since then there have been several books, journal special issues, conferences, and research programmes, as well as numerous articles devoted to the discussion and promotion of energy justice. Explicitly interdisciplinary in nature,[2] the concept has attracted the attention not only of legal scholars, but also geographers, sociologists, philosophers, political scientists, and others.[3]

Energy justice scholars argue that 'the global energy system is replete with extreme injustices and asymmetries',[4] which are to be found throughout the energy lifecycle, from production to transportation to consumption and waste disposal, and in relation to all energy forms. Injustices can arise both from having *too much* energy (the environmental and social burdens imposed by waste, over-consumption, and pollution) and from *not having enough* energy (lack of access to modern forms of energy, under-consumption, and poverty).[5] Thus energy justice is proposed as a key organizing concept for academic research into energy issues, providing 'an opportunity to develop new crosscutting social science research agendas on exploring where injustices occur [and] developing new processes of avoidance and remediation'.[6]

But the ambitions of energy justice scholars are not purely academic.[7] Energy justice is also recommended as a guiding principle for energy decision-makers at all

[1] The first use of the concept in an academic context was in L. Guruswamy, 'Energy Justice and Sustainable Development' (2010) 21 *Colorado Journal of International Environmental Law and Policy* 231, although there were some earlier (albeit limited) uses in activist literature—see R.J. Heffron and D. McCauley, 'The Concept of Energy Justice Across the Disciplines' (2017) 105 *Energy Policy*, 658 at 659.

[2] Heffron and McCauley, ibid., at 662.

[3] N. Creutzfeld, et al., *ESRC Just Energy: Literature Summaries: Energy Justice* (2018), available at: https://esrcjustenergy.files.wordpress.com/2018/12/literature-summaries-energy-justice.pdf, last accessed 30 December 2019.

[4] B.K. Sovacool and M.H. Dworkin (eds), *Global Energy Justice: Problems, Principles, and Practices* (Cambridge University Press, 2014) 377.

[5] B.K. Sovacool, et al., 'Energy Decisions Reframed as Justice and Ethical Concerns' (2016) 1 *Nature Energy*, 1 at 1.

[6] K. Jenkins, et al., 'Energy Justice: A Conceptual Review' (2016) 11 *Energy Research and Social Science*, 174 at 176. See also D. McCauley, *Energy Justice: Rebalancing the Trilemma of Security, Poverty and Climate Change* (Palgrave Macmillan, 2018) at v.

[7] See Heffron and McCauley, (n 1), at 661–2.

Aileen McHarg, Energy Justice In: *Energy Justice and Energy Law.* Edited by Íñigo Del Guayo, Lee Godden, Donald N. Zillman, Milton Fernando Montoya, and José Juan González, Oxford University Press (2020). © The Several Contributors.
DOI: 10.1093/oso/9780198860754.003.0002

levels—from regulators and policy makers, to energy firms, to individual consumers[8]—and, it is claimed, can supply energy law as a legal discipline with a unifying normative underpinning that it has hitherto lacked.[9] For its proponents, the practical implications of energy justice are radical. For Heffron et al., it offers a new way of balancing the familiar energy trilemma of security, affordability, and sustainability according to principles of justice and equity, rather than economic efficiency.[10] Similarly, Sovacool et al. argue that '[t]he incorporation of considerations of justice into energy policy-making will alter how we view entire energy systems, with concerns such as equity and equality of distribution becoming more predominant, while other concerns, such as profit-maximisation, receding (sic) in importance', requiring the development of 'new business models and regulatory paradigms'.[11]

What we might call the 'ethical turn' in energy law and policy thus appears to be highly significant, both in terms of ushering in new ways of thinking about energy systems and their relationship to fundamental questions of social ordering and political values and also—at least potentially—in terms of its practical implications for their organization and governance. This chapter aims to assist in understanding the ethical turn in two main ways. First, it seeks to account for the rise to prominence of energy justice and to understand what its advocates hope to achieve. Second, it explores what is meant by energy justice, elucidating the dimensions of justice employed in the literature, the theories of justice which are advanced, and who are to be regarded as the agents of energy justice (in other words, how the concept is to be operationalized in practice). The chapter concludes by assessing the potential and current limitations of energy justice as a guiding principle for the future development of energy law and policy.

II. Why Energy Justice?

Many of the issues which concern energy justice scholars have been discussed for some time, without being specifically labelled as questions of 'energy justice'.[12] For example, promoting universal access to energy systems was a key motivation for the post-war expansion of electricity and gas grids in Europe and North America, while securing access to modern energy services for all has been acknowledged as being central to the achievement of the Millennium Development Goals adopted by the United Nations in

[8] See, e.g., Sovacool and Dworkin, (n 4), at 25–6.

[9] R.J. Heffron and K. Talus, 'The Evolution of Energy Law and Energy Jurisprudence: Insights for Energy Analysts and Researchers' (2016) 19 *Energy Research and Social Science*, 1 at 8–9. See also R.J. Heffron, et al., 'A Treatise for Energy Law' (2018) 11 *Journal of World Energy Law and Business*, 34 at 42, where energy justice is proposed as one of seven core principles of energy law.

[10] R.J. Heffron, et al., 'Resolving Society's Energy Trilemma through the Energy Justice Matrix' (2015) 87 *Energy Policy*, 168 at 169.

[11] B.K. Sovacool, et al., 'New Frontiers and Conceptual Frameworks for Energy Justice' (2017) 105 *Energy Policy*, 677 at 689.

[12] K. Jenkins, et al., 'Energy Justice: A Policy Approach' (2017) 106 *Energy Policy*, 631 at 631.

2000.[13] The oil crises of the 1970s focused attention on questions of equity and intergenerational justice in relation to allocation of scarce resources,[14] as well as raising the profile of issues of affordability and fuel poverty. Similarly, the social and environmental injustices caused by energy developments, such as hydroelectric dams or resource extraction operations, have been widely recognized and debated.[15]

However, the sustained focus on energy justice can be attributed to a boom in social science scholarship on energy issues—again over the past decade—in a field hitherto dominated by engineers and economists.[16] Social scientists have sought to foster a fuller, more human-centred understanding of energy systems as more than merely technical mechanisms for the delivery of units of energy at the lowest possible cost.[17] Instead, emphasis is placed upon the fundamental importance of access to adequate energy services—and of the circumstances in which energy is produced, transported, consumed, and disposed of—to fulfilment of the conditions of human flourishing.[18] Thus, 'how we distribute the benefits and burdens of energy systems is pre-eminently a concern for any society that aspires to be fair'.[19]

In addition, social scientists emphasize the complexity of energy decision-making, as involving psychological, behavioural, ethical, and socio-political aspects, as well as technical and economic considerations.[20] Hence, Sovacool et al. point out that:

> Energy system interventions are about more than technology and economic development; they are about political power, social cohesion, and even ethical and moral concerns over equity, due process, and justice. Energy systems can be reconceived as a political, deliberative challenge involving the satisfaction of competing preferences; a social dilemma pitting, at times, the climatic and development goals of energy security or improved resilience against the pressing needs of marginalized and vulnerable populations; and a moral quandary revolving around how energy burdens and benefits are fairly, or unfairly, disseminated.[21]

The increased social scientific interest in energy issues can in turn be attributed to two main, interconnected factors. The first is a rejection of—or disillusionment with—the

[13] Y.O. Omorogbe, 'Promoting Sustainable Development through the Use of Renewable Energy: the Role of Law', in D.N. Zillman, et al. (eds), *Beyond the Carbon Economy: Energy Law in Transition* (Oxford University Press, 2008), 41–5.

[14] See, e.g.,I. Illich, *Energy and Equity* (Calder and Boyars Ltd, 1974); D. Maclean and P.G. Brown (eds), *Energy and the Future* (Rowman and Littlefield Pub. Inc., 1983).

[15] E.g., the displacement of 1.3 million people, the loss of archaeological and cultural sites, and ecological changes caused by the construction of the Three Gorges Dam in China, or the widespread environmental despoliation and human abuses consequent upon oil extraction in the Niger Delta.

[16] See B.K. Sovacool, 'What Are We Doing Here? Analysing Fifteen Years of Energy Scholarship and Proposing a Social Science Research Agenda' (2014) 1 *Energy Research and Social Science*, 1; G. Frigo, 'Energy Ethics: A Literature Review' (2018) 6 *Relations: Beyond Anthropocentrism*, 177.

[17] See Sovacool, et al. , (n 5), at 4.

[18] R. Gillard, et al., 'Advancing an Energy Justice Perspective of Fuel Poverty: Household Vulnerability and Domestic Retrofit Policy in the UK' (2017) 29 *Energy Research and Social Science*, 53 at 54.

[19] See Sovacool, (n 16), at 15.

[20] See Frigo, (n 16), at 178.

[21] See Sovacool et al., (n 5), at 5.

promise of neo-liberal energy policies that satisfactory energy decisions can be made through the operation of impersonal market forces. Energy justice scholars point to the failure of neo-liberalism to deliver an effective and balanced, long-term energy system.[22] Moreover, the persistence of oligopoly and monopoly, as well as an ongoing heavy regulatory presence, underlines the continued importance of human decision-making. As Sovacool and Dworkin put it:

> Utility managers, system operators, business leaders and ordinary consumers do not function merely like automatons that rationally calculate price signals and change their behavior to optimize benefits and minimize costs. Instead, they are embroiled in a complicated social and cultural environment that is shaped by and helps to shape technological changes, rituals, behaviors, values, attitudes, emotions, and interests.[23]

The second important factor is the global transition towards a low-carbon energy system. Again, the extensive government intervention necessary to secure the energy transition has re-emphasized the importance of political choices in the design and development of energy systems, and hence of the criteria according to which they are made. Indeed, addressing perceived injustices has often proved to be instrumentally necessary as a condition of securing public acceptance of low carbon energy policies. This has helped to focus attention on[24] those left behind by the energy transition (i.e. workers and communities dependent upon fossil fuel industries),[25] as well as those excluded from its benefits and/or who bear a disproportionate share of its burdens (such as communities which bear the amenity costs of low carbon generation, without sharing its financial benefits,[26] or which are affected by new power lines, whilst themselves being unable to access the grid).[27] Energy justice scholars point out that 'simply decarbonizing the *status quo* … is not energy justice'.[28] As Eisenberg states:

> a world with low carbon emissions does not somehow transform into a utopia. A shift to a clean-energy economy stands to perpetuate or exacerbate current patterns of inequity. Those patterns could specifically relate to low-carbon industries, for instance, through land theft to develop wind and solar farms, forced labor to extract the natural resources necessary to create solar panels, or impositions of health hazards from

[22] See McCauley, (n 6), at 3.

[23] See Sovacool and Dworkin, (n 4), at 363.

[24] See, e.g., N. Healy and J. Barry, 'Politicizing Energy Justice and Energy System Transitions: Fossil Fuel Divestment and a "Just Transition"' (2017) 108 *Energy Policy*, 451.

[25] See, e.g., Healy and Barry, ibid.; J. Bethem, 'Life within Energy Policy' (2018) 6 *Relations: Beyond Anthropocentrism*, 69 at 79–81; A.M. Eisenberg, 'Just Transitions' (2019) 92 *Southern California Law Review*, 273.

[26] See, e.g., A. McHarg, 'Community Benefit Through Community Ownership of Renewable Generation in Scotland: Power to the People?', in L. Barrera-Hernandez, et al. (eds), *Sharing the Costs and Benefits of Energy and Resource Activity: Legal Change and Impact on Communities* (Oxford University Press, 2016).

[27] See, e.g., the substantial public opposition to the Beauly to Denny transmission line in Scotland T. Brian, R. Dent, and R. Jackson, *Beauly to Denny: Report of the Public Local Inquiry* (Scottish Government, 2009).

[28] See Healy and Barry, (n 24), at 457. See also McCauley, (n 6), at 69.

> biomass fuels. The patterns could also arise in other contexts in the low-carbon world, such as through inequitable access to clean energy.[29]

Thus, she argues, 'the shift to a low-carbon economy is an opportunity to rectify the injustices of the fossil fuel economy, and to not do so, or to allow inequalities to worsen, would itself effectuate injustice'.[30]

A further way in which the energy transition is important in understanding the rise of energy justice is through the increased prominence it has given to the environmental aspects of energy production and use, and hence to environmental law and regulation. In fact, there is general agreement that the concept of energy justice developed out of earlier debates about environmental and climate justice.[31] According to Bickerstaff et al., the concept of energy justice provides a way of bounding and separating out energy-specific issues from the broader concerns of environmental and climate justice discourses,[32] although it also enables focus on consumption and access issues, and not merely the environmental injustices arising from energy production and transportation. Jenkins argues that this makes energy justice a smaller scale and more strategically impactful concept than either environmental or climate justice.[33] She also claims that, because energy justice, in contrast to environmental and climate justice, has largely developed as an academic rather than activist concept, this gives it greater conceptual rigour and clarity, which in turn increases its likelihood of successfully influencing policy.[34]

This greater exposure to environmental law and justice discourses has also proved to be influential with energy lawyers, who have been inspired to supply their own discipline with a set of philosophical precepts similar to those underpinning environmental law—its own 'moral compass'[35]—and for whom notions of justice have obvious appeal. Co-option and development of the concept of energy justice helps to signal the maturing of energy law as a distinct legal discipline.[36] The emphasis on *energy* justice promises to supply a set of normative principles suitable to the specific circumstances and challenges of the energy industries, whilst the stress on energy *justice* emphasizes the relative autonomy of energy law from developments in energy practice,[37] and hence that it has its own contribution to make to the successful resolution of problems posed by energy systems.[38]

29 See Eisenberg, (n 25), at 282.

30 Ibid., at 280.

31 D. McCauley, et al., 'Advancing Energy Justice: the Triumvirate of Tenets' (2013) *International Energy Law Review*, 107 at 107.

32 K. Bickerstaff, et al., 'Introduction: Making Sense of Energy Justice', in K. Bickerstaff, et al. (eds), *Energy Justice in a Changing Climate* (Zed Books, 2013), at 2. Note, McCauley and Heffron have subsequently attempted to re-integrate energy justice with environmental and climate justice under the umbrella term of 'Just Transition',D. McCauley and R. Heffron, 'Just Transition: Integrating Climate, Energy and Environmental Justice' (2018) 119 *Energy Policy*, 1.

33 K. Jenkins, 'Setting Energy Justice Apart from the Crowd: Lessons from Environmental and Climate Justice' (2018) 39 *Energy Research and Social Science*, 117 at 119.

34 Ibid. at 119–20.

35 See Heffron and Talus, (n 9), at 4–5.

36 Ibid. at 2.

37 See Heffron, et al., (n 9), at 36.

38 See ibid. at 4.

III. What is Energy Justice?

Given the academic origins of energy justice, it is reasonable to expect a high degree of theoretical sophistication in the development and use of the concept, as well as critical reflection on the challenges of its deployment in practice. In this section, I discuss, first, the particular forms (or 'dimensions') and theories of justice employed by energy justice scholars. In other words, what analytical distinctions do they draw when discussing energy justice, and what normative theories do they advance as to what constitutes justice or injustice in relation to the outcomes of energy decision-making? I also consider the range of decision-makers who are, or might be, subject to obligations to act in accordance with principles of justice (the 'agents' of energy justice), and some of the practical issues which arise in seeking to operationalize the concept.

A. The Dimensions of Energy Justice

Justice is a multi-faceted concept. It may be concerned with the substance of how people are treated, or the procedures by which decisions affecting them are made. It may be backwards- or forwards-looking: concerned either with how the circumstances in which people find themselves arose; or focused upon the impact of those circumstances in terms of people's ability to flourish and realize their goals. It may be assessed over different temporal and geographical scales. And it may be concerned with the treatment of individuals, or of the groups to which they belong, or even of non-human subjects.

The dimensions of justice most frequently discussed in the literature on energy justice are the 'triumvirate of tenets' identified by McCauley et al. in 2013.[39] These are:

1. *Distributive* justice, which concerns both the 'distribution of costs, or how the hazards and externalities of the energy system are disseminated throughout society' and the 'distribution of benefits, or how access to modern energy systems and services is distributed throughout society'.[40]
2. *Procedural* justice, which Walker and Day define, following the Aarhus Convention,[41] as requiring access to information about energy issues, meaningful participation in energy decision-making, and access to legal procedures for obtaining redress or challenging decision-making processes.[42]

[39] See McCauley, et al., (n 31).
[40] See Sovacool, et al., (n 5), at 4.
[41] Convention on Access to Information, Public Participation in Decision-Making and Access to Justice in Environmental Matters, 2161 UNTS 450, 1998.
[42] G. Walker and R. Day, 'Fuel Poverty as Injustice: Integrating Distribution, Recognition and Procedure in the Struggle for Affordable Warmth' (2012) 49 *Energy Policy*, 69 at 72.

3. *Recognition* justice, which requires acknowledgement of and respect for 'the various needs, rights and experiences'[43] of those affected by energy decisions (for example, the greater amounts of energy required to satisfy the basic needs of particular social groups, such as elderly or disabled people),[44] and for attention to be paid to 'which parts of society are privileged or ignored'[45] (for example, the tendency to dismiss those opposed to wind farm developments as NIMBYs).[46]

To these three tenets, Heffron and McCauley add a fourth—*restorative* justice—which they define as a duty to rectify injustices arising from energy decision-making.[47] However, a range of other justice concepts can also be found in the literature. For instance, the idea of *corrective* justice may be employed to demand that those who harm the environment through energy-related activities be made to take responsibility for their actions,[48] or that those whose rights or legitimate expectations are overridden by the transition to a low carbon energy system be compensated for their losses.[49] Notions of *inter-generational* justice are invoked to insist that attention is paid not merely to the consequences of energy decision-making for current populations (*intra-generational* justice), but also to the effects on future generations of, for instance, atmospheric pollution or resource depletion.[50] Ideas of *international* or *global* justice are used to demand that we view questions of energy justice on a global scale and not merely on a national scale, for instance that we should work to secure universal access to modern energy services, and to ensure that the risks associated with energy production and use are not exported from wealthy countries to poorer ones.[51] This may be regarded as one aspect of a broader notion of *spatial* justice, which emphasizes the geographic dimensions of inequality and inequity, both within and beyond nation states, highlighting, for instance, the 'clear geographic patternings associated with energy poverty, as well as the geographically embedded and contingent nature of its underlying causes'.[52] Finally, some authors argue that attention should also be paid to *inter-species* equity and other *non-anthropocentric* notions of justice (such as *bio-centrism* and *eco-centrism*).[53]

These various dimensions of energy justice are often assumed either to relate to different aspects of energy decision-making,[54] or to be complementary and mutually reinforcing.[55] For instance, Gillard et al. argue that recognition injustice (lack

[43] See Gillard, et al., (n 18), at 54.
[44] See, e.g., ibid., at 54–5.
[45] See McCauley, (n 6), at 18.
[46] See Jenkins, et al., (n 6), at 177.
[47] See (n 1), at 660–1. In subsequent work, restorative justice replaces recognition justice as the third of a new 'triumvirate of tenets', see McCauley and Heffron, (n 32), at 1.
[48] See, e.g., Sovacool, et al., (n 5), at 4; J.D. Schneider, 'Review of: L. Guruswamy (ed.), International Energy and Poverty: The Emerging Contours' (2016) 37 Energy Law Journal , 193 at 195.
[49] See, e.g., Eisenberg, (n 25), at 308.
[50] See, e.g., Sovacool and Dworkin, (n 4), chapter 9.
[51] See, e.g., Sovacool and Dworkin, (n 4), *passim*; McCauley, (n 6), chapter 1.
[52] S. Bouzarovski and N. Simcock, 'Spatializing Energy Justice' (2017) 107 *Energy Policy*, 640 at 640.
[53] See, e.g., Sovacool, et al., (n 11), at 680–3; G. Frigo, 'Energy Ethics: Emerging Perspectives in a Time of Transition' (2018) 6 *Relations: Beyond Anthropocentrism*, 7 at 18.
[54] See McCauley, (n 6), at 90.
[55] See Gillard, et al., (n 18), at 54.

of recognition or mis-recognition) is manifested in two ways: 'through social structures and institutions that ignore, misrepresent or reinforce inequalities, and through social processes that limit possibilities for expression and ostracise minorities'.[56] In other words, lack of recognition of the needs or interests of specific groups tends to lead to them being under-represented in debates and policy decisions, and hence to the perpetuation or exacerbation of the inequalities they face.[57] Similarly, Heffron and McCauley claim that restorative justice provides a 'uniting aim' of energy justice, because it forces decision-makers to engage with justice concerns and to consider the full range of issues identified by other justice principles, as these identify the areas where restorative action would be required and the costs involved in doing so.[58]

Clearly, however, it cannot always be the case that the different dimensions of justice co-exist harmoniously; sometimes they will be in tension or conflict with one another—something that is not always fully acknowledged in the energy justice literature. For instance, procedural justice may sometimes be in tension with distributive and recognition justice. An emphasis on participation and voice may serve to further empower the already powerful and articulate at the expense of vulnerable groups, and it may be particularly difficult to give adequate recognition to the needs and interests of those distant in time and space, such as future generations or international groups.[59] Similarly, apparently fair procedures may have the effect of legitimizing substantively unjust results, for instance where disadvantaged communities are empowered to 'choose' to host a nuclear waste disposal site through a competitive bidding process. There are also important trade-offs and tensions between *intra-* and *inter-*generational justice. For instance, Sovacool et al. point out that protecting the interests of future generations would suggest slow depletion rates for natural resources, whereas considerations of intra-generational distributive justice might require us to maximize the use of resources to facilitate access for the poor and vulnerable.[60] Similarly, while it is obvious that global responsibility for energy-related climate change is unevenly distributed, it might be argued that we all share a responsibility to future generations to mitigate further harms.

From a legal perspective, however, perhaps the most important potential conflict is that between distributive justice and corrective justice. While creative legal action to vindicate the rights and legitimate expectations of those harmed by energy decision-making may sometimes be used to improve distributive outcomes, the role of (unequally distributed) property rights in land, or in licences and concessions may act as a significant limit on the ability of governments and regulators to reorganize energy systems in the interests of distributive justice. Consideration of how such conflicts should be resolved is a surprising omission from a discourse which is proposed as a guiding principle for energy law.

[56] Ibid., at 55.
[57] Ibid., at 54.
[58] See Heffron and McCauley (n 32), at 660.
[59] See Jenkins, et al., (n 6), at 178.
[60] Sovacool, et al., (n 5), at 4.

B. Theories of Energy Justice

Theories of justice can help us to make sense of, and to resolve, conflicts and uncertainties as to what justice requires in particular contexts. Theories of justice offer differing interpretations of what constitutes, for example, distributive justice or procedural justice. For instance, distributive justice theories propose a range of different distributive principles (rights, needs or welfare, utility, desert), each of which may be interpreted in different ways (what counts as a right; what needs are morally relevant; how is utility to be measured; what behaviour is morally deserving, and deserving of what?).[61] Particular justice theories may prioritize certain dimensions of justice over others. For instance, libertarian theorists such as Nozick or Hayek argue that it does not make sense to talk of social or distributive justice; for them, we can only meaningfully talk of justice or injustice in relation to individual actions, and so distributional patterns are just provided that they have come about as a result of transactions freely entered into, however unequal or otherwise 'unfair' they appear to be.[62] Theories of justice also help to guide us in determining which temporal frames or spatial scales are relevant, and how to prioritize conflicting rights, needs, interests, and so on.

Different theories of justice may offer substantially different answers to particular energy-related questions. For instance, a desert-based theory might conclude that prosumers deserve to be rewarded for their contribution to the reduction of overall carbon emissions, even if green subsidies have a regressive effect on the energy poor and are thus contrary to a needs-based understanding of distributive justice. Similarly, rights-based or utilitarian theories might give radically different answers to the question of whether electricity and gas grids ought to be extended to remote, sparsely-populated areas.

So, which theories of justice do energy justice scholars advance?

In their 2014 book, *Global Energy Justice*, Sovacool and Dworkin draw upon a range of different justice theories in the Western philosophical tradition to illustrate and offer solutions to particular problems of the global energy system. In later work, Sovacool et al. draw further inspiration from non-Western theories.[63] Although Sovacool and Dworkin acknowledge that the theorists they discuss do not always give compatible answers to justice problems,[64] they claim that justice is pluralist,[65] and that 'the concept of justice may be less important for what it *is* than for what it *does*'.[66] In other words, 'the concept of justice is a tool with multiple functions'.[67] These include improving

[61] See generally, J. Lamont and C. Favor, 'Distributive Justice', in E.N. Zalta (ed.), *Stanford Encyclopaedia of Philosophy* (Stanford, 2017), available at https://plato.stanford.edu/archives/win2017/entries/justice-distributive; D. Miller, *Political Philosophy: A Very Short Introduction* (Oxford University Press, 2003), chapter 5.

[62] See Sovacool and Dworkin, (n4?), at 273–9; Lamont and Favor, ibid., at section 7.

[63] Sovacool, et al., (n 11), at 678–80.

[64] Sovacool and Dworkin (n 4), at 18, 355. See also Sovacool, et al., (n 11), at 680–3.

[65] Sovacool and Dworkin (n 4), at 374; see also S. Fuller and D. McCauley, 'Framing Energy Justice: Perspectives from Activism and Advocacy' (2016) 11 *Energy Research and Social Science*, 1 at 6; McCauley, (n 6), at 29; Jenkins, et al., (n 6), at 180.

[66] Sovacool and Dworkin(n 4), at 10.

[67] Ibid.

decision-making, providing standards of justification beyond individual preferences, and helping to secure greater acceptance of decisions. Nevertheless, from these diverse theoretical foundations, Sovacool and Dworkin claim to derive eight principles of energy justice: the promotion of availability; affordability; due process; access to information; sustainability; intra-generational equity; inter-generational equity; and responsibility.[68] To these eight principles, Sovacool et al. add a further two: resistance to injustice; and intersectionality.[69]

While the principles presented may have a certain intuitive appeal, it is fair to say that they are poorly grounded, and the links between particular theories of justice and the energy policy prescriptions derived from them are sketched with only the broadest of brushes. The lack of coherence between the different justice theories discussed is also problematic from a functional perspective. First, it runs contrary to the central purpose of the concept of justice, which—according to Miller—is to treat individuals in a non-arbitrary way; this requires, at a minimum, consistency of treatment both between people and over time.[70] To invite people to decide energy issues in terms of justice, rather than some other standard such as efficiency, does not in fact achieve justice in this formal sense if justice theories are treated as a pick and mix from which decision-makers can choose at will. Secondly, lack of coherence limits the persuasive power of arguments about energy justice. For instance, a libertarian who is convinced by Sovacool and Dworkin's appeal to Nozick to argue for an end to energy subsidies[71] is unlikely to be convinced by their appeal to Rawlsian welfare liberalism to justify social pricing.[72] Finally, without a robust theoretical foundation, the appeal to justice as a set of decision-making tools is likely to be met with the response, 'why these tools, and not others?' This is particularly unsatisfactory where energy justice is offered as an alternative to market-based decision-making, since the free market is underpinned by its own theory of justice (i.e. one which emphasizes individual freedom and choice, and the belief that free competition maximizes social utility).

Other scholars do make greater efforts to ground their claims about energy justice in a coherent philosophy. The most frequently invoked theories are the arguments of welfare liberals like Rawls and Sen to the effect that primary goods (including access to energy) should be distributed in such a manner as to secure the greatest benefit to the worst off (Rawls) or to afford each individual equal capability to achieve valued functioning, including the ability to live a fulfilling life, as well as to satisfy basic human needs (Sen).[73] This is often combined with an appeal to cosmopolitan justice theories, to insist that energy justice be addressed on a global scale.[74]

[68] Ibid., at 366–71.
[69] See Sovacool, et al., (n 11), at 687–8.
[70] See Miller, (n 61), at 76.
[71] Sovacool and Dworkin (n 4), chapter 8.
[72] Ibid., chapter 7.
[73] See, e.g., Walker and Day, (n 42), at 70; Gillard, et al., (n 18), at 54; McCauley, (n 6), at 11–17.
[74] See, e.g., Heffron, et al., (n 10), at 170; Sovacool and Dworkin, (n 4), at 372–3; Sovacool, et al., (n 5), at 1, 2, 4; McCauley, (n 6), at 13, 39.

These theories are, of course, controversial. For example, though inspired by Rawls' theory of justice, Rawls himself rejected the cosmopolitan claim that it makes sense to address distributive justice questions on a global scale, arguing for a narrower understanding of international justice, based on a more limited set of obligations to respect fundamental human rights and to assist people in countries without well-ordered systems of government.[75] Guruswamy bases his call for international action to help what he calls the 'energy-oppressed poor' on this narrower understanding of international justice,[76] while Schneider argues that appeals for global energy justice would make more practical headway if based on utilitarian arguments that all nations benefit from alleviating economic deprivation.[77]

The fact that justice theories are controversial is not, of course, a reason to reject the claims of energy justice scholars. Hall rightly notes that universal understandings of justice are difficult to attain because they require 'shared interpretations of the right or good'.[78] Moreover, to dismiss calls for change on the basis that there is no consensus is, implicitly, to defend the justice of the status quo.[79] Nevertheless there are still a number of questions that need to be addressed and fully worked through before there can be said to be a fully-developed and comprehensive theory of energy justice.

Important issues include:

1. How are energy needs to be understood, and what relevance do matters like cultural factors affecting levels of energy use[80] and the role of individual choice have for the determination of basic needs?
2. What implications do welfarist principles have for the organization of energy systems: how much role is there for the operation of energy markets; are principles other than need (such as utility, desert, or inter-generational equity) relevant to energy consumption decisions beyond the basic minimum?
3. How relevant are principles of distributive justice to energy justice questions other than issues of access and affordability? Does equality demand public ownership of energy resources? Is the amelioration of environmental harms best understood as involving questions of distributive rather than corrective justice?
4. How far should property rights and other vested interests be regarded as a legitimate brake on energy system reforms?

[75] J. Rawls, *The Law of Peoples* (Harvard University Press, 1999). See generally M. Blake and P.T. Smith, 'International Distributive Justice', in E.N. Zalta (ed.), *The Stanford Encyclopedia of Philosophy* (Stanford, 2015), available at: https://plato.stanford.edu/archives/spr2015/entries/international-justice/; Miller, (n 61), chapter 7.

[76] See (n 1), at 258–65.

[77] See Schneider, (n 48), at 195–6.

[78] S.M. Hall, 'Energy Justice and Ethical Consumption: Comparison, Synthesis and Lesson Drawing' (2013) 18 *Local Environment*, 422, at 428–9; see also McCauley (n 6), at 90.

[79] Lamont and Favor, (n 61), section 1.

[80] See, e.g., Bouzarovski and Simcock (n 52), at 644, point out that energy poverty may be particularly stigmatizing in places such as the US where high levels of energy consumption is the norm, or in Scandinavian countries where a high value is placed on having a 'cosy' home. On the other hand, accommodation of such cultural norms may perpetuate global inequality in the use of energy resources and legitimize over-consumption.

C. The Agents of Energy Justice

As was noted in the Introduction, energy justice is intended to be more than an academic discourse, providing a critical standard against which to measure current energy decision-making. It is also intended to *change* the way in which those decisions are made in practice.[81] Indeed, as was also noted above, one of the advantages claimed for energy justice over environmental and climate justice is its greater potential for influencing policy; the latter two discourses being regarded as having failed to make much practical impact.[82] A fully-developed theory of energy justice thus needs to consider *to whom* energy justice arguments are directed, and *how*, and *to what extent*, justice-related considerations can be embedded in practical decision-making. Practical implementation needs to be addressed not simply as a question of political *strategy*; as Jenkins recognizes, 'even with ... well planned tools, energy justice is likely to encounter contested, tricky and political dilemmas and resistances'.[83] Practical considerations also need to feed back into the development of conceptual and normative arguments about energy justice, as persuasive normative precepts have to take into account the limits of what is practically possible, and to be sensitive to the constraints imposed by other, particularly institutionally-based, accounts of what constitutes legitimate decision-making.

Nevertheless, this aspect of energy justice is also under-developed. As Jenkins et al. note, the discussion has tended to be abstract,[84] with only limited and patchy attention paid to questions of practical realization. To whom, then, might energy justice be addressed—who are the actors or agents who will effectuate energy justice (or continue to perpetrate injustices)—and what barriers might need to be overcome to ensure that they act in accordance with principles of justice?

1. Legislators, Regulators, and Policy-makers

The most obvious set of agents of energy justice are legislators, regulators, and other policy-makers; reflecting its social science origins, energy justice is a heavily policy-oriented discourse. The issues which arise here concern, first, how to motivate policy-actors to respond to energy justice concerns. Secondly, and of particular relevance for lawyers, it is necessary to consider what legal, structural, and governance reforms might help to ensure that decision-makers *can* and *do* focus on considerations of justice.[85] This might include, for instance, reform of regulators' statutory duties; new institutional structures to ensure a more holistic view of energy decision-making; and/or new structures and procedures for representing and consulting affected interests.

[81] See, e.g., Sovacool and Dworkin, (n 4), at 356; Jenkins, (n 33), at 120.

[82] Heffron and McCauley, (n 1), at 662.

[83] See Jenkins, (n 33), at 120.

[84] See Jenkins, et al., (n 12), at 633.

[85] Ibid., at 632. For consideration of these questions in a related context, see A. McHarg, 'Regulating for Sustainable Electricity Market Outcomes in Britain: Asking the Law Question' (2013) 30 *Environmental and Planning Law Journal*, 289.

Thirdly, work is required to identify what policy tools, processes, and approaches are best able to capture the nuances of energy justice questions, in particular complex issues of recognition justice. For example, in their review of fuel poverty policy in the UK, Gillard et al. point out that well-meaning but overly-simplistic policies are ineffective in reaching a large percentage of the fuel poor and that poorly-targeted policies may actually increase rather than reduce distributive injustice.[86]

Heffron et al. have proposed the adoption of an 'energy justice metric' to be used in decision-making about the development of energy infrastructure.[87] This, they argue, would allow the justice implications of particular infrastructure proposals to be costed and fed into existing cost-benefit analysis models. It would include consideration, for example, of the political costs and benefits associated with energy security, costs imposed in terms of public health impacts and environmental pollutions, impacts on the cost of energy, loss of amenity, the risk of fatal accidents, and so on. However, the difficulties with this kind of technocratic, cost-benefit approach are very well known,[88] in particular the challenges of ascribing monetary values to questions of justice and problems of incommensurability, as well as the risk of impact assessments becoming no more than 'tick-box' exercises, which fail to dislodge pre-existing decision-making mindsets. In addition, cost-benefit analysis involves a utilitarian approach to decision-making which is at odds with the rights-based approaches that the authors have advanced in other work,[89] and which also does not seem to take account of demands for procedural and recognition justice.

If the challenges of embedding energy justice in policy-making at national level are significant, they become even more severe at the global level. Heffron et al. call for the adoption of due process at all levels of energy decision-making, including the global,[90] but a major limitation on the implementation of cosmopolitan theories of energy justice is that there are currently no comprehensive institutions of global governance[91] and of course, very strong objections in the anti-globalization literature to their adoption.[92] Taking cosmopolitan accounts of energy justice seriously thus requires attention to what legal instruments and structures would be necessary to deliver them, as well as how far it is possible—and legitimate—to overcome current barriers to global decision-making, especially those rooted in state sovereignty.

2. Energy Businesses

The definition of 'energy decision-makers' is drawn widely by energy justice scholars to include not only formal policy-makers, but also a range of other actors, including

[86] See Gillard, et al., (n 18), at 55, 57–8.
[87] See Heffron, et al., (n 10), at 172–5.
[88] See, e.g., R. Baldwin, M. Cave, and M. Lodge, *Understanding Regulation: Theory, Strategy and Practice* (Oxford University Press, 2nd edn., 2011), ch 15.
[89] See, e.g., McCauley, (n 6), at 11–17.
[90] See Heffron, et al., (n 10), at 170.
[91] See Jenkins, et al., (n 12), at 631.
[92] See, e.g., M.B. Steger, *Globalization: A Very Short Introduction* (Oxford University Press, 4th edn., 2017), chapters 4 and 8.

those running or working in energy-related businesses.[93] Although businesses operate within a framework of laws and regulations which already embody judgements about what is the 'just' or otherwise appropriate way for them to behave, these almost invariably leave considerable freedom for energy firms to act justly or unjustly. Justice-relevant decision-making may include, for example, high level decisions about how and where to invest in energy infrastructure; firm-level policies about the treatment of vulnerable customers; as well as 'on the ground' decisions to be made by individual employees, for instance about how best to respond to a potential grid overload.[94]

Again, there are important questions to be addressed about how and to what extent private businesses can be induced to act ethically, especially when maximizing profits for shareholders is seen, in some quarters, as the overriding moral imperative for firm managers,[95] and hence there is a risk that businesses might engage in what might be termed 'justice-washing'—that is, the adoption of the language of energy justice, while actually continuing to act unjustly.[96] There are extensive academic debates on corporate social responsibility[97] which energy justice scholars need to engage with, as well as to consider whether alternative, not-for-profit business models might create more supportive conditions for the pursuit of energy justice.[98]

3. Individuals

The prospect that individuals may not only be the beneficiaries of greater energy justice, but should themselves be regarded as agents of energy justice opens up further interesting debates. Hall draws attention to ideas of 'ethical consumption', which suggest that, once basic energy needs are satisfied, individuals may have moral duties, for instance, to use less energy or use it more efficiently, to favour less polluting energy sources, or to avoid energy suppliers which engage in unethical business practices.[99]

One question to be addressed here is if these are indeed moral obligations, or rather whether individuals engaging in such practices are acting in a morally heroic manner—that is, going beyond that which can reasonably be required of them. A second question is how to encourage ethical energy consumption, which is especially challenging for invisible, intangible, and instrumental products like electricity and gas.[100] Jenkins et al. suggest that improved information disclosure might be a way of encouraging more ethical and sustainable consumption practices.[101] Hall, however, argues that information strategies alone are not particularly effective in changing behaviour.[102] She

[93] Sovacool, et al., (n 5), at 1.
[94] See Sovacool and Dworkin, (n 4), at 1–3.
[95] See M. Friedman, 'The Social Responsibility of Business is to Increase its Profits', *The New York Times Magazine*, 13 September 1970, available at: http://umich.edu/~thecore/doc/Friedman.pdf.
[96] For examples, see Sovacool, et al., (n 11), at 686–7.
[97] For an overview, see J. Moon, *Corporate Social Responsibility: A Very Short Introduction* (Oxford University Press, 2014).
[98] See R. Hiteva and B Sovacool, 'Harnessing Social Innovation for Energy Justice: A Business Model Perspective' (2017) 107 *Energy Policy*, 631.
[99] See Hall, (n 78).
[100] Ibid., at 431.
[101] See Jenkins, et al., (n 6), at 178.
[102] See Hall, (n 78), at 432.

does, though, suggest that advancing duty-based ethical theories, which focus on motivations for ethical behaviour rather than upon distributional outcomes, might be a more fruitful avenue for energy justice scholars hoping to influence individuals' energy choices.[103]

4. Courts

A final set of potential agents of energy justice is the courts. Curiously, although Sovacool et al. include 'jurists' in their list of energy decision-makers,[104] there has been no sustained discussion of the role of the courts in advancing energy justice. This is a major omission from the literature, given the proposed role for energy justice as (one of) the guiding principle(s) for the future development of energy law.

As already noted, access to the courts is regarded as an aspect of procedural justice,[105] but what substantive duties on judges (if any) flow from energy justice principles? Do the courts themselves have a duty to facilitate access to justice, for instance by applying caps on litigation expenses as required by the Aarhus Convention for environmental litigation?[106] What scope is there for 'energy justice litigation', akin to climate change litigation? How creative should the courts be, taking account of principles of the Rule of Law and Separation of Powers, in developing new causes of action against governments and businesses to compensate victims of energy injustice and/or to advance distributive, procedural, and recognition justice in energy decision-making? And how realistic is it to expect the development of a single, global set of guiding principles for energy law, given jurisdictional pluralism, varying patterns of litigation, the pull of precedent, and the myriad context- and case-specific factors which influence judicial decisions in particular disputes?

IV. Conclusion

The ethical turn in energy scholarship is an important and highly-suggestive development, albeit one which is yet to make much impact in practice. Energy justice scholars are right to call our attention to the many injustices which are embedded within or are perpetrated by existing energy systems, and to argue for more holistic and human-centred energy decision-making, which understands energy as a socially-embedded phenomenon calling for a politically- and morally-informed response and not merely a technological or economic one.

However, as this brief survey has sought to show, there is a long way to go before energy justice moves beyond a 'motivational call to arms'[107] to become a coherent and fully developed philosophy or set of principles capable of guiding energy law and policy.

[103] Ibid., at 433.
[104] See Sovacool, et al., (n 5), at 1.
[105] See text accompanying (n 42).
[106] See (n 41), Article 9(5).
[107] See Fuller and McCauley, (n 65), at 3.

Admittedly, the intellectual demands of developing such a theory are great—requiring engagement with centuries of reflection on what justice requires, and decades of academic debate on related questions such as the conditions of effective policy-making, the merits of globalization, the meaning of corporate social responsibility, or the limits of legitimate judicial creativity. Nevertheless, while the energy justice literature is still in its infancy, claims about the greater academic rigour and clarity of the concept, as compared to the related ideas of environmental and climate justice, do not always stand up to scrutiny. The discipline is marked by academic hyper-activity and hyper-innovation, seemingly driven by the desire to stake a claim in an exciting new field, rather than to engage in the hard intellectual labour of developing properly grounded and defensible theoretical claims or thinking through the implications of securing just energy decisions in practice. Nevertheless, this means that there is much interesting work to be done, and a great deal for energy lawyers in particular to get their teeth into.

3

Energy Poverty and Energy Access

A Legal Analysis

Íñigo del Guayo

I. Introduction

Energy has become an important tool in the fight against global poverty. This is because access to energy services is directly related to a better quality of life for humans: countries with lower poverty rates have a greater energy consumption. This chapter deals with energy poverty and energy access, and there is at first instance the need to clarify the distinction, if any, between both concepts. We should also inquire about the meaning of another group of concepts used within international or national legal and/or policy documents, such as fuel poverty, energy vulnerability, energy equity, and energy affordability.

Energy justice and energy poverty have become central and paramount issues of energy transition towards a sustainable energy system and they have a growing importance within international literature.[1] Within the wider concept of energy distributive justice (understood as the equitable distribution of the benefits and burdens of energy activities) energy poverty is also a key issue. The fight against energy poverty is one of the core issues of distributive justice nowadays. This chapter also reviews other approaches to energy poverty, not so directly connected with distributional issues, but with other branches of energy justice, in particular social justice, recognizing that energy injustice in the form of energy poverty cannot be separated from other social ills, such as subordination based on caste, race, gender, or indigeneity.[2]

II. Energy Poverty Within an International Context

The United Nations' 2030 Agenda for Sustainable Development was adopted in 2015 by 193 of its members, offering seventeen Sustainable Development Goals (SDGs)

[1] B.K. Sovacool and M.H. Dworkin (eds), *Global Energy Justice. Problems, Principles, and Practices* (Cambridge University Press, 2014) and A. Halff, B.K. Sovacool, and J. Rozhon (eds), *Energy Poverty. Global Challenges and Local Solutions* (Oxford University Press, 2014).

[2] See Chapter 1 within this book.

Íñigo del Guayo, Energy Poverty and Energy Access In: *Energy Justice and Energy Law*. Edited by Íñigo Del Guayo, Lee Godden, Donald N. Zillman, Milton Fernando Montoya, and José Juan González, Oxford University Press (2020).
DOI: 10.1093/oso/9780198860754.003.0003

to 'transform our world'.[3] These SDGs include eradicating poverty and hunger, and ensuring access to affordable, clean energy. Energy is a crucial part of people's daily life, therefore access to it will be a determining factor in people's quality of life. Sustainable Development Goals number 1 ('No poverty': SDG1), and, in particular, number 7 ('Affordable and Clean Energy': SDG7) deal with the issues analysed in this chapter. The goals contained in SDG7 specifically refer to the need of ensuring 'access to affordable, reliable, sustainable and modern energy for all'. This chapter addresses the ideas contained in SDG7. They provide an introduction to the distinction between energy access and affordability (or fuel poverty),[4] and connect with the so-called 'energy trilemma' of security, efficiency, and sustainability, in relation to energy poverty.[5] The international organization 'Sustainable Energy for All' (SEforALL) works to help a faster achievement of SDG7. There are other regional initiatives of the same nature, such as the so-called 2017 winter package of the EU, which refers to 'clean energy for all'.[6]

III. Conceptual Clarification

A. The Three Meanings of Energy Poverty

The expression energy poverty has a variety of meanings, all or most of them with legal implications. In general, one should accept that energy poverty is the user's perspective of energy justice.[7] In most instances, energy poverty becomes identified with fuel poverty in the sense of the lack of affordability to pay monthly energy bills for electricity and/or gas at dwellings. However, energy poverty has also two other meanings: (i) the use of polluting fuels; and (ii) the lack of energy efficiency (i.e. excessive use of energy to meet energy needs). In these meanings, poverty is not linked to low incomes (affordability), but rather to other meanings of 'poor': unsatisfactory, pitiable, lacking, underachieving and so on. Is there a fourth meaning of energy poverty in the sense of lack of (physical) access to the energy resource? Even though energy access and energy poverty are different, sometimes they become identified, particularly in the media, as including within energy poverty the lack of access to energy (i.e. the lack of infrastructure giving access to the energy resource).

[3] United Nations, 'Transforming our world: The 2030 Agenda for Sustainable Development', Resolution adopted by the General Assembly on 25 September 2015 A/Res/70/1, http://www.un.org/ga/search/view_doc.asp?symbol=A/RES/70/1&Lang=E, accessed 14 July 2019 (hereafter SDG).

[4] See section III.B.

[5] See section VII.A.

[6] https://ec.europa.eu/energy/en/topics/energy-strategy-and-energy-union/clean-energy-all-europeans, accessed 14 July 2019. See Catherine Redgwell and Lavanya Rajamani, Chapter 4 within this book.

[7] See Aileen McHarg, Chapter 2 within this book.

B. Energy Access and Energy Poverty: Two Similar But Different Concepts

There is an inextricable link between poverty and access to energy. Both go hand in hand. Where there is poverty, there is no access or low access to energy, and where there is no access or low access to energy, there is poverty. This is why the lack of access to energy tends to be identified with energy poverty. Actually, the International Energy Agency (IEA) defines energy poverty with the following wording: 'a lack of access to modern energy services. These services are defined as household access to electricity and clean cooking facilities (e.g. fuels and stoves that do not cause air pollution in houses)'.[8] When the reason for not having access is the lack of financial resources to build the infrastructure needed, then there is an obvious argument to build a wide concept of energy poverty covering both the lack of (physical) access to infrastructure and the lack of affordability (or fuel poverty).

However, energy poverty and energy access are different things.

There is energy access when consumers can actually reach the energy source, be it electricity or other fuel. There is fuel poverty when consumers cannot afford their electricity or/and gas bills. In general terms many people living in developing countries do not have access to energy resources (lack of access would therefore be the main form of energy poverty in those countries), whereas in Western societies energy poverty mainly defines the form of fuel poverty. Combining access and affordability, we can identify four different situations.

First, under ideal circumstances, consumers should enjoy access to energy and should be able to pay for it. However, that is not always the case and this is where the difference between energy access and energy poverty (in the sense of 'fuel poverty') lies and can be easily perceived.

Second, there is an extreme situation when individuals have no access to energy and could not pay for it if they did have access. This is certainly the case of many people in underdeveloped regions of the world.

Third, there is the opposite situation when individuals have the financial means to pay for the energy they need, but they do not have access to energy. This situation does not seem to be as frequent as the first one, but one can imagine a new urban development where the new group of dwellings is not properly connected to the electricity network, nor to the gas one. The situation in which there is not fuel poverty but there is not access to energy is also conceivable in the case of rich societies, but who have difficult access to the resource. This was the case of Western societies, which suffered for decades difficulties in accessing oil and gas resources from remote places (in the case of the USA, the oil sands and shale gas revolutions have changed that).

Fourth, some consumers may have access to energy, since they can reach the energy source, but they might be unable to pay for it when they suffer from fuel poverty. This

[8] https://www.iea.org/about/glossary/e/, accessed 15 July 2019.

fourth situation explains why there are consumers who suffer energy poverty in developed countries.

Taking into account those four situations, it could be possible, from an economic point of view, to cover the concepts of access and affordability (the reverse side of fuel poverty), under the wider concept of 'meeting energy demand'. Access will guarantee demand insofar as consumers can actually reach the energy resource, but only if access is supplemented by affordability, demand would be fully satisfied.

There is a clear connection between energy access and energy poverty, in the sense of the use of polluting fuels: for example, the EU is deploying efforts towards 'clean energy for all'[9] (i.e. efforts to facilitate access to energy sources which do not harm the environment).

The IEA is mainly focused on energy access. Its *World Energy Outlook 2018* stresses that the number of people without electricity access fell below 1 billion for the first time in 2017, and that the number of people without access to clean cooking facilities has been gradually declining, but still amounted to 2.7 billion people globally in 2017. The IEA is of the opinion that to provide 'universal electricity for all, decentralised systems, led by solar PV in off-grid and mini-grid systems, is the least-cost solution for three-quarters of the additional connections needed'. However, 'grid extension has still a role to play, especially in urban areas'. Access to 'clean cooking relies primarily on the deployment of LPG, natural gas and electricity in urban areas and a range of technologies in rural areas'.[10]

IV. Fuel Poverty and its Indicators

A. British Pioneering in the Definition of Fuel Poverty

When is there fuel poverty? The first indicator of energy poverty was proposed by Boardman in 1991,[11] who considered energy poverty to exist when there was a 10 per cent (or more) share for energy expenditures in a household's income. For many years, that was the only available 'definition'. The British *Warm Homes and Energy Conservation Act 2000* was a pioneer in providing a legal definition of energy poverty and stated that a person is to be regarded as living in fuel poverty if he is a member of a household living on a lower income in a home, which cannot be kept warm at reasonable cost. One year later, and using the indicator of Boardman, the 'UK Fuel Poverty Strategy 2001' defined a fuel poor household as one that cannot afford to keep adequately warm at reasonable cost, because it needs

[9] Under the umbrella of 'clean energy for all' the European Commission submitted a package of draft Directives and Regulations in 2017, the so-called 'Winter Package', which won approval in 2018: https://ec.europa.eu/energy/en/topics/energy-strategy-and-energy-union/clean-energy-all-europeans, accessed 14 July 2019.

[10] https://www.iea.org/energyaccess/, accessed 15 July 2019.

[11] B. Boardman, *Fuel Poverty: From Cold Homes to Affordable Warmth* (Belhaven Press, 1991).

to spend more than 10 per cent of its income on all fuel use and to heat its home to an adequate standard of warmth.[12] The *Energy Action Scotland 2016* defines fuel poverty of a household in similar terms, and adds that if over 20 per cent of income is required, then this is termed as extreme poverty.[13] The method that links income to expenditure is used in England, also by means of the low-income high cost (LIHC) indicator. Under this indicator, a household is considered to be fuel poor if it has required fuel costs that are above average (the national median level), and were it to spend that amount, it would be left with a residual income below the official poverty line.[14]

B. Alternative Indicators of Fuel Poverty

Two other approaches exist to measure fuel poverty. The first approach compares the level of domestic energy services achieved versus a pre-defined standard. It measures indoor temperatures and identifies households unable to guarantee an adequate indoor thermal regime. This approach is usually based on standards fixed by the World Health Organization (WHO). According to those standards, a satisfactory heating regime for vulnerable households is 23°C in the living room and 18°C in other occupied rooms. For other households it is 21°C in the living room and 18°C in other occupied rooms.[15] Temperatures in the higher end of the range are often recommended for population subgroups physically vulnerable to cold (e.g. elderly, infirm, or children) and for the main living room. The disadvantage of this method is that indoor temperature surveys (and of other energy services) are almost non-existent.

The second alternative approach relies on a household's self-assessment of its living conditions. It is often implemented through three indicators: (i) inability to keep the house adequately warm; (ii) arrears on utility bills; and (iii) presence of a leaking roof, damp walls, floors or foundation, or rot in window frames or floor. These are all attributes related to what is consensually considered a basic life necessity by over 95 per cent of the EU population. This is the only approach that currently allows comparison across EU Member States.[16]

[12] https://webarchive.nationalarchives.gov.uk/+/http:/www.berr.gov.uk/files/file16495.pdf, accessed 15 July 2019.

[13] There is a pending Bill at the Scottish Parliament on the issue, the *Fuel Poverty (Target, Definition and Strategy) (Scotland) Bill 2018*.

[14] Department for Business, Energy & Industrial Strategy, *Annual Fuel Poverty Statistics Report, 2018 (2016 Data)* (London, 2018). See H. Thomson and C. Snell, 'Quantifying the Prevalence of Fuel Poverty across the European Union' (2013) 52 *Energy Policy*, 563.

[15] WHO, *Health Impact of Low Indoor Temperatures: Report on a WHO Meeting: Copenhagen 11–14 November 1985* (WHO: Regional Office for Europe, 1987).

[16] J.D. Healy, *Housing, Fuel Poverty, and Health: A Pan-European Analysis* (Ashgate Publishing, 2004) and S. Bouzarovski, 'Energy Poverty in the European Union: Landscapes of Vulnerability' (2014) 3 *Wiley Interdisciplinary Reviews: Energy and Environment*, 276. The information within this paragraph about the two alternative methods has been extracted (or quoted) from S. Tirado-Herrero, 'Energy Poverty Indicators: A Critical Review of Methods' (2017) 26 *Indoor and Built Environment*, 1018.

V. Poverty and Energy Poverty

Poor people cannot afford not only energy services, but also other basic services (housing, water, transport, etc.). From this perspective, one may argue that fuel poverty is nothing but one particular (and relevant) aspect of poverty, among other possible ones. Fuel poverty (or the absence of energy affordability) is currently an issue even in developed countries, notwithstanding there is universal and reliable access to modern energy services. This could be an argument in favour of accepting that energy poverty is a specific form of poverty distinct from any other else. However, fuel poverty in developed countries is only a signal that the number of poor people is growing in said countries, due mainly to the consequences of the financial and economic crisis, which started in 2008. The other two meanings of energy poverty (the use of polluting fuels and the lack of efficiency) explain why energy poverty is not a mere variation of poverty. With regard to efficiency, the 'UK Fuel Poverty Strategy' (2001) concluded that a household could be suffering from energy poverty not only due to low incomes and high-energy costs, but also due to energy inefficiency.[17] In relation to the use of polluting fuels, this kind of energy poverty is not linked to low income. Consequently, energy poverty (other than fuel poverty) is not an aspect of poverty. Income or fuel poverty is a key driver but not the sole cause or even a necessary condition for energy poverty.

VI. Energy Poverty and Vulnerability

The gas and electricity industries are 'network bound industries'. Consequently, every electricity and gas consumer is a vulnerable consumer, since consumption is dependent on a physical connection.[18] Consumers will be supplied if and when the owner of the network wants and at the price the energy company wants. That is precisely why those industries must be regulated, to protect consumers from the monopolistic power of the energy company. Within that context, consumers' protection is a traditional part of energy law. However, in recent times a new concept of a vulnerable consumer has emerged, and that is the consumer who cannot afford to pay for his or her energy bills.[19] Addressing this problem exceeds the ordinary boundaries of consumption law

[17] https://webarchive.nationalarchives.gov.uk/+/http:/www.berr.gov.uk/files/file16495.pdf, accessed 15 July 2019.

[18] In some texts of the EU, vulnerability is a condition of all consumers of electricity. In point 9 of the European Charter on the Rights of Energy Consumers, it is stated that the existence of monopolies in the electricity sector limits the freedom of choice and the possibilities of changing suppliers, aggravates the lack of information and 'therefore, increases the vulnerability of consumers': European Parliament Resolution of 19 June 2008, *Towards a European Charter on the Rights of Energy Consumers*. The European Parliament refers to the *Communication from the Commission. Towards a European Charter on the Rights of Energy Consumers*, Brussels: COM(2007)386 final, Brussels, 5 July 2007.

[19] For a comprehensive meaning of the concept, see C. Graham, 'Ofgem, Reforming Regulation and Vulnerability' (2017) 21 *Utilities Law Review*, 154–158.

(governmental rules protecting consumers within a bilateral relationship and, thus, within the scope of commutative justice) and enters the realm of a new energy justice paradigm, which encompasses the exigencies of distributive justice. Additionally, contemporary law tends to include within consumers' rights not only the right of access to energy, whatever form it may adopt, but particularly the right of access to clean or sustainable energy.

The fight against energy poverty is something different from the protection of vulnerable customers, but in reality, they are difficult concepts to separate. Both concepts normally go together. However, energy poverty is somewhat wider than the vulnerability of some electricity customers. Just as a vulnerable customer is in a situation of energy poverty, so is a customer whose consumption is inefficient and for that reason their consumption is more expensive than normal. Energy inefficiency could be understood, in certain circumstances, as a form of energy poverty.

VII. Energy Poverty and the Three Objectives of Energy Policy

A. The Energy 'Trilemma': Security, Efficiency, and Sustainability

In almost every single country in the world, national energy policy pursues three key objectives: security, economic efficiency, and sustainability.[20] This constitutes a traditional 'trilemma' for governments, which must balance its three components, for the sake of prosperity and competitiveness. The goals contained in SDG7 specifically refer to the need of ensuring access to affordable, reliable, sustainable, and modern energy.[21] The goals contained in SDG7 provide a convenient introduction to the issues discussed in this chapter. It shows that access and affordability are so closed that they both tend to be included in a wide meaning of energy poverty: there is energy poverty either if a human being has no access to the energy resource or if, once he or she gets access, cannot afford to pay for the said resource.[22]

Depending on democratic decisions taken in each country, there are times in which security may be pursued at the expense of the other two aims, and vice versa. Whereas from 1980 to 2000 economic efficiency (by means of liberalization and privatization)

[20] To pick only one example among hundreds, we read about Turkish energy policy, the following statements: 'To reduce the risks arising from energy supply security and to ensure that energy is produced and used more efficiently parallel to the significant increase in energy demand, the formation of free market conditions and the development of a competitive investment climate became the key strategies. (. . .) And finally, there has to be affordable, reliable and environmental friendly energy supply all over the country to have sustainable environment': S. Erdongan, A. Gedikli, and S.Y. Genç, 'An Overview of Turkey's National Energy Policies', in S.S. Koç, A. Orhan, and S.Y. Genç (eds), *Politico-Economic Evaluation of Current Issues* (Cambridge International Academics, 2018), 162.

[21] See section II.

[22] An analysis of energy poverty in the sense of lack of access is contained in C.J.K. Sandoval, 'Energy Access is Energy Justice: the Yurok Tribe's Trail-blazing Work to Close the Native American Reservation Electricity Gap', in R. Salter, C.G. Gonzalez, and E.A.K. Warner (eds), *Energy Justice. US and International Perspectives* (Elgar, 2018), 166 (hereafter Salter, et al., *Energy Justice*).

was maximized over security and sustainability, in present times (particularly after the *2015 Paris Agreement*[23]) environmental sustainability is the main driver of legal reform: the world must fight climate change.

B. Energy Poverty and the Energy 'Trilemma'

We may draw a parallelism between the three meanings of energy poverty, and those three policy objectives. Trying to connect energy poverty with one of the three energy policy objectives is not an intellectual diversion, but rather a prerequisite to answer key constitutional and legal questions: who is to guarantee accessibility and/or affordability? Who is expected to put an end to energy poverty: governments and regulators or markets and companies? The fact that energy poverty is linked to one or other policy objective has juridical consequences, since legal instruments to achieve, say, energy security differ from those capable of promoting energy sustainability.

It is difficult to say which policy objective is linked to energy poverty in the sense of fuel poverty. Energy security provides governments with a reason to regulate, to intervene, and to interfere in free markets. Energy (economic) efficiency provides governments with reasons to fight against all those obstacles, which hinder economic freedom of energy actors (producers and consumers). There are arguments that fuel poverty is connected to both energy security and economic efficiency.

If one of the tasks of governments is to guarantee that energy supply is reliable and that consumers can have access to energy (and pay for it) whenever they need it (energy being a basic means of life), in the case of citizens who suffer fuel poverty, governments are obliged to take legal and financial steps to help those citizens. Fuel poverty is, therefore, a component of energy security. This conclusion is reinforced when considering the close links between energy poverty and access, so strong that sometimes energy poverty is defined to be the lack of access to energy. Public and private efforts to have access to the energy source, within or without the country's boundaries, are a clear component of energy security.

There are also arguments in favour of considering fuel poverty as part of economic efficiency. Let us start by referring to those energy policies of liberalization and privatization promoted by the World Bank and the International Monetary Fund under the so called *Washington Consensus* (1989). Within that policy framework was the assumption that competition within energy markets should manage to lower energy prices, because of the free market, and prices will precisely reflect how much a consumer is ready to pay for the supply of energy. In other words, there are consumers who suffer fuel poverty because of two economic inefficiencies. On the one hand, prices may be artificially too high due to the abuse of the dominant position by energy monopolies or oligopolies. On

[23] 21st session of the Conference of the Parties (COP 21) to the United Nations Framework Convention on Climate Change (UNFCCC) and the 11th session of the Meeting of the Parties to the Kyoto Protocol (CMP 11), Paris 2015, at https://unfccc.int/sites/default/files/english_paris_agreement.pdf, accessed 15 July 2019.

the other hand, final prices may include not only costs related to the supply of energy, but also inefficient or abusive regulatory costs. By promoting free energy markets, governments will be directly fighting those inefficiencies and indirectly fighting energy poverty. Energy poverty is, therefore, a component of energy economic efficiency.

Two of the meanings of energy poverty (the use of polluting fuels and the lack of energy efficiency) are clearly linked to the third energy policy, that of environmental sustainability. There are, of course, arguments to link those two meanings with the other two policy objectives. For example, the more efficiency we gain, the less dependent a country is on foreign supplies and the more secure it becomes. The use of polluting fuels influences negatively on efficiency, since there are externalities, which energy prices do not always reflect properly and, hence, the system is inefficient in economic terms. Notwithstanding those arguments, it seems evident that those two meanings of energy poverty have to do mainly with sustainability.

The above exercise of attaching the fight against energy poverty to one or several of the three components of the 'energy trilemma' can be compared with some academic endeavours of identifying to which of the eight core principles of energy justice, energy poverty relates. The eight core principles of justice are: (i) availability; (ii) sustainability; (iii) affordability; (iv) due process; (v) transparency and accountability; (vi) intra-generational equity; (vii) inter-generational equity; and (viii) responsibility. Principles (i) (availability), (iii) (affordability), and (vi) (intra-generational equity) 'require the eradication of energy poverty and the provision of high quality energy services on an equitable basis to all'.[24] The call for an 'intra-generational equity' is a call for a fair distribution of the benefits of energy resources among citizens. Principles ii (sustainability) and vii (inter-generational equity) would be related to energy poverty in the use of polluting fuels.

C. Brief Remarks on Efficiency and Poverty

There are two important caveats to bear in mind when reading the expression energy efficiency in policy and/or legal documents.

First, energy efficiency has a technical as well as an economic meaning. In technical terms, energy efficiency improves when less energy is consumed to achieve the same output. In economic terms, there is energy efficiency when prices reflect the optimal allocation of the resource. Energy efficiency, in technical terms, is part of the third objective (sustainability) of the 'trilemma', since the reduction of consumption contributes to a healthy environment.

Second, economic efficiency cannot be restricted to allocative efficiency, which is optimized in free markets under bilateral transactions, but one must also consider distributive efficiency, measuring if and how well richness is distributed among all. In the field

[24] The eight core principles of energy justice and the quotation are extracted from Salter, et al., *Energy Justice* (n 22) 3.

of energy, allocative efficiency is reached in energy markets' transactions (informal or organized pools), whereas distributive efficiency is the result of a proper regulation of said markets. Private law and commutative justice are linked to allocative efficiency, and public law and distributive justice are linked to distributive efficiency. The consequence of this with regard to energy poverty is that we are not to contrast (energy) economic efficiency against public aid to consumers to guarantee energy affordability. From a liberal point of view, the optimal allocation of resources (i.e. allocative efficiency) is only reachable within free competitive markets. Fighting fuel poverty usually means governmental interference in markets, including public subsidies or/and the prohibition to cut off energy supply to some consumers unable to pay their bills. This interference must be avoided in accordance with liberal economists, since it distorts competition and ultimately hinders allocative efficiency. However, economic efficiency is both allocative and distributive. Consequently, guaranteeing that every citizen has a share in the resource by means of some public instruments outside energy markets is not necessarily inefficient per se, insofar as it satisfies distributive efficiency and keeps the disturbance of free markets to a limit.

VIII. Energy Poverty and Energy Justice

A. Which Justice to Fight Against Poverty?

The consequences of Hurricane Charley in 2004, in terms of the sky-rocketing increase of the price of a number of essential products, lead some academics to discuss the legitimacy of a number of laws passed by the Florida legislature to prohibit abusive prices. Opponents to said laws said they interfere with free markets, which promote well-being and respect individual freedom. People in favour of those laws argued the general well-being was harmed when there are exorbitant prices in difficult times, and measuring the general well-being must include the suffering of those who cannot afford to satisfy their basic needs in an emergency. Supporters of the laws against abusive prices also argued that free markets are not always truly 'free'. Besides those considerations about markets and general well-being, they were angry against people who behaved like a buzzard towards those who had lost everything in the hurricane. This last argument adopts a moral conception of justice: outrage grows when somebody gets what he or she does not deserve. How far should avarice go to take advantage of those suffering due to the hurricane? This discussion leads to the two main conceptions of justice: one based on virtue, one based on liberty. Justice based on virtue is something of ancient times, and is rooted in the conception of justice of Aristotle and Thomas Aquinas. Justice based on liberty is the main current stream of thinking of modernity, in accordance with Kant. Justice principles defining our rights are not to be based in any particular vision of virtue. On the contrary, a just society respects the freedom of each one to choose its own vision of a good life.[25]

[25] M.J. Sandel, *Justice. What's the Right Thing to Do?* (Farrar, Straus and Giroux, 2009), 11.

With regard to energy, there are important specificities of this commodity (which is simultaneously a service) which pushes into a special consideration of how justice principles operate in the sector. In the energy sector there would be elements to defend that the fight against poverty relies on a conception of justice based on both liberty and virtue. Individuals suffering from energy poverty cannot be considered truly free, since they lack a basic element to have a decent life and make truly free choices. Energy poverty can be rooted in a mistaken regulatory framework, which allows energy companies to make profits they do not deserve, at the expense of vulnerable consumers.

B. Energy Poverty and Distributive Justice

The cry for justice in the energy sector and, particularly, for the eradication of energy poverty is based on a substantive (or moral) concept of justice. There is a lack of justice whenever there is a human being who has no access to the energy resource or no ability to pay for energy services. He or she has neither one nor the other. One of the fundamentals of that assessment is that every individual has the right to energy insofar as clean energy services are an essential part of a decent life and, thus, of human dignity.[26]

It has been noted that 'energy justice is composed of three central tenets, namely distributive, procedural, and recognition justice. Distributive justice examines the allocation of the costs and benefits of the energy system across society'.[27] Therefore, the quest for access to clean energy for all is rooted in distributive justice. Equitable distribution of the costs and benefits of energy resources is the core element of distributive justice. In a global energy system distributive justice concerns are related also to an equitable distribution of costs and benefits across space (i.e. among nations) and time (i.e. among generations).[28] If every citizen has the right to a proportion of the energy resources with which its nation is allotted (within its boundaries or imported from abroad), the lack of affordability to pay the electricity and/or gas bills (i.e. fuel poverty) represents a direct attack to distributive justice.[29]

[26] See section IX.A. The European Commission recognizes that energy poverty affects living conditions and health: 'A Framework Strategy for a Resilient Energy Union with a Forward-Looking Climate Change Policy. Energy Union', *Communication from the Commission to the European Parliament, the Council, the European Economic and Social Committee, the Committee of the Regions and the European Investment Bank*, COM (2015) 80 final, Brussels, 25 February 2015, 12.

[27] The definition is taken from Salter, et al., *Energy Justice* (n 22) 3.

[28] B.K. Sovacool and M.H. Dworkin (eds), *Global Energy Justice. Problems, Principles, and Practices* (Cambridge University Press, 2014) , 13.

[29] For an extensive analysis of how property rights regimes guarantee 'that the distribution of wealth will not be equal; some will get richer than others', see J.W. Hamilton and N. Bankes, 'Different Views of the Cathedral: The Literature on Property Law Theory', in A. McHarg, B. Barton, A. Bradbrook, and L. Godden (eds), *Property and the Law in Energy and Natural Resources* (Oxford University Press, 2010), 19. There are several references in that chapter to the so-called 'Lockean proviso', as contained in J. Locke, *Second Treatise of Government*, Project Gutenberg eBook, available at http://www.gutenberg.org/ebooks/7370. It is there that we read the following statement by Locke: everyone has 'an equal right to the earth and its natural produce'.

Basically, there are two different approaches to fight fuel poverty: one favours direct public intervention to help citizens to pay their energy bills, whereas the other one favours a more holistic group of instruments to help poor people to escape from poverty by themselves, and, hence, from fuel poverty. Whereas the first approach represents distributive justice, as such, the second approach focuses on commutative justice. There are several ways to fight fuel poverty in a distributive justice context: community ownership, price capping (to guarantee energy affordability); among measures to protect consumers, some are directly addressed to fight energy poverty, particularly measures to protect vulnerable consumers, by means of establishing public service obligations (PSOs). These PSOs may have several versions, but there are two main ones: (i) subsidies (or a discount on the bill) to help a particular group of vulnerable consumers; and (ii) governmental control over prices to keep them within a limit, so that they do not become abusive prices.[30] Commutative justice represents an equality between two parties within a bilateral transaction, as opposed to distributive justice, meaning the proportional share of each person in accordance with a distributive criterion.[31] Commutative energy justice is achieved within transactions between producers and consumers at a certain price, which matches the intersection between supply and demand. By helping people to escape from poverty by themselves, rather than paying their energy bills, governments would be helping distributive equity to take place in contractual transactions, and there will be no need of direct public intervention.

IX. The Fight Against Energy Poverty Through Law

The hesitation about which energy policy objective is linked to energy poverty[32] brings to the forefront the existence of two confronting legal and/or institutional approaches to the problem of fuel poverty.

A. Energy Access and Affordability as a Human Right

The concepts of energy access and energy poverty are directly linked to the right to energy, as a fundamental human right. There is no stand-alone right to energy in present times, but it is obvious how essential energy is for a decent standard of living.[33] There is room for future recognition of such a human right. In current times there would be arguments to include the right to energy within the right to health or/and a healthy

[30] See section IX.B.
[31] For an in depth discussion of both types of justice, see E.J. Weinrib, *The Idea of Private Law* (Oxford University Press, 2012).
[32] See section VII.B, second paragraph.
[33] Salter, et al., *Energy Justice* (n 22) 6.

environment. Recent academic contributions have recognized the potential of the human rights impact assessment framework in energy access projects. Notwithstanding the increase of investment in energy projects in developing countries—aimed to solve the lack of access to energy of millions of people—those projects have involved human rights violations.[34]

B. Legal Approaches Related to Energy Security

The first approach connects fuel poverty to energy security, something that has legal consequences. Fuel poverty as part of energy security is rooted in the original idea, widely spread among continental European countries, of energy services as public services. By creating a public institution enjoying monopolistic rights, and charging it with the task of performing a public service, governments try to assure the constant delivery of the (energy) service, with no interruption and under equal conditions to everybody. This is expressed, in French, under the three 'laws' of the public service: *loi de la regularitè, loi de la continuité, et loi de la egalité* (the law of regularity, the law of continuity, and the law of equality). Within the *public service* tradition law must guarantee a secure and reliable energy supply to every single consumer. But this aim is frustrated when some consumers cannot afford the price of its energy. In this situation, there are two options. The law may impose upon energy companies the obligation to supply the energy, under certain circumstances, even when the consumers do not pay (and the price will be paid by the energy company at its own expense, with a simultaneous decrease of its income). Once there is a public decision not to allow companies to cut off supply when some consumers cannot afford to pay their bills, one key question arises: who is (or are) to pay the bills of those consumers who cannot afford to pay their bills? One option is that companies bear the cost, as a PSO. Alternatively, law may require that either the rest of the consumers or taxpayers finance the costs, which consumers in fuel poverty do not pay. This latter alternative seems to be better linked with distributional justice than the former one. This approach leads to the establishment of subsidies in favour of consumers suffering fuel poverty. In some jurisdictions a special 'bonus' has been introduced in favour of vulnerable consumers, in the form of a discount of their bill. In those countries where the discount is to be borne by energy companies, there is an obvious risk that companies pass the difference onto the rest of the consumers, thus distorting the retail market. Consequently, it seems better also for a transparent electricity market that the 'bonus' is borne by the taxpayers. At the end, it can be argued that fuel poverty is not really rooted in the energy system itself (fuel

[34] D.S. Olawuyi, 'Energy (and Human Rights) for All: Addressing Human Rights Risks in Energy Access Projects', in Salter, et al. (n 22) 73; Y.V. Cárdenas and P. Urteaga-Crovetto, 'The Concept of Global Justice and Its Contribution towards Better Understanding and Resolving Natural Resource Conflicts', in A. Manirabona and Y.V. Cárdenas (eds), *Extractive Industries and Human Rights in an Era of Global Justice: New Ways of Resolving and Preventing Conflicts* (LexisNexis, 2019).

poverty is only an aspect of poverty), and, hence, it is a 'social benefit' rather than an 'electricity benefit'.[35]

Some international institutions are not in favour of subsidies. The World Energy Council (WEC), for example, recognizes that in developing countries there is a combination of low gross domestic product and low energy equity (i.e. low accessibility and affordability). Consequently, they must strike a balance between ensuring energy affordability and creating the investment conditions to support infrastructure expansion. In this situation, governments are tempted to introduce subsidies. The WEC is of the opinion that in the short term, subsidies may be vital for lower-income consumers. Subsidies may also help to promote economic and social programmes. However, the final assessment of the WEC about energy subsidies is negative, since they can be costly to deploy, are contentious to remove, and tend to decrease overall performance on the energy trilemma over the long term (case studies demonstrate how long-term subsidies erode profitability of utilities, stall improvements in energy infrastructure, and stimulate inefficient energy use).[36]

In the EU and in many other countries, protection against energy poverty (in its triple dimension) takes place mainly by means of the imposition of PSOs upon electricity and gas companies. In accordance with EU law, PSOs may relate to security, including security of supply, regularity, quality, and price of supplies and environmental protection, including energy efficiency, energy from renewable sources, and climate protection.[37] The wording of EU law illustrates how the EU attaches the fight against energy poverty to PSOs. In turn, PSOs are related to the three meanings of energy poverty: security of supply (regularity of supplies); affordability (price of supplies); and sustainability (efficiency, renewable energies, and climate protection). There is a difference between electricity and gas in the EU with regard to the so-called *universal service*. The 2009 EU Electricity Directive states that all household electricity customers, and, where Member States deem it appropriate, small enterprises, enjoy *universal service*, that is the right to be supplied with electricity of a specified quality within their territory at reasonable, easily and clearly comparable, transparent, and non-discriminatory

[35] The EU 2009 Electricity Directive seems to be in favour of a system which helps vulnerable consumers within a social system scheme (rather than by means of electricity prices). It states that support to vulnerable consumers must not impede the effective opening of the market set or market functioning. The European Commission has expressly shown its preference to a protection through the general welfare system: 'Energy poverty can only be tackled by a combination of measures, mainly in the social field and within the competence of authorities on the national, regional or local levels. When phasing out regulated prices, Member States need to propose a mechanism to protect vulnerable consumers, which could preferably be provided through the general welfare system. If provided through the energy market, it could be implemented through schemes such as a solidarity tariff or as a discount on energy bills. The cost of such schemes needs to be covered by non-eligible consumers collectively. Hence, it is important that such a system is well targeted to keep overall costs low and to limit the distortions deriving from regulated prices (e.g. not increase further tariff deficits in Member States)': *A Framework Strategy for a Resilient Energy Union with a Forward-Looking Climate Change Policy. Energy Union, Communication from the Commission* (n 26) 13.

[36] World Energy Council, *World Energy Trilemma 2016*, published by the World Energy Council (2016) in partnership with Oliver Wyman.

[37] Article 3, 2, of both the Directive 2009/72/EC of the European Parliament and of the Council of 13 July 2009 concerning common rules for the internal market in electricity and repealing Directive 2003/54/EC, and of the Directive 2009/73/EC of the European Parliament and of the Council of 13 July 2009 concerning common rules for the internal market in gas and repealing Directive 2003/55/EC: both at OJ (2009) L 211/55.

prices. The Directive does also state that Member States must impose on distribution companies an obligation to connect customers to their network, under terms fixed by the Directive itself.[38] A key concept in EU law is that of vulnerability, since Member States must act appropriately to protect end customers and, in particular, to ensure adequate protection of vulnerable customers (a concept which is to be defined by each of the Member States). The concept of vulnerable consumer can refer to energy poverty and, among other things, to the prohibition of disconnection of these customers in critical periods.[39]

C. Legal Techniques Related to Economic Efficiency

The second legal and/or institutional approach to the problem of fuel poverty connects it to energy economic efficiency, and particularly with allocative efficiency, rather than with distributive efficiency.[40] The ideology behind this approach will favour economic growth to fight fuel poverty: if there is economic growth, there will be decent jobs and energy supplies would become affordable to all individuals and their families.

This seems to be the approach of the IEA. The second of the four main areas of work of the IEA is economic development (supporting free markets to foster economic growth and eliminate energy poverty). The most relevant idea here is that the IEA thinks that economic development (actually, free markets) is a way of fighting energy poverty, and of eliminating it.[41]

A similar, but different, approach is that of the WEC, which defines energy sustainability based on three core dimensions: energy security, energy equity, and environmental sustainability. Energy equity entails accessibility to energy and affordability of energy supply across the population. In other words, it entails the guarantee of 'energy access' and the fight against 'fuel poverty' (insofar as affordability means that consumers have sufficient means to pay their energy bills). Advancing energy access and addressing affordability (which the WEC considers to be two different things) are two

[38] Article 3, 3, of the 2009 Electricity Directive.

[39] Article 3, 7, of the 2009 Electricity Directive. See further, H. Vedder, M. Roggenkamp, A. Ronne, and I. del Guayo, 'UE Energy Law', in M. Roggenkamp, C. Redgwell, A. Ronne, and I. del Guayo (eds), *Energy Law in Europe. National, EU and International Regulation* (3rd ed, Oxford University Press, 2016), paragraphs 4.209–4.212. See S. Pye, A. Dobbins, et al., 'Energy Poverty and Vulnerable Consumers in the Energy Sector Across the EU: Analysis of Policies and Measures' (2015) 2 Policy Report, at http://www.insightenergy.org, accessed 15 July 2019. In Spain, due to the increasing number of consumers unable to pay their monthly electricity bills at the time of the economic crisis (2008–2016), Parliament created a social bonus, as a means of helping vulnerable electricity consumers. Additionally, the prohibition to cut off the supply of electricity, even when the bill is unpaid, to the so-called 'severe vulnerable consumers' was introduced in 2017: See I. del Guayo, 'Consumidores vulnerables en el sector eléctrico, lucha contra la pobreza energética y el bono social' (2016) 203 *Revista de Administración Pública*, 343. See M. Roggenkamp and L. Diestelmeier, Chapter 10 within this book.

[40] See section VII.C.

[41] http://www.iea.org/about/ourmission/, accessed 15 July 2019. The three other areas of focus of the IEA are: first (i), energy security (promoting diversity, efficiency, flexibility, and reliability for all fuels and energy sources); third (iii), environmental awareness (analysing policy options to offset the impact of energy production and use on the environment, especially for tackling climate change and air pollution) and; fourth (iv), working closely with partner countries, in particular emerging economies, to find solutions to shared energy and environmental concerns.

of the five focus areas, which the WEC identifies to accelerate energy transition.[42] For the WEC, expanding infrastructure is the only way (mainly in developing countries) to support energy access. It is interesting to note that, actually, investing in infrastructure is the only way, for the WEC, to support *advanced energy security, reliability, and access*. This wording clearly shows how the WEC connects access and security of supply, and, therefore, energy poverty with the lack of access. There is the need to promote private investment in infrastructure by means of regulatory changes, to lower business costs and increase competitiveness. However, the WEC is aware that solely expanding infrastructure is not enough to guarantee access. Efforts must also be made to promote distributed generation (solar and wind) in rural and/or remote communities that cannot currently be cost-effectively connected to the grid. Governments must put in force innovative mechanisms enabling affordable access for people. Examples are pay as you go business models and mobile banking solutions to promote the take-up of renewable-powered energy services. It must be noted that the WEC says *affordable access*, illustrating the links between access and affordability (which is the reverse side of energy poverty). In summary, the WEC tends to think that affordability is better achieved by means of infrastructure investment, which, in turn, depends on market conditions.

Beside access and affordability, the other focus areas, identified by the WEC to accelerate energy transition, are: (i) transforming energy supply; (ii) improving energy efficiency and managing demand; and (iii) decarbonizing the energy sector. The last two connect with two of the meanings of energy poverty, since the energy poverty also means poor energy efficiency standards, as well as the use of polluting fuels.[43]

X. Conclusions

There are three main meanings of energy poverty: fuel poverty, the lack of energy efficiency, and the use of polluting fuels. Affordability is the reverse side of fuel poverty. Energy access (accessibility) is a prerequisite of energy affordability (insofar as access means the physical connection between the energy resource and the consumer by means of the proper infrastructure). If there is no access, there is no energy. This is why there is a wider concept of energy poverty covering both the lack of access and the lack of affordability. There can be access, but fuel poverty, and there can be no access but no fuel poverty. The way to solve the lack of energy access is investment in new infrastructure. By allowing people suffering from energy poverty to build their own energy infrastructure using renewable energies (mainly solar and wind), the system is fighting against three modalities of energy poverty: (i) energy poverty as lack of access; (ii) energy poverty as fuel poverty; and (iii) energy poverty as the use of polluting

[42] The other three areas are: (i) transforming energy supply; (ii) improving energy efficiency and managing demand; and (iii) decarbonizing the energy sector.

[43] World Energy Council, *World Energy Trilemma 2016* and *World Energy Trilemma Index 2018*, published by the World Energy Council (2018 and 2016, respectively) in partnership with Oliver Wyman.

fuels. Fighting energy poverty is an exigence of energy justice, namely of distributive justice. Due to the evolution of the energy system, energy poverty is a distinct version of poverty. The protection of consumers and vulnerable consumers is a traditional part of energy law, but generally as part of procedural or commutative justice. However, new trends locate that area of law within distributive justice. There are several legal instruments to overcome energy poverty, one being the potential creation of a new human right: that of access to affordable and clean energy. The most common legal techniques have to do with the so-called 'energy trilemma'. Depending on which component of the trilemma energy poverty is related, some legal means will be used, in favour of other ones. When energy poverty is considered to be part of energy security, the way to address poverty is usually the imposition of PSOs upon companies. These encompass the prohibition to cut off the supply to certain customers, even if they do not pay their bill, as well as the setup of a subsidies regime. When energy poverty is considered to be part of energy (allocative) efficiency, the focus will be put on two other aspects of the problem: on the one hand, in energy access, and, hence, in investment in new infrastructure; on the other hand, in economic growth to help people to be able to pay for their own energy needs.

4

And Justice for All? Energy Justice in International Law

Catherine Redgwell and Lavanya Rajamani*

A just global energy system is one that is safe, reliable, fair, affordable, and also sustainable for current and future generations and the natural world. Importantly, energy justice also necessitates an energy path forward that is restorative, or minimizes and reverses the cumulative impacts of energy systems at local, regional, and global levels. This includes adverse impacts on the planet's ecosystems and on the communities disproportionately burdened by the impacts of energy production, distribution, and consumption.[1]

I. Introduction: Defining Energy Justice in an International Context

While most of the existing literature on energy justice is situated in the domestic context, connections with the international or global dimension are frequently made. As Salter et al. emphasize, 'energy justice' intersects with environmental justice, human rights, climate justice,[2] and indigenous rights,[3] all of which clearly have international legal dimensions.[4] Sovacool et al. define energy justice 'as a *global* energy system that fairly disseminates both the benefits and costs of energy services, and one that contributes to more representative and impartial energy decision-making'.[5] Their understanding is based

* Some parts of this chapter draw on C. Redgwell, 'Sustainable Development of National Energy Resources: What has International Law Got to Do with It?' (2017) 8 *Journal of Sustainable Development Law and Policy*, 1 and C. Redgwell, 'Sustainable Use of Natural Resources', in L. Krämer and E. Orlando (eds), *Principles of Environmental Law: Elgar Encyclopedia of Environmental Law Series* (Edward Elgar, 2018), vol 6.

[1] R. Salter, C. Gonzalez, and E. Warner, 'Energy Justice: Frameworks for Energy Law and Policy', in R. Salter, C. Gonzalez, and E. Warner (eds), *Energy Justice: US and International Perspectives* (Edward Elgar, 2018), 1, 2 (hereafter Salter, et al,. *Energy Justice*).

[2] D. McCauley, *Energy Justice: Re-Balancing the Trilemma of Security, Poverty and Climate Change* (Palgrave Macmillan, 2018), vi (hereafter McCauley, *Energy Justice*).

[3] See also K. Bickerstaff, G. Walker, and H. Bulkeley, 'Introduction: Making Sense of Energy Justice', in K. Bickerstaff, G. Walker, and H. Bulkeley (eds), *Energy Justice in a Changing Climate: Social Equity and Low-Carbon Energy* (Zed Books, 2013), 1, 2(hereafter Bickerstaff, et al., *Energy Justice*).

[4] Salter, et al., *Energy Justice* (n 1), 4.

[5] B. Sovacool, R. Heffron, D. McCauley, and A. Goldthau, 'Energy Decisions Reframed as Justice and Ethical Concerns' (2016) 1 *Nature Energy*, 1, 4 (emphasis added) (hereafter Sovacool, et al., *Energy Decisions Reframed*).

Catherine Redgwell and Lavanya Rajamani, And Justice for All? Energy Justice in International Law In: *Energy Justice and Energy Law*. Edited by Íñigo Del Guayo, Lee Godden, Donald N. Zillman, Milton Fernando Montoya, and José Juan González, Oxford University Press (2020). © The Several Contributors. DOI: 10.1093/oso/9780198860754.003.0004 on the application of notions of distributional and procedural justice alongside 'cosmopolitan' interpretations of equity and fairness,[6] and as such chimes with the four broad themes of distributional justice around which this book is organized.[7] More particularly, each of the eight core principles of their energy justice framework has an international dimension. The principles are: availability, sustainability, affordability,[8] due process, transparency and accountability, intra-generational equity, inter-generational equity, and responsibility.[9] Many of these principles are frequently emphasized and have distinct echoes in international energy law and policy, ranging from the Sustainable Development Goals (SDGs)[10] to the revised core principles of the International Energy Agency (IEA).[11] Sustainability in particular imports requirements of fairness and equity when sharing among states, intra-generationally and inter-generationally, the benefits and burdens of energy resource exploration and exploitation. The focus of this chapter is on locating energy justice in international law drawing on several of these core principles of energy justice reflecting strong distributional justice elements, namely: sustainability (Parts II and III), the intersection with human rights (Part III), intra-generational and inter-generational equity, and the related concept of common but differentiated responsibilities (CBDR), in particular in the climate change regime (Part IV), while Part V concludes.

II. Locating the Core Principles of Energy Justice in International Law: Towards a Sustainable Energy Future

'Sustainability' as a core principle of energy justice may roughly be encapsulated in the admonition that 'energy resources should not be depleted too quickly'.[12] Sustainability of energy resources has a relatively recent and chequered history, as does the development of sustainable development itself in international law.[13] While many of the

However, this is as much a definition of the *goal* of energy justice as it is a definition of it, with subsequent elaboration of their energy justice decision-making framework: see text at (n 8). Moreover, 'global' does not necessarily mean 'international' in the legal sense.

6 Ibid.

7 See United Nations Sustainable Development Goals Knowledge Platform https://sustainabledevelopment.un.org/sdg7 accessed 18 September 2019 and editors' Introduction to this book, in Chapter 1.

8 See also McCauley, *Energy Justice* (n 2) 6–9, emphasizing the themes of accessibility, availability, and sustainability (6–9) in his discussion of three 'core themes or tenets' of global energy justice' distribution, recognition, and procedural justice (13–17). This triumvirate approach is echoed in the energy justice 'trilemma' he identifies of energy security, energy poverty, and climate change.

9 Ibid., 5, Table 2: 'Energy justice decision-making framework'. This framework is intended to provide a constructive bridge between conceptual theory and energy practices, decision-making, and public choices.

10 See, e.g., SDG 7 (energy), discussed in the Introduction to this book, in Chapter 1.

11 Today the IEA's four main areas of focus are energy security, economic development (including elimination of energy poverty), environmental awareness, and global engagement; see further IEA, 'Our Mission' http://www.iea.org/about/ourmission/ accessed 16 September 2019 (hereafter IEA, 'Our Mission')

12 Sovacool, et al., *Energy Decisions Reframed* (n 5), 5.

13 See generally V. Barral, 'The Principle of Sustainable Development', in L. Krämer and E. Orlando (eds), *Principles of Environmental Law: Elgar Encyclopedia of Environmental Law Series* (Edward Elgar, 2018), vol 6, 103; P. Birnie, A. Boyle, and C. Redgwell, *International Law and the Environment* (OUP, 3rd edn, 2009), 115–27 (hereafter Birnie, et al., *International Law and Environment*); P. Sands and J. Peel, *Principles of International Environmental Law* (OUP, 4th edn, 2018), 217–29 (hereafter Sands and Peel, *Principles of IEL*); and specifically in

elements of sustainable development are autonomous concepts, the legal status of sustainable development as an umbrella concept is debated and 'no easy answer can be given to the question whether international law now requires that all development should be sustainable, or if so, what that would mean in specific terms'.[14] Nonetheless its impact on the evolution of international law can be seen in the *Gabčíkovo-Nagymaros* case, where the International Court of Justice (ICJ) referred to the 'need to reconcile economic development with protection of the environment [which] is aptly expressed in the concept of sustainable development'.[15] This invocation of, and reliance upon, the concept of sustainable development is a clear illustration of what Viñuales describes as the 'architectural function' performed in international law by principles in shaping 'a norm, a treaty (or an identifiable part of it), or a legally linked set of treaties'.[16]

Sustainable development—'development that meets the needs of the present without compromising the ability of future generations to meet their own needs'[17]—reflects notions of justice and equity including: the integration of economic and environmental development; the sustainable utilization of natural resources; and the equitable allocation of resources within the present generation and between present and future generations (inter- and intra-generational equity). The procedural elements of sustainable development comprise: cooperation between states; environmental impact assessment; and public participation in environmental decision-making and access to information. The integration of economic and environmental development engages customary international environmental law, notably the duty of prevention and vigilance, and to conduct an environmental impact assessment,[18] as well as 'new norms and standards' ... 'set forth in a great number of instruments'.[19] These instruments include multilateral environmental agreements such as those relating to climate change, in particular the 2015 Paris Agreement, that are relevant to energy use, and energy justice. These treaties, and the practice under them, are constantly evolving, and will continue to pose increasingly concrete sustainability demands on states. Thus, many energy resource development decisions are today 'sustainability constrained'.[20] Such constraints

the energy context, C. Redgwell, 'Sustainable Development of National Energy Resources: What Has International Law Got To Do With It? (2017) 8 *Journal of Sustainable Development Law and Policy*, 1.

[14] Birnie, et al., *International Law and Environment* (n 13) 125, and references contained therein.

[15] Case concerning *Gabčíkovo-Nagymaros Project (Hungary v Slovakia)* (Judgment) [1997] ICJ Rep 7, [140] (hereafter *Hungary v Slovakia*); see also Case concerning Pulp Mills on the River Uruguay (*Argentina v Uruguay*) (Provisional Measures) [2006] ICJ Rep 113, [80] and (Judgment) [2010] ICJ Rep 14, [177] (hereafter *Argentina v Uruguay* 2010). In the Indus Waters Kishenganga Arbitration (*Pakistan v India*) (Partial Award) [2013] PCA https://pcacases.com/web/sendAttach/1681 [450] (hereafter *Pakistan v India*), the tribunal recognized sustainable development as a principle.

[16] J. Viñuales, 'The Rio Declaration on Environment and Development: A Preliminary Study', in J. Viñuales (ed.), *The Rio Declaration on Environment and Development: A Commentary* (OUP, 2015), 21.

[17] World Commission on Environment and Development, *Our Common Future* (1987), 43; however, this definition 'begs elaboration' (Birnie, et al., *International Law and Environment* (n 13) 120.

[18] *Pakistan v India* (n 15) [450].

[19] *Hungary v Slovakia* (n 15) [140].

[20] R. Higgins, 'Natural Resources in the Case Law of the International Court', in A. Boyle and D. Freestone (eds), *International Law and Sustainable Development: Past Achievements and Future Challenges* (OUP, 1999), 111, citing N. Schrijver, *Sovereignty over Natural Resources: Balancing Rights and Duties* (CUP, 1997), 164–8. These constraints are evident in dispute settlement, with an observable shift in focus in the cases involving natural resources

are all the more urgent and important given the strong linkages between sustainable energy exploitation and consumption and combatting climate change, safeguarding food production, and ensuring access to secure energy supplies as part of sustainable development.[21]

However, in the international legal context, while interconnected, *sustainable* utilization does not mean *equitable* utilization.[22] While the former implies a balancing of interests, it does not equate with equal division of resources. It rests on the foundation of shared sovereignty and is of particular resonance for shared resources such as international watercourses—not energy resources.[23] In any case, the obligation of 'sustainable use of natural resources' is highly contextualized and has no single fixed meaning.[24] This follows logically from the fact that the legal status of natural resources varies according to whether the resource is under the sovereignty of one state, shared by several states, or held in common for the benefit of all. Mainly, however, energy resources fall into this first category, with elements of the third only in respect of the common heritage of mankind principle applying to deep seabed mineral resources.[25]

Nonetheless, attempts to distil core common elements have been made, notably by the International Law Association (ILA) in the 2002 New Delhi Principles of International Law relating to Sustainable Development, which emphasizes the 'duty of States to ensure sustainable use of natural resources'.[26] The relevant ILA Committee observed that:

> the level and obligation of conservation required in the sustainable use of any particular natural resource will vary in light of all circumstances, though as a matter of the general obligation, a State is expected to act in accordance with precaution and due diligence and in the interests of the long-term sustainability of the resource *and the benefit of their peoples*.[27]

brought by states before the ICJ 'from disputes about concessions and control of natural resources to disputes about sustainability and the limits of resources use': Higgins, ibid.

[21] See IEA, 'Our Mission' (n 11).

[22] M. Alberton, 'Environmental Principles in Maritime and Fresh Water Agreements', in L. Krämer and E. Orlando (eds), *Principles of Environmental Law: Elgar Encyclopedia of Environmental Law Series* (Edward Elgar, 2018), vol 6, 524–37. The 'interconnectedness between equitable and reasonable utilization of a shared resource and the balance between economic development and environmental protection that is the essence of sustainable development' was noted by the ICJ in *Argentina v Uruguay* 2010 (n 15) [177].

[23] See further C. Redgwell and L. Rajamani, 'Energy Underground: What's International Law got to do with it?', in D. Zillman, A. McHarg, A. Bradbrook, and L. Barrera-Hernandez (eds), *The Law of Energy Underground—Understanding New Developments in Subsurface Production, Transmission, and Storage* (OUP, 2014), 118–19. Thus, for example, '[t]here is no international legal obligation to jointly develop straddling fields, though international courts and tribunals have been consistent in encouraging such development': ibid., 119.

[24] See further C. Redgwell, 'Sustainable Use of Natural Resources', in L. Krämer and E. Orlando (eds), *Principles of Environmental Law: Elgar Encyclopedia of Environmental Law Series* (Edward Elgar, 2018), vol 6, 115 (hereafter Redgwell, *Sustainable Use*).

[25] D. French, 'From the Depths: Rich Pickings of Principles of Sustainable Development and General International Law on the Ocean Floor—the Seabed Disputes Chamber's 2011 Advisory Opinion' (2011) 26 *International Journal of Marine and Coastal Law*, 525–68.

[26] The Declaration is annexed to Resolution 3/2002, ILA Report of the Seventieth Conference (New Delhi, 2002), 22 (hereafter ILA Report 2002). The 2012 Sofia Guiding Statements added an insightful gloss to this. ILA Report of the Seventy-Fifth Conference (Sofia, 2012), 821.

[27] ILA Report 2002 (n 26) (emphasis added). For further analysis see Redgwell (n 24).

This last observation resonates with the early articulations of permanent sovereignty over natural resources (PSNR), one of the general principles 'at the core of international law relating to sustainable development'.[28] Paragraph 1 of the 1962 Declaration on Permanent Sovereignty over Natural Resources expressly refers to peoples, as well as nations:

> The right of peoples and nations to permanent sovereignty over natural resources must be exercised in the interest of their national development and the well-being of the people concerned.[29]

Historically, the evolution of the principle of PSNR commenced with an acknowledgement of both state and peoples' rights to these resources.[30] While subsequent soft law and treaty iterations of PSNR have omitted reference to 'peoples',[31] and it cannot be considered part of the customary law articulation of this principle, it *does* form part of the collective right of peoples to self-determination.[32] This has led some to argue that 'peoples' have a dual character as both subject and beneficiary of the principle of PSNR and the consequences for, inter alia, the assertion of rights over (the state's) natural resources.[33] The sustainable use of natural resources is thus instrumental (and intergenerational) in ensuring the well-being of present and future generations. But this is not a passive vertical relationship: principles of international law relating to sustainable development include respect for human rights, both substantive and participatory (e.g., public participation and access to information and justice are included in the ILA Delhi Principles[34]) and good governance norms. In relation to indigenous peoples, there is the added protection of the UN Declaration on the Rights of Indigenous Peoples which requires free, prior, and informed consent of indigenous peoples before the approval of any project affecting their lands, territories, or resources, including the extraction or exploitation of mineral, water, or other resources.[35] Some of these concepts have been given contemporary salience in references to a 'social license to operate' and in direct benefit sharing arrangements[36] which extend far beyond the alleged 'trickle

[28] ILA Report 2002 (n 26) 389. Also recognized in judicial decisions, e.g. Case Concerning Armed Activities on the Territory of the Congo (*Democratic Republic of the Congo v Uganda*) (Judgment) [2005] ICJ Rep 168.

[29] UNGA Res 1803 (XVII), 14 December 1962.

[30] Compare UNGA Resolution 545 (VI), 5 February 1952 and UNGA Resolution 1803 (VII) 1962 ('the right of peoples and nations') with UNGA Resolution 3281 (XXIX) 1974 ('every State').

[31] Treaty articulations now use the exclusive 'sovereign right(s) of States' framing: see, e.g., Principle 21 of the 1972 Stockholm Declaration; Principle 2 of the Rio Declaration; Article 193 of the 1982 UN Convention on the Law of the Sea; Article 3 of the Convention on Biological Diversity; Article 18 of the Energy Charter Treaty.

[32] See G. Triggs, 'The Rights of Indigenous Peoples to Participate in Resource Development: An International Legal Perspective' and C. Redgwell, 'The International Law of Public Participation: Protected Areas, Endangered Species, and Biological Diversity', in D. Zillman, A. Lucas, and G. Pring (eds), *Human Rights in Natural Resource Development: Public Participation in the Sustainable Development of Mining and Energy Resources* (OUP, 2002), 123 (hereafter Triggs, *Rights of Indigenous Peoples*) and 187.

[33] See further D. Dam-De Jong, *International Law and Governance of Natural Resources in Conflict and Post-Conflict Situations* (CUP, 2015), 49–50.

[34] See Redgwell, *Sustainable Use* (n 24).

[35] UNDRIP, Arts 19, 29(2), 32(2). See also ILO Convention No. 169, Art. 15(1).

[36] See C. Redgwell, *Intergenerational Trusts and Environmental Protection* (Juris, 1999), 25–30 (trust funds) (hereafter Redgwell, *Intergenerational Trusts*).

down' effect of conventional petroleum profits' taxes, rents, and royalties accruing to the state and used for public benefit.[37] More questionable is whether benefit sharing may also serve as a bridge between the environmental and human rights accountability of multinational corporations, particularly in relation to indigenous peoples and local communities.[38]

III. Seeking Energy Justice in International Law: A Human Rights Approach

As noted above, there is a clear link between human rights law and energy justice,[39] including the core principles of due process and accountability. Substantive human rights may be invoked to challenge energy production or consumption as impairing a substantive human right to private life or to a clean/healthy/satisfactory environment; but this is a double-edged sword, as rights may also be invoked to defend such activities as the legitimate enjoyment of a substantive right such as the right to property.[40] Such rights may be individual or collective.[41] Procedural human rights are also of increasing relevance in securing, inter alia, access to information, participation in decision-making,[42] and access to energy justice.

Surveying the international landscape, there are relatively few examples of human rights challenges to the sustainability of energy projects, and which explicitly invoke the principle of sustainable development. This is no doubt in part owing to its 'normative uncertainty ... and an absence of standards for judicial review'.[43] A rare example, specifically in the energy context, is the Ogoniland case where the African Commission on Human and Peoples' Rights found that the right of peoples freely to dispose of their own natural resources had been violated, as had their right to 'ecologically sustainable development'.[44] Article 24 of the African Charter on Human and

[37] See generally L. Barrera-Hernandez, B. Barton, L. Godden, A. Lucas, and A. Rønne (eds), *Sharing the Costs and Benefits of Energy and Resource Activity: Legal Change and Impact on Communities* (OUP, 2016), and in particular the contribution by Yinka Omorogbe, 'Resource Control and Benefit Sharing in Nigeria', 259–77 (hereafter Omorogbe, 'Resource Control').

[38] See, inter alia, E. Morgera, 'Benefit-sharing as a Bridge between the Environmental and Human Rights Accountability of Multinational Corporations', in B. Boer (ed.), *Environmental Law Dimensions of Human Rights* (OUP, 2015), chapter 2.

[39] See, e.g., Damilola Olawuyi, 'Energy (and human rights) for all: addressing human rights risks in energy access projects' in Salter, et al., *Energy Justice* (n 1) 73, which includes the example of the West African Gas Pipeline considered further below.

[40] See further C. Redgwell, 'Property Law Sources and Analogies in International Law', in A. McHarg, B. Barton, A. Bradbrook, and L. Godden (eds), *Property and the Law in Energy and Natural Resources* (OUP, 2010), 100,105–7.

[41] See, e.g., Triggs, *Rights of Indigenous Peoples* (n 32).

[42] A cautionary note should be sounded here for, as Bickerstaff, et al. observe, while 'participation [is] a key trope of a fair decision-making process and outcome ... too often these efforts to involve publics have centred on expressions of concerns in relation to decisions being made at the downstream stages in innovation and policy processes': Bickerstaff, et al., *Energy Justice* (n 3), 5. See also M. Lee, C. Armeni, J.d. Cendra, S. Chaytor, S. Lock, M. Maslin, C Redgwell, and Y. Rydin, 'Public Participation and Climate Change Infrastructure' (2013) 25 *Journal of Environmental Law*, 33–62.

[43] Birnie, et al., *International Law and Environment* (n 13), 126.

[44] The Social and Economic Rights Action Center and the Center for Economic and Social Rights v Nigeria, ACHPR Communication 155/96 (2002) [52]–[55].

Peoples' Rights provides that '[a]ll peoples shall have the right to a generally satisfactory environment favourable to their development'.[45] The African Charter combines this recognition of a substantive right with recognition of an *actio popularis*, thus reducing the obstacle of standing to enforce the substantive right. Given the environmental impact of energy activities, a potentially more fertile source of case law is human rights challenges to energy activities on the basis of impairment of the right to a particular quality of environment. Although under general human rights law there is only limited express recognition of a substantive right to environment, there is extensive recognition of this right at the regional[46] and national level.[47] Since 2012, Special Rapporteurs under mandate from the Human Rights Council[48] have prepared a series of reports mapping how human rights bodies have applied human rights norms to environmental issues.[49] In 2018, the first Special Rapporteur while presenting a set of Framework Principles that summarized human rights obligations in relation to the environment,[50] recorded 'strong evidence of the converging trends towards greater uniformity and certainty in the understanding of human rights obligations relating to the environment'.[51] Both the Special Rapporteurs on Human Rights and the Environment appointed thus far have advocated the adoption of a substantive human right to the environment through a resolution or a treaty.[52] And, indeed, there are increasing references to human rights in the context of international environmental instruments. The 2015 Paris Agreement became the first multilateral environmental agreement to contain an explicit reference to human rights, albeit in its preamble,[53] and this has led to an increasing emphasis within the climate change regime on procedural rights. Thus, for instance, parties are encouraged to provide information on the 'planning processes' that led to their nationally

[45] African Charter on Human and Peoples' Rights (adopted 27 June 1981, entered into force 21 October 1986) 1520 UNTS 217 Art. 24.

[46] In addition to the African Charter, ibid, the right to environment, with differing formulations, finds expression in the Additional Protocol to the American Convention on Human Rights in the Area of Economic, Social and Cultural Rights (adopted 17 November 1988, entered into force 16 November 1999) Art. 11(1); the Convention on Access to Information, Public Participation in Decision-Making and Access to Justice in Environmental Matters (adopted 25 June 1998, entered into force 21 October 2001) 2161 UNTS 447 (Aarhus Convention) Art. 1; the Arab Charter on Human Rights (adopted 22 May 2004, entered into force 15 March 2008) 12 IHRR 893, Art. 38; and the Association of Southeast Asian Nations (ASEAN) Human Rights Declaration (adopted 18 November 2012) [28(f)]. See generally J.G. Merrills, 'Environmental Rights', in D. Bodansky, J. Brunnée, and Ellen Hey (eds), *Oxford Handbook of International Environmental Law* (OUP, 2007) (hereafter Merrills, *Environmental Rights*); A. Boyle, 'Human Rights and the Environment: Where Next?', in B. Boer (ed.), *Environmental Law Dimensions of Human Rights* (OUP, 2015), chapter 7; and J. Knox and R. Pejan (eds), *The Human Right to a Healthy Environment* (CUP, 2018).

[47] See D. Boyd, 'Catalyst for Change: Evaluating Forty Years of Experience in Implementing the Right to a Healthy Environment', in J. Knox and R. Pejan (eds), *The Human Right to a Healthy Environment* (CUP, 2018), 17.

[48] Human Rights Council Res 19/10 (12 March 2012).

[49] See John Knox, 'Report of the Independent Expert on the issue of human rights obligations relating to the enjoyment of a safe, clean, healthy and sustainable environment: Mapping Report' (30 December 2013) UN Doc A/HRC/25/53.

[50] John Knox, 'Report of the Special Rapporteur on the issue of human rights obligations relating to the enjoyment of a safe, clean, healthy and sustainable environment' (24 January 2018) A/HRC/37/59, annex (hereafter 'Framework Principles').

[51] Ibid. [9].

[52] UN Doc A/73/188, 19 July 2018, [46]–[48].

[53] Paris Agreement, preambular recital 11.

determined contributions, including on public participation, as well as engagement with local communities and indigenous peoples.[54] In a similar vein, the parties to the Biodiversity Convention have adopted guidelines on environmental and social assessment and on consultation with indigenous peoples and local communities.[55]

Notwithstanding these advances, the recognition of a direct 'right' to a clean and healthy environment at the international level remains uncommon, with some scholars continuing to question its value and utility. Merrills, for example, questions whether the recognition of new rights such as the right to a healthy/clean/satisfactory environment is needed when account is taken of what is already in place. He even notes that 'the violation of the collective right to a "general satisfactory environment" found by the African Commission on Human and Peoples' Rights in *The Social and Economic Rights Action Centre and the Centre for Economic and Social Rights v Nigeria* was accompanied by so many other individual and collective rights as to add relatively little to the decision'.[56]

Recognition of indirect environmental rights is more prevalent, namely, through existing rights such as the right to private, home, and family life[57] or the right to life[58] and to the preservation of health and well-being. This is in evidence at the international, regional, and national level. The European Court of Human Rights (ECtHR) has developed an extensive jurisprudence in this area in the last three decades, starting with the landmark case of *Lopez Ostra v Spain*.[59] In the context of the right to life, the ECtHR has held that states have not just a negative obligation of non-interference but a *positive* obligation to act to enforce, for instance, zoning legislation and emission limit requirements that could protect life,[60] and to provide information to protect against the risk even of natural disasters such as mudslides[61] and flash floods.[62] Much of the jurisprudence of the Inter-American Court and Commission on Human Rights in the context of the environment has been in relation to the rights of indigenous peoples to the use and enjoyment of their lands,[63] with implications for the fairness and benefits of energy exploitation. The Inter-American Court's 2017 advisory opinion is, however, of broader application. The court highlighted the interdependence and indivisibility between human rights, the environment, and

[54] UNFCCC, Decision 4/CMA.1, 'Further guidance in relation to the mitigation section of decision 1/CP.21', FCCC/PA/CMA/2018/3/Add.1, 19 March 2019, Annex I, section 4 (a)(i).

[55] See E. Morgera, 'Dawn of a New Day? The Evolving Relationship between the Convention on Biological Diversity and International Human Rights Law' (2018) 53 *Wake Forest Law Review*, 101.

[56] *The Social and Economic Rights Action Centre and the Centre for Economic and Social Rights v Nigeria* (2003) 10 IHRR 282, discussed by Merrills, *Environmental Rights* (n 46). See also A. Boyle, 'Human Rights and the Environment: Where Next?' (2012) 23 *European Journal of International Law*, 614.

[57] See, e.g., Article 8 of the ECHR read with *López Ostra v Spain* App no 16798/90 (ECtHR, 9 December 1994) and the string of cases that follow.

[58] See, e.g., Article 2 of the ECHR read with *Oneryildiz v Turkey* App no 48939/99 (ECHR, 30 November 2004) and the string of cases that follow.

[59] *López Ostra v Spain*, App no 16798/90 (ECtHR, 9 December 1994).

[60] *Fadeyeva v Russia*, App no 55723/00 (ECtHR, 9 June 2005).

[61] *Budayeva v Russia*, App no 15339/02 (ECtHR, 20 March 2008).

[62] *Kolyadenko v Russia*, App no 17423/05 (ECtHR, 28 February 2012).

[63] See, e.g., *Kichwa Indigenous People of Sarayaku v Ecuador*, Series C no 245 (IACtHR, 27 June 2012) and *Saramaka People v Suriname*, Series C no 172 (IACtHR, 28 November 2007).

sustainable development, and cast both negative and positive duties on the state in relation to the right to life, as extended to protect against 'illegal pollution of the environment in a manner that affects the conditions allowing for a decent life'.[64] The court also, in a potentially far-reaching move, indicated that the responsibility of states under the American Convention extends to actions within their territory or control that cause transboundary environmental harm, and thus affects the rights of individuals outside its geographical borders.[65]

It is in the human rights context that we also see a significant role for non-state actors (NSAs). While this is principally observable in the vertical enforcement by individuals of rights against the state, increasingly there are attempts to apply human rights in a horizontal manner.[66] Domestically the picture varies from state to state. For example, litigation under the United States Alien Tort Claims Act has been pursued by NSAs seeking to challenge the activities of, inter alia, energy companies as violating customary principles of [international] environmental and human rights law—the example of *Kiobel* springs to mind—albeit none has succeeded in surmounting obstacles to the exercise of jurisdiction by the US courts.[67] In the related context of climate justice, claims are increasingly being brought against major fossil fuel companies for their disproportionate role in causing climate change. Of particular significance is the case brought by Greenpeace and others against fifty large fossil fuel companies, characterized as the 'Carbon Majors', before the Philippines Human Rights Commission.[68] In the wake of numerous climate-linked disasters, the petitioners requested the Commission to investigate the responsibility of these companies for violations or threats of violations

[64] *Advisory Opinion on Environment and Human Rights*, No OC/23-17 (IACtHR, 15 November 2017).

[65] Ibid.

[66] UN Sub-commission on the Promotion and Protection of Human Rights, 'Norms on the Responsibilities of Transnational Corporations and other Business Enterprises with respect to Human Rights' E/CN.4/Sub.2/2003/12/Rev.2, 26 August 2003, https://digitallibrary.un.org/record/501576 accessed 16 September 2019. See also Chapter II of the OECD's revised Guidelines for Multinational Enterprises (2000) http://www.oecd.org and the UN Global Compact (2000) http://www.unglobalcompact.org, both requiring respect for human rights based on existing international standards. Such soft instruments reflect the input of one category of NSAs in seeking to regulate the conduct of another—MNEs. Guiding Principles on Business and Human Rights: Implementing the United Nations 'Protect, Respect and Remedy' Framework, (2011) A/HRC/17/31, endorsed by the Human Rights Council by HRC Res 17/4 (16 June 2011); in the energy context see the analysis by R. Lindsay, R. McCorquodale, L. Blecher, J. Bonnitcha, A. Crockett, and A. Sheppard, 'Human Rights Responsibilities in the Oil and Gas Sector: Applying the UN Guiding Principles' (2013) 6 *Journal of World Energy Law and Business*, 2–65. S. Murphy, 'Taking Multinational Corporate Codes of Conduct to the Next Level' (2005) 43 *Columbia Journal of Transnational Law*, 489 and E. Morgera, *Corporate Accountability in International Environmental Law* (OUP, 2009).

[67] *Kiobel v Royal Dutch Petroleum*, 133 S Ct 1659 (Supreme Court of the United States, 2013). See e.g. M. Bastile, 'The Long View on *Kiobel*: A Muted Victory for International Legal Norms in the United States?' 13–19; J. Nolan et al., 'Beyond *Kiobel*: Alternative Remedies for Sustained Human Rights Protection' 48–54 in 'Agora: Reflections on *Kiobel*' (2013) 107 *American Journal of International Law*, 829 and P.D. Mora, 'The Alien Tort Statute After Kiobel: The Possibility for the Unlawful Assertions of Universal Civil Jurisdiction Still Remains' (2014) 63 *International and Comparative Law Quarterly*, 699 and, more generally, H.H. Koh, 'Separating Myth from Reality about Corporate Responsibility Litigation' (2004) 7 *Journal of International Economic Law*, 263.

[68] On the initial petition see Greenpeace, Petition Requesting for Investigation of the Responsibility of the Carbon Majors for Human Rights Violations or Threats of Violations resulting from the Impacts of Climate Change <http://climatecasechart.com/non-us-case/in-re-greenpeace-southeast-asia-et-al/?cn-reloaded=1> accessed 16 September 2019; on the outcome see Isabella Kaminski,' Carbon Majors Can Be Held Liable for Human Rights Violations, Philippines Commission Rules', Climate Liability News, 9 December 2019 <https://www.climateliabilitynews.org/2019/12/09/philippines-human-rights-climate-change-2/> accessed 2 January 2020; and more generally see J. Peel and H. Osofsky, 'A Rights Turn in Climate Change Litigation?' (2018) 7 *Transnational Environmental Law*, 37.

of human rights resulting from the impacts of climate change. The Commission conducted its inquiry over three years and found that the 'Carbon Majors' played a clear role in anthropogenic climate change, and could be held liable for its impacts. These are among the examples of the various transnational and international conduits that litigants may pursue in their quest for energy and climate justice, and the core principle of accountability in particular.

Human rights standards may also be enforced indirectly through loan conditionality, often in the context of large energy infrastructure projects. In its lending practices, and as set forth in its Operational Guidelines, the World Bank requires conformity with certain International Labour Organization (ILO) conventions, including on forcible resettlement of populations.[69] Additionally, NSAs in the borrower country may seek internal review by the Inspection Panel of the bank's failure to comply with its own policies and procedures on environmental and human rights protection, and general project oversight. An example is the West African Gas Pipeline Project where requesters in Ghana and Nigeria alleged non-compliance by the bank with a number of operational guidelines.[70] 'Standing' for the complaint flowed from an investment guarantee to Ghana through the International Development Association (IDA) and political risk insurance to the West African Pipeline Company (WAPCo) through the Multilateral Investment Guarantee Agency (MIGA). The panel's report set forth a damning context for the development of the oil industry in Nigeria that has bolstered economic development but with 'adverse effects on the livelihood and environment of communities living in the production areas and near the pipelines' and with social and political conflict rooted in the 'inequitable social relations that underlie the production and distribution of profits from oil, and its adverse impact on the fragile ecosystem of the Niger Delta'.[71] The panel found numerous instances of non-compliance by the bank indeed the panel may have been influenced by the context of petroleum developments in Nigeria in examining the diligence of the bank in adhering to its own policies and procedures. The bank's board of directors responded (including through measures to improve resettlement and compensation and to improve transparency through information disclosure). However, the Inspection Panel is not an adjudicative body and it does not have the power to propose remedial measures, issue injunctions, stop the project, or award financial compensation for any injury suffered.

[69] Operational Guidance on Environment Impact Assessment 4.0; see also the discussion in Triggs, *Rights of Indigenous Peoples* (n 32).

[70] Investigation Report: Ghana: West African Gas Pipeline Project, World Bank Inspection Panel, Report No. 42644-GH, 25 April 2008. The Panel assessed compliance with Operational Policies and Procedures on: environmental assessment; involuntary resettlement; poverty reduction; economic evaluation of investment operations; project supervision; and World Bank Policy on Disclosure of Information. OP 4.12 on Involuntary Resettlement, for example, requires the avoidance of development-induced displacement where feasible and has as one of its objectives that 'resettlement activities should be conceived and executed as *sustainable development programs*, providing sufficient investment resources to enable persons displaced by the project to share in the project benefits' (emphasis added).

[71] Ibid. For an assessment of the benefits that can accrue from petroleum exploitation against the backdrop of the Nigerian experience, see Omorogbe, 'Resource Control' (n 37), 259.

IV. Energy Justice and Equity in International Law: Intra- and Inter-generational Equity and Common but Differentiated Responsibilities

While the arguments explored above suggest that there is currently little foundation for arguing a duty of optimum or sustainable use of non-living energy resources,[72] distributional obligations may nevertheless arise within, and between, generations with respect to such resource use.

Both inter-generational and intra-generational equity have been identified by many authors—and by the Intergovernmental Panel on Climate Change (IPCC)—as an integral element of the broader principle of sustainable development,[73] which can be 'seen as encompassing an international understanding of intra-generational (as well as inter-generational) equity in its effort to strike a fair balance between the often conflicting goals of economic development and environmental protection'.[74] Inter- and intra-generational equity are central to the definition of sustainable development.[75] Sands identifies categories of principles inherent in the concept of sustainable development (including equity and consideration of the needs of future generations) and those drawn from other areas of international law providing assistance in achieving it (including CBDR).[76] A strong sustainability approach is arguably more consistent with inter-generational equity given the emphasis upon maintaining certain 'critical natural stock—such as the climate system and biodiversity—[that] cannot be replaced by human-made capital and must be maintained'.[77] This is a task transcending the climate regime. As the IPCC concludes, 'designing a successful climate policy may require going beyond a narrow focus on mitigation and adaptation, beyond the analysis of a few co-benefits of climate policy, and may instead require "mainstreaming" climate issues into the design of comprehensive [sustainable development] strategies, including at local and regional levels'.[78]

[72] V. Lowe, *International Law* (OUP, 2007), 24; see also J. Harrison and E. Morgera, 'Article 61', in A. Proelss (ed.), *United Nations Convention on the Law of the Sea: A Commentary* (C.H. Beck/Hart/Nomos, 2017), 482 observing that the conservation and management of living resources obligations of the coastal state in the EEZ contained in UNCLOS, Art. 61 apply only to living resources with no equivalent provision for non-living resources.

[73] See, e.g., P. Sands, 'International Law in the Field of Sustainable Development' (1994) LXV *British Year Book of International Law*, 303 (hereafter Sands, *International Law*); E. B. Weiss, 'In Fairness to Future Generations and Sustainable Development' (1992) 8 *American University International Law Review*, 19 (hereafter Weiss, *In Fairness*, 1992); Redgwell, *Intergenerational Trusts* (n 36), 42. IPCC WG III contribution to the 5AR, 'Climate Change 2014: Mitigation of Climate Change', chapter 4 'Sustainable Development', section 4.2.2, 14 (hereafter IPCC WG III, 'Climate Change 2014') noting that 'Equity *between* generations underlies the very notion of [sustainable development]'. See also UNFCCC, Art. 3(4), which lays out the general right to promote sustainable development.

[74] D. Shelton, 'Equity', in D. Bodansky, J. Brunnée, and E. Hey (eds), *Oxford Handbook of International Environmental Law* (OUP, 2007), 642 (hereafter Shelton, *Equity*).

[75] See (n 13).

[76] Sands, *International Law* (n 73).

[77] IPCC WG III, 'Climate Change 2014' (n 73) section 4.2.1.1.

[78] Ibid., at section 4.2.1.2.

The principle of inter-generational equity[79] defines the rights and obligations of present and future generations with respect to the use and enjoyment of natural and cultural resources, inherited by the present generation and to be passed on to future generations in no worse condition than received.[80] This applies both to the diversity of the resources and general quality of the environment that is passed on.[81] The principle is often linked with notions of fairness and distributive justice.[82] It 'articulates a principle of fairness among generations in the use and conservation of the environment and its natural resources'.[83]

Inter-generational equity has been extensively addressed in legal doctrine and pioneered within it by Edith Brown Weiss since her classic 1989 work *In Fairness to Future Generations*.[84] In her more recent analyses, she articulates the three elements of the principle of inter-generational equity as: (i)'non-discriminatory access to the Earth and its resources'; (ii)'comparable options (reflected in the diversity of resources)'; and (iii)'comparable quality in the environment'.[85] This 2013 articulation of the principles demonstrates a subtle shift from her articulation in *In Fairness to Future Generations* which used 'conservation' in place of 'comparable'. This recent phrasing conveys a more accurate sense of an equitable balancing of the needs of present and future generations.[86] Moreover, as the case studies employed underscore (including the generational issues arising from radioactive waste disposal), the 'resources' in question are both living and non-living.

From these three basic principles are derived five 'duties of use': (i) the duty to conserve resources; (ii) the duty to ensure equitable use; (iii) the duty to avoid adverse impacts; (iv) the duty to prevent disasters, minimize damage, and provide emergency assistance; and (v) the duty to compensate for environmental harm.[87] Climate change evidences all three types of inter-generational problem which may arise in the use of planetary resources: (i) reduced or barred access to the use and benefit of resources passed on from previous generations; (ii) depletion of resources for future generations; and (iii) degradation in the quality of resources available for future generations.[88] Implementation

[79] See, generally, E.B. Weiss, *In Fairness to Future Generations: International Law, Common Patrimony, and Intergenerational Equity* (Transnational Publishers, 1989) (hereafter Weiss, *In Fairness*, 1989); and Redgwell, *Intergenerational Trusts* (n 36).

[80] Given current climate change predictions, this seems unlikely for the present generation.

[81] Weiss, *In Fairness*, 1989 (n 79).

[82] See further discussion by J. Brunnée, 'Climate Change, Global Environmental Justice and International Environmental Law', in J. Ebbesson and P. Okowa (eds), *Environmental Law and Justice in Context* (CUP, 2009), 316–32 (hereafter Brunnée, *Climate Change*). Distributive justice is also one of the two key elements of CBDRRC as 'a manifestation of equity': P. Cullet, 'Principle 7: Common but Differentiated Responsibilities', in J. Viñuales (ed.), *The Rio Declaration on Environment and Development: A Commentary* (OUP, 2015), 231 (hereafter Cullet, *Principle 7*).

[83] E.B. Weiss, 'Inter-generational Equity' (February 2013) *Max Planck Encyclopedia of Public International Law* (hereafter Weiss, *Inter-generational Equity*) and Shelton, *Equity* (n 74) 642.

[84] Weiss, *In Fairness*, 1989 (n 79). In contrast, intra-generational equity is only lightly explored in the doctrine with greater attention paid to supporting concepts such as CBDR.

[85] Weiss, *Inter-generational Equity* (n 83) paragraph 7.

[86] Viñuales and Dupuy categorize principles of international environmental law according to their function as 'prevention' or as 'balance', with CBDR and inter-generational equity discussed under the latter: J. Viñuales and P.M. Dupuy, *International Environmental Law* (CUP, 2nd edn, 2018), chapter 3 (hereafter Viñuales and Dupuy, *International Environmental Law*).

[87] Weiss, *In Fairness*, 1989 (n 79) 51–60; for analysis see Redgwell, *Intergenerational Trusts* (n 36) chapter 4.

[88] Redgwell, *Intergenerational Trusts* (n 36), 54 and, generally, E.B. Weiss, 'Conservation and Equity Between Generations', in T. Buergenthal (ed.), *Contemporary Issues in International Law: Essays in Honour of Louis B. Sohn* (Engel, 1984), 245–89.

of these principles in the climate change context requires measures to prevent rapid changes in climate and to prevent or mitigate damage, and measures to assist countries in adapting to climate change.[89] Needless to say, the climate change regime, a product of dysfunctional politics, is only partially able to implement these principles.

Notions of trusteeship at the international level, expressed in terms of inter-generational equity, build on the use of equity[90] 'as a basis upon which to provide standards for allocating and sharing resources and for distributing the burdens of caring for the resources and the environment in which they are found'.[91] The climate regime in particular is imbued with equitable considerations, flowing inter alia from the recognition in Article 3(1) UNFCCC of the obligation to protect the climate system for the benefit of present and future generations 'on the basis of equity' and 'in accordance with their common but differentiated responsibilities and respective capabilities'.[92] Article 3 may be viewed as supporting the legitimate expectation of future generations of equitable access to planetary resources, and the concomitant obligation of the present generation as trustee of these resources to ensure that future options are not unduly constrained. Moreover, intra-generational equity[93] is clearly recognized in the incorporation of common but differentiated responsibilities and respective capabilities (CBDRRC)[94] as a complement to differentiated responsibility for historical/current contributions to climate change, and in the explicit acknowledgement in Article 4(7) that it is for developed states to shoulder the greater burden in restoring the global patrimony.[95] The UNFCCC also contains preambular recitals that recognize that developing country emissions are low in per capita terms, and that their share of the global emissions will grow to meet their social and development needs.[96] Article 3(1), read with other provisions of the UNFCCC, thus clearly incorporates notions of both intra- and inter-generational equity, and the principle of CBDRRC as an expression of intra-generational concerns.

[89] E.B. Weiss, 'Climate Change, Intergenerational Equity and International Law: An Introduction' (1989) 15 *Climatic Change*, 327, 330.

[90] See Shelton, *Equity* (n 74). Brunnée notes that when equity is used in conjunction with justice, it is correctly limited to matters of distributive justice, the broader notion of justice also embracing corrective justice and procedural justice: Brunnée, *Climate Change* (n 82) 319.

[91] Weiss, *Inter-generational Equity* (n 83). Accordingly, she asserts that '[t]his use of equity provides a foundation for the principle of intergenerational equity'. IPCC WG III states that 'Equity *between* generations underlies the very notion of [sustainable development]': IPCC WG III, 'Climate Change 2014' (n 73) chapter 4, section 4.2.2, 14.

[92] 1771 UNTS 107. The general principles contained in the UNFCCC apply to its 1997 Kyoto Protocol, 37 ILM (1998) 22 and the 2015 Paris Agreement, 12 December 2015, C.N.92.2015.TREATIES-XXVII.7.d.

[93] See Sands, *International Law* (n 73); Weiss, *In Fairness*, 1992 (n 73), 19; Redgwell, *Intergenerational Trusts* (n 36), 42.

[94] L. Rajamani, 'Common but Differentiated Responsibilities', in L. Krämer and E. Orlando (eds), *Principles of Environmental Law: Elgar Encyclopedia of Environmental Law Series* (Edward Elgar, 2018), vol 6, 291–302; L. Rajamani, *Differential Treatment in International Environmental Law* (OUP, 2006) (hereafter Rajamani, *Differential Treatment*); Cullet, *Principle 7* (n 82), 229–44; C. Stone, 'Common but Differentiated Responsibilities in International Law' (2004) 98 *American Journal of International Law*, 276–301; Sands and Peel, *Principles of IEL* (n 13), 244–9.

[95] See generally Rajamani, *Differential Treatment* (n 94). On shifting patterns of differentiation under the climate regime see Cullet, *Principle 7* (n 82), 232; L. Rajamani, 'The Changing Fortunes of Differential Treatment in the Evolution of International Environmental Law' (2012) 88 *International Affairs*, 605 (hereinafter Rajamani, *Changing Fortunes*); and L. Rajamani, 'Ambition and Differentiation in the 2015 Paris Agreement: Interpretive Possibilities and Underlying Politics' (2016) 65 *International and Comparative Law Quarterly*, 493–514.

[96] FCCC, preambular recital 3.

The 2015 Paris Agreement strengthens and nuances the application of the CBDRRC principle in the climate change regime. It contains references to the CBDRRC principle in a preambular recital,[97] and in provisions relating to the purpose of the agreement,[98] progression,[99] and long-term low greenhouse gas (GHG) emission development strategies.[100] The most significant of these references is in Article 2 that sets the temperature goal and frames the implementation of the entire agreement. All references to the CBDRRC principle in the Paris Agreement, however, are accompanied by the phrase 'in light of different national circumstances'. This qualification—which represents a compromise arrived at between the United States and China[101]—arguably introduces a dynamic element to the interpretation of the principle (CBDRRC-NC). As national circumstances evolve, so too will the CBDR of states.[102]

The CBDRRC principle, more broadly, 'constitutes a means of translating the concept of intra-generational equity to the inter-State level, and the South-North context in particular, with a view to attaining sustainable development'.[103] Despite some elision of the concepts of intra-generational equity and CBDRRC,[104] the former is a broader concept addressing disparities between states. Indeed, in the climate change regime developing countries have long argued for a much wider notion of equity that encompasses arguments based on fairness, justice, equality (for equals), affirmative action, redistribution, and restoration.[105] Proposals by developing countries for 'equitable access to sustainable development',[106] the 'principle-based reference framework',[107] the 'carbon budget',[108] and 'international climate justice tribunal'[109] are inspired by this wider notion of equity rather than a narrow construction of CBDRRC. And, there are several references to equity even in the 2015 Paris Agreement including in: two preambular recitals—one in the context of CBDRRC[110] and another in the context of human rights;[111] Article 2(2) in the context for implementation of the Paris Agreement; Article 4(1) in the context of mitigation ambition; and Article 14 in the context of the Global Stocktake, a process to assess collective progress towards the long-term goals of the

[97] Paris Agreement, preambular recital 3.
[98] Ibid., Art. 2.2.
[99] Ibid., Art. 4.3.
[100] Ibid., Art. 4.19.
[101] See The White House, US–China Joint Announcement on Climate Change, Beijing, China, 12 November 2014 (Office of the Press Secretary, 11 November 2014) [2].
[102] See L. Rajamani, 'Guiding Principles and General Obligation (Article 2.2 and Article 3)', in D. Klein, et al. (eds), *The Paris Agreement on Climate Change: Analysis and Commentary* (OUP, 2017), 131.
[103] E. Hey, 'Common but Differentiated Responsibilities', in *Max Planck Encyclopedia of Public International Law* (February 2011).
[104] See, e.g., Viñuales and Dupuy, *International Environmental Law* (n 86), 71.
[105] Discussed in Rajamani, *Differential Treatment* (n 94), chapter 5.
[106] UNFCC, Decision 1/CMP.6, The Cancun Agreements: Outcome of the work of the Ad Hoc Working Group on Further Commitments for Annex I Parties under the Kyoto Protocol at its fifteenth session, 15 March 2011, UN Doc. FCCC/KP/CMP/2010/12/Add.1, [6]. See also BASIC experts, 'Equitable Access to Sustainable Development: Contribution to the Body of Scientific Knowledge' (2011).
[107] Submission by Swaziland on behalf of the African Group under Workstream I of the ADP, 8 October 2013.
[108] Submission of the Plurinational State of Bolivia, Proposal on the Compound Index of Countries' Participation in the Global Emissions Budget under the Convention applicable to all Parties, 20 November 2014.
[109] Intended Nationally Determined Contribution from the Plurinational State of Bolivia, 12 October 2015.
[110] Paris Agreement, preambular recital 3.
[111] Ibid., preambular recital 11.

agreement. There are also references to the related notions of 'equitable access to sustainable development',[112] poverty eradication,[113] and climate justice.[114] Equity, it is thus clear, is central to the implementation of the Paris Agreement—this can be inferred from the references to equity in the context of the 'purpose' of the agreement and mitigation ambition. Further, since it is referred to in the context of the Global Stocktake, equity could have a central role in the evolution of the climate regime.

Equity and CBDR have taken various forms in the climate change regime such as financial assistance, capacity-building, and transfer of technology.[115] While differentiation with respect to central obligations such as that found in the 1997 Kyoto Protocol—such that developed countries have GHG mitigation obligations and developing countries do not—is rare,[116] and has not been replicated in the Paris Agreement, facilitation of financial and technical assistance are amongst the most frequent forms of differential treatment found in treaties.[117] Interestingly, the Paris Agreement represents a step change from the UNFCCC and Kyoto Protocol in relation to differentiation. The Paris Agreement operationalizes the CBDRRC-NC principle not by tailoring commitments to categories of Parties, but by tailoring differentiation to the specificities of the issue area—mitigation, adaptation, finance, technology, capacity-building, and transparency. In effect, this has resulted in different forms of differentiation in different areas, and in arguably diluting the differentiation in favour of developing countries, an enduring site of conflict in the climate negotiations.

The ability of the climate change regime to successfully address the threat of climate change has fundamental implications for equity—between and within nations and peoples. These are implications not just in relation to the impacts of climate change, which are highly differential and disproportionate to the contributions of some states to climate change, but also in relation to the burdens of regulation, which may fall on developing countries that are already struggling to meet social, development, and energy access goals. Notwithstanding some blurring of the lines between the categories of developed and developing countries, there are persistent inequalities between those living in developed and developing countries.[118] And, many developing countries have yet to provide energy access to all their citizens. An estimated 1.1 billion people, 14 per cent of the world's population, do not have access to electricity,[119] and while rapid gains are being made in countries like India,[120] an estimated 700 million people, predominantly

112 Ibid., preambular recital 8.

113 Ibid., preambular recital 8, Arts 2.1, 4.1, and 6.8.

114 Ibid., preambular recital 13.

115 See Article 12 in the IUCN's *International Covenant on Environment and Development*, Environmental Law & Policy Paper No. 31 Rev. 3 (4th edn, 2010) 55.

116 See Rajamani, *Changing Fortunes* (n 95).

117 Cullet, *Principle 7* (n 82), 239. See further C. Redgwell, 'Facilitation of compliance', in J. Brunnée, M. Doelle, and L. Rajamani (eds), *Promoting Compliance in an Evolving Climate Regime* (OUP, 2012), 177–93.

118 See B. Milanovic, *The Haves and the Have-Nots: A Brief and Idiosyncratic History of Global Inequality* (Basic Books, 2011), 115–19, finding that if country averages are broken down into actual incomes received by people in each country 'practically all people living in a richer country are better off than all people living in a poorer country' and that the 'poorest Americans are better off than two-thirds of the world population'.

119 IEA, *Energy Access Outlook 2017*, 11 (hereafter IEA 2017).

120 India has provided access to 500 million since 2000, and is expected to reach universal electricity access in the early-2020s, with renewables accounting for about 60 per cent of those who gain access. See IEA 2017 (n 119), 13.

in sub-Saharan Africa, are projected to remain without electricity in 2040.[121] For many developing countries, the burden of addressing energy poverty is crippling. While they have the opportunity to do so in sustainable ways, there are potential cost implications, and the climate regime can only provide a fraction of the assistance needed, thus placing the burden primarily on these nations.

Moreover, the 'nationally determined contributions' that states have submitted under the Paris Agreement thus far, are wholly inadequate. UNEP's *Emissions Gap Report* finds that 'pathways reflecting current NDCs imply global warming of about 3°C by 2100, with warming continuing afterwards'.[122] The IPCC notes that different levels of warming have different implications for equity, that is, 'in the comparative distribution of benefits and burdens for specific states, persons, or generations, and in terms of their likely impacts on sustainable development and poverty'.[123] At the higher levels of warming likely under current Nationally Determined Contributions (NDCs), inequities between and among nations and peoples will be exacerbated.

V. Conclusion

While the foregoing does not constitute an exhaustive survey of international law, elements of energy justice, as reflected in the eight core principles identified in part I of the chapter, are clearly found within it. Whether it is the 'sustainability constrained' exercise of PSNR, transparency and accountability of international organizations, or the equitable distribution of the benefits and burdens of tackling climate change within and between generations, there is increasing evidence of the core principles of energy justice emerging in international law and policy. But two observations are called for. The first is that it is by no means clear that energy justice in international law has any distinctive content or substance beyond serving as a useful label for identifying those principles and rules of international law with distributional effect which operate, inter alia, in an energy context. The second is that even where principles with intended distributional effect are present in international law, their application is imperfect and enforcement—especially of 'soft norms'—problematic in the state-centric system of international law. The latter point is well illustrated by the inability of the climate change regime fully to implement intra- and inter-generational equity and the dilution of CBDRRC as an expression of intra-generational concern under the Paris Agreement. That said, as the revised mission statement of the IEA attests, there is a clear direction of travel in incorporating, however imperfectly, elements of energy justice in international energy law and policy.

[121] IEA, *World Energy Outlook 2018*, 5.
[122] UNEP, *Emissions Gap Report 2018: Executive Summary* (2018), 4.
[123] IPCC 1.5°C Report, chapter 1, 55.

PART III

PROCEDURAL JUSTICE, COMMUNITY PARTICIPATION, AND RESTORATIVE JUSTICE

5

Community Energy and a Just Energy Transition

What We Know and What We Still Need to Find Out

*Annalisa Savaresi**

I. Introduction

The search for the means to deliver the energy transition has brought to the fore the potential to engender transformative change through grassroots innovation and new forms of social and policy experimentation.[1] In this fast-moving landscape, law- and policy-makers have in recent years adopted measures to stimulate decentralized renewable energy generation, with the involvement of local and rural communities, who have thus become protagonists of the energy transition.

In the EU, the communication 'Clean Energy for All Europeans'[2] and the 2030 Climate and Energy Framework envision a central role for citizens in the energy transition. The term 'community energy' has recently made its debut in EU law and policy documents to identify situations in which communities own, in whole or in part, infrastructure for the generation of renewable energy, regardless of the type of technology deployed. The recasts of the Renewable Energy[3] and Electricity Directives[4] for the first time ask all Member States to promote and facilitate the development of renewable energy community projects that provide 'environmental, economic or social community benefits for its shareholders or members or for the local areas (…) rather than financial profits'.[5]

* This piece builds on A. Savaresi, 'The Rise of Community Energy from Grassroots to Mainstream: The Role of Law and Policy' (2019) 31 *Journal of Environmental Law* 487; and on the author's contribution to P.V. Herrejon and A. Savaresi, 'Wind Energy, Benefit-Sharing and Indigenous Peoples: Lessons from the Isthmus of Tehuantepec, Southern Mexico' (2020) *Oil, Gas & Energy Law Journal* (OGEL) https://www.ogel.org/journal-advance-publication-article.asp?key=604 accessed 30 July 2019.

[1] J.P Tomain, *Clean Power Politics: The Democratization of Energy* (Cambridge University Press, 2017).

[2] European Commission, 'Communication from the Commission to the European Parliament, the Council, the European Economic and Social Committee, the Committee of the Regions and the European Investment Bank, Clean Energy for All Europeans' (2016).

[3] Directive 2018/2001 of the European Parliament and of the Council on the promotion of the use of energy from renewable sources, [2018] OJ L328/82 [Recast Renewables Directive], Article 22.

[4] Directive 2019/944 of the European Parliament and of the Council on common rules for the internal market for electricity [2019] OJ L 158/125 [Recast Electricity Directive], Article 16.

[5] Recast Renewables Directive, Article 2.16; and Recast Electricity Directive, Article 2.11.

Annalisa Savaresi, Community Energy and a Just Energy Transition In: *Energy Justice and Energy Law.* Edited by Íñigo Del Guayo, Lee Godden, Donald N. Zillman, Milton Fernando Montoya, and José Juan González, Oxford University Press (2020). DOI: 10.1093/oso/9780198860754.003.0005

The mainstreaming of community energy, however, requires significant structural adjustment to governance systems built around large-scale energy production and distribution. The recasts of the Electricity and Renewables Directives largely leave it to national law- and policy-makers to find the means for mainstreaming community energy. So far, however, only a handful of 'pioneer' EU Member States—Denmark, Germany, and the UK—have accrued significant experience grappling with the regulatory complexities associated with mainstreaming of community energy. And even though community energy has been widely studied already and much is now known about how community energy happens, who participates and why, the literature converges on the need to understand what community energy does in practice, what material changes it has produced, and on whether and how community energy can meaningfully contribute to just energy transitions.[6] In particular, there is no firm empirical basis to suggest that, when communities own renewable energy generation infrastructure, this automatically translates into environmental, economic, or social community benefits. Instead, the literature remains largely reliant on 'anecdotal evidence from a small number of case studies' for evidence of the benefits of community energy.[7]

The imminent implementation of the Renewables and the Electricity Directives in the EU makes it crucial to systematically assess the practice of community energy, to understand when it actually delivers societal benefits and whether, and how it contributes to a just energy transition. Capturing and sharing the lessons learned from both success and failure in those Member States that have pioneered the mainstreaming of community energy could therefore not be more timely. Yet to date, no comprehensive study of how to mainstream community energy, while delivering multiple societal benefits has been carried out.

The vast majority of the literature on community energy has been produced by scholars from sociology and human geography, using a case-study approach. There is therefore a need to analyse the practice of community energy more systematically, to make sense of the justice questions analysed in this book[8] in relation to community energy.

So far legal scholarship has scantly examined the matter of community energy. I have already highlighted a series of knowledge gaps and blind spots concerning the role of law and policy in mainstreaming community energy.[9] These knowledge gaps concern: how the scope of community energy activities is defined (i.e. what may be considered a community energy project); how the benefits of these activities may be

[6] F. Mey and M. Diesendorf, 'Who Owns an Energy Transition? Strategic Action Fields and Community Wind Energy in Denmark' (2018) 35 *Energy Research & Social Science*, 108; A.L. Berka and E. Creamer, 'Taking Stock of the Local Impacts of Community Owned Renewable Energy: A Review and Research Agenda' (2018) 82 *Renewable and Sustainable Energy Reviews*, 3400; L. Gorroño-Albizu, K. Sperling, and S. Djørup, 'The Past, Present and Uncertain Future of Community Energy in Denmark: Critically Reviewing and Conceptualising Citizen Ownership' (2019) 57 *Energy Research & Social Science*, 101231; E. Creamer, et al., 'Community Renewable Energy: What Does It Do? Walker and Devine-Wright (2008) Ten Years On' (2019) 57 *Energy Research & Social Science*, 101223.

[7] Creamer, et al. (n 6) .

[8] See Introduction, Chapter 1 in this book.

[9] A. Savaresi, 'The Rise of Community Energy from Grassroots to Mainstream: The Role of Law and Policy' (2019) 31 *Journal of Environmental Law*, 487.

measured, reported, and assessed; and how to distribute the benefit and burdens associated with community projects in a fair and equitable way.

Building upon that work, this chapter scrutinizes evidence from selected EU Member States that have pioneered the mainstreaming of community energy through the lens of justice theories. The aim is to probe the sometimes uncritical assumptions about community energy, highlighting the complex, layered, conflicting justice claims that underlie its mainstreaming. In order to do this, the chapter distils a set of distributive, procedural, and restorative justice questions associated with community energy, and considers the way in which they have been addressed, drawing on examples from Denmark, Germany, and the UK. The chapter concludes with a reflection on what we know and what we still do not know about community energy's potential to deliver a just energy transition.

II. Conceptualizing Community Energy

Law and policy documents on community energy typically define community energy projects as those where communities own, in full or in part, energy generation plants.[10] The notion of community energy in regulatory practice, therefore, does not merely entail that local residents be heard in relation to energy projects, or receive so-called benefit packages, but rather it centres on the communities' partial or total ownership and management of renewable energy generation plants.

This understanding is manifest in the recasts of the Renewables and Electricity Directives, adopted in 2018 and 2019, respectively, as part of the EU's 2030 Climate and Energy Framework. For the first time, the Directives require EU Member States to enable communities to produce, consume, store, and sell renewable energy without being subject to unjustified or discriminatory conditions or procedures.[11]

The criteria to define community energy that are listed in the Directives revolve around the nature of shareholders and the purpose of the endeavour. The Directives bundle together projects whose shareholders or members are natural persons, local authorities, including municipalities, or Small and Medium Enterprises (SMEs).[12] As a result, rather diverse entities fall within the scope of the notion of community energy drawn up by the Directives, such as, for example, a biomass power plant partially owned and run by a local council, or a wind farm wholly owned by a remote island community.

Quite crucially, the Directives state that community energy projects are expected to provide 'environmental, economic or social community benefits for its members or the local areas where it operates, rather than financial profits'.[13] The Directives are however

[10] See, e.g., UK Government, Department of Energy and Climate Change, *Community Energy Strategy* (2014), 47; Scottish Government, *Community Energy Policy Statement* (2015), 6.

[11] Recast Renewables Directive, Article 22.1.

[12] Recast Renewables Directive, Article 2.16; and Recast Electricity Directive, Article 2.11.

[13] Recast Renewables Directive, Article 2.15; and Recast Electricity Directive, Article 2.11.

silent on how the benefits that community energy projects are expected to deliver may be measured, reported, and assessed.

The Directives instead merely require Member States to adopt 'enabling frameworks to promote and facilitate' renewable energy communities, by removing unjustified regulatory and administrative barriers.[14] The main elements of these enabling frameworks and the related implementation measures will have to be reported in updates of Member States' integrated national energy and climate plans and progress reports.[15]

The Directives, therefore, do not attempt to solve the many intricate regulatory questions associated with mainstreaming of community energy,[16] which are left to Member States to address. The Directives do, however, point to a set of factors—such as capacity-building, access to information, finance, and markets—that have been crucial in the practice of those Member States with greater regulatory experience with the mainstreaming of community energy.

The picture emerging from these pioneer Member States is fragmented. Denmark was arguably the original pioneer of community energy and has a large number of wind cooperatives. The historically important role of the community sector in Denmark's energy transition has been widely reported in the literature, but has faltered in recent years.[17] From a historical perspective Denmark provides insights into the underlying conditions shaping the development of community energy from a thriving to a declining sector.[18]

Germany's transformative experience with community energy—which reportedly delivers a large share of the renewable energy in the country—became an international success story and a blueprint for others. Since the reform of the feed-in tariff system however, the community sector has lost pace and struggles to adapt to the new policy.[19] The German case is therefore interesting for exploring how a strong and well-established sector is continuing to develop with the support of local authorities, while grappling with challenges associated with costs and a changing regulatory environment.

The UK's community energy sector is young and modest, compared with that of Denmark and Germany. The bulk of the progress—both in terms of policy and infrastructure—has taken place in Scotland, where the Scottish Government has made a concerted effort to establish a supportive environment for communities to take ownership of energy projects. This experience has been widely studied and has produced some of the most innovative and interesting scholarship on community energy in recent years, with Scotland becoming a veritable living lab to experiment new solutions to mainstreaming community energy, in the face of highly volatile subsidies from the

[14] Recast Renewables Directive, Articles 21.6 and 22.4; and Recast Electricity Directive, Article 16.1.
[15] Recast Renewables Directive, Articles 21.6 and 22.5.
[16] These are analysed in Savaresi (n 9).
[17] See Mey and Diesendorf (n 6).
[18] See for example Gorroño-Albizu, Sperling, and Djørup (n 6).
[19] F.W. Geels, et al., 'The Enactment of Socio-Technical Transition Pathways: A Reformulated Typology and a Comparative Multi-Level Analysis of the German and UK Low-Carbon Electricity Transitions (1990–2014)' (2016) 45 *Research Policy*, 896.

UK Government.[20] Consequently, the UK case provides an interesting opportunity to consider the implications of the mainstreaming community energy in a regulatory environment where experience with the cooperative model and local authority's powers are limited.

III. Justice Questions Associated with Community Energy

Writing on policy change for public engagement with energy infrastructure, Cowell and Devine Wright note that the energy transition requires decisions about which issues are open for contestation, and at which stage in the policy and decision-making process. In turn, this process requires balances to be struck between different dimensions of justice, in the light of the situations that certain energy infrastructures create.[21]

Energy justice scholarship identifies a set of fundamental questions on how the benefits and burdens of transitioning are shared; who is involved in decision-making processes and how; and how are any wrongs remedied and/or compensated.[22] So far legal scholarship has selectively looked at these questions, largely focusing on procedural justice, and without specifically considering community energy.[23]

In relation to community energy, justice considerations translate into *procedural* questions over who participates in decision-making in relation to projects and how; how community membership is determined and by whom; and how communities' capabilities to engage in renewable generation are built. On *distributive* justice, the matter is instead whether and how the benefits of renewable energy generation are shared within a given community and with entities beyond the community. Finally, from the perspective of *restorative* justice, the question is how negative impacts are redressed, both within and without a given community.

These questions tend to intersect with one another, and indeed the distinction between them is often artificial. Equally, the answers to these questions do not come from law only, or from one single law or policy instrument. Instead, and rather typically, these answers come from the interplay of energy, environmental, land, planning, property, and human rights law. With this fundamental caveat in mind, the next sections consider the main procedural, distributive, and restorative justice associated

[20] See e.g., the analysis in B. Slee and J. Harnmeijer, 'Community Renewables: Balancing Optimism with Reality', in G. Wood and K. Baker (eds), *A Critical Review of Scottish Renewable and Low Carbon Energy Policy* (Palgrave Macmillan, 2017); A. McHarg, 'Community Benefit Through Community Ownership of Renewable Generation in Scotland: Power to the People?', in L. Barrera-Hernandez, et al. (eds), *Sharing the Costs and Benefits of Energy and Resource Activity* (Oxford University Press, 2016).

[21] R. Cowell and P. Devine-Wright, 'A "Delivery-Democracy Dilemma"? Mapping and Explaining Policy Change for Public Engagement with Energy Infrastructure' (2018) 20 *Journal of Environmental Policy & Planning*, 499, 514.

[22] See, e.g., K. Jenkins, et al., 'Energy Justice: A Conceptual Review' (2016) 11 *Energy Research & Social Science*, 174, 166–7.

[23] With the sole exception of McHarg (n 20).

with community energy and how they may be answered, drawing on examples from Denmark, Germany, and the UK.

A. Procedural Justice

The matter of decision-making on the generation of renewable energy has received much attention in the literature.[24] Less literature exists on the specific procedural justice questions associated with community energy.[25] It seems clear however that, even though community projects are expected to overcome public resistance to the development of renewable energy generation plants, they raise procedural justice questions, both in relation to those included in project ownership, as well as those who are not.[26] In response, this section unpacks these questions, considering how community membership is defined, who can partake in projects and how.

The criteria to define the scope of community membership in a project are paramount in understanding its procedural justice implications. In this connection, the literature often distinguishes between communities 'of place' to indicate those who happen to live in the area where a project is developed; and communities 'of interest', to indicate those who choose to actively engage with a project.[27] The literature reports how both typologies of community engage in the generation of renewable energy.[28]

It is furthermore important to distinguish between, on the one hand, proactive shared ownership, that is, when a community takes the initiative and establishes a joint venture with a commercial developer; and reactive shared ownership, that is, when members of a given community are offered the possibility to purchase shares in a project led by a commercial developer.

When a community initiates a project, it is in principle free to define the boundaries of community membership, in the context of a process of self-identification.[29] Self-identification is widely recommended as best practice in natural resource

[24] See, e.g., M. Aitken, S. McDonald, and P. Strachan, 'Locating "Power" in Wind Power Planning Processes: The (Not so) Influential Role of Local Objectors' (2008) 51 *Journal of Environmental Planning and Management*, 777; C. Armeni, 'Participation in Environmental Decision-Making: Reflecting on Planning and Community Benefits for Major Wind Farms' (2016) 28 *Journal of Environmental Law*, 415.

[25] N. Simcock, 'Exploring How Stakeholders in Two Community Wind Projects Use a "Those Affected" Principle to Evaluate the Fairness of Each Project's Spatial Boundary' (2014) 19 *Local Environment*, 241; N. Simcock, 'Procedural Justice and the Implementation of Community Wind Energy Projects: A Case Study from South Yorkshire, UK' (2016) 59 *Land Use Policy*, 467; B. van Veelen and C. Haggett, 'Uncommon Ground: The Role of Different Place Attachments in Explaining Community Renewable Energy Projects' (2017) 57 *Sociologia Ruralis*, 533; E. Creamer, et al., 'Community Energy: Entanglements of Community, State, and Private Sector' (2018) 12 *Geography Compass*, e12378; B. van Veelen, 'Negotiating Energy Democracy in Practice: Governance Processes in Community Energy Projects' (2018) 27 *Environmental Politics*, 644.

[26] As noted for example in Aitken, McDonald, and Strachan (n 24).

[27] The elaboration of these notions is attributed to the classic works by H.F. Kaufmann, 'Towards an Interactional Concept of Community' (1959) 38 *Social Forces*, 8; and K.P. Wilkinson, *The Community in Rural America* (Greenwood, 1991). See, e.g., M. Brennan, J. Birdger, and T.R Alter, *Theory, Practice, and Community Development* (Routledge, 2013) 41.

[28] See, e.g., G. Bristow, R. Cowell, and M. Munday, 'Windfalls for Whom? The Evolving Notion of "Community" in Community Benefit Provisions from Wind Farms' (2012) 43 *Geoforum*, 1108, 1109.

[29] For example, the Community Empowerment (Scotland) Act, Part 1, 1.11 defines community as including 'any community based on common interest, identity or geography'.

management.[30] Thus, in the energy context, a community initiating a renewable energy generation project may decide, for example, to restrict membership to those residing in an island, or in a housing estate.

Some forms of renewable energy generation postulate access to natural resources, such as water (in case of hydro power) or land (in case of wind power). This in turn means that only those communities that already have access to these resources, or who can get access to them, may partake in energy projects. In this connection, Scotland provides a unique example of a community right to buy land, even in cases where the land owner is unwilling to sell.[31] This is subjected to the requirement that the land is 'wholly or mainly abandoned or neglected' or somehow managed in a way that is detrimental to a community's 'environmental well-being'; [32] or that the acquired land be used to 'further sustainable development'.[33]

The availability of support and/or of public/private finance for community projects is another factor significantly conditioning the scope of community membership.[34] For instance the policies on eligibility for funding for community energy may significantly contribute to determine the scope of those willing and able to be involved in projects. Over the years, dedicated forms of support for the development of community-owned renewable energy generation plants have been created in Denmark, the UK, and Germany.[35]

Criteria concerning eligibility to access support or other incentives may also influence the choice of legal form shaping community endeavours—most typically, co-operatives, trusts, foundations, or community owned companies.[36] For example, for a variety of historical and sociological reasons, associated also with favourable funding conditions,[37] the cooperative model has historically been predominant in Denmark,[38] and is presently widespread in Germany,[39] but is not as frequently used in the UK.

[30] See, e.g., the definition of local community in the context of the 1992 Convention on Biological Diversity, Report of the Expert Group Meeting of Local Communities Representatives, UN Doc UNEP/CBD/WG8J/7/8/Add.1 (2011)—as analysed in A. Savaresi, 'The International Human Rights Law Implications of the Nagoya Protocol', in E. Morgera, M. Buck, and E. Tsioumani (eds), *The 2010 Nagoya Protocol on Access and Benefit-sharing in Perspective* (Martinus Nijhoff, 2013), 75–8.

[31] See McHarg (n 20), 307; M.M. Combe, 'The Environmental Implications of Redistributive Land Reform' (2016) 18 *Environmental Law Review*, 104.

[32] Community Empowerment (Scotland) Act (2015) section 74.

[33] Land Reform (Scotland) Act (2016) Part 5.

[34] As suggested also in B. Barton and M. Goldsmith, 'Community and Sharing', in L. Barrera-Hernandez, et al. (eds), *Sharing the Costs and Benefits of Energy and Resource Activity: Legal Change and Impact on Communities* (Oxford University Press, 2016), 31–2.

[35] See Savaresi (n 9), 15.

[36] See, e.g., C. Haggett and M. Aitken, 'Grassroots Energy Innovations: The Role of Community Ownership and Investment' (2015) 2 *Current Sustainable/Renewable Energy Reports*, 98, 101; Slee and Harnmeijer (n 20), 49.

[37] R. Bolton, T. Foxon, and S. Hall, 'Energy Transitions and Uncertainty: Creating Low Carbon Investment Opportunities in the UK Electricity Sector' (2016) *Environment and Planning C: Government and Policy*, 1387, 12; C. Nolden, 'Governing Community Energy—Feed-in Tariffs and the Development of Community Wind Energy Schemes in the United Kingdom and Germany' (2013) 63 *Energy Policy*, 543, 548.

[38] See, e.g., B.K Sovacool, 'Energy Policymaking in Denmark: Implications for Global Energy Security and Sustainability' (2013) 61 *Energy Policy*, 829, 30; C. Banet, 'Enabling the Crowdfunding of Energy Projects', in L. Barrera-Hernandez, et al. (eds), *Sharing the Costs and Benefits of Energy and Resource Activity: Legal Change and Impact on Communities* (Oxford University Press, 2016), 334.

[39] See, e.g., E. Schmid, et al., 'Imagine All These Futures: On Heterogeneous Preferences and Mental Models in the German Energy Transition' (2017) *Complete Energy Research & Social Science*, 45, 35.

In the case of reactive ownership, legislation often plays a major role in determining the scope of community. Danish law, for example, imposes on developers an obligation to offer a 20 per cent ownership stake to those living at a distance of 4.5 km from the energy project site.[40] If the shares are not sold, they may be offered to other local residents. This is however not a collective right, and it only benefits individuals.[41] The fact that shares are offered for sale further limits the scope of community only to those with the financial means to make a purchase.[42] Availability of financial capital therefore crucially determines who gets involved in a project.[43]

The approach embedded in Danish law has inspired similar measures in the UK. In 2015 the UK introduced a 'community electricity right' giving 'individuals resident in a community or groups connected with a community, or both' (*sic*), the right to buy a stake in new commercial renewable projects that are either located in the community (in the case of land-based projects), or adjacent to the community (in the case of offshore projects).[44] The community electricity right was introduced with the understanding that a voluntary approach would be tested first, and that regulatory powers would be exercised only if the voluntary approach did not deliver the hoped for results.[45] While these regulatory powers are yet to be exercised, the relevant factors for identifying those entitled to benefit from the community energy right include: distance from the facility; the number of residents; and administrative boundaries.[46] Therefore, in the UK, like in Denmark, a geographical criterion for determining community membership seems to have prevailed.

This focus on so-called communities of place is clearly associated with a desire to address social acceptance and to counter local resistance to the development of projects. This geographical focus however raises the question of whether and how communities of interest may or should be included in project ownership. At least in principle, project shares could be offered to all those willing to engage, rather than just local residents. Indeed, experience with equity-based crowdfunding—that is, with investors purchasing an equity stake in the form of securities in a project or a commercial company[47]—suggests that there may be considerable financial opportunities to be seized by expanding the boundaries of ownership beyond the local level. Moreover, while historically law and policy have resorted to geographical criteria to determine the scope of community membership, a more flexible approach to the definition of community seems to be progressively emerging, with nuancing between 'host' and 'less immediate' communities.[48]

[40] Denmark, Promotion of Renewable Energy Act (2008), sections 13–17.

[41] As noted also in A. Rønne, 'Opposition to Wind Farms and Possible Responses of the Legal System', in L. Barrera-Hernandez, et al. (eds), *Sharing the Costs and Benefits of Energy and Resource Activity: Legal Change and Impact on Communities* (Oxford University Press, 2016), 185.

[42] Ibid. 186.

[43] As noted also in Slee and Harnmeijer (n 20), 51.

[44] Infrastructure Act (2015), paragraphs 38–9. The parallel with Danish law is highlighted also in McHarg (n 20), 302.

[45] UK Government, Department of Energy and Climate Change, Infrastructure Bill: The Community Electricity Right Policy Brief (2014).

[46] Infrastructure Act (2015), schedule 6.

[47] See Banet (n 38), 51.

[48] See, e.g., Bristow, Cowell, and Munday (n 28); Barton and Goldsmith (n 34).

With specific regard to decision-making on community energy, a fundamental distinction needs to be drawn between *intra*-community relations, between those involved in a given project; and *extra*-community relations, between the community, local residents, and other stakeholders who are not involved in a given project.

At the *intra*-community level, limited evidence exists of how communities take decisions, and what processes exist to ensure legitimacy and fairness in intra-community decision-making processes. The legal form of community endeavours may determine some aspects of communities' internal organization. For example, legislation on cooperatives may require following certain decision-making processes. Other issues, nevertheless, are likely to be left entirely to the self-organization of communities. While this margin of discretion chimes with empowerment and self-governance narratives, it may underlie conflict and exclusion that commences from the beginning of a project, when the scope of community is defined, and continues with day-to-day decision-making.[49]

The matter of *extra*-community relations is comparatively better regulated, as a result of public participation requirements in environmental decision-making. Like any other development, in fact, community energy projects are subjected to screening and approval in the context of planning processes.[50] Depending on their size, community projects may also be subjected to an environmental impact assessment (EIA). EIAs and planning procedures, therefore, are important means for the public to have a say on whether or not a community project ought to be carried out, its siting, and design.

As mentioned above, even though broadly speaking community energy policies are expected to better involve local communities in decision-making, they are not immune from raising procedural justice questions, both in relation to those who are not included in project ownership, as well as those who are included. Evidence of community projects that have engendered a remarkable degree of opposition certainly exists. One eloquent example is the Viking Energy project in Shetland, Scotland. A joint venture between the local community and a utility company, this large-scale, shared ownership community project was authorized in 2007 with the aim of setting 103 wind turbines around Shetland, generating a potential output of up to 457 megawatts, one of the largest in the UK. Twelve years on, however, the project has attracted a flurry of public opposition and litigation—instigated on the basis of legislation concerning the protection of bird habitats,[51] and on the rights of local crofters[52]—and the project remains far from completion.

Finally, project ownership often requires communities to collaborate or even take the lead in the establishment and/or management of renewable energy generation plants.

[49] As noted e.g. by Aitken, McDonald, and Strachan (n 24); Simcock (n 25).

[50] As reported for example in H.T. Anker and M.L. Jørgensen, 'Mapping of the Legal Framework for Siting of Wind Turbines' (Department of Food and Resource Economics, University of Copenhagen) IFRO Report, 239, 8.

[51] This specific dispute is now concluded. See UK Supreme Court, *Sustainable Shetland v The Scottish Ministers* [2015] UKSC 4. See McHarg (n 20), 314.

[52] Decision of the Scottish Land Court, Viking Energy Wind Farm LLP (Applicant) v Crofters having rights in the Common Grazings of the Townships of Sandwick, Sweening & Laxo and Other Common Grazings (Respondents), Case reference SLC 31/16, 5 September 2018.

This in turn presupposes a set of capabilities that can either be already embedded in a community, or, conversely, be engendered by means of external support. The matter of external support has attracted specific attention especially in the UK.

Energy production in the UK has long been a highly centralized corporate affair.[53] The adoption of community energy policies in the UK[54] was therefore coupled with the creation of intermediaries supporting communities in interactions both with authorities and corporate actors.[55] The literature describes these intermediaries as organizations 'connecting local projects with one another' as well as 'with the wider world' thus helping to generate a 'shared institutional infrastructure' and knowledge transfer to sustain projects.[56]

The literature reports how these intermediaries have appeared 'in waves' in the UK; with a decisive acceleration in recent years, as a result of the adoption of renewable energy targets at the EU, national, and subnational levels.[57] The plethora of actors presently working with community energy in the UK is diverse and includes intermediaries established by national and subnational governments, as well as non-governmental organizations and private sector professionals.[58] These actors have played a prominent role in community energy projects. Far from being mere neutral brokers providing a shared institutional infrastructure and enabling knowledge transfer, however, intermediaries have increasingly played an active role in community energy projects, thus becoming 'framers and coordinators' of community action,[59] professional services providers, and even project partners. This phenomenon became particularly evident in the aftermath of changes in UK renewable energy subsidies, which prompted some intermediaries to step in and become project co-owners and shareholders, in order to ensure the continued viability of community projects.[60]

While intermediaries have been crucial capacity-builders in contexts where the ability of communities to engage in renewable energy generation is limited, the interests of the community and the intermediaries do not necessarily align. Therefore, there is much scope to better understand when they are mere brokers or, rather, when such intermediaries become the actual drivers of community action. A related question is whether intermediaries genuinely empower communities to make their own choices,

[53] S. Hall, T.J Foxon, and R. Bolton, 'Financing the Civic Energy Sector: How Financial Institutions Affect Ownership Models in Germany and the United Kingdom' (2016) 12 *Energy Research & Social Science*, 5, 8; McHarg (n 20), 298.

[54] For England, see: Department of Energy and Climate Change, Community Energy Strategy (2014); and Community Engagement for Onshore Wind Developments: Best Practice Guidance for England, 2014. For Scotland, see: Scottish Government, Community Energy Policy Statement (2015); and Good Practice Principles for Shared Ownership of Onshore Renewable Energy Developments (2015).

[55] E.g. for England, the Centre for Sustainable Energy; for Scotland, Community Energy Scotland and Local Energy Scotland.

[56] See T. Hargreaves, et al., 'Grassroots Innovations in Community Energy: The Role of Intermediaries in Niche Development' (2013) 23 *Global Environmental Change*, 868, 870.

[57] Ibid., 870 and 872.

[58] Ibid.

[59] Ibid., 876.

[60] As discussed in the presentation by Andy Lyle (Locogen) 'Shared Ownership Lessons' 2017 edition of the Scottish Government's Community and Renewable Energy Scheme Conference, Stirling—notes on file with the author.

or rather merely pass onto them packages of ready-made solutions. An even more crucial justice question concerns whether safeguards exist to ensure that these intermediaries do not take advantage of their position to push for outcomes that favour them over the community. These questions raise a set of complex procedural justice considerations on intra-community decision-making processes and who has voice in these decisions.

B. Distributive Justice

Community energy has been portrayed as a solution to energy poverty, [61] and more broadly, a means to address distributive justice questions associated with the energy transition.[62] Yet, in and of themselves community energy projects raise specific distributive justice questions concerning the sharing of the benefits of community activities.

One of the trickiest questions associated with the mainstreaming of community energy is access to the energy grid and the lack of flexibility in extant governance and infrastructure arrangements concerning the distribution of energy. While community self-consumption does not necessarily require grid connection, many community projects need to be connected to the electricity grid and sell energy on the market, and to be financially viable. Multiple scenarios can be envisioned in this respect and different regulatory approaches have been experimented with in practice.[63]

Communities' statutory access to the electricity grid is provided in Denmark, Germany, and the UK,[64] but this may happen at a cost that in practice hinders the commercial viability of projects. The UK is a case in point, with communities required to bear the costs of connection to the grid, including a share of costs for network reinforcement.[65] The effect has been to hinder projects in marginal areas that are characterized by great renewable energy generation potential and high rates of energy poverty, like the Scottish isles.[66] Therefore, the technical question of grid access is intimately associated with deeper distributive justice questions. Better outcomes have reportedly been achieved in Denmark and Germany, where grid operators take charge of expansion and upgrade costs.[67] In Germany, community energy has engendered momentum for the re-communalization of electricity grids.[68] However, the high costs associated with the

[61] See, e.g., R.W. Saunders, R.J.K. Gross, and J. Wade, 'Can Premium Tariffs for Micro-Generation and Small Scale Renewable Heat Help the Fuel Poor, and If so, How? Case Studies of Innovative Finance for Community Energy Schemes in the UK' (2012) 42 *Energy Policy*, 78. See Chapter 10 in this book.

[62] See, e.g., Jenkins, et al., (n 22), 177.

[63] M. Mendonca, *Feed-in Tariffs: Accelerating the Deployment of Renewable Energy* (Earthscan, 2012), 30–5.

[64] As discussed in Savaresi (n 9), 503.

[65] Connection and Use of System Code (2014) section 2.14. See also Ofgem, Community Energy Grid Connections Working Group Report (2014) 2.

[66] House of Commons Scottish Affairs Committee, The renewable energy sector in Scotland, 2016, 82–8.

[67] Electricity Supply Act (2017) paragraph 67.

[68] Hall, Foxon, and Bolton (n 53), 10; T. Moss, S. Becker, and M. Naumann, 'Whose Energy Transition Is It, Anyway? Organisation and Ownership of the Energiewende in Villages, Cities and Regions' (2015) 20 *Local Environment*, 1547, 1558.

connection of small scale projects have raised concerns over the efficient allocation of financial resources for the energy transition.[69]

The other core distributive justice question associated with community energy concerns benefit-sharing. Similarly to others,[70] the renewable energy sector has in recent years seen a shift from scenarios where communities are treated as passive benefits recipients, towards 'ongoing social contract(s)'[71] that provide a 'genuine two-way street and a fair exchange' rather than 'a token payment'.[72] Local residents have therefore been progressively involved in the determination of what benefits they receive to various degrees in all surveyed countries. Intermediaries have played an important role in the design of benefit-sharing templates and, more generally, in engendering community capacity to negotiate benefits.[73]

Some law-makers have developed guidelines on community benefits.[74] There is however a great deal of variation in practice amongst states, and even within the same state. The UK, for example, has taken a voluntary approach to benefit-sharing,[75] which is not a formal requirement, though it is largely expected in practice.[76] Scotland has moreover created a registry of community benefits and adopted guidelines on what benefits should consist of, as well as how they should be determined, placing specific emphasis on dialogue with communities, but leaving it to developers to identify who these may be.[77]

In spite of their widespread uptake, the literature reports that benefit-sharing arrangements tend to be perceived as a bribe to secure project approval and/or minimize public resistance from local communities.[78] Some literature points to opportunities associated with greater institutionalization of benefits,[79] as well as with their framing in more positive terms,[80] even though evidence emerging from Denmark does not necessarily corroborate this proposition.[81]

[69] Geels, et al., (n 19), 904.

[70] See, e.g., the discussion of developments in biodiversity law in L. Parks, 'Challenging Power Asymmetries from the Bottom Up? Community Protocols and the Convention on Biological Diversity at the Global/Local Crossroads' (Social Science Research Network 2016) https://papers.ssrn.com/abstract=2884965 accessed 24 March 2017.

[71] ClientEarth, 'Community Power Report' (ClientEarth 2016) 123 .

[72] Scottish Parliament's Economy, Energy and Tourism Committee, Report on the achievability of the Scottish Government's renewable energy targets, SP Paper 220, 2012, 243.

[73] As reported for example in Bristow, Cowell, and Munday (n 28), 1115.

[74] As discussed in Savaresi (n 9); and P.V. Herrejon and A. Savaresi, 'Wind Energy, Benefit-Sharing and Indigenous Peoples: Lessons from the Isthmus of Tehuantepec, Southern Mexico' (2020) *Oil, Gas & Energy Law Journal* (OGEL) https://www.ogel.org/journal-advance-publication-article.asp?key=604 accessed 30 July 2019.

[75] See UK Government, Department of Energy and Climate Change, Benefits Best Practice Guidance, 2014.

[76] As noted in McHarg (n 20), 306.

[77] See Scottish Government, Good Practice Principles for Community Benefits from Onshore Renewable Developments, 2015, 6–7. See also Scottish Government, Good Practice Principles for Community Benefits from Offshore Renewable Developments, 2015.

[78] See, e.g., B.J.A. Walker, D. Russel, and T. Kurz, 'Community Benefits or Community Bribes? An Experimental Analysis of Strategies for Managing Community Perceptions of Bribery Surrounding the Siting of Renewable Energy Projects' (2017) 49 *Environment and Behavior*, 59.

[79] Ibid.

[80] See, e.g., D. Rudolph, C. Haggett, and M. Aitken, 'Community Benefits from Offshore Renewables: The Relationship between Different Understandings of Impact, Community, and Benefit' (2017) *Environment and Planning C: Politics and Space*, 10 .

[81] M.L. Jørgensen, 'Compensation Schemes and Distributive Fairness in Wind Energy Projects' (2017) (European Environmental Law Forum Annual Conference, Copenhagen) http://law.au.dk/fileadmin/Jura/dokumenter/forskning/EELF/MARIE_LEER__31.08.pdf accessed 26 July 2018. See discussion in Savaresi (n 9).

The recasts of the RES and Electricity Directives expect community energy projects to provide benefits, but do not elaborate on how these should be defined, quantified, monitored, or distributed. As noted above, while some law-makers have developed voluntary guidance on benefits from renewable energy generation projects, this is not specific to community projects. And while benefit-sharing arrangements are widespread in the practice of renewable energy generation, little evidence exists of how decisions on who benefits, how, and of the criteria used to identify benefits and beneficiaries in community energy projects.[82]

With community energy, benefit-sharing assumes both an extra-community and an intra-community dimension. At the intra-community level, it is up to communities to choose how to distribute benefits, though intermediaries can be important in steering community practice. While community energy policies are often based on the assumption that communities of place may place greater emphasis on long-term, collective benefits, this assumption is not necessarily corroborated by evidence.[83] Indeed, little systematic information and research exists on intra-community benefit-sharing arrangements.

At the extra-community level, the question of benefit-sharing resurfaces in relation to those who are not part of a given community, but are affected by a renewable energy project. Also here, an overall lack of data seems to exist on whether and how benefit-sharing arrangements in community energy projects differ from those in non-community owned projects. Once more, the fact that community projects deliver better outcomes in terms of distributive justice seems to be assumed. The imminent implementation of the Renewables and the Electricity Directives therefore calls for greater assessment of the practice of community energy in pioneer states, to understand when community projects actually deliver societal benefits, and when they do not.

C. Restorative Justice

Renewable energy generation raises burden-sharing and restorative justice questions that are not too dissimilar to those associated with the development of any infrastructure. For example, the establishment of hydroelectric dams may affect pre-existing water uses and the rights and interests of those using a given water basin for fishing, irrigation, recreational purposes, and other uses. The same may be said, *mutatis mutandis*, about onshore wind and its impacts on existing land uses, including species and habitat conservation. Reported human rights abuses associated with renewable energy

[82] V. Brummer, 'Community Energy – Benefits and Barriers: A Comparative Literature Review of Community Energy in the UK, Germany and the USA, the Benefits It Provides for Society and the Barriers It Faces' (2018) 94 *Renewable and Sustainable Energy Reviews*, 187.

[83] Bristow, Cowell, and Munday (n 28), 1199; van Veelen and Haggett (n 25).

generation are on the rise and include: killings, threats, intimidation; land grabs; inadequate working conditions; and encroachment of indigenous peoples' land and livelihoods.[84]

Law and policy play a particularly important role in recalibrating the balance between societal interests in the context of the development of renewable energy generation plants. Before a project is approved, EIA and planning processes provide opportunities to debate potential burden-sharing arrangements.[85] When a project has been approved, negative impacts, such as reduced quality of life, may be mitigated by means of compensation, obtained through the exercise of tort or public law remedies.

Innovative solutions have been experimented with in Denmark, where a semi-automatic mechanism for the compensation for the loss of value of real estate exists. Thus Danish law requires those developing new wind energy generation plants to compensate those affected *before* a project is developed, and only if the loss is of a certain entity.[86] As Rønne notes, this arrangement is problematic, as it conveys the impression that wind farms are a source of nuisance by default.[87] Another problematic aspect is the adequacy of compensation provided, as well as the fact that receiving compensation at this stage does hinder subsequent legal action.[88]

Burden-sharing considerations are closely interconnected with the protection of a series of human rights, most saliently the right to respect for one's private family life, as well as the right to property.[89] States' obligations to adopt measures protecting against violations of these rights encompass harm caused by private actors. States however also enjoy a great deal of discretion in striking a balance between societal interests.[90]

In the context of community projects, burden-sharing arrangements have both an intra, as well as an extra-community dimension. With regard to the latter, community projects raise burden-sharing questions like any other project. The matter is to understand whether burden sharing is less problematic, or easier to carry out in relation to community projects. Even less is known about intra-community burden sharing. Beyond the remit of what is prescribed by law, burden sharing is a matter for internal community decision-making, upon which no reflection seems to exist in the literature.

While the literature optimistically portrays community energy as a means to address human rights concerns associated with the expansion of the production of renewable energy,[91] the evidence produced in support of this assertion is anecdotal. This is therefore another area where further, rigorous investigation would seem in order to assess whether community projects deliver 'just' outcomes for communities. An analysis of

[84] A. Signorelli and E. Horvath, 'Fast & Fair Renewable Energy: A Practical Guide for Investors' (Business & Human Rights Resource Centre, 2019) https://www.business-humanrights.org/en/fast-fair-renewable-energy-a-practical-guide-for-investors accessed 31 July 2019; Herrejon and Savaresi (n 74).

[85] As observed also in Anker and Jørgensen (n 50), 8.

[86] Promotion of Renewable Energy Act, Part 2.

[87] As suggested also in Rønne (n 41), 188.

[88] As noted for example in Jørgensen (n 81).

[89] See, e.g., the use of human rights arguments against the establishment of a wind farm before the European Court of Human Rights in *Fägerskiöld v Sweden*, Application no 37664/04 Admissibility.

[90] Report of the Special Rapporteur on the issue of human rights obligations relating to the enjoyment of a safe, clean, healthy and sustainable environment (2016) A/HRC/31/52, 66.

[91] See Signorelli and Horvath (n 84), 8.

litigation associated with community projects, for example, could provide a clearer picture of when and how burden sharing associated with community projects is contested, and whether and how this differs from non-community driven projects.

Finally, broader burden-sharing considerations are associated with the cost of producing energy at the community level, and whether and how this is captured in energy prices. In Germany, for example, the widespread uptake of renewable energy has engendered unexpected perverse outcomes for the cost of electricity, placing financial burdens on lower income households, and benefitting upper income ones.[92] Measures to address this inefficiency have recently been put in place, resulting in a slowdown in the uptake of community energy.[93]

IV. Conclusion

This chapter probes the sometimes uncritical assumptions about community energy, highlighting the complex, layered, conflicting justice claims that underlie its mainstreaming. It explores how legal scholarship is a key means to make sense of that complexity and, eventually to translate justice claims into practice, highlighting areas for further research.

On procedural justice, this chapter has shown that there is a host of questions, which rather than being resolved, merely assume new nuances in the context of community energy. One crucial interrogative in this connection is how community membership itself is defined. Regulatory experience thus far shows that geography has been a predominant criterion. Yet, no one single paradigm exists and greater reflection is needed on how to define community membership; and on whether greater attention ought to be paid to communities of interest, as opposed to communities of place. More generally, this chapter has evidenced that little data exists on decision-making in and on opposition to community projects. Greater understanding of the role of intermediaries would furthermore be in order to understand whether and how community agency is constrained by the involvement of brokers, and the justice considerations associated with this intervention.

On distributive justice, this chapter has analysed questions concerning access to the grid and benefit-sharing. It revealed that apparently technical questions underlie deeper justice interrogatives associated with energy governance arrangements. Similarly, on benefit-sharing, while community energy is often portrayed as a means to move communities beyond a passive role, the assumption that it delivers more equitable outcomes largely remains to be proved. Yet, little specific research on benefit-sharing arrangements associated with community projects exists and there seems to be much scope to further investigate what benefits community projects deliver and to whom.

[92] P. Grösche and C. Schröder, 'On the Redistributive Effects of Germany's Feed-in Tariff' (2014) 46 *Empirical Economics*, 1339.

[93] REN21, 'Renewables 2018 Global Status Report' (REN21, 2018), 41 http://www.ren21.net/gsr-2018/ accessed 8 August 2018.

On restorative justice, this chapter has queried whether community energy is an efficacious means to equitably share the burdens associated with the development and operation of renewable energy generation plants. It suggests that burden sharing takes on new facets in the context of community energy, which remain to be fully explored. An analysis of litigation associated with community projects would likely provide greater understanding of whether and how these restorative justice questions are addressed.

In sum, this chapter has shown that the suitability of community energy to deliver in terms of equity and justice is oftentimes assumed, rather than tested and proved. With states all over the world looking to engender the energy transition, greater scholarly enquiry into the justice implications of community agency in renewable energy generation is in order. This chapter has reflected on what we know, what we still do not know and suggested directions in which future enquiry could venture. The answers to the questions it raised cannot come from legal scholarship alone. While law plays an important role in setting the frame in which justice questions emerge and are resolved, it is but a small piece in a complex puzzle, whose resolution postulates interdisciplinary collaboration. Moving forward, greater interdisciplinary and transdisciplinary thinking seems necessary to connect, build, and improve extant knowledge on how to deliver the societal benefits of community energy envisioned in the recasts of the EU's 2030 Climate and Energy Framework.

6

Electricity Network Tariffs Regulation and Distributive Energy Justice

Balancing the Need for New Investments and a Fair Energy Transition

Catherine Banet

I. Introduction

The purpose of this chapter is to investigate how the regulation by law of electricity distribution network tariffs can accommodate the concomitant needs of new investments and distributive energy justice to ensure a fair energy transition for both operators and energy consumers.

The electricity prices paid by final consumers are commonly structured around three main components: the energy cost, that is, the price of electricity generation, trade, and supply; network charges, for both transmission or distribution; and taxes and other surcharges, including Value Added Tax (VAT), various tax contributions, and support measures.

Network charges relate to the costs of using the networks to transport electricity. For public networks, they are usually fixed by the competent authorities through tariff regulation to ensure fair access and avoid any abuse of dominant position by operators in a position of natural monopoly. They are therefore termed 'network tariffs'. The regulation of network charges also aims to provide a careful balance between the coverage of grid maintenance, operation and development costs for the operator, and a fair access price for the grid users, both electricity producers and consumers. Network tariffs represent the main source of revenues for network operators, and a cost recovery shortfall may put them in a difficult financial situation or cause them to refuse new requests from users. The share of the network charges in the electricity bill vary from country to country, ranging from 20 to 40 per cent according to the International Energy Agency (IEA) estimates.[1] For example, in 2018, network charges for household electricity bills represented 27 per cent in France[2] and 25 per cent in Norway.[3]

[1] International Energy Agency, *Re-powering Markets* (2016), 210.
[2] Source: CRE.
[3] Source: NVE.

Catherine Banet, Electricity Network Tariffs Regulation and Distributive Energy Justice In: *Energy Justice and Energy Law*. Edited by Íñigo Del Guayo, Lee Godden, Donald N. Zillman, Milton Fernando Montoya, and José Juan González, Oxford University Press (2020).
 DOI: 10.1093/oso/9780198860754.003.0006

It is expected that electricity consumers, both households and large consumers, will face an increase in grid costs associated with their consumption in the years to come due to the need for investments in grid infrastructures. Both ageing infrastructures and new production/consumption patterns that rely increasingly on distributed and alternative sources will require transmission and distribution operators (TSOs and DSOs) to make significant financial investments.[4] In particular, DSOs are in the front line of the energy transition and distribution network tariff design will be the focus of this chapter. Ninety per cent of variable renewable energy generation is already connected to the distribution grid.[5] New consumption patterns related to local flexibility management, demand response, aggregation, batteries, electrification of transport, and peer-to-peer trading are among the factors adding complexity to the traditional tasks of the DSOs. All these new tasks may represent business opportunities for DSOs, but they also add a financial burden which is not always reflected in the structure of network tariffs. This requires a reconsideration of the remuneration model of the DSOs, including the provision of incentives to make them rely on new factors such as flexibility and not only on investments where appropriate.

Traditionally, the network costs are transferred to final consumers, who will bear the financial burden. This is added to a continuous increase during the past decade of the contribution to renewable energy source (RES) support as part of the tax component of the bill. The application of network tariffs to new renewable energy generators feeding the grid has also varied. This raises a fundamental question of distributive energy justice, where final consumers will have to pay higher electricity prices to finance the energy transition, while not always being incentivized or rewarded for a change in consumption behaviour under current legislation. Customers may react to the changing network tariff parameters by adapting consumption, developing prosumption, or even storing electricity. Therefore, network tariff structure could send signals to consumers and enable them to adapt their use of the network (consumer empowerment). With a correct tariff design, network costs may even be reduced due to the optimization of investments and a more efficient use of distribution networks.

In the framework of the energy transition, the existing tariff structures are being challenged. Therefore, a reflection has started in several jurisdictions to address the need for revising distribution network tariff structure(s) in order to ensure a fair transfer of costs between primarily DSOs and electricity producers and consumers. It aims at developing the right incentives through tariff regulation. This chapter reviews theory and practice of distribution network tariff regulatory reforms at EU-level and in selected European countries in the context of the energy transition, focusing on residential consumers. It starts by detailing the components of network tariffs (section II) and the common principles governing their design (section III). It then reviews the guiding principles proposed for the re-design of network tariff structure with the

[4] For a discussion on the fundamental changes in how distribution networks are used, see Council of European Energy Regulators (CEER), 'The Future Role of DSOs' A CEER Conclusions Paper, Ref. C15-DSO-16-03 (2015).

[5] European Commission, Proposal for a Directive on common rules for the internal market in electricity (recast), COM(2016) 864 final/2, 23 February 2017, at 6.

purpose of balancing the need for new investments and a fair energy transition. Next, the question of the need for coordination and even harmonization of network tariff structure is raised, looking at the attempts made through the EU Clean Energy Package for all Europeans to advance a common methodology (section IV). Finally, the chapter discusses aspects of procedural justice when tariff structures are subject to adjudication and judicial review (section V). The chapter ends with some concluding remarks (section VI).

II. Understanding Electricity Network Tariff Components and Their Effects on Distributive Energy Justice

A. General Definition of Network Tariff Components

Tariff structures can generally be organized according to two alternatives: volume-based tariff and capacity-based tariff. In practice, many hybrid models exist, and offer a combination of these two. They also integrate some fixed components. Additional variables, such as customer categories and other mechanisms to recover grid costs, will also affect grid tariff design. The effects on distributive energy justice will vary accordingly.

1. Volumetric Network Tariff

A volumetric tariff is based on the volume of electricity consumed by the final customer and is expressed in €/kWh. The customer is charged for the electricity—the commodity—consumed (consumption-based tariffs). A majority of European countries apply tariff models based on volume or having a dominant volume component.

Volumetric tariffs can be designed according to several alternatives. They can be proportionate, progressive, degressive, or based on time-of-use. The choice of alternative will depend on the status of the market as well as technology deployment. These models are notably easier to implement with traditional metering systems. If the volume tariffs are proportionate, consumers pay per kWh or m^3 consumed, irrespective of volume level. If they are progressive, the tariffs per kWh will increase proportionately with an increasing consumption level. At the opposite end of the spectrum, degressive tariffs per kWh will decrease with an increasing consumption level. If based on time-of-use, volume tariffs will reflect the available capacity in the grid and are intended to move consumption from peak time (with high tariffs) to off-peak times (with lower tariffs). A day/night tariff may also be applied, even without smart meters, whereas more complex peak and off-peak tariffs will require smart metering.[6]

This model has both advantages and disadvantages for the DSO and consumers in terms of distributive energy justice. Volumetric tariffs provide good incentives for

[6] European Federation of Local and Regional Energy Companies (CEDEC), 'Distribution Grid Tariff Structures for Smart Grids and Smart Markets' Position Paper (2014) (hereafter CEDEC, 'Distribution Grid Tariff Structure').

customers to adjust their behaviour by reducing or relocating energy consumption during the day, as well as using energy efficient appliances. With self-generation and self-consumption, customers feed less electricity into the grid. Consequently, less electricity will be transported to the grids connecting those types of customers. Having a tariff based on volume consumed seems advantageous for those final customers, but can create important financial uncertainty and balancing challenges for DSOs, in particular in a scenario of massive solar photovoltaic (PV) deployment.

2. Capacity-based Network Tariff

A capacity tariff is based on the capacity of the connection to the grid. It reflects peak load, with the consequence that consumers with high peak loads pay high network costs. Currently, there is a general support for moving towards more capacity-based tariffs so as to better adapt to the changes in the energy system and reflect operating expenses (OPEX).

The most common design options for capacity tariff are to be flat, variable, or dependent on the time of use (TOU). If the capacity tariff is flat, a fixed fee will be charged according to the connection capacity (kVA) or the measured capacity (kW). If the capacity tariff is variable, different tariffs will apply to the different capacity levels. A capacity tariff based on the TOU will vary to reflect the available capacity in the grid (with peaks and off peaks), and will require a smart meter.[7]

In terms of distributive energy justice, several reports stress the degressive effect that capacity tariffs can have on the price per kWh, with the result that small consumers will proportionally pay more and be those who are impacted most. However, DSOs will find the model advantageous as it will better reflect varying capacity usage of the grid. It may reduce their costs related to grid capacity management.[8]

3. Fixed Components

Fixed components are independent of individual consumption factors, such as demand or consumption. They are expressed in €/point of delivery.

4. Multiple Component Tariffs

Multiple component tariffs are hybrid solutions combining elements from both capacity and volume-based tariff models, with fixed and/or variable components. Examples of such hybrid models applied to industrial customers can be found in Belgium, France, the Netherlands, and Italy.

The organization CEDEC has conducted a comparative analysis of the volume and capacity models, measuring their performance based on the extent to which they respect the guiding principles of tariff structures (see section below) on the one hand; on the other hand, they achieve general policy objectives (energy markets, climate policies, and security of supply). CEDEC concludes that, 'apparently, capacity driven

[7] CEDEC, 'Distribution Grid Tariff Structure', 4.
[8] CEDEC, 'Distribution Grid Tariff Structure'.

tariffs bring the most appropriate answer to the guiding principles for tariff setting'; while 'volume driven tariffs are more in line with the formulated energy and climate policy objectives.'[9] Therefore, hybrid tariffs with multiple components could be the most appropriate solutions to balance these apparently contradictory effects.

B. Examples of National Network Tariff Regulation and Distributive Effects

The structure of network tariffs varies widely within Europe. It reflects both historical energy policy choices, the set-up of the energy system, and the pace at which network users and operators react to new technologies.

In Italy, more than 150 DSOs operate the distribution grid and report data to the regulator, who in turn is competent for setting the distribution tariffs. The regulation defines different tariff classes corresponding to different customer types (household, commercial) as well as the voltage levels (low, medium, high, and extra high). For all types, the distribution network tariff consists of the three above mentioned components: a flat component, a capacity component at connection point (€/kW), and a progressive energy or volume component (€/kWh). The volume component will be more predominant for household consumers (66 per cent) than for industrial tariffs (17 per cent). Another feature is that the tariffs are not geographically differentiated.

In France, the operation of the distribution grid is dominated by one main company, Enedis (95 per cent), but many local distribution companies are operating at lower levels. The French Energy Code provides for the criteria and methodology for elaborating the distribution tariffs. It defines their elaboration and approval procedure. Details regarding implementation are determined and set by the Energy Regulatory Commission (CRE) and/or by Decree. The acronym of the network tariff model for electricity networks and related installations is TURPE (*tarifs d'utilisation des réseaux publics d'électricité*). There is not one, but several TURPE-tariffs, according to the type of installation (distinguishing source and location) and the type of network user. The methodology for setting the tariffs must be based on transparent, non-discriminatory criteria.[10] The elaboration of tariffs shall reflect three main principles: (i) the 'postage stamp' tarification principle (*timbre-poste*), which means that the same tariff applies whatever the distance of transportation;[11] (ii) the same tariffs apply to the whole French territory (so-called *péréquation tarifaire*);[12] and (iii) the operating costs covered are those corresponding to the costs of an efficient operation. For each update of the tariffs, the TSO and the main DSOs will submit provisional trajectories.

[9] CEDEC, 'Distribution Grid Tariff Structure', 10–11.

[10] Article L.341-2, Energy Code (France).

[11] In accordance with Article 14.1 of Regulation (EC) nr. 714/2009, which provides that 'charges shall not be distance-related'.

[12] Article L. 121-1, Energy Code (France).

In Norway, more than 130 DSOs operate the distribution grid, traditionally comprising a regional grid (33–132 kV) and a distribution grid (up to 22 kV). The distribution grid is itself divided into high-voltage and low-voltage segments. Distribution tariffs have traditionally been mostly volume-based (70 per cent) with some fixed components. They are fixed by the DSOs in accordance with the criteria and the methodology defined by law and supplemented by guidance from the Norwegian Water Resources and Energy Directorate (NVE). The tariffs must be set in a non-discriminatory manner, but can include some differentiation based on objective and verifiable criteria. Another fundamental principle of optimal tariff design is that all grid users should pay a price that is equal to the short-term marginal cost incurred through their use of the grid. The marginal loss can be positive or negative, depending on whether changes in electricity fed into or tapped from the grid increase or decrease the energy loss. For small energy customers, the legislation defines two main components of the network tariffs that also apply to producers, that is, the energy component (NOK/kWh) and the fixed component (NOK/year).[13] The energy component, or usage-dependent energy component, corresponds to compensation for the energy losses in the network system. The energy component for producers who feed into the distribution grid is set based on marginal losses in the network system as a whole. The energy component from the distribution grid may therefore be used to cover a share of the other fixed costs of grid operation. The energy component is not sufficient to cover all grid operation costs and must therefore be supplemented by a fixed component (about 30 per cent of the network tariff).[14] Grid operators use other tariff components to cover the remaining costs and to provide a fair return on grid investments in the form of a fixed charge. The fixed component is paid by metering point, and the metering data is used to adjust the fixed component.[15] There are ongoing discussions in Norway about moving forward towards a more capacity-based model.

The Netherlands appears almost as an exception, since there is no volumetric component in the distribution network for households.[16] This situation results from a reform implemented in 2009, whereby the system transitioned from mainly volume-based tariffs (at 77 per cent), to a capacity-based tariff. The invoice differences for household customers caused by the introduction of the capacity tariffs were neutralized as much as possible through the energy tax, termed the 'neutralization tax'. The principle of the tariff structure is set by the Minister of Economic Affairs. The tariff principles are further detailed by the National Regulatory Authority (NRA) in a 'tariff code' based on a proposal by DSOs after consultation with other stakeholders.

[13] Customers with an installed capacity exceeding a set limit, e.g. over 80 or 125 amperes, or customers with an expected annual consumption exceeding 100,000 kWh, usually have a capacity charge (NOK/kW) in addition to the fixed and energy charges. The capacity charge is based on used capacity within defined periods of time.

[14] Source: SSB. For a comparison with other Nordic countries, see Nordic Energy Regulators (NorREG), 'Tariffs in Nordic countries—survey of load tariffs in DSO grids', Report 3/2015, Annex 4.

[15] See Regulations on metering and settlement (Norway).

[16] The volumetric component appears again for large industrial consumers. See M. Mulder and B. Willems, 'The Dutch retail electricity market' (2019) 127 *Energy Policy*, 228–39.

C. Network Tariffs and Other Tools to Recuperate Distribution Network Costs

Network tariffs for the use of the networks are the main but not the only way for operators to recover their costs. In addition to the network tariff charge on the consumer's electricity bill, distribution network costs can be recovered via connection charges, taxes, regulated services, and contractual arrangements with industrial customers and generators.[17] In most cases, they will be recovered by a combination of network tariffs and connection charges.[18] These variables will differ according to the user groups, for example, industrial or residential customers, generation or consumption, traditional consumers or prosumers. The complex equation between these multiple parameters is normally calculated by the NRA. This combination of tools to recuperate distribution network costs makes it even more complex for NRAs to ensure distributive justice.

III. How Principles of Network Tariff Design Address Distributive Justice

When discussing the regulation of the electricity grid, a distinction should be made between the regulation of distribution networks in general and the regulation of network tariffs in particular. Network tariffs are *tools* that contribute to the fulfilment of more general objectives. The challenge is to send incentives through network tariffs that will be consistent with the overall objectives of network regulation, and, beyond that, energy policy objectives. Historically, a core objective defined for distribution network regulation has been and still is to ensure quality of service, sufficient investment, and non-discriminatory access.[19] Network tariffs should aim at optimal use and development of the grid. Over time, other guiding principles have been added, such as fairness.

A. The Principles of Good Tariff Design

A review of the abundant literature on tariff design enables to identify the following principles of good tariff design: a tariff should be cost-reflective, enable infrastructure and operational cost-efficiency, enable revenue adequacy, be transparent, and be fair.

[17] Electricity Distribution Network Tariffs CEER Guidelines of Good Practice, 23 January 2007, Ref. C16-DS-27-03, page 6.

[18] T. Schittekatte and L. Meeus, 'Introduction to Network Tariffs and Network Codes for Consumers, Prosumers, and Energy Communities' (2018) *European University Institute*, Technical Report (Florence), 3 (hereafter Schittekatte and Meeus, 'Introduction to Network Tariffs and Network Codes').

[19] IEA, 'Re-powering markets', 207.

1. Cost-reflectiveness

By being cost-reflective, tariffs should reflect the cost that network users impose on the system and that are incurred by the operator when serving them. They should provide appropriate incentives to avoid unnecessary costs.[20] This principle requires a clear identification of the costs to be reflected and communication of them to the users imposing those costs. Consumers thereby have the opportunity to adapt their behaviour; such as moving their consumption to a certain time of day, or investing in energy saving appliances, or producing their own renewable energy. In the absence of cost-reflectiveness, grid users will not perceive the correct trade-off between using the network and adjusting production/consumption.[21] For the DSOs and the NRAs, this will require identifying the cost drivers, such as investments, operation and maintenance costs, and also energy losses. It might not be possible to recover all grid costs through tariffs, and this should be adjusted for through other supplementary mechanisms, as explained above.[22]

2. Infrastructure and Operational Cost-efficiency

According to this principle, network tariffs should contribute to reducing infrastructure costs by reducing or shifting peak demand, as well as reducing operational—including administrative—costs.

3. Cost Recovery

Network tariffs should ensure full recovery of all allowed network costs that have been efficiently incurred.[23] They should also enable a reasonable return on capital. This results in a balancing exercise between costs and reasonable return on capital. What is considered to be reasonable return on capital will usually be regulated and a revenue cap set.

4. Non-discriminatory

In principle, network tariffs should be non-discriminatory, meaning that there should be no undue discrimination among network users.[24] Indeed, tariffs should aim to ensure equal treatment for all customers , and all users of the network should contribute to cost recovery. Therefore, some countries apply network charges on generation, including at the distribution level. The extent to which a non-discriminatory tariff achieves distributive justice can be subject to debate, because, under certain circumstances, a difference in treatment serves to repair a difference of situation and would therefore appear to be fairer as long as it does not provide an unjustifiable advantage for the beneficiaries and a greater burden on the other users. Therefore, exemptions from

[20] CEER, 'Guidelines Good practice Tariffs', 7.
[21] Schittekatte and Meeus, 'Introduction to Network Tariffs and Network Codes', 7.
[22] See section II.C.
[23] Schittekatte and Meeus, 'Introduction to Network Tariffs and Network Codes', 10; CEER 'Guidelines Good Practice Tariffs', 7.
[24] CEER 'Guidelines Good Practice Tariffs', 7.

network tariffs, in part or in full, or a differentiated network tariff reflecting different types of users, may be justified.

5. Transparency, Simplicity, and Predictability

The three separate but related criteria of transparency, simplicity, and predictability contribute to good governance in network tariff policy. When the methodology for calculating tariffs is transparent, it will contribute to a better understanding of the allocation of costs between the different users, and will help to prevent any non-justifiable preferential or discriminatory treatment.

The tariff design should be simple so as to enable customers to understand the purpose and structure of the tariff—and thus to respond to its signals—as well as to contribute to implementation. Simplicity in network design may prove to be demanding to achieve, in particular with the new dynamics observed in the energy system. As pointed out in section II.A, there is a wide variety of design solutions for network tariffs. Tariffs have also become increasingly differentiated, with more and more hybrid systems having multiple components, with the view of better reflecting the diversity of users and thereby contributing towards energy justice. The diversity of network users will only continue to increase as the energy system diversifies. A simple methodology for network tariffs could help to decrease the risk of perceived injustice among network users, and in particular among households. It will facilitate the implementation of the tariffs and the achievement of its different objectives. A simple methodology for network tariffs will also support the principle of cost-efficiency, as users will better understand the basis for the tariffs, enabling them to adjust their use of the network. Simplicity of network design enhances accessibility to all user categories.

With a predictable regime for network tariffs, network users can better estimate the costs of their network use. The tariff may represent a lower burden on energy consumers as it will also enable DSOs to better plan grid operation and development that adheres to a sound economic model. Predictability is nevertheless challenged as a principle of good network design by the changing nature of the energy system. As changes are happening more rapidly and to a greater extent than before, network tariffs will also need to evolve and adapt.[25] Maintaining a predictable network tariff structure will also be a complex task for the NRAs and the DSOs.

6. Fairness as a Necessary Balance of Interests

Fairness is recognised as one of the guiding principles of good network tariff design. A central requirement will be to strike the right balance between different interests and different objectives. The concept of fairness in network tariff design has been debated by the economic theory, with reference to the other affiliated concepts of distributive effects, transparency, and graduality.[26] In that sense, fairness encompasses the objectives defended by the principles of cost-reflectiveness, non-discrimination, transparency,

[25] CEER 'Guidelines Good Practice Tariffs', 2017, 7.
[26] Schittekatte and Meeus, 'Introduction to Network Tariffs and Network Codes', 12.

simplicity, and predictability, but adds a distributional dimension with elements of affordability.

Being fair may require network tariffs to be even more differentiated, and even sometimes discriminatory to compensate for an unfair situation at the outset. For example, not all customer usages of the network are flexible, and consumption may not be reduced or relocated. Similarly, the different purposes for using the network are not easily categorized without being discriminatory. Certain uses may appear to be unnecessary (e.g. charging expensive electricity-powered recreational appliances), while others will be vital for the users (e.g. medical appliances, work equipment). As pointed out by some authors, higher network tariffs would be neither fair nor have an effect on consumption.[27] Moreover, network tariff structures should not distort market signals intended to indicate when it is efficient for individual power plants to run.

National methodologies for network tariffs very commonly include some differentiation parameters aimed at ensuring fairness. One way to do this is to distinguish between different categories of customers by defining them in terms of different tariff classes. A tariff class will refer to a customer segment or category. It may be defined by voltage level (kV) as a measure of capacity, by customer types (e.g. household or industrial), by geographical locations (definition of zones), or by type of metering solutions (e.g. whether metered or unmetered and type of meter). A recent study, performed for the European Commission, reveals that in the EU, tariff classes are mostly defined by voltage level.[28] At the same time, cross-subsidization between consumer groups should be avoided.

Distribution network tariffs can also take into account the different types of charging base. The charging base will reflect individual variables such as varying volumes and time-of-use, and could include flat rate and non-linear rates.[29]

A point of divergence in national legislation is whether the tariff should be uniform or should differ between locations within the national territory. For example, in France, the legislation requires that the network tariff shall be uniform throughout the whole national territory in accordance with the notion of 'territorial solidarity', which is defined in the Energy Code. Likewise, the 'postage stamp' principle aims to ensure that the price does not take into account the distance covered by the energy between the production site and the consumer site, reflecting 'individual solidarity'.

In the context of the energy transition, with a more diverse and complex energy system, one may wonder whether the meaning of fairness in network tariff design has changed. One might also remark that achieving fairness in network design has become an increasingly complex exercise.

[27] Ibid.

[28] Refe, Mercados, and Indra, 'Study on tariff design for distribution systems', Final Report, prepared for Directorate-General for Energy (28 January 2015), 7 (hereinafter Refe, 'Study on tariff design').

[29] Under a flat rate tariff, all consumers pay the same unit price regardless of capacity reached or volume consumed. A non-linear tariff differentiates unit prices according to capacity or volume consumed.

B. Safeguards: Unbundling Requirements and the Role of National Regulatory Authorities (NRAs)

Two legal requirements indirectly serve as safeguards for good network tariff design, namely: the unbundling requirement and the role of the NRAs in determining network tariff methodology.

First, the unbundling requirements aim at: (i) preventing DSOs from abusing their natural monopoly position over the distribution network in the situation where they are part of a vertically integrated undertaking; and (ii) preventing market distortion through cross-subsidization. Unbundling requirements can take several forms (legal, ownership, and functional unbundling) and be applied vertically or horizontally. At EU level, the Electricity Directive defines minimum requirements in terms of legal unbundling of distribution activities from other activities not related to distribution where the DSO is part of a vertically integrated undertaking.[30] Ownership unbundling can also be applied. Finally, functional unbundling requirements in terms, inter alia, of management separation and independent and effective decision-making will influence the manner in which network tariffs are designed. Notably, the basis for cost recovery calculation and optimal operation of the grid should be the focus of the DSO when considering the design and calculation of network tariffs.

Second, the NRAs should play an active role in elaborating the methodology for network tariffs. Indeed, to ensure that the DSO will not abuse its position of natural monopoly, the DSO itself should not set the tariff for using the network —although it often can make proposals—and should be regulated. The methodology criteria for network design are often already defined in the legislation. The NRA will apply those criteria when elaborating the tariffs. In some countries, the NRA and the DSOs share the responsibility for designing, with the NRA setting overall principles and ensuring compliance, while the DSOs propose the exact tariff structure. The NRA will notably assess the revenue a DSO can expect—often with a cap—and will ensure that overall policy objectives are taken into consideration. In this sense, the NRA is a more appropriate entity to address concerns such as energy justice than the DSOs themselves, and will thereby serve as a safeguard. This also presupposes that those considerations and policy objectives are defined in the national legislation.

Under EU law, the Electricity Directive provides that the NRA 'shall' have the duty of fixing and approving distribution tariffs or their methodologies, on the basis of transparent criteria.[31] The independence that the NRAs shall have in setting and approving tariffs works as an important safeguard, that the European Commission is eager to see implemented. As an example, in 2018, the European Commission referred Germany to the European Court of Justice of the EU (CJEU) for not having ensured that the rules concerning the powers and independence of the NRA were fully respected, and

[30] Article 26, Electricity Directive 2009/72/EC and Article 35, Electricity Directive (EU) 2019/944.
[31] Article 37, Electricity Directive 2009/72/EC and Article 59.1, Electricity Directive (EU) 2019/944.

in particular the full discretion that the regulator enjoys in setting network tariffs and other terms and conditions for access to networks and balancing services. The details of network tariff setting were laid down to a large extent in detailed regulations adopted by the federal government, and not enough left to the discretion of the NRA.[32]

The 2019 recast of the Electricity Directive contains a precise list of policy objectives which 'shall' guide the action of NRAs, including in the matter of tariff design and approval. Article 58 of the Directive (EU) 2019/944 refers, inter alia, to the objectives of: promoting a competitive, flexible, secure, and environmentally sustainable internal market for electricity within the Union, and effective market opening for all customers and suppliers; helping to achieve, in the most cost-effective way, the development of secure, reliable, and efficient non-discriminatory systems that are consumer-oriented; ensuring that customers benefit through the efficient functioning of their national market, helping to ensure a high level of consumer protection; helping to achieve high standards of universal service and of public service in electricity supply, contributing to the protection of vulnerable customers. These objectives are not the only ones defined in Article 58 and the Electricity Directive in general, but they specifically target consumers' interests, which was indeed one of the focus areas for the whole 'Clean Energy Package for All Europeans'. The long list of ambitious objectives provided in the Directive proves the complexity of the task given to the NRAs when balancing those different interests in the elaboration of network tariffs.

C. Re-designing Electricity Tariff Structure for Increased Fairness: Possible Legal Approaches

1. Balancing Interests in the Re-design of Network Tariffs

Traditionally, consumers and other grid users have relied exclusively on the network for their electricity supply. Network costs have therefore been mainly recovered to reflect network usage through a volume-based charge. With the changes currently taking place in the energy system, network costs are more driven than before by the growth of embedded generation, demand response, and use of flexibility. Consequently, DSOs face a higher volume and revenue risk.[33] DSOs are increasingly exposed to volume risk because of lower than expected demand. Indeed, many European countries have been experiencing significant reductions in energy usage.[34] For consumers, new energy production, storage, and saving solutions change the volume of electricity consumed on the grid. Both DSOs and consumers expect that network tariffs reflect these new realities and provide for a fair balance of interests. Therefore, there is a general consensus

[32] European Commission, Press Release IP/18/4487, 19 July 2018.

[33] Centre for Competition Policy, 'Designing distribution network tariffs that are fair for different consumer groups', report for BEUC, 2018, 13.

[34] According to Eurelectric, total distributed energy fell by 6.8 per cent in Spain and 8.6 per cent in Italy between 2011 and 2014. Source: Eurelectric, 'Network Tariffs—A Eurelectric Position Paper', 2016.

on the need to move from volumetric tariffs to capacity-based tariffs—often with TOU tariffs—which will better reflect the main drivers of network costs.

Network tariffs are identified by the Agency for the Cooperation of Energy Regulators (ACER) as a key instrument and an area of further action.[35] According to ACER, 'distribution tariff structures will be reviewed to ensure the efficient use of distribution networks, including through an assessment of whether the costs imposed on networks by their usage at peak times should be reflected in tariffs'.[36] One step in that direction has been the publication by the Council of European Energy Regulators (CEER) of Guidelines of Good Practice for Distribution Network Tariffs.

Re-designing network tariffs in the context of the energy transition does not mean starting from scratch. It will be necessary to build on existing models and the principles of good tariff design. The novelty will be the increased complexity of the task as the number of parameters and objectives increases. Proposing a whole new structure may negatively affect the customers who made investments based on the previous tariffs and would be perceived as unfair. Those challenges can be accommodated by setting transition periods or temporary exemption regimes, but this will also increase the complexity of tariff implementation.

Thereafter, not all consumers will become active, and tariffs should certainly incentivize consumers, but not penalize those who are not in a situation to invest in new smart energy solutions. Therefore, network tariffs should reflect fairness between active and passive domestic consumers. Similarly, fairness should be applied along the voltage chain, and cost allocation should be balanced between voltage levels. The 'cascading principle' in terms of payment of distribution network tariffs has been proposed as a solution.[37]

Even more fundamentally, changes in grid structures (central vs decentralized grids; unbundling and end of vertically integrated companies) and ownership (public vs private) raise the question of ascertaining whether the grid still delivers a social good that requires socializing its costs.

2. Possible Legal Principles and Regulatory Approaches in Network Tariff Re-design

The question for law makers is to ascertain which regulatory approach to pursue. Based on the reforms engaged so far, a preliminary list of legal principles of network tariff re-design can be identified and are presented below. If these are not principles per se, the mechanisms identified below can serve as benchmark regulatory approaches.

In accordance with the hierarchy of legal norms (lex superior), general objectives are best set in the legislation as they will serve as guidance for NRAs in the elaboration of tariff methodologies and supervision. Those general objectives will also serve the interpretation of tariff provisions in case of judicial review.[38] Objectives of energy justice,

[35] ACER, 'Energy Regulation: A bridge to 2025' Conclusions Paper (2014).
[36] Ibid.
[37] Schittekatte and Meeus, 'Introduction to Network Tariffs and Network Codes', 13.
[38] See section V.

consumer protection, and core principles of good tariff design should therefore be defined at the level of the law.

Methodology components for tariff setting can also be defined directly in the law or by administrative decision, and a clear legal basis in the legislation is preferable. Likewise, the rights of DSOs and the different 'system users' should be clearly set by the legislation.[39] The definition of a 'duty to consult' interested parties on proposed network tariffs and/or methodology is also common practice in several countries.[40] It derives from general public consultation obligations and permits a better assessment of the needs of the load, proposed solutions and in fine reinforces the acceptability of network tariffs.

The structure of the distribution tariffs needs to be regularly updated, and this need will become more important in the future. A rapidly changing energy system and technological developments will require regular updates of the tariff structures.[41] This will require regulatory flexibility and legal innovation. Long legislative processes for amending tariff methodologies are not well suited for addressing those rapid changes, and the idea of using a 'regulatory toolbox' and 'Guidance of best practice' is gaining momentum, as reflected by ACER in its 'Bridge to 2025' Paper. A toolbox could rank the different tariff options according to policy objectives and desired effects.

IV. Need for Coordination and Even Harmonization: Towards a Common Tariff Methodology?

A common approach to tariff methodology may be needed for several reasons. First, it can help in sharing best practices. Second, it may be necessary in the event of integrated markets such as the European internal energy market. The EU is taken hereafter as an example of the discussions on harmonization of network tariff methodology, the question being to ascertain whether harmonization is desirable in the EU context, and if yes; which level of harmonization is the most adequate and consistent with EU law principles. As a starting point, it must be recalled that distribution grid tariffs are the competence area of the Member States, implemented by the NRAs. Their structure will consequently vary from country to country, including within the EU. Meanwhile, certain provisions of secondary EU law already harmonize some criteria of distribution network tariff design. Those questions have been discussed in the framework of the Clean Energy Package for All Europeans.

[39] See section V.

[40] See also Article 37.12, Electricity Directive 2009/72/EC. The 'duty to consult' on proposed distribution tariffs is for example defined in the French Energy Code, Article L. 341-3.

[41] Certain tariff structures, including e.g. elements of time-of-use tariffs, will be dependent on the use of IT/digital tools such as smart meters.

A. EU Harmonized Provisions on Principles of Distribution Network Tariffs

The EU legal framework already contains a series of requirements related to the design of network tariffs in line with the principles identified above. General requirements are derived from primary EU law, while more specific network tariff design criteria are defined in the Electricity Directive, the Electricity Regulation, and the Energy Efficiency Directive.

Primary EU law contains general provisions which are relevant for network tariff design. Internal market rules will apply when national measures represent, or may represent, direct or indirect barriers to trade. The principle of non-discrimination in network tariff design finds legal basis in treaty provisions on competition. For example, exemption from network tariffs has been an issue for consideration under state aid rules. The European Commission reached in 2018 a negative decision against a German measure fully exempting certain large German electricity users from network charges in 2012–2013. The costs incurred by the exemption were financed by a special levy imposed on final electricity consumers. Because electricity consumers were obliged to pay the surcharge under German law and the German State has control over the funds, the measure constituted state aids, and could not be justified. The European Commission requested changing the regime and ordered the recovery of the illegal aid perceived.[42]

The Electricity Directive and the Electricity Regulation contain a series of requirements on the design principles for distribution network tariffs. The Directive requires that tariffs for access to networks should be transparent and non-discriminatory.[43] They shall be cost-reflective, and take into account the long-term, marginal, avoided network costs from distributed generation, demand-side management measures[44] and enable active consumption.[45] Based on the objective of consumer protection, all European industry and commerce, including small and medium-sized enterprises, and all citizens of the Union, should be able to enjoy 'reasonable tariffs', for reasons of fairness, competitiveness, and job creation. The interests of the DSOs are protected by provisions on remuneration and the need to allow the necessary investments in the networks.[46] The Directive requires NRAs to ensure that, when fixing or approving network tariffs and methodologies, DSOs are provided with appropriate incentives '... to increase efficiencies, foster market integration and security of supply and support the related research activities'.[47] The CJEU can conduct a judicial review of those provisions and Case C-771/18, Commission v Hungary, is a case to follow. In this case, the Commission has brought Hungary before the court after it found that Hungarian law excluded certain

[42] SA.34045—Exemption from network charges for large electricity consumers (§19 StromNEV) in Germany, 28 May 2018.

[43] Recital 32, Directive 2009/72/EC.

[44] Recital 36, Directive 2009/72/EC.

[45] Article 15, Directive 2009/72/EC.

[46] Article 37.6(a), Electricity Directive 2009/72/EC.

[47] Article 37.8, Electricity Directive 2009/72/EC.

types of costs from the calculation of network electricity tariffs, in violation of the principle of cost recovery of tariffs provided for in the Electricity Regulations. In addition, the Commission found that Hungary adopted amendments to its energy legislation which jeopardize the right of market operators to a full judicial review of the national regulator's decisions on network tariffs.[48]

The Energy Efficiency Directive 2012/27/EU requires Member States and their NRAs to respect a series of requirements when developing distribution tariffs, that is: provide incentives for grid operators to enable energy efficiency improvement measures at the level of network users;[49] permit components of tariff structures with a social aim;[50] and ensure that network tariffs allow suppliers to improve consumer participation in system efficiency, including demand response.[51] The Directive also requires Member States to ensure that network tariffs fulfil a series a criteria set out in Annex XI to the Directive, also taking into account the relevant network codes and guidelines. Inter alia, Annex XI requires that network tariffs may support dynamic pricing for demand response measures by final customers, such as time-of-use tariffs; critical peak pricing; real time pricing; and, peak time rebates.

B. The Clean Energy Package for all Europeans and Further Harmonization Attempts

In its original proposal for revised Electricity Directive and Regulation, the European Commission developed several arguments in favour of further harmonization of distribution network tariffs. The Commission notably argued that: uncoordinated national policies concerning the principles for distribution tariffs may distort the internal market; distributed generation or energy storage services will face very different incentives to participate in the market; new technologies and energy services will be increasingly traded across borders; and 'uncoordinated national policies concerning the principles for distribution tariffs may distort the internal market to an extent that distributed generation or energy storage services will be under very different incentives to participate in the market'.[52] Market fragmentation was identified as another risk.[53] In the proposal for revised Electricity Regulation, the Commission proposed to include the harmonization of distribution tariff structures on the list of network codes or guidelines.[54] This would have resulted in the possibility of drafting a network code on distribution network tariffs.

48 European Commission, Press Release IP/18/4487, 19 July 2018.

49 Article 15.1, Directive 2012/27/EU, as amended.

50 Article 15.3, Directive 2012/27/EU.

51 Article 15.4, Directive 2012/27/EU.

52 COM(2016) 864 final/2.

53 The risk of market fragmentation as a consequence of the lack of harmonized tariff methodology is also referred to in Article 18.9 of the Electricity Regulation (EU) 2019/943.

54 COM(2016) 864 final/2.

Any proposal for EU harmonization must comply with the necessity and subsidiarity principles. In the present case, several stakeholders challenged the need for a harmonized approach. Notably, CEER opposed the idea, arguing that: costs vary between different systems, both within and between Member States, making tariffs difficult to harmonize at EU level; ownership of distribution grids vary, and so the underlying economic model; generation and consumption patterns vary widely between countries; and finally, there are differences between the degrees of interconnection.[55]

C. The Compromise Solution Adopted in the Revised Electricity Regulation

Article 18 of the Electricity Regulation (EU) 2019/943 contains the most detailed provisions on tariff methodologies, supplementing the general criteria defined in the Electricity Directive. Those provisions must be applied without prejudice to the provisions of the Energy Efficiency Directive, to which they refer.[56]

Article 18 enounces a series of general principles for tariff design, that both reiterate and elaborate on the principles defined in the Electricity Directive and the Energy Efficiency Directive. Charges for use of networks[57] shall be cost-reflective, transparent, reflect actual costs incurred in accordance to an efficient operation of the network, and shall take into account the need for network security and flexibility. They shall be applied in a non-discriminatory manner. The Regulation also requires ('shall') that the charges for use of the network do 'not include unrelated costs supporting unrelated policy objectives'.[58] This requirement narrows the scope of the objectives that can be reflected in network tariff regulation. Furthermore, Article 18 requires ('shall') that use of network charges be elaborated in such a way that they do not discriminate, positively or negatively, against producers or consumers. They shall not discriminate either against energy storage or aggregation, and shall not create disincentives for self-generation, self-consumption, or for participation in demand response.[59] These provisions refer directly to the new production and consumption patterns observed in the energy system, and translate distributive energy concerns relevant for network tariff regulation.

Article 18 provides for some few general requirements as to the possible content of tariff methodology. It both repeats general principles, such as cost-reflectiveness,[60] infrastructure, and operation cost-efficiency,[61] and introduces two new possible methodology

[55] CEER, 'Distribution and Transmission Network Tariffs and Incentives' (2017) *CEER White Paper Series*, (paper # I).
[56] Article 18.1, Regulation (EU) 2019/943.
[57] Often, when referring to charges for the use of networks, both the Electricity Directive and the Electricity Regulation also refer to charges for related network reinforcements. The present chapter only refers to charges for use of networks.
[58] Article 18.1, Regulation (EU) 2019/943.
[59] Article 18.1, Regulation (EU) 2019/943.
[60] Article 18.2 and 18.7, Regulation (EU) 2019/943.
[61] Article 18.8, Regulation (EU) 2019/943.

components. First, the level of the tariffs applied to producers and/or final customers 'shall provide locational signals at Union level'.[62] The Regulation does not explain how this requirement can be applied, but one can interpret it as a way by which to promote the European dimension in the assessment of cost-efficiency, and to send signals to both producers and consumers, to the extent that they can relocate. Second, the Regulation provides that national distribution network tariff methodologies 'may' introduce 'performance targets' for assessing DSO cost effectiveness and operative efficiency.[63] The idea of introducing 'performance indicators' was already promoted in a 2015 study for the European Commission.[64]

However, the Electricity Regulation does not harmonize the methodology components themselves. The compromise reached resulted in a minimum solution on this point.[65] Within a very short time frame (by 5 October 2019), ACER had to provide a 'best practice report on transmission and distribution tariff methodologies' which had to cover eight mandatory points: (a) the ratio of tariffs applied to producers and tariffs applied to final customers; (b) the costs to be recovered by tariffs; (c) time-differentiated network tariffs; (d) locational signals; (e) the relationship between transmission tariffs and distribution tariffs; (f) methods to ensure transparency in the setting and structure of tariffs; (g) groups of network users subject to tariffs including, where applicable, the characteristics of those groups, forms of consumption, and any tariff exemptions; and (h) losses in high, medium, and low-voltage grids. [66] ACER shall update the report at least every two years. The methodology components listed focus on the types of signals that can be used for the different types of system users as well as the incentives used for DSOs. They can contribute to distributive energy justice by levelling the playing field between the different system users, by insisting on the ability of those users to react to signals (transparency) and by insisting on cost-recovery through tariffs (cost-basis).

Beyond the information value of this report, NRAs will be obliged to take it into consideration when fixing and approving network tariffs or their underlying methodologies. This requirement is relatively weak in terms of enforcement, since the Commission will hardly start infringement proceedings for lack of implementation of this provision. This requirement must therefore be seen as a first step towards a more coordinated approach between Member States in terms of tariff methodology. It will also certainly contribute to the elaboration of the 'regulatory toolbox' as a regulatory approach.[67]

[62] Article 18.3, Regulation (EU) 2019/943.
[63] Article 18.8, Regulation (EU) 2019/943.
[64] Refe, 'Study on tariff design', 7.
[65] See comments in section IV.B.
[66] Article 18.9, Regulation (EU) 2019/943. ACER submitted its report on transmission tariff methodologies on 23 December 2019: ACER, 'Practice report on transmission tariff methodologies in Europe' (2019). ACER is to deliver another report dedicated to distribution tariff structures in the near future.
[67] See section III.C.2.

V. Procedural Justice and Network Tariffs Adjudication

The legal basis for network tariff principles and methodology can be found in different instruments. Network tariff design principles and methodology are usually defined in legislation and implementing acts. Tariff methodology and specific tariff setting decisions can be adopted by NRAs (administrative decisions). Finally, DSOs will apply the methodology in their contractual arrangements with system users.

Access to dispute settlement mechanisms and judicial review for challenging the legality of the network tariff will vary according to the type of legal act in question, but most jurisdictions define some basic rights for operators and network users in terms of dispute resolution and access to justice. It is beyond the scope of this chapter to review the question of procedural justice applied to network tariffs in detail, but some general observations can be made.

First, most legislation has provisions for dispute settlement mechanisms, either in general terms or specifically for network tariffs. In the EU context, the Electricity Directive requires NRAs to act as the dispute settlement authorities when an affected party wants to complain against a DSO in relation to that operator's role, which includes implementation of network tariffs.[68] The Electricity Directive refers explicitly to the right to complain concerning a decision on tariff methodologies.[69]

Second, most legal systems ensure a system of judicial review for administrative decisions. The EU Electricity Directive refers to the right to judicial review of NRAs' decisions, including tariffs. The right of market operators to a full judicial review of the NRAs' decisions on network tariffs is subject to current legal proceedings in a case brought by the European Commission against Hungary.[70]

Third, when reviewing the legality of the tariff decisions, the point will often be to know the extent to which the tariff complies with the principles and methodology defined in law.[71] One issue courts could be confronted with is the intensity of the judicial review in such cases, and, in particular, how far they aim to go in the interpretation of the tariff methodology. Another general point is to ascertain which principles the judicial review should be based on, and whether it should be limited to the objectives of network tariff setting or if it should extend to broader objectives of energy policy, and even climate and social policy. It can be noted that the 2019 Electricity Directive provides that NRAs can require DSOs to change their terms and conditions if they are not in accordance with the tariff principles defined in Article 18 of the 2019 Electricity Regulation.[72]

[68] Article 37.11, Directive 2009/72/EC and Article 60.1 Directive (EU) 2019/944.
[69] Article 60.3, Directive (EU) 2019/944.
[70] Case C-771/18, European Commission v Hungary, action brought on 7 December 2018.
[71] For example, the interpretation of network tariffs structure and methodology has been subject to judicial review in France, with a decision which resulted in the review of the tariffs by the NRA. See the judgment by *Conseil d'État*, 9th and 10th Chambers jointly, 09 March 2018, case 407516.
[72] Article 60, Directive (EU) 2019/944.

Finally, network tariff adjudication could have a reparative justice dimension when the NRA or the court can decide on compensatory measures if the final distribution tariffs or methodologies deviate from the provisional tariffs or methodologies proposed by the DSOs. This situation is foreseen by the EU Electricity Regulation.

VI. Conclusion

As demonstrated by this chapter, there is a basic distinction between the principles for network design and the tariff methodology. This distinction is reflected in the legislation itself. The example of the EU shows that it is possible to agree on general common principles, but it is more difficult to agree on a harmonized approach to tariff methodology.

Tariff structure is important in terms of giving correct signals/incentives for energy efficiency (consumption), investment efficiency, and choice between different energies. The general trend followed at the moment is to move towards capacity-based tariffs, with the intention of better reflecting OPEX. In any case, tariffs must follow a clear structure (volume- or capacity-based or a combination), must follow the design principles, and must help to fulfil the objectives of energy, climate, or even social policy.

Distribution tariffs are tools used to achieve a series of goals. However, they cannot solve all problems and achieve all policy goals at the same time, particularly in the more complex energy system of the energy transition. They must be seen as a part of a regulatory puzzle, where their design reflects the objectives set for them. As put by CEER, 'there are other tools and mechanisms to achieve wider goals'.[73] They primarily give signals, provide incentives, and enable cost recovery.

Finally, distributive energy justice considerations in the context of network tariffs have a specific meaning. In the electricity transport networks, electricity consumers are seen as 'system users', together with producers. This makes a difference in both terminology and regulatory approach. In the context of EU legislation, distributive energy justice considerations relate primarily to, on the one hand, the fair treatment of the different 'system users', and, on the other hand, the fair balance of interests between general policy goals, operation and development of the systems, DSOs' financial situations and users' rights. Thus, there appears to be a clear distinction between general consumer protection issues and distributive energy justice issues for active/responsive consumers, that is, consumer empowerment. Distribution network tariff principles do not aim at consumer protection, but at ensuring a fair balance of interests. Energy transition aspects are directly integrated in that balancing exercise by the recognition of new ways to use or not use the network.

[73] CEER Guidelines of Good Practice for Distribution Network Tariffs, 2017, 7.

7

Collaborating with Underserved Communities to Contribute to Decarbonization in the United States

LeRoy Paddock and Achinthi Vithanage

I. Introduction

In the United States and in many other countries, vulnerable communities are often disproportionately impacted by both the direct and indirect impacts of energy production and use. These communities are frequently referred to as 'underserved' communities for a variety of reasons including limited access to health care and healthy foods that result in residents being more vulnerable to environmental hazards. Underserved communities frequently have significantly less political influence than wealthier communities and therefore may not be provided with the same level of environmental protection as more affluent and politically connected communities.[1] Many underserved communities are also at most risk from climate change. At the same time, financial conditions may limit the ability of residents and business owners in underserved communities to benefit from energy efficiency opportunities, distributed renewable energy sources such as solar, and low carbon technologies like electric vehicles (EVs). These conditions create issues of distributional justice that involve both the additional burdens of traditional energy production as well as lack of access to the benefits of clean energy and energy efficiency. They also implicate questions of procedural justice related to the ability of underserved communities to have a real voice in what is occurring in their communities. Together, these circumstances limit the ability of underserved communities to contribute to decarbonization efforts that are important to reducing risks in their communities.

This situation presents an important question of energy justice. Benjamin Sovacool and Michael Dworkin in their book *Global Energy Justice* define an 'energy-just' world as 'one that equitably shares both the benefits and the burdens involved in energy production and consumption of energy services, as well as one that is fair in how it treats people and communities in energy decision-making'.[2] A closely related concept is the

[1] See M. Lavelle and M. Coyle, 'Unequal Protection: The Racial Divide In Environmental Law A Special Investigation' (1992) 15 *National Law Journal*, https://www.ejnet.org/ej/nlj.pdf accessed 1 July 2019
[2] B.K. Sovacool and M.H. Dworkin, *Global Energy Justice* (Cambridge University Press, 2014), 5.

LeRoy Paddock and Achinthi Vithanage, Collaborating with Underserved Communities to Contribute to Decarbonization in the United States
In: *Energy Justice and Energy Law.* Edited by Íñigo Del Guayo, LeRoy Godden, Donald N. Zillman, Milton Fernando Montoya, and José Juan González, Oxford University Press (2020). © The Several Contributors. DOI: 10.1093/oso/9780198860754.003.0007

ability of underserved communities to play a central role in solving the problems discussed above. This issue is at least partially captured in the idea of 'equitable development'. Equitable development 'is driven by … clear expectations that the outcomes from development need to be responsive to underserved populations and vulnerable groups, in addition to using innovative design strategies and sustainable policies'.[3] Another related idea is that of 'energy democracy' or 'energy sovereignty' which 'envisions a "right" of peoples and communities to make their own decisions on energy systems that are in line with their own circumstances'.[4]

This chapter explores ways for collaborating with underserved communities that can help reduce pollution burdens, better distribute the benefits associated with energy efficiency improvements and new technologies such as distributed generation and EVs, and provide underserved communities with a larger voice in helping to chart their energy future thereby helping to alleviate energy injustices. The chapter does so by examining the work of a community-based energy non-profit organization, Elevate Energy, that is playing a key programme administration and advocacy role in energy justice work in the State of Illinois, by exploring the growing deployment of 'community solar' projects, and by surveying how underserved communities can reap equitable benefits from energy efficiency programmes and the growing use of EVs. In examining these areas we also explore how community-based solutions can advance the idea of equitable development and energy democracy.

II. Disproportionate Burdens and Benefits

The residuals of energy production especially from coal-fired power plants include a suite of conventional pollutants such as sulphur dioxide, nitrogen oxides, and particulate matter that are known to cause serious health problems. In addition, these power plants emit a variety of air toxics including heavy metals such as mercury which have contributed to the need to issue fish advisories in many lakes and streams across the country, often having a disproportionate impact on subsistence fisher folk.[5] A study by the National Association for the Advancement of Colored People (NAACP) of 378 coal-fired power plants in the U.S. found that a disproportionately high number of low-income households and people of colour live within a three mile radius of coal-fired power plants.[6] As a result, energy justice advocates have argued for equitable access to

[3] U.S. Environmental Protection Agency, 'Equitable Development and Environmental Justice' https://www.epa.gov/environmentaljustice/equitable-development-and-environmental-justice accessed 8 April 2019.

[4] R. Salter, C.G. Gonzalez, and E.A. Kronk Warner, 'Energy Justice: Frameworks for Energy Law and Policy' in R. Salter, C.G. Gonzalez, and E.A. Kronk Warner (eds), *Energy Justice: US and International Perspectives* (Edward Elgar Publishing, 2018), 9–10 (hereafter *Energy Justice*).

[5] See, e.g. N.E. Selin and A. Giang, 'Are Tighter EPA Controls on Mercury Pollution Worth It?' (9 February 2016) *The Conversation* https://theconversation.com/are-tighter-epa-controls-on-mercury-pollution-worth-it-53551 accessed 7 March 2019.

[6] NAACP, *Coal Blooded: Putting Profits before People* (2016), 15 https://www.naacp.org/wp-content/uploads/2016/04/CoalBlooded.pdf accessed 9 July 2019. While a significant number of coal-fired power plants have closed in recent years, the study does demonstrate that low income communities and communities of colour have been disproportionately affected by pollution from energy production.

and participation in distributed renewable generation programmes to allow all communities to be 'part of our national transition to clean energy'.[7] They also seek 'inclusive policies to afford relief to low-income families spending a "disproportionate amount" of their household income on energy'.[8]

Transportation fuels can also have serious disproportionate impacts on underserved communities. Diesel emissions, primarily from trucks along highway corridors, have proven to be the largest source of air toxics in many low-income and communities of colour in major cities such as Los Angeles.[9] Prolonged exposure to air pollution from vehicle emissions can cause respiratory illness, headaches, and other ailments. Having to deal with these medical issues can be costly, taking time away from productive employment and consequently, diminishing quality of life. They also have a compounding effect on a community's ability to withstand acute environmental pressures, such as heat waves. Thus, the health benefits associated with improved air quality are significant to the overall well-being of overburdened populations.

The direct impact of pollution from power production and mobile sources are not the only environmental issues disproportionately affecting underserved communities. These communities are also often among the most vulnerable to climate change. The impacts may include increased flooding from erratic weather patterns because low-income housing may be more common in flood plains,[10] excess heat exposure because the cost of air conditioning may be prohibitive, storm vulnerability of less expensive housing such as mobile homes, greater exposure to climate-influenced disease in part because of poor access to health care or nutrition, and other climate impacts on food production.[11] Electrifying transportation is a key element of reducing this exposure since mobile sources of air pollution are now the largest sources of carbon dioxide emissions in the U.S.[12]

Further, energy costs for underserved communities can consume a disproportionately high percentage of their budget. In the U.S. energy costs are viewed as 'affordable' if they are six per cent or less of household income. While higher income families may spend as little as one per cent of their income on energy, one study found that some lower income families spend as much as twenty per cent of their income on energy.[13]

[7] Grid Alternatives, et al., 'Low-Income Solar Policy Guide' (2016), 7 http://www.lowincomesolar.org/wp-content/uploads/2016/03/Low-Income-Solar-Policy-Guide_3.11.16.pdf accessed 3 April 2019.

[8] Uma Outka, 'Fairness in the Low-carbon Shift: Learning from Environmental Justice' in *Energy Justice* (n 4), 29.

[9] See South Coast Air Quality Management District, *Multiple Air Toxics Study III* (September 2008) ES-7 http://www.aqmd.gov/docs/default-source/air-quality/air-toxic-studies/mates-iii/mates-iii-final-report-(september-2008)/final-report-executive-summary.pdf?sfvrsn=10 accessed 1 July 2019.

[10] See S. Mervosh, 'Unsafe to Stay, Unable to Go: Half a Million Face Flood Risk in Government Homes' (11 April 2019) *New York Times* https://www.nytimes.com/2019/04/11/us/houston-flooding.html accessed 1 July 2019.

[11] See National Oceanic and Atmospheric Administration, *Fourth National Climate Assessment, Chapter 14: Human Health* (2018) https://nca2018.globalchange.gov/chapter/14/ accessed 1 July 2019.

[12] 'Transportation Replaces Power in U.S. as Top Source of CO2 Emissions' (4 December 2017) *Yale Environment 360* https://e360.yale.edu/digest/transportation-replaces-power-in-u-s-as-top-source-of-co2-emissionsaccessed 1 July 2019.

[13] See A. Chandler, 'Where the Poor Spend More Than 10 Percent of Their Income on Energy', (8 June 2016) *The Atlantic* https://www.theatlantic.com/business/archive/2016/06/energy-poverty-low-income-households/486197/ accessed 10 March 2019; See also E.L. Hoffman, 'Preserving America's Affordable Rental Housing: The CRA Case' (21 May 2018) *National Housing Trust* https://www.nationalhousingtrust.org/news-article/preserving-america%E2%80%99s-affordable-rental-housing-cra-case accessed 1 July 2019.

Further, electric energy costs may be a factor in rising rental costs for housing for low-income families.[14] As a result, it is important to find ways that underserved communities can both reduce costs and contribute to efforts to mitigate climate change to help minimize climate impacts on their communities. However, these communities face several important obstacles to achieving this outcome. First, the communities often must deal with other critical challenges such as access to healthy food or health care that can command more attention than climate challenges. Finding ways to reduce these risk factors while also supporting communities in addressing climate issues can reduce overall risk and make communities more climate resilient.[15] Further, underserved communities may not have the assets needed to invest in energy efficiency measures even though the investment may be quickly offset by cost savings. This problem may be even more acute for investments in distributed renewable energy generation equipment such as solar panels or new technologies such as EVs. Many low-income residents are not home-owners and must rely on landlords to make the investments in energy efficiency and distributed renewable energy generation without raising rents to the point where they are no longer affordable. The communities may also lack political influence in shaping programmes that can provide them with the resources needed to contribute to climate mitigation and reduced energy costs, as well as bringing new opportunities for employment to their communities.

The economic benefits of electrified transportation to already overburdened communities could be substantial, although the current barriers to EVs in underserved communities must be addressed as discussed in section VI. According to the Union of Concerned Scientists, 'using electricity to power a vehicle is almost always cheaper than using gasoline', and customers will have better odds with stable electricity prices and reliability in power supply when compared to gasoline, which can fluctuate with international market influence.[16] At the same time, EVs render certain vehicle maintenance costs, such as oil changes, redundant and offer performance advantages over diesel-based vehicles.[17]

On the benefits side of the equation, Roger Colton has argued that 'Energy use reduction programs can and should be viewed as an environmental amenity that should be equitably distributed, not merely as a response to environmental burdens that should be avoided'.[18] Having the ability to utilize energy efficiency improvements and

[14] See H.L. Schwartz, A.E. Curtright, C. Ogletree, E. Thornton, and L. Jonsson, *Energy Efficiency as a Tool for Preservation of Affordable Rental Housing* (Rand Corporation, 2018), 9–10 https://www.rand.org/content/dam/rand/pubs/research_reports/RR2200/RR2293/RAND_RR2293.pdf accessed 1 July 2019.

[15] See J.R. Gibson, 'Why Climate Change and Equity Matter for Climate Change: An Interview with Chione Flegal of PolicyLink' (13 February 2018) *Union of Concerned Scientists*https://blog.ucsusa.org/jamesine-rogers-gibson/why-climate-change-and-equity-matter-for-infrastructure-an-interview-with-chione-flegal-of-policylink accessed 10 March 2019.

[16] Union of Concerned Scientists, *Going from Pump to Plug: Adding Up the Savings from Electric Vehicles* (2017), 1 https://www.ucsusa.org/sites/default/files/attach/2017/11/cv-report-ev-savings.pdf accessed 7 July 2019.

[17] Ibid., 2.

[18] See Roger Colton, 'The Equities of Efficiency: Distributing Energy Use Reduction Dollars', in *Energy Justice* (n 4), 113

low-carbon technologies helps build a community's ability to cope with climate change. As Professor Alice Kaswan has noted

> The capacity to cope is a function of such factors as a community's financial and social resources, access to health care, and geographic mobility ... Decreasing social vulnerability requires adaptation measures to reduce the underlying sensitivity to harm and enhance the impacted communities' resilience to harm after it has occurred.[19]

To achieve equity and enhance the ability of communities to cope with climate change may require differentiated treatment. Professor Kaswan has observed

> Adaptation policies that attempt to treat everyone the same, regardless of the underlying demographic characteristics, will result in substantial inequality given underlying differences. To achieve equitable adaptation, adaptation policies must explicitly address the demographics of affected populations and target interventions to address the needs of the most vulnerable populations.[20]

Achieving energy justice requires a focus on whether outcomes are equitable rather than providing an equal amount of resources for all communities; some communities will need more resources than others to achieve a similar outcome.[21] The following sections discuss ways for achieving more equitable outcomes for underserved communities.

III. Elevate Energy

Elevate Energy is an energy non-profit organization that works in Chicago and throughout the State of Illinois and surrounding states. Its mission is to provide 'smarter energy use for all'.[22] The organization focuses on designing and implementing programmes 'that reduce costs, protect people and the environment, and ensure the benefits of clean and efficient energy use reach those who need them most' in order to 'create a world in which everyone has clean and affordable heat, power, and water in their homes and communities—no matter who they are or where they live'.[23] The organization expects that by doing so it will 'significantly mitigate the climate crisis and improve the economic health of communities'.[24] Elevate Energy initially targeted energy efficiency and dynamic pricing as its principal areas of work but added renewable energy because it was already working in buildings in underserved communities. Its

[19] A. Kaswan, 'Domestic Climate Change Adaptation and Equity in the United States' (2012) 42 *Environmental Reporter News & Analysis*, 11125–6.
[20] Ibid., 11139.
[21] See Colton (n 18), at 126.
[22] See Elevate Energy https://www.elevateenergy.org/about/ accessed 1 April 2019.
[23] Ibid.
[24] Ibid.

portfolio now includes community solar projects.[25] Elevate Energy contracts with the utility companies to implement energy efficiency improvements, providing assistance both to private building owners and a wide range of non-profit organizations including day care centres, community organizations, and churches.[26]

In Chicago, Elevate Energy emphasizes energy efficiency in small apartment buildings, typically four stories or less in height, that are according to Elevate Energy 'naturally affordable'. The buildings make up a significant percentage of low-income housing in the city and have typically not received a great deal of attention since most are tenant occupied and the landlords have not had strong incentives to make energy efficiency improvements. The buildings often use old, inefficient steam boilers for heating. Energy efficiency work related to heating systems is particularly important in Chicago because of the comparatively high cost of natural gas and the cold winters.[27]

Community-focused organizations like Elevate Energy can play an important intermediary role in providing access to energy efficiency and alternative energy resources for underserved communities by advocating for legislation and programmes that can meet the needs of underserved communities and by providing the expertise needed to carry out programmes once they have been created. For example, Elevate Energy staff were directly involved in drafting the Future Energy Jobs Act (FEJA) discussed below and were consulted during negotiations on the legislation. The organization employs a staff of 125 that range from community organizers, to technical experts, to programme managers, to community development professionals. This broad expertise allows the organization to help coordinate coalitions to develop new legislation, manage low-income assistance programmes for the state's large electric utilities, work with communities to ensure they have a strong voice in implementing programmes, integrate energy issues into local community development initiatives, conduct energy efficiency audits, contract for and manage efficiency improvements and community solar projects, and conduct evaluations of programmes.[28] By doing so, non-profit organizations like Elevate Energy can support community efforts to improve energy efficiency and gain access to renewable energy that would otherwise be very difficult for other organizations or individuals to accomplish.

Elevate Energy is administering the Illinois Solar for All programme created by the FEJA for the Illinois Power Agency. The Illinois Solar for All also incentivizes community solar installations, including placing solar panels on old industrial sites (referred to in the U.S. as 'brownfields' sites) to allow low-income renters access to renewable energy.[29] Elevate Energy is also working in Illinois' coal country to retrain out-of-work coal field workers, citizens returning from incarceration, and foster-care alumni to install and maintain solar panels.[30] Community solar projects are discussed in more detail in section V of this chapter.

[25] Ibid.
[26] Interview with Elevate Energy staff, 5 December 2018 (Notes on file with author).
[27] Ibid.
[28] Ibid.
[29] Ibid.
[30] Ibid.

IV. Future Energy Jobs Act

The State of Illinois, in 2007, enacted the Illinois Power Agency Act establishing an Energy Efficiency Standard that required electric utilities to achieve a two per cent reduction in energy use through energy efficiency each year beginning in 2015.[31] In 2011 the Illinois Energy Infrastructure Modernization Act allowed electric utilities to include in their electricity rates, investments of $2.6 billion in smart grid technology including the deployment of smart meters.[32] These laws set the stage for an innovative new energy programme that would take into account the needs of underserved communities. The Illinois FEJA[33] adopted in 2016 included in its 'Findings' that the 'state should encourage: the adoption and deployment of cost-effective distributed energy resource technology and devices', 'provide incentives for electric utilities to achieve the [state's] energy savings goals', and that 'low-income customers should be included within the state's efforts to expand the use of distributed generation technologies and devices'.[34]

Among the key elements of the Act are:

- An increased emphasis on energy efficiency requiring Illinois electric companies to reduce demand by as much as 21.5 per cent by 2030.
- Performance bonuses to incentivize electricity companies to exceed annual energy savings targets so that utilities are no longer rewarded only for selling more electricity.
- A requirement that a minimum of $25 million be spent each year by electric utilities exclusively on programmes to increase energy efficiency of low-income households.
- The state's first community solar programme that includes $750 million to support a Solar for All programme in low-income communities with programmes to train low-income community members to work in the solar industry.
- Rate caps that ensure the cost of the energy efficiency, community solar, and zero emissions credit programmes do not significantly raise electricity costs for consumers.[35]

A diverse 'Clean Jobs Coalition'[36] involving a significant number of community organizations, including those organized by Elevate Energy, labour, environmental organizations, businesses, and government supported the FEJA. This coalition helped create

[31] Ibid.
[32] Illinois Public Act 097-0616, S.B. 1652 (2011).
[33] Illinois Public Act 099-0906.
[34] Illinois Public Act 099-0906, SB 2814, section 1.
[35] See N. Magrisso, 'Future Energy Jobs Bill: A Path for Illinois to a Bright Clean Energy Economy' (5 December 2016) *Natural Resources Defense Council* https://www.nrdc.org/experts/nick-magrisso/future-energy-jobs-bill-path-illinois-bright-clean-energy-economy accessed 1 July 2019.
[36] See Illinois Clean Jobs Coalition http://ilcleanjobs.org accessed 20 June 2019.

broad bi-partisan support for the Act in significant part because it resulted from a collaborative effort by a wide range of energy stakeholders[37]. The Act doubled the energy efficiency spending required of the state's two main public utilities and through the Solar for All programme that includes incentives for community solar projects and job training programmes for residents of underserved communities.[38] The Act also allows utilities to count energy efficiency savings from natural gas usage towards the energy efficiency goal prioritizing natural gas efficiency in low-income communities.[39]

Anne McKibbin, Policy Director for Elevate Energy, observed that FEJA requires

> utilities convene a low-income energy efficiency advisory committee to 'assist in the design and evaluation of the low-income energy efficiency programs' that includes 'representatives from community-based organizations' (Public Act 99-906) ... [T]his advisory committee will help remedy a 'procedural injustice' in how energy efficiency programs have been created and evaluated (Pino 2018). The committee, called the Income Qualified Energy Efficiency Advisory Committee, will serve as a forum for underserved communities to have input into ComEd's and Ameren's new low-income energy efficiency programs, providing utilities with valuable insights into how their programs are working on the ground, and where changes may be needed to ensure program goals are fully realized.[40]

She also pointed out that 'coalition members are also deeply interested in workforce development and, specifically, ensuring that trained low-income and minority individuals are hired by contractors and that small, diverse contractors can grow their businesses, become utility trade allies, gain consistent business, and hire more members of their communities'.[41]

The workforce development issue has been particularly challenging. The FEJA does not contain workforce development provisions for energy efficiency work even though the Solar for All provisions of the Act does include workforce development language. Even for the Solar for All programme there is concern that many of the early job opportunities will be in communities outside of the low-income areas that may be hard for members of the low-income communities to travel to even though they have received the training in solar installation and maintenance.[42] These workforce issues play a critical role in the energy justice/equitable development/energy democracy discussions because the jobs allow a community to play a direct role in determining its energy future and can provide the income needed to reduce multiple risks including inadequate health care and poor nutrition.[43]

[37] See L. Goldberg and A. McKibbin, *Breakthroughs in Equity and Energy in Illinois* (American Council for an Energy Efficient Economy, 2018), 13-2–13-7 https://www.elevateenergy.org/wp/wp-content/uploads/Breakthroughs-in-Equity-and-Energy-in-Illinois.pdf accessed 3 April 2019.

[38] Ibid., 13-1.

[39] Ibid., 13-8.

[40] Ibid., 13-10.

[41] Ibid., 13-10.

[42] Interviews (n 26).

[43] Ibid.

Creating energy-focused non-profits that are able to work with low-income communities to develop and implement energy justice initiatives that provide more access to efficiency improvements and to renewable energy generation is one way to facilitate energy justice. Creative, stakeholder-supported legislation that provides critical resources to support energy efficiency programmes, community solar projects and job training is another key to making progress in both of these areas. The next sections of this chapter explore other ways to support community solar programmes in underserved communities and conclude with a discussion of EVs in the context of underserved communities.

V. Community Solar

The falling cost of solar energy technology and growing acceptance of both the economic and climate change benefits of sourcing electricity needs through renewable energy have stimulated rapid expansion in the U.S. solar energy market.[44] Whether those benefits are being accrued by all communities equally and equitably is an emerging issue. A recent study discovered significant racial and ethnic disparities in rooftop solar installations across the country based on national census data.[45] The equity implications of these findings are heightened by increasing awareness of the disproportionate energy burdens and difficult economic circumstances shared by people of colour in underserved communities.[46] Contrary to popular sentiment,[47] addressing past energy injustices through renewable energy opportunities is not necessarily a given outcome. As Deborah Sunter puts it,

> When it comes to rooftop solar, there are a lot of economic benefits ... and so unlike the fossil fuel industry, where energy injustice was attributed to exposure to negative consequences like pollution, with rooftop PV the injustice is more that certain communities are missing out on these economic benefits.[48]

[44] See E.F. Merchant, 'US Surpasses 2 Million Solar Installations as Industry Looks to "Dominate" the 2020s' (9 May 2019) *Greentech Media* https://www.greentechmedia.com/articles/read/u-s-solar-installations-top-2-million#gs.lfoghl accessed 20 June 2019; and J. Rogers and L. Wisland, 'Renewables: Energy You Can Count On—Solar Power on the Rise' (August 2014) *Union of Concerned Scientists* https://www.ucsusa.org/sites/default/files/attach/2014/08/Solar-Power-on-the-Rise.pdf accessed 20 June 2019.

[45] D.A. Sunter, S. Castellanos, and D.M. Kammen, 'Disparities in Rooftop Photovoltaics Deployment in the United States by Race and Ethnicity' (2019) 2 *Nature Sustainability*, 71, 72 (hereafter Sunter, Castellanos, and Kammen): 'In national census tracts with the same median household income, communities with over 50 per cent black residents have 69 per cent less rooftop solar installed than tracts with no racial or ethnic majority whilst majority white communities have 21 per cent more rooftop solar installed than tracts with no racial or ethnic majority.'

[46] 'Green Causes Are Not Always Colorblind: Racial Disparity in Energy Issues' (5 March 2018) *Chester Energy & Policy Blog* https://chesterenergyandpolicy.com/2018/03/05/green-causes-are-not-always-colorblind-racial-disparity-in-energy-issues/ accessed 7 July 2019.

[47] A. Haddon, 'Intersections: 5 Ways Renewables Can Address Environmental Racism' (9 February 2017) *Schneider Electric Perspectives* https://hub.resourceadvisor.com/renewable-energy/intersections-5-ways-renewables-can-address-environmental-racism-2 accessed 7 July 2019.

[48] E.F. Merchant, 'Report Finds Wide Racial and Ethnic Disparities in Rooftop Solar Installations' (14 January 2019) *Greentech Media* https://www.greentechmedia.com/articles/read/report-finds-wide-racial-and-ethnic-disparities-in-rooftop-solar?utm_medium=email&utm_source=Daily&utm_campaign=GTMDaily#gs.4kiphw accessed 7 July 2019.

The lack of home ownership,[49] the high number of multi-unit dwellers, and disproportionately low 'seeding' rates[50] in underserved communities, as well as limited financing options available to members of these communities together pose major barriers to solar access. This inequity issue is exemplified by situations where minority organizations, like the Florida chapter of the National Association for the Advancement of Colored People, have opposed local incentives for rooftop solar systems, arguing that the incentives would result in higher electricity bills for low-income households in order to subsidize solar energy assets that those same households are unlikely to be able to afford.[51] The solution to achieving better distribution of the multiple benefits associated with solar energy adoption is to find new ways that underserved communities can gain access to the benefits of solar energy. Community-driven energy projects, like community solar, can be one element of a solar solution.

Community solar, sometimes referred to as shared solar, refers to local solar facilities that provide power and/or financial benefit to, or are owned by, multiple community members.[52] Pursuing this kind of programme addresses multiple energy justice issues. First, the Community solar model enables solar energy access to renters, multi-unit housing dwellers, and home-owners whose properties are unsuitable for onsite solar facilities.[53] Pooling financial resources as a community makes it a more financially affordable option allowing individual community members to participate through smaller payments.[54] The community solar model also promotes a shared sense of responsibility over the shared asset, yet it has the added flexibility of using a subscription model, which allows subscriptions to be easily transferred.[55] Further, any investment in a solar energy asset is a sustainable long-term investment, with increased cost savings to the community members over time. A reduced reliance on greenhouse gas (GHG) emitting fossil fuels can also help reduce climate change impacts on underserved communities.

While accessibility and affordability are improved with the community solar model, it is not without financial constraints. Accessing capital to fund community solar projects to benefit underserved communities can be an obstacle at the outset.[56]

[49] Sunter, Castellanos, and Kammen (n 45).

[50] 'Seeding' refers to a feedback loop where early adopters of solar energy assets, known as 'seed' customers, compel others in the community to adopt. Ibid.

[51] While competing environmentalist groups suggested that utility donations to the minority organization may have played a part in this opposition, the underlying issue of inadequate minority inclusion in solar energy programmes remains. E. Halper, 'Minority Groups Back Energy Companies in Fight Against Solar Power' (9 February 2015) *LA Times* https://www.latimes.com/nation/la-na-solar-race-20150209-story.html accessed 7 July 2019.

[52] J. Coughlin, et al., 'Guide to Community Solar: Utility, Private, and Non-profit Project Development' (2010) U.S. Department of Energy, 2 https://www.nrel.gov/docs/fy11osti/49930.pdf accessed 5 July 2019.

[53] T. Figel, et al., 'Low-Income Solar Policy Guide' (11 March 2016) GRID Alternatives, Vote Solar & Center for Solar Inclusion, 15 http://www.lowincomesolar.org/wp-content/uploads/2016/03/Low-Income-Solar-Policy-Guide_3.11.16.pdf accessed 7 July 2019 (hereafter Figel, et al.).

[54] United States Department of Energy, Office of Energy Efficiency and Renewable Energy, 'Community and Shared Solar' https://www.energy.gov/eere/solar/community-and-shared-solar accessed 7 July 2019.

[55] Ibid.

[56] GTM Research (now Wood Mackenzie), 'The Vision for U.S. Community Solar: A Roadmap to 2030 and Beyond' (July 2018), 9 (hereafter GTM Research).

Community solar advocates emphasize the need for explicit policy focus on serving low-income communities.[57] Policymakers can turn to a host of strategies targeted towards disproportionately burdened communities, such as seed funding, solar facility carve outs, job training programmes, project ownership, siting preferences, and incentives[58] to promote community solar investment in underserved communities. Ensuring that community representatives are also at the policy-determining table through strategic deliberative processes is a necessary precondition to assuring procedural justice.[59] Whether it is for siting purposes or related employment training, collaborating with local communities and organizations when making those decisions will add to the transparency and visibility of the community solar project.[60] In doing so, community solar and the policies enabling their uptake, can promote an approach to solar energy deployment that advances the idea of equitable development and energy democracy. A recent Department of Energy (DOE) funded project, Accelerating Low-Income Financing and Transactions for Solar Access Everywhere[61], partners with a host of organizations, including Elevate Energy,[62] which share deep experience in energy services and community building, to survey and identify community solar models that best serve low-income communities.[63]

A small-scale community solar project in the state of Minnesota, MN Community Solar, and a research study surveying community respondents involved,[64] provide some insight into the importance of community collaboration in achieving energy justice goals. With a capacity of forty kilowatts, the MN Community Solar project is a partnership between Xcel Energy, a Minneapolis-based energy utility, a local business providing the host site for the installation, the city of Minneapolis, several solar installers and contractors, and local community subscribers. The study reinforced the value of consumer trust in peers and near-peers exceeding that of experts when it comes to new technology adoption. It revealed that investor-owned utility representatives and local installers were regarded with suspicion while information from neighbours and affinity groups garnered greater confidence and trust.[65] Additionally, if the community solar project is owned or operated by a community member organization and spatially proximate to the community, a greater sense of connection was found to be present among

[57] Figel et al., (n 53), 15–16.

[58] GTM Research (n 56), 10.

[59] N. Blascsok, 'Energy Justice: Bringing People Back to the Heart of Energy Decisions' (2 March 2018) *Sussex Energy Group Blog* http://blogs.sussex.ac.uk/sussexenergygroup/2018/03/02/energy-justice-bringing-people-back-heart-energy-decisions/ accessed 6 July 2019.

[60] Figel, et al., (n 53), 16.

[61] U.S. Department of Energy, 'SETO FY2018–Photovoltaics' (2018) *Solar Energy Technologies Office* https://www.energy.gov/eere/solar/seto-fy2018-photovoltaics accessed 26 June 2019.

[62] Other partners include non-profits Groundswell, Southface Institute, and Clean Energy Works. See Groundswell, 'Groundswell-led Collaboration Begins Research to Expand Solar Access for Low-Income Communities, Funded by U.S. Department of Energy' (8 June 2019) *Groundswell* https://groundswell.org/groundswell-led-collaboration-begins-research-to-expand-solar-access-for-low-income-communities/ accessed 25 June 2019.

[63] P. Athey, 'DOE Funds Research to Boost Solar for Low-Income Families' (7 June 2019) *E&E News* https://www.eenews.net/eenewspm/2019/06/07/stories/1060511627 accessed 25 June 2019.

[64] M. Peters, et al., 'Community Solar Initiatives in the United States of America: Comparisons with—and Lessons for—the UK and Other European Countries' (October 2018) 121 *Energy Policy*, 355–64.

[65] Ibid., 360.

community members.[66] This suggests that community ownership in a solar energy asset and utilizing neighbourhood or public assets for a community solar project may secure greater community acceptance and participation with a project.[67]

Nevertheless, this is not conclusive that there are fewer benefits for community solar projects that are distantly located to those communities securing the projects' benefits. A recent community solar project spearheaded by two partners at the Nixon Peabody law firm demonstrates how strong partnerships can still be formed with local communities despite spatial distance. Sparked by a realization that solar installations in the District of Columbia had primarily been sited in the city's most affluent areas, the two partners sought a creative solution to deliver solar energy benefits to underserved communities.[68] They formed an independent non-profit called New Partners Community Solar Corporation that utilized favourable solar regulations and incentives, corporate and D.C. government funding, pro-bono legal assistance from the law firm, and the rooftop of their leased office premises to install a 182-kilowatt solar energy system. Power produced at the firm's location was then turned into dollar equivalents by the local utility, Pepco, and delivered as solar credits to the Trinity Plaza affordable housing community in D.C. For residents at Trinity, installing solar panels on their buildings would not have been possible due to unsuitable roof conditions and storm water runoff rules.[69] As an underserved community facing disproportionately high energy burdens, this community solar project brought cost savings[70] with added benefits[71] for Trinity residents. While the project's success is certainly attributable to the tenaciousness and creativity of the two lawyers, it is also tied to the collaborative partnership developed at the outset with the non-profit D.C. housing developer, Mission First Housing Group, and the benefitting residents of the Trinity Plaza community.

VI. Electric Vehicles

Under the 2030 Agenda for Sustainable Development, countries, including the U.S., committed to adopting policies that promoted, inter alia, 'universal access to affordable, reliable, sustainable and modern energy services' as well as 'sustainable transport

[66] Ibid., 361.

[67] Ibid.

[68] J.W. Moyer, 'How a D.C. Law Firm Installed Solar Panels to Help Low-income People Save on Utilities' (11 May 2018) *The Washington Post* https://www.washingtonpost.com/local/a-dc-law-firm-looks-to-the-sun-to-help-apartment-dwellers-pay-utility-bills/2018/05/10/e302b5aa-4fd5-11e8-b292-edc09f8f590a_story.html?utm_term=.bc7e29e682a0 accessed 6 July 2019.

[69] Ibid.

[70] Residents received credits ranging from $20–$50 per month. Ibid. The project provides each affordable housing tenant with approximately $250 per year in energy billing credits. A. McClain, 'Solar Rooftop Panel Program Expanded to More Commercial Buildings in Washington, DC' (9 August 2017) *Nixon Peabody* https://www.nixonpeabody.com/en/news/press-releases/2017/08/09/solar-rooftop-panel-program-expanded-to-more-commercial-buildings-in-washington-dc accessed 6 July 2019.

[71] Costs savings would have alleviated financial stress for low-income households, likely providing greater choice in income expenditure on other necessities, like medical care, rent, and child-related expenses.

systems'.[72] Many have interpreted this to require a transition to an electrified transportation system supported by renewable energy sources,[73] aligning with the low GHG emissions development encouraged under the Paris Agreement.[74]

The U.S., like several other countries,[75] has begun to focus on broader adoption of EVs. This effort is constrained at present by the high cost of most EVs and the need to create a widely deployed charging infrastructure. Energy justice issues are also beginning to feature in vehicle electrification discussions. While underserved communities have a great deal to gain as a result of lower exposure to air pollutants from deployment of EVs powered by renewable energy, they have few opportunities to directly benefit from EVs due to their high cost and limited charging infrastructure locations. This is a significant distributional justice issue. How a transition to EVs occurs and whether underserved communities are involved in its decision-making processes will be key to realizing the full range of EV benefits.

This section focuses on EVs and how their use can alleviate historic energy injustices. While the potential benefits of EVs are limited by new and existing barriers for vulnerable communities, this section also surveys EV programmes and policies that are designed to reach underserved communities and concludes that preventing new forms of energy injustice arising in the EV space will require collaborative and democratic solutions.

A. Driving Out the Barriers to EVs

Renewable energy-driven EVs benefit underserved communities in two important ways: they reduce exposure to air pollutants and help mitigate climate change. Yet, clear benefits alone are seldom enough to bring underserved communities along on the EV 'ride'. Even at this early stage, financial, cultural, situational, opportunity, legal, and policy barriers, have presented themselves, hampering access to EVs by underserved populations.

While consumers with higher incomes are well placed to take advantage of the long-term cost savings of EV use, the upfront costs remain a serious entry barrier

[72] United Nations General Assembly Resolution 70/1, 'Transforming Our World: The 2030 Agenda for Sustainable Development' (21 October 2015) ¶27 https://www.un.org/en/development/desa/population/migration/generalassembly/docs/globalcompact/A_RES_70_1_E.pdf accessed 6 July 2019.

[73] For instance, the UN Environment Assembly's Air Quality Resolution and its global Electric Mobility Programme supports fifty countries and cities to develop electric mobility as part of a vision for a cleaner transport sector. UN Environment, Why Does Electric Mobility Matter? https://www.unenvironment.org/explore-topics/transport/what-we-do/electric-mobility/why-does-electric-mobility-matter#_msocom_1 accessed 6 July 2019.

[74] United Nations Framework Convention on Climate Change (UNFCCC), Paris Agreement, (12 December 2016) Article 2(1)(b) https://unfccc.int/sites/default/files/english_paris_agreement.pdf accessed 6 July 2019.

[75] Countries like China, France, Germany, Iceland, India, Netherlands, and the United Kingdom, have proposed future bans on new sales of internal combustion engine vehicles; see Center for Climate Protection, *Survey of Global Activity to Phase Out Internal Combustion Engine Vehicles* (2018) https://climateprotection.org/wp-content/uploads/2018/10/Survey-on-Global-Activities-to-Phase-Out-ICE-Vehicles-FINAL-Oct-3-2018.pdf accessed 16 July 2019. Sri Lanka, Denmark, Egypt, and Costa Rica have proposed complete bans on all fossil-fuel vehicles with varying effective dates: see Coltura, 'Gasoline Vehicle Phaseout Advances Around The World' https://www.coltura.org/world-gasoline-phaseouts accessed 16 July 2019.

for moderate-income consumers, let alone those with lower incomes.[76] Noting that non-electric car ownership amongst low-income consumers is already lower than amongst high-income consumers,[77] EV ownership is unlikely to be affordable to low-income populations even if EV prices match their non-electric counterparts. Under the American Taxpayer Relief Act of 2012, the U.S. government provides a limited tax credit of up to $7,500 to encourage the purchase of EVs,[78] however most low-income consumers are unable to benefit since they will typically not incur the tax liability needed to take advantage of the credit. There are state or local tax incentives[79] but few are directed to support EV ownership by underserved community members.[80]

In some instances, policies designed to encourage build out of EV charging infrastructure could adversely affect underserved communities. For instance, some states permit investment costs of transportation electrification to be passed along to consumers through electricity rates. Massachusetts' state legislation allows a utility to recover costs for infrastructure deployment provided that it 'is in the public interest, meets a need regarding the advancement of EVs in the commonwealth and does not hinder the development of the competitive electric vehicle charging market'.[81] While such laws foster EV infrastructure development, they place an additional burden on low-income communities through higher electricity costs.

EV charging infrastructure may be difficult to develop in underserved communities for a variety of reasons including outdated building codes that prevent or complicate placing charging stations, the fact that Multi-unit Dwellings (MuDs), which are often home to underserved populations, provide little to no accommodation for EV charging spaces,[82] and potential complex negotiations of easements or licenses with landlords to enable access to charging units. These problems are compounded by situational barriers such as costly electrical upgrades needed to support charging infrastructure with little incentive for apartment owners to undertake the upgrades without raising rents.

Awareness by underserved community members of EV options, benefits, and opportunities is low[83] and EV marketing gives little attention to underserved communities. Elected public officials may similarly lack familiarity with available EV incentives for

[76] D. Burlison, 'Making EVs Possible for Low-Income Drivers' (30 November 2018) *Sustainable America* https://sustainableamerica.org/blog/making-evs-possible-for-low-income-drivers/ accessed 6 July 2019.

[77] National Equity Atlas, 'Car Access in the United States' (2018) https://nationalequityatlas.org/indicators/Car_access accessed 6 July 2019.

[78] Public Law 112-240, s 403; 26 U.S. Code Sec. 30.

[79] G.E. Miller, 'Electric & Hybrid Tax Credits by State (Updated 2019)' (21 April 2019) *20SomethingFinance* https://20somethingfinance.com/electric-hybrid-tax-credits-by-state/ accessed 16 July 2019.

[80] See, e.g., California's Clean Vehicle Rebate Project which provides sizable rebates to low- and moderate-income consumers to buy or lease a new EV: https://cleanvehiclerebate.org/eng/income-eligibility accessed 16 July 2019.

[81] Massachusetts General Laws, c 25A, s 16(f).

[82] L. Davis, 'Apartments Rarely Come with Access to Charging Stations. But Electric Vehicles Need Them' (27 July 2018) *The Conversation* https://theconversation.com/apartments-rarely-come-with-access-to-charging-stations-but-electric-vehicles-need-them-100296 accessed 6 July 2019.

[83] See International Council on Clean Transportation, 'Expanding Access to Electric Mobility in the United States' (December 2017), 14 https://www.theicct.org/sites/default/files/publications/Expanding-access-electric-mobility_ICCT-Briefing_06122017_vF.pdf accessed 20 June 2019.

underserved communities.[84] Raising awareness among members of underserved communities about opportunities to acquire affordable EVs and gain access to EV charging infrastructure, as well as the new job opportunities that EVs are creating,[85] will be important in growing the number of EVs in underserved communities.

B. Producing Collaborative and Democratic Solutions

The plethora of barriers cropping up to hinder or prevent EV adoption in underserved communities suggests that new forms of energy injustices are already occurring. In a 2018 report, the Lawrence Berkeley National Laboratory highlighted how critical it is for government decision making to 'appropriately capture equity and risk mitigation considerations at the outset, rather than scrambling later to rectify problems created by early actions'.[86] Considering the relative infancy of the EV industry, it is an opportune moment for action.

An important starting point is data collection to identify EV infrastructure gaps that lead to inequities. In allocating a portion of public benefit funds from the Exelon–Pepco merger in the Washington, D.C. and Maryland service territory to support an analysis of the gaps in EV charging infrastructure, the Maryland Public Service Commission made data gathering a priority for achieving the state's goal of having 300,000 zero emission vehicles on roads by 2025.[87] A gap analysis that specifically focuses on underserved communities could assist with siting EV charging infrastructure in locations that meet equity and access goals.[88]

These equity considerations are beginning to take hold when thinking about EV deployment. The Transportation Electrification Accord outlines eleven principles for 'how transportation electrification can be advanced in a manner that benefits all utility customers'.[89] While there is no express reference to assisting underserved populations, the accord calls for EV load management that accounts for the interests of all electricity customers (Principle 7), mapping and EV charging station signage for all (Principle 9), and places expectations on utilities to engage with all stakeholders in developing rate designs, infrastructure deployment programmes, and education and outreach efforts that benefit all utility customers (Principle 10).[90] Though the accord is a voluntary

[84] See Guest Author, '5 Steps for Making Electric Vehicles Benefit All' (24 October 2016) *Environmental Defense Fund* http://blogs.edf.org/energyexchange/2016/10/24/5-steps-for-making-electric-vehicles-benefit-all/ accessed 6 July 2019.

[85] The EV Infrastructure Training Program is an industry collaborative that ensures EV training opportunities are available and accessible to low-income communities. See https://evitp.org/training accessed 6 July 2019.

[86] P.B. Jones, J. Levy, J. Bosco, J. Howat, and J.W. Van Alst, 'The Future of Transportation Electrification: Utility, Industry and Consumer Perspectives' (2018) *Berkeley Labs Report*, 73 http://eta-publications.lbl.gov/sites/default/files/feur_10_transportation_electrification_final_20180813.pdf accessed 6 July 2019 (hereafter Jones, Levy).

[87] Maryland Public Service Commission, 'Letter Order Regarding Most Favored Nations Funding to Support Public Conference 44 Electric Vehicles Work Group Activities' Case No. 9361, Order No. 88128 (6 October 2017) https://webapp.psc.state.md.us/newIntranet/AdminDocket/NewIndex3_VOpenFile.cfm?FilePath=//Coldfusion/AdminDocket/PublicConferences/PC44//78.pdf.

[88] Jones, Levy (n 86), 97.

[89] The Transportation Electrification Accord https://www.theevaccord.com/ accessed 6 July 2019.

[90] Ibid.

standard, it has secured signatures from 114 international, national, regional, state, and local entities including vehicle manufacturers, electric utilities, infrastructure and technology companies, consumer advocates, and public interest groups;[91] and represents an important shift in mindset amongst key players in the EV space. Strengthened and consistent application of Principle 10 and dedicating collaboration efforts towards meaningfully engaging underserved communities in the EV conversation would heighten the equity and access benefits being sought and simultaneously chip away at distributional energy injustices.

For EVs, equal access to resources may not lead to equitable outcomes. Instead it is important to focus on what types of programmes will result in equitable access to EVs and EV infrastructure given the differences in the barriers faced by underserved communities. New programmes, rate designs, and cost allocations premised on equity considerations can promote positive outcomes for these communities.[92] Several emerging laws and policies are beginning to support EVs in underserved communities. For instance, New Hampshire state legislation prohibits an owner or operator of a charging station from requiring a subscription fee for use of a charging station which may be cost-prohibitive for underserved community members,[93] and requires charging stations to support multiple payment options.[94] Some states use funding from administrative settlements[95] or litigation settlements such as the Volkswagen diesel fraud case to help fund charging infrastructure in underserved communities.[96] At the same time, jurisdictions like New Mexico encourage charger deployment in low-income areas through utility cost recovery criteria in new legislation.[97] Finally, Maryland has a policy that requires landlords to set aside space for EV charging in Multiple Unit Housing developments.[98]

As such laws and policies are introduced to eliminate existing, and prevent future, distributive energy injustices, implementing bodies will need to ensure procedural injustices are avoided in the process. Indeed, consumer advocates like the National Consumer Law Center, call for community consultation by utilities and energy regulators when

[91] The Transportation Electrification Accord, About https://www.theevaccord.com/about accessed 6 July 2019.

[92] Jones, Levy (n 86), 97.

[93] New Hampshire Senate Bill 575, SB 575-FN—AS AMENDED BY THE HOUSE, 236:134 Prohibitions and Restrictions (III) (2018) https://legiscan.com/NH/text/SB575/2018 accessed 6 July 2019.

[94] Ibid., 236:133 Operation of Electric Vehicle Charging Stations; Signage (VI).

[95] In 2015 Pacific Gas & Electric agreed with the California Public Utilities Commission to a three-year pilot programme to accelerate deployment of EV charging stations, of which at least 15 per cent had to be located in the most disadvantaged communities in PG&E's service territory: *Pacific Gas and Electric Co.* (2016) Cal. P.U.C. Dec. No. 16-12-065.

[96] For example, the Oregon Department of Environmental Quality is using 15 per cent of the Volkswagen diesel litigation mitigation fund to build EV charging infrastructure with a focus on rural and low-income communities. See Oregon Executive Order 17-21 (2017).

[97] House Bill 521 (2019) and New Mexico Statutes 62-3; see also U.S Department of Energy, Office of Energy Efficiency and Renewable Energy, Alternative Fuels Data Center https://afdc.energy.gov/laws/all?state=NM accessed 25 June 2019.

[98] Maryland's Public Service Commission passed a proposal for a statewide EV portfolio which included reservations for EV infrastructure deployment for low-income communities in MUD housing: see Maryland Public Service Commission, Order No. 88997, Case No. 9479 https://www.psc.state.md.us/wp-content/uploads/Order-No.-88997-Case-No.-9478-EV-Portfolio-Order.pdf accessed 25 June 2019.

considering how electrification could address existing inequalities in transportation.[99] Southern California Edison's Charge Ready Pilot Programme is one example of a collaborative effort with businesses, local governments, and community organizations, to deploy EV charging stations within its service territory.[100] Importantly, 50 per cent of the Charge Ready sites to date have been situated 'within communities that are most heavily impacted by pollution and most vulnerable to its effects'.[101] Thus there is a participatory role to be played by these communities in implementing infrastructure siting policies and programmes.

For those members of underserved communities interested in EV ownership, incentive programmes in the form of vouchers, rebates, or financing assistance are already being utilized in some communities. For example, California state law established the Charge Ahead California Initiative which directs the California Air Resources Board to use some of the funding generated through the state's GHG cap-and-trade programme to create equity programmes that increase access to clean transportation in underserved communities.[102] These programmes include an Enhanced Fleet Modernization Program 'Plus-Up' Program that gives low-income participants an assortment of vouchers, charging equipment incentives for public transit and car-sharing to help transition from older polluting car models to clean technology vehicles; and the Low-Income Financing Assistance Pilot Project that provides financing options for low-income clients to purchase EVs and install home chargers.[103] Oregon's EV rebate structure[104] provides funding for low and moderate income purchasers/lessees who live in areas with elevated concentrations of air pollution.[105] Designing state-funded programmes in this manner ensures that benefits are spread to low-income consumers for a more holistic EV transition.

Policies that support affordable car-sharing services rather than car ownership could also help meet the needs of underserved community members who do not view EV ownership as a priority or possibility. BlueLA, created through a California Air Resources Board grant to the City of Los Angeles, pilots EV car-sharing in low-income communities in the city. Recognizing that working families may only need access to an EV for point-to-point use, BlueLA enables drivers to have the flexibility of depositing the vehicle at a public transportation hub and not have to return it to its

[99] D. Iaconangelo, 'Chargers in "Disadvantaged" Areas Face Pushback' (21 May 2019) *E&E News* https://www.eenews.net/energywire/2019/05/21/stories/1060368973 accessed 25 June 2019.

[100] M. Baumhefner, 'Proposal to Charge Electric Cars in Southern California Gets the Green Light' (14 January 2016) *Natural Resources Defense Coucil* https://www.nrdc.org/experts/max-baumhefner/proposal-charge-electric-cars-southern-california-gets-green-light accessed 6 July 2019.

[101] Southern California Edison, 'Charge Ready Pilot Final Report: Results and Findings' https://www.edison.com/content/dam/eix/documents/innovation/charge-ready-final-report-summary.pdf accessed 6 July 2019.

[102] California SB 1275 (Vehicle retirement and replacement: Charge Ahead California Initiative) https://leginfo.legislature.ca.gov/faces/billTextClient.xhtml?bill_id=201320140SB1275 accessed 6 July 2019.

[103] Charge Ahead California, 'Leading with Equity' (undated) http://greenlining.org/wp-content/uploads/2017/01/Charge-Ahead_Equity-Fact-Sheet_v10.pdf accessed 6 July 2019.

[104] Go Electric Oregon, 'Incentives & Rebates' https://goelectric.oregon.gov/incentives-rebates accessed 6 July 2019.

[105] Sierra Club & Plug In America, 'AchiEVe: Model State & Local Policies to Accelerate Electric Vehicle Adoption' (Version 2.0, June 2018) https://www.sierraclub.org/sites/www.sierraclub.org/files/blog/EV%20Policy%20Toolkit.pdf accessed 6 July 2019.

original pick-up location.[106] Developed in partnership with a committee of community organizations,[107] the community-invested car-sharing programme increased the mobility of underserved communities in a collaborative and sustainable way.

Other alternatives to EV ownership may also produce more energy just outcomes. Partly in response to campaigns by environmental justice advocates for alternate electrification programmes[108] and partly due to underutilization of chargers in low-income areas in other projects,[109] Duke Energy Corporation opted for a programme funding chargers for electric school buses and public transportation in North Carolina rather than reserving a segment of its chargers for low-income residents.[110] This experience points out the importance of collaborating with underserved communities to find solutions that work for each community. In some communities promoting EV ownership may be the best answer while in others EV-sharing may be preferred, while in others the electrification of buses and transit may provide the best local solution.

VII. Conclusion

Fossil fuel-based electric energy production and use in transportation have resulted in disproportionate impacts in underserved communities, particularly because of the heightened risk these communities face. This risk is further exacerbated by the adverse implications of a carbon-saturated planet that increasingly has an impact on these communities in inequitable ways. Further, many underserved communities are unable to access the benefits that flow from increased energy efficiency, local generation of renewable energy, and the use of EVs. In fact, some approaches to these measures can increase costs to underserved community members who are least able to afford these increases. It is therefore critical that in pursuing more sustainable energy policies underserved communities be part of the conversation and that their voices are able to help shape outcomes. Energy-focused non-profit organizations like Elevate Energy can strengthen the voices of underserved communities and help organize the resources needed to allow communities' members to realize the benefits of energy efficiency and locally-generated renewable energy. Laws such as the Illinois FEJA, that was designed based on collaboration with community organizations and provides resources to underserved communities, can play a central role in lowering both risk and costs through programmes specifically designed to meet the needs of underserved communities. Similarly, well-designed community solar programmes can provide

[106] R. Spachek, 'New L.A. Car-sharing Service Aims to Serve Low-income Neighborhoods' (9 June 2017) *Los Angeles Times* https://www.latimes.com/business/la-fi-bluela-20170609-story.html accessed 6 July 2019.

[107] BlueLA, *About BlueLA*, https://www.bluela.com/about-bluela accessed 6 July 2019.

[108] D. Iaconangelo, 'Chargers in "Disadvantaged" Areas Face Pushback' (21 May 2019), *E&E News* https://www.eenews.net/energywire/2019/05/21/stories/1060368973 accessed 25 June 2019.

[109] One of Duke Energy Corp.'s pilot projects in Florida, which placed 10 per cent of its new chargers in low-income areas, found low utilization of those chargers.

[110] D. Iaconangelo, 'Duke Plans Largest Utility EV Investment Ever in Southeast' (2 April 2019) *E&E News* https://www.eenews.net/energywire/stories/1060139181/ accessed 25 June 2019.

more just outcomes by increasing access for underserved communities to renewable technologies. Those programmes need to engage underserved communities to meet community needs and provide resources that make community solar affordable. The programmes can also help build community resilience by bringing job training and job opportunities to underserved communities. Finally, electrified transportation efforts that are supported by state laws, that are based on community consultations, and that either bridge the affordability gap for EVs and address the barriers to EV infrastructure in underserved communities, or provide alternative approaches to using EVs such as through EV car-sharing or EV-based public transportation can lower risks for underserved communities and provide more equitable access to the benefits of electrification.

8

Energy Justice Along the 'New Silk Road'

Balancing Investors' and Consumers' Rights in Central Asia

*Anatole Boute**

I. Introduction

Central Asia—that is, the post-Soviet region composed of Kazakhstan, Uzbekistan, Kyrgyzstan, Tajikistan, and Turkmenistan—holds massive energy reserves.[1] Yet, most Central Asian utilities struggle to guarantee the secure and reliable operation of their energy systems. The use of outdated installations, in combination with the strong growth and inefficiency of energy consumption, jeopardizes the balance of energy supply and demand.[2] Interruptions of energy supply, in particular in the winter when energy is most needed, are a cause of social hardship.[3]

One of the main reasons explaining energy insecurity in Central Asia is that energy tariffs are set far below cost-recovery levels. With artificially low energy prices, utilities suffer financial losses and are not in a position to service debt. For instance, the World Bank has repeatedly warned Kyrgyzstan that exceptionally low energy tariff levels 'do not allow the sector entities to recover cash expenses let alone long run marginal costs of power supply' and as a result the 'power sector may face fatal failures leading to extended outages, further impeding the country's economic development, and deteriorated quality of life for the population'.[4]

Given its energy riches and strategic location in the Eurasian heartland, Central Asia is a central component of China's Belt and Road Initiative or 'New Silk Road'—the large-scale infrastructure initiative that aims to enhance the regional and

* This chapter builds on A. Boute, *Energy Security Along the New Silk Road: Energy Law and Geopolitics in Central Asia* (Cambridge University Press, 2019). The research underlying the completion of this chapter benefited from support by the HK Research Grants Council General Research Fund Project 14608118.

[1] BP, *BP Statistical Review of World Energy* (67th edition, 2018) http://www.bp.com/en/global/corporate/energy-economics/statistical-review-of-world-energy.html accessed 16 July 2019.

[2] S. Grunwald, 'Central Asia Regional Economic Cooperation: Power Sector Regional Master Plan' (Asian Development Bank, 2012) http://www.adb.org/projects/documents/central-asia-regional-economic-cooperation-power-sector-regional-master-plan-tacr accessed 16 July 2019.

[3] See, e.g. D. Fields, et al., 'Tajikistan's Winter Energy Crisis: Electricity Supply and Demand Alternatives' (World Bank, 2013) https://openknowledge.worldbank.org/handle/10986/15795 accessed 16 July 2019.

[4] World Bank, 'Kyrgyzstan: Electricity Supply Accountability and Reliability Improvement Project' (World Bank, 2013) http://documents.worldbank.org/curated/en/120001468091788636/pdf/787360PID0Init024020130 0Box377347B.pdf accessed 16 July 2019.

Anatole Boute, Energy Justice Along the 'New Silk Road' In: *Energy Justice and Energy Law.* Edited by Íñigo Del Guayo, Lee Godden, Donald N. Zillman, Milton Fernando Montoya, and José Juan González, Oxford University Press (2020).
DOI: 10.1093/oso/9780198860754.003.0008

international integration of the Chinese economy.[5] Besides launching infrastructure projects aimed at securing external energy supplies to China (e.g. the Central Asia–China gas pipeline), China invests in power stations and transmission lines in order to enhance energy supply in the Central Asian countries themselves.[6] Central Asia is also of key strategic importance for Russia, being located within its 'sphere of influence'.[7] Chinese and Russian investments are a welcome source of capital and technology to help address Central Asia's urgent infrastructure requirements. At the same time, the Belt and Road Initiative and Russia's external investment policy are increasingly scrutinized,[8] and criticized for creating a relation of unsustainable dependency on external debt.

In this context, domestic energy market reforms are urgently needed to restore the financial viability of energy utilities and limit the perceived geopolitical risks associated with dependency on external donors. In particular, it is essential for the Central Asian states to reform energy tariffs in order to gradually achieve cost-recovery energy price levels. However, tariff reforms are highly unpopular, raise questions of social protection, and threaten social peace in the region. Despite low energy tariffs, energy poverty affects an important segment of the Central Asian population.[9] With an important part of the Central Asian population already struggling to meet its energy needs, the implementation of tariff increases to finance the necessary investments in energy security risks stoking civil unrest. Most notably, the decision of the Kyrgyz government to increase electricity prices in 2010 was one of the key contributing factors to the second Kyrgyz Revolution.[10] In a context of energy poverty and tight budgetary constraints, what legal and regulatory options could Central Asian states select to restore their utilities' financial viability without jeopardizing the affordability of energy supply?

[5] National Development and Reform Commission (NDRC), 'Vision and Actions on Jointly Building Silk Road Economic Belt and 21st-Century Maritime Silk Road' (2015) http://en.ndrc.gov.cn/newsrelease/201503/t20150330_669367.html accessed 16 July 2019; NDRC and NEA of China, 'Vision and Actions on Energy Cooperation in Jointly Building Silk Road Economic Belt and 21st-Century Maritime Silk Road' (2017) https://eng.yidaiyilu.gov.cn/zchj/qwfb/13754.htm accessed 16 July 2019.

[6] See, e.g., S. Lain, 'The Potential and Pitfalls of Connectivity along the Silk Road Economic Belt', in M. Laruelle (ed.), *China's Belt and Road Initiative and its Impact in Central Asia* (The George Washington University, Central Asia Program, 2018), 1, 3.

[7] D. Trenin, 'Russia's Spheres of Interest, Not Influence' (2009) 32 *The Washington Quarterly*, 3.

[8] See, e.g., A. Cooley, *Great Games, Local Rules: The New Great Power Contest in Central Asia* (Oxford University Press, 2012); M. Laruelle (ed.), *China's Belt and Road Initiative and its Impact in Central Asia* (The George Washington University, Central Asia Program, 2018); M. Laruelle and S. Peyrouse, *The Chinese Question in Central Asia: Domestic Order, Social Change, and the Chinese Factor* (Hurst Publishers, 2012); T. Fingar (ed.), *The New Great Game: China and South and Central Asia in the Era of Reform* (Stanford University Press, 2016).

[9] See, e.g., A. Balabanyan, et al., 'Keeping Warm: Urban Heating Options in the Kyrgyz Republic' (World Bank, 2015), 27, http://www.worldbank.org/en/news/feature/2015/02/25/urban-heating-options-for-the-kyrgyz-republic accessed 16 July 2019; A. Balabanyan, et al., 'Keeping Warm: Urban Heating Options in Tajikistan' (World Bank, 2015), 17, https://openknowledge.worldbank.org/handle/10986/22088 accessed 16 July 2019.

[10] D. Wood, 'Electricity Plays Key Role in Kyrgyzstan Uprising' (19 April 2010) *World Resources Institute* http://www.wri.org/blog/2010/04/electricity-plays-key-role-kyrgyzstan-uprising accessed 16 July 2019; J. Nichol, 'The April 2010 Coup in Kyrgyzstan and its Aftermath: Context and Implications for U.S. Interests' (2010) *Congressional Research Service*, 5, http://fas.org/sgp/crs/row/R41178.pdf accessed 16 July 2019; A. Bohr, 'Revolution in Kyrgyzstan—Again' (2010) *House Russia and Eurasia Programme Paper 03/10* http://www.chathamhouse.org/sites/files/chathamhouse/public/Research/Russia%20and%20Eurasia/0410pp_kyrgyzstan.pdf accessed 16 July 2019.

This chapter starts by examining the principle of cost recovery under Central Asian law and demonstrates that, by imposing on energy utilities the financial cost of social protection, the Central Asian governments act in breach of the legal basis that governs tariff regulation. Paradoxically, artificially low energy tariffs exacerbate the problems of energy poverty and insecurity by encouraging consumption and trapping consumers in high energy dependency. Courts can contribute to the popular acceptance of tariff reforms by shifting the blame of tariff increases away from the government. At the same time, courts have to enforce consumers' procedural rights in the tariff regulation process. Public participation in tariff regulation can help consumers understand the necessity of tariff reforms. This requires a transparent and open discussion on the real causes of utilities' financial troubles, including the endemic corruption that affects the functioning of the Central Asian energy companies. Implementing tariff reforms is necessary to restore the economic viability of the Central Asian energy systems, and to secure energy supply without increasing national dependency on foreign aid.

II. Investors' Economic Rights

The regulation of energy tariffs is a common mechanism for ensuring that the charges for natural monopoly services remain reasonable and that consumers are protected against 'exploitation at the hands of [monopolistic] companies'.[11] However, the risk for the utilities is that tariffs are set below cost-recovery levels.

In most Central Asian countries, the tariff regulator is legally obliged to balance the interests of energy consumers and energy companies.[12] This obligation implies that, in principle, the government cannot jeopardize the financial viability of the utilities by imposing on them the cost of social protection policies.[13] Central Asian law requires the regions' governments to determine tariffs that reflect the real cost of energy supply.[14] Non cost-recovery tariffs must be accompanied with adequate subsidies to compensate utilities for the resulting financial losses.[15] The regulation of the energy sector must ensure the utilities' economic independence.

Given exceptionally low energy prices in the region, tariffs must be increased in order to reach cost-recovery levels, ensure the economic independence of utilities and,

[11] *Munn v. Illinois*, United States Supreme Court, 94 U.S. 113, 94 U.S. 134 (1876); *FPC v. Hope Nat. Gas Co.*, United States Supreme Court, 320 U.S. 591, 320 U.S. 612 (1944).

[12] Article 4, Tajik Energy Law, 29 November 2000, No. 33; Article 17, Kyrgyz Natural Monopoly Law, 8 August 2011, No. 149; Article 4, Uzbek Natural Monopoly Law, 19 August 1999, No. 815-I; Article 15, Turkmen Electricity Law, 16 August 2014, No. 104-V.

[13] See more generally A. Boute, *Russian Electricity and Energy Investment Law* (Brill Nijhoff, 2015), 192–4.

[14] Article 21, Kyrgyz Electricity Law, 28 January 1997, No. 8; Articles 7 and 10, Turkmen Electricity Law; Article 15-1, Kazakh Natural Monopoly Law, 9 July 1998, No. 272-I. See, also, Article 6, Uzbek Natural Monopoly Law, 19 August 1999, No. 815-I; Order of the Tajik Anti-monopoly Authority on the Determination, Approval and Introduction of Natural Monopoly Tariffs, 5 October 2011, No. 107.

[15] Article 15, Tajik Natural Monopoly Law, 5 March 2007, No. 235; Article 21, Kyrgyz Electricity Law; Order of the State Agency for the Regulation of the Fuel-Energy Complex under the Kyrgyz Government on the Method for the Determination of the Production Cost Price and the Formation of Heat Tariffs, 14 March 2016, No. 2. See, also, Order of the Kazakh Minister of Economy on Temporary Reduction Coefficients for Electricity Transmission Tariffs, 31 July 2015, No. 581.

in particular, enable them to finance the necessary investments to restore the supply–demand adequacy.

A. Cost Recovery in Kyrgyzstan

Tariff increases in Kyrgyzstan are of symbolic relevance for tariff reforms in Central Asia, given that the introduction of higher prices helped trigger the 2010 Kyrgyz Revolution. The neighbouring countries, and indeed the new Kyrgyz administration, are worried to repeat the same mistake and risk social unrest. Nevertheless, in 2014, less than four years after the 2010 revolution, the Kyrgyz government again decided to increase energy prices.

The government increased residential electricity tariffs by more than 70 per cent, but crucially limited this tariff increase to the electricity that households consume above a generous quantity of subsidized electricity.[16] Moreover, the government raised tariffs for industrial consumers at double the level of households' social tariffs and announced yearly tariff increases of 7 per cent. These tariff increases are justified based on the necessity to ensure sufficient financial revenues to reconstruct the obsolete energy infrastructure, and thereby to avoid a collapse of the energy system. However, given the exceptionally low level of prices in the country and large investment requirements in the Kyrgyz energy sector, much higher tariff increases are needed to ensure the financial sustainability of the Kyrgyz energy sector.[17]

Similarly, in the natural gas sector, tariffs remain below cost-recovery levels. Low tariffs eventually resulted in the financial collapse of Kyrgyzgas (the former Kyrgyz utility) which triggered the transfer of Kyrgyzgas to the Russian energy company Gazprom. The Kyrgyz government continues to set natural gas tariffs below cost recovery levels, now effectively imposing on Gazprom the cost of 'affordable' gas supply. According to Gazprom's official website, 'the tariff determined for "Gazprom Kyrgyzstan" is unprofitable and does not cover the costs of purchasing, transporting and storing natural gas. The "Gazprom" corporation directly covers the cost deficit'.[18]

Kyrgyz gas consumers for the moment benefit from subsidized energy at the expense of Gazprom. However, there is a geopolitical cost to Gazprom's generosity, namely, Kyrgyzstan's dependence on Russia for its gas supplies and Kyrgyzstan's commitment to interrupt the restructuring of its gas sector.[19]

[16] Decree of the Kyrgyz Government on the Approval of the Medium-term Electricity and Heat Tariff Policy (2014–2017), 20 November 2014, No. 660.

[17] In 2015, the World Bank estimated that heat tariffs covered around 13 per cent to 50 per cent of the real cost of heat supply. See A. Balabanyan, et al., 'Keeping Warm: Urban Heating Options in the Kyrgyz Republic' (World Bank, 2015), 23.

[18] Gazprom Kyrgyzstan, 'Tarify' (2017) http://kyrgyzstan.gazprom.ru/services/tarif/ accessed 16 July 2019.

[19] Kyrgyz–Russian Agreement on Cooperation in the Field of Gas Transportation, Distribution and Sale in Kyrgyzstan, 23 July 2013 (*Soglashenie o sotrudnichestve v sfere transportirovki, raspredeleniia i realizatsii prirodnogo gaza na territorii Kyrgyzskoi Respubliki*) http://www.conventions.ru/view_base.php?id=2103 accessed 16 July 2019.

B. Cost Recovery in Tajikistan

In Tajikistan, electricity tariffs only cover 'a fraction of long run marginal costs and [are] among the lowest in the world'.[20] The 2015 financial audit of the Tajik electricity utility 'Barki Tojik' raised concerns 'about the Group's ability to continue as a going concern. Unless the Company continues to receive financial support from its shareholder [the Tajik Government] and other related companies as well as from its bankers, it may be unable to continue operating'.[21]

The government adopted a new tariff policy in May 2017 aimed at gradually restoring the financial viability of the Tajik electricity sector.[22] The new tariff policy represents an important step in the transition to cost-recovery tariff regulation. The Tajik government committed to ensuring the financial autonomy of the electricity utility, by bringing tariffs to cost-recovery levels, including a sufficient return on investment to attract capital for the development of the energy infrastructure.

C. Cost Recovery in Uzbekistan

In Uzbekistan, the national electricity utility Uzbekenergo benefits from very high indirect subsidies in the form of gas supplies at discounted prices.[23] Domestic gas prices have increased steadily since 2008, but remain far from export price parity.[24] By discounting the price of primary energy supplies to its power plants, Uzbekistan thus forgoes gas export revenues.[25] The affordability of electricity supply comes at the expense of the gas sector and the public budget.

D. Cost Recovery in Kazakhstan

Kazakhstan partly liberalized its wholesale electricity market. In principle, wholesale electricity market prices are formed on the basis of the forces of supply and

[20] World Bank, *Key Issues for Consideration on the Proposed Rogun Hydropower Project* (World Bank, 2014), 17, <http://pubdocs.worldbank.org/en/339251488268367141/World-Bank-Note-Key-Issues-for-Consideration-on-Proposed-Rogun-Hydropower-Project-eng.pdf> accessed 16 July 2019.

[21] Baker Tilly Klitou and Partners SRL, 'Consolidated Financial Statements of Barki Tajik Holding for the Year Ended 31 December 2015' http://barqitojik.tj/en/activity/finansy-i-audit/auditorskie-otchety/196903/ accessed 16 July 2019.

[22] Decree of the Tajik Government on the Concept of Electricity Tariff Regulation, 27 May 2017, No. 259.

[23] A. Kochnakyan, et al., 'Uzbekistan Energy/Power Sector Issues Note' (World Bank, 2013) http://documents.worldbank.org/curated/en/2013/06/18882686/uzbekistan-energy-power-sector-issues-note accessed 16 July 2019; Asian Development Bank, 'Uzbekistan: Talimarjan Power Project' (Asian Development Bank, 2010), 7, http://www.adb.org/sites/default/files/project-document/64346/43151-02-uzb-rrp.pdf accessed 16 July 2019.

[24] World Bank, 'Uzbekistan: Scaling Up Energy Efficiency in Buildings' (World Bank, 2016), 12, https://openknowledge.worldbank.org/handle/10986/25093 accessed 16 July 2019.

[25] A. Kochnakyan, et al., 'Uzbekistan Energy/Power Sector Issues Note' (World Bank, 2013), 8, http://documents.worldbank.org/curated/en/2013/06/18882686/uzbekistan-energy-power-sector-issues-note accessed 16 July 2019.

demand. In practice, the Kazakh government continues to subject electricity prices to stringent limits (caps).[26] Although in theory electricity prices are supposed to enable power producers to recover both operating and capital expenses, in practice the price caps often make it difficult for producers to recover more than their operating costs.

In the electricity retail sector, retail tariffs should enable energy suppliers to recover their costs (e.g. the cost of purchasing electricity on the wholesale market).[27] However, artificially low prices threaten retail suppliers with bankruptcy.[28]

Similarly, in the gas sector, Kazakh law recognizes the right of gas producers to sell the gas they produce at cost-recovery price levels (including a 10 per cent return on investment),[29] but strict price limits barely enable the producers to recover their costs.

The utilities' financial problems are most acute in the heating sector. For social reasons, heat tariffs are kept artificially low, but the resulting financial losses are only partially subsidized by the city administration.[30]

E. Cost Recovery in Turkmenistan

Turkmenistan is notorious for its generous energy subsidies, but it has not been able to escape the pressure to reform its energy tariffs, at least to some extent. The prices that consumers have to pay over and above a minimum quantity of free electricity are subject to carefully calibrated tariff increases.[31] The government has also increased the price of natural gas.[32] However, absolute prices remain exceptionally low and well below export price parity, which indicates the sensitivity of tariff increases, in a country endowed with massive natural gas resources.

[26] Article 12-1, Kazakh Electricity Law, 9 July 2004, No. 588-II; Order of the Kazakh Minister of Energy on the Rules for the Determination of the Estimated Tariff and the Approval of the Maximum and Individual Tariffs, 20 February 2015, No. 105; Order of the Kazakh Minister of Energy on the Approval of Maximum Electricity and Capacity Tariffs, 3 July 2015, No. 465.

[27] Order of the Kazakh Minister of National Economy on the Approval of Price Formation Rules on Socially Significant Markets, 1 February 2017, No. 36.

[28] M. Aldayarov, I. Dobozi, and T. Nikolakakis, 'Stuck in Transition: Reform Experiences and Challenges Ahead in the Kazakhstan Power Sector' (World Bank, 2017), 38, http://www.worldbank.org/en/country/kazakhstan/publication/kazakhstan-power-sector-note accessed 16 July 2019; 'Energetiki pokazyvaiut ubytki vtoroi kvartal podriad', *Kapital,* 15 January 2018, https://kapital.kz/economic/66062/energetiki-pokazyvayut-ubytki-vtoroj-kvartal-podryad.html accessed 16 July 2019.

[29] Article 15, Kazakh Gas Law, 9 January 2012, No. 532-IV.

[30] Y. Zhang, et al., 'Synthesis Report: Unlocking Energy Efficiency Potentials in Cities in Kazakhstan' (World Bank, 2018), 10, http://documents.worldbank.org/curated/en/267161521612788850/Synthesis-report-unlocking-energy-efficiency-potentials-in-cities-in-Kazakhstan accessed 16 July 2019.

[31] 'Konets zemnogo raia: v Turkmenii otmeniat l'goty na gaz, vodu i elektroenergiiu' (2015) *Regnum*, https://regnum.ru/news/1970829.html accessed 10 December 2018; 'V Turkmenistane povyshaiutsia tseny na elektroenergiiu', 23 November 2014, *Infobad*, http://infoabad.com/novosti-turkmenistana/v-turkmenistane-povyshayutsja-ceny-na-yelektroyenergiyu.html. accessed 10 December 2018.

[32] G. Berdymukhamedov, 'Naseleniiu Turkmenistana vpervye za 20 let podniali tarify na gaz' (1 February 2014) *Pronedra* https://pronedra.ru/gas/2014/02/01/tarify-na-gaz-turkmenistan/ accessed 16 July 2019.

III. The Role of Courts in Enforcing Cost-Recovery Tariffs

Surprisingly, given the concerns regarding the independence of the Central Asian judiciary[33] and the central role of the state in all sectors of the energy industry, courts have played a role in enforcing investors' economic rights. In particular, the Kazakh Supreme Court helped to entrench the utilities' right to cost-recovery tariffs by ruling that energy tariffs must enable the utilities to achieve financial viability, and ensure the reliable functioning of the energy infrastructure.[34] Setting energy tariffs below cost-recovery levels is illegal, unless the government compensates utilities for the economic losses that result from artificially low tariff levels.[35]

In addition to the requirement of cost recovery, the lower courts referred to the risk of collapse of the energy systems to justify the annulment of artificially low energy prices. According to the Almaty Economic Court, 'the introduction of a compensating [i.e. lower] tariff will have negative consequences for the uninterrupted supply of energy to the city of Almaty'.[36] By imposing economic losses on energy utilities, artificially low prices present 'a threat for the safe functioning of heat production installations and the uninterrupted energy supply'.[37] Similarly, the Economic Court of the Karaganda Region annulled an electricity tariff decision by referring to the disruptive effect it would have on planned maintenance works,[38] and thus energy security.

By ruling that artificially low prices violate utilities' economic rights, courts can contribute to the public acceptability of urgently needed tariff reforms. Governments are no longer to blame for the unpopular tariff increases that result from judicial decisions annulling artificially low energy prices.

IV. Social Protection through Consumption Subsidies

According to their constitution, all Central Asian republics are 'social states'.[39] The Central Asian constitutions recognize the right to housing, health, life in a healthy

[33] World Bank, 'Judicial Independence Index' (2017) https://govdata360.worldbank.org/ accessed 16 July 2019.

[34] *Karaganda Electricity Distribution Company v. Department of the Kazakh Anti-monopoly Agency in the Karaganda Region*, Kazakh Supreme Court, 3 February 2011, No. 3g-365-11; *Zhezkazgan Electricity Distribution Company v. Department of the Kazakh Anti-monopoly Agency in the Karaganda Region*, Kazakh Supreme Court, 9 April 2014, No. 3gp-224-14; *Pavlodarenergosbyt v. Department of the Kazakh Anti-monopoly Agency in the Pavlodar Region*, Kazakh Supreme Court, 3 February 2011, No. 3r-365-11; *Sunkar-1 v. Kazakh Agency for the Regulation of Natural Monopolies*, Kazakh Supreme Court, 12 January 2012, No. 3g-228-12.

[35] *Arlan-Trans-Astana v. Kazakh Ministry of Transport and Communication*, Kazakh Supreme Court, 27 April 2016, No. 3gp-291-16.

[36] *Almaty Power Production Company v. Kazakh Anti-monopoly Agency*, Economic Court of the City of Almaty, 12 July 2012, No. 2-3950/12, confirmed by Almaty City Court (Appeal), Decision of 15 September 2012, No. 2a-5006.

[37] Ibid.

[38] *Zhezkazgan Electricity Distribution Company v. Department of the Kazakh Anti-monopoly Agency in the Karaganda Region*, Economic Court of the Karaganda Region, 5 March 2013, confirmed by Kazakh Supreme Court, Decision of 9 April 2014, No. 3gp-224-14.

[39] Article 1, Constitution of the Republic of Kazakhstan, 30 August 1995; Article 1, Constitution of the Republic of Tajikistan, 6 November 1994; Article 1, Constitution of the Republic of Kyrgyzstan; Article 14,

environment, and social protection of the most vulnerable members of society.[40] Although the Central Asian constitutions do not explicitly recognize a right to affordable energy, the recognition of this right finds support in the other social rights of the constitution (e.g. right to housing, health, and life in a healthy environment).[41] In contemporary society, access to modern and sustainable energy services is indispensable to decent housing and health conditions,[42] particularly in the Central Asian climate. The social state provisions of the Central Asian constitutions have been reflected in the region's natural monopoly and energy laws that aim to ensure a 'socially acceptable' supply of energy.[43]

A. Consumption Subsidies

As seen above, the Central Asian states currently ensure the affordability of energy supply by keeping prices below cost-recovery levels. Besides the negative implications for utilities and the public budget, keeping prices low for all consumers is a highly inefficient way of ensuring social protection because most of the benefits will be captured by upper-income groups that typically consume more energy.[44]

Providing direct subsidies to vulnerable consumers is a more transparent way of helping consumers who struggle to meet their energy needs with cost-recovery tariffs. By contrast to artificially low prices for all energy consumers, direct subsidies target vulnerable consumers only. This limits the burden of social protection on the public budget.

The two poorest countries in the region, Tajikistan and Kyrgyzstan, provide targeted social assistance to vulnerable consumers regarding the payment of electricity.[45]

Constitution of Uzbekistan, 15 December 1992, No. 247; Article 5, Constitution of Turkmenistan, 18 May 1992, No. 691-XII.

[40] Article 28, Kazakh Constitution; Articles 39 and 98, Uzbek Constitution; Article 9, Kyrgyz Constitution; Articles 1 and 57, Tajik Constitution; Article 5, Turkmen Constitution.

[41] A. Bradbrook and J. Gardam, 'Placing the Access to Energy Services Within a Human Rights Framework' (2006) 28 *Human Rights Quarterly*, 389.

[42] World Health Organization, 'Fuel for Life: Household Energy and Health' (World Health Organization, 2006) http://www.who.int/indoorair/publications/fuelforlife/en accessed 16 July 2019.

[43] Article 1, Tajik Natural Monopoly Law; Articles 1 and 4, Kyrgyz Natural Monopoly Law; Article 4, Kyrgyz Electricity Law, 28 January 1997, No. 8; Articles 8 and 10, Turkmen Electricity Law, 16 August 2014, No. 104-V; Article 4, Uzbek Electricity Law, 30 September 2009, No. 3RU-225.

[44] D. Coady, et al., 'How Large Are Global Energy Subsidies?' (International Monetary Fund, 2015), 4, http://www.imf.org/en/Publications/WP/Issues/2016/12/31/How-Large-Are-Global-Energy-Subsidies-42940 accessed 16 July 2019.

[45] Tajik Law on Targeted Social Assistance, 24 February 2017, No. 1396; Decree of the Tajik Government on Reinforcing Social Assistance of Vulnerable Families and Citizens, 1 August 2008, No. 379; Decree of the Tajik Government on the Continuation and Introduction of a Pilot Mechanism of Targeted Social Assistance for Vulnerable Families and Citizens, 3 July 2014, No. 437.

However, due to fiscal constraints, the government focuses on the 'extreme poor only'.[46] In Kyrgyzstan, direct social subsidies are limited to veterans, invalids, and inhabitants of remote mountain areas.[47] Large groups of poor households that are not included in these categories, yet need more energy than the minimum social threshold, are left without direct social assistance.

In Kazakhstan, the only direct social subsidies that exist are the subsidies to facilitate the access of vulnerable consumers to general communal services.[48] Regional authorities are charged with the provision of social support to vulnerable consumers,[49] but face significant budget constraints. Their ability to cope has deteriorated as a result of the economic difficulties facing Kazakhstan since the collapse of world oil prices in 2014.

As the energy inefficiency of the Central Asian economy demonstrates, subsidizing energy consumption gives no incentives to households and industries to use energy frugally.[50] By increasing consumers' energy dependency, subsidies have the adverse effect of undermining the affordability of the energy supply in the long term. In the event of future increases of energy prices, energy-inefficient users will be exposed to far more severe financial consequences than users who have implemented efficiency-improvement measures.

B. Volume-differentiated Tariffs

An alternative approach to direct consumption subsidies is to entitle household consumers to a certain quantity of energy at preferential tariffs, and to increase the price of energy above that social threshold.[51] The advantage of this approach is that, by restricting the quantity of energy subject to subsidized prices, governments avoid incentivizing consumers to use energy wastefully above the social threshold.

Turkmenistan has adopted the most extreme form of social tariff: free energy supply. This social scheme applies only to a limited quantity of energy, well below the average level of energy consumption. Above this limit, energy tariffs apply, albeit at very preferential rates.[52]

Kyrgyzstan entitles household consumers to a social tariff for a quantity of electricity that corresponds to the consumption of an average Kyrgyz household (excluding the

[46] World Bank, 'Tajikistan: Nurek Hydropower Rehabilitation Project Phase 1' (World Bank, 2017), 6, http://documents.worldbank.org/curated/en/691071494036135802/pdf/Tajikistan-PAD-04142017.pdf accessed 16 July 2019.

[47] See Kyrgyz Law on Veterans, 8 May 1996, No. 14; Kyrgyz Law on Rights and Guarantees of Compensation for Inhabitants of Mountain Regions, 28 June 1996, No. 33; Kyrgyz Law on the Social Protection of Invalids, 17 April 1991, No. 421-XII.

[48] Article 97, Kazakh Law on Housing Relations, 16 April 1997, No. 94.

[49] Article 31, paragraph 14, Kazakh Law on Local Administration, 23 January 2001, No. 148.

[50] A. Bauer, et al., 'Macroeconomic, Environmental, and Social Implications', in B. Clements, et al., (eds), *Energy Subsidy Reform: Lessons and Implications* (International Monetary Fund, 2013), 18.

[51] R. Bacon, E. Ley, and M. Kojima, 'Subsidies in the Energy Sector: An Overview' (World Bank, 2010), 13, http://siteresources.worldbank.org/EXTESC/Resources/Subsidy_background_paper.pdf accessed 16 July 2019.

[52] Decree of the President of Turkmenistan on the Approval of the Electricity Tariff, 4 November 1996, No. 2855.

use of electricity for heating purposes).[53] Above this guaranteed quantity of subsidized electricity, prices increase significantly.

The supply of a minimum quantity of electricity at preferential tariffs should ensure that households' basic electricity needs can be afforded. Moreover, the higher tariff levels that apply above the social limit should incentivize consumers to improve the efficiency of their energy use. At the same time, the steep tariff increase above the normative limit represents a form of cross-subsidy which, at least partially, compensates utilities for the lost revenues that result from the social tariffs.

Volume-differentiated tariffs are an important reform measure towards energy justice in Central Asia. However, given exceptionally low prices and the very high energy intensity in the region, these measures are insufficient to reorganize the energy industry towards financial sustainability.

V. Energy Efficiency for Energy Justice

Subsidies are needed to protect vulnerable consumers, but this should not increase the pressure on Central Asia's energy systems. Reducing energy consumption is often the most effective way to shield consumers from the impact of tariff reforms.[54] Ideally, subsidies need to be redirected towards the financing of energy-efficiency-improvement measures. External donors have a role to play in this process, but foreign support can come at the expense of strategic influence.

A. Energy Efficiency Subsidies

Central Asia's laws on energy efficiency provide a legal basis for the provision of direct subsidies to finance efficiency improvements in the residential sector.[55] Moreover, the Central Asian states in principle recognize the importance of a 'right to energy savings',[56] that is, a right for utilities to continue to benefit from existing tariff levels to recover the capital expenses of energy-saving measures. Although this right postpones the benefits of cost reductions for consumers, their medium- and long-term interest is served if utilities improve the efficiency of their operations, and thereby reduce the operating cost of

[53] Decree of the Kyrgyz Government on the Approval of the Medium-term Electricity and Heat Tariff Policy (2014–2017), 20 November 2014, No. 660. See, also, S. Moiseeva, 'Gosagentstvo po TEK otvetilo na kritiku limita potrebleniia elektrichestva' (5 December 2014) *Vechernyi Bishkek* http://www.vb.kg/doc/295976_gosagentstvo_po_tek_otvetilo_na_kritiky_limita_potrebleniia_elektrichestva.html accessed 16 July 2019; D. Iusupova, 'Turdubaev ob"iasnil ustanovlennyi limit potrebleniia elektrichestva' (27 October 2014) *Vechernyi Bishkek* http://www.vb.kg/doc/291355_tyrdybaev_obiasnil_ystanovlennyy_limit_potrebleniia_elektrichestva.html accessed 16 July 2019.

[54] See, European Commission, Energy Policy for Consumers, 11 November 2010, SEC (2010), 1407 final, at 14.

[55] Article 23, Tajik Energy Efficiency Law, 19 September 2013, No. 1018; Article 17, paragraph 7, Kazakh Energy Efficiency Law, 13 January 2012, No. 541-IV; Article 23, Kyrgyz Energy Efficiency Law, 7 July 1998, No. 88. See, also, Articles 17 and 18, Uzbek Energy Efficiency Law, 25 April 1997, No. 412-I.

[56] Decree of the Kyrgyz Government on the Medium-term Strategy for the Development of the Kyrgyz Electricity Sector for 2012–2017, 28 May 2012, No. 330.

energy supply. However, with exceptionally low energy tariffs, the region's governments are struggling to release sufficient resources to implement an ambitious efficiency subsidization policy.

B. The Role of External Donors

External donors, including multilateral development banks, have a role to play in compensating for the social impact of tariff reforms by investing in energy efficiency improvement measures.

A successful example is the tariff reform in the Pamir (Gorno-Badakhshan) Autonomous Region of Tajikistan. The Agha Khan Foundation, in cooperation with the International Finance Corporation (World Bank), manages the electricity network in the region based on a concession agreement that sets out how international financing is used to compensate the concessionaire for the financial losses resulting from preferential tariffs in the region.[57] The Concession Agreement obliges the Pamir Energy Company (the holder of the Pamir electricity concession) to provide electricity at 'Socially Protected Tariffs' that are lower than the 'Maximum Average Price' (or the cost-recovery price) the company is authorized to charge based on the Concession. The Tajik government must pay to the Pamir Energy Company the difference between the Maximum Average Price and the Socially Protected Tariffs upon provision of the electricity service. The World Bank, with the support of donors (e.g. the Swiss Confederation), assists the government in meeting these social protection costs.[58]

Multilateral development banks also support investments in energy efficiency improvements. An area of focus is the pumped irrigation sector. Around 30 per cent of national electricity supply is used for agricultural purposes in Uzbekistan, Turkmenistan, and Tajikistan.[59] Given that electricity is one of the main operating costs of pumped irrigation, electricity tariffs are an important determinant of the economic viability of water-intensive crops (e.g. cotton) in semi-arid Central Asia.[60] To support the production and export of these agricultural products, Uzbekistan, Tajikistan, and Kyrgyzstan

[57] A. Markandya and R. Sharma, 'Tajikistan: Reducing Poverty through Private Infrastructure Services—The Pamir Private Power Project' (World Bank, 2004) http://documents.worldbank.org/curated/en/468511468778533007/pdf/307980TJ0Pamir0Power01see0also0307591.pdf accessed 16 July 2019; World Bank and International Finance Corporation, 'Pamir Private Power Project' (World Bank, 2002), 18, http://projects.worldbank.org/P075256/pamir-private-power-project?lang=en accessed 16 July 2019.

[58] Development Credit Agreement (Pamir Private Power Project) between Republic of Tajikistan and International Development Association, 3 July 2002, http://projects.worldbank.org/P075256/pamir-private-power-project?lang=en accessed 16 July 2019; Grant Agreement between the Republic of Tajikistan (the Recipient), represented by the Government of Tajikistan (the Government) and the International Development Association, 24 February 2003, http://projects.worldbank.org/P075256/pamir-private-power-project?lang=en accessed 16 July 2019.

[59] International Energy Agency, 'Statistics for Electricity and Heat' (2015) http://www.iea.org/statistics/electricity/ accessed 16 July 2019.

[60] C. Burt, 'The Costs of Irrigation Inefficiency in Tajikistan' (World Bank, 2017) http://documents.worldbank.org/curated/en/116581486551262816/The-costs-of-irrigation-inefficiency-in-Tajikistan accessed 16 July 2019.

set exceptionally low electricity tariffs for irrigation pumps.[61] This results in the wasteful use of water and electricity, with consequences for both the availability of water resources and the adequacy of electricity supply and demand.[62] Charging the real cost of electricity for pumped irrigation would provide a strong incentive to modernize the irrigation systems and encourage more frugal electricity and thus water use. However, in view of the economic importance of the agricultural sector for the Central Asian economies and its high dependence on pumped water,[63] the governments of Uzbekistan, Tajikistan, and Kyrgyzstan are reluctant to transition towards cost-reflective electricity prices for irrigation. Similarly to residential consumption, improving the efficiency of the pumped irrigation infrastructure is needed to facilitate the acceptability of irrigation tariff increases. By investing in the modernization of the Central Asian pumped irrigation sector, multilateral development banks are indirectly contributing to the acceptance of energy tariff reforms in the region.[64]

In the same vein, China, Russia and other strategic investors in the region could contribute to the affordability and security of energy supply in Central Asia by redirecting their investments towards energy efficiency improvements. However, as highlighted by existing studies on Eurasian energy relations, foreign aid can come at the expense of strategic influence.[65] Foreign aid does therefore not replace the necessity of domestic energy tariff reforms.

VI. Procedural Justice to Break the Vicious Tariff Circle in Central Asia

As highlighted by the 2010 Kyrgyz Revolution, the feasibility of energy tariff reforms depends on public acceptance. Given the sensitivity of energy pricing in the former Soviet Union[66] and in particular the 'sense of entitlement associated with the legacy of

[61] The subsidization of the agricultural sector through low electricity prices for irrigation pumps is not unique to Central Asia. See, e.g. Lucio Monari, 'Power Subsidies: A Reality Check on Subsidizing Power for Irrigation in India' (World Bank, 2012) https://openknowledge.worldbank.org/handle/10986/11350 accessed 16 July 2019.

[62] S. Devarajan, et al., 'MENA Economic Monitor: Corrosive Subsidies' (World Bank, 2014),18, http://documents.worldbank.org/curated/en/922481468275944547/MENA-economic-monitor-corrosive-subsidies accessed 16 July 2019.

[63] Centre of Hydro-meteorological Service of Uzbekistan, 'Third National Communication of the Republic of Uzbekistan under the UNFCCC' (2016), 109, https://unfccc.int/process-and-meetings/transparency-and-reporting/reporting-and-review-under-the-convention/national-communications-and-biennial-update-reports-non-annex-i-parties/national-communication-submissions-from-non-annex-i-parties accessed 16 July 2019.

[64] World Bank, *Uzbekistan: South Karakalpakstan Water Resources Management Improvement Project* (World Bank, 2014), 3, http://documents.worldbank.org/curated/en/2014/05/19546240/uzbekistan-south-karakalpakstan-water-resources-management-improvement-project accessed 16 July 2019; World Bank, 'Kyrgyzstan: Second On-farm Irrigation Project' (World Bank, 2013) http://documents.worldbank.org/curated/pt/574881468278086245/Kyrgyz-Republic-Second-On-Farm-Irrigation-Project accessed 16 July 2019; World Bank, 'Kazakhstan: Second Irrigation and Drainage Improvement Project' (World Bank, 2009) http://documents.worldbank.org/curated/en/2009/11/11345959/kazakhstan-second-irrigation-drainage-improvement-project accessed 16 July 2019.

[65] See (n 8).

[66] C. von Hirschhausen and P. Opitz, 'Power Utility Re-Regulation in East European and CIS Transformation Countries (1990–1999): An Institutional Interpretation' (2001) 246 *Discussion Papers of DIW Berlin German Institute for Economic Research* https://ideas.repec.org/p/zbw/tubsem/20017.html accessed 16 July 2019;

the socialist social compact',[67] tariff reforms cannot be implemented unless a consensus is built.[68] The case for energy tariff reform needs to be made and its long-term benefits for consumers explained.[69] Public consultations on energy tariff reforms are often advocated as ways of improving the transparency and accountability of tariff decisions.[70] Kyrgyzstan, Tajikistan, and Kazakhstan have procedures in place to involve their citizens in the adoption of energy tariff policies.[71] In principle, public participation should build support for energy tariff reforms by 'increasing public awareness about the rationale for energy tariffs reforms'.[72]

However, the organization of public consultations on energy tariff regulation remains a contentious issue in Central Asia.[73] An open and transparent discussion on the financial troubles of utilities would involve discussing corruption and the misappropriation of funds within utilities. Energy theft, overstatement of losses, and inflation of costs negatively affect the financial performance of individual utilities and the economic efficiency of the energy sector as a whole.[74] However, the ownership and control by the government of the energy utilities, almost by definition, link the government to the mismanagement of the utilities.

In 2014, the Kyrgyz judiciary annulled the new energy tariff policy of the government by ruling that the public consultation that preceded the adoption of the policy did not engage in a sufficiently open discussion of the real issues at stake.[75] This judicial decision was thus based on procedural impropriety, in particular the failure to organize a proper public consultation. Non-compliance with the procedural requirement of public consultation constituted a 'fundamental breach' of Kyrgyz law that could be

D. Tkachenko, 'Reguliruemye tarify na energiiu: bor'ba za kopieki v administrativnom poriadk' (2009) *Energetika i Pravo*.

[67] J. Lampietti and N. Junge, 'Europe and Central Asia Power Sector Reform', in A. Coudouel, A. Dani, and S Paternostro (eds), *Poverty and Social Impact Analysis of Reform* (World Bank, 2006), 213.

[68] D. Otorbaev, Prime Minister of Kyrgyzstan, Letter of Policy Development to Jim Yong Kim, President of the World Bank Group, 23 December 2014, http://documents.worldbank.org/curated/en/385351468088467926/pdf/933900PGD0P15200900IDA0R20150000201.pdf accessed 16 July 2019.

[69] See, e.g. T. Alleyne, et al., 'Reforming Energy Subsidies: Lessons from Experience', in B. Clements, et al., (eds), *Energy Subsidy Reform: Lessons and Implications* (International Monetary Fund, 2013), 23–42.

[70] See, e.g. United Nations Economic Commission for Europe, 'Analysis of National Case Studies on Policy Reforms to Promote Energy Efficiency Investments' (United Nations, 2015), 7, http://www.unece.org/fileadmin/DAM/energy/se/pdfs/geee/pub/ESE.44_ECE.ENERGY.97.pdf accessed 16 July 2019; N. Abdyrasulova and N. Kravsov, *Electricity Governance in Kyrgyzstan: An Institutional Assessment* (Civic Environmental Foundation UNISON, 2009), 24–7 and 33–5.

[71] Article 22, Kyrgyz Law on Normative Legal Acts, 20 July 2009, No. 241; Article 17, Kyrgyz Natural Monopoly Law; Article 8, Tajik Natural Monopoly Law; Article 17, paragraph 2, Kazakh Natural Monopoly Law.

[72] World Bank, 'Kyrgyz Republic: Energy Sector Development Policy Operation' (World Bank, 2014) http://documents.worldbank.org/curated/en/731181523025372363/Kyrgyz-Republic-Energy-Sector-Development-Policy-Operation accessed 16 July 2019.

[73] See, more generally, Organization for Economic Cooperation and Development, 'Regulatory Policy in Kazakhstan: Towards Improved Implementation' (Organization for Economic Cooperation and Development, 2014), 73–80, http://www.oecd.org/countries/kazakhstan/kazakhstan.htm accessed 16 July 2019.

[74] J. Halpern, C. Kenny, and E. Dickson, 'Deterring Corruption and Improving Governance in the Electricity Sector' (World Bank, 2009) http://documents.worldbank.org/curated/en/301391468329462782/Deterring-corruption-and-improving-governance-in-the-electricity-sector-a-sourcebook accessed 16 July 2019.

[75] *Toktakunov N.A., Sultanov M.T. v. Government of Kyrgyzstan*, Interregional Bishkek Court, Judgment of 29 September 2014; and Kyrgyz Supreme Court, 16 June 2015, No. AD-1539/14 mbs3.

rectified only by annulling the decree with retroactive force and requiring the government to start the regulatory process anew.

The annulment of a government tariff decree by the Kyrgyz judiciary demonstrates that the courts can play a role in enforcing consumers' rights in the energy sector, despite the general perception that the Central Asian judiciary is weak.[76] The importance of the Kyrgyz decision must be understood against the historical background of the 2010 Kyrgyz Revolution that was, at least to a certain extent, triggered by the lack of transparency that affected the decision by the administration to increase prices. The court avoided the politically controversial question of what affordable energy means, but contributed to the transparency and thus the acceptability of tariff reforms on the basis of procedural grounds.

VII. Conclusion

The case of Central Asia highlights the difficulty of transitioning from hidden subsidies (i.e. artificially low energy prices) to transparent financial arrangements (i.e. cost-recovery tariffs, with public support for vulnerable consumers). Subsidies are needed to help consumers to obtain access to energy under reasonable conditions, but it is counterproductive to subsidize the consumption of energy. To escape from this trap, it is essential to subsidize energy-efficiency improvements instead of energy end use. Given the high capital expenditures of energy-efficiency-improvement measures and limits to the state budget in Central Asia, external donors and foreign investments have an important role to play in the transition of the Central Asian energy sector to financial sustainability. However, foreign aid can come at the expense of dependency and strategic influence.

Tariff reforms are needed in order to avoid increasing dependency on foreign aid and strategic investments. In the short term, tariff increases to cost-recovery levels can threaten the affordability of energy supply, in particular for the most vulnerable consumers. However, in the long term, it is in the interest of consumers that the utilities have the financial capacity to invest in the modernization of the energy infrastructure. To the benefit of the long-term affordability and security of energy supply, as well as the protection against foreign strategic influence, it is necessary to reform energy tariffs by carefully balancing the interests of consumers and investors. Procedural justice is an important dimension of this reform process.

First, the legal requirement of 'cost-recovery' tariff regulation shall protect utilities against tariff decisions shifting onto utilities the financial burden of affordable and secure energy supply. Despite concerns on limited judicial independence in Central Asia, courts have a role to play in the protection of utilities' economic rights, and the public acceptance of tariff reforms. In particular, by ruling that artificially low prices violate

[76] According to World Bank, 'Judicial Independence Index' (2017), https://govdata360.worldbank.org/, Kyrgyzstan's judiciary is the weakest in the region (in comparison to Tajikistan, Kazakhstan, and Uzbekistan).

utilities' economic rights, courts can shift the blame of unpopular tariff increases away from the governments.

Furthermore, the legal requirement of public consultation can help gain popular support for necessary tariff reforms by involving consumers in the decision-making process and explaining the unsustainability of existing price levels. Similarly to investors' rights, courts have an important role to play in enforcing consumers' procedural rights and so contribute to the acceptability of urgently needed reforms.

PART IV

CONSUMERS AT THE FRONTLINE OF A NEW ENERGY JUSTICE

9

State Protection of Energy Consumers

Between Human Rights and Private Sector Regulation

*Hanri Mostert and Tjakie Naude**

I. Introduction

Legal systems differ across the world. So do energy markets. The constant, though, is that end-consumers need to access energy supply, and to enjoy protection within the energy market, regardless of whether energy is to be accessed as a state-provided resource or as one available on the open market. This chapter explores the role of the state in protecting end-consumers within different energy market models.

The indigent and affluent have notable disparity of opportunity in accessing clean, affordable, and reliable energy,[1] and its accompanying economic potential. The more onerous the generation, transmission, and distribution, the greater the likelihood of consumer vulnerability.[2] Noting (but because of scope constraints not engaging with) existing scholarship on consumer vulnerability,[3] we accept that potential vulnerability concerns all energy consumers, but that some factors—poverty included—render some consumers hyper-vulnerable.[4]

* We gratefully acknowledge the research assistance of Analisa Ndebele and Hannah Massyn and the financial support of the National Research Foundation and the University of Cape Town. Opinions expressed here, and errors made should not be attributed to these individuals or institutions.

[1] Y. Omorogbe, 'Universal Access to Modern Energy Services: The Centrality of the Law', in Y. Omorogbe and A.O. Ordor (eds), *Ending Africa's Energy Deficit and the Law: Achieving Sustainable Energy for All in Africa* (Oxford University Press, 2018), 10–11 (hereafter Omorogbe, *Universal Access*); International Energy Agency, 'Energy Access Outlook 2017' (2017) *International Energy Agency* https://www.iea.org/publications/freepublications/publication/WEO2017SpecialReport_EnergyAccessOutlook.pdf accessed 18 July 2018. A. Eberhard, O. Rosnes, M. Shkaratan, and H. Vennemo, *Africa's Power Infrastructure: Investment, Integration, Efficiency* (World Bank Publications, 2011), 5; H. Corder and T. Andzenge, 'Regulation as a Catalyst for the Electrification of Africa', in Y. Omorogbe and A.O. Ordor (eds), *Ending Africa's Energy Deficit and the Law: Achieving Sustainable Energy for All in Africa* (Oxford University Press, 2018), 71–3.

[2] B. Sovacool, R. Sidortsov, and B. Jones, *Energy, Security, Equality and Justice* (Routledge, 2014), 85–6 (hereafter Sovacool, et al., *Energy*); Omorogbe, *Universal Access* (n 1), 10.

[3] E.g. Sovacool, et al., *Energy* (n 2) generally S. Bouzarovski, 'Understanding Energy Poverty, Vulnerability and Justice', in S. Bouzarovski (ed.), *Energy Poverty: (Dis)Assembling Europe's Infrastructural Divide* (Palgrave Macmillan, 2018), 17–22 (hereafter Bouzarovski, *Understanding Energy Poverty*); S.M. Baker, J.W. Gentry, and T.L. Rittenburg, 'Building Understanding of the Domain of Consumer Vulnerability' (2005) 25 *Journal of Macromarketing*, 128–39; M. Gallardo, 'Identifying Vulnerability to Poverty: A Critical Survey' (2018) 32 *Journal of Economic Surveys*, 1074–105.

[4] See especially Bouzarovski, *Understanding Energy Poverty* (n 3), 20–1 who highlights the plight of the unemployed, the elderly, and the disabled.

Hanri Mostert and Tjakie Naude, State Protection of Energy Consumers In: *Energy Justice and Energy Law.* Edited by Íñigo Del Guayo, Lee Godden, Donald N. Zillman, Milton Fernando Montoya, and José Juan González, Oxford University Press (2020). © The Several Contributors. DOI: 10.1093/oso/9780198860754.003.0009

Three consumer concerns, highlighted in Sustainability Development Goal (SDG) 7's formulation of 'access to affordable, reliable, sustainable and modern energy for all' stand out:

(i) First, energy supply must be constant and reliable, lest 'energy drudgery'[5] jeopardize productivity and wealth-creating potential. Access to energy is measured by the available sources of the energy, the infrastructure and technology available to convert such energy into electricity, mechanical and cooking power and the rate of electrification.[6]
(ii) Second, energy must be affordable. Vulnerability can be influenced by, for example, particular energy pricing models or particular types of subsidies available to designated groups.[7]
(iii) Third, energy sources must be sustainable. Current energy needs must be managed such that future generations can still meet theirs.[8]

These are potential points of vulnerability for energy end-consumers. For indigent users of energy, vulnerability is compounded where the above concerns converge.[9] The purpose of this chapter is to seek understanding of how different legal systems address such vulnerability, and which protective mechanisms are invoked.

The analysis compares jurisdictions on a spectrum of energy market models. On the one end, there are markets dominated by virtual state monopolies. Both supply and consumer protection take on a different shape in such jurisdictions, compared to those on the other end of the spectrum, where distribution of energy to end-consumers is privatized. Between these poles are various intermediate positions, with jurisdictions in different stages of privatizing their energy supply and adapting their consumer protection measures accordingly. The South African example highlights the issues experienced in a state-dominated system of supply and distribution. The EU is the opposite. To demonstrate the variations within privatized markets, and the degree to which privatization can be implemented successfully, we consider the Australian and Nigerian models of energy supply and end-consumer protection.

II. State-supply Models

The dominant model of energy market organization in Sub-Saharan Africa is still state-run, centralized, vertically integrated, monopolistic utilities for energy generation,

[5] The indirect costs of generating, transporting, and harnessing energy from inefficient solid fuels. Sovacool, et al., *Energy* (n 2), 94–8; B.K. Sovacool and M.H. Dworkin, *Global Energy Justice: Problems, Principles, and Practices* (Cambridge University Press, 2014), 225–30.

[6] See Omorogbe, *Universal Access* (n 1), 9–10.

[7] See Bouzarovski, *Understanding Energy Poverty* (n 3), 21.

[8] S. Krumdieck, 'Introduction to Sustainable Energy', in C.F. Kutscher, J.B. Milford, and F. Kreith (eds), *Principles of Sustainable Energy Systems* (CRC Press, 3rd edn, 2018), 3–6.

[9] N. Simcock, H. Thomson, S. Petrova, and S. Bouzarovski, *Energy Poverty and Vulnerability: A Global Perspective* (Routledge, 1st edn, 2017), 249; Omorogbe, *Universal Access* (n 1), 10.

transmission, distribution, and supply networks.[10] These state-run supply networks primarily utilize non-renewable resources[11] to generate power for distribution by a central national grid.[12]

Vertically integrated systems beget particular types of consumer vulnerability.[13] Interruption of supply might, for example, result from problems in generation, transmission, or distribution, and impact varying numbers of affected consumers, duration of interruptions, and remedial costs.[14] Distribution processes seem particularly susceptible to interruptions,[15] although they are usually shorter and less costly than outages resulting from generation or transmission failures.[16]

A. Lack of Applicable Consumer Protection Rules

State-supply systems barely ever have detailed rules on the protection of end-consumers of electricity (e.g. detailed billing).[17] The need for protection in state-supply systems is motivated differently from systems where supply functions have been privatized.[18] In state-supply systems, energy consumers must find recourse to administrative remedies, such as just administrative action,[19] or protection of fundamental or human rights.[20]

[10] P. Lucas, A. Dagnachew, and A. Hof, 'Towards Universal Electricity Access in Sub-Saharan Africa: A Quantitative Analysis of Technology and Investment Requirements' (2017) *Policy Report, PBL Netherlands Environmental Assessment Agency*, 6 https://www.pbl.nl/en/publications/towards-universal-electricity-access-in-sub-saharan-africa accessed 2 February 2019 (hereafter Lucas, et al., 'Towards Universal Electricity Access'); A. Eberhard, 'Competition and Regulation in the Electricity Supply Industry in South Africa' (Paper prepared for the Competition Commission) (2000), 3 https://www.gsb.uct.ac.za/files/Electricity_competion_in_SA-Eberhardt.pdf accessed 19 February 2019.

[11] N. Avila, J.P. Carvallo, B. Shaw, and D.M. Kammen, *The Energy Challenge in Sub-Saharan Africa: A Guide for Advocates and Policy Makers: Part 1: Generating Energy for Sustainable and Equitable Development* (Oxfam Research Backgrounder Series, 2017), 8 (hereafter Avila, et al., *The Energy Challenge*).

[12] J. Ifediora, 'Solving the Energy Poverty Problem in sub-Saharan Africa' (27 September 2017) *Council on African Security and Development* https://www.casade.org/solving-the-energy-poverty-problem-in-sub-saharan-africa/ accessed 13 January 2019; Lucas, et al., 'Towards Universal Electricity Access' (n 10), 6.

[13] M. Edimu, *Using Probability Density Functions to Analyze the Effect of External Threats on the Reliability of a South African Power Grid* (unpublished PhD (ElecEng) thesis), (University of Cape Town, 2013) 3–4, 17–18.

[14] I.A. Masembe, *Benefits of Smart Grid Technology in South Africa* (unpublished MSc (Eng) thesis), (University of Cape Town, 2013) 5 (hereafter Masembe, *Benefits*).

[15] Ibid., 5.

[16] Ibid.

[17] J. Kapika and A. Eberhard, *Power Sector Reform and Regulation in Africa: Lessons from Kenya, Tanzania, Uganda, Zambia, Namibia and Ghana* (HSRC Press, 2013), 2, 4–5; M. Kojima and C. Trimble, *Making Power Affordable for Africa and Viable for its Utilities* (World Bank, 2016), 29–30 (hereafter Kojima and Trimble, *Making Power Affordable*).

[18] D. Pudney, 'Benefits of Privatising the Electrical Distribution Sector' (29 March 2018) *EE Publishers* https://www.ee.co.za/article/privatisation-of-electricity-utilities-can-improve-financial-viability-customer-service.html accessed 9 July 2019 (hereafter Pudney, 'Benefits of Privatising'); Kojima and Trimble, *Making Power Affordable* (n 17), 4, 33–7.

[19] *Afriforum NPC & Others v Eskom Holdings SOC Limited & Others* [2017] 3 All SA 663 (GP) [23], [26], [68] (hereafter *Afriforum*); Pudney, 'Benefits of Privatising' (n 18).

[20] *Afriforum* (n 19), [23], [26].

Among models of state-supplied energy,[21] South Africa exemplifies the potential problems well. Its national power utility, the parastatal Eskom,[22] dominates the generation[23] of electricity and has a monopoly over transmission.[24] More than 40 per cent of the electricity generated by Eskom is sold to municipalities, which then on-sell it to end-consumers.[25] The National Energy Regulator of South Africa (NERSA) has licensed most municipalities to distribute electricity to consumers.[26] Despite electricity distribution being a municipal function,[27] Eskom also acts as the distributor in certain areas.[28] These areas often struggle to integrate planning, resulting in delayed implementation and maintenance of distribution infrastructure.[29]

[21] For example, Zambia's vertically integrated State-owned utility ZESCO (discussed by A.D. Owen, *Policy Report on the Electricity Sector in Zambia* (report prepared by Energy Studies Institute of the National University of Singapore for Freedom to Create 2016) 9) and SNEL, the monopolistic national utility of the Democratic Republic of Congo (DRC), as discussed by Promethium Carbon, *Report: Electricity Market Reform in Southern Africa* (2016), 17.

[22] Estimated to have an installed energy generation capacity of nearly 63 per cent of the total generation capacity in Sub-Saharan Africa. Eskom, 'Medium-Term System Adequacy Outlook: 2017–2022' (2017), 10; KPMG, 'Sub-Saharan Africa Power Outlook' (2014), 6; E. Teljeur, F. Sheik, T. Kolobe, and D. da Costa, 'Electricity Supply Industry Restructuring: Options for the Organisation of Government Assets' (2016) *Trade & Industrial Policy Strategies and Business Leadership South Africa*, 1 (hereafter Teljeur, et al., 'Electricity Supply').

[23] Generating ± 95 per cent of South Africa's electricity demand. Private generators, municipalities, and other redistributors generate only a small percentage. See Development Bank of Southern Africa, 'Infrastructure Barometer 2012: Progress in Infrastructure Development Since Democracy' (2012) https://www.dbsa.org/EN/About-Us/Publications/Documents/Infrastructure%20Barometer%202012.pdf accessed 7 June 2019; ESI Africa, 'Embedded Generation in South Africa' (8 January 2014) *ESI Africa* https://www.esi-africa.com/top-stories/embedded-generation-in-south-africa/ accessed 8 July 2019; South African Local Government Association, 'Status of Small Scale Embedded Generation (SSEG) In South African Municipalities' (2017), 4–5 (hereafter SALGA, 'Status of SSEG').

[24] This may change in the near future. C. Ramaphosa, '2019 State of the Nation Address' (South African Government, 7 February 2019) https://www.gov.za/speeches/president-cyril-ramaphosa-2019-state-nation-address-7-feb-2019-0000 accessed 9 July 2019 announced that Eskom will be unbundled into three entities to deal respectively with the generation, transmission, and distribution. Moreover, the Independent System and Market Operator ('ISMO') Bill (Government Gazette No. 34289 of 13 May 2011) was introduced in 2012, withdrawn in 2014, and revived again in 2018 (Notice 87 of 2019, Government Gazette No. 42237 of 20 February 2019 (hereafter GG 42237). Should it be passed, a newly established State-owned body will be responsible for buying electricity from generators and independent power producers (IPPs). ISMO Bill s 4(3)(a–g). This statutorily established body—the Independent System and Market Operator SOC Ltd—would also be mandated with selling electricity to consumers and distributors at a wholesale tariff. ISMO Bill s 3, s 4(3)(j). These innovations will effectively terminate Eskom's dominance of the electricity production system. It is unclear whether the government intends to pursue the goals in the ISMO Bill further. See further GG 42237; Parliamentary Monitoring Group, 'Call for Comments: Independent System and Market Operator Bill, 2019 (Private Member's Bill)' (20 February 2019) https://pmg.org.za/call-for-comment/806/ accessed 7 July 2019.

[25] SALGA, 'Role of Municipalities' (n 26), 2. The remainder is sold directly to some large consumers, i.e. industry and mines. Eskom, 'Integrated Report 2016', 9; Statistics South Africa, 'Electricity: Big Business for Municipalities' (Stats SA, 10 July 2017) http://www.statssa.gov.za/?p=10186 accessed 8 July 2019; Masembe, *Benefits* (n 14), 5.

[26] Under Electricity Regulation Act (ERA) 4 of 2006 s 8(a) (hereafter ERA 2006), municipalities, private individuals, or corporate entities feeding privately generated electricity into the public grid require a licence issued by NERSA. Political and financial reasons often make such licenses difficult to obtain. South African Local Government Association, 'The Role of Municipalities as a Service Authority for Electricity Provision' (Paper prepared by SALGA for the AMEU Committees, October 2014), 4–5 (hereafter SALGA, 'Role of Municipalities'). H. Trollip, A. Butler, J. Burton, T. Caeto and, C. Godinho, *Energy Security in South Africa* (MAPS, 2014), 18; Statistics South Africa, 'Tracking Municipal Revenue and Expenditure' (Stats SA, 29 March 2018) http://www.statssa.gov.za/?p=11049 accessed 9 July 2019.

[27] Schedule 4b, Constitution of the Republic of South Africa, 1996 (hereafter Constitution); White Paper on Energy, 1998.

[28] The South African–German Energy Partnership, *The Electricity Distribution Industry in Germany and South Africa—A Review of Policy and Regulation* (2018), 14 (hereafter SAGEP, *Electricity Distribution*).

[29] Ibid., 4, 14.

Regulatory uncertainty prevails in South Africa's electricity sector.[30] Its electricity retail markets are becoming fragmented.[31] Since 2007, South Africa has been plagued by intervals of rolling blackouts (known as 'loadshedding'[32]): the response to Eskom's inadequate generation capacity, in an attempt to avert the collapse of the grid.[33] The aging energy infrastructure is prone to failures and is inadequate to cater for regional needs.[34] An upturn in urbanization, coupled with increasing poverty and electricity theft, also pose challenges for municipalities distributing power.[35] Several municipalities are strapped for cash, under-resourced, and poorly managed, often failing to pay for their Eskom supply.[36] Due to pervasive non-payment problems,[37] Eskom is owed billions.[38] To collect arrears, Eskom interrupted electricity supply to over forty municipalities.[39] This deliberate disruption resulted in litigious action,[40] with concomitant cost to the taxpayer. The litigation highlighted the brokenness of the distribution, supply, and billing systems.[41]

End-consumers bear the consequences of the blackouts, which affect productivity and economic activity immensely.[42] Nevertheless, there are hardly any specific or detailed rules protecting end-consumers of electricity.

The generic rules for consumer protection, in the Consumer Protection Act[43] (CPA), do not cater for questions specific to access to energy. Section 5(8)(c) and (d) of the CPA render the act applicable to state-provided goods. Section 1 of the CPA includes gas, water, and electricity in its definition of 'goods'. This would make the CPA's provisions

[30] T. Murombo, 'Regulating Energy in South Africa: Enabling Sustainable Energy by Integrating Energy and Environmental Regulation' (2015) 33 *Journal of Energy and Natural Resources Law*, 4, 339.

[31] SAGEP, *Electricity Distribution* (n 28), 4.

[32] See H. Mostert and H. van Niekerk, 'Disadvantage, Fairness, and Power Crises in Africa: A Focused Look at Energy Justice', in Y. Omorogbe and A.O. Ordor (eds), *Ending Africa's Energy Deficit and the Law: Achieving Sustainable Energy for All in Africa* (Oxford University Press, 2018), 48–9.

[33] *Afriforum* (n 19) [68–70].

[34] A. Eberhard, 'Electricity Blackouts in South Africa: Proximate and Ultimate Causes & Recommendations for the Future' (University of Cape Town, 14 February 2007), 3–4 and 7 http://pmg-assets.s3-website-eu-west-1.amazonaws.com/docs/2007/070214eleblackouts.pdf accessed 10 April 2019.

[35] SAGEP, *Electricity Distribution* (n 28), 4.

[36] See (nn 39–41).

[37] See, e.g., *Darries and others v City of Johannesburg and others* 2009 (5) SA 284 (GSJ) (hereafter *Darries*).

[38] *Eskom group interim results for the six months ended 30 September 2018* (Eskom, 28 November 2018), 15.

[39] Eskom relied in this regard on s 21(5) ERA. In *Afriforum* (n 19) this strategy was challenged when Afriforum (a non-profit company) and other businesses, including a private hospital group, sought declaratory orders that Eskom may not interrupt electricity supply to any local authority as a means of collecting arrears. See further (n 40–41).

[40] The applicants in *Afriforum* (n 19) argued that s 21(5) ERA is unconstitutional [34–35], [59]. In the alternative, they argued, Eskom must exhaust all other internal remedies against defaulting municipalities, and must approach the court [35] before cutting electricity supply for debt collection. The applications were moot, as Eskom withdrew its decisions to interrupt supply to the defaulting municipalities [120–123]. The court nevertheless pronounced on the constitutionality of s 25(1) ERA, in view of the contention that Eskom does not require judicial oversight to interrupt electricity supply. The court did not rule on the issue of no-interruption-without-court-order, though, because it was concerned about the legal costs involved and because it regarded *ex post facto* judicial review of Eskom's administrative actions as sufficient oversight [148–154].

[41] *Afriforum* (n 19) records how one of the applicant businesses, who received and faithfully paid for more than 50 per cent of the electricity supplied to a particular municipality, and whose business activities was the backbone of the local community, settled to pay Eskom directly, bypassing the municipality. This settlement was made an order of court [27].

[42] For a study on the retail sector, see, e.g., A. Goldberg, *The Economic Impact of Load Shedding: The Case of South African Retailers* (MBA thesis), (University of Pretoria, 2015), 89–100.

[43] Consumer Protection Act 68 of 2008 (hereafter CPA).

on 'goods' rather than 'services' applicable: while 'consumer's rights to demand quality service'[44] is likely not to apply to electricity, presumably section 55 read with section 56 of the CPA, on 'consumer's right to safe, good quality goods' and 'implied warranty of quality' would apply.

The remedies for defective goods—refund, repair, or replacement within six months [45]—are as inappropriate and/or inadequate as the remedies for defective services—proportionate refund or repair[46]—to deal with the problems experienced by electricity end-consumers.[47] The remedies for damages[48] seem equally inappropriate. It is uncertain whether the remedy for damage caused by defective 'goods'[49] apply to pure economic loss caused by defective, hazardous goods.[50]

City of Johannesburg v National Consumer Commission[51] demonstrates some of the anomalies. No provision in the CPA assists energy consumers with the level of detail required in the billing process. The National Consumer Commission (NCC) accordingly had to deal with numerous utility consumer complaints, inter alia, about billing.[52] The NCC issued compliance notices[53] to the City of Johannesburg, which the National Consumer Tribunal (NCT) set aside on procedural grounds,[54] avoiding a decision on the applicability of the CPA's provisions on right to quality services,[55] and on the city's complaints handling process.[56] This case indicates, first, that electricity is not covered by existing fair pricing rules,[57] as electricity rates are fixed by NERSA.[58] Moreover, using estimates in calculating what consumers owe for electricity and water appears not to be prohibited by the CPA's provisions on unfair prices and practices.[59]

The CPA thus seems largely inadequate to address the issues experienced by electricity end-consumers. NERSA itself is, however, a member of the Consumer Protection Forum. Its 'Guidelines for Electricity Resale'[60] provide electricity consumers with

[44] CPA (n 43), s 54.

[45] Ibid. s 56.

[46] Ibid. s 54.

[47] In *City of Johannesburg v National Consumer Commission* NCT/2667/2011/101 (P); NCT/2081/2011/101(1) (P) [2012] ZANCT 6 (30 March 2012) (hereafter *Johannesburg v NCC*) the NCT deemed it unnecessary to decide the varied application of the rules for 'goods' and 'services' to electricity, even though the City raised the argument [126 et seq].

[48] CPA (n 43), s 61.

[49] Ibid. s 61.

[50] Section 61(5) states that harm for which a person may be held liable in terms of this section 'includes' death, injury, illness, loss of or physical damage to any propery and 'any economic loss that results from' the listed forms of harm above..

[51] *Johannesburg v NCC* (n 57).

[52] For example, errors on water and electricity accounts, non-provision of accounts in respect of services used, refunds owed, faulty water, and electricity meters and the charging of reconnection fees when consumers were cut off.

[53] Relying, inter alia, on the right to quality service in s 54 CPA (n 43).

[54] Particularly as these complaints were not individually investigated by NCC before compliance notices were issued. *Johannesburg v NCC* (n 47) [101–102], [130–132], [137–143].

[55] CPA (n 43), s 54.

[56] In relation to the City's complaints handling process, the NCT held that this point did not need to be decided given that there was no proper investigation by the NCC into the NCT's complaints handling process *Johannesburg v NCC* (n 47) [123ff].

[57] For example, CPA (n 43), s 48.

[58] Under section 48 CPA (n 43), unfair prices in consumer contracts are prohibited.

[59] *Johannesburg v NCC* (n 47) [116ff], [122].

[60] The National Energy Regulator of South Africa, *Guidelines on Electricity Resale* (NERSA, 2016) (hereafter NERSA, *Guidelines*).

dispute resolution mechanisms, with NERSA as potential mediator.[61] The guidelines apply, however, only to a small group of 'resellers'—mostly sectional title bodies corporate and home owners' associations—who can distribute electricity at a profit.[62] It excludes Eskom and municipal distributors, who are licenced by NERSA. As such, its provisions have limited impact. The alternative for electricity end-consumers is to rely on the judicial machinery enforcing 'public law rights' in terms of the Constitution and the Promotion of Administrative Justice Act (PAJA).[63]

B. Recourse to Public Law Remedies

South African municipalities are constitutionally compelled to provide basic services (e.g. electricity).[64] By way of supplementation, the Housing Act,[65] compels municipalities to 'take all reasonable and necessary steps within the framework of national and provincial housing legislation and policy' to ensure provision of 'economically efficient' services, also electricity.[66] Low-income consumers may apply to local authorities for rebates on, inter alia, electricity services.[67] The PAJA[68] further presents mechanisms[69] promoting the right to procedural fairness which have been employed in litigation to protect energy consumers.[70] These imply, at least, that adequate notice and a chance to make representations be given to persons affected by potential disconnections brought on by municipalities defaulting on their payments to Eskom.[71]

Nevertheless, it is still an open question whether the provision of basic services (e.g. electricity) gives rise to fundamental right. The courts[72] have already heard the

[61] Ibid., 1, 12.

[62] Ibid., IV; Eskom, *Communication to Resellers on the Nersa "Guidelines on Electricity Resale" Document* (2017), 1.

[63] *Joseph & Others v City of Johannesburg & Others* 2010 (4) SA 55 CC (9 October 2009) (hereafter *Joseph*). The *a quo* decision (reversed on appeal) was reported as *Darries* (n 37).

[64] Constitution (n 27), ss 152 and 153.

[65] Housing Act 107 of 1997. See *Darries* (n 37), [5].

[66] Housing Act (n 65), s 9(1)(a)(iii). In *Afriforum* (n 19) it was argued that Eskom cannot directly or indirectly violate the purported constitutional right to electricity by preventing municipalities from fulfilling their constitutional duty [74].

[67] City of Cape Town, *Credit Control and Debt Collection Policy* (City of Cape Town Bylaws, May 2019) http://resource.capetown.gov.za/documentcentre/Documents/Bylaws%20and%20policies/Credit%20Control%20and%20Debt%20Collection%20Policy.pdf accessed 8 July 2019.

[68] Promotion of Administrative Justice Act 3 of 2000 (hereafter PAJA).

[69] Section 3 of PAJA (n 68) provides every person the right to procedurally fair administrative action where their rights are 'materially and adversely' affected. Section 4 provides the same right to those administrative actions which 'materially and adversely affects' the public. Section 6(2)(a)(iii) allows judicial review of administrative action where the person who took it was 'biased or reasonably suspected of bias'—one way in which administrative action may be procedurally unfair, while section 6(2)(c) allows judicial review of administrative action where 'the action taken was procedurally unfair'.

[70] See, e.g., *Darries* (n 37) which considered the question whether it is lawful and constitutional for a municipality to disconnect electricity supply to a residence 'without complying with the recognised components of the right to procedural fairness as envisaged by the PAJA and the Constitution and without considering the circumstances of the residents affected' [4]. Also *Afriforum* (n 19), where the question became moot when Eskom withdrew its decisions to enforce settlement of arrears from defaulting municipalities by interrupting supply and undertook to follow due process under PAJA.

[71] *Afriforum* (n 19) [120–123].

[72] E.g. in *Afriforum* (n 19).

argument that electricity supply is indispensable in realizing the constitutional right to sufficient water and health care services.[73] This came from a private hospital group with an unblemished payment record which would have been affected by Eskom's deliberate disconnecting of defaulting municipalities.[74] The Court acknowledged that such disconnections will affect, inter alia, 'the constitutional rights to dignity, practicing of a trade, occupation or profession, property and housing'.[75] Loadshedding-induced limitations on individual rights may, nevertheless, be salvaged under the Constitution's general limitations clause,[76] given the 'compelling national interest in Eskom's financial sustainability' and any proportional safeguards implemented.[77]

Litigious challenge is a rather cumbersome manner of accessing consumer protection, especially where, (as in South Africa) there are so many indigent energy consumers.[78] Also, the courts' capacity to effect energy consumer protection is limited to the matters brought before them. Mostly only otherwise intractable matters end up in the courts. So far, these pertained to interruptions in or disconnection of power supply and non-payment. For example, in *Joseph v City of Johannesburg*[79] the South African Constitutional Court (CC) was asked to intervene when power supply to a particular rental housing building was terminated because of non-payment by the landlord.[80] Those affected—the tenants—diligently had been paying their dues to the landlord, who did not settle the building's utility bills. This illustrates on a small scale the same problems also experienced at municipal level, where those punished for energy debt by disconnection are not necessarily the ones who contributed to the non-payment problem. In *Joseph*[81] the tenants could not rely on any contractual right to electricity between them and the supplier, City Power. The contract was between the landlord and City Power. The landlord's failure to pay City Power resulted in the tenants' electricity supply being terminated.

In *Joseph*, rather than recognizing a fundamental right to electricity implied in the constitutional right to housing,[82] the CC afforded affected residents a 'public law right'[83] to receive basic services like electricity, balanced against the local authority's right to collect arrears.[84] Practically, this finding required the local authority to give fourteen days' advance notice of the intention to cut power supply to a building's residents,[85] and

[73] Constitution (n 27), ss 27 and 24. *Afriforum* (n 19), [70].
[74] *Afriforum* (n 19), [67], [71].
[75] Ibid. [136].
[76] Constitution (n 27), s 36.
[77] *Afriforum* (n 19), [156].
[78] 43 per cent of South Africans cannot access 'adequate, reliable, safe and environmentally benign energy'. L. Baker and J. Phillips, 'Tensions in the Transition: The Politics of Electricity Distribution in South Africa' (2019) 37 *Environment and Planning C: Politics and Space*, 177–96; Sustainable Energy Africa, *State of Energy in South African Cities* (SEA, 2015), 51.
[79] *Joseph* (n 63), the appeal to *Darries* (n 37).
[80] *Joseph* (n 63), [1].
[81] Ibid., [2].
[82] Ibid., [32]. For criticism see D. Bilchitz, 'Citizenship and Community: Exploring the Right to Receive Basic Municipal Services in Joseph' (2010) 3 *Constitutional Court Review*, 45–78 (hereafter Bilchitz, 'Citizenship').
[83] *Joseph* (n 63), [40].
[84] Ibid., [51].
[85] Ibid., [61].

to allow them a chance to make submissions.[86] Specifically citing the dictates of administrative justice,[87] the CC relied on considerations underpinning the ideas of procedural and participatory justice in reaching its findings. [88]

Mkontwana v Nelson Mandela Metropolitan Municipality,[89] severely criticized for its outcome,[90] involved almost the converse of *Joseph*, although the inequities arising were equally obvious. In attempting to sell land, a landowner was beholden to a provision requiring clearance of utility levies before transfer could be effected, [91] which meant that the landowner ultimately had to pay for the electricity usage of unlawful occupiers on the land.[92]

The problem before the court, time and again, is how to understand the relationship between the state and citizens as regards provision of basic services. Bilchitz[93] argues that this is not a purely commercial relationship: the consumer is not the customer of the state-as-service-provider, because the state is not (nor should be) driven by commercial self-interest.[94] The relationship also cannot be framed as a social contract[95] between the state and its citizens (even though the objectives of the relationship may be social):[96] '[T]he strong private law overtones' in this approach fail to motivate the duty to provide basic services satisfactorily.[97] Instead, 'relationality' and *ubuntu*—the indigenous notion of empathy or humaneness—should underlie the relationship between the state and its subjects in relation to, inter alia, provision of basic services.[98] For Bilchitz, the bottom line is that 'the government has a responsibility to provide services and the people have the right to receive them'.[99]

Bilchitz builds this argument on the *Joseph* judgment. There, the unfairness was patent: it should not be permissible to terminate power supply *to paying tenants*, without so much as a notice, just because *a delinquent landlord* did not settle the utility bills. For an energy consumer to be left without recourse under such circumstances is unreasonable, even if there is no direct relationship between the consumer and the state. This is especially so where the atate is responsible for all aspects of energy provision. That distribution is outsourced to a (delinquent) landlord makes no difference.

Bilchitz' argument casts administrative law approaches to disconnection of supply in a new light. In *Resilient Properties (Pty) Ltd v Eskom Holdings Soc Ltd*,[100] an interim order was sought, prohibiting Eskom from terminating electricity supply to a

86 Ibid., [62–63].
87 Ibid., [43–45].
88 Ibid., [46].
89 *Mkontwana v Nelson Mandela Metropolitan Municipality* 2005 (1) SA 530 (CC) (hereafter *Mkontwana*).
90 Bilchitz, 'Citizenship' (n 82).
91 *Mkontwana* (n 89), [15].
92 Ibid., [33], [75].
93 Bilchitz, 'Citizenship' (n 82).
94 Ibid., 58–9.
95 Ibid., 60–2.
96 Ibid., 62.
97 Ibid.
98 Ibid., 66–7, 69.
99 Ibid., 66.
100 *Resilient Properties (Pty) Ltd v Eskom Holdings Soc Ltd* 2019 (2) SA 557 (GJ) (hereafter *Resilient Properties*).

delinquent (non-paying) local authority. The court identified disconnection for non-payment as an administrative action.[101] Eskom knew that a humanitarian disaster would ensue[102] from terminating supply, hence the court found Eskom's decision to terminate 'not rationally connected to the purpose' for which it was empowered to terminate supply.[103] The court refused to accept that Eskom's ability to terminate electricity supply extended to making decisions that would result in a widespread human catastrophe.[104] Recognizing that it would be a country-wide disaster if Eskom was not paid for providing electricity, the court weighed the 'short-term consequences for the community' as more immediately drastic.[105]

III. Privatized Supply Models

Energy markets are 'liberalized' when the vertically integrated State-owned Enterprises (SOEs) are unbundled to create wholesale and retail markets.[106] This is often coupled with introduction of an independent regulator and privatization of state-owned entities, to allow market forces to create a more efficient electricity supply.[107] In liberalized markets, companies seek to provide essential utility services at lower costs.[108] Competition is thus promoted and the possibility of private investment into the sector increased.[109]

Liberalized markets bring about another set of consumer concerns, alongside various responses. Consumer protection rules differ from one system to another on the issue of 'switching'—in how far they promote competition by affording consumers the necessary information and rights to switch easily between suppliers. Differing levels of social affluence also affect how consumer protection rules cater for protecting hyper-vulnerable consumers' access to electricity as against energy companies.

The following sections discuss the EU, Australia, and Nigeria briefly, as systems with privatized electricity distribution. They demonstrate the different responses to hyper-vulnerability. One response is to foster competition among electricity suppliers, and supplement with social grants. Another is to write obligations towards vulnerable consumers into the laws regulating private electricity suppliers.

101 PAJA (n 68), s 6, read with Constitution (n 27), s 33. See *Resilient Properties* (n 100), [74–75].

102 Inter alia, because water supply and sewerage systems would collapse and old-age homes and healthcare affected.

103 *Resilient Properties* (n 100) [79].

104 Ibid., [78].

105 Ibid., [48].

106 D. Hall and T.A. Nguyen, 'Electricity Liberalisation in Developing Countries' (2017) 17 *Progress in Development Studies*, 2, 99 (hereafter Hall and Nguyen, 'Electricity Liberalisation').

107 Ibid.

108 C. Morris, 'Privatisation of Public Services is Failing, says Think Tank' (10 August 2017) *Energy Transition: The Global Energiewende* https://energytransition.org/2017/08/privatization-of-public-services-is-failing-says-think-tank/ accessed 18 April 2019 (hereafter Morris, 'Privatisation').

109 PWC, 'Africa Power and Utilities Sector Survey' (2015), 27 https://www.pwc.com/gx/en/utilities/publications/assets/pwc-africa-power-utilities-survey.pdf accessed 18 June 2018.

A. European Union (EU)

Liberalized, privatized, and deregulated markets are a hallmark of many energy systems in Europe.[110] As the position in the EU is also discussed elsewhere in this book,[111] and due to space constraints, this chapter does not focus on any individual EU Member States, but only considers the Proposal for the Recast Electricity Directive,[112] which contains detailed rules and reduces cross-subsidization of hyper-vulnerable consumers by more affluent consumers. The proposed Directive's envisaged system exemplifies a model that promotes competition as a means to protect vulnerable consumers. This policy choice is supplemented by specific rules on billing, which supports consumers' freedom of choice and access to information to make informed energy decisions.

In societies as affluent as the EU, social nets (e.g. unemployment grants) help residents to obtain electricity from private electricity suppliers. Private energy suppliers hence need not be coerced to provide free access to hyper-vulnerable consumers. Although 'social security systems should be the primary means of addressing energy poverty',[113] the recently proposed Directive on Common Rules for the Internal Electricity Market[114] permits Member States 'to regulate prices temporarily to assist and protect energy-poor or vulnerable consumers'.[115] Direct cross-subsidization is not allowed: certain categories of consumers[116] should not be bearing the cost of price interventions supporting others explicitly.[117]

The proposed Directive is also against price setting for electricity, because of its frequently detrimental consequences, such as 'accumulation of tariff deficits, limitation of consumer choice, poorer incentives for energy saving and energy efficiency investments, lower standards of service, lower levels of consumer engagement and satisfaction, and restriction of competition, as well as to there being fewer innovative products and services on the market'.[118] Member States are directed to make electricity affordable by other means, the clear policy preference being for competition amongst service providers in a 'fully liberalised, well-functioning retail market'.[119] Competition law and policy should be used to ensure effective competition.[120]

[110] L. Ilie, A. Horobet and C. Popescu, 'Liberalisation and Regulation in the EU Energy Market' (2007) *Munich Personal RePEc Archive* https://mpra.ub.uni-muenchen.de/6419/1/ accessed 18 June 2018. SAGEP, *Electricity Distribution* (n 28), 17.

[111] See Chapter 10, in this book.

[112] European Parliament legislative resolution of 26 March 2019 on the proposal for a directive of the European Parliament and of the Council on common rules for the internal market in electricity (recast) (COM(2016)0864 – C8-0495/2016 – 2016/0380 (COD)) (hereafter 'EU Recast Electricity Directive').

[113] 'Parliament makes EU electricity market cleaner and more consumer-friendly' (*News European Parliament*, 26 March 2019) http://www.europarl.europa.eu/news/en/press-room/20190321IPR32108/parliament-makes-eu-electricity-market-cleaner-and-more-consumer-friendly accessed 29 March 2019 (hereafter 'Parliament makes EU electricity market cleaner').

[114] 'EU Recast Electricity Directive' (n 112).

[115] 'Parliament makes EU electricity market cleaner' (n 113).

[116] Presumably those with a higher income.

[117] 'EU Recast Electricity Directive' (n 112), Recital 25.

[118] Ibid., Recital 22.

[119] 'EU Recast Electricity Directive' (n 112), Recital 22.

[120] Ibid., Article 5(1).

Any price setting for electricity 'should be carried out only as public service obligations ... subject to specific conditions' as the Directive determines.[121] Such price setting should be for limited time periods,[122] for example, 'where supply is severely constrained, causing significantly higher electricity prices than normal, or in the event of a market failure where interventions by regulatory authorities and competition authorities have proven to be ineffective'.[123]

The proposed Directive acknowledges that Member States may take differing measures to protect vulnerable consumers, also for disconnection.[124] Vulnerability may include factors relating to 'income levels, the share of energy expenditure of disposable income, the energy efficiency of homes, critical dependence on electrical equipment for health reasons, age or other criteria'.[125] In particular, consumers in remote areas should be protected.[126]

The proposed Directive requires that suppliers inform consumers on alternatives to disconnection in advance, including 'prepayment systems, energy audits, energy consulting services, alternative payment plans, debt management advice or disconnection moratoria'.[127] Member States are particularly encouraged to invest in making housing more energy-efficient.[128]

The proposed Directive does not set out all rights of consumers who buy electricity. It leaves most of such regulation to the cross-sectorial law (e.g. on unfair contract terms).[129] However, it expects some 'basic contractual rights' of customers to be certain.[130] Consumers should have access to a checklist that dispenses practical information about consumer rights. Moreover, the information to be contained in contracts with end-consumers is prescribed. Also, key terms must be summarized prominently, 'in concise and simple language'.[131]

Some specific details on supporting consumers' freedom of choice are included. Amendment of contractual terms affecting household customers require at least one month's notice, alongside provision of reasons. Such customers should be free to terminate if they do not accept the amended terms.[132] To assist consumers to compare offers and to switch suppliers, the Directive restricts the use of switching fees[133] and requires Member States to provide an independent, easy-to-access comparison tool.[134] Bills must provide 'comparisons with an average normalised or benchmarked final customer in the same user category' and a link to the comparison tool.[135] To avoid

[121] Ibid., Recital 22, Article 5.
[122] Ibid., Recital 23, Article 5(4).
[123] Ibid., Recital 23.
[124] Ibid., Recital 58.
[125] Ibid., Article 28.
[126] Ibid., Article 28.
[127] Ibid., Article 10(11).
[128] Ibid., Recital 58–60.
[129] Ibid., Recital 30.
[130] 'EU Recast Electricity Directive' (n 112), Recital 30.
[131] Ibid., Article 10.
[132] Ibid., Article 10(4).
[133] Ibid., Recitals 32, 33.
[134] Ibid., Recital 35, Article 14.
[135] Ibid., Recital 48. Schedule 1 sets out the minimum requirements for bills.

information overload on bills, only a 'limited number of important items of information' should be reflected on the electricity bill. This information must be 'necessary to enable consumers to regulate their energy consumption, compare offers and switch suppliers'.[136]

The proposed Directive further implicitly seeks to strengthen access—and thus competition—by providing that 'citizen energy communities' may generate and supply energy for the benefit of their members.[137] These communities are legal entities with the primary purpose of providing economic and other benefits to their members, rather than to generate profits.[138] The implication of this provision may be that more traditional energy supply companies have to lower their prices if they wish to discourage such local communities from generating their own electricity.

B. Australia

Australia, another example of a fairly affluent society with a liberalized and largely privatized market, has detailed rules granting rights to hyper-vulnerable consumers against energy suppliers. Electricity generators 'are owned by a mix of public and private entities'[139] who bid to supply electricity to a notional 'pool'.[140] A central authority, the Australian Energy Market Operator, then transmits this supply, allocated from the lowest bid, until demand is met.[141] Consumers buy electricity from private electricity retail suppliers,[142] who are obliged by law to assist hyper-vulnerable consumers. There are minimum and maximum market price caps determined with reference to the consumer price index.[143]

The government only sets retail electricity prices in some states in Australia. However, the Australian Energy Regulator (AER)[144] regulates 'network costs and sets the price that distributors can charge for transporting electricity to homes and businesses' and 'approves the price that distributors can charge for access to gas pipelines'.[145] The AER's website provides information for consumers, inter alia, about their rights against energy retailers.[146] The AER also has an online price comparison tool.[147] Where the government does not set retail prices, information guidelines must ensure that

[136] Ibid.
[137] Ibid., Article 16.
[138] See the definition of 'citizen energy community' in Article 2(11). 'EU Recast Electricity Directive' (n 112).
[139] Z. Hilson and A. Cunsolo, 'Electricity Regulation in Australia: Overview Q&A' (1 October 2018) *Thomson Reuters Practical Law*, 6 (hereafter Hilson and Cunsolo, 'Electricity Regulation').
[140] Ibid., 2.
[141] Ibid.
[142] Ibid., 1–2.
[143] Ibid., 2.
[144] Ibid., 8.
[145] Australian Energy Regulator, 'About energy bills_2' https://www.aer.gov.au/consumers/my-energy-bill accessed 26 March 2019 (hereafter Australian Energy Regulator).
[146] Accessible at <www.aer.gov.au> accessed 26 March 2019.
[147] Australian Energy Regulator (n 145).

consumers have sufficient information through advertisements to compare the prices of different retailers.[148]

Australia's National Energy Retail Law (NERL) forms part of the 'national energy customer framework', together with the National Energy Retail Rules (NERR), the latter promulgated by the Australian Energy Market Commission.[149] NERL contains requirements for customer contracts, disconnection procedures, the relationship between supplier and customer, and hardship policies.[150] There are small variations amongst states and territories in the consumer protection rules. Some states have not yet implemented the law.[151]

The NERL provides for designated retailers in particular areas to offer their services to 'small customers'[152] at standing-offer prices under a standard contract conforming to prescribed model terms and conditions.[153] Small customers may also enter into market retail contracts with suppliers, where prices may be lower than those in the standard contract, and where terms may differ. A minimum set of prescribed terms aimed at customer protection must nevertheless be included.[154]

The detailed NERR apply where states have implemented the NERL.[155] Among others, the 173 rules plus an extensive list of model terms and conditions for retail contracts[156] afford consumers the right to fair contracts with easily understandable, clear terms and conditions.[157] Also, consumers are entitled to clear and detailed information on bills, including a comparison of electricity usage with other households in the area, the estimated date of the next scheduled meter reading and reference to concession schemes; as well as actual meter readings as far as possible, but at least annually.[158] Where estimates are used, they must be based on historical metering data for the specific customer; where no data exists, the standard is average energy usage by a comparable customer over the relevant period.[159]

Consumers are further protected in that 'the small customer' can only be disconnected from the prepayment meter system, on weekdays between 10 a.m. and 3 p.m.,[160] when it is presumably easier to top up and reconnect. They must be given four days' notice of retailer-planned interruptions.[161]

The NERR contain provisions on flexible payment options,[162] payment plans, and advice on energy efficiency and government concession programmes for customers

[148] National Energy Retail Law (South Australia) Act 2011, ss 61–63 (hereafter 'NERL'); see Hilson and Cunsolo, 'Electricity Regulation' (n 139), 24.

[149] Hilson and Cunsolo, 'Electricity Regulation' (n 139).

[150] Ibid., 24. Latest consolidated version: 17, of 1 February 2019, available at https://www.aemc.gov.au/sites/default/files/2019-01/NRR%20-%20v17.PDF accessed 26 March 2019 (hereafter NERR).

[151] See NERR (n 150), 1.

[152] Residential customers and small business users.

[153] 'NERL' (n 148), Schedule 1, ss 22, 25. Model terms and conditions in Schedule 1 to the NERR (n 150).

[154] NERR (n 150), Schedule 1, ss 33–37.

[155] See NERR (n 150), 1.

[156] Ibid.

[157] Schedule 1 to the NERR (n 150) contains plain-language model terms and conditions for retail contracts.

[158] NERR (n 150), Rule 20.

[159] Ibid., Rule 21.

[160] NERR (n 150), Rule 129.

[161] Ibid., Rule 59C.

[162] Ibid., Rule 32ff.

who are struggling to pay bills.[163] Similarly, there are provisions on replacement of prepayment meters with standard ones for struggling customers.[164] Hardship customers may not be charged security deposits. These can also be waived for other customers, except in stipulated circumstances, for example, an unsatisfactory credit history.[165]

Where energy contracts are for a fixed term, switching will incur an exit price.[166] The NERR prescribe a ten-business day cooling-off period after conclusion of a new energy supply contract.[167] Charges for early termination may not exceed the reasonable costs to the retailer caused by early termination, and may not recover lost profits. The manner of calculating termination charges must be set out in the contract.[168]

There are specific provisions for customers with medically induced vulnerability. In particular, the NERR provides that consumers may register life support status with their energy supplier. They must then be notified four days in advance of maintenance-related planned power interruptions.[169] Prepayment meter contracts may not be concluded in respect of life support customers[170] and premises housing a life support customer may also not be 'de-energised'.[171]

Low-income consumers may also apply for concessions from state authorities. For example, in South Australia, certain low-income residential customers can receive a concession of $223 to cover electricity and gas payments.[172] Some cardholders—for example, pensioners, totally and permanently incapacitated persons, extremely disabled persons, and asylum seekers with low incomes—are also eligible for concessions.[173] Moreover, eligible consumers can apply to receive 18 per cent off electricity usage and supply charges, flexible payment options and no fees, for example, in relation to late payment or exit fees.[174]

Though the Australian energy market, like the EU, is liberalized, the policy approaches towards protecting vulnerable consumers are very different in these two jurisdictions. As indicated, the EU's focus seems increasingly to be on reducing energy costs by fostering competition in the energy retail industry. Australia's approach is to tighten the bolts on retailers with strict compliance requirements as concerns vulnerable

[163] Such hardship policy must be approved by the AER. 'NERL' (n 148) ss 43–45, NERL. Whilst the consumer complies with the payment plan, debt recovery may not be commenced against them. NERR (n 150), Rules 71–76.

[164] NERR (n 150), Rule 141.

[165] Ibid., Rule 40.

[166] AER, 'Switching Retailers' https://www.aer.gov.au/consumers/switching-retailers accessed 26 March 2019.

[167] NERR (n 150), Rule 47; see also AER, 'Comparing Offers' https://www.aer.gov.au/consumers/switching-retailers/comparing-offers accessed 26 March 2019. This cooling-off right may be exercised either orally or in writing. NERR (n 150), Rule 47(4).

[168] NERR (n 150), Rule 49A.

[169] National Energy Retail Amendment, 'Strengthening Protections for Customers Requiring Life Support Equipment Rule 2017 No. 3' https://www.aemc.gov.au/sites/default/files/content/a4094ca5-dc6a-4dfb-bbe7-8aa9a3baa831/Life-Support-rule-change-RRC0009-Final-Rule-For-Publication.pdf accessed 26 March 2019. NERR (n 150), Rules 123–126.

[170] 'NERL' (n 148), s 59.

[171] NERR (n 150), Rule 124B.

[172] South Australian Government, 'Energy Bill Concessions' https://www.sa.gov.au/topics/care-and-support/financial-support/concessions/energy-bill-concessions accessed 27 March 2019.

[173] Ibid.

[174] South Australian Government, 'Energy Concession Discount Offer' https://www.sa.gov.au/topics/care-and-support/financial-support/concessions/energy-bill-concessions/energy-discount-offer accessed 27 March 2019.

consumers. Which approach is preferable is an open question. The decade between 2007/2008 and 2017/2018 saw significant price increases in Australian energy: 56 per cent for residential customers.[175] One reason is 'the gaming of the system by generators'.[176] A recent Retail Electricity Pricing Enquiry by the Australian Competition and Consumer Commission (ACCC) recommended ways to boost competition amongst retailers, lower costs, and enhance customer outcomes,[177] for example, through a 20 per cent market share cap for any one participant in any National Energy Market region and across the National Energy Market as a whole.[178]

C. Nigeria

Some studies show that liberalization and unbundling have not necessarily yielded the anticipated results in the African context (yet): nineteen African countries noted an increase in electricity tariffs where liberalization of the market was promoted.[179] This necessarily creates a cautionary mood in African policy spheres.[180] We consider Nigeria[181] here, as an example of an African country that is attempting to meet growing energy demands by deregulating and liberalizing its electricity market.[182]

Nigeria's electricity market is an example of incomplete privatization and insufficient consumer protection. Nigeria's Electric Power Sector Reform Act of 2005 created the Nigerian Electricity Regulatory Commission (NERC), as an independent regulator. The Act contains sections on 'Consumer Protection and Licensee Performance Standards'.[183] They provide for NERC to develop consumer protection standards, codes of practice, and procedures on the following topics: 'customer service'; 'complaint handling'; 'assistance to special needs customers such as the blind or disabled, elderly or severely ill'; 'customers who have difficulty in paying bills'; 'applying for electricity service'; 'disconnection of customers in breach of their agreements'; and 'information to be provided to consumers'.[184]

175 Hilson and Cunsolo, 'Electricity Regulation' (n 139), 2.

176 Ibid.

177 Ibid., 27.

178 Ibid., 28.

179 Making Africa's Power Sector Sustainable: Stakeholders' Policy Dialogue Forum Addis Ababa, Ethiopia, (15–16 December 2005) https://sustainabledevelopment.un.org/content/documents/addis_psr_policy_statement.pdf accessed 18 June 2018. See also M. Ncube and C.L. Lufumpa, *Infrastructure in Africa: Lessons for future development* (Policy Press, 2017) See also E. Teljeur, M. Chetty, and M. Hendriksz, 'Africa's Prospects for Infrastructure Development and Regional Integration: Energy Sector', in M. Ncube and C.L. Lufumpa (eds), *Infrastructure in Africa: Lessons for Future Development* (Policy Press, 2017), ch 6, in particular 189–207.

180 Hall and Nguyen, 'Electricity Liberalisation' (n 106), 105; Teljeur, et al., 'Electricity Supply' (n 22), 6.

181 S. Amadi, 'The Rule of Law Approach to Regulating Electricity Supply in Nigeria' (2017) 8, *Journal of Sustainable Development Law and Policy*, 2, 26–7 (hereafter Amadi, 'Regulating Electricity').

182 A. Eberhard, K. Gratwick, E. Morella, and P. Antmann, *Independent Power Projects in Sub-Saharan Africa: Lessons from Five Key Countries* (World Bank, 2016), xli–xliii; K.A. Folly, 'Electricity Deregulation: Where Are We?' (2017) *Africa's Power Journal* https://www.esi-africa.com/electricity-deregulationwhere-are-we/ accessed 18 July 2018.

183 Electric Power Sector Reform Act of 2005, ss 80 and 81(hereafter ESPRA 2005).

184 Ibid., s 80(1).

Contrary to the position in the latest EU Directive, in Nigeria cross-subsidization of poorer consumers by the more affluent is clearly envisaged. The Act provides for a Power Consumer Assistance Fund, used to 'subsidise underprivileged consumers' to which other customers contribute, and the Rural Electrification Fund.

The Act requires the establishment of 'standards for compensation to consumers who do not enjoy regular power supply'.[185] However, NERC has apparently not developed standards and codes on all these topics yet. Its website only lists four documents under the topic 'documents that concern Customer Service regulations, standards and procedures, tariffs and general electricity issues'.[186] NERC's website also contains a summary of consumer rights and obligations.[187]

First, the document titled Customer Service Standards of Performance for Distribution Companies, 2007;[188] provides for short time periods within which faults must be rectified,[189] new connections installed,[190] and reconnection made after payment of arrears.[191] It also provides for notice periods for interruption due to maintenance[192] and requires actual meter readings at least every three months.[193] Some circumstances, for example, those of an 'exceptional nature beyond the control of the Distribution Company', exempt the latter from compliance.[194] Such companies report to the Commission on their performance.[195]

Second, the document entitled Connection and Disconnection Procedures for Electricity Services, 2007,[196] requires, inter alia, that disconnection for non-payment can generally only take place at least three months after non-payment, and pursuant to a written warning stipulating contact details where customers can seek assistance with payment.[197] Vulnerability is addressed to some degree in that disconnection for non-payment may not occur and reconnection must occur where 'the customer has applied for assistance from the Power Consumer Assistance Fund or some other customer welfare mechanism recognised by the Commission'.[198] The company may further not disconnect supply 'where it is aware that a life support machine is in use'.[199]

[185] ESPRA 2005 (n 183), s 80(3).

[186] See Nigerian Electricity Regulatory Commission, 'Consumer Affairs'. https://nerc.gov.ng/index.php/library/documents/Consumer-Affairs/ accessed 21 March 2019 (hereafter 'NERC Documents'). These are also the only documents posted on a major electricity supplier's website: BEDC Electricity, 'Customer Service Standards of Performance for Distribution Companies' http://bedcpower.com/customer-service-standards-of-performance-for-distribution-companies/ accessed 21 March 2019.

[187] Nigerian Electricity Regulatory Commission, 'Consumer Rights & Obligations' https://www.nercng.org/index.php/home/consumers/consumer-rights-obligations accessed 21 March 2019.

[188] Customer Service Standards of Performance for Distribution Companies, GN 71 in the Official Gazette of the Federal Republic of Nigeria, No 102, vol 94 of 21 December 2007 (hereafter Customer Service Standards).

[189] Ibid., Regs 1, 6, 9.

[190] Ibid., Reg 2.

[191] Ibid., Reg 7.

[192] Ibid., Reg 4.

[193] Ibid., Reg 10.

[194] Ibid., Reg 11.

[195] Ibid., Reg 12.

[196] 'Connection and Disconnection Procedures for Electricity Services', GN 72 in the Official Gazette of the Federal Republic of Nigeria, No 103, vol 94 of 21 December 2007 (hereafter Connection and Disconnection Procedures).

[197] Ibid., Reg 5.

[198] Connection and Disconnection Procedures (n 196), Reg 10(e), 12(1)(b).

[199] Ibid., Reg 10(2).

A disconnection notice must be left at the premises which, inter alia, informs the consumer what to do to obtain reconnection.[200] When a customer requests disconnection, the company must first confirm the consent of the other occupants thereto.[201]

Third, the document entitled Meter Reading, Billing, Cash Collections and Credit Management for Electricity Supplies Regulations, 2007[202] affirms the duties of distribution companies. When the company is unable to obtain a meter reading, it must notify the consumer to provide a reading, or otherwise estimate a reading following an approved methodology.[203] Bills must contain prescribed information, for example, previous and present meter readings, and whether they were estimated, actual, or the customer's own.[204] Customers anticipating difficulties with settling their bill on time may contact the company, who must offer an arrangement to pay outstanding dues.[205] Fourth, the website has a document about 'Customer Complaints Handling: Standards and Procedures'.[206]

Despite the detail that the framework legislation envisages, Nigeria's consumer protection rules are insufficient to promote competition between private suppliers when compared with the EU and Australian rules considered above. The accurate billing rules have not prevented over-charging,[207] due to the widespread use of estimates and ineffective dispute resolution. [208] Nor does available documentation guarantee sufficient information and rights to facilitate switching between suppliers on the basis of more competitive offers. There is no effective enforcement of consumer rights, as service failures are rampant[209] and power outages frequent. Recourse to more general rules of consumer protection has also been unavailable: the generally applicable Federal Competition and Consumer Protection Act was only signed into law in 2019.

For Nigeria, privatization has not (yet) brought the expected benefits of increased competition.[210] Amadi's scathing analysis of the Nigerian power reform decries the fact that 'a contract-based trading had not been established' by the time of privatization. [211] Moreover, Onyi-Ogelle highlights the divestment from the power sector that has taken place after liberalization.[212] A lack of diversified supply means monopolies effectively continue to rule various aspects of energy provision.[213] Corruption appears to be the cause of some of the problems.[214] In addition, government has interfered with NERC,

200 Ibid., Reg 9.
201 Ibid., Reg 8.
202 Meter Reading, Billing, Cash Collections and Credit Management for Electricity Supplies Regulations, GN 73 in the Official Gazette of the Federal Republic of Nigeria, No 104, vol 94 of 21 December 2007 (hereafter Meter Reading).
203 Ibid., Reg 1.
204 Ibid., Reg 4(3) read with the schedule.
205 Meter Reading (n 202), Reg 14.
206 'NERC Documents' (n 186).
207 Amadi, 'Regulating Electricity' (n 181), 31.
208 Amadi, 'Regulating Electricity' (n 181), 31.
209 Ibid., 30.
210 Ibid., 31.
211 Ibid., 43.
212 O. Onyi-Ogelle, 'The Implications of Legal Reform in the Nigeria Power Sector' (2016) 10 *African Research Review*, 279, 280 (hereafter Onyi-Ogelle, 'Implications').
213 Amadi, 'Regulating Electricity' (n 181), 31.
214 Ibid., 31; Onyi-Ogelle, 'Implications' (n 214), 280–8.

inter alia, by forcefully removing the first commissioners in 2009 and only reappointing new commissioners in December 2010.[215]

Nigeria's example shows that the failure of liberalization in energy markets may be attributable to failures of governance more broadly. Governance failures will impact on the implementability of legislative measures to protect energy consumers, which then have to be addressed by other means. Unsurprisingly, responses then fall back on state intervention, even in the privatized context.[216] Amadi argues that the regulator must not only correct market failure, but also protect human rights, including the social and economic rights of residents.[217] However, no particular alternative pathways are suggested. The extent to which NERC has promoted access to electricity by vulnerable consumers thus remains unevaluated.

IV. Concluding Assessment

The analysis above suggests that the type of consumer protection system operative in a particular context is influenced by the role of the state in the supply of electricity to end-consumers. The notion of the empathetic state applies regardless of whether supply is monopolized or electricity distribution is privatized. The idea of the empathetic state embodies the tenets of social, procedural/participatory, and distributive/restorative justice which this book harnesses in developing a theory of energy justice.

Privatization seems like a solution, where—as in South Africa—the vertically integrated power market is on the verge of collapse and power outages are rampant, due to the lethal mix of insufficient generation and transmission resulting from growing demand and aging infrastructure,[218] corruption, and a culture of non-payment. Where states are weaker, or societies poorer, however, introducing distributed generation may exacerbate vulnerability.[219] Those unable to invest in private electricity generation are hit hardest by access issues caused by, for example, ageing infrastructure.[220]

Nigeria's experience with liberalizing its energy market illustrates that, absent 'strong normative and legal frameworks for a robust regulatory regime',[221] privatization of energy markets holds no promise of better service delivery.[222] This may motivate countries with large indigent contingents to continue with policy routes that place the public sector in control of energy provision.[223] In systems like these, the mechanisms of public law—human rights and administrative justice remedies—can provide claims to protection by the state where the legal frameworks for energy consumer protection fall

215 Amadi, 'Regulating Electricity' (n 181), 30.
216 See, e.g., Ibid., 43.
217 Ibid., 47.
218 Avila, et al., *The Energy Challenge* (n 11), 8.
219 SAGEP, *Electricity Distribution* (n 28), 17.
220 SAGEP, *Electricity Distribution* (n 28), 17.
221 Amadi, 'Regulating Electricity' (n 181), 32.
222 Ibid., 31.
223 Hall and Nguyen, 'Electricity Liberalisation' (n 106), 2.

short. As indicated, however, remedies in the public law realm often come with concerns about hampered access to justice.

The rules of jurisdictions with privatized energy distribution systems—such as Nigeria, the EU, and Australia—demonstrate the policy choices that need to inform a state's decision to liberalize its power market. Clearly, the more liberalized the market is, the greater the need for detailed rules to protect consumers, for example, to facilitate easy and informed switching between suppliers. In these contexts, the empathetic state manifests in the regulatory frameworks for protecting vulnerable consumers.

In addressing concerns about policy direction on how to protect vulnerable consumers, the EU and Australian examples show two different responses. In the EU, the approach is to promote competition among service providers to lower energy prices. Coupled with a strong social state structure, vulnerable consumers are supported through mechanisms such as social grants.[224] The Australian approach is one of detailed regulation of the market, with specific and detailed provisions protecting those consumers who are financially or medically vulnerable.

Mechanisms addressing hypervulnerability may include price control, the establishment of other social security safety nets to assist energy affordability to low-income consumers, obliging government to invest in making housing more energy-efficient,[225] and cross-subsidization of hyper-vulnerable consumers by more affluent consumers. To ensure sufficient access to electricity, hyper-vulnerable consumers clearly need active, direct state intervention, or regulatory direction-giving. Here, it seems, the type of consumer protection at work is influenced by the degree of affluence of the community it seeks to serve. In more affluent societies (e.g. the EU) it seems more likely that hyper-vulnerable consumers like the indigent can be protected through means other than the rules on electricity supply.

Privatization seems better suited to contexts where the population is generally wealthier, and where the state can maintain the infrastructure by means other than having to rely on archaic grid tariff systems. In such systems there is a greater likelihood of sufficient state resources being available to enforce consumer protection rules and to enable real competition between suppliers.

The options gleaned from our four brief jurisdictional studies do not suggest a binary solution to electricity consumer issues as either public-law or private-law driven. Instead, state-involvement seems imperative to protect vulnerable consumers, whether through human-rights and administrative-justice based approaches, or through detailed consumer rules.

An approach not dealt with in any of the jurisdictions we considered above is found in the call for the re-municipalization of public services.[226] Some argue that local

[224] S. Pye and A. Dobbins, *Energy Poverty and Vulnerable Consumers in the Energy Sector across the EU: Analysis of Policies and Measures* (Insight_E, 2015), v-vii.

[225] See (n 113).

[226] D. Hall, E. Lobina, and P. Terhorst 'Re-municipalising Municipal Services in Europe' (2012) *Public Services International Research Unit* https://www.psiru.org/reports/re-municipalisation-europe.html accessed 11 July 2019.

ownership is more desirable than privatization[227] and that municipalities or local government structures need to regain control over the generation and distribution of electricity.[228] This argument assumes that, unlike the private sector, which focuses on increasing profits, municipalities' main concern is providing quality services and returning profits into the municipal budget.[229] The German energy market exemplifies the benefits of re-municipalization of energy provision.[230]

Arguments favouring re-munipalization of energy supply essentially support the devolution of governance to the local level. They assume that governance structures are in place and functioning well. The example of South Africa above, and to some extent even the Nigerian experience, should show, however, that it cannot simply be assumed that governance structures are as robust as needed for such a devolved model to work; not on the local level, and not even on the national level. In South Africa, Eskom has displayed a persistently poor record of governance, as have the failings of municipalities entrusted with the distribution of electricity. These problems beget further problematic behaviour on the part of electricity consumers and their middlemen. In such systems, a hybrid model which does not create a monopoly for generation and distribution, but involves private suppliers as well as a State-owned Enterprise, may induce more efficiency at the state level, which may reduce the need for loadshedding. However, even partial privatization of electricity distribution will require detailed rules and robust enforcement measures such as those of the EU and Australia.

Ultimately, the state is at centre stage in dealing with energy-consumers' concerns from a context in which the majority of the people affected can by typified as poor. Where the state then is weak or failing, or captured by corruption, consumer vulnerability is exacerbated. Privatization alone will not address the problem: where competition laws are weak or consumer rules are not properly enforced, and where sufficient action is not taken against corruption, privatization will not have sufficiently positive outcomes for consumers. Even in privatized systems, the generation of cleaner energy must be strategized carefully where indigence is widespread.

[227] Morris, 'Privatisation' (n 108).
[228] Ibid.
[229] Ibid.
[230] Ibid.

10

Energy Market Reforms in the EU

A New Focus on Energy Consumers, Energy Poverty, and Energy (in)Justice?

*Martha Roggenkamp and Lea Diestelmeier**

I. Introduction

The position of end-consumers in the European energy market has changed drastically over the last few decades. This change is primarily due to the process of market liberalization, that is, a market based on the principle of free movement of goods, services, persons, and capital without obstacles to competition, but more recently also as a result of the need to increase the consumption of renewable energy sources (RES) in order to meet the 2020 and subsequent 2030 and 2050 goals.[1] Whereas in the European Union (EU) the process of market liberalization started in 1988 when the European Commission presented its Working Document on the internal energy market (IEM),[2] it has been substantiated by the introduction of a wide range of EU laws since 1996.[3] Energy consumers play a specific role in the process of EU market liberalization. The assumption is that a liberalized and competitive market provides energy consumers with a free choice of supply and supplier and, accordingly, consumers become part of a process that should result in lower energy prices and improved quality of service. Gradually, energy consumers have been transformed from being merely 'captive' customers to becoming 'active' customers.[4]

One of the key issues in the process of market liberalization is the extent to which these principles should apply equally to all energy consumers, and/or whether a distinction

* The authors would like to thank Louis Sandiford, LLM Energy and Climate Law, for his assistance in preparing this chapter.

[1] The Third Energy and Climate Package of 2007 provided for an EU target of 20 per cent renewable consumption in 2020. In 2014, the European Council agreed on a new EU-wide binding target for renewable energy of at least 27 per cent in 2030. On 28 November 2018, the Commission presented its strategic long-term vision that the EU should be climate neutral by 2050. See http://ec.europa.eu/energy/en/topics/energy-strategy-and-energy-union, last visited 9 September 2019.

[2] Commission of the European Communities, Communication 'The Internal Energy Market', Brussels 2 May 1988, COM(88) 238 final (hereafter *The IEM*).

[3] The first directive entered into force in 1996 as Directive 96/92/EC concerning common rules for the internal market in electricity [1996] OJ L 77/20 (hereafter *1996 Electricity Directive*), and was amended in 2003, 2009, and 2019. See in more detail section II.

[4] Whereas *The IEM* (n 2), 4, identified in 1988 that 'some energy end-uses [. . .] inevitably involve virtually captive markets', the 2019 Electricity Directive introduces the concept of 'active' customer.

Martha Roggenkamp and Lea Diestelmeier, Energy Market Reforms in the EU In: *Energy Justice and Energy Law*. Edited by Íñigo Del Guayo, Lee Godden, Donald N. Zillman, Milton Fernando Montoya, and José Juan González, Oxford University Press (2020). © The Several Contributors. DOI: 10.1093/oso/9780198860754.003.0010

needs to be made between different types of consumers. It is crucial to ask: is it necessary to distinguish between large and small consumers, industrial and household consumers, and/or active and vulnerable consumers? Implicit within this is an evaluation of whether all energy consumers can act effectively in the competitive market setting—if they cannot, then how can this be remedied? And if they can act effectively, why place limits on competition? The approach thus far has been to treat specific categories of consumers differently in order to ensure energy justice and to protect against energy poverty. EU law therefore requires Member States (MS) to take appropriate measures to protect small (household) consumers, whilst also providing adequate safeguards to protect vulnerable customers.[5] Despite an EU legal framework on the protection of energy consumers, energy poverty and energy injustice are still present throughout the EU.[6] While the need to protect small consumers has been explicitly recognized within EU energy law since 1996, the existence of energy poverty was not acknowledged in statute until the 2009 Electricity and Gas Directives. Both Directives include the concept of energy poverty in an identical recital, recognizing energy poverty as a 'growing problem' and requiring MS to take action via the implementation of social policies and/or energy efficiency improvements.[7] The Directive on the internal electricity market was reformed in 2019 and further develops the role of small consumers by enabling them to participate to a greater extent in the market. Consumers' ability to stimulate competition by being more 'active' regarding their purchasing choices, alongside the potential for them to exert pressure on producers by themselves generating electricity for private use, is viewed by the EU as pivotal to these ends.[8] Recital 4 of the 2019 Electricity Directive envisages a market wherein '*citizens take ownership of the energy transition, benefit from new technologies to reduce their bills and participate actively in the market, and where vulnerable consumers are protected*'.[9] Energy consumers are thus expected to benefit from the reforms of the 2019 Electricity Directive as they can expect to benefit financially from participating in the market by means of new technologies (as buyers and sellers), whilst also benefitting from increased consumer protections—with vulnerable customers singled out as requiring additional support. This twofold role, however, also suggests that consumers, in particular small consumers, might develop into two categories. One category of consumers who are able to 'take ownership of and benefit from new technologies' (for example, consumers who produce energy and have access to battery storage), and another category of consumers who are less able to invest in such technologies and thus being more at risk of falling into energy poverty.

[5] Directive (EU) 2019/944 on common rules for the internal market in electricity [2019] OJ L 158/125 (hereafter *2019 Electricity Directive*), Article 28(1); Directive (EU) 2019/692 concerning common rules for the internal market in natural gas [2019] OJL 117/1 (hereafter *2019 Gas Directive*) Article 3(3).

[6] Agency for the Cooperation of Energy Regulators (hereafter *ACER*) and Council of European Energy Regulators (hereafter *CEER*), 'Annual Report on the Results of Monitoring the Internal Electricity and Natural Gas Markets in 2017: Consumer Empowerment Volume' (ACER/CEER 2018), 5 (hereafter ACER/CEER, 'Annual Report for 2017').

[7] Directive 2009/72/EC concerning common rules for the internal market in electricity [2009] OJ L 211/55 (hereafter *2009 Electricity Directive*) recital 53; Directive 2009/73/EC concerning common rules for the internal market in natural gas [2009] OJ L 211/94 (hereafter *2009 Gas Directive*) recital 50.

[8] *2019 Electricity Directive* (n 5), recital 10.

[9] Ibid., recital 4.

Moreover, against the background of energy poverty being recognized as being a form of energy injustice, this discrepancy might cause the risk of distributional and social injustices among small customers in the EU.[10]

Considering the above, this chapter will focus on the position of small (predominantly household) energy consumers in the EU. For this purpose, it is necessary to present briefly the process of energy market liberalization in the EU, and the types and roles of consumers identified under EU law (section II). Following on from this, the chapter will present an overview of the current legal framework governing consumer protections for small/household energy customers generally in the EU (section III). Moving from theory to practice, the chapter will then look at how vulnerable customers are currently protected in the EU, with examples of how existing EU legislation has been implemented at MS level (section IV). This is then followed by an analysis of the EU energy market reform and how it addresses this potential discrepancy between participation (consumer empowerment) and protection of small consumers in the energy sector (section V). Concluding, this chapter elaborates on the question of whether this requires a new focus on energy poverty and injustice in EU energy law (section VI).

II. The Role of Consumers in a Liberalized Energy Market

The current role of consumers in the energy market and the ensuing legal challenges cannot be understood without some background on the development of the energy market and the role of consumers in the process of market liberalization. The most recent energy market reform of 2019 again emphasizes the role of energy consumers in the liberalized energy market, and aims to increase their level of market integration. This is achieved through enabling new forms of participation, and subsequently, the creation of new categories of consumers.

A. Process of Market Liberalization

The first energy market liberalization reforms were introduced at the end of the 1980s, with the process beginning in earnest with the passing of the first Directive on the internal electricity market in 1996 (followed by a Directive on the internal gas market in 1998).[11] These Directives were reformed in 2003,[12] 2009,[13] and 2019.[14] Moreover,

[10] G. Walker and R. Day, 'Fuel Poverty as Injustice: Integrating Distribution, Recognition and Procedure in the Struggle for Affordable Warmth' (2012) 49 *Energy Policy*, 69.

[11] *1996 Electricity Directive* (n 3); Directive 98/30/EC concerning common rules for the internal market in natural gas [1998] OJ L 204/1 (hereafter *1998 Gas Directive*).

[12] Directive 2003/54/EC concerning common rules for the internal market in electricity [2003] OJ L 176/37 (hereafter *2003 Electricity Directive*); Directive 2003/55/EC concerning common rules for the internal market in natural gas [2003] OJ L 176/57 (hereafter *2003 Gas Directive*).

[13] *2009 Electricity Directive* (n 7); *2009 Gas Directive* (n 7).

[14] *2019 Electricity Directive* (n 5); *2019 Gas Directive* (n 5). The regulatory reform of the *2019 Gas Directive* is far more limited than the reform of *2019 Electricity Directive*. There is, for example, no reference to 'active' consumers.

several other Directives governing, inter alia, the use of RES[15] and Regulations governing cross-border electricity and gas trade supplemented the liberalization process.[16] The latter Regulations are relevant as the EU not only aims to liberalize MS' energy markets, but at the same time also aspires to integrate these markets into one single market.

In seeking to create one IEM, drastic alterations to the very structure of the energy market became necessary. The network-bound energy sector has for several decades been organized around the concept of public undertakings or undertakings assigned with a de facto or de jure task of general economic interest, that is, the supply of electricity and/or gas to end-consumers 24/7.[17] Hence, these undertakings (utilities) were generally exempted from the rules of free movement and competition in order to enable them to fulfil this particular task assigned to them. Market liberalization, however, required that this approach should be changed. EU policy thus aimed to (i) apply more stringently the key principles of free movement and competition as established by the TFEU (primary law); and (ii) to implement secondary legislation (e.g. Directives and Regulations) based on the same principles. In other words, the same principles apply to these public undertakings *ex ante* via Directives and Regulations, as well as *ex post* (via e.g. dispute settlement and merger control procedures).

It follows from the above that the Directives governing energy market liberalization aim to further competition within the EU energy market. When assessing the legal instruments governing the network-bound energy sector, it is necessary to distinguish between the grid and those who are connected to the grid. Whereas the grid is considered a natural monopoly and thus needs to be regulated in order to avoid any abuse of that monopoly position, those who are connected to the grid (producers and consumers) should in a liberalized market be given the opportunity to freely operate in that market.[18] Energy producers should thus be exempted from any exclusive rights regarding the production and sale of their products.[19] Similarly producers as well as consumers should be able to act (to buy and to sell) in a competitive market. Indeed, energy market liberalization in the EU is based on the concept of energy consumers having a

[15] Most recently through Directive (EU) 2018/2001 on the promotion of the use of energy from renewable sources [2018] OJ L 328/82 (hereafter *2018 Renewable Energy Directive*).

[16] For electricity: Regulation (EC) 714/2009 on conditions for access to the network for cross-border exchanges in electricity [2009] OJ L 211/15, amended by Regulation (EU) 347/2013 on guidelines for trans-European energy infrastructure [2013] OJ L 115/39 and Regulation 543/2013 on submission and publication of data in electricity markets [2013] OJ L 163/1.

For gas: Regulation (EC) 715/2009 on conditions for access to the natural gas transmission networks [2009] OJ L 211/36, amended by Commission Decision 2010/685/EU [2010] OJ L 293/67, Commission Decision 2012/490/EU [2012] OJ L 231/16, Regulation (EU) 347/2013 on guidelines for trans-European energy infrastructure [2013] OJ L 115/39, Commission Decision (EU) 2015/715 [2015] OJ L 114/9 and Regulation (EU) 2018/1999 on the Governance of the Energy Union and Climate Action [2018] OJ L 328/1 (hereafter *2018 Governance Regulation*).

[17] Consolidated Version of the Treaty on the Functioning of the European Union [2012] C 326/01 (hereafter *TFEU*), Article 106.

[18] *The IEM* (n 2): 'Monopolies of electricity distribution to consumers' and 'Exclusive rights of the use of distribution and interconnecting transmission systems, particularly insofar as this affects consumers' ability to obtain supplies from sources other than their allotted distributor' were both identified as 'suggested priorities to address'.

[19] Ibid., 66: 'Decompartmentalization of the natural gas networks' is listed under 'suggested priorities in the natural gas sector'.

free choice of supply, meaning that they (in principle) can switch supplier and be part of a process that leads to lower energy prices and better services.[20] In order to achieve this goal, energy networks and network activities had to be separated (i.e. unbundled) from the commercial activities (i.e. production and supply).[21]

B. Types of Consumers pre-2019

While the EU has sought to grant specific rights to energy consumers, access to these rights has not always been universal. EU legislation long utilized the term 'eligible consumer' as a means of specifying who was to be entitled to freely choose their supplier and conclude supply contracts—with ineligible customers having no such rights at EU-level. By specifying minimum consumption thresholds, the 1996 Electricity Directive and the 1998 Gas Directive only required MS to open up their markets to large consumers.[22] However, these thresholds were merely minimum requirements, and therefore the degree to which markets were opened was not fully harmonized. The legal reforms of 2003 put an end to this approach, establishing that all non-household customers were to become eligible consumers (for the purposes of the establishing rights contained in the Directives) as of July 2004, and subsequently all customers (including households) were to become eligible by July 2007.[23] The legal reforms of 2009 did not change the concept of eligible customers and restated that all customers are eligible—something that in effect rendered the term 'eligible' redundant. All references to eligible customers were finally removed in the 2019 Electricity Directive.[24] However, as one distinction ceased to be, a new one came into existence, with the Directive introducing a new category of consumers, namely 'active customers' (see further below in section II.C).

While all consumers are now entitled to freely choose their supplier, there are still a number of different categories of customers (with different applicable protective legal frameworks) at EU level. The most general distinction made is that between *'wholesale or final customers'*.[25] Whereas wholesale customers are customers purchasing electricity and/or gas for the purpose of resale,[26] final customers purchase them for own use.[27]

For the purpose of this chapter, the category of 'final customers' is particularly pertinent. From a technical perspective, the types of final customers can generally be distinguished by two characteristics, namely the quantity of consumption (volume) and

[20] *2019 Electricity Directive* (n 5), recital 11.

[21] Under EU law there are several unbundling regimes. See, inter alia, M.M Roggenkamp, et al., *Energy Law in Europe—National, European and International Regulation* (Oxford University Press, 3rd edn, 2016) (hereafter Roggenkamp, *Energy Law in Europe 3rd edn*).

[22] *1996 Electricity Directive* (n 3), Article 19(1) and Article 19(2); *1998 Gas Directive* (n 11), Article 18(2).

[23] *2003 Electricity Directive* (n 12), Article 21(1); 2003 Gas Directive (n 12), Article 23(1).

[24] Please note that this distinction still exists in the Gas Directive.

[25] *2019 Electricity Directive* (n 5), Article 2(1); *2009 Gas Directive* (n 7), Article 2(24).

[26] Ibid., Article 2(2); ibid., Article 2(29).

[27] Ibid., Article 2(3); ibid., Article 2(27).

the size of the connection (capacity). This translates, into the categorization of 'large' and 'small' consumers. The energy market Directives define these categories as *'non-household customers'* and *'household customers'*. A non-household customer is '[. . .] *a natural or legal person who purchases electricity / natural gas that is not for own household use*, [the electricity Directive additionally explicates:] *including producers, industrial customers, small and medium-sized enterprises, businesses and wholesale customers*'.[28] Household customers are defined as *'customers purchasing natural gas / electricity for his own household consumption*, [the electricity Directive additionally explicates:] *excluding commercial or professional activities*'.[29] The latter category may nevertheless include small enterprises if these enterprises employ less than fifty persons and their annual turnover or balance sheet does not exceed EUR 10 million. Clearly, the legislation does not seek to make distinctions based on technical differences alone (large versus small consumption), instead seeking to infer the purpose for which the energy is required. Whereas non-household customers are final customers and use energy for commercial purposes, household customers are consuming energy for the purpose of private and individual well-being. This distinction is relevant as the protective legal framework aims to provide safeguarding measures exclusively for the latter purpose. The specific measures are further outlined in section III below.

C. 2019: An Expanded Role for Consumers

In addition to these pre-existing distinctions, the 2019 Electricity Directive provides for an additional class of consumers by institutionalizing the phenomenon widely referred to as 'prosumers'.[30] Prosumers are ordinarily understood as being consumers who also produce electricity.[31] This particular category of consumers had not previously been explicitly recognized at an EU level and therefore uncertainty existed as regards the rights and protections that would enable these prosumers across the EU to participate in the market. This changed with the introduction of the 2019 Electricity Directive, which uses the term 'active customers' instead of 'prosumers' and defines the class as follows:

> *'active customer' means a final customer, or a group of jointly acting final customers, who consumes or stores electricity generated within its premises located within confined boundaries or, where permitted by a MS, within other premises, or who sells self-generated*

[28] Ibid., Article 2(5); ibid., Article 2(26).

[29] Ibid., Article 2(4); ibid., Article 2(25).

[30] Sometimes also referred to as 'self-consumers', see for different regulatory approaches on prosumers for example C. Banet, 'Prosumer Legislation in Norway—A First Step for Empowering Small Energy Consumers'; L. Diestelmeier and D. Kuiken, 'Legal Framework for Prosumers in the Netherlands'; and M. Lang, 'Prosumer Legislation in Germany', in M.M. Roggenkamp and C. Banet (eds) *European Energy Law Report XII* (Intersentia, 1st edn, 2018).

[31] N. Šajn, *Electricity 'Prosumers'* (European Parliament Research Service, 2016).

electricity or participates in flexibility or energy efficiency schemes, provided that those activities do not constitute its primary commercial or professional activity;[32]

That the term 'active customers' was preferred to 'prosumers' gives insight into the minds of legislators in this area. As the definition makes clear, the class is far wider than 'consumers who also produce electricity'. Besides producing electricity, being an active customer may entail storing electricity or participating in energy efficiency schemes. The legal reform can therefore be seen as enabling prosumers to become market participants also by means of demand flexibility, that is, the process where consumers act upon incentives to adjust their demand. Through this, active customers may be able to contribute to the development of new markets for demand flexibility, which becomes increasingly important for the integration of RES.[33] However, with past experiences having shown that not all consumers are even able to participate in the market, it must be questioned whether the restructuring of the EU energy market to include a new tier (with high entry costs) atop the existing market may exacerbate rather than mitigate these issues. Such concerns are often expressed in the 'utilities death spiral' argument.[34] These arguments contend that, as those who can save money invest in technology that allows them to save money, the price differences (as the customer base dwindles) become more and more pronounced. Within the context of demand flexibility, it can be readily identified that participation in the market is likely to require initial investments, meaning that poor and vulnerable customers are at risk of being excluded from these markets and reaping subsequent benefits. As this chapter argues, this might require a new focus on energy poverty and energy (in)justice. The following section outlines the legal framework on the protection of energy consumers.

III. EU Legal Framework on the Protection of Energy Consumers

While the liberalization of the energy sector granted consumers a central role by giving them the freedom to choose their supplier, it also required explicit protection measures to be put into place for those consumers who may be at risk due to an inequality of bargaining power within the energy sector. This is especially the case for small (household) customers, who—in spite of a liberalized market setting, which theoretically should provide competitive market prices and better services—remain in a weak negotiating position and are therefore considered to be in need of a protection regime. The EU legal framework thus requires MS to implement several instruments in this regard. As a general rule MS are called upon to ensure high levels of consumer protection and thus to take measures to increase transparency as regards contractual terms and conditions,

[32] *2019 Electricity Directive* (n 5), Article 2(8). The moniker 'renewables self-consumers' is preferred within the *2018 Renewable Energy Directive* (n 5), Article 2(14).

[33] M. Kubli, M. Loock, and R. Wüstenhagen, 'The Flexible Prosumer: Measuring the Willingness to Co-create Distributed Flexibility' (2018) 114 *Energy Policy*, 540.

[34] W. Boyd, 'Public Utility and the Low-Carbon Future' (2014) 61 *UCLA Law Review*, 1614, 1675.

and to establish adequate dispute settlement mechanisms.[35] In addition, some specific instruments apply, which range from specific protections under EU energy law to general EU consumer protection law. These will be discussed in the following subsections.

A. EU Energy Law: Public Service Obligations

One of the most prominent measures for protecting energy consumers, which was introduced in the first set of Directives, is the option for MS to impose public service obligations (PSO) on electricity and gas undertakings, that is, undertakings which carry out a task that can be defined as a general economic interest, such as the continuous and non-discriminatory supply of energy to small customers.[36] Such PSOs may relate to security, including security of supply, regularity, quality, and price of supplies and environmental protection, including energy efficiency, energy from renewable sources, and also climate protection. They have to be clearly defined, transparent, non-discriminatory, and verifiable and at the same time guarantee equality of access for EU undertakings to national consumers.[37]

Several MS made use of the opportunity to apply a PSO in order to regulate the price of energy supply for small consumers (through retail tariffs) in order to ensure that these consumers would never be in a position that they would pay tariffs they could not afford. Examples of such regulated supply tariffs based on a PSO can, amongst others, be found in Denmark, France, and Spain.[38] However, regulated supply tariffs have a negative impact on market liberalization efforts as they foreclose competition and consumers have no incentive to switch between suppliers. As an effort to further competition, the 2019 Electricity Directive now explicitly requires that supply prices (as a general rule) should be market-based.[39] The only instance in which an exception to this rule may be made is for the benefit of 'energy poor or vulnerable household customers'—and even in such instances any public interventions must pass a strict five-stage test essentially assessing the necessity and proportionality.[40]

B. EU Energy Law: Universal Service and Supplier of Last Resort

The 2003 Electricity Directive introduced some additional protections for small customers. MS were required to ensure that all household customers and, if appropriate, small enterprises, shall enjoy universal service, which is defined as the right to be supplied with electricity of a specified quality within their territory at reasonable, easily,

[35] *2019 Electricity Directive* (n 5), Article 26 and *2009 Gas Directive* (n 7), annex I, 1(f).
[36] This provision was included in Article 3 of the Electricity and Gas Directives from 1996/1998 until 2009.
[37] This passage is replicated verbatim in *2019 Electricity Directive* (n 5), Article 9(2).
[38] See chapters on Denmark, France, and Spain in: Roggenkamp, *Energy Law in Europe 3rd edn* (n 21).
[39] *2019 Electricity Directive* (n 5), Article 5.
[40] Ibid., Article 5(4).

and clearly comparable and transparent prices. Moreover, distribution companies have the obligation to connect (all) customers to their network under regulated terms, conditions, and tariffs.[41] In addition, the Directives provide that MS may appoint a supplier of last resort (SoLR).[42] However, in the absence of a definition of what a SoLR entails, MS have in practice applied this concept in two different manners. The concept of SoLR can refer to the concept of a default supplier and as such be used by MS in situations where customers have not chosen a specific supplier, or as an alternative supplier in case an existing supplier is no longer able to supply, for example, due to bankruptcy or the revocation of a supply licence. Whereas several examples can be found of MS applying a SoLR as a default supplier,[43] examples of SoLR acting in cases of suppliers going bankrupt can only be found in the Netherlands, Belgium, Germany, and the UK.[44] The 2019 Electricity Directive changes little with regards SoLR(s), a tacit (though not express) approval of the many ways in which MS have chosen to utilize the SoLR structure.

C. EU Consumer Protection Law

The provisions governing consumer protection in the Electricity and Gas Directives cannot be considered in isolation, as Directive 2011/83/EU (amending Directive 93/13/EEC) on Consumer Rights[45] also provides rules on the protection of energy consumers.[46] This Directive is based on the principle of maximum harmonization, and thus prevents MS from enacting or maintaining stricter rules.[47] Although sector-specific measures (such as those included in the Electricity Directive) apply without prejudice to Directive 2011/83/EC, the provisions of the general Consumer Protection Directive would still prevail in the rather unlikely case of a conflict.[48] In practice the situation can be even more complicated, as in addition to the EU Directives and domestic consumer protection legislation, national civil laws (which often contain general rules on the conclusion of contracts and the principle of good faith) must also be considered.

This complexity became evident in *RWE Vertrieb v Verbraucherzentrale Nordrhein-Westfalen*,[49] wherein the European Court of Justice (ECJ) examined the compatibility of

[41] *2009 Electricity Directive* (n 7), Article 3(3); replicated in *2019 Electricity Directive* (n 5), Article 27(1).

[42] *2009 Gas Directive* (n 7), Article 3(3); *2019 Electricity Directive* (n 5), Article 27(1).

[43] ACER/CEER, 'Annual Report for 2017' (n 6), 11.

[44] R. van 't Hoft, 'Regulating Security of Energy Supply for End Consumers—A Comparative Overview', in M.M. Roggenkamp and C. Banet (eds) *European Energy Law Report XI* (Intersentia, 1st edn, 2017), 317–45.

[45] Directive 2011/83/EU on consumer rights [2011] OJ L 304/64 (hereafter *2011 Consumer Rights Directive*)

[46] The *2011 Consumer Rights Directive* applies as of 13 June 2014 and replaces Directive 85/577/EEC to protect the consumer in respect of contracts negotiated away from business premises [1985] OJ L 372/31, Directive 93/13/EEC on unfair terms in consumer contracts [1993] OJ L 95/29, Directive 97/7/EC on the protection of consumers in respect of distance contracts [1997] OJ L 144/19 and Directive 1999/44/EC on certain aspects of the sale of consumers goods and associated guarantees [1999] OJ L 171/12.

[47] See for the different harmonization methods Chapter 5 section C5 of M. Roggenkamp, et al., (eds), *Energy Law in Europe—National, EU and International regulation* (OUP, 1st edn, 2001).

[48] B. Jan Drijber, 'EU Case Law Applying to the Energy Sector and the Protection of Consumers, Environment and Investments: A Review', in M.M. Roggenkamp and H. Bjornebye (eds) *European Energy Law Report X* (Intersentia, 1st edn, 2014), 11–27.

[49] *RWE Vertrieb AG v Verbraucherzentrale Nordrhein-Westfalen e.V.* [2013] ECLI:EU:C:2013:180 (hereafter *RWE Vertrieb v Verbraucherzentrale Nordrhein-Westfalen*)

price variation clauses with the general rules on consumer protection contained within Directive 93/13/EEC (now Directive 2011/83) and the 2003 Gas Directive. Generally, Article 1(2) of Directive 93/13/EEC stated that contractual terms which reflect mandatory, statutory, or regulatory provisions of national law are not subject to the Directive, as there is a presumption that the national legislature struck a balance between all the rights and obligations of the parties to a certain category of contracts. However, that this principle does not always prevail was proven in *RWE Vertrieb v Verbraucherzentrale Nordrhein-Westfalen*, highlighting a resistance on the part of the ECJ to narrow the scope or effect of the Consumer Protection Directive. Although this case dealt with gas supply contracts, it has a wider application and potentially also applies to electricity contracts owing to the basis of the ruling being that energy consumers are in a weak position vis-à-vis suppliers both as regards bargaining power and level of knowledge.

IV. Identifying Energy Poverty and Protecting Vulnerable Customers

The above has shown that a special regime applies to small customers in order to protect them from possible market abuses. However, in practice, these consumers' circumstances may differ, and they are faced with a variety of challenges. Some will be able to act in a liberalized market, while others will only be able to do so to a lesser extent or not at all. The latter category is often regarded as vulnerable customers. Such small and vulnerable customers may be more prone to 'energy poverty'.

A. Vulnerable Customers

The 2003 Energy Market Directives added a requirement for MS to '*take appropriate measures to protect final customers, and shall in particular ensure that there are adequate safeguards to protect vulnerable customers, including measures to help them avoid disconnection*'.[50] As the concept of vulnerable customer is not clearly defined at EU level, MS have a discretionary power to establish their own definitions. Monitoring reports on the implementation of the concept of 'vulnerable customers' at MS level conclude that the concept depends on a wide range of factors such as socio-demographic attributes, for example, age or health status, or circumstances, such as single parenthood or unemployment.[51] An indication of the breadth of these discrepancies can be illustrated by contrasting the share of vulnerable customers within each MS (9.9 per cent of French consumers were considered 'vulnerable' in 2016 compared to 0.7 per cent in Poland and 0.8 per cent in Hungary),[52] as well as the wide variety of measures deemed necessary to

[50] *2003 Electricity Directive* (n 12), Article 3(3); 2003 Gas Directive (n 12), Article 3(5).
[51] ACER and CEER, 'Annual Report on the Results of Monitoring the Internal Electricity and Natural Gas Markets in 2016' (ACER/CEER 2017), 36 (hereafter ACER/CEER, 'Annual Report for 2016'.
[52] Ibid., 35.

protect vulnerable customers.[53] Besides defining the concept of a vulnerable customer, each MS must also 'take appropriate measures, such as providing benefits by means of their social security systems to ensure the necessary electricity supply to such vulnerable customers, or to provide support for energy efficiency improvements'.[54] Such measures '*shall not impede the effective opening of the market [. . .] or market functioning and shall be notified to the Commission [and] [. . .] may include measures to be taken within the general social security system*'.[55]

The 2019 Electricity Directive appears to take a step further in a definitional sense, setting out in Article 28(1) the factors that ought to be considered when defining the range of the class: '*The concept of vulnerable customers may include income levels, the share of energy expenditure of disposable income, the energy efficiency of homes, critical dependence on electrical equipment for health reasons, age or other criteria.*' It is doubtful, however, whether the guidance set out in Article 28(1) of the 2019 Electricity Directive will be sufficient to corral MS into updating their definitions. The only aspects of the passage that act as binding obligations on MS are to 'take appropriate measures' and to 'define the concept of vulnerable customers'. The guidance in the sentence following is only that (wording like 'may include' and 'or other criteria' are the death knell for enforceability), and indeed directly contradicts the 2014 Vulnerable Consumer Working Group (VCWG) Guidance Document. The Guidance Document pushed for the class to be defined more by reference to circumstances rather than socio-demographic properties, stating that an approach which '*seeks to avoid assumptions that particular "groups" of consumers are by definition vulnerable, such as old people*' should be avoided.[56]

The discrepancy between definitions can best be illustrated by comparing the definitions of two neighbouring MS, the UK and Ireland. UK energy regulator Ofgem's definition of vulnerability broadly follows the VCWG Guidance Document, with reference to a combination of circumstances and characteristics, avoiding assumptions of vulnerability within particular groups:

> *Our definition of vulnerability is when a consumer's personal circumstances and characteristics combine with aspects of the market to create situations where he or she is: (a) Significantly less able than a typical consumer to protect or represent his or her interests in the energy market; and/or (b) Significantly more likely than a typical consumer to suffer detriment, or that detriment is likely to be more substantial.*[57]

In Ireland, meanwhile, explicit references to characteristics (as a sole qualifier) continue to exist:

[53] ACER/CEER, 'Annual Report for 2017' (n 6), 16.
[54] *2019 Electricity Directive* (n 5), Article 28(2).
[55] *2019 Electricity Directive* (n 5), Article 28(2); *2009 Gas Directive* (n 5), Article 3(4).
[56] Vulnerable Consumer Working Group (hereinafter *VCWG*), 'Vulnerable Consumer Working Group Guidance Document on Vulnerable Consumers, November 2013' (*VCWG* 2014), 7, 11.
[57] Office of Gas and Electricity Markets (hereinafter *Ofgem*), 'Consumer Vulnerability Strategy' (*Ofgem* 2013), 4.

> *a household customer who is: (a) critically dependent on electrically powered equipment, which shall include but is not limited to life protecting devices, assistive technologies to support independent living and medical equipment, or (b) particularly vulnerable to disconnection during winter months for reasons of advanced age or physical, sensory, intellectual or mental health. Advancing age is taken to be a person of pensionable age (66 years or above) living alone, with another vulnerable person or with minors.*[58]

One may note that while Queen Elizabeth II may not be considered a vulnerable customer in the UK, she would be considered vulnerable in Ireland (if living alone or with only her husband).

B. Energy Poverty

As mentioned previously, energy poverty is considered a 'growing problem' within the EU, with the issue of energy poverty already acknowledged in the 2009 Directives. Recitals 50 and 53 of the 2009 Gas Directive and the 2009 Electricity Directive clearly state that MS should '*[. . .] take appropriate measures, such as formulating national energy action plans [. . .] providing for support for energy efficiency improvements, to address energy poverty where identified, including in the broader context of poverty*'.[59] The 2019 Electricity Directive goes a step further, emphasizing the need for a stronger focus on energy poverty and vulnerable customers compared to its predecessor. It includes various new recitals and articles acknowledging the existence of energy poverty among vulnerable customers.[60]

Article 29 of the 2019 Electricity Directive requires MS to (i) define a set of criteria for the purposes of measuring energy poverty; (ii) continuously monitor the number of households in energy poverty; and (iii) report on the evolution of energy poverty and measures taken to prevent it to the Commission every two years as part of their Integrated National Energy and Climate Progress Reports, in accordance with Article 21 of the 2018 Governance Regulation. This provision overlaps with Article 3(3)(d) of the 2018 Governance Regulation, which requires MS to identify the numbers of customers in energy poverty and therefore are required to '[. . .] *establish and publish a set of criteria, which may include low income, high expenditure of disposable income on energy and poor energy efficiency*'.The focus on economic aspects (when establishing and publishing a set of criteria) is noteworthy, and indicates which aspects are considered pertinent when defining energy poverty—solely economic, none social. More generally, the above passage also showcases the 2019 Electricity Directive's recognition of the need to introduce measures to reduce energy poverty. However, when read in conjunction with other provisions of the 2019 Electricity

[58] S.I. No. 463/2011 European Communities (Internal Market in Electricity and Gas) (Consumer Protection) Regulations of 2011 s 2(1).

[59] *2009 Electricity Directive* (n 7), recital 53; *2009 Gas Directive* (n 7), recital 50.

[60] *2019 Electricity Directive* (n 5), recital 59 and recital 60.

Directive (namely those that remove some of the previous weapons in a MS's arsenal to protect consumers, such as the phasing out of regulated retail prices via a PSO), a clear dichotomy emerges. It appears that while the EU is extremely eager to get to grips with the problem of energy poverty, it no longer countenances interferences in the market to achieve this goal. This broadly follows the EU's approach across other areas of energy law,[61] wherein market-based solutions have been strongly preferred to State-led solutions.

In order to take measures against energy poverty, it is necessary to identify and measure it. Although the 2019 Electricity Directive attempts to provide more clarity regarding the concept and the extent of energy poverty in the EU, getting to grips with how to define and address the issue is still a major challenge as the concept of energy poverty is multifaceted, may vary across MS, and cannot be captured by a few indicators.[62] Energy poverty, or fuel poverty, is in practice a complex interaction between issues like high energy bills, poor energy efficiency, and low income. Moreover, these factors are likely to amplify each other and thereby further create conditions exacerbating energy poverty.[63] Attempts to capture the extent of energy poverty throughout the EU have shown significant differences between MS both with regard to the definition and the severity of the problem.[64] As of 2017, only five MS national regulatory authorities reported as having a definition for energy poverty.[65]

V. EU Energy Market Reform: Extending Consumer Empowerment

The reforms of the EU energy market legislation (more specifically the 2019 Electricity Directive and the 2018 Renewable Energy Directive) reiterate the important role of energy consumers for a liberalized market. In addition to the existing empowerment of consumers, which primarily consists of their right to switch supplier, the new Directives aim to incentivize consumers to participate in the market not only as consumer, but also as producer, demand-response service provider, or energy community member. This may raise the level of participation in the market, offering new benefits to consumers. However, as this chapter argues, this might also require a new focus on energy poverty and vulnerable customers. The following sections outline the ways in which consumers can participate in the market, varying from switching to developing energy communities

[61] Such as in capacity auctions for cross-border (interconnector) capacity.

[62] Íñigo del Guayo, Chapter 3 of this book.

[63] S. Pye and A. Dobbins, 'Energy Poverty and Vulnerable Consumers in the Energy Sector Across EU: Analysis of Policies and Measures' (2015) INSIGHT_E, 16.

[64] H. Thomson and C. Snell, 'Quantifying the Prevalence of Fuel Poverty Across the European Union' (2013) 52 *Energy Policy*, 563–72.

[65] ACER/CEER, 'Annual Report for 2017' (n 6), 17.

A. Switching Procedures

One of the key elements of market liberalization is the right of consumers to choose their supplier and thus also to switch suppliers. In order to facilitate switching, special measures have been introduced to ensure that small (household) consumers can switch without unnecessary obstacles. These measures are twofold. Firstly, they provide as a basic rule that all consumers have the right to a contract with a supplier. Secondly, they govern the switching process, which entails that one supply contract is replaced by a contract with another supplier. As the market liberalization evolved, the provisions governing the supply contract and the switching process have been expanded. Hence, the number of provisions in the 2019 Electricity Directive has increased.

The supply contract governs the relationship between consumer and supplier. It therefore needs to specify the identity and address of the supplier regardless of the MS where it is registered, the services they provide, the duration of the contract, information on tariffs, maintenance charges and compensation, and refund mechanisms.[66] All conditions need to be fair and well known in advance,[67] and there should be adequate notice of any intention to modify the contract.[68] Moreover, consumers need to be offered a wide and non-discriminatory choice of payment methods, including prepayment methods.[69] The 2019 Electricity Directive also contains a requirement for suppliers to prominently display on each bill issued the end date of the contract (if applicable); the final customer's switching code.[70] As the right of consumers to switch supplier is essential for the development of a competitive market, the directives try to minimize any barriers to switching. Switching is not only promoted by providing transparency as regards the contractual conditions but also by providing consumers with independent information on the available energy supply offers. MS are therefore required to inform small consumers of at least one independent comparison tool (e.g. a website).[71] MS are required to ensure that such a switching process should take place within a reasonable time. This means that the total duration of the process should not exceed three weeks from the date of the customer's request.[72] Last but not least, when changing supplier, customers will not be charged for changing supplier[73] and are entitled to receive a final closure account.[74]

Despite the acknowledgement that switching supplier is essential for the development of a competitive market, switching rates (on the whole in the EU) have been rather low, with wide variations between MS. In 2017, the highest switching rate of

[66] *2019 Electricity Directive* (n 5), Article 10(3); *2009 Gas Directive* (n 7), annex I, 1(a).
[67] Ibid., Article 10(2); ibid., annex I, 1(a).
[68] Ibid., Article 10(4); ibid., annex I, 1(b).
[69] Ibid., Article 10(6); ibid., annex I, 1(d).
[70] Ibid., annex I, 1.2(f). No equivalent provision was introduced by the *2019 Gas Directive*.
[71] *2019 Electricity Directive* (n 5), Article 14 and annex I, 1.2(i).
[72] See also recital 34, which also states that by the year 2026 the technical switching process should be completed within 24 hours on any working day.
[73] *2019 Electricity Directive* (n 5), Article 10(8); *2009 Gas Directive* (n 7), annex I, 1(e).
[74] Ibid., Article 10(12); ibid., annex I, 1(j).

household consumers for electricity was reported by Norway (18.8 per cent) and the lowest was in Bulgaria (0.002 per cent). Within the gas market, the highest switching rate could be found in the United Kingdom (18.6 pre cent), while Luxembourg had the lowest switching rate (0.18 per cent).[75] With more people being removed from regulated tariffs (as detailed in III.A) and the additional requirements in the 2019 Electricity Directive, it can be expected that the number of customers switching suppliers may begin to increase.

B. Extended Market Participation: 'Active Customer' and 'Citizen Energy Communities'

One of the most prominent (and more novel) approaches taken by the 2019 Electricity Directive to foster consumer empowerment is by enabling their participation in the market not only as consumers, but also as 'active customers' or via 'citizen energy communities' (CEC).[76] Neither concept existed before in EU legislation. Their emergence in the reform of 2019 can not only be explained by the aim to further empower consumers, but also by the need to find new solutions to integrate increasing amounts of variable RES in the system. Matching variable RES with consumption requires demand flexibility. Demand flexibility can be defined as the ability to adjust consumption according to a specific signal, for example a financial incentive to consume or not consume electricity at a specific time.[77] The 2019 Electricity Directive combines the aim of furthering liberalization by empowering consumers via, for example, demand-response schemes and CECs, and the aim to accelerate energy transition by integrating RES efficiently in the system.

Incentivizing demand-flexibility also of small (household) customers is one of the objectives of the 2019 Electricity Directive[78] and reflected in the potential activities of 'active customers' and CECs. One of the possible activities of 'active customers' is explicitly mentioned as *'participat[ing] in flexibility or energy efficiency schemes'*. While this is not explicitly mentioned for CECs, the potential activities, atop of generation, distribution, supply, and consumption, are very broad, that is, *'[. . .] aggregation, energy storage, energy efficiency services or charging services for electric vehicles or provide other energy services'*. This opens new dimensions for consumers to participate in the market, and thus to gain potential empowerment beyond the possibility of switching supplier.

However, both 'active customers' and CECs are not defined as being purely commercially driven actors. 'Active customers' are not allowed to have their activities as *'primary commercial or professional activity'* and a CEC is, inter alia, defined as an entity which:

75 CEER, 'Performance of European Retail Markets in 2017' (CEER 2018) 31–3.

76 *2019 Electricity Directive* (n 5), Article 2(8) and 2(11). For'active customers' see section II.C of this chapter, and for energy communities see Annalisa Savaresi, Chapter 5 of this book.

77 Smart Grid Task Force—Expert Group 3—Regulatory Recommendations for Smart Grids Deployment, 'Regulatory Recommendations for the Deployment of Flexibility' (2015), 12.

78 *2019 Electricity Directive* (n 5), recital 39.

> […] *has for its primary purpose to provide environmental, economic or social community benefits to its members or shareholders or to the local areas where it operates rather than to generate financial profits;* […][79]

While the exact implementation is again left to MS, it is clear that CECs may prove vital not only as regards electricity generation and supply, but as a vehicle for fulfilling a broader purpose—one which may also very well relate to 'environmental, economic or social community benefits'. This relates the dimension of empowerment to that of potential protection via communities. The next section focuses on the relation between empowerment and protection.

C. Relation between Empowerment and Protection

The 2019 Electricity Directive includes potential new drivers for consumer empowerment beyond switching suppliers. However, it also creates further distinctions within the group of customers, 'active' and 'passive' customers; and members of a CEC, and those who are not members. Subsequently, this might result in new challenges regarding the appropriate protection level for these different categories.

The 2019 Electricity Directive clearly strives to ensure that '*all customer groups (industrial, commercial and households)* […] *have access to the electricity markets to trade their flexibility and self-generated electricity*'.[80] However, even if all customers had access to the market, their ability to trade their flexibility depends on the technologies at their disposal or CEC membership. As such, participation in demand-response schemes and CEC membership presupposes an investment of time, expertise, and money from the consumer. This raises the question whether the provisions for 'activating' consumers and CECs are promoting an inclusive approach or whether vulnerable customers might be excluded from these new forms of participation.

It is clear that a customer, or 'active customer' with more flexibility technologies (for example an electric vehicle, a home battery, different 'smart home devices', and own generation) has a higher-quality flexibility profile than a customer who does not have access to such technologies. In an electricity sector which implements dynamic prices for household customers (and where regulated retail prices are abolished), customers with a low-quality flexibility profile might thus be placed at a considerable disadvantage in benefitting from the 'activating' aspirations of the 2019 Directive. Indeed, they may even increasingly suffer from peak pricing, which they are unable to escape due to an inability to vary demand in the same manner as other final customers. As a consequence, a fragmented market may emerge, with different tiers correlating with the range of technologies at final customers' disposal. In such a system, customers can be distinguished based on their ability to engage in demand-response schemes, determined by

79 *2019 Electricity Directive* (n 5), Article 2(11).
80 *2019 Electricity Directive* (n 5), recital 39.

their 'flexibility profile'. The question then is whether the existing categorization of customers is in fact useful in an electricity sector which steers towards the integration of demand flexibility. This question is especially relevant for guaranteeing the protection of vulnerable customers and the prevention of energy poverty, as the need for protection might be considerably different among the different categories.

Yet, as the 2019 Electricity Directive phases out the option for MS to protect consumers by implementing regulated retail prices (see section IV.B) it also opens another possible approach to protection via empowerment, that is, a community energy approach:

> *[. . .] Community energy can also advance energy efficiency at household level and help fight energy poverty through reduced consumption and lower supply tariffs. Community energy also enables certain groups of household customers to participate in the electricity markets, who otherwise might not have been able to do so. Where they have been successfully operated such initiatives have delivered economic, social and environmental benefits to the community that go beyond the mere benefits derived from the provision of energy services. [. . .]*[81]

There is a distinct possibility that this could include the protection of vulnerable customers and the prevention of energy poverty. However, as this is not enshrined in the definition (but left as an option at the discretion of the MS) there is no guarantee that MS will take this approach. Against the background of these new developments, the following section discusses whether the energy market reform in the EU also requires a new focus on energy poverty and (injustice).

VI. Conclusion—A New Focus on Energy Poverty and Energy (in)Justice?

This chapter has analysed the roles of small (household) consumers in a liberalized EU energy market. Consumer rights and protections vary across MS. Similarly, the concept of vulnerable customers differs per MS. Finally, it has been noted that the phenomenon of 'prosumers' has found its way into EU energy law. These prosumers may, however, still be classified as vulnerable customers, and so there is a potential conflict between consumer participation and protection of small consumers in the energy sector. This twofold role also suggests that consumers, in particular small consumers (which generally includes households), might develop in two categories, one which is able to 'take ownership of and benefit from new technologies' and another category which is not able to do so and remains vulnerable to or even suffers from energy poverty. The question is whether the renewed focus on energy poverty and injustice in the 2019 Electricity Directive sufficiently addresses this issue. Follow-up issues are, for example, whether

[81] *2019 Electricity Directive* (n 5), recital 43.

'active' and thus 'fully empowered' customers are in need of the same protections as consumers who remain passive; or whether members of a CEC can rely on protection beyond the community, for example through a SoLR. Essentially, the opening of new categories of 'empowered' consumers also requires rethinking the relevant protection regime. It remains to be seen how the MS implement the new provisions and whether emerging realties result in adequate legal responses.

11

Energy Justice and Energy Transition in Australia

From Remote Access to Consumer Protection

Lee Godden

I. Introduction: Energy Transition and Distributive Justice in Australia

Australia, as a major energy exporting nation in the world, presents a complex picture in terms of energy justice. Australia has an abundance of energy resources for renewable energy development and traditional fossil fuels.[1] Despite its high level of fossil fuel exploitation, Australia's national government made very weak commitments under the Paris Agreement.[2] National climate and energy law and policy currently centre on voluntary emission reductions and support for fossil fuel resource exploitation. Nonetheless, in some subnational jurisdictions a robust climate change platform is driving energy transition.[3] The result is a geographically skewed distribution of renewable energy transition across the nation. This chapter looks at the patchwork of energy transition in Australia through the lens of energy justice. The analysis focuses first on distributive justice and explores the equity of the distribution of benefits and burdens in energy transition. Secondly, and integrated with that theme, the analysis examines how issues of social justice could inform the energy transition, including the recognition that energy injustice cannot be separated from poverty and discrimination based on factors such as class, race, gender, or indigeneity.[4]

The chapter provides a framing for the distributive and social justice components of energy justice, an overview of the legal frameworks that govern energy access, distribution, and consumer protection within Australia, before examining two representative

[1] See Australian Government, Department of the Environment and Energy, 'Australian Energy Statistics, Table O Electricity Generation by Fuel Type 2017–18 and 2018' (March 2018), https://www.energy.gov.au/publications/australian-energy-statistics-table-o-electricity-generation-fuel-type-2017-18-and-2018>accessed 26 August 2019.

[2] Paris Agreement (22 April 2016) United Nations Framework Convention on Climate Change (entered into force 4 November 2016), https://unfccc.int/process-and-meetings/the-paris-agreement/the-paris-agreement accessed 26 August 2019. See also Australian Government, Department of Foreign Affairs and Trade, 'Australia's Intended Nationally Determined Contribution to a New Climate Change Agreement' (August 2015).

[3] See, e.g., Climate Change Act 2017 (Vic).

[4] C. Hogan and B. Salt, 'The Rise of Energy Poverty in Australia' (KPMG, December 2017) 8, https://assets.kpmg/content/dam/kpmg/au/pdf/2017/census-insights-energy-poverty-australia.pdf accessed 26 August 2019 (hereafter Hogan and Salt, The Rise of Energy Poverty in Australia).

Lee Godden, Energy Justice and Energy Transition in Australia In: *Energy Justice and Energy Law.* Edited by Íñigo Del Guayo, Lee Godden, Donald N. Zillman, Milton Fernando Montoya, and José Juan González, Oxford University Press (2020).
DOI: 10.1093/oso/9780198860754.003.0011

case studies. The first considers access to energy for remote Aboriginal communities in the Northern Territory to investigate the racial dimensions of energy provision. Remote Aboriginal communities experience high degrees of energy poverty and long-term poor health and social outcomes.[5] The Australian Renewable Energy Agency (ARENA) has funded pilot solar projects in remote Aboriginal communities to address this disparity. By contrast, energy affordability, consumer protection, and information transparency have become political drivers for energy market reforms in the highly urbanized, south-eastern part of the continent.[6] An Australian 2016 demographic analysis identified that lower income households proportionally spend more on energy.[7] In this region, electricity supply is governed by the National Electricity Market (NEM).[8] Governments have introduced measures to 'intervene' to correct market failures in the energy market under policies that seek to reduce 'price gouging by corporate energy providers'.[9] This chapter considers the legal and normative frameworks that have produced both a mismatch of energy benefits and burdens in remote Australia and an energy consumer 'squeeze' in southern Australia.

II. Energy Justice in Australia

The distribution of energy disadvantage within Australia closely reflects general socio-economic patterns and pockets of structural inequality and discrimination within the nation.[10] Thus, access to energy for remote communities, especially Aboriginal peoples living on traditional country, remains well below the standards of energy access and affordability in much of Australia. The experience of these communities is clearly inconsistent with achieving the United Nations Sustainable Development Goals. This position persists despite a long-standing national policy agenda to 'Close the Gap' to change the structural disadvantage of Aboriginal communities with respect to housing, employment, and health—all areas where energy access is critical. Ironically, many communities live in areas where energy resources are plentiful and where an energy transition toward renewables is underway.[11] This paradox of energy poverty in the midst of plenty highlights inequalities, which in other jurisdictions have been identified as a form of racial and cultural discrimination.[12]

[5] See, e.g., Y. Paradies, R. Harris, and I. Anderson, 'The Impact of Racism on Indigenous Health in Australia and Aotearoa: Towards a Research Agenda' (Discussion Paper No 4), (Cooperative Research Centre for Aboriginal Health, 2008).

[6] L. Chester, 'The Impacts and Consequences for Low-Income Australian Households of Rising Energy Prices Department of Political Economy' (The University of Sydney, October 2013), 7.

[7] Hogan and Salt, The Rise of Energy Poverty in Australia (n 4), 6–7.

[8] The NEM is the connected power system spanning the eastern seaboard of Australia and its associated energy market and legal frameworks.

[9] S. Elsworth, 'Energy Bill Gouge Finally Loses Power', *The Herald Sun* (30 June 2019), 21.

[10] Hogan and Salt, The Rise of Energy Poverty in Australia (n 4), 5–6.

[11] Northern Territory Government, 'Northern Territory: Roadmap to Renewables' (September 2017), https://roadmaptorenewables.nt.gov.au/?a=460760 accessed 26 August 2019.

[12] See Paddock, Chapter 7 in this book.

In the more highly urbanized south-east of Australia, energy justice considerations largely register as the relative disadvantage of consumers to cheaper electricity and gas prices, or the capacity of communities to access the increasing level of solar and wind renewable energy. Governments are now more willing to exert influence on the liberalized energy market, although still generally do so in line with market-based philosophies. The consumer protection market reforms have occurred in the context of divisive conflicts over climate change and energy policies in Australia over the last decade.[13] Rarely though are the underlying structural inequities of market-driven energy systems scrutinized at a policy level; nor is there a coherent framework for determining energy justice.

A. Energy Resources in Australia

Australia is an energy-rich nation. Australia's continuing export of fossil fuels, particularly coal, has global distributive justice implications in terms of climate change impacts.[14] The fossil fuel industry however is regarded as critical to Australia's economy, due to heavy dependence on transnational trade in energy exports, and in providing substantial employment, in economically depressed regional areas.[15] Australia, from 2009, developed an extensive climate law regime with a carbon pricing mechanism which was subsequently dismantled in 2014.[16] Initiatives in the land sector and some carbon market features were retained albeit with reduced capacity for market trading. As a result, companies have faced few legal obligations under Australian law to reduce their greenhouse gas emissions.[17]

Moreover, the earlier state-based fossil fuel generation profile has left a legacy whereby the majority of Australia's population of approximately 25 million remains linked to large power stations and a centralized grid. Currently, electricity production still relies predominantly on coal (63 per cent), with natural gas fired generation (20 per cent) and renewable generation (16 per cent) making up the remainder.[18] Australia's vast land mass means that significant network infrastructure is necessary for power supply and distribution across the country.[19] Australia has an 'unambitious' Renewable Energy Target

[13] I. Millar and S. Whitehead, 'Climate Change Law in Australia—A History and the Current State of Play' (2018) 92 *Australian Law Journal*, 756, 756 (hereafter Millar and Whitehead, 'Climate Change Law in Australia').

[14] D. Karoly, *Climate Litigation Workshop* (Melbourne Law School, The University of Melbourne,2019).

[15] For an alternative view, see A. Cahill, *Bridging the Divide: Uniting Regional Communities for Climate Action* (Australian-German Climate and Energy College, The University of Melbourne,2019) (hereafter Cahill, *Bridging the Divide*).

[16] Millar and Whitehead, 'Climate Change Law in Australia' (n 13), 763.

[17] E. Aydos and S. Rudolph, 'Climate Policy Made "Down Under": The Political Economy of a New Carbon Market in Australia' (2018) 4 *Carbon & Climate Law Review*, 304, 312.

[18] Australian Government, Department of the Environment and Energy, 'Australian Energy Update 2018' (August 2018), 22, https://www.energy.gov.au/sites/default/files/australian_energy_update_2018.pdf accessed 26 August 2019.

[19] A. Kallies, 'A Barrier for Australia's Climate Commitments? Law, the Electricity Market and Transitioning the Stationary Electricity Sector' (2016) 39 UNSW Law Journal, 1547 (hereafter Kallies, 'A Barrier for Australia's Climate Commitments?')

(RET)[20] and is still developing its legal frameworks to support effective energy transition.[21] Nonetheless, there has been significant investment in renewable generation. Rooftop solar installations are increasing rapidly.[22] There are differential rates of uptake among socio-economic groups, and noticeable spatial variation in access across the country.[23] Emerging research suggests that there are significant disparities within the Australian population in terms of both access to renewable energy and its utilization for household energy.[24] Further, although the penetration of renewables in urban residential areas is accelerating, there is limited off-grid renewable energy development, principally in regional areas. Australian research institutions are actively investigating the potential for hydrogen to operate in renewable energy generation or as an energy export.[25] Given the energy resources in the country and the technological development, the inequalities of access and utilization of energy do not derive principally from energy scarcity.[26] Quintessentially, the disparities are of a distributive and social justice character.

III. Normative Frameworks for Energy Justice

Before considering energy law and regulation in Australia it is helpful to articulate how the normative content of energy justice is understood in application to Australia. An indication of the maturing of energy law has been the attempt to provide a coherent normative framework for energy law, building on the idea of energy justice.[27] Normative objectives resonate beyond energy law's instrumental focus, typically referencing climate change imperatives and energy democracy to argue for a transition to renewables as a transformation of society.[28]

Calls for bottom-up movements acknowledge that addressing energy justice will require wider structural change in societies. Earlier chapters in this book provide guidance on the general concepts and key themes pertaining to energy justice.[29] Here, the

[20] J. Prest and G. Soutter, 'The Future of Australia's Federal Renewable Energy Law' (2018) 92 *Australian Law Journal*, 799, 799.

[21] L. Godden and A. Kallies, 'Smart Infrastructure: Innovative Energy Technology, Climate Mitigation, and Consumer Protection in Australia and Germany', in D. Zillman, et al., (eds), *Innovation in Energy Law and Technology: Dynamic Solutions for Energy Transitions* (Oxford University Press, 2018), 391–411.

[22] Clean Energy Council, *Clean Energy Australia Report 2019* (4 April 2019), 4, https://assets.cleanenergycouncil.org.au/documents/resources/reports/clean-energy-australia/clean-energy-australia-report-2019.pdf accessed 26 August 2019.

[23] Hogan and Salt, The Rise of Energy Poverty in Australia (n 4), 6–8.

[24] Australian Competition and Consumer Commission, *Restoring Electricity Affordability and Australia's Competitive Advantage: Retail Electricity Pricing Inquiry—Final Report* (June 2018), vii(hereafter Australian Competition, *Restoring Electricity Affordability and Australia's Competitive Advantage*).

[25] See CSIRO, 'National Hydrogen Roadmap', https://www.csiro.au/en/Do-business/Futures/Reports/Hydrogen-Roadmap accessed 26 August 2019.

[26] Cahill, *Bridging the Divide* (n 15).

[27] See Aileen McHarg in Chapter 2 of this book.

[28] D. Fairchild and A. Weinrub, 'Introduction', in D. Fairchild and A. Weinrub (eds), *Energy Democracy: Advancing Equity in Clean Energy Solutions* (Island Press, 2017), 1 (hereafter Fairchild, *Energy Democracy: Advancing Equity in Clean Energy Solutions*).

[29] See chapters 1, 2, 3, and 4 of this book.

focus is on examining how general justice theories might have explanatory purchase in understanding critical questions of energy justice within Australia.

A. Distributive and Social Justice in Energy Justice

Social justice and distributive justice have been the focus of analysis and philosophical inquiry. John Rawls' *Theory of Justice* is well known. It has provided an institutional and legal approach to distributive justice.[30] Rawls argues that justice is fundamentally a question of the just distribution of primary social and economic goods, including legal rights and forms of wealth (property). Rawls outlines a thought experiment where people contemplate the just arrangement of primary goods in a future society from an 'original position'.[31] In this original position one does not know what future position the person will hold in that society (for example, rich or poor) or what skills and expertise they may draw on. Rawls asserts that we would all agree that primary social goods should be distributed equally, unless the inequality is to everyone's advantage. Given that energy access is integrally linked to social and economic 'goods', in following Rawls' approach there would likely be agreement that there should be equality in the distribution of access to energy.

There may be less consensus about when an unequal distribution will be to everyone's advantage. On this basis, Rawls has been critiqued as adopting a utilitarian stance whereby the overall wealth or social goods of a society may be increased by denying or limiting access to primary goods (necessities) to some sectors of society. In effect, this exclusion from primary goods may work on the basis of class, gender, race, ethnicity, or other discriminatory factors. Hypothetically, we could apply such an approach in Australia by limiting energy access to some groups, for example by limiting public investment in energy infrastructure. This may enhance overall national Gross Domestic Product but leaves vulnerable communities at a considerable disadvantage—breaching the ideas of equality and fairness upon which presumptively a theory of distributive justice is based.

Patently there is not equality in the distribution of social goods in most societies. Energy access and use can be characterized by significant disparities in a society. Accordingly, other theorists have critiqued Rawls' attempt to separate justice from the actual conditions pertaining in a society. In this light, distributive justice is not merely a matter of ensuring putatively equal distributions of primary socio-economic goods (for example, energy benefits), but in facilitating such distributions in a manner which enables individuals and communities to lead flourishing lives. Amartya Sen's scholarship is associated with the idea that distributive justice should advance individual capabilities.[32] This approach identifies what is needed to transform the primary goods of a

[30] J. Rawls, *A Theory of Justice* (rev edn, Harvard University Press, 1999); J. Rawls, *Justice as Fairness: A Restatement*, (ed.) E. Kelly (Harvard University Press, 2001) (hereafter Rawls, *A Theory of Justice*).

[31] Rawls, *A Theory of Justice* (n 30), chapter 3.

[32] A. Sen, *The Idea of Justice* (Harvard University Press, 2011) (hereafter Sen, *The Idea of Justice*).

society (such as energy access and use) into a fully functioning social life. The focus is to facilitate normative objectives beyond the physical distribution of energy assets. Sen highlights the inadequacies of Rawls' approach as it does not seek to redress current inequalities in the distribution of social goods.[33] Sen's focus on existing inequalities aligns with social justice theories that examine how factors such as class and indigeneity influence the distribution of primary goods such as energy.[34]

Commentators have used energy justice concepts to articulate a relationship between energy law and climate policy.[35] Central to this relationship is the promotion of a decentralized renewable energy model that 'advances ecosystem health, economic sustainability, and social justice through the empowerment of our communities'.[36] This approach distinguishes procedural and substantive justice.[37] 'Procedural justice implies that only procedures and rules of social processes can be just, while result-based justice refers to fair outcomes of social processes.'[38]

B. Distributive Justice Approaches in Australia

A similar transformational approach in Australia directed to environmental justice is offered by Chief Justice Brian Preston of the New South Wales Land and Environment Court.[39] Preston argues that environmental justice comprises three interlinked yet distinct concepts: 'distributive justice, procedural justice and justice as recognition'.[40] These three elements are applicable to energy justice, either as a subset of environmental justice, or preferably, as its own distinct agenda for a sustainable, transformative approach.

For Preston, distributive justice concerns the distribution of environmental goods (or benefits) and environmental burdens. It is to be advanced by giving substantive rights to members of the community (justice as recognition) that are to share in environmental benefits, and to 'prevent, mitigate, remediate or be compensated for environmental burdens' (such as pollution).[41] Three questions are to be answered:

- Who are the members of the community of justice to whom distributive justice is due?
- What are the environmental benefits and burdens to be distributed?
- What are the principles or criteria of distribution to be applied?[42]

[33] Ibid., 18–9.
[34] See also M. Nussbaum and A. Sen (eds), *The Quality of Life* (Oxford University Press, 1993); M. Nussbaum, *Frontiers of Justice: Disability, Nationality, Species Membership* (Harvard University Press, 2006).
[35] See, e.g. International Energy Agency, World Energy Outlook 2015 https://www.iea.org/weo/energyandclimatechange/accessed 26 August 2019.
[36] Fairchild, *Energy Democracy: Advancing Equity in Clean Energy Solutions* (n 28), 15.
[37] Ibid., 5.
[38] Ibid.
[39] B. Preston, 'Access to Environmental Justice: The Effectiveness of the Law' (LSAANZ Conference, University of Wollongong, 15 December 2018) (hereafter Preston, 'Access to Environmental Justice').
[40] Ibid., 1.
[41] Ibid.
[42] Ibid., 2.

Preston draws on a capability model:

> Just arrangements should be assessed ... in how distributions of benefits and burdens affect the capabilities of members of the community of justice to achieve valuable functionings (both activities and states of existence or being).[43]

Procedural justice is significant for examining how distributive choices about energy are made and what may influence those choices. Procedural justice can be advanced by assigning rights to information, participation, and review processes 'before a court or tribunal to challenge decision-making or impairment of substantive or procedural rights'.[44] These ideas are long-established pillars of open government in environmental law.[45] Inclusive decision-making procedures are a precondition for distributive justice. Decision-making in energy law in Australia (and in many countries) is rarely subject to broad participatory requirements or judicial or merits review beyond the immediate energy project—and then only indirectly in terms of its distributional ramifications.

This chapter adopts Preston's analysis in combination with Sen's capability approach by which to examine energy justice in Australia: highlighting the fundamental question of justice as recognition.[46] The law plays both a substantive and normative role—for example, it allows the formal designation of substantive rights to individuals and organizations.[47] Critically, Preston argues that the law will often narrowly designate the community of justice.[48] The narrowness of that designation is evident in terms of who and what is valued in energy governance, and by the limited opportunity to challenge these embedded arrangements. Preston makes the telling observation that the law favours 'consuming users of the environment over non-consuming users and devalues some individuals, groups or communities compared to others'.[49] In energy, the law clearly favours consumption over non-consumptive values—the difficulties in achieving Sustainable Development Goal 7 reflect such an orientation.

C. Frameworks for Distributive and Social Justice in Energy

The models that seek to advance energy justice draw on a wide range of legal, 'soft law', and non-legal measures. Potentially relevant frameworks include: energy legislation; national electricity rules; human rights instruments; consumer protection and competition laws; and, increasingly, non-government legal actions in the absence of

[43] Ibid.
[44] Ibid., 3.
Ibid., 2.
[45] L. Godden, J. Peel, and J. McDonald, *Environmental Law* (2nd edn, Oxford University Press, 2019), chapter 2 (principles of environmental law) (hereafter Godden, *Environmental Law*).
[46] Preston, 'Access to Environmental Justice' (n 39), 3, 5.
[47] See T. Campbell, *Rights: A Critical Introduction* (Routledge, 2006), chapter 2.
[48] Preston, 'Access to Environmental Justice' (n 39), 3, 5.
[49] Ibid., 1.

comprehensive energy policy and regulation. Despite the transition to renewable energy sources in Australia, the underlying patterns of distributive, racial, and structural inequalities in respect of energy have not been markedly altered by the technological and regulatory transformation around renewable energy. Energy policy is rarely acknowledged to be a decisive influence in socio-economic outcomes, except around political sensitivities such as consumer pricing.[50] Moreover, the dominant policy agenda in Australia readily attributes lower energy prices with fossil fuel energy sources.[51] The challenge is to ensure that in moving to renewable technologies that energy justice outcomes are not subsumed under divisive political positions. In this regard, Preston's central questions are crucial around identifying the energy benefits and burdens to be distributed, and the basis for that distribution to occur; queries that require an understanding of how energy law and governance is organized within Australia.

IV. Legal Frameworks for Energy Governance

In Australia, most energy laws have a statutory basis with specific regimes developed through national energy policy platforms; particularly competition reforms that restructured the conventional state energy utilities in the 1990s. Australia's fossil fuel abundance, and its contribution to substantial economic output,[52] is reflected in energy law and regulation, albeit modified by liberalized energy markets. Energy legislation, until relatively recently, has developed in isolation from the normative models of energy justice. The path dependency on fossil fuels remains an obstacle to implementing successful energy transition policies. Nonetheless, several subnational governments have expansive energy transition and climate change laws.[53] States such as South Australia and Victoria have legislation setting long-term emission reduction targets.[54] In Victoria, the objective is to reach zero net emissions by 2050 and to set an ambitious energy transition agenda.[55] The Victorian government has mainstreamed climate change decision-making and facilitated the closure of a major power plant.[56] The policy and legal framework also engages with the distributional impacts of the introduction of

[50] See Victoria State Government, 'Victorian Government Final Response to the Independent Review of the Electricity & Gas Retail Markets in Victoria' (2018), 4, https://www.energy.vic.gov.au/__data/assets/pdf_file/0034/396583/Independent-and-Bipartisan-Review-of-the-Electricity-and-Gas-Retail-Markets-in-Victoria.pdf accessed 26 August 2019 (hereafter Victorian Government, Final Response to the Independent Review).

[51] See conservative party leader Scott Morrison taking lumps of coal into Federal Parliament to argue for retention of fossil fuels in the energy sector: E. Hunt, 'Scott Morrison and Ray Hadley Laugh About Coal Prop: "Great Stunt"', (13 February 2017) *The Guardian* https://www.theguardian.com/australia-news/2017/feb/13/scott-morrison-and-ray-hadley-laugh-about-coal-prop-great-stunt accessed 26 August 2019.

[52] L. Fahey, '"Lock the Gate": Accessing Private Land for Energy' (2015) 34 *Australian Resources and Energy Law Journal*, 226.

[53] Climate Change Act 2017 (Vic) (n 3).

[54] Ibid.; Climate Change and Greenhouse Emissions Reduction Act 2007 (SA).

[55] A. Calabro, S. Niall, and A. Skarbek, 'The Victorian Climate Change Act: A Model' (2018) 92 *Australian Law Journal*, 814, 816.

[56] Ibid.

transformative energy 'solutions'.[57] Earlier carbon trading legislation at a national level also sought to address the regressive impact of these measures on vulnerable groups in Australian society.[58] While patchy in terms of its implementation across the country, the inclusion of legislative objectives and financial measures to address the social equity implications of energy provision reveal an ongoing concern by Australian policy makers.

A. Sustainability and Energy Justice

To date, sustainability has been the main vehicle in Australian law for developing principles consistent with energy justice. As with many countries, international law was a major driver for the adoption of sustainable development and nascent ideas of energy justice in Australia.[59] 'Ecologically sustainable development' appears in the statutory purposes of much Australian legislation pertinent to energy justice,[60] and it was a guiding principle for Australia's previous forays into carbon pricing legislation.[61] Rarely, due to the balancing formula embedded in the sustainable development concept, will the principle require the institution of substantive legal rules to guide decision-making to require a discrete normative outcome of sustainability (or energy justice).[62] The lack of substantive enforceable obligations suggests it is a form of procedural justice (i.e. a duty on decision makers to consider impacts).[63] Notably, Australia does not have constitutional protection of environmental rights; let alone formalized 'rights to sustainable energy'.

B. The Distributive and Social Justice Implications of Climate Litigation

Doctrinal areas of law such as the tort of negligence[64] continue to be important in achieving social justice via climate litigation and promotion of energy transition.[65] Climate litigation has focused on public interest matters designed to prompt government policy to more adequately meet multilateral instruments, such as the Paris

[57] See, e.g., Victoria State Government, Department of Environment, Land, Water and Planning, 'Victoria's Climate Change Framework' (2016), 29 https://www.climatechange.vic.gov.au/victorias-climate-change-framework accessed 26 August 2019.

[58] Clean Energy Act 2011 (Cth) now repealed.

[59] S. Bruce, 'International Law and Renewable Energy: Facilitating Sustainable Energy for All?' (2013) 14 *Melbourne Journal of International Law*, 18.

[60] See generally Godden, *Environmental Law* (n 45), 61–4.

[61] Clean Energy Act 2011 (Cth) (n 58), s 3.

[62] Godden, *Environmental Law* (n 45), 69–70.

[63] Preston, 'Access to Environmental Justice' (n 39), 1–2, 11–14.

[64] T. Baxter, 'Urgenda-Style Climate Litigation Has Promise in Australia' (2017) 32 *Australian Environment Review*, 70.

[65] J. Peel and H. Osofsky, *Climate Change Litigation: Regulatory Pathways to Cleaner Energy* (Cambridge University Press, 2015).

Agreement.[66] Australia is a prominent jurisdiction in climate actions,[67] although most actions comprise challenges to energy project impact assessments and development approvals.[68] In a landmark decision in 2019, the *Rocky Hill case*,[69] the NSW Land and Environment Court confirmed a planning authority refusal to allow a new open-cut coal mine near Gloucester.[70] That decision was grounded upon negative climate change *and* social impacts.[71] Yet the decision occurred in the context of several contemporary unsuccessful legal challenges to coal mine developments.[72] In the Rocky Hill judgment, the court found a causal connection between the proposed mine and climate change: holding that the project's cumulative greenhouse gas emissions would contribute to the global total of emissions concentrations in the atmosphere.[73] In establishing this link, the court looked to the benefits and burdens that such a mine would impose, particularly for future generations.[74] It favoured distributive justice outcomes in seeking to reduce environmental burdens at a global and local scale. By contrast, the dismissal of community-based and native title challenges to the approvals in the Adani trajectory of climate litigation,[75] gave priority to short-term economic benefits. The very different distributive and social justice outcomes that ensue in the wake of public interest climate litigation highlight the need for legislative reform to more consistently achieve these normative objectives.

Litigation underway in Australia under a social justice theme relates to: carbon risk disclosure by companies;[76] fossil fuel divestment by superannuation funds;[77] and the failure of organizations to take into account climate change impacts that have exacerbated extreme events.[78] Thus, there are a diverse set of legal measures in play to advance energy transition, even given the vacuum in national policy and legal measures. Many measures have implicit social and distributive justice impacts relating to the distribution patterns of energy access and benefits.

66 UN Environment and Columbia Law School, 'The Status of Climate Change Litigation: A Global Review' (May 2017), 8.

67 Ibid., 5, 11.

68 J. Bell-James and S. Ryan, 'Climate Change Litigation in Queensland: A Case Study in Incrementalism' (2016) 33 *Environmental and Planning Law Journal*, 515.

69 *Gloucester Resources Ltd v Minister for Planning* [2019] NSWLEC 7.

70 J. Bell-James, 'Landmark Rocky Hill Ruling Could Pave the Way for More Courts to Choose Climate over Coal', (11 February 2019) *The Conversation* http://theconversation.com/landmark-rocky-hill-ruling-could-pave-the-way-for-more-courts-to-choose-climate-over-coal-111533 accessed 26 August 2019.

71 *Gloucester Resources Ltd v Minister for Planning* (n 69), [270], [422].

72 See the judicial review challenges to the Carmichael (Adani) coal mine in Queensland: Environmental Law Australia, 'Carmichael Coal ("Adani") Mine Cases in Queensland Courts', http://envlaw.com.au/carmichael-coal-mine-case/.

73 *Gloucester Resources Ltd v Minister for Planning* (n 69) [486]–[525].

74 Ibid., [415]–[416], [669].

75 See Environment Protection Biodiversity Conservation Act 1999 (Cth) judicial review actions and the native title action: Environmental Law Australia (n 72).

76 S. Venuti and M. Wilder, 'Obligations on Australian Companies to Address Climate Change' (2018) 92 *Australian Law Journal*, 789, 790.

77 See Commonwealth Courts Portal, 'Applications for File: Mark McVeigh v Retail Employees Superannuation Pty Ltd ACN 001 987 739' (2019), https://www.comcourts.gov.au/file/Federal/P/NSD1333/2018/actions accessed 26 August 2019. See, e.g., *McVeigh v Retail Employees Superannuation Pty Ltd* [2019] FCA 14.

78 A. Forester, A. Macintosh, and J. McDonald, 'Transferable Lessons for Climate Change Adaptation Planning? Managing Bushfire and Coastal Hazards in Australia' (2013) 30 *Environmental and Planning Law Journal*, 469.

C. Human Rights

Human rights frameworks offer another model for examining embedded distributive and social justice energy issues. There is a growing link between the human rights framework and climate/energy justice.[79] Australia's human rights framework however has limited integration into energy law. Australia is a party to the major human rights instruments at international law.[80] Human rights principles, aligned to social justice, are pertinent in relation to climate change impacts upon vulnerable communities. A group of Torres Strait Islanders, who live on islands in north-eastern Australia, are bringing a complaint under the International Covenant on Civil and Political Rights[81] to the United Nations Human Rights Committee against the Australian government on the basis of that government's limited action on climate change.[82] The complaint relates to the rising sea levels on the islands, that threaten the Torres Strait Islanders' rights to culture, the right to a family, and the right to life, and the government's failures to institute effective mitigation nationally, as well as adaptation measures on the islands.

V. Energy Justice and Remote Communities in the Northern Territory

While there has been overt recognition of the social justice implications of climate change for Indigenous communities, there has not been clear acknowledgement of distributive and social justice implications of energy access for Indigenous Australians. Energy access governed by state and territory laws[83] remains problematic for these communities—at times unavailable, unaffordable, or unsustainable.

The Northern Territory is the least populated area in Australia. Much of the territory is held by Traditional Owners under either the Aboriginal Land Rights (Northern Territory) Act 1976 (Cth) or claimed under the Native Title Act 1993 (Cth). A significant number of Aboriginal communities still live on traditional country in locations remote from major centres and reticulated energy supply. The provision of energy, health, and water services to these communities has been substandard for many years, with governments sometimes failing to meet basic service provision. Consequently, the standard of living in these communities lags well behind mainstream Australia.

[79] See Annalisa Savaresi, Chapter 5 in this book.

[80] International Covenant on Civil and Political Rights (16 December 1966) 999 UNTS 171 (entered into force 23 March 1976); International Covenant on Economic, Social and Cultural Rights (16 December 1966) 999 UNTS 3 (entered into force 3 January 1976). See also United Nations Universal Declaration of Human Rights, UNGA Res 217A(III) (10 December 1948); United Nations Declaration on the Rights of Indigenous Peoples, UNGA Res 61/295 (13 September 2007).

[81] International Covenant on Civil and Political Rights (n 80).

[82] See Client Earth, 'Climate Threatened Torres Strait Islanders Bring Human Rights Claim against Australia' (12 May 2019) https://www.clientearth.org/press/climate-threatened-torres-strait-islanders-bring-human-rights-claim-against-australia/ accessed 26 August 2019.

[83] Electricity Industry Act 2004 (WA); Electricity Reform Act 2000 (NT); Electricity Act 1994 (Qld).

Low-income, large-family households that are highly susceptible to energy poverty constituted the highest proportion of households in Australian Indigenous communities.[84] These communities clearly lack a just arrangement of primary social goods. More critically, the situation clearly fits Sen's approach which requires us to identify and address existing inequality as these communities are prevented from using energy 'goods' to enhance their individual and communal capabilities.[85] There have been long-standing calls for more investment in culturally-appropriate economic development in these communities.[86] In this context, the chapter examines two Northern Territory energy transition projects with very different answers in respect of those questions. The first is an expansion of solar energy availability in remote communities, and the other is an unconventional gas project on traditional country.

A. Energy Transition in the Northern Territory

Remote Aboriginal communities in Northern Australia were too remote to be connected to the conventional power grids that were concentrated upon the urban population centres in the south. The relevant governments compromised by installing diesel generators in remote communities as a substitute for an energy grid.[87] These diesel generators have proved to be neither cost effective nor reliable for remote communities. In many instances the price of delivering diesel to these communities is greater than the price of the diesel itself.[88] Renewable energy technologies would seem a solution, but implementation of wind or solar projects still requires considerable funding.

While much of the formal legislation supporting energy transition at a national scale has been dismantled, two significant funding initiatives to support the transition to renewable energy were retained.[89] One of those initiatives is ARENA, a statutory agency established in 2012.[90] ARENA seeks to achieve an 'affordable and reliable renewable energy future' by providing funding to reduce the cost of renewable energy technologies and increasing the clean energy supply.[91] The return on investment for ARENA is not limited to financial profits but can include, for example, 'knowledge sharing' requirements imposed on funding recipients.[92] ARENA previously provided

[84] Hogan and Salt, The Rise of Energy Poverty in Australia (n 4), 6.

[85] Sen, *The Idea of Justice* (n 32).

[86] L. Strelein, et al., 'AIATSIS Submission—Inquiry into the Opportunities and Challenges of Engagement with Traditional Owners in the Economic Development of Northern Australia' (March 2019), https://aiatsis.gov.au/publications/products/aiatsis-submission-inquiry-opportunities-and-challenges-engagement-traditional-owners-economic-development-northern-australia accessed 26 August 2019.

[87] The Australian government has recently announced it may introduce microgrids for remote communities, Paul Osborne, 'Remote communities power up on $50m plan', The Katherine Times, March 27 2019.

[88] T. Yusaf, S. Goh, and J.A. Borserio, 'Potential of Renewable Energy Alternatives in Australia' (2011) 15 *Renewable and Sustainable Energy Reviews*, 2214.

[89] M. Miller, 'Climate Finance and Financial Markets in Australia: The CEFC and ARENA' (2018) 92 *Australian Law Journal*, 822, 823 (hereafter Miller, 'Climate Finance and Financial Markets in Australia').

[90] Australian Renewable Energy Agency Act 2011 (Cth).

[91] Miller, 'Climate Finance and Financial Markets in Australia' (n 89), 823.

[92] Ibid.

finance to off-grid renewable energy for mine projects in remote Australia. [93] More recently, ARENA has helped fund a pilot series of solar projects in remote Aboriginal communities.

1. The Daly River Project

The deployment of solar power to provide 'environmentally friendly, reliable energy' in the Northern Territory is now advancing rapidly.[94] In September 2018, Nauiyu (Daly River), a largely Aboriginal community, became the first town to meet the Territory government's 50 per cent clean energy target. The community is located 200 kilometres from the capital city of Darwin. The community now runs on solar power alone during daylight hours, with savings of almost 400,000 litres of diesel fuel per year resulting in emissions reductions and financial benefits. The project was constructed by Indigenous Essential Services,[95] with over half of the funding provided by ARENA,[96] as part of a Power Water Corporation Solar Energy Transformation Program, which is installing solar power in remote communities. The SETUP scheme, as of April 2019, has introduced solar power into twenty-five remote communities. It aims to reduce diesel use and to provide benefits to communities and their environment.[97] The local Aboriginal community at Daly River see an identification between the sustainable energy outcomes and their community well-being. Nauiyu elder Miriam-Rose Ungunmerr saw the project as fitting with the community's traditional way of life: 'We've always been people that look after nature and now it's amazing with having solar—it's in that mindset of ours in a traditional sense. It's also going to help nature in the long run.'[98]

2. The Northern Territory and Unconventional Gas Projects

While solar projects are advancing renewable energy access for remote communities in the Territory, the region simultaneously is being opened up to unconventional gas exploitation.[99] The Northern Territory government placed a moratorium on shale gas fracking and unconventional gas developments in the jurisdiction. While the moratorium was in place, the Territory government conducted a major scientific inquiry

[93] Ibid., 828.

[94] Australian Government, Australian Renewable Energy Agency, 'NT Solar Energy Transformation Program', https://arena.gov.au/projects/northern-territory-solar-energy-transformation-program/ accessed 25 August 2019.

[95] Indigenous Essential Services Pty Ltd is a not-for-profit subsidiary of the Northern Territory Power and Water Corporation that services twenty major remote towns, fifty-two remote communities, and fifty-seven outstations. See Power and Water Corporation, *Indigenous Essential Services Pty Ltd Annual Report* (2013), 5–6 http://www.territorystories.nt.gov.au/jspui/handle/10070/256400 accessed 26 August 2019.

[96] Australian Government, Australian Renewable Energy Agency (n 94).

[97] PowerWater Northern Territory, https://www.powerwater.com.au/about/news-and-media/news/2019/remote-community-roll-out-of-solar-power-complete accessed 26 August 2019.

[98] N. Cranenburgh, 'Remote Communities Finding Success with Renewable Energy Tech' (30 January 2018) *Create Digital* https://www.createdigital.org.au/remote-communities-renewable-energy/ accessed 26 August 2019.

[99] See K. Vowles, 'Petroleum Legislation Amendment Bill 2018 (NT) First Reading Speech' (Legislative Assembly of the Northern Territory, 29 November 2018) https://legislation.nt.gov.au/api/sitecore/Bill/SC_OtherDoc?itemId=700d6c12-41f0-470f-a9bb-272da2d7466c&type=SpeechBody accessed 24 August 2019

into the impacts of unconventional gas production.[100] The subsequent report provided the basis for lifting the moratorium. The Territory's Chief Minister gave as a rationale that the industry would create jobs, but he insisted that the regulatory regime would be tightly enforced.[101] Many Aboriginal groups did not support the findings of the report.[102] Nonetheless, in mid-2018, the Territory government announced amendments to the petroleum legislation and associated laws to allow shale gas projects across 51 per cent of the Northern Territory.[103] The issue sharply divided local communities.[104] The decision to allow shale gas projects is regarded by some community members as impinging on 'the health, climate and culture of Aboriginal communities and Territorians who are the most threatened by fracking'.[105]

Previously, Traditional Owners in the Territory had sought an injunction and reversal of a fracking approval on Aboriginal land near Mataranka Hot Springs, an area of significant cultural heritage. The Northern Territory government had granted shale gas exploration licences across the region, including a permit over 6,500 square kilometres of Aboriginal land, to Minerals Australia and Jacaranda Minerals in March 2015.[106] Under the Aboriginal Land Rights (Northern Territory) Act 1976 (Cth), Aboriginal owners can veto mining, but this must occur at the exploration phase. The grant of the licence created deep divisions within the Maratanka Aboriginal land trust community, with some individuals indicating that they were not adequately consulted about the scale and risks of a shale gas project.[107] Whether there has been free, prior, and informed consent to agreements that allow the shale gas exploitation to proceed highlights the need for an interplay between procedural and substantive energy justice.

3. Procedural and Distributive Justice

Effective consultation, as procedural justice, is a prerequisite to ensuring that the respective benefits and burdens of energy projects can be assessed by Aboriginal communities, and to better facilitate distributive and social justice outcomes. If we adopt Preston's questions as a benchmark, then it is conceivable to argue that the benefits gained through an energy transition to renewable energy, such as solar installations, may better enhance Aboriginal community well-being and allow for more community capacity-building than unconventional gas projects where most of the benefits typically do not accrue locally. Thus, while unconventional gas extraction is often argued to

[100] See *The Scientific Inquiry into Hydraulic Fracturing in the Northern Territory: Final Report* (27 March 2018), https://frackinginquiry.nt.gov.au/inquiry-reports/final-report accessed 26 August 2019.

[101] '"Betrayed": Aboriginal Communities React to Decision to Allow Fracking in Half of NT' (17 April 2018) *NITV* https://www.sbs.com.au/nitv/article/2018/04/17/betrayed-aboriginal-communities-react-decision-allow-fracking-half-nt accessed 26 August 2019.

[102] In April 2019, the government opened the first environment management plan for onshore shale gas exploration drilling for public comment.

[103] The Petroleum Legislation Amendment Bill 2017 (NT) and Petroleum Legislation Amendment Act 2019 (NT) gave effect to key recommendations from *The Scientific Inquiry Final Report* (n 100).

[104] '"Betrayed"' (n 101).

[105] Seed Indigenous Youth Climate Network National Director Amelia Telford, quoted in '"Betrayed"' (n 101).

[106] The mineral companies are largely owned by one of Australia's wealthiest individuals.

[107] See 'Mataranka', http://dontfracktheterritory.org/community/mataranka/ accessed 18 July 2019.

be a transition energy source, such arguments need to be tested more stringently in relation to securing energy for Aboriginal peoples on traditional country in remote Australia.

VI. Consumer Protection in Liberal Energy Markets in Australia

A. The National Energy Market

Redressing energy poverty in remote and more densely-populated regions in Australia remains a critical distributive and social justice issue. Studies have revealed that some of the poorest households in non-metropolitan regions in states such as Victoria pay substantially higher prices for energy than households in the most affluent suburbs of the capital city.[108] The National Energy Market (NEM) which operates in south-eastern Australia has undergone progressive market liberalization with private operators now predominant.[109] In NEM areas, electricity supply is governed by the National Electricity Law (NEL).[110] Due to federal constitutional arrangements for energy, the national market was set up through the Council of Australian Governments (COAG), an executive policy forum comprised of state and federal ministers.[111] Several NEM institutions operate under the COAG. The Australian Energy Market Operator (AEMO) oversees and facilitates the wholesale electricity market and has a role in national transmission network planning. The Australian Energy Market Commission (AEMC) is responsible for rule-making and market development. A body of energy regulation (see the National Energy Retail Law (South Australia) Act 2011 (SA)) specifically deals with retail energy supply.[112] The Australian Energy Regulator (AER)[113] enforces market rules and regulates networks, including regulating distribution costs to the residential and business sectors and distribution charges regarding access to gas pipelines.[114] The AER also promotes consumer information transparency, including through online price comparison tools.[115] The National Energy Customer Framework (NECF)[116]

[108] A. Carey and B. Preiss, 'Victorian Households on Standard Energy Offers Losing Hundreds a Year' (16 August 2018) *The Age* https://www.theage.com.au/politics/victoria/victorian-households-on-standard-energy-offers-losing-hundreds-a-year-20180815-p4zxoh.html accessed 26 August 2019.

[109] L. Chester, 'The Privatisation of Australian Electricity: Claims, Myths and Facts' (2015) 26 *Economic and Labour Relations Review*, 218.

[110] National Energy Retail Law (South Australia) Act 2011 (SA) pts 2, 5.

[111] Kallies, 'A Barrier for Australia's Climate Commitments?' (n 19).

[112] National Energy Retail Law (South Australia) Act 2011 (SA) (n 110). The relevant provisions of the law in relation to consumer protection and market process are set out by Mostert and Naude, Chapter 9 in this book.

[113] The functions of the AER with respect to energy retail markets is outlined by the Australian Government Australian Energy Regulator, 'Retail Markets', https://www.aer.gov.au/retail-marketsaccessed 2 August 2019.

[114] Australian Government, Australian Energy Regulator, 'My Energy Bill', https://www.aer.gov.au/consumers/my-energy-bill accessed 26 August 2019.

[115] For discussion in relation to vulnerable consumers see Mostert and Naude, Chapter 9 in this book.

[116] The NECF is comprised of the National Energy Retail Law, the National Energy Retail Regulations, and the National Energy Retail Rules. The AER is responsible for NECF monitoring and enforcement. See Australian Government, Department of the Environment and Energy, 'National Energy Customer Framework', https://www.energy.gov.au/government-priorities/energy-markets/national-energy-customer-framework accessed 26 August 2019.

operates in conjunction with the Australian Consumer Law.[117] The NECF comprises a governing framework for the retail sale of electricity and gas to residential and small business energy customers, comprising measures such as an energy ombudsman, guaranteed service level schemes, and community service obligations.[118] The NEM institutional framework relies on mirror legislation promulgated in South Australia and subsequently adopted in jurisdictions participating in the NEM. The NEM is in slow transition away from fossil fuels.

B. Energy Stress and Consumer Protection

In this liberalized, national electricity market, electricity prices for domestic consumers have risen sharply since 2007.[119] Chester in 2013 identified two forces at play: increasing energy use in Australian households, and escalating energy prices.[120] While some policy makers are quick to attribute rising costs to renewable energy market penetration in the electricity sector, research has identified it as only one of several contributing factors.[121] The Australian Competition and Consumer Commission (ACCC) noted '[a]nother major factor in wholesale [electricity] prices has been the significant shortages in competitively priced gas at a time when gas-powered generation would often be the logical source of replacement of lost coal-fired capacity. Gas prices have "doubled or tripled in recent years".'[122] As coal-fired power is removed from the electricity generation profile there is growing reliance on gas generation to maintain reliable and secure supply.[123]

Concerns around energy justice in the NEM-regulated areas relate to relative energy poverty due to the high proportionate cost of energy supply for low-income households and individuals.[124] In other jurisdictions, the term fuel poverty is used.[125] Such concerns resonate with a capabilities approach to distributive justice, in that '[t]he well-being, health and lifestyle of low-income Australian households are suffering from the cumulative effects of ever-increasing electricity bills over a sustained period of many years which has compounded the circumstances of ... vulnerable households'.[126]

While the NECF and the National Electricity Retail Law provide relatively robust consumer protections, continuing concerns about relative deprivation due to lack of

[117] *Competition and Consumer Act 2010* (Cth) sch 2 (the Australian Consumer Law covers areas such as unfair contract terms, misleading and deceptive conduct, and product safety and liability).

[118] For an overview of NECF see Australian Enegery Market Commission (2019), https://www.aemc.gov.au/regulation/energy-rules/national-energy-retail-rules/national-energy-customer-framework, accessed 30 January 2019.

[119] Chester found that 'the average increase in Australian household electricity prices from 2007 to 2013 was nearly 83%': Chester, 'Impacts and Consequences for Low-Income Australian Households' (n 6), 7.

[120] Ibid., 11.

[121] Regarding price escalation, see Australian Competition and Consumer Commission (n 24) 4–23, 32–7.

[122] Ibid., viii.

[123] Ibid., 60–5.

[124] Chester, 'Impacts and Consequences for Low-Income Australian Households' (n 6), 15.

[125] European Commission, EU Energy Poverty Observatory, 'Urban Fuel Poverty' (17 July 2019), https://www.energypoverty.eu/news/urban-fuel-poverty accessed 26 August 2019.

[126] Chester, 'Impacts and Consequences for Low-Income Australian Households' (n 6), 7.

affordable energy are driving further initiatives designed to ensure the national energy laws better reflect energy justice. The moves to distance governments (and the political process) from utility ownership, regulation, and energy price setting as part of a privatization and deregulatory agenda are recognized now as limiting government accountability in protecting energy consumers.

Australian governments therefore are actively 'intervening' to correct market failures in the liberalized energy market under policies that seek to reduce 'price gouging by corporate energy providers'.[127] The premise that increasing competition among energy providers and distributors will necessarily have consumer benefits has proved problematic. Governments typically work through areas of law such as consumer protection to achieve distributive and social justice. Established measures to assist low-income households with energy affordability are rebates, concessions, and temporary government financial assistance.[128] Recent legal and policy reform has focused also on enhancing competition between energy distributors and retailers, the fairness and transparency of energy contracts, as well as boosting consumer information as to the 'cheapest' energy plan.[129] A wider challenge remains to more effectively integrate distributive and social justice models into energy laws. In Preston's designation, it requires energy consumers to have substantive rights to energy at affordable prices.[130]

C. Energy Market Reviews in the National Electricity Market

The challenges of balancing liberalized energy markets in transition with consumer protection can be understood by examining two major reviews of the operation of energy markets in Australia in the last few years. The Commonwealth government commissioned the ACCC to conduct a national inquiry into retail electricity pricing.[131] There was a slightly earlier review in Victoria.[132] Both reviews occurred in the context of escalating electricity and gas prices and acknowledgement of the regressive effect on low-income households and individuals.[133] There are other financial pressures too, as Australians have a very high level of household debt.[134] In metropolitan areas some households severely limit expenditure, including on basic 'goods' such as energy supply.[135] The growing division in Australian society between energy 'haves' and

[127] N. Perpitch, 'Power Retailer Synergy Accused of Price-Gouging Customers up to $100 Million' (3 April 2019) *ABC News* https://www.abc.net.au/news/2019-04-03/power-retailer-synergy-found-to-have-overcharged-customers/10967182 accessed 26 August 2019.

[128] Chester, 'Impacts and Consequences for Low-Income Australian Households' (n 6), 11.

[129] See the Victorian Energy Compare website; ibid., 7.

[130] See Mostert and Naude, Chapter 9 in this book.

[131] Australian Competition, *Restoring Electricity Affordability and Australia's Competitive Advantage* (n 24).

[132] The Victorian government initiated the bipartisan *Independent Review of the Electricity and Gas Retail Markets in Victoria* in November 2016. See (n 50).

[133] Hogan and Salt, The Rise of Energy Poverty in Australia (n 4), 7, note that 'Large low-income households, most exposed to energy poverty, live in the struggle-town suburbs of our biggest cities'.

[134] S. Letts, 'Households Wealth Drops $260b in Just Three Months as Debt Hits a Record 200pc of Income' (29 March 2019) *ABC News* https://www.abc.net.au/news/2019-03-28/australian-household-wealth-down-260-billion-in-december-quarter/10950242 accessed 26 August 2019.

[135] Australian Competition, *Restoring Electricity Affordability and Australia's Competitive Advantage* (n 24), xi.

'have-nots' represents a redrawn class and income disparity that highlights the class dimensions of energy justice in Australia.[136] The political sensitivity of this energy divide is evident in government responses to the reviews, where the rhetoric of consumer empowerment and 'fair go' is prominent.[137]

1. ACCC Retail Pricing Inquiry

The ACCC inquiry undertook a detailed examination of the NEM price escalation. It examined prices in the retail, distribution, and wholesale generation sectors, as well as considering the costs imposed by environmental regulation and energy transition measures.[138] The Inquiry found several factors contributed to the price escalation, including: increasing concentration of ownership of entities in the generation sector; network infrastructure costs; the operation of the RET in distorting investment; and generous solar feed-in tariffs.[139] The Inquiry also scrutinized consumer pricing practices by energy retailers, stating that '[r]etailers have made pricing structures confusing and have developed a practice of discounting which is opaque and not comparable across the market. Standing offers are priced excessively to facilitate this practice, leaving inactive customers paying far more than they need to for electricity'.[140] As well as recommendations to enhance competition in the wholesale market and distribution sectors, the ACCC directed specific attention to reforms in the retail market, acknowledging that increased competition had not forced down prices. The ACCC recommended: replacement of an energy contract 'standing offer' by a lower-priced 'default offer' to be priced no higher than a level determined by the regulator; greater transparency in energy price information; tighter price monitoring via a marketwide regulator; funding to raise awareness of energy pricing comparators; and increased civil penalties for non-compliance by electricity retailers. In terms of vulnerable consumers, the ACCC recommended streamlining and extension of the electricity concession scheme.[141] A set of ministerial principles subsequently were designed to inform rule changes relating to consumer protection regulation. These recommendations included: reduction of regulatory complexity; a focus on consumer outcomes; consumer access to information and resources to make informed decisions; the promotion of fair and reasonable treatment of consumers in engagement with market participants; reduction of the risk of inequity in outcome between consumers in the retail market; and supporting vulnerable consumers to increase their participation in the market.[142] Many of these reforms are now reflected in the NECF.

[136] ACCOS, 'Energy Prices as Share of Disposable Income—A Problem for Low-Income Households' (June 2019) https://www.acoss.org.au/wp-content/uploads/2019/06/ACOSS-briefing-note_energy-prices-as-share-of-disposable-income.pdf accessed 26 August 2019.

[137] Australian Competition, *Restoring Electricity Affordability and Australia's Competitive Advantage* (n 24), iv; Victorian Government, Final Response to the Independent Review (n 50), 4.

[138] Australian Competition, *Restoring Electricity Affordability and Australia's Competitive Advantage* (n 24), 2.

[139] Ibid., ii–xiv.

[140] Ibid., v.

[141] Ibid., xxiii.

[142] Ibid., xxiv;see Mostert and Naude, Chapter 9 in this book.

2. Victorian Retail Energy Market Review

Similar findings and recommendations arose from Victoria's review. Several submissions to the Review raised concerns about energy justice. The Brotherhood of St Laurence, a well-respected charitable NGO, made a submission which highlighted the lack of affordable electricity as energy injustice:

> Central to our approach is—energy is an essential service. Without the services energy enables—heating, cooling, lighting, entertainment—households' health, wellbeing, social and economic participation are all put at risk ... We know the numbers of disconnections have increased—forcing some households to go without energy, at the same time we know other households trade off paying their energy bills with other needs such as buying food or participation in school excursions ... [143]

The dismay at households having to trade off necessities against energy bills highlights how the NGO perceived affordable energy as integral to a capacity-based approach to energy justice. In turn, the charity identified the retail electricity markets as requiring specific attention:

> The retail charges component of energy bills have largely escaped detailed attention. We can only surmise this is because as retail markets have been deregulated and market indicators have suggested competition is working the assumption has been made that the outcomes will be better for consumers. We are concerned that the market has failed to deliver on its full potential. Energy retailers rather than consumers are capturing too much of the value in the market. Changes are needed.[144]

The submission expressly identified the measures used by electricity retailers that were distorting the prices paid by consumers and undermining the Victorian government energy concession scheme.[145] Since that submission, the Brotherhood of St Laurence, in association with community-based welfare organizations, have continued to identify the growing number of Australian households at risk of energy stress.[146] Energy is clearly conceived of as a primary social good that brings benefits, well-being, and a quality of life—and exclusion from these benefits compromises distributive and social justice values. Australian governments are alive to the sensitive political territory where core 'Australian' social values are threatened.

The Victorian government responded quickly,[147] stating that '[t]he Government has heard loud and clear that the deregulated retail energy market is not working

[143] Brotherhood of St Laurence, 'Submission to the Review of Electricity and Gas Retail Markets in Victoria' (March 2017) https://www.energy.vic.gov.au/__data/assets/pdf_file/0031/69466/Brotherhood-of-St-Laurence-Submission-includes-attachment.pdf accessed 26 August 2019.

[144] Ibid., 3.

[145] Ibid.

[146] ACOSS and Brotherhood of St Laurence, 'Energy Stressed in Australia' (October 2018) https://www.acoss.org.au/wp-content/uploads/2018/10/Energy-Stressed-in-Australia.pdf accessed 26 August 2019.

[147] Victorian Government, Final Response to the Independent Review (n 50).

effectively'.[148] All of the Victorian Review's recommendations were accepted and the view that energy was an essential service was clearly reiterated. The centrepiece reform was to 'abolish costly standing offers and require energy retailers to offer a fair price for energy — called the Victorian Default Offer'.[149] Reinforcing a central tenet of energy market reforms in Australia, the response proclaimed that the reforms 'will make energy markets simpler and fairer, improving access to affordable energy for all Victorians'.[150]

The ultimate legislation set a mandatory requirement for energy retailers to provide a basic service offer,[151] with prices no greater than a regulated price set by the Essential Services Commission (ESC).[152] The basic service offer also imposed an obligation of supply on energy providers. Another tranche of reforms related to 'empowering consumers'. The reforms centred on billing information to consumers, including requirements for readily understandable information about costs, and marketing reforms, including a requirement that providers notify customers of the 'best deals'.[153] Victorian energy consumers, as part of recommendations around energy price comparisons, were offered monetary bonuses to check an online energy comparator tool.[154] The reforms set default offer requirements and 'fair' terms.[155] The ESC was directed to review the Energy Retail Code. The Victorian government directed a range of initiatives designed to promote personal energy savings, and a consumer energy data hub,[156] as well as working with the Commonwealth government to introduce a 'Consumer Data Right'.[157]

The Review recommendations specifically addressed low-income and vulnerable energy consumers with recommendations targeted to improving access to information and support for people facing energy hardship, including a review of energy retailers' hardship provisions and an energy brokerage scheme. [158] Finally, the Review highlighted the need for strong market supervision, requiring the Victorian ESC to monitor and report on the competitiveness and efficiency of the Victorian retail energy markets.[159]

[148] For an analysis of Energy Retail Law reforms, see Mostert and Naude, Chapter 9 in this book.
[149] Victorian Government, Final Response to the Independent Review (n 50), 5; Energy Legislation Amendment (Victorian Default Offer) Bill 2019 (Vic).
[150] Ibid., 4.
[151] Ibid., 5; Energy Legislation Amendment (Victorian Default Offer) Act 2019 (Vic) cls 4, 12.
[152] Essential Services Commission, 'Making the Most of the Victorian Default Offer' (2018) https://www.esc.vic.gov.au/making-most-victorian-default-offer accessed 26 August 2019.
[153] Victorian Government, Final Response to the Independent Review (n 50), 6; Essential Services Commission, 'It's Your Energy Victoria' (2018) https://www.esc.vic.gov.au/its-your-energy accessed 26 August 2019 (hereafter Essential Services Commission, 'It's Your Energy Victoria'). Services Commission, 'Energy Rights Campaign Survey Overview' (2018) https://www.esc.vic.gov.au/electricity-and-gas/inquiries-studies-and-reviews/electricity-and-gas-retail-markets-review-implementation-2018/energy-rights-campaign-survey-overview accessed 26 August 2019.
[154] Victorian Government, Final Response to the Independent Review (n 50), 7; Essential Services Commission, 'The Essential Services Commission and Your Energy Rights' (2018) https://www.esc.vic.gov.au/essential-services-commission-and-your-energy-rights.
[155] Victorian Government, Final Response to the Independent Review (n 50), 8.
[156] Ibid., 9.
[157] Treasury Laws Amendment (Consumer Data Right) Bill 2018 (Cth); Treasury Laws Amendment (Consumer Data Right) Bill 2019 (Cth).
[158] Victorian Government, Final Response to the Independent Review (n 50), 10–13.
[159] Ibid., 14.

3. From Consumer Protection to Energy Rights

While the clarion call to ensure energy justice and to strictly regulate the retail energy market resonates through the Victorian government's response to the Review, the new regulatory and financial measures for consumer protection and containment of electricity costs have largely been consistent with a deregulated state. Nonetheless, the ESC website proclaims its more proactive role, stating that it does not just regulate energy but promotes 'your energy interests'.[160] Yet, despite a comprehensive package of reforms centred on consumer energy rights, overall, the legislative scheme does not represent a fundamental restructuring of energy provision in liberalized markets.[161] It is interesting in this context to note the language of energy rights that has emerged from the generic concepts of consumer protection, information access and transparency, competition policy, and contract regulation based around unfair terms that featured in the Victorian review of retail energy markets. Further, while there is a focus on protecting highly vulnerable energy consumers, the legislative reforms are addressed to the entire energy sector (although the retail sector is a specific focus). The reforms, like the NECF, offer 'energy rights' that are only able to be materially realized given the accompanying reforms and directives to the institutional structures that govern energy market operation.

VII. Conclusion

By comparison with the Victorian legislative and financial packages to address distributive and social justice disparities in energy, the Northern Territory solar project measures directed to remote Aboriginal communities are ad hoc, and essentially of an executive/funding character. They are not embedded in a comprehensive distributive justice package that identifies energy burdens on consumers and seeks to 'even up' the relationship between energy providers and energy consumers—despite Aboriginal households being identified as among the most vulnerable of energy consumers in Australia.[162] Instead, the projects represent a small 'intervention' largely made possible through technological energy transition rather than any significant redistribution of energy benefits and burdens. The benefits ensuing to these remote communities through energy transition need to be offset against the burdens that will shift to other Aboriginal communities in the Territory as unconventional gas extraction and fracking are instigated over a land mass where a large proportion of the land is held under various forms of Aboriginal 'tenure'. Further, this extraction will provide ready access to gas for energy consumers in markets far distant from where the energy burdens are located. Thus, while the transition to gas may accrue abstract benefits at a global scale,

[160] Essential Services Commission, 'It's Your Energy Victoria' (n 153).

[161] Z. Gillam, 'A Basic Service Offer is a Quick Fix for the Energy Mess' (20 August 2018) *The Age* https://www.theage.com.au/national/victoria/a-basic-service-offer-is-a-quick-fix-for-the-energy-mess-20180817-p4zy78.html accessed 26 August 2019.

[162] Hogan and Salt, The Rise of Energy Poverty in Australia (n 4), 7.

the existing energy injustice on a racial basis in the Northern Territory remains largely intact.

A robust model of energy justice needs to consider justice as recognition—to make explicit who (and on what criteria) shares in the benefits and burdens of the distribution of primary energy 'goods' in Australia. In the NEM-governed areas of the south-east, there is a growing acknowledgement of a substantive right to energy (and perhaps even to affordable energy as a regulatory determined quantum). The reforms centred on regulated service provision and prices are recently implemented, so it is difficult yet to judge their effectiveness. Even so, to achieve energy justice in Australia will require moving beyond a narrowly defined concept of sustainable development to include a more holistic model that comprehensively engages the political, social, economic, and legal factors at play.

PART V

ACCESS TO ENERGY, POVERTY, AND DISTRIBUTIVE JUSTICE

12

Energy Justice and the Design of Climate Change Legislation

Avoiding Regressive Measures

Barry Barton and Jennifer Campion

I. Introduction

Energy justice can be debated in the abstract but at some stage one asks, as one does with any question of justice, whether our laws can be arranged to produce results that are more just, and to avoid results that are less just. We ask that question in relation to laws and policies that attempt to mitigate climate change, reducing the emissions of greenhouse gases. Although there is extensive literature on equity *between* states in their contributions to climate change mitigation, less consideration has been given to advancing equity and energy justice *within* states as they struggle to choose and enact legislation to address climate change.

We are pulled different ways to combat climate change and to avoid adverse effects on low-income households. Energy poverty may or may not describe the situation of low-income households, but it is not necessary to use that concept to analyse energy justice and the avoidance of adverse effects on the poor. Nor is it necessary to state the matter as one of energy access, which is the subject of Goal 7 of the United Nations Sustainable Development Goals of 2015, and which can be seen as being in tension with Goal 13, combatting climate change. However energy justice concerns the distribution of wealth and income; one of the most basic questions of social justice in any society. It seems desirable to ask what we can do to make sure that climate change policies advance energy justice.

Our specific concern within energy justice is the distributional effect of different climate change mitigation policies, and in particular whether policies are progressive or regressive in their effects on the wealth and income of individuals and households. We need climate change policies to be effective and efficient; but we also need them to be equitable. The matter has not been as thoroughly analysed as one might expect; much of the existing literature focuses on a policy's efficacy as an instrument to meet national targets, implicitly leaving questions of household well-being to the social welfare system. We believe that effects on households must be more central than that in climate change policy making.

Barry Barton and Jennifer Campion, Energy Justice and the Design of Climate Change Legislation In: *Energy Justice and Energy Law.* Edited by Íñigo Del Guayo, Lee Godden, Donald N. Zillman, Milton Fernando Montoya, and José Juan González, Oxford University Press (2020). DOI: 10.1093/oso/9780198860754.003.0012

Our analysis is rooted in the politics and economics of distribution; the distribution of wealth or income in society, between the rich, the middle-income households, and the poor. We adopt the conventional terminology of economic and policy literature; policies that improve the situation of low-income households relative to high-income houses are 'progressive' and policies that do the opposite are 'regressive'. Policies that affect both equally are 'proportionate'. This terminology has long been used in the analysis of policies in fields such as taxation.[1] From an energy justice point of view we are keen to avoid policies with regressive characteristics. There are sound reasons for doing so; it advances fairness and justice; it actually improves the effectiveness of policies in some circumstances, as we shall see; and it increases political acceptance. Climate change is always a political challenge. As the recent Australian election showed, it is divisive and it can be decisive.[2] If significant numbers of voters are alienated because policy measures seem to penalize low-income and middle-income households, and impose relatively light burdens on high-income households, then the politics of envy will be hard to resist.

Our analysis draws particularly on thinking about the issues in economics, and seeks to make interdisciplinary connections to improve our law-making. In particular we use reviews carried out by Garnaut,[3] McInnes,[4] and Zachmann, Fredriksson, and Claeys,[5] because of their particular focus on distributional questions. Garnaut, who carried out an influential study in Australia, concentrated mainly on emissions trading systems; McInnes concentrated on other policy measures, while Zachmann and colleagues made a broad review of the literature and noted a number of research gaps. These reviews and other literature find that many policy options have the potential to be regressive in effect, so there is a substantial challenge to be met. But as Zachmann and colleagues point out, doing nothing will harm everyone, and low-income households in particular; 'non-action cannot be the answer'.[6]

Two points can be addressed briefly before we proceed to consider the various policy options. The first is the international dimension. As we noted above there is an extensive literature on equity between states,[7] but in considering equity within states, our main problem, we find that the effect of policies in different countries is often

[1] For example, D.M. Suits, 'Measurement of Tax Progressivity' (1977) 67 *American Economic Review*, 747.

[2] For example, D. Cave, 'It Was Supposed to Be Australia's Climate Change Election. What Happened?', *New York Times* (online edition, 19 May 2019) accessed 20 December 2019.http://www.nytimes.com.

[3] R. Garnaut, *The Garnaut Climate Change Review: Final Report* (Cambridge University Press, 2008) (hereafter Garnaut, *Garnaut Climate Change Review*).

[4] G. McInnes, 'Understanding the Distributional and Household Effects of the Low-Carbon Transition in G20 Countries' (Final Report, 2017) available http://www.oecd.org accessed 11 July 2019 (hereafter McInnes, 'Distributional and Household Effects of the Low-Carbon Transition'). As to price measures, McInnes addresses energy, transport and carbon taxation, although not emissions trading schemes.

[5] G. Zachmann, G. Fredriksson, and G. Claeys, *The Distributional Effects of Climate Policies* (Bruegel, 2018) (hereafter Zachmann, et al., *Distributional Effects of Climate Policies*).

[6] Ibid., 7.

[7] See, e.g., P. Baer, 'Equity, Greenhouse Gas Emissions, and Global Common Resources', in S. Schneider, et al., (eds), *Climate Change Policy: A Survey* (Island Press, 2002); B. Metz, 'International equity in climate change policy' (2000) 1 *Integrated Assessment*, 111–26; S. Vanderheiden, 'Climate Change Mitigation, a Problem of Injustice', in *World Social Science Report 2013: Changing Global Environments* (OECD, 2013) https://sciencepolicy.colorado.edu accessed 11 July 2019; M.B. Richards, E. Wollenberg, and D. van Vuuren, 'National Contributions to Climate Change Mitigation from Agriculture: Allocating a Global Target' (2018) 18 *Climate Policy*, 1271–85.

different.[8] For developed countries, evidence suggests that in many cases climate policies are regressive.[9] This is because low-income households 'display higher expenditure for carbon intensive goods to satisfy basic needs like heating and transportation'.[10] The result is that low-income households would lose a higher share of their consumption than high-income households. Losing a given percentage of income is a more serious concern for poorer households with narrow margins to live on, even if in absolute terms they pay less for climate policy. However, for developing countries, the profile of the consumption of carbon-intensive goods across income groups may mean that climate policies have a progressive direct effect. This is because the poorer households are not the primary consumers of those carbon-intensive goods, so a climate policy that removes such subsidies would be expected to be progressive because it would affect high-income households more than proportionately.[11] For example, Nigeria's petrol subsidy is considered highly regressive,[12] so a climate policy that involved its removal would be expected to result in a progressive outcome.

The second point concerns time. Climate change itself is likely to affect the distribution of incomes, reducing the income of poor households relative to others, but most of its effects will not come for some decades.[13] On the other hand, policies to mitigate climate change may also adversely affect the income of households, especially low-income ones, but the effect comes sooner. The question of the distribution of costs and benefits over time, over present and future generations, is a difficult one; how does one evaluate present-day action in relation to future effects, and how does one value uncertain future damage?[14] Strictly speaking the analysis of progressive and regressive characteristics needs to be projected over time to be accurate.[15] But the more immediate political problem is that policy measures may impose costs in the short term that weigh particularly on middle-income and low-income households, even if the measures are for their long-term good.[16]

[8] McInnes, 'Distributional and Household Effects of the Low-Carbon Transition' (n 4), 15, makes a brief but valuable analysis of some of the literature on this point.

[9] A.M. Bento, 'Equity Impacts of Environmental Policy', (2013) 5 *Annual Review of Resource Economics*, 181–96; A.M. Bento, L.H. Goulder, E. Henry, M.R. Jacobsen, and R.H. von Haefen, 'Distributional and Efficiency Impacts of Gasoline Taxes: An Econometrically Based Multi-Market Study' (2005) 95 *American Economic Review*, 282–7; M. Wier, K. Birr-Pedersen, H.K. Jacobsen, and J. Klok, 'Are CO2 Taxes Regressive? Evidence from the Danish Experience' (2005) 52 *Ecological Economics*, 239–51.

[10] T.D. Nguyen, O. Edenhofer, G. Grimalda, M. Jakob, D. Klenert, G. Schwerhoff, and J. Siegmeier, 'Policy Options for a Socially Balanced Climate Policy' (17 March 2017) *G20 Insights* http://www.g20-insights.org accessed 11 July 2019.

[11] A. Dennis, 'Household Welfare Implications of Fossil Fuel Subsidy Reforms in Developing Countries' (2016) 96 *Energy Policy*, 597–606.

[12] I. Soile and X. Mu, 'Who Benefit Most from Fuel Subsidies? Evidence from Nigeria' (2015) 87 *Energy Policy*, 314–24. Similarly, progressive policies are anticipated as a result of the application of carbon price policies in China and India: M. Brenner, M. Riddle, and J.K. Boyce 'A Chinese Sky Trust?: Distributional Impacts of Carbon Charges and Revenue Recycling in China' (2007) 35 *Energy Policy*, 1771–84; A. Datta, 'The Incidence of Fuel Taxation in India' (2010) 32 *Energy Economics*, S26–33.

[13] Garnaut, *Garnaut Climate Change Review* (n 3), 385.

[14] M.A. Cohen, D. Fullerton, and R.H. Topel (eds), *Distributional Aspects of Energy and Climate Policies* (Edward Elgar, 2013): a compilation of papers from a 2010 seminar exploring issues implicit in climate change proposals in the US Congress and the assertion that the proposals would adversely affect low-income households.

[15] R.J. Lazarus, 'Super Wicked Problems and Climate Change: Restraining the Present to Liberate the Future' (2009) 94 *Cornell Law Review*, 1153, at 1157.

[16] J. Boston, 'Climate Change Policy' in Hayward (ed.) *New Zealand Government and Politics* (6th ed, OUP, 2015). See also D. Held and A. Hervey, 'Democracy, Climate Change and Global Governance: Democratic Agency

II. Carbon Pricing: The Effects of Carbon Taxes, Emissions Trading Schemes, and Fuel Taxes

Carbon pricing refers generically to policy instruments that put a price on carbon dioxide emissions, whether it be in the form of carbon taxes, emissions trading schemes, or fuel taxes. (For example, British Columbia in Canada has a Carbon Tax Act;[17] and the European Union has a large Emissions Trading System established under Directives.)[18] The price instrument is generally regarded as a very efficient policy measure, sending a signal right through the economy but allowing individual companies and people to choose how to respond to it. Nearly all G20 countries have implemented, or are considering implementing, some form of carbon pricing.[19] However there is a risk that the price signal will not fall equitably in society. The *gilets jaunes* ('yellow vests') movement in France emerged in response to the rising fuel taxes which the government introduced with the intention of encouraging the use of more environment-friendly vehicles. According to the *gilets jaunes*, rising fuel prices hit workers who depend on cars to get to and from work, particularly those who live in the countryside. In their view, the policy disproportionately affected the rural poor, in contrast to the city-dwelling 'elite'. There is a risk of a social backlash against price measures if they seem unfair.[20]

A number of analysts such as Garnaut conclude that the price effects of an emissions trading scheme are likely to fall heavily on low-income households.[21] Scheme participants such as petrol companies and electricity companies are often able to pass price increases straight through to consumers, especially if there is low price elasticity and few options available to consumers. Zachmann, Fredriksson, and Claeys come to a similar conclusion. Lower-income households spend a larger share of their income on emissions-intensive products such as heat and power, and are less able to switch to less emissions-intensive substitutes.[22] There is much evidence to support this conclusion.[23]

and the Policy Issue', in D. Held, A. Hervey, and M. Theros (eds), *The Governance of Climate Change: Science, Economics, Politics and Ethics* (Polity Press, 2011).

[17] Carbon Tax Act, SBC 2008 c 40.

[18] Directive 2003/87/EC of the European Parliament and of the Council of 13 October 2003 establishing a system for greenhouse gas emission allowance trading within the Union and amending Council Directive 96/61/EC, as amended several times: see https://ec.europa.eu/clima/policies/ets_en#Legislative_history, accessed 15 July 2019.

[19] World Bank and Ecofys, *State and Trends of Carbon Pricing* (World Bank, 2018), available online from: https://openknowledge.worldbank.org.

[20] S. Tagliapietra and G. Zachmann, 'Des politiques climatiques plus justes sont possibles' (14 December 2018) *Le Monde* http://www.lemonde.fr; P. Botsford, 'Climate Justice: French "Gilet Jaunes" Protests Provide Lessons for Countries Transitioning to Low-carbon Economies' (February/March 2019) *IBA Global Insight* http://www.ibanet.org/ accessed 11 July 2019.

[21] Garnaut, *Garnaut Climate Change Review* (n 3), 385.

[22] Zachmann, et al., *Distributional Effects of Climate Policies* (n 5), 32. Carbon prices also affect returns to capital and labour as factors of production, and the effects are likely to be slightly progressive although the pattern is a mixed one.

[23] See the discussion in Zachmann, et al., *Distributional Effects of Climate Policies* (n 5) on this point, but see also the discussion by S. Carattini, M. Carvalho, and S, Fankhauser, for the Grantham Institute: 'How to make carbon taxes more acceptable' (Grantham Institute Policy Report, December 2017) http://www.lse.ac.uk/GranthamInstitute accessed 11 July 2019.

Lower-income households use less electricity and gas than rich ones, but not that much less (demand is inelastic), and they have fewer choices in the housing market and less chance of buying modern appliances. On the European Union Emissions Trading System (ETS) Zachmann et al. identify specific problem features that transfer wealth from governments and households to firms.[24] One is the cheap but sometimes worthless international credits that corporations are sometimes allowed to use; another is the undue allocation of free allowances to trade-exposed industries, which can take the profits when they can impose the carbon charge on customers; and another is indirect-cost compensation for electricity-intensive firms. Even apart from equity considerations, these features can all be regarded as weaknesses in the design of ETS systems, but the equity dimension is striking when an ETS treats households and small businesses as captive default participants who are obliged to carry the costs while other sectors do not. Free allocation of credit units in an ETS is another problem; equity demands that they should more often be auctioned and not grandparented for free.

Other price instruments present similar problems. Feed-in tariffs provide an advantageous price for wind and solar electricity, but they are strongly regressive if they are paid for by households but not energy-intensive industries.[25] This can happen if households are not entitled to exemptions to the higher prices that are available to industrial companies.[26]

But law reformers and policy makers have choices. Garnaut observes that emissions trading schemes are not intended to make large, arbitrary transfers of wealth, especially regressive changes in income distribution.[27] There is a clear duty for the government that designs the scheme also to ensure distributive efficiency and to address the social welfare implications of the scheme on those people who are most affected and least able to respond. Zachmann et al. make the same point. Policy makers can choose to rebalance electricity and gas tariffs that supply energy at much higher prices to households than to industrial consumers.

Equally, there are positive elements in price instruments. Price pressure through an energy tax may be less regressive than energy efficiency standards (which are considered below).[28] A carbon tax may skew costs more towards high-income households than do clean energy credits, which are strongly skewed towards those households.[29] McInnes believes that the widespread concern that energy taxes and carbon taxes are regressive mainly stems from country-specific studies that are not always generalizable.[30] Studies on the effects of gasoline taxes in the United States, for example, have been carried out where there is high average income, high vehicle ownership, long

[24] Zachmann, et al., *Distributional Effects of Climate Policies* (n 5), 78.
[25] Ibid., 9, 78, 93.
[26] P. Grösche and C. Schröder, 'On the Redistributive Effects of Germany's Feed-in Tariff' (2014) 46 *Empirical Economics*, 1339–83.
[27] Ibid., 393.
[28] A. Levinson, 'Energy Efficiency Standards are More Regressive than Energy Taxes: Theory and Evidence', (Working Paper 22956) (2016) *National Bureau of Economic Research*.
[29] Ibid., 212.
[30] McInnes, 'Distributional and Household Effects of the Low-Carbon Transition' (n 4), 14.

commuting distances, and limited public transport. A tax on cooking gas in India is found to be regressive for urban middle-expenditure groups, but strongly progressive in rural areas. There is a great deal of context and complexity to take into account.

III. Recycling Revenues from Putting a Price on Carbon

A number of researchers conclude that price policies can be made much more progressive in their effect by recycling the income that is derived under the policy.[31] In an emissions trading scheme, the revenue from sales or auctions of units is one such source; in a carbon tax scheme, the revenue is even more readily identifiable. McInnes makes an overview that shows that if a significant part of revenue is handed back then negative distributional effects can avoided.[32] The revenue can be used to provide lump sum transfers or fuel payments to low-income households; increased benefit payments using existing social support schemes; or targeted social tariffs for energy utility billing. The recycling of revenues to households can offset the potential regressive distributional effects of climate policy.[33] Switzerland currently does this via a 'carbon dividend' paid to households, which is proportionately more valuable to lower-income households since all households receive the same amount.[34] Alternately, a 'revenue neutral' approach can be taken, which would use the revenues from carbon pricing to reduce existing 'distortionary taxes', such as income tax.[35] California recycles revenue from smog abatement fees, vehicle registration fees, equipment plate fees, and cap-and-trade auction proceeds, and does so on a large scale; in the 2015–16 year it distributed US$127,810,300 to clean vehicle owners and lessees.[36]

Williams, Gordon, Burtrow, Carbone, and Morgenstern find that the initial regressive effect of carbon taxes depends greatly on how the carbon tax revenue is used.[37] Lump sum rebates to households are effective for this purpose, benefitting the first three income quintiles; but using the revenue to reduce labour income taxes is also effective. Governments can also make use of funds that are released through the removal of a subsidy, and redeploy them to promote development goals in health care, education,

[31] Garnaut, *Garnaut Climate Change Review* (n 3), 386 et seq; Zachmann, et al., *Distributional Effects of Climate Policies* (n 5), 88.

[32] McInnes, 'Distributional and Household Effects of the Low-Carbon Transition' (n 4), 18.

[33] T.D. Nguyen, O. Edenhofer, G. Grimalda, M. Jakob, D. Klenert, G. Schwerhoff, and J. Siegmeier, 'Policy Options for a Socially Balanced Climate Policy' (17 March 2017) *G20 Insights* http://www.g20-insights.org accessed 11 July 2019.

[34] For a recent consideration of the Swiss carbon dioxide levy, see L. Ott and S. Weber, 'The Impact of CO2 Taxation on Swiss Households' Heating Demand' (IRENE Working paper 18-09) (University of Neuchatel Institute of Economic Research, 21 December 2018).

[35] D. Klenert, G. Schwerhoff, O. Edenhofer, and L. Mattauch, 'Environmental Taxation, Inequality and Engel's Law: The Double Dividend of Redistribution' (2016) *Environmental and Resource Economics*, 1–20, as cited in: T.D. Nguyen, O. Edenhofer, G. Grimalda, M. Jakob, D. Klenert, G. Schwerhoff, and J. Siegmeier, 'Policy Options for a Socially Balanced Climate Policy' (17 March 2017) *G20 Insights* http://www.g20-insights.org accessed 11 July 2019.

[36] Clean Vehicle Rebate Project, *Final Report Fiscal Year 2015–2016*, (Center for Sustainable Energy. Prepared under Grant G-15-LCTI-01 for the California Air Resources Board).

[37] R.C. Williams III, H. Gordon, D. Burtrow, J.C. Carbone and, R.D. Morgenstern, 'The Initial Incidence of a Carbon Tax Across Income Groups' (2015) 68 *National Tax Journal*, 195.

and infrastructure.[38] Garnaut recognizes that there is a case for coal-producing regions to obtain special support for employment and structural assistance.[39]

It seems very arguable that schemes to recycle revenue must be regarded as essential and integral components of climate change law and policy. They cannot be regarded as luxuries or mere political devices.

IV. Consumer Fuel Subsidies

Subsidies for fossil fuel consumers are a particularly challenging question; and so is their removal. Where they exist they are enormously popular and they make it easier for low-income households to meet their energy needs for cooking, transport, and farming.[40] But they increase the amount of the fossil fuel that is consumed, beyond normal market conditions, and so they increase greenhouse gas emissions. They are also expensive, and there is a global trend to reduce them.[41] The over-consumption and market distortion can produce energy shortages. In Myanmar (Burma), fixed prices for electricity, diesel, and petrol have resulted in shortages when those prices fall below international market levels.[42] However if these shortcomings lead to the removal of subsidies without appropriate measures being put in place, there is a risk of adverse effects on low-income households that rely upon the subsidies.[43]

Fuel subsidies are prone to being captured by people who were not intended to be the beneficiaries. For example, a recent study of Indian subsidies found that, of the US$22.5 billion spent on fossil fuel subsidies in 2010, less than US$2 billion benefitted the poorest 20 per cent of the population.[44] The story seems to be a common one wherever incentives are poorly designed. Instead of subsidising the fuel, the policy measure can be devised to subsidize a household, and in doing so it can target the subsidy accurately for the households that really need it. In 2016, India introduced a direct cash transfer scheme for residential kerosene consumers and launched a programme to raise kerosene prices progressively.[45] Indonesia is removing electricity subsidies,

[38] A. Dennis 'Household Welfare Implications of Fossil Fuel Subsidy Reforms in Developing Countries' (2016) 96 *Energy Policy*, 597–606; K. Siddig, A. Aguiar, H. Grethe, P. Minor, and T. Walmsley, 'Impacts of Removing Fuel Import Subsidies in Nigeria on Poverty' (2014) 69 *Energy Policy*, 165–78.

[39] Garnaut, *Garnaut Climate Change Review* (n 3), 396.

[40] B. Sovacool, 'Reviewing, Reforming, and Rethinking Global Energy Subsidies: Towards a Political Economy Research Agenda', (2017) 135 *Ecological Economics*, 150–63.

[41] Their total global cost to governments in 2017 is estimated at more than $300 billion, although the figure has been declining due to reforms in a number of countries: International Energy Agency, *World Energy Outlook 2018*, 55, 110.

[42] B. Sovacool, 'Reviewing, Reforming, and Rethinking Global Energy Subsidies: Towards a Political Economy Research Agenda', (2017) 135 Ecological Economics, 150–63, at 156.

[43] N.D Rao, 'Kerosene Subsidies in India: When Energy Policy Fails as Social Policy' (2012) 16 *Energy for Sustainable Development*, 35–43; K. Siddig, A. Aguiar, H. Grethe, P. Minor, and T. Walmsley, 'Impacts of Removing Fuel Import Subsidies in Nigeria on Poverty' (2014) 69 *Energy Policy*, 165–78.

[44] M. Lockwood, 'Fossil Fuel Subsidy Reform, Rent Management and Political Fragmentation in Developing Countries' (2015) 20 *New Political Economy*, 475–94.

[45] International Energy Agency, *World Energy Outlook 2018*, 111.

leaving customers in lower-income brackets eligible for subsidies and promoting efficient appliances.[46]

V. Transport Generally and Electric Vehicles Specifically

Policies for emission reductions from transport policies, and the promotion of electric vehicles (EVs) in particular, offer clear examples of how equity and distribution can be promoted or neglected. In many G20 countries transport affordability is central to the lives of low-income households, which can spend 10 per cent to 12 per cent on public transport where it is available, and where it is not they may be 'forced' into car ownership, and can commit as much as 50 per cent of household expenditure to transport.[47] Depending on the settlement pattern of the region where they live, low-income households may have few opportunities to reduce private vehicle use. Long commutes can be a way of life for people in precarious employment. The likely result is that a transport fuel charge will be strongly regressive. In an urban population, however, or in a less wealthy country, it can be progressive. The land transport policy picture also depends on the availability of transport options such as active transport (walking and cycling) and public transport. On the other hand, carbon charges on air transport are very likely to be progressive in effect.[48] Also capable of producing progressive effects is the 'feebate' system where a fee is charged when a high-emissions vehicle is registered and a rebate is given for a low-emission vehicle, the revenue from the fees paying for the rebates.[49]

If we turn more specifically to EVs we find some striking issues in policy design. In New Zealand, the Road User Charges Act 2012 has been used to exempt EV owners from paying the road user charge which funds the construction and maintenance of the road transport system.[50] The incentive does not bring down the size of the initial investment, so the purchaser must be able to afford the higher capital cost of the EV before getting access to the annual savings. This is common in EV incentives globally. In the United States, EVs are encouraged by a federal income tax credit for purchasers, ranging between US$2,500 and US$7,500 depending on the size of the vehicle battery.[51] The key point is that the credit is not refundable, so it is of little benefit to people who have low tax liabilities. The Congressional Budget Office estimated that for the tax year 2011, only about 20 per cent of potential tax filers had a federal income tax liability of US$7,500 or more, and only about 40 per cent had liability of US$2,500 or more, to set

[46] International Energy Agency, *Energy Efficiency 2018*, 155.

[47] McInnes, 'Distributional and Household Effects of the Low-Carbon Transition' (n 4), 7.

[48] Zachmann, et al., *Distributional Effects of Climate Policies* (n 5), 39.

[49] J. German and D. Meszler, *Best Practices for Feebate Program Design and Implementation* (International Council for Clean Transportation, 2010); B. Barton and P. Schütte, 'Electric Vehicle Law and Policy: a Comparative Analysis' (2017) 35 *Journal of Energy and Natural Resources Law*, 147.

[50] Road User Charges (Exemption Period for Light Electric RUC Vehicles) Order 2012. For a typical car driver driving 14,000 km the charge is NZD 812 per annum.

[51] 26 USC § 30D; the credit survived the tax reform of 2017. It is restricted to the first 200,000 vehicles sold by each manufacturer in the US.

off against the credit.[52] A later study showed that taxpayers with adjusted gross income under US$75,000 (the bottom 80 per cent of filers) received little more than 10 per cent of the credit money; those over US$75,000 (the top income quintile) received about 90 per cent of it, and the average credit amount for those over US$200,000 was three times as high as the amounts received in any other category.[53] The incentive could have been organized differently. If it had been a fully-refundable credit, low-income taxpayers could have claimed its full value, receiving any surplus as a refund. If it had been structured as a direct point-of-purchase rebate it would have benefitted all purchasers. [54] There was no coherent economic rationale for making these credits non-refundable.[55] The incentive need not have been designed to benefit the wealthy and stay out of reach of the poor.

In contrast, California has a rebate system that was originally $2,500 for battery EVs and $1,500 for plug-in hybrid EVs for all purchasers, but was modified in 2016 with a cap for high-income households and an extra rebate for low-income households.[56] (The rebate is under the Clean Vehicle Rebate Project, which is funded under several different laws.)[57]

Modelling research has compared a flat rebate of this kind with one that is based on a progressive rate schedule that varies with purchaser income. The progressive rate rebate would result in the same number of EVs being sold, but more cost-effectively (programme cost per additional vehicle of $22,743 rather than $30,017) and with much greater allocative equity.[58] Adding a price cap of $60,000 on the vehicles eligible would further increase programme cost-effectiveness ($21,349) and would dramatically reduce the overall cost of the programme.

The first point that one can take from these examples, which are quite typical EV incentives, is that climate change incentives can be designed with greater and lesser

[52] Congressional Budget Office, *Effects of Federal Tax Credits for the Purchase of Electric Vehicles* (September 2012), 25: for the tax year 2011, with tax filers including people who do not file because they were below the income threshold. The CBO also found that the credit may have little effect because of the pressure that corporate average fuel efficiency standards put on vehicle manufacturers.

[53] S. Borenstein and L.W. Davis, 'The Distributional Effects of US Clean Energy Tax Credits' (2016) 30 *Tax Policy and the Economy*, 191 at 205, 209, 211. They find that this credit is more concentrated in the higher income categories than other clean energy credits, but that such credits generally, as tax 'expenditures', are much more concentrated there than other tax credit and deduction policies.

[54] Many studies show that this is the most effective kind of incentive: K. Gallagher and E. Muehlegger, 'Giving Green to Get Green? Incentives and Consumer Adoption of Hybrid Vehicle Technology' (2011) 61 *Journal of Environmental Economics and Management*, 1.

[55] S. Borenstein and L.W. Davis, 'The Distributional Effects of US Clean Energy Tax Credits' (2016) 30 *Tax Policy and the Economy*, 191 at 218.

[56] California Environmental Protection Agency, Air Resources Board, *Proposed Fiscal year 2015–16 Funding Plan for Low Carbon Transportation Investments and the Air Quality Improvement Program* (California Clean Vehicle Rebate Project, 2015) http://www.cleanvehiclerebate.org accessed 6 March 2019. The cap is $150,000 gross annual income for single filers, $204,000 for head-of-household filers, $300,000 for joint filers. The $2,000 rebate increase is available where the household income is not greater than 300 per cent of the federal poverty level. (All references in this paragraph are to US dollars.)

[57] California Alternative and Renewable Fuel, Vehicle Technology, Clean Air and Carbon Reduction Act of 2007, c 750 Cal Statutes 2007 (AB 118) amending the California Health and Safety Code and Vehicle Code and the Greenhouse Gas Reduction Fund created pursuant to §16428.8 of the Government Code of California.

[58] J.R. DeShazo, T.L. Sheldon, and R.T. Carson, 'Designing Policy Incentives for Cleaner Technologies: Lessons from California's Plug-in Electric Vehicle Rebate Program' (2017) 84 *Journal of Environmental Economics and Management*, 18. The schedule modelled was: income less than $25,000, rebate of $7,500; $25,000–$50,000, rebate of $5,000; $50,000–$75,000, rebate of $2,000; over $75,000, no rebate. (All US dollars.)

degrees of allocative equity. Incentives need not only help the well-to-do to buy EVs;[59] they need not be regressive and wasteful. Any extra complexity in linking an incentive to household income must be weighed against the benefits of reducing inequity and waste in the use of public funds.

The second point is that paying attention to allocative equity can often produce greater efficacy and greater programme cost-effectiveness. DeShazo observes that emission reductions will be greater if incentives reach low-income consumers, because they tend to drive more polluting vehicles, drive them further, and exhibit less propensity to buy clean vehicles; low-income households are more likely than high-income ones to be influenced by the existence of an incentive. Poorly-designed policies transfer public funds to wealthy vehicle buyers who would have bought low-emissions vehicles anyway.[60]

VI. Energy Efficiency Measures

Energy efficiency actions are among the most effective policy measures that can be taken to reduce greenhouse gas emissions.[61] They can improve performance in many fields of energy supply and demand, such as housing, appliances, lighting, heating and cooling, and transport, in residential, industrial, and commercial situations. They offer substantial co-benefits in health, pollution reduction, economic growth, and energy security.[62] Many energy efficiency improvements pay for themselves even without taking the climate and environmental benefits into account; they are what can be called cost-negative.[63] They should benefit low-income households, but their uptake is often slow. Low-income households lack the capital to make an investment that will pay off over time; they are very adverse to risk when a mistake could be ruinous. They often do not have the leeway in their lives to alter their circumstances, and their energy use patterns are controlled by where they live, what kind of house they live in, what kind of work they can get, what kind of appliances they can afford, and how often they can update them. Policy measures must be adapted to these realities. For example a subsidy scheme to buy better appliances may fail if low-income households still cannot pay their share of the project. A scheme that pays the full cost may be more successful. Such energy efficiency schemes are a prime opportunity for recycling revenues from carbon charges. They can therefore be very progressive in their distributional effect. There has been criticism of energy efficiency policies for being more regressive than carbon charges,

[59] M. Nilsson and B. Nykvist, 'Governing the Electric Vehicle Transition—Near Term Interventions to Support a Green Energy Economy' (2016) 179 *Applied Energy*, 1360.

[60] J.R. DeShazo, 'Improving Incentives for Clean Vehicle Purchases in the United States: Challenges and Opportunities' (2016) 10 *Review of Environmental Economics and Policy*, 149 at 160–2.

[61] International Energy Agency, *Energy Efficiency 2018: Analysis and Outlooks to 2040* (2018).

[62] International Energy Agency, *Capturing the Multiple Benefits of Energy Efficiency* (2014), 97.

[63] K. Gillingham, A. Keyes, and K. Palmer, 'Advances in Evaluating Energy Efficiency Policies and Programs' (2018) 10(1) *Annual Review of Resource Economics* 511–32. The authors note that energy efficiency policies typically have more political support than policies to limit emissions directly.

for example if standards or pricing put purchases and investments out of reach of low-income households, even if they are not very efficient investments.[64] However standards and pricing mechanisms are only some of the options available to improve energy efficiency. Much depends on the design of the policy.

VII. Energy Efficiency in Rental Housing

Energy efficiency in the energy performance of rental housing is worth particular scrutiny from an equity point of view. If energy performance can be improved, energy losses and greenhouse gas emissions will be lower, and major health co-benefits can be reaped when a house is warm and dry. Rental housing is a particular problem from an equity point of view, because low-income households tend to be renters rather than owner-occupiers.[65] The same has been found for flats in multi-owner buildings in the United Kingdom.[66] Rental housing is often older, colder, and poorer in quality than owner-occupied housing. Rental housing energy efficiency presents a well-known market failure, the principal-agent problem of split incentives; the landlord is responsible for the fabric of the building and for furnaces and heaters, but the tenant pays the utility bills and experiences the living conditions.[67] Landlords have little incentive to invest in insulation and efficient appliances (they usually doubt that they can obtain higher rental returns if they do) and tenants have little incentive to make improvements to a property that they do not own, and indeed where housing is hard to find many tenants prefer to minimize their dealings with the landlord. The default rule in some common law countries is that the law does not imply any warranty of habitability in a lease of a dwelling house, and this includes insulation;[68] but legislatures have usually changed the rule to reflect different norms.

However it has often been a struggle to put good energy efficiency measures into place for rental housing. Building code rules are no use because they are aimed at new builds, not the existing housing stock. Conventional policy instruments may not be effective, such as where an insulation subsidy programme encounters inertia among both landlords and tenants—the split incentive problem at work, even where the programme in theory makes the work a worthwhile investment.[69] Some conventional

[64] A. Levinson, 'Energy Efficiency Standards Are More Regressive Than Energy Taxes: Theory and Evidence' (2019) 6 *Journal of the Association of Environmental and Resource Economists*, S7–S36. Levinson criticizes the invariable habit of law makers to reject economists' advice that pollution taxes are more efficient than standards; but the reason is very likely to be the political difficulty of introducing a new tax.

[65] B. Barton, 'A Warm and Dry Place to Live: Energy Efficiency and Rental Accommodation' (2013) 19 *Canterbury Law Review*, 1; S. Borenstein and L.W. Davis, 'The Distributional Effects of US Clean Energy Tax Credits' (2016) 30 *Tax Policy and the Economy*, 191 at 205.

[66] S. Bright and D. Weatherall, 'Framing and Mapping the Governance Barriers to Energy Upgrades in Flats' (2017) 29 *Journal of Environmental Law*, 203 at 213.

[67] Adrian Bradbrook was a pioneer in this field: 'The Development of Energy Conservation Legislation for Private Rental Housing' (1991) 8 *Environmental and Planning Law Journal*, 91. Also B. Barton, 'Energy Efficiency and Rental Accommodation: Dealing with Split Incentives' in P. Babie and P. Leadbeter (eds), *Law as Change: Engaging with the Life and Scholarship of Adrian Bradbrook* (University of Adelaide Press, 2014).

[68] *Southwark London Borough Council v Mills* [2001] 1 AC 1, 17.

[69] B. Barton, 'A Warm and Dry Place to Live: Energy Efficiency and Rental Accommodation' (2013) 19 *Canterbury Law Review*, 1.

policy instruments are deliberately unavailable to landlords and their tenants. The largest of the United States federal tax credits available to households is the Non-business Energy Property Credit.[70] It assists with purchases of energy-efficient insulation, windows, furnaces, and air conditioning. But it is only available to home owners; neither renters nor landlords are eligible.[71] The same goes for the Residential Energy Efficient Property Credit for solar panels, solar hot water, and fuel cells, although there is a parallel programme for commercially owned systems. Further, neither credit is refundable. The result is that taxpayers with adjusted gross incomes below $20,000 receive 1 per cent of all the tax credit dollars available under these schemes; those over $75,000 (the fifth quintile) receive about 60 per cent of them.[72] Borenstein and Davis observe that the main causes of this tilting of incentives strongly toward upper-income tax filers may be the non-refundability of the credits and their unavailability to renters, but liquidity constraints and credit costs are probably also substantial barriers.

Efforts to put energy efficiency measures in place for rental housing have often been tentative. They are often overshadowed by the difficult politics of compelling landlords to pay for improvements. Information disclosure measures have been widely used to provide tenants with advice about the energy performance of a dwelling, even though tenants can only use it if the housing supply situation is one where they have real choices and market power.[73] In the United Kingdom, it was hoped that the Green Deal programme would help finance rental and owner-occupier improvements alike, but it was not successful.[74] In New Zealand, the Residential Tenancies Act 1986 was amended in 2016 and 2017 to prescribe insulation, heating, ventilation, and weatherproofing requirements for rental properties. In contrast England and Wales have relied on prescribing standards of energy efficiency as demonstrated by an energy performance certificate, under the Energy Act 2011 and regulations; but their introduction has been equally gradual.[75] A landlord may not rent out a property that fails to reach the required level of energy efficiency without making improvements, but the principle in the Act is one of no cost to the landlord,[76] and if the property cannot be brought up to standard with improvements under that principle it can be rented out anyway. Although that rule may change, a reluctance to make landlords pay to produce better energy outcomes is very evident.

[70] US Internal Revenue Code, 26 US Code §25C; S. Borenstein and L.W. Davis, 'The Distributional Effects of US Clean Energy Tax Credits' (2016) 30 *Tax Policy and the Economy*, 191.

[71] 26 U.S. Code § 25C. S. Borenstein and L.W. Davis, 'The Distributional Effects of US Clean Energy Tax Credits' (2016) 30 *Tax Policy and the Economy*, 191 at 194; they note that there is no equivalent programme available to landlords.

[72] S. Borenstein and L.W. Davis, 'The Distributional Effects of US Clean Energy Tax Credits' (2016) 30 *Tax Policy and the Economy*, 191 at 211. (All references in this paragraph are to US dollars.)

[73] On such measures in Australia and the EU, see B. Barton, 'A Warm and Dry Place to Live: Energy Efficiency and Rental Accommodation' (2013) 19 *Canterbury Law Review*, 1.

[74] S. Bright and D. Weatherall, 'Framing and Mapping the Governance Barriers to Energy Upgrades in Flats' (2017) 29 *Journal of Environmental Law*, 203 at 219. They show that it is a struggle to deliver even basic energy-efficiency improvements in such owner-occupied housing.

[75] Energy Efficiency (Private Rented Property) (England and Wales) Regulations 2015, SI 2015/962, under the Energy Act 2011 (UK).

[76] Energy Act 2011 (UK) s 43(4).

Once again, it is evident that the policy options and legal design for energy and climate change include some measures that grapple with distributional equity, and others that completely ignore it, or indeed seem calculated to produce inequity. Once again we can observe that the question of efficacy is important as well as that of justice; the rental share of the housing stock is too large to ignore if we want to produce change.

VIII. Concluding Remarks

Even the brief inquiry that this chapter has been able to make demonstrates that we can take the concept of energy justice and apply it in a very concrete manner to the laws that we might make to combat climate change. Understanding distributional effects on wealth and income, and the progressive and regressive consequences of policy options, is essential if we are to attain higher levels of energy justice. We argue that equity is important in national law as well as international law, where it has been much discussed. At the same time, the discussion of energy poverty, which has usually had a national focus, can be expanded to become a discussion of how to create laws that avoid energy injustices. We find that we can make a productive cross-pollination across disciplines by drawing on economic analysis, while recognizing that law and public policy analysis may put more emphasis on social and distributive justice as values to be pursued for their own sake.[77]

It is discomforting to find that much of analysis of climate change policies concludes that they have regressive characteristics, with undue adverse effects on the less wealthy in society. Zachmann, Fredriksson, Claeys, and Levinson are particularly challenging. However McInnes is a valuable antidote; she stresses that many of the studies that have been done about various taxes, charges, subsidies, and incentives are very context-specific. What is regressive in one situation or in one country may be very progressive in another. We must be on guard against generalizations that are based on a weak evidentiary foundation. We must also take heed of the caution that a number of analysts express about the preliminary nature of research in the field. Zachmann and colleagues record their surprise that for the European ETS, an enormous policy instrument, there has been no comprehensive analysis to quantify its total distributional effect.[78] McInnes identifies a number of shortcomings in the existing research and gaps that need to be filled.[79] Many studies concentrate on the impact of a single measure on expenditure and income; many are static analyses that do not take behavioural changes into account; many focus on expenditure and income and not on impacts on household welfare, mobility, health, and social inclusion. There are few studies of geographic distributional effects or of comparisons between countries.

[77] The economic analysts we have referred to have tackled the question of how the burden is shared, but not all do; the Stern Report, for example, says very little about the matter: N. Stern, *The Economics of Climate Change* (Cambridge University Press, 2007).

[78] Zachmann, et al., *Distributional Effects of Climate Policies* (n 5), 83.

[79] McInnes, 'Distributional and Household Effects of the Low-Carbon Transition' (n 4), 14.

But doing nothing is not the answer. We need to make efforts to devise policies that are not regressive, or are less regressive, and we must make sure that there is a path forward for low-income households in tackling climate change as much as high-income ones. 'Action for climate and growth needs to be inclusive.'[80] We find that in addition to ethical and justice arguments there is a basic efficacy argument; policies that do not bring meaningful change for low-income families are, generally, less successful.[81] In some sectors, such as road transport, they have high levels of carbon emissions, which cannot be ignored if society's overall reduction effort is to be successful. We must also remember that equity and distributional effects are a concern for society as a whole, not only the lowest quintile. The many middle-income households, with their many votes, are also needed on board, confident that everyone is shouldering a fair share of the burden. To be stable through multiple political cycles, climate laws depend on widespread support in society.

We have choices. Much depends on careful policy design. We can avoid the worst examples of regressive legislation, some examples of which we have discussed. We can give priority to emissions sources, such as air transport, where action is likely to have progressive effects.

We should give special attention to policy measures that allow climate taxes and other revenues to be recycled into income-targeted assistance for households. Revenue recycling is often identified as the feature that can turn a policy's effects from regressive to progressive. The implication may be that we should favour policy options that offer such revenue for recycling; thus, if we have an emissions trading scheme, auctioning credits in a way that produces revenue can be used to increase distributional justice. Similarly a feebate scheme recycles revenue and finds a way to make low-emissions choices affordable.

There is a convincing argument that distributional justice should be an inherent component of climate change law and policy; distribution and social equity should not be regarded as a different sphere of policy. Climate change law should not be developed in isolation from its social context. If designed carefully, it should be capable of producing a triple dividend:[82] reduced emissions, economic growth through recycled tax revenue, and an equity dividend as well.

[80] Ibid., 7.

[81] J.R. DeShazo, 'Improving Incentives for Clean Vehicle Purchases in the United States: Challenges and Opportunities' (2016) 10 *Review of Environmental Economics and Policy*, 149; T.G. Reames, M.A. Reiner and, M.B. Stacey, 'An Incandescent Truth: Disparities in Energy-efficient Lighting Availability and Prices in an Urban U.S. County' (2018) 218 *Applied Energy*, 95–103.

[82] McInnes, 'Distributional and Household Effects of the Low-Carbon Transition' (n 4), 20.

13

Meanings of Energy Poverty in the South American Context

A Regional Overview

*Milton F. Montoya and others**

I. Energy Poverty Characteristics in the Latin American Context

The Latin American and Caribbean region went from 61 per cent energy coverage to 94 per cent energy coverage in 2016 according to the data provided by the World Bank on energy access.[1]Likewise, during 2016 in different inhabited areas, 98 per cent of the population living in urban areas had energy and 86 per cent of the population in rural areas had energy.[2] According to the International Energy Agency (IEA) projections, only 1 per cent of the Latin American population (four million people) will not have access to energy by 2020.[3] This means that by 2020 the region will be close to having universal energy access for its population. Bearing in mind the experiences in achieving universal access in developing countries such as Thailand and China, the last fifteen percentage of access is the hardest and most difficult to cover. During a twenty-year period these countries went from 30 per cent coverage to 90 per cent coverage and spent a further twenty years in giving energy access to the 10 per cent that remained.[4] However, today we are in a position where new technological solutions are put in place with growing accessible costs that would mean an easier coverage for the last 10 per cent for Latin America's case.

* This article is the result of a co-authorship between a variety of Latin American experts on the topic. Milton F. Montoya and Daniela Aguilar Abaunza are the co-authors of '*Energy Poverty in Colombia*'; Daniel Gutierrez Rivera wrote the section about '*Energy Poverty in Chile*'; Juan Justo Bautista and Liber Martin are the co-authors of '*Energy Poverty in Argentina*'; Ignacio Herrera Anchustegui is the author of '*Energy Poverty in Venezuela*'; Alberto Cairampoma Arroyo and Paul Villegas Vega wrote the section about '*Energy Poverty in Peru*' and Marina Motta Benevides Gadelha is the author of *Energy Poverty in Brazil*'. These countries were chosen because represent a significant percentage of the energy consumption in Latin America in comparison to other countries such as Ecuador, Paraguay, Uruguay or Bolivia which due to their comparative smaller size were not included in this study.

[1] The World Bank, 'Access to Electricity' https://data.worldbank.org/indicator/EG.ELC.ACCS.UR.ZS?locations=ZJ accessed 14 August 2019

[2] International Energy Agency, 'Energy Access Outlook 2017: From Poverty to Prosperity' (2017) https://www.iea.org/publications/freepublications/publication/WEO2017SpecialReport_EnergyAccessOutlook.pdf accessed 14 August 2019.

[3] Ibid., 41.

[4] Ibid., 30.

Milton F. Montoya and others, Meanings of Energy Poverty in the South American Context In: *Energy Justice and Energy Law*. Edited by Íñigo Del Guayo, Lee Godden, Donald N. Zillman, Milton Fernando Montoya, and José Juan González, Oxford University Press (2020).
 DOI: 10.1093/oso/9780198860754.003.0013

Another special feature in the Latin American region concerning energy poverty is the process of urbanization that has been accompanied by increasing urban poverty, also reflected in energetic terms. As opposed to other regions in the world, poverty in Latin America has been found primarily in great cities and urban areas, even exceeding rural poverty. The causes underlying this phenomenon are related to an increase in rural migration to urban areas as well as to the insufficient capability of cities to absorb the increased population.[5] This migration process can be voluntary or forced. These types of migration hold true for the Colombian case where the internal conflict has made certain populations prone to energy poverty and marginality.

For Latin America's case, there is a shortage of literature on energy poverty. However, we may highlight CEPAL's (Economic Commission for Latin America and the Caribbean)research where there is a methodological exercise to define energy poverty for Latin America's context. CEPAL and the doctrine for the region consider that the British definition of energy poverty mentioned by del Guayo in Chapter 3 is restricted and cannot be applied to Latin America.[6] We will underscore two criticisms towards this definition. First, when it refers itself to heating as the barometer to measure energy poverty it ignores the weather and geographical differences in the region. This variable implies that heating is not considered as a basic need and is understood more as a luxury item.[7] This is why other yardsticks should be taken into account such as food refrigeration, cooking, lighting, and entertainment. These variables are fundamental when defining energy poverty within the Latin American context.

A second criticism underscores that the fixed percentage of use (10 per cent) is not adequate for the Latin American context where due to the weather differences already mentioned there are different patterns in the energy consumption throughout the region.[8]

This is how the CEPAL proposed the concept 'Energy poverty at the homes' and a method of meeting energy absolute needs. For the CEPAL a home is in energy poverty when people inhabiting it do not meet their energy absolute needs; needs related to a series of satisfactions and economic goods, which are considered essential in the set place and time according to the social and cultural conventions[9]. This definition has two components. One is the fixed or absolute component, absolute needs where no matter the cultural or historical context are stable such as the needs of subsistence, protection, entertainment, creation, and pleasure. The second component varies and it depends on the cultural and social perceptions of how to meet these needs. To summarize,

[5] Comisión Económica para América Latina y el Caribe, 'Contribución de los servicios energéticos a los objetivos de desarrollo del milenio' (2009) https://www.cepal.org/es/publicaciones/3720-contribucion-servicios-energeticos-objetivos-desarrollo-milenio-la-mitigacion-la accessed 14 August 2019 (hereafter CEPAL, 'Contribución de los servicios energéticos a los objetivos de desarrollo del milenio').

[6] See Chapter 3 in this book.

[7] X.L. Romero, *Pobreza energética en el Caribe insular* (1st ed, Universidad Externado de Colombia, 2015) 16

[8] CEPAL, 'Contribución de los servicios energéticos a los objetivos de desarrollo del milenio'(n 5).

[9] Ibid., 16.

for example, access to energy has a different meaning if it is in an indigenous protected area or a smallholder farm area as opposed to the meaning it would have for a great city exposed to changing weather or stable weather and the consumption patterns that reflect such heterogeneity.

II. Energy Poverty in Colombia

The concept of energy poverty has been used several times by the Constitutional Colombian Court referring to situations of interruption of energy, as we will discuss in this chapter. According to the Constitutional Court, a person or a family fulfils the conditions of energy poverty when they are incapable of paying for a minimum quantity of electricity to meet their domestic needs or when they are forced to spend an excessive portion of their income to pay for the electricity bill.[10] The aforementioned might imply debt or reduction of expenditure on health, education, or food in order to cover the payment of the electric service.

On the other hand, the Unit of Mining Energy Planning (UPME) proposed the need of developing a methodology to clearly define the parameters to calculate the level of energy poverty and at the same time define the concept for the Colombian case. The definition taken into account by the Energy National Plan 2015 is under the parameters presented by the CEPAL and discussed in section A.[11] We analyse energy poverty in Colombia in this section.

A. Access to Energy

Colombia has one of the best indexes of access to electricity in the region. According to numbers from the IEA[12] in 2017, 97 per cent of the population had access to electricity; this means that only 1.5 million people were not covered by the energy service. Likewise, the rural electrification rate in 2017 was 84 per cent and the urban rate was 100 per cent.[13] In the year 2015, in order to cook, 70 per cent of the population had liquefied petroleum gas (LPG) or natural gas, 10 per cent electricity but 20 per cent of the population still cooked with wood or coal.[14] In this context the energy demand grew considerably, between 1975 and 2008 by 78.2 per cent.[15]

[10] Corte Constitucional de Colombia, 'Ruling T-761' (11 December 2015) http://www.corteconstitucional.gov.co/relatoria/2015/T-761-15.htm accessed 14 August 2019 (hereafter Ruling T-761 of 2004).

[11] Unidad de Planeación Minero Energética, 'Plan Energético Nacional. Ideario Energético' (2015), https://biblioteca.minminas.gov.co/pdf/Plan%20energetico%20Nacional%202050.pdf accessed 14 August 2019(hereafter UPME, 'Plan Energético Nacional').

[12] International Energy Agency, 'Access to Electricity', https://www.iea.org/sdg/electricity/accessed 14 August 2019.

[13] Ibid., 1.

[14] UPME, 'Plan Energético Nacional' (n 11).

[15] C. Poveda and P. Martínez, 'Trends in Economic Growth, Poverty and Energy in Colombia: Long-run and Short-run Effects' (2011) *Energy System*, 2, 290.

B. Electricity Affordability and Protection to Vulnerable Users

Law 142 of 1994 and Law 143 of 1994 not only introduced competition in the electricity sector, but also detailed measures with a strong social vision to reduce energy poverty.[16] The fundamental instrument in this regard is subsidies for low-income populations. In this sense, the electricity bill is proportional to the level of income, where high-income, commercial, and industrial users, subsidize in part low-income users. There are also subsidies for natural gas, water, sewage, sanitation, and rural telephony. The subsidies depend on the position in a stratification scheme, which consists of six strata, according to the dwelling and its location. Strata four and five subsidize levels one, two, and three.

However, the disproportion between subsidized sectors and taxpayers has created a budget deficit, which is currently being debated. For instance, approximately 60 per cent of electricity demand belongs to strata one and two, 23 per cent belongs to stratum three, in contrast with only 4 per cent of taxpayers in strata five and six.[17] In this regard, the energy planning authority UPME has recommended the progressive clearing of the subsidized percentage and the elimination of the subsidy to stratum three.[18]

C. Quality of the Electricity Service

In terms of quality, the resolution CREG 097 of 2008 and the Resolution CREG 067 of 2010 regulate the quality of energy supply. Service quality indexes are defined in terms of the duration and frequency of service interruptions, with the network operator being obliged to ensure this quality. The incentive mechanism to ensure quality implies that the distribution charge increases or decreases according to the guaranteed quality, and compensates the worst served users. At this point, it is recognized that smart meters allow consumers to interact with the price and better manage their consumption and also allow the participation of users in demand response programmes, where they participate in programmed disconnections in exchange for economic incentives and reductions in their bills.

The interruption of electricity supply is part of the sanctions imposed on the user for the failure to pay for the electricity bill.[19] However, jurisprudence of the Constitutional Court has considered multiple times, and for special cases, that such interruptions are not constitutionally permissible when they violate fundamental rights. It is the case of public facilities and 'subjects of special constitutional protection'. As for the suspension of service in public facilities, the Constitutional Court through the action for protection (*acción de tutela*) has recognized that the right to a decent life of people living in

[16] CEPAL, 'Contribución de los servicios energéticos a los objetivos de desarrollo del milenio'(n 5).
[17] UPME, 'Plan Energético Nacional' (n 11).
[18] UPME, 'Plan Energético Nacional' (n 11).
[19] Colombia Congress, Law 143 of 1994, Article 6.

penitentiary and prison centres,[20] hospitals,[21] and schools,[22] is violated when facing an interruption of electricity.

With respect to 'subjects of special constitutional protection' this terms refers to people who, due to their particular physical, psychological, or social condition, deserve positive state action for the purpose of achieving real and effective equality.[23]In this case, the Constitutional Court has indicated that although access to electricity does not constitute an autonomous fundamental right, exceptionally and in connection with other rights such as the right to a dignified life, health and personal integrity, it can be protected through the 'action of protection'.[24]Likewise, the action for protection has been admissible in cases of individuals with special constitutional protection, when the company providing the service fails to comply with its obligation to suspend the supply after three unpaid billing periods, accumulating a large debt.[25]

D. Legal Challenges

The efforts that Colombia has carried out to universalize the electricity service are considerable. Plans to provide energy and normalize it, accompanied with funds that collect important resources to develop projects to provide energy have been successful as shown by the data. Larger efforts in rural areas and especially in post-conflict areas are vital to build lasting peace. This construction needs to integrate new social sectors and needs government presence in the regions through the correct provision of public services.

The fight against energy poverty does not only consist in universalizing access or the connectivity in the system but also requires that the users are capable of paying for the service. This is why the stratum and subsidies scheme has been the cornerstone to fight against energy poverty in Colombia, helping the most vulnerable sectors in paying for their public services including electricity. Even if the current subsidy scheme may not be sustainable, it is important to expand the base of the payers without reducing the percentage of the subsidy or the subsidized sectors. In this case, it is important to reassess the payment exemption of the industrial sector because it generates strong inconsistencies in the taxing area as well as in fiscal sustainability and social equity. It is important that the industrial sector also helps the Solidarity Fund to benefit the most vulnerable population and that the national budget continues to contribute in a fair

[20] Corte Constitucional de Colombia 'Ruling T-881' (17 October 2002) http://www.corteconstitucional.gov.co/relatoria/2002/t-881-02.htm accessed 14 August 2019.

[21] Corte Constitucional de Colombia 'Ruling T-1205'(2 December 2004) http://www.corteconstitucional.gov.co/relatoria/2004/t-1205-04.htm accessed 14 August 2019 (hereafter Ruling T-1205 of 2004).

[22] Corte Constitucional de Colombia 'Ruling T-380' (31 August 1994) http://www.corteconstitucional.gov.co/relatoria/1994/t-380-94.htm accessed 14 August 2019.

[23] Corte Constitucional de Colombia 'Ruling T-167' (11 March 2011) http://www.corteconstitucional.gov.co/relatoria/2011/T-167-11.htm accessed 14 August 2019. Corte Constitucional de Colombia 'Ruling T-167' (11 March 2011) http://www.corteconstitucional.gov.co/relatoria/2011/T-167-11.htm accessed 14 August 2019.

[24] Ruling T-1205 of 2004, (n 21).

[25] Ruling T-761 of 2004, (n 10).

ratio to these subsidies. As several authors have said, a cut on the public expenditure could not only reduce economic growth but also increase the population in poverty.[26]

III. Energy Poverty in Chile

The preparation of an energy policy for Chile in 2050 contained in decree 148 of the Ministry of Energy of 2016, establishes the central guidelines for the development of a reliable, sustainable, inclusive, and competitive energy sector. This is one of the goals to ensure universal and equitable access to modern, reliable, and affordable energy services for the entire population by the year 2050.[27]

Along these lines, the United Nations Development Programme (UNDP) prepared a report, hereinafter UNDP Report ('Energy Poverty: analysis of international experiences and learning for Chile'), from the year 2018. In this report, they identify the elements that determine the phenomenon of energy poverty in Chile based on a comparative analysis of the subject and various processes to define what energy poverty is, bringing forth its dimensions in Chile according to the context and national variables.[28]

The 2018–2022 Energy Route of the Ministry of Energy of Chile establishes as the first of its mega-commitments that of creating a map of the country's energy vulnerability, identifying families that do not have electricity and other energy services, with the purpose of shortening existing gaps.[29]

A. Access to Energy

As indicated in the UNDP Report, it is clear that in the designing of the concept of energy poverty, various dimensions must be understood which will allow for the sustainable and balanced development of a country, satisfy the energy needs of the population, and ensure the environmental sustainability. In this line, we highlight the broad definition of the UNDP report on energy poverty '*as the absence of options to access adequate, affordable, safe, reliable and environmentally friendly energy. This with the aim of achieving sustainable development, both economically and humanly*'.[30]

Access to electricity is almost universal, thanks to the implementation of electrification and rural energization programmes carried out by the Government.[31]

[26] Ruling T-1205 of 2004, (n 21).

[27] Ministerio de Energia—Gobierno de Chile, 'Energía 2050—Política Energética de Chile', http://www.energia.gob.cl/sites/default/files/energia_2050_-_politica_energetica_de_chile.pdf accessed 14 August 2019.

[28] United Nations Development Programme, *Energy Poverty: Analysis of International Experiences and Learning for Chile* (2018) (hereafter UNDP, *Energy Poverty: Analysis of International Experiences and Learning for Chile*).

[29] Ministerio de Energia—Gobierno de Chile, 'Ruta energética 2018-2022: Liderando la modernización con sello ciudadano' (2018) <http://www.energia.gob.cl/rutaenergetica2018-2022.pdf accessed 14 August 2019.

[30] UNDP, Energy Poverty: Analysis of International Experiences and Learning for Chile (n 28), 18.

[31] Subsecretaria de Desarrollo Regional y Administrativo, 'Programa de Electrificación Rural-PER: Contrato de Prestamos 1475/OC-CH', http://www.subdere.gov.cl/documentacion/programa-de-electrificaci%C3%B3n-rural-contrato-de-pr%C3%A9stamo-1475oc-ch accessed 14 August 2019.

B. Electricity Affordability and Protection to Vulnerable Users

In the 2018–2022 Energy Route of the current government of Chile, important legal initiatives related to energy poverty are contemplated, which partially take over four associated items. The first, and most relevant one, is related to the reform of the electric power distribution segment, which aims to modernize the regulation of the sector, having as its main axis the improvement of the security and quality of the supply of electric power. The aim is to have flexible regulation incorporating technological innovation, which establishes the appropriate incentives in terms of quality of service in the distribution segment in order to achieve long-term public policy objectives to reduce the unavailability times of electricity supply.

The second initiative is related to the regulation of solid biofuels, such as firewood and its derivatives, which aims to establish the technical specifications for its application, as well as the conditions and requirements for its commercialization, especially in rural areas.

The third initiative refers to an announcement made by the Ministry of Energy to prepare a proposed Climate Change Law, in conjunction with the Ministry of Environment, which will aim to generate an institutional framework on the subject, defining the various environmental management instruments that allow the implementation of a strategy to reduce greenhouse gas emissions.

Finally, the Ministry of Energy, following the global trends of change in energy, initiated a binding process of decarbonization of the national energy matrix, including the preparation of a plan and timetable for the withdrawal or reconversion of coal-fuelled power plants.

C. Quality of the Electricity Service

Regarding the reliability of energy, according to annual reports of reliability of the electrical systems, and in comparison with other member countries of the Organisation for Economic Cooperation and Development (OECD),[32] the quality of energy supply in Chile is deficient, due to the fact that end-customers suffer cuts for several hours, possibly longer, and even days, without access to supply. It is for this reason that, through public energy policies, by 2050 no region of the national territory will have more than an hour on average of lack of access to electric supply per year.

[32] SAIDI (System Average Interruption Duration Index). We understand reliability as the quality of an electrical system determined by sufficiency, safety. and quality of service, according to Article 225 letter R of the General Electric Services Law. California Public Utilities Commission, 'Electric System Reliability Annual Reports' http://www.cpuc.ca.gov/general.aspx?id=4529 accessed 14 August 2019.

D. Legal Challenges

Taking into account what has been described so far, Chile has a well-defined public energy policy, which establishes the general guidelines in relation to what should be understood by energy poverty, how to address its associated problems, as well as its objectives, commitments, and goals.

The Chilean energy policy defines the concept of energy poverty from a broad standpoint, including aspects that allow having an adequate, affordable, safe, reliable, and environmentally friendly energy usage.

Likewise, the national energy policy identifies great deficiencies in terms of energy poverty, pointing out the deficit in service quality of energy supply to final customers, the strong thermal component of the electricity matrix, and the indiscriminate use by the population of polluting fuels. The great challenge for Chile will be that its elaborate public energy policy is correctly executed through the various legal initiatives.

IV. Energy Poverty in Argentina

Argentina has an electric coverage rate of 99.3 per cent of the population.[33] Sixty per cent of households are connected to natural gas networks and use this fuel for cooking and heating. Considering natural gas and LPG, the proportion of families that use gas is 97 per cent. The remaining 3 per cent of households still use firewood for cooking, that is, more than one million people.[34]

In this framework, this section briefly describes the evolution of the energy poverty profile in the last two decades. In the first stage, which runs from 2002 to 2016, the main challenges in this area were related to structural poverty, with a foremost role of those sectors that lacked connection to the networks and were forced to get energy supply through more expensive and insecure means. Lacking access to networks results in deprivation, or much higher prices, for the disadvantaged since they must pay market prices, normally much higher, for alternative packed fuels. In 2016, the energetic poor profile added grid users, who, due to a significant increase in tariffs, are compromised in their capacity to pay utility bills. In the last two years, the network customer went from being a privileged stakeholder to share with the informal user a place in the picture of energy poverty.

[33] Presidencia de la Nación Argentina, 'Objetivos de Desarrollo Sostenible. Informe país Argentina' (2018) https://www.argentina.gob.ar/sites/default/files/informe-ods-todo.pdf accessed 14 August 2019.

[34] G. Jacinto and S. Carrizo, 'Energía y pobreza en la Argentina' (2018) 3 *Petrotecnia*, 23.

A. Access to Energy: Affordability and Protection to Vulnerable Users

Starting in 2002—a year of deep national crisis—and for more than a decade, the energy policy implemented in Argentina was characterized by the presence of high consumption subsidies that resulted in a significant reduction in customers' costs, especially those of the metropolitan area of Buenos Aires.[35] Insofar as subsidies were focused on consumption, groups that lacked access to grids were excluded from these benefits, either because of the precariousness of their homes or the simple absence of such infrastructure[36]. Under this model, low-income people did not have access to subsidized natural gas or electricity, which benefitted the population with medium and high incomes[37].

In that decade, poverty ranged around 20–30 per cent of the inhabitants—after reaching peaks of 50 per cent in 2002/2003[38]—and at least one in four people were deprived of adequate housing and energy services. This situation deepened in areas of maximum precariousness and vulnerability, such as informal settlements, inhabited by almost three million people, most without formal access to electricity or natural gas grids.

In the context of lack of access to networks in urban areas, electricity is obtained through unauthorized connections —highly unsafe and intermittent—while the lack of natural gas is supplied with LPG cylinders, whose shortcomings in terms of supply and sufficiency usually require supplementation with firewood, coal, or kerosene[39]. The caloric unit of LPG has a price several times higher than the equivalent of natural gas. The combination of this high cost with the low value of residential tariffs ended up configuring a clear case of transfer of income to consumers with greater resources.[40]

So, in this period, energy poverty was characterized by the existence of 'excluded consumers', understood as those individuals who do not have access to the utility grids for reasons beyond their control and, in particular, for suffering structural conditions of socio-economic disadvantage. 'Excluded consumers' are those out of the network and who pay proportionally much more than the formal customer to cover this lack of access.

From a perspective of real equality, aid should be targeted only to the most needy sectors of society, in order to avoid the distortions involved in recognizing them

[35] Where a third of the country's population lives.

[36] G' Bravo, R' Kozul, and R. Landaveri, 'Energy Access in Urban and Peri-urban Buenos Aires' (2008) 12 *Energy for Sustainable Development*, 56–72 (hereafter Bravo, 'Energy Access in Urban and Peri-urban Buenos Aires').

[37] J.H.I. Dyner and J. Cherni, 'Electricity Market Reform in Argentina: Assessing the Impact for the Poor in Buenos Aires' (2005) 13 *Utilities Policy*, 1–14.

[38] Observatorio de la Deuda Social Argentina, Universidad Católica Argentina, *Incidencia de la Indigencia y la Pobreza por Ingresos a partir de la Encuesta de la Deuda Social Argentina* (2010–2018) http://bibliotecadigital.uca.edu.ar/repositorio/investigacion/incidencia-indigencia-pobreza-ingresos-2018.pdf accessed 14 August 2019.

[39] Bravo, 'Energy Access in Urban and Peri-urban Buenos Aires'(n 36), 12.

[40] Corporación Andina de Fomento (ed.), 'Energía: una visión sobre los retos y oportunidades en América Latina y el Caribe. Aspectos sociales del acceso a la energía' (2013) https://repositorio.cepal.org/bitstream/handle/11362/1505/1/Energia_CAF_CEPAL.pdf accessed 14 August 2019.

indiscriminately (error by inclusion) or insufficiently (error by exclusion). For its granting, objective conditions must be verified whose permanence over time is subject to monitoring.

In 2016, consumption subsidies began to be sharply cut to reduce the fiscal deficit and this led to a significant increase in public utility tariffs and fuel prices. The combination of these decisions with a strong inflationary process led to a new era of energy poverty in which network users, who were previously privileged actors, are now added to the picture. Recent studies based on the income criterion show that more than half of the households in the metropolitan area of Buenos Aires are energy poor, since they allocate more than 10 per cent of their disposable income—after food—to satisfy their basic energy needs. It is estimated that almost 30 per cent of households are severely energy poor, since they must allocate more than 10 per cent of their total income to the payment of those services.[41] In this way, the new depiction of energy poverty is characterized by the incorporation of formal consumers and the deepening of informal ones' difficulties in procuring sources of supply.

B. Legal Challenges

The worsening of the chronic scenario of energy poverty in Argentina coexists with the development of an increasingly sophisticated legal framework to fight it. Argentine law provides different remedies that allow judicial provisions of universal access to basic services.

First, the operational right of access to energy services is supported by the International Covenant on Economic, Social and Cultural Rights, which enjoys constitutional status in Argentina. According to the interpretation of its international enforcement bodies, to which the national Supreme Court ascribes,[42] 'all beneficiaries of the right to adequate housing should have sustainable access to natural and common resources, safe drinking water, energy for cooking, heating and lighting, sanitation and washing facilities, means of food storage, refuse disposal, site drainage and emergency services' and 'personal or household financial costs associated with housing should be at such a level that the attainment and satisfaction of other basic needs are not threatened or compromised. Steps should be taken by States parties to ensure that the percentage of housing-related costs is, in general, commensurate with income levels'.[43]

As it is known, under this international treaty, 'a minimum core obligation to ensure the satisfaction of, at the very least, minimum essential levels of each of the rights is

[41] Centro de Economia Politica Argentina, 'Efecto de los incrementos tarifarios en los hogares de la Región Metropolitana: una mirada desde la pobreza energética' (2017) https://www.centrocepa.com.ar/informes/173-efecto-de-los-incrementos-tarifarios-en-los-hogares-de-la-region-metropolitana-una-mirada-desde-la-pobreza-energetica.html accessed 14 August 2019.

[42] CSJN, *CEPIS* [2016] Decision 339:1077.

[43] Committee on Economic, Social and Cultural Rights, 'General Comment N° 4, The Right to Adequate Housing, (art. 11 (1) of the Covenant)' (1991) https://tbinternet.ohchr.org/_layouts/15/treatybodyexternal/Download.aspx?symbolno=INT%2fCESCR%2fGEC%2f4759&Lang=en accessed 14 August 2019.

incumbent upon every State party'.[44] Furthermore, the 'Protocol of San Salvador', additional to the American Convention on Human Rights in the Area of Economic, Social and Cultural Rights states that 'Everyone shall have the right to live in a healthy environment and to have access to basic public services' (Article 11). All these provisions support the enforceability of primary conditions of access to services such as electricity, gas, and water in the home, at affordable prices.

In parallel, Article 42 of the National Constitution enshrines the right of public utility users 'to the protection of their health, safety and economic interests'. In the words of the Supreme Court, this clause shows that 'users and consumers are particularly vulnerable subjects to which the framers decided to protect in a special way'.[45]

In the last fifteen years, energy poverty in Argentina went from having its epicentre in the group of informal consumers to now including those consumers connected to networks, who experience increasing difficulties to pay for the service. Since direct, indirect, and cross subsidies have proven to be inherent to not only electricity or LPG services, but to the entire energy matrix, affecting especially those who lack grid access, they need to be redesigned and oriented towards effectively reducing energy poverty, while meeting other energy policy goals like efficiency.

Individual and collective litigation for grid expansion, quality standards, and fair taxation may help in reducing the gap but cannot replace public policy and genuine investment. Moreover, the high cost of the energy transition already implemented by Argentina without defining clearly who will pay for it not only is unfair but also triggers major conflicts between the involved actors in the coming years. This worsening of the situation coexists with a legal framework that empowers excluded groups to claim essential levels of coverage before courts. It is one more chapter in the eternal effectiveness gap of the sophisticated Latin American rights model.

V. Venezuela's Twist to Energy Poverty and Political Control: Gasoline Subsidies

The Venezuelan outlook on energy poverty is different from the other Latin American countries studied in this chapter. While most of these countries address energy poverty through subsidies in the provision of electricity, and partially to gas, Venezuela's traditional approach has been to use gasoline as a political and economic tool to deal with the energy poor.

Venezuela's bane and boon are its hydrocarbon richness.[46] The extraction, refinement, and trade of petroleum products (oil and gas and its refined subproducts) constitute about 98 per cent of Venezuela's exports, amounting to about

[44] Committee on Economic, Social and Cultural Rights, 'General Comment N° 3, The Nature of States Parties' obligations, (Art. 2, Para. 1, of the Covenant)' (1990) https://tbinternet.ohchr.org/_layouts/15/treatybodyexternal/Download.aspx?symbolno=INT%2fCESCR%2fGEC%2f4758&Lang=en accessed 14 August 2019.

[45] CSJN, *Ledesma*, 2008, *Decisions*, 331:819; *Unión de Usuarios y Consumidores*, 2014, *Decisions*, 337:790; *Prevención*, 2017, *Decisions*, 340:172.

[46] Venezuela has the largest proven oil reserves in the world with 302 billion barrels. US Energy Information Administration, 'Venezuela' https://www.eia.gov/beta/international/analysis.php?iso=VEN accessed 14 August 2019.

US$32 billion.[47] Despite this, non-official sources estimate that 90 per cent of Venezuelans 'now live in poverty'[48] due to the devastating economic crisis, that has ravaged Venezuela's economy in the last years.[49]

Different governments have used 'oil money' for decades to support the energy poor, along with electricity subsidies. The Venezuelan State has fixed and subsidized gasoline and diesel prices, making them the cheapest in the world,[50] with an estimated cost of US$0.000001 in 2017.[51] These subsidies have been granted to control politics and public discontent by creating a sense of popular ownership over Venezuela's natural resources and limiting the impact of poverty, for example by keeping transportation costs very low.[52] In the past, gasoline price increases have led to riots, massacres, and protests, such as 'El Caracazo' of 1989,[53] and more recently from 2016 onwards.

Gasoline subsidies for all end users, traced back over more than three decades, show that the executive power decided to artificially control gasoline prices through a subsidy, keeping them well below any international price. For example, in 1989, President Pérez's government increased gasoline prices by 101 per cent,[54] and again in 1990.[55] Gasoline prices were, once again, raised in 1996 by the Caldera Government up to 500 per cent.

Yet, despite the use of subsidies for gasoline, Venezuela lacks a coherent, comprehensive, and well-thought out energy poverty policy. Admittedly, in the last years President Maduro's government's measures and declarations might be read as modifying the schemes of general energy subsides to benefit only 'the most needed [poorer] users and the productive sectors to incentivize' as it happens with electricity,[56] or even to eliminate gasoline subsidies altogether.[57]

[47] OPEC, 'Venezuela Facts and Figures', https://www.opec.org/opec_web/en/about_us/171.htm accessed 14 August 2019.

[48] REUTER, 'Venezuelans report big weight losses in 2017 as hunger hits'<available at https://www.reuters.com/article/us-venezuela-food/venezuelans-report-big-weight-losses-in-2017-as-hunger-hits-idUSKCN1G52HA. Compare this with the latest data from the Venezuelan National Statistic Institute (from 2018), claiming that just 19.7 per cent of households were 'poor'. Instituto Nacional de Estadística, 'Indicadores de Necesidades Básicas Insatisfechas *1999–2018*' http://www.ine.gov.ve/index.php?option=com_content&view=category&id=104&Itemid=45# accessed 14 August 2019.

[49] For 2018 the IMF estimated an inflation of 1.37 per cent million. The estimation for 2019 I of 10 million per cent. International Monetary Fund, 'Inflation rate, average consumer prices—Venezuela', https://www.imf.org/external/datamapper/PCPIPCH@WEO/WEOWORLD/VEN accessed 14 August 2019.

[50] The February 2019 prices for gasoline in Venezuela were, according to the official rate of US$0.01 per litre, well behind the US$0.13 per litre of Sudan and more than a hundred times cheaper than the world average of US$1.09. Global Petrol Prices, 'Gasoline prices, liter-25 March 2019' https://www.globalpetrolprices.com/gasoline_prices/ accessed 14 August 2019.

[51] BBC News Mundo, 'Qué es y cómo funciona el carnet de la patria que permitirá seguir comprando gasolina a precio subsidiado en Venezuela', (14 August 2018), https://www.bbc.com/mundo/noticias-america-latina-45182511 accessed 14 August 2019.

[52] R. Linkohr, 'La política energética latinoamericana: entre el Estado y el mercado' (2006) 204 *Nueva Sociedad*, 90; G. Fontaine, *Petropolítica: una teoría de la gobernanza energética* (FLACSO-IEP, 2010).

[53] For some literature on this event see, inter alia: J.H. Martínez, 'Causas e interpretaciones del Caracazo'(2008) Historia Actual Online 16, at 85; P. Vásquez Lezama, 'El Caracazo (1989) y la tragedia (1999): Economía moral e instrumentalización política del saqueo en Venezuela' (2012) *Cuadernos Unimetanos*, 30 at 14.

[54] Resolution of the Ministry of Energy and Mines fixing the prices of fuel (OJ [1989] N 4.076).

[55] P. Luzardo, *El Proceso de Ajuste y los Precios Estatales: Un Análisis del Mercado Interno de la Industria Petrolera Venezolana* (1993). Universidad del Zulia / Venezuela / Cuadernos Latinoamericanos; ISSN: 1690-7582; https://produccioncientificaluz.org/index.php/cuadernos/article/view/14675/14652 (accesed 03 January 2020).

[56] Article 66 of the Organic Law of the System and Electric Service (OJ [2010] N. 39.573).

[57] BBC News Mundo, 'Maduro anuncia el fin de la gasolina casi gratis para todos en Venezuela' (14 August 2018) https://www.bbc.com/mundo/noticias-america-latina-45177965 accessed 14 August 2019.

A. Access to Energy: Subsidizing Gasoline Prices in Venezuela—Policy and Legal Basis

It is not easy to find the legal base for Venezuela's subsidies to gasoline or a policy to address energy poverty, not even within the 'Plan of the Motherland 2013–2019'.[58] Nevertheless, Venezuelan legislation clarifies that the activities of 'supply, storage, transport, distribution and retail sale of the derived hydrocarbon products designated by the Executive Power [...]' constitute public service obligations, including the retail of gasoline. As a public service obligation, it 'must be assumed by the State, tending to satisfy general or collective needs, in compliance with a constitutional or legal obligation, and towards which private parties do not have a right to carry them out "freely" ',[59] under the competence of the Public National Power.[60]

Designating gasoline retailing as a public service obligation allows the Executive Power to 'fix the prices of derived hydrocarbon products and to adopt measures to ensure the supply, service efficiency and prevent its interruption'.[61] A similar price prerogative applies to the electricity supply, as the service shall be provided under conditions of 'efficiency, co-responsibility, solidarity, equity and economic sustainability, contributing to the achievement of the most amount of happiness possible',[62] and allowing for subsidies to the energy poor.[63]

B. Terminating the Subsidy Scheme, Cheap Gasoline for Political Support, or Just a Failed Attempt?

Not even oil-rich Venezuela can subsidize gasoline to all users forever and especially at those price levels. The ongoing economic and (now political) crisis in Venezuela led President Maduro in February 2016 to increase gasoline prices for all users by 1.328 per cent for 91 octanes and 6.000 per cent for 95 octanes.[64] This was the first

[58] Hugo Chávez, 'Propuesta del Candidato de la Patria Comandante Hugo Chávez Para la gestión Bolivariana socialista 2013–2019', see paragraphs 3.1.12–3.1.14. http://www.siteal.iipe.unesco.org/sites/default/files/sit_accion_files/siteal_venezuela_0467.pdf accessed 14 August 2019.

[59] A.R. Brewer-Carías, 'El Régimen Constitucional De Los Servicios Públicos En Venezuela' (2002) http://allanbrewercarias.net/Content/449725d9-f1cb-474b-8ab2-41efb849fea2/Content/I,%201,%20857.%20EL%20REGIMEN%20CONSITUCIONAL%20DE%20LOS%20SERVICIOS%20PUBLICOS%20_BRASIL%20CURITIBA_2002.pdf accessed 14 August 2019 (hereafter Brewer, 'El Régimen Constitucional De Los Servicios Públicos En Venezuela').

[60] Article 156 (29), of the Constituion of the Bolivarian Republic of Venezuela, 2009, N 5.908 Extraordinary.

[61] Article 60 of the Organic Law of Hydrocarbons, 2006, N. 38.492. See also Recital 2 of the Administrative Resolution issued by the Ministry of the Popular Power for Petroleum and Mines N. 015 of 18 February 2016 fixing fuel prices, 2016, No. 40.851.

[62] Organic Law of the System and Electric Service (2010), Article 10.

[63] Organic Law of the System and Electric Service (2010), Article 66.

[64] J. Wattles and P. Gillespie, 'El precio de la gasolina en Venezula aumentó 6.000% ... pero sigue siendo la más barata del mundo' (18 February 2016) CCN en Español, https://cnnespanol.cnn.com/2016/02/18/

gasoline price increase since 1996. The prices at the time were the equivalent to about US$0.00003 and 0.000005, respectively, per litre according to the official exchange rate.[65] In spite of this increase, Venezuela's gasoline continued and continues to be the cheapest gasoline in the world. This price increase would mean savings of around US$800 million as acknowledged by Maduro.[66] Popular protest followed, particularly due to the impact on public transportation prices and the effects on the poorest in the country.[67]

Despite the protests, the Executive Power found it to be insufficient. In July 2018, President Maduro declared another price increase, this time to equate them to the 'prices set in international markets', in an unprecedented measure in Venezuela, and terminating, at least on paper, the subsidy policy for gasoline in the country for all users.[68] According to this announcement, all users would have had to pay about US$1 per gasoline litre.

This came with a caveat that can be read as either an attempt to implement some form of energy-poverty policy concerning the gasoline subsidy—following the electricity example—or, and perhaps more likely, as a measure of political control. Maduro's regime would impose a two-year phasing out scheme to progressively phase out gasoline subsidies.[69] During the scheme, only those holders of a 'Card of the Motherland' would benefit from discounted gasoline prices and only those without this 'Card' would have to pay for gasoline at 'international prices'.[70] This 'Card of the Motherland' is an identity document issued by the government according to socio-economic status and need for financial support that works based on a QR code. About seventeen million Venezuelans could theoretically benefit from this discount according to the data of the government. The 'Card of the Motherland' is associated with political affiliation to Maduro's political party,[71] and which opponents to the regime can have either no access, or may not wish to obtain one. Thus, it is no surprise that the measure was seen as a move to further oppress the opposition and, at the same time, force popular pledging to the regime in

el-precio-de-la-gasolina-en-venezuela-aumento-6-000-pero-sigue-siendo-la-mas-barata-del-mundo/; Noticias RCN, 'Maduro anunció aumento del precio de la gasolina en Venezuela por primera vez en 20 años'(17 February 2016), https://noticias.canalrcn.com/internacional-america/maduro-anuncio-aumento-del-precio-gasolina-venezuela-primera-vez-20-anos accessed 14 August 2019.

[65] V. Salmerón, 'Los volátiles escenarios de la gasolina' (August 2018) https://prodavinci.com/los-volatiles-escenarios-de-la-gasolina/ accessed 14 August 2019.

[66] La Prensa, 'Venezuela: ¿por qué Nicolás Maduro aumentó el precio de la gasolina?' (19 February 2016) https://laprensa.peru.com/actualidad/noticia-venezuela-que-nicolas-maduro-aumento-precio-gasolina-58457 accessed 14 August 2019.

[67] BBC News Mundo, 'Venezuela: mueren dos policías en protestas en San Cristóbal' (30 March 2016) https://www.bbc.com/mundo/noticias/2016/03/160329_venezuela_policias_san_cristobal_dp accessed 14 August 2019.

[68] Ibid., at 1.

[69] Deutsche Welle (DW), 'Fin de la gasolina barata en Venezuela' (17 August 2018) https://www.dw.com/es/fin-de-la-gasolina-barata-en-venezuela/a-45123175 accessed 14 August 2019.

[70] Brewer, 'El Régimen Constitucional De Los Servicios Públicos En Venezuela' (n 59), 37.

[71] J. Magdaleno, 'Escenarios en la encrucijada venezolana' (2018) 274 *Nueva Sociedad*, 156.

exchange for cheap gasoline,[72] a strategy used already for years when it comes to access to food.[73]

Despite these announcements, the termination of the subsidy has not taken place. In fact, the change of prices never occurred.[74] It remained a non-executed promise (or threat), and no official reason for the abrupt change was given. One can speculate that the lifting of the subsidy did not take place due to the political cost for the regime, or simply (and as it occurred) because the government found no way to implement the system in any reliable way, or perhaps it was just incompetence.[75]

C. Legal Challenges and Concluding Remarks

Venezuela's 'energy twist' to alleviating energy poverty has consisted of subsidizing gasoline prices for all end users for more than thirty years, making it the cheapest in the world—and by a large margin. Gasoline subsidies have become part of the Venezuelan idiosyncrasy; a 'sacred right' of Venezuelans as 'owners' of the oil riches, and a political tool to manage discontent. Thus, gasoline subsidies are less about energy poverty and more about energy populism. This is also palpable in the scant regulation of energy poverty. The legal basis, legal method, and content of the rules shifts in accordance to political needs and it reveals the existence of an opaque and unpredictable system based on a mix of laws, presidential decrees, and administrative provisions.

Prompted by the ongoing and devastating economic crisis, it is only recently that a sketch of energy poverty policy and rules has started to emerge in Venezuela, for example with the 'Green Band' system in electricity, or the announced but retracted gasoline price subsidies based on socio-economic indicators. Yet, compared to the energy poverty treatment given by other countries in the region, the Venezuelan poverty

[72] BBC News Mundo, 'Qué es y cómo funciona el carnet de la patria que permitirá seguir comprando gasolina a precio subsidiado en Venezuela' (14 August 2018) https://www.bbc.com/mundo/noticias-america-latina-45182511; ABC, 'Maduro exige "el carnet de la patria" para obtener gasolina' (30 July 2018) https://www.abc.es/internacional/abci-venezuela-racionara-gasolina-traves-carnet-patria-201807301021_noticia.html; El Universal, 'INTT reiteró que sin el carnet de la patria no habrá subsidio de la gasolina' (19 August 2018)http://www.eluniversal.com/politica/18189/intt-sin-carnet-de-la-patria-no-hay-subsidio-de-la-gasolina accessed 14 August 2019.

[73] J.R. López Padrino, 'Carnet de la Patria: Herramienta de Control Social' (1 March 2018) *Tal Cual Digital* http://talcualdigital.com/index.php/2018/03/01/26519/ accessed 14 August 2019.

[74] See, e.g., the news discussing this lack of price increase and the reigning 'status-quo'. C.S. Meneses, 'El precio de la gasolina aumentó de facto y no por decreto' (18 December 2018) http://cronica.uno/el-precio-de-la-gasolina-aumento-de-facto-y-no-por-decreto/ (accessed 14 August 2019); ABC, 'Largas colas un día antes de la subida del precio de la gasolina en Venezuela' (24 September 2018) https://www.abc.es/internacional/abci-largas-colas-antes-subida-precio-gasolina-venezuela-201809241249_noticia.html accessed 14 August 2019.

[75] El Nacional, 'Venta de gasolina con carnet de la patria empezó con fallas en Táchira' (5 September 2018) http://www.el-nacional.com/noticias/servicios/venta-gasolina-con-carnet-patria-empezo-con-fallas-tachira_250559; El Carabobeño, 'Biopago de gasolina con Carnet de la Patria en todo el país desde el 24 de septiembre', (21 September 2018) https://www.el-carabobeno.com/biopago-de-gasolina-con-carnet-de-la-patria-en-todo-el-pais-a-desde-el-24-de-septiembre/ accessed 14 August 2019.

rules appear as less sophisticated, under-developed, and with a focus on gasoline as an energy resource.

However, recent blackouts show an increasing concern about energy access. Venezuela (Caracas and eighteen out of twenty-seven states) experienced a series of constant power cuts from March to July of 2019. The government states that those blackouts are a product of cyber attacks directed by the opposition and the Donald Trump administration.[76] However, non-governmental studies affirm that such blackouts are a consequence of the lack of maintenance and investment on the management of the electricity grid, inappropriate planning, and corruption.[77]

VI. Energy Poverty in Peru

Energy in Peru is a basic element for the economic and social development of the country. The growth of the energy industry has been a determining factor for the sustainability of the provision of services in favour of both the citizens and investment projects of varying scales.[78]

The Peruvian regulatory framework has evolved to the point that it provides opportunities for the private sector to participate in different parts of the energy industry. However, the private sector has prioritized its participation in activities that may provide bigger financial profits.

A. Access to Energy

Two favourable consequences of the energy policy applied in the 1990s were the coverage increase and quality improvement of the energy services.[79] However, they also evidenced that the proposal to insert private parties in the provision of services was not enough to make basic energy services universal.

Even though universal access has been an objective within the reforms taken by the Law of Electrical Concessions[80], it is only since 2001 with the law creating the Electrical Social Compensation Fund (FOSE) that the first measures to ensure the access to low-income people have been adopted. The proposed formula that is still being used is the application of a crossed subsidy between those who have high electricity consumption and those who have a lower one.

[76] El Pais, ' El colapso del sistema eléctrico venezolano sume de nuevo a gran parte del país en la oscuridad' (23 July 2019) https://elpais.com/internacional/2019/07/23/america/1563833322_780396.html accessed 14 August 2019.

[77] Dinero, 'Estas son las verdaderas causas del apagón en Venezuela' (3 September 2019) https://www.dinero.com/internacional/articulo/por-que-se-fue-la-luz-en-venezuela-en-2019/268147 accessed 14 September 2019.

[78] A. Cairampoma, 'El servicio universal en el sector eléctrico peruano: análisis del marco regulatorio desde la perspectiva de la experiencia de la Unión Europea' (2012) *Revista de Derecho Administrativo*.

[79] V. Vega, *Los Títulos habilitantes en la Transmisión de Electricidad* (Pontifical Catholic University of Peru, 2017).

[80] Executive Power, Electrical Concession Law, Law Decree 25844 (1992).

B. Electricity Affordability and Protection to Vulnerable Energy Users

In 2010, the National Energy Policy of Peru 2010–2040[81] was approved, which states the goal of universal access to electric supply after recognizing the relevance of the energy services for the country. Thus, one of the guidelines for the stated goal is to reach total coverage of electric and hydrocarbon supply. It is during this stage that the need to create a special system to achieve universal access started to take shape.

Against this backdrop, it must be noted that the attempt to provide universal energy services was focused essentially on providing electricity, setting aside options such as promoting residential natural gas consumption. Because of this, and in accordance with the National Energy Policy, Law No. 29852 was approved in 2012,[82] creating the Energy Social Inclusion Fund (FISE).

The goals of FISE, always with a focus on vulnerable populations, are the mass use of natural gas (residential and automobile), the compensation for the development of new supplies in the energy frontier and social compensation and advocacy for access to liquid petrol gas both in urban and in rural areas. FISE is also in charge of managing a compensation mechanism for residential electrical tariffs (cross-subsidy).

In 2013 the Universal Access to Energy Plan 2013–2022 was approved.[83] This plan outlines the mechanisms to be used for universal access to energy and rural energization, which are: (i) Advertising Program for the Mass Use of Natural Gas; (ii) Advocating and/or Compensating for Access to Fuels; (iii) Development Programs of New Supplies in the Energy Frontier; and (iv) Programs and Improvement of Rural Energy Use.

C. Quality of the Service

Despite the state having a competent regulatory framework to perform the activities needed for the universal access of the electricity supply, the results were not as expected. Consequently, in 2015 the Technical Responsibility Areas (ZRT) were created, which outline the geographical areas to achieve universal access to electrical service, which preferably consider the borders of the Regions where the relevant distribution dealerships act.

Later, in 2017, the ZRTs were outlined for the territory. Since then the distribution companies are required to participate in the advertising, planning, and supervision of

[81] Supreme Decree 064-2010-EM, Presidency of the Republic approves the National Energy Policy of Peru 2010–2040.

[82] Law 29852 (3 April 2012). Law that creates the Energy Security System in Hydrocarbon and the Energy Social Inclusion Fund.

[83] Ministry of Energy and Mines, Approves the Universal Access to Energy Plan 2013–2022, Ministerial Edict 203-2013-MEM/DM.

the electrification projects that are proposed within their ZRTs. Furthermore, the distribution dealers have the priority when it comes to carrying out the electrification projects in their ZRTs.

D. Legal Challenges

It is important to note that within the Peruvian legal system, the electricity and natural gas distribution dealership is responsible for marketing, an activity that up to now has not been available to free competition. Otherwise, the proposal for ZRTs would not have been possible or, in any case, would have had a different layout.

Currently, in the framework of the proposed objectives for 2021—the Bicentennial of the Republic—the Ministry of Energy and Mines (governing body of the energy sector) has two priority goals, one linked to electricity services and the other to natural gas.[84]

The goal related to electricity service is based on providing electricity service to 100 per cent of the population living in rural areas, which would mean closing the 18.5 per cent gap and benefitting 420 thousand families.

The second goal is to have one and a half million households connected to the natural gas networks, which would translate to 18 per cent of households in the country and five million inhabitants who would benefit from this service. In order to achieve that, an investment of $600 million is needed. As the numbers may hint, Peru is closer to achieving universal service in public electricity service than in natural gas, a field where there is still plenty to be done.

Lastly, within the framework of the Peruvian proposal to achieve universal service related to energy services, the Draft Regulation of the General Rural Electrification Law was published in 2019, which sets guidelines of complementarity, subsidiarity, sustainable development and technological adaptation, and diversification.

VII. Energy Poverty in Brazil

According to the United Nations (UN), in Brazil, there is no official line of poverty and extreme poverty. However, in view of this absence, it is possible to consider that the extreme poverty line most recommended for measuring poverty in Brazil comes from Decree No. 8.794, of June 29 2016[85], which defines income criteria for the transfer

[84] Ministry of Energy and Mines Determines the Technical Responsibility Areas that cover the entire national territory and the thirteen Electricity Distribution Companies in charge of said areas, Ministerial Edict 511-2017-MEM/DM. Diario Oficial El Peruano, 7 December 2019. https://busquedas.elperuano.pe/normaslegales/determinan-zonas-de-responsabilidad-tecnica-zrt-que-cubren-resolucion-ministerial-no-511-2017-memdm-1594094-1/ (Accesed 10 October 2019).

[85] United Nations in Brazil, 'Thematic documents. Eradication of poverty: end poverty in all its forms, everywhere' https://busquedas.elperuano.pe/normaslegales/determinan-zonas-de-responsabilidad-tecnica-zrt-que-cubren-resolucion-ministerial-no-511-2017-memdm-1594094-1/ accessed 14 August 2019 (hereafter UN, 'Thematic documents. Eradication of poverty: end poverty in all its forms, everywhere').

of social benefits. According to Article 1 of the aforementioned Decree, families in extreme poverty are those that receive monthly family incomes per capita of up to R$85.00;[86] the poor families, on the other hand, are those with individual monthly income of up to R$170.00.[87]

Using the criteria adopted by the World Bank, which considers poor those persons with daily incomes below US$5.5[88]—or R$635.80per month per purchasing power parity—the Brazilian Institute of Geography and Statistics (IBGE) presented data showing that in 2017, in Brazil, there were 54.8 million people living below the poverty line—2 million more than in 2016. This means that the proportion of the population living in poverty rose from 25.7 per cent to 26.5 per cent, according to the Synthesis of Social Indicators (SIS), released in December 2018.[89] [90]

With regard to the distribution of the poor in rural and urban areas, data from the report 'Rural Poverty in Latin America and the Caribbean' published by the Food and Agriculture Organization of the United Nations (FAO) show a positive impact on poverty reduction and a decrease in the number of rural people who are prevented from consuming the basics for feeding themselves. In Brazil, in 1990 there were 71 per cent of people suffering from deprivations of all kinds in rural areas, and this percentage dropped to 29 per cent in 2014.[91]

Among the states of the federation, the largest proportion of the poor are in Maranhão, with more than half the population, 54.1 per cent, and in Alagoas, with almost half (48.9 per cent) of its inhabitants receiving less than US$5.5 per day.[92]

A. Access to Energy, Electricity Affordability and Quality of the Electricity Service

In Brazil, there are persons who do not use energy because they do not have access to it, that is, because they are deprived of supply, and also there are individuals who resort to fraud or to theft to obtain energy.[93]

[86] Equivalent to 22 USD WITH 0590 CENTS. Estadao, 'Economy section' https://economia.estadao.com.br/indicadores-economicos/moedas/conversor-de-moedas accessed 14 August 2019 (hereafter Estadao, 'Economy section').

[87] Equivalent to US$44.1180. Ibid.

[88] Receiving less than US$3.20 a day reflects the poverty line in low-middle-income countries, while US$5.50 (around R$20.45) per day is the standard line for middle-high income countries.

[89] Brazilian Institute of Geography and Statistics, 'Synthesis of Social Indicators—SIS' https://www.ibge.gov.br/estatisticas-novoportal/sociais/populacao/9221-sintese-de-indicadores-sociais.html?=&t=downloads accessed 14 August 2019.

[90] It is important to point out that IBGE made use of a criterion that includes many more people than that adopted by Decree No. 8.794, dated 29 June 2016, which considers poor people living up to US$1.47 per day, if the current exchange rate is adopted.

[91] The Food and Agriculture Organization of the United Nations (FAO), http://www.fao.org/home/en/.

[92] UN, 'Thematic documents. Eradication of poverty: end poverty in all its forms, everywhere' (n 85), 23.

[93] M. Hallack and B. Marcoje, 'Pobreza, ineficiência energética e gato: três pilares de um desafio' (2017), http://gesel.ie.ufrj.br/app/webroot/files/IFES/BV/hallack1.pdf accessed 14 August 2019.

Thus, if in Brazil about 99.7 per cent of the households receive electricity,[94] this number is misleading because: (i) it does not consider clandestine connections and fraud;[95] (ii) it does not show the efficiency of appliances connected to homes; (iii) it does not measure energy underutilization; and (iv) it ignores the fact that 47 per cent of Brazilians do not receive an adequate electricity service.[96] There is, therefore, underreporting of energy poverty in Brazil, which, since unknown, will not be properly fought.

B. Legal Challenges

The lack of access to energy, under consumption, inefficiency of equipment, and the theft of energy are particular features of Brazilian energy poverty, whose solution will not be achieved only by the Social Electricity Tariff (TSSE), regulated by Law No. 12,212 of 20 January 2010 and Decree No. 7,583, dated October 13 2011, which is characterized by discounts on the tariff applicable to the residential class of electricity distributors for low-income families, indigenous families, and quilombos.

The solution involves an even greater diversification of the Brazilian energy matrix,[97] subsidies for the acquisition of efficient equipment, and real subsidies or even a free supply of solar energy equipment through energy efficiency programmes, since a residential system currently costs between R$15 thousand[98] and R$25 thousand[99] and still requires a lot of physical space[100]—that is absolutely inaccessible to the poorest.[101]

[94] Brazilian Institute of Geography and Statistics, 'Brazilian indicators for the objectives of sustainable development. Indicator 7.1.1—Percentage of population with access to electricity', https://www.ibge.gov.br/pt/inicio.html accessed 14 August 2019.

[95] In 2015, the non-technical losses (synonymous with theft of energy) from the fifty-nine main Brazilian electricity distributors were 5 per cent of the energy available in the distribution networks, corresponding to more than 15 million megawatt hours (MWh), the equivalent of the consumption of all consumers in the state of Santa Catarina in one year. Instituto Acende Brasil, 'White paper 18: commercial losses and delinquency in the electricity sector', http://www.acendebrasil.com.br/media/estudos/2017_WhitePaperAcendeBrasil_18_PerdasInadimplencias.pdf accessed 14 August 2019.

[96] Brazilian Institute of Consumer Protection, 'Idec points out the low quality of energy services in Brazil', https://idec.org.br/idec-na-imprensa/idec-aponta-baixa-qualidade-dos-servicos-de-energia-no-brasil accessed 14 August 2019.

[97] 'Brazil has the most renewable energy matrix in the industrialized world with 45.3% of its production from sources such as water resources, biomass and ethanol, as well as wind and solar energy.' Government of Brazil, 'Energy matrix', http://www.brasil.gov.br/noticias/meio-ambiente/2010/11/matriz-energetica accessed 14 August 2019.

[98] Equivalent to US$3.892,76.

[99] Equivalent to US$6.487,94.

[100] ISTOÉ, 'Aneel opens discussion on subsidies to solar energy', https://istoe.com.br/aneel-abre-discussao-sobre-subsidios-a-energia-solar/ accessed 14 August 2019.

[101] It is worth remembering that the northeast concentrates the largest percentage of people living in poverty, 44.8 per cent, equivalent to 25.5 million people. Brazilian Institute of Geography and Statistics, 'Indicadores Sociales' https://www.ibge.gov.br/estatisticas/sociais/populacao/9221-sintese-de-indicadores-sociais.html?%253f=&t=downloads accessed 14 August 2019. In addition, it is the region with the highest solar incidence and lower interannual variability of solar incidence, which implies greater stability in the production of solar energy throughout the year. E. Pereira, F. Martins, A. Gonçalves, and R. Costa, 'Atlas brasileiro de energia solar' (2nd edn, 2017), http://ftp.cptec.inpe.br/labren/publ/livros/Atlas_Brasileiro_Energia_Solar_2a_Edicao.pdf accessed 14 August 2019.

It is also necessary to establish targets of access to electric power and national electrification programmes; to include energy generation and distribution in rural electrification plans and programmes and adopt quality standards for products and services.[102]

VIII. Conclusions

The definition of energy poverty for Latin America is wide and considers more components to take into account than those considered by the widespread UK definition. Then, the definition applicable to Latin America takes into account more complex factors recognizing not only weather and geographical differences in the region but also the variety of cultural and social perceptions over energy needs and consumption.

In the case of Colombia, the efforts that the country has carried out to universalize the electricity service are considerable. Plans to normalize the provision of energy, accompanied with funds that collect important resources to develop projects to supply energy have been successful. However, larger efforts in rural areas and especially in post-conflict areas are vital to build lasting peace especially for post-conflict related areas. Besides, the role of the Constitutional Court has been vital in defining energy poverty and protecting vulnerable populations to guarantee the provision of minimum services.

Chile has established a national energy policy defining energy poverty, identifying the great deficiencies such as a deficit in service quality, the strong thermal component of the electricity matrix, and the indiscriminate use by the population of polluting fuels. The great challenge for Chile will be that its elaborate public energy policy is correctly executed.

In the case of Argentina, the high cost of energy transition is worsening the chronic scenario of energy poverty, which coexists with the development of an increasingly sophisticated legal framework to fight it. Argentine law provides different remedies that allow judicial enforcement for universal access to basic services. Such legal framework begins from the incorporation of international law, to constitutional provisions and Supreme Court decisions over the principle of progressive taxation applicable to public utility bills.

In the case of Venezuela, a sketch of energy poverty policy and rules has started to emerge, due to the ongoing and devastating economic crisis. A serious discussion about what energy poverty means, in an energy-rich but economically ravaged country, needs to happen; but severe electricity blackouts are increasingly taking place in vast areas of Venezuela, including the capital, Caracas.

Peru enacted a law that creates the FOSE[103] incorporating cross-subsidies between those who have high electricity consumption and those who have a lower one. In terms

[102] K. Skierka, C. Singer, A. Leopold, C. Miller, W. Brent, and S. Rebekah. *Decentralized Renewables: From Promise to Progress*. (Power for all, 2017) https://policy.practicalaction.org/resources/publications/item/decentralized-renewables-from-promise-to-progress accessed 14 August 2019.

[103] Congress of the Republic (2001). Law that creates the Electrical Social Compensation Fund, Law 27510.

of energy access, there is the General Rural Electrification[104] in charge of implementing electrification projects in rural areas, isolated and border towns. Among the objectives for 2021 are providing universal access to electricity for rural areas and connecting more users to natural gas networks. Peru is closer to achieving universal service in public electricity service, but not in natural gas, a field where there is still plenty to be done.

Finally, in Brazil, the TSSE is characterized by discounts on the tariff applicable to the residential class of electricity distributors for low-income families, indigenous families, and quilombos. This instrument is not enough to tackle the lack of access to energy, under consumption, inefficiency of equipment, and the theft of energy.

[104] Congress of the Republic (2006). General Rural Electrification Law, Law 28749.

14

The Challenges of Rural Electrification in Canada

*Alastair Lucas**

I. Introduction

Developed countries are not immune to energy justice problems. Focusing on Canada, this chapter aims to identify and assess the legal techniques used in three different provincial and territorial jurisdictions to address the challenge that has been posed by rural electrification (RE). The jurisdictions discussed are, Alberta, Ontario, and Yukon; the latter one of Canada's northern territories.

An historical approach is used to show RE evolution in these jurisdictions after 1910. To structure this historical investigation the areas examined include: (1) how the jurisdiction identifies the problem of RE (long distances, high capital costs, sparse population); (2) the nature of the discourse (equal access to basic goods, justice, cross subsidization); (3) the range of solutions canvassed including alternative legal structures and tools; and (4) changes over time.

These issues are explored as matters of energy justice. Distributive justice (equitable distribution of the benefits and burdens of energy activities) is particularly important in view of the focus on public electricity services. To what extent were the needs of rural populations addressed in circumstances of relatively greater urban political and economic power? Social justice (energy injustice cannot be separated from other social ills, such as poverty and discrimination) is another perspective for RE issues. It is classic discrimination against agrarian citizens by relatively wealthier urban counterparts. Agrarian populations can also be seen as subject to quasi-colonial exploitation, consistent with C. B. Macpherson's thesis concerning western Canadian farmers in the early settlement period.[1] This approach will provide opportunity for comparison among the Canadian provinces and territory over more than a century. However, focus in Ontario and Alberta will be on the RE formative period to approximately 1975.

The issues are framed as challenges that face or have faced developed countries. However, the ultimate objective is to identify mistakes to avoid and opportunities to seize. Therefore, the last section is devoted to lessons learned.

* The author acknowledges Professor Nigel Bankes' research question contributions.

[1] C.B. Macpherson, *Democracy in Alberta: Social Credit and the Party System* (University of Toronto Press, 2nd edn, 1962), 7 (hereafter Macpherson, *Democracy in Alberta*).

Alastair Lucas, The Challenges of Rural Electrification in Canada In: *Energy Justice and Energy Law.* Edited by Íñigo Del Guayo, Lee Godden, Donald N. Zillman, Milton Fernando Montoya, and José Juan González, Oxford University Press (2020). DOI: 10.1093/oso/9780198860754.003.0014

II. Rural Electrification

A. Identifying the Problem

In Ontario, Alberta, and Yukon, there are relatively distinct eras of RE. However, there are differences, largely for reasons of timing and pace of European settlement. Yet, every jurisdiction has addressed similar RE problems during settlement, informed by geography and the course of settlement in that jurisdiction. The major issues include long distances, relatively sparse populations, and high capital costs. Other common issues include the relative quality of rural life and public vs private power. In this section, the order for addressing the issues is based on the historical timeline; thus: Ontario, Alberta, Yukon.

1. Distances and Sparse Populations

From an early twentieth-century perspective, long distances seem to be an obvious impediment to rural electric service.[2] It was an era when road transportation was rudimentary—roads were poor, and the first motor vehicles were just appearing. Railway service was limited. Network services require relatively large and concentrated populations to justify infrastructure investment. Thus, long distances should be thought of as distances between large urban centres, where electricity generation and distribution first occurred, and widely distributed rural towns and villages, and most problematically, individual farms. This problem was particularly acute in hinterland jurisdictions with challenging geography like Yukon where electrical service was slow to develop, even in smaller population centres.[3] Ontario developed earliest, with Southern Ontario becoming Canada's most urbanized region. Major development in Alberta occurred a century later as European settlement spread across plains highly suitable for intensive agriculture. Yukon essentially began with the 1898 Klondike gold rush. It became a significant mining jurisdiction, though population in the territory has remained small. Mountainous northern terrain meant small agricultural potential. For Yukon First Nations, settlement encroachment on traditional lands was largely limited to natural resources development.

2. High Capital Costs

In these circumstances, capital costs of electric transmission infrastructure were bound to be considered high. This was true for potential private electricity providers. It was equally true for governments that considered rural electric service. Government choices involved balancing other potential public services and welfare. In both cases,

[2] H. Hampton, *Public Power* (Insomniac Press, 2003), 62–3 (hereafter Hampton, *Public Power*).

[3] See Yukon Energy Corporation, 'The History of Power in Yukon', online: https://yukonenergy.ca/about-us/news-events/the_history_of_power_in_yukon (accessed 23 December 2019).

the target population was relatively poor farmers always at the mercy of unpredictable weather and markets.

Early public RE proposals faced a series of economic obstacles. These included high construction and electricity transmission costs in conditions of relative national and provincial economic uncertainty. Technology was rudimentary. Even the populist Ontario United Farmers government first elected in 1919, did not, when faced with high costs, rush into public RE. Private utilities were even more reluctant to invest.

The staples economy[4] that developed around natural resource industries including agriculture shaped the relative economic position of farmers. Reliance on a staples economy risks resource depletion including agricultural soil quality, and vulnerability to global market fluctuations.[5]Agriculture was a special case in the western Canadian settlement period. Unlike other resource industries, early capitalism could not account for the labour of farmers themselves[6] within a family homestead model. The result, it was said was that farmers were exploited in a 'quasi colonial'[7] manner. This contradiction in capitalist commodity production created pressure on responsible governments to fill the gap by compensating for agricultural labour. RE was one compensatory item.

Macpherson's quasi colonial thesis can be viewed now through a distributive justice lens. It is an historian's perspective on implications for a particular group of the manner in which a period of human settlement unfolded. But it can also highlight the inequitable distribution of electricity benefits and burdens faced by rural Canadians.

For Yukon, the context was not merely quasi colonial; the territory was one of Canada's domestic colonies. So RE had to develop in the context of national factors—particularly natural resource exploitation; this resource development was seen as part of nation building—with all Canadians having a stake. However, remoteness and geography meant particularly high costs for energy provision.

3. Quality of Rural Life

A closer look reveals that that these geographical and capital cost issues did not capture the related underlying problem in all jurisdictions. This was a matter of living standards—essentially one of equity—for rural citizens relative to their urban counterparts. In the early settlement era, class and European origins, and political and economic power divisions were clearly visible. All of this became acute by the end of the Second World War when four out of five Canadian farms still lacked electricity.

Thus, RE should be viewed in a context in which provincial governments found it necessary to court increasingly unhappy rural voters[8] and municipalities[9]. Electrification

[4] E. Hughes, A. Kwasniak, and A. Lucas, *Public Land and Natural Resource Law in Canada* (Irwin Law, 2016), 102–6(hereafter Hughes, Kwasniak and Lucas, *Public Land Law*).

[5] Ibid., citing M. Howlett and K. Brownsey, *Canada's Resource Economy in Transition* (Emond Montgomery, 2008), 21–3.

[6] D. Schulze, *The Politics of Power: Rural Electrification in Alberta, 1920–1989* (Department of History Thesis) (McGill University, 1989), 24 (hereafter Schulze, *Politics of Power*).

[7] Macpherson, *Democracy in Alberta* (n 1).

[8] K. Fleming, *Power at Cost* (McGill-Queen's University Press, 1992), 13; Hampton, *Public Power* (n 2), 42.

[9] Ibid., 7.

represented a tangible improvement in their lives—in their farming operations, but perhaps most significantly in their personal and family lives. Radio, phonographs, washing machines, and electric irons would go a long way toward closing the gap between them and urban residents.[10]

Government responses to these problems varied. Following early private utility activity, Ontario created the Hydro-Electric Power Commission (HEPC) in 1911.[11] The objective was to provide power as widely as possible and thereby to address rural–urban wealth and quality of life disparities. Population concentration was rapidly increasing and distances, at least in southern Ontario, were less problematic than western prairie distances. Though not initially a commission priority, this set the stage for government supported RE through the public power commission vehicle.

The commission's 'power at cost' motto proved attractive.[12] Adam Beck, the dynamic and long-serving HEPC Chair conceived the idea of marketing the advantages of electric power to rural residents. Competition with earlier established private power companies was intense. Beck's 'Hydro Circus', launched in 1912, saw covered wagons bearing the latest electrical devices touring the province, exhibiting at agricultural fairs and visiting individual farms. It was, reputedly, the world's first government sponsored campaign to systematically bring electricity to large rural areas. It made a huge impression, not just in Ontario, but also in the United States, where it helped inspire the US RE campaign that came along some twenty years later as part of President Franklin Delano Roosevelt's New Deal[13] in which the government introduced policies and programmes to counter the poverty and overall economic weakness of the Great Depression. Included was the Tennessee Valley Authority whose mandate was developing hydroelectric facilities to supply cheap electricity. The New Deal, like HEPC's RE initiatives, addressed distributional inequalities in periods of major economic slowdown.

However, it became apparent that while some labour-saving devices were attractive for farm operations, overall results were disappointing. Municipal electric power with rural extensions was the route to developing financially viable distribution systems. Otherwise, rural rate subsidies became necessary since there was little incentive for private producers in an unregulated market. Another factor in Ontario was that electricity generated with natural gas produced in Ontario remained private and competed with provincial public hydro. More broadly, continued debate over 'power at cost' vs the rural consumer preference for stable uniform power rates, reflected the rural–urban divide based on major relative differences in economic power.[14]

Yukon electricity development (which occurred more recently), while initially a mixed public and private system, became primarily a federal and territorial government project. In Alberta, by contrast, private investor-owned utilities developed the

[10] Ibid., 61.
[11] Ibid., chapter 1.
[12] Ibid., 11.
[13] Hampton, *Public Power* (n 2), 59; see M. Dubofsky, *The Law and the New Deal* (Garland, 1990) (hereafter Dubofsky, *New Deal*).
[14] Ibid., 62.

provincial electrical system. This had significant consequences for the pace and legal techniques used or debated for RE and it presents contrasts when compared with Ontario and Yukon. However, a constant in all of the jurisdictions has been the real and perceived high capital costs of RE.

This perception meant continued lack of electricity service for rural residents. For these residents, lack of electricity would be felt as injustice—inability to share these modern benefits, including commercial and lifestyle opportunities, with urban counterparts. There would be distributive justice failure.

4. Private vs Public Power and Redressing Energy Poverty

In the 1930s and 1940s, Alberta sought to accommodate farmers while leaving capital cost risk to the private sector. Governments of very different political stripes passed various statutes with the objective of easing farmers' financial burdens (including the cost of electrifying farms), particularly in the dark days of the depression.[15] But governments were cautious, and for farmers it never seemed to be enough.[16]

In Ontario the push for 'power at cost' overwhelmed private producers, who mounted an offensive early in the commission's history.[17] The energy poverty of rural residents was taken seriously by governments. However, even the populist United Farmers government delayed public RE. The government first created a fund to cover 50 per cent of rural power line construction and maintenance[18], and then added a loan fund in 1930. A uniform rate for rural electrical service was set in 1944.

Alberta's counterpart agrarian populist government, the United Farmers of Alberta (UFA) elected in 1921, studied various public rural power alternatives, including new hydroelectric development, to supply electricity to municipalities.[19] The latter plan encountered federal opposition; but ultimately private utility Calgary Power's Ghost River hydroelectric development was approved in 1928. These events raised the profile of rural electricity in a very much-underserved rural Alberta. Schulze notes that,

> Before 1928 the possibility of rural electrification hardly seems to have entered the debate on hydro-electric development in Alberta ... But in the late 1920s, as electric power became an important political issue in a number of provinces whose governments considered public ownership, its rural applications began to receive consideration as well.[20]

A complicating factor in Alberta was that provincial public lands, including coal and hydro resources, had remained vested in the federal government when the province was created in 1905. It was not until 1930 that the federal government transferred these

15 E.G. Ontario, 'Flat Power Rates'; Fleming, *Power at Cost* (n 8); Alberta Social Credit Statutes (nn 50, 51).
16 Schulze, *Politics of Power* (n 6), 67.
17 Hampton, *Public Power* (n 2), 42, 46.
18 Ibid., 26.
19 Schulze, *Politics of Power* (n 6) 30–1.
20 Ibid., 35..

resources to the province under the Natural Resources Transfer Agreement.[21] This slowed the approval of hydroelectric projects with which RE had come to be associated.

One result was that wealthy farmers simply went out and acquired electricity service themselves from Calgary Power.[22] In the period before its election loss in 1935, the UFA moved gradually toward public power ownership including discussions about taking over Calgary Power. Yet it continued to renew Calgary Power's water licences and approvals.

The populist Social Credit government that took office in 1935 affirmed private power production. Schulze summed up the context as follows: '... rural electrification offered to farmers the possibility of so dramatic a change in living conditions that it was guaranteed a return to the political agenda.'

Yet, for the Social Credit government the priority was efficiency, and private power development provided the answer. There would be no public power. However, the debate about public RE did not die. We can speculate on whether a public power choice at this stage of Alberta's development would have more completely met rural resident energy concerns.

Eventually, private power was assured after the long tenure Social Credit government carried out a referendum on public or private power in 1948. Citizens supported private power by a narrow margin. This set the course for Alberta's private utility model, under which continued RE pressure spawned the extensive Rural Electrification Association (REA) Coop sector that exists today.[23] Alberta remains Canada's only private electric power jurisdiction.

For rural residents, positive energy justice outcomes can now be seen. But, for example, Alberta's RE co-operative sector remains vigilant. It is in present day remote communities, particularly indigenous communities, where energy justice issues remain, even as renewable energy technologies open off-grid electricity opportunities.

Meanwhile, in rural Alberta, the push for electrification strengthened after the Second World War. The world had changed and so had farmers' expectations. For rural residents, the question was not if they would be electrified, but when. Government response, with other priorities and voting patterns in mind, was cautious. In priority terms, major issues concerned the agricultural industry, particularly marketing matters, and the rapidly developing oil and gas industry. This prompted piecemeal government action on electrification, with establishment of an Alberta Power Commission, and the commissioning of a report on RE.[24]

Yet rural pressure remained strong with some farmers weighing wait time and direct action and opting for their own gasoline or wind-powered electric systems. A small number of rural electricity co-operatives sprang up, answering the social equity need.[25]

[21] Given constitutional status by the *British North America Act, 1930*, 20-21 Geo. V, c 26 (UK).

[22] Schulze, *Politics of Power* (n 6), 52.

[23] Alberta Power Market, Rural Electrification Associations (August 2019) https://albertapowermarket.com/2017/05/15/rural-electrification-associations-unique-distributors-of-electricity-in-alberta/ accessed 17 September 2019.

[24] Schulze, *Politics of Power* (n 6), 63.

[25] Ibid., 67.

When the government requested the two private power companies to initiate a RE programme with service at a uniform rate and government subsidies to the utilities, the utilities pushed back. They pleaded excessive cost and proposed that farmers should organize co-operatives to fund, with government subsidies, the rural distribution facilities, and receive service from the companies at lower rates.[26] This was the origin of the Rural Electricity Associations (REAs) that remain the core of Alberta's RE. Further legislation[27], amendments, beginning in 1975, to the broader energy regulatory statutes, defined service areas for REAs and provided that REAs could provide service only to 'members'.[28]

B. The Discourse—Energy Justice

The key interests—rural residents, governments, power companies, and provincial citizens generally—perceived the problem of RE differently. These interests carried the discourse; but it depended in each of Alberta, Ontario, and Yukon, on the era and on economic and political conditions. The implications for energy access and addressing distributive inequalities were strong in certain periods in each jurisdiction.

1. Economic Perspectives

Economic issues, particularly the relatively high cost of RE, were more stark in recently settled, sparsely populated, agriculturally-dependent Alberta than in Ontario. Yukon's sparse population, territorial 'colonial' status, and hinterland mining economy made the economics of RE even more challenging for residents outside the mining communities. Rural residents in all three provinces saw the full cost of service as prohibitive, prompting calls for subsidies. Urban residents worried about public financial burdens entered the public policy debates. Private power companies simply said that for them, RE presented a less than compelling business case. The implications of this are plain. Markets would, in theory, rule, with rural residents likely feeling injustice. Even if private power rates were set by public utility regulators, the power balance might still favour the urban-centred private sector.

2. Nation Building

The focus of nation building was on staples. This was natural for a country like Canada with European settler beginnings and a nineteenth-century wave of western settlement that overwhelmed indigenous inhabitants. Natural resource industries were the builders. Thus, major mines, forestry projects, oil and gas (in the West) and power

[26] Central Alberta Rural Electrification Association (CAREA), Application for a Declaration Under the Hydro and Electrical Energy Act, Alberta Utilities Commission Decision, July 4 2012, paragraph 19–20.

[27] Enabling legislation was passed in 1948: see ibid. paragraph 21–22 and Alberta *Rural Utilities Act*, RSA 2000 c. R-21.

[28] Ibid., paragraph 21–31, and the decision in the CAREA Application (n 26) which confirmed that REAs do not have customer priority where REA and private utility service areas overlap.

dams were seen as nation-building activities. Electricity generally was in this category, particularly commercially useful electricity. This early capitalist pressure also favoured urban power development. Rural electricity supported the agricultural sector; but farms were remote and dispersed. The result was that by comparison, for example, with the natural resources sectors, agriculture did not fully share these nation-building benefits.[29]

Another aspect of nation building concerns the periods of recovery following the 1930s depression and the post-war recovery periods, particularly the global economic surge that followed the Second World War. The Great Depression put a halt on major public investment in RE. In these dark days, it was well understood that electricity was not only beyond the economic reach of most farmers, but also largely beyond the capability of provincial and local governments.[30] As conditions improved in the 1940s, and particularly post-Second World War, rural communities saw electrification as an important element of economic and social recovery. It provided more opportunities and allowed them to participate in the benefits of economic development from which they had been largely excluded.

Governments were bombarded by voter pressure on all sides. The agricultural sector was an urgent priority. However, the export nature of agriculture within the Canadian federal system created complexities. Discussion emerged about federal government responsibility for agricultural development; or lack thereof.

Threads of this discourse prompted community discussion about local action and self-help. It was these ideas that would bear fruit in the form of REAs and co-operatives, particularly in Alberta. This was intended to pressure unresponsive governments and create market strength for negotiations with power utilities.

3. Distributive Justice

Rural residents did not view electrification simply as a set of economic issues. They considered themselves to be entitled democratically to be accommodated. This included having energy needs met. The 'quasi colonial exploitation'[31] felt by farmers loomed large since it defined the nature of the agriculture business. Farmers were increasingly squeezed by marketing, transportation, and even farm machinery monopolies. These views can be seen as grounded in distributive justice[32] ideas, or simply as a matter of equity based on fundamental human dignity. As noted above, context mattered. In the Depression and immediate pre-Depression period, electricity was not essential for prairie agriculture, which centred on large-scale grain and livestock farming, rather than the dairy and poultry operations more common in Ontario, which could benefit greatly from electrical service.[33]

[29] For discussion of inequitable benefits and burdens distribution in remote Australian Aboriginal communities, see Lee Godden, Chapter 11 in this book.
[30] Ibid.
[31] Macpherson, *Democracy in Alberta* (n 1).
[32] J. Rawls, *A Theory of Justice* (Belknap, 1971), 207.
[33] Schulze, *Politics of Power* (n 6), 54.

C. Solutions Canvassed

The perceived problems with RE in the provinces of Alberta and Ontario, and the Yukon territory, and the discourse that emerged, prompted a range of ideas about solutions. The three main approaches were: (i) governments would establish public utilities to deliver rural power at reasonable prices; (ii) governments would provide subsidies to rural citizens in the form of direct subsidies or mandated rural power prices; and (iii) private utilities would deliver rural electrical service. Historical and developing economic and political conditions made these ideas more or less attractive in each of the three jurisdictions.

1. Public Utilities

In Ontario, after creation of the HEPC in 1906, the commission's 'Power at Cost' motto and aggressive commitment to RE created early public comfort with public electric service. Private utilities were overshadowed. In 1974 the HEPC became Crown Corporation Ontario Hydro.[34] However, by the late 1990s democratic governance ideas were changing. Focus was on collaborative industry–government regulator and even self-regulation models.[35]

In 1998 Ontario implemented an electricity market and, with the ultimate goal of complete privatization, reorganized Ontario Hydro into power generation (Ontario Power Generation), electricity service (Hydro One), electrical system operator, electrical safety, and electricity finance components.[36] This was a response to an Ontario Hydro debt crisis and power rate increases resulting from aggressive expansion and the high cost of refurbishing nuclear generating stations. Today, Ontario Power Generation (OPG) produces about half of the electricity generated in the province.

On the transmission and service side, Hydro One began as a form of Crown Corporation, but since 2015 was in a privatization process. This was completed in 2017 with the government owning just under 50 per cent of the common shares.[37] Hydro One has encountered difficulty with rural area transmission with new, mostly renewable, electricity coming into the grid. Through all of this, public power was the RE driver and the large extent of public hydro ownership and service remains significant to the present. This shows the strong attention in Ontario to equitable energy access over a considerable time period.

[34] *Power Commission amendment Act*, S.O. 1973, c. 57.

[35] See N. Gunningham and D. Sinclair, *Leaders and Laggards: Next Generation Environmental Regulation* (Greenleaf, 2002).

[36] *Energy Competition Act, 1998*, S.O. 1998, c. 15.

[37] A. Morrow, 'Hydro One: Ontario's Privatization Plan Explained' (3 June 2015) *The Globe and Mail*; (updated, 15 May 2018) (accessed 23 December 2019). https://www.theglobeandmail.com/news/politics/hydro-one-ontarios-privatization-plan-explained/article24743446/. W. Rice, 'Ontario First Nations were offered and now hold 2.4% of outstanding Hydro One common shares', (CBC News, posted 4 January 2018) https://www.cbc.ca/news/indigenous/ontario-first-nations-hydro-one-shares-1.4473126 accessed 17 September 2019.

Before the Second World War the HEPC pushed a policy of rural extensions from municipal and regional systems, a policy that continued after the war. The next step was establishment of rural power districts, followed by a third step, a province-wide network of rural transmission lines, and eventually a uniform rural power rate.[38] This was an element of a broader objective—creating a complete Southern Ontario grid,[39] a goal that was considered by government to be self-evident—not a matter for public consultation.

Alberta's debate about RE was introduced above. Tight government budgets made the government-owned utility approach unattractive, particularly to the conservative Social Credit government, and even to the populist agrarian UFA government. Two lessons emerged. One is that in tight economic conditions, private commercial action or involvement becomes attractive to governments, and public vs private, investor-owned, utility solutions become a subject of political debate, pitting fiscal conservatives against those citizens concerned with distributive justice. A second lesson is that in this context, RE becomes a subset of the public vs private issues for electricity supply and distribution generally in the province. This may, as Alberta illustrates, take its colour from the province's political alignment and the course of political issues during the early years of provincial electrification debates.

Yukon is an example of a mixed public–private regime. Population centres were small and remote, so that the entire electrification problem was essentially rural. Yukon Electric, a private electricity company was established in 1901. Much later, in 1948, the federal government created the Northern Canada Power Commission with a mandate to build and operate major hydroelectric plants. This mandate was devolved to Yukon and vested in the publicly owned utility Yukon Energy Corporation (YEC). Today, YEC generates nearly all power in the territory and transmits power to one third of customers outside the capital, Whitehorse. Yukon Electric (now ATCO Yukon) purchases power from YEC and delivers it to Whitehorse and two thirds of rural communities.[40] The latter includes only a minority of First Nations communities.

2. Power Subsidies

Subsidies for RE were used in all three jurisdictions. Ontario's HEPC adopted consumer subsidies when extension of municipal grids proved too costly. This continues today through Hydro One's Rural or Remote Rate Protection Program. However, there is controversy about the high cost of connecting remote First Nations, and with cross-subsidy support from ratepayers generally. The debate is the classic one of who pays—ratepayers or taxpayers?[41]

[38] Fleming, *Power at Cost* (n 8), chapters 3, 4.
[39] Ibid., 24.
[40] Yukon Energy Corporation https://yukonenergy.ca/ accessed 5 September 2019.
[41] See B. Hill, 'Ontario energy minister refuses to release data on rural electricity rates' (8 December 2016) *Global News* https://globalnews.ca/news/3004254/energy-minister-refuses-to-release-data-on-rural-electricity-rates/ (accessed 23 December 2019); ; B. Hill, 'Ontario hydro customers could pay $650 million to connect remote First Nations communities' (14 November 2016) *Global News* https://globalnews.ca/news/3065508/ontario-hydro-customers-could-pay-650-million-to-connect-remote-first-nations-communities/ (accessed 23 December 2019).

Alberta also used subsidies, though to a minor extent. The province resolutely continued to support a private electricity market. However, even the private utilities felt the pressure. They responded by encouraging and supporting REAs, the model that took root and fostered RE. Subsidy support came from a government REA revolving fund. Government clarified the roles and responsibilities of REAs.[42]

In Yukon, RE consumer subsidies come directly from government agencies.[43] There is also a RE local improvement levy for ratepayers who benefit from electrical power line extensions.[44]

3. Private and Public Utility Ownership and Rural Electrification Associations

As discussed above, Ontario's first electricity was provided by private companies and municipal power utilities. After its 1906 establishment, the HEPC faced competition with these electricity providers.[45] In this early period, remote and powerless First Nations communities simply were not considered. Eventually, the commission grew into Ontario Hydro and public support coalesced behind the idea of a provincial public electric utility.

At the end of the Second World War, with the Alberta public–private debate continuing and the resulting default private electrical service, only 4 per cent of farms were electrified. The 1948 plebiscite confirmed the private utility ownership policy. Farm community response was to act cooperatively by creating REAs to fund district electrification. REAs raised half of the needed funds, and a government loan programme provided the remainder.[46] By 1961, 87 per cent of rural citizens had access to electricity.[47]

4. Legal Tools, Approaches, and Constraints

a) Legislation and corporate forms

Relevant legal tools included new legislation, legislative amendments, and regulatory rules. In addition, novel legal institutions were developed. In Ontario, the HEPC was created under a specially designed statute, not simply as an emanation of the Ontario government. Distributive energy justice in the form of addressing a persistent standard of living gap between rural and urban citizens drove HEPC's RE push. However, after HEPC's 1906 creation, achieving its widely available and affordable public power mandate was not a given. There was concerted opposition by the province's private power industry. The decisive decision by HEPC under its Chair, Adam Beck, was to work with Ontario municipalities. HEPC's statute allowed municipalities to enter into power supply contracts with HEPC.[48] Thus in the 1907 municipal elections, nineteen

[42] *Roles and Responsibilities Regulation*, 2003, Alta Reg 169/2003.

[43] Yukon Energy, Rural Electrification and Telecommunications Program (15 August 2019) http://www.community.gov.yk.ca/property/ruralelec.html accessed 17 September 2019.

[44] *Rural Electrification Local Improvement Tax Regulations*, 2008, YOIC 2008/63.

[45] Fleming, *Power at Cost* (n 8), 52–3, chapter 2.

[46] Alberta Culture and Tourism, Electricity and Alternative Energy, Rural Electrification in Alberta (15 August 2019) https://yukonenergy.ca/customer-service/programs/rural-electrification-and-telecommunications-program accessed 17 September 2019.

[47] Ibid.

[48] Hampton, *Public Power* (n 2), 46.

municipalities included referenda on proposed power supply contracts. All nineteen were successful and subsequently, amendments to the HEPC Act removed the basis for industry legal challenges based on arguments that municipal power supply contract power was limited and that there was de facto expropriation of private power property.[49] This cemented the concept of public power in Ontario and provided the institutional cohesion to advance RE beyond the stringing of individual lines.

In Alberta, RE associations were unique non-profit constructs that bridged the public–private power divide (see below). They permitted local citizens to manage RE projects and design rural electric systems for wide-spaced farms with illumination and electric machinery (such as milking machines) needs, and not simply take what private utilities with urban models had to offer. At the same tine this arrangement permitted the overall private power system in the province to continue.

b) Constitutional powers and constraints

In the mid-1930s RE was not a specific objective of the Alberta Social Credit government's radical citizen credit scheme. Yet RE prospects would undoubtedly have benefitted from Social Credit plans for reduction of public debt, and limits or prohibitions on personal debt and mortgage foreclosure proceedings to protect farmers and citizens generally. Derided as based on loony economics, the Social Credit 'model' can be seen as a system to protect vulnerable citizens. RE would fit the model, being a social welfare policy for providing broad access to electricity. However, the problem for the Alberta Government turned out to be constitutional jurisdiction.

This 'social credit' plan was based on the theories of C. H. Douglas. His idea was to enhance purchasing power by subsidizing producers or allocating industrial profits to consumers. A series of bills introduced in the Alberta Legislature, the *Alberta Social Credit Act* and the *Agricultural Land Relief Act* provided for advancing credit in the form of 'Alberta Treasury Certificates' to agricultural and manufacturing businesses, and for consumer dividends. The legislation defined the concept of 'Alberta Credit', as 'the unused capacity of the industries and people of the province to produce wanted goods and services'.[50] This was to be determined annually by a Provincial Credit Commission and deposited in a Provincial Credit Account to be used for provincial public purposes.

At a stroke, the system would create the mechanism to balance the provincial budget and restore financial security to citizens while vanquishing the predatory banks. Taxes were to be imposed on banks and bank securities converted to 'credits'.[51] An *Accurate News Act*[52] required newspapers to publish unaltered government statements when required to do so by the Social Credit Board created by the *Alberta Social Credit Act*.

Unfortunately for the Alberta Government, the social credit bills were 'reserved' by the provincial Lieutenant Governor to have their validity determined by the federal Governor General. It was an unprecedented use of the federal government's

[49] Ibid.
[50] *Alberta Social Credit Act*, Alberta Legislature, Reserved Bill, 1937 (Third Session), s. 2 (a).
[51] *Alberta Bank Taxation Act*, Alberta Legislature, Reserved Bill, 1937 (Third Session).
[52] *Bill 9, Alberta Legis 1937 (Third Sess.).*

constitutional power of disallowance. The Governor General, with advice from the federal cabinet, referred the bills to the Supreme Court of Canada for constitutional determination.

The court declared three key bills to be unconstitutional[53]—beyond the legislative jurisdiction of the province under the *Constitution Act, 1867*. Essentially, the Supreme Court held that the legislation was within the exclusive federal legislative power in relation to 'Banking and Bills of Exchange',[54] and 'the Regulation of Trade and Commerce'[55] under *the Constitution Act, 1867*. The Judicial Committee of the Privy Council (then Canada's final Appeal Court) supported the Supreme Court.[56]

This result dashed the hopes of Alberta's government and supportive citizens. For the struggling government and rural residents, RE hopes now rested on private power development where there was little action until after the Second World War . The Social Credit party's frugal base balked at RE costs, leaving the initiative in the hands of private electric utilities. This meant a retreat from potential energy justice gains by rural Albertans.

5. Changes Over Time

The discussion above shows that from the early twentieth century, RE was seen differently as circumstances changed in Canada and in the specific jurisdictions. There was an important social justice dimension. Changing rural population conceptions of social justice saw perceptions of electricity access advance from mere dreams of better lives, to electricity as essential for social equity between urban and rural populations. The most significant factors were technological, economic, and political. Transmission technology became more efficient, as did generating technology. The latter was significant in Ontario, as large and small hydroelectric projects were completed. Hydro development was also important in mid-twentieth century Alberta.

Government changes reflected different objectives and ideologies. Yet, political shifts often changed relatively little in the RE push. For example, once United Farmers parties in both Ontario and Alberta formed governments, they did not put a high priority on public RE programmes. Social ideas also changed. Notably, quality of life aspirations strengthened in rural society. Rural citizens became more sensitive to urban–rural gap issues—matters of social justice that included equal access to affordable electricity.

Starting points were significant. Southern Ontario was a more populous, more compact and relatively wealthier region than Alberta when RE prospects emerged in the early twentieth century. Yukon was still at the exploration stage. These early starting points tended to produce policy lock-in. Thus while Ontario's political and economic conditions changed, the populace continued to view the idea of public power favourably

[53] *Reference Re Alberta Statutes*, [1938] SCR 100; *Reference Re Alberta Debt Adjustment Act*, [1942] SCR 31, Aff'd [1943] AC 356 (Privy Council); *Reference Re Alberta Land Relief Act*, [1938] 4 DLR 28 (SCC).

[54] *Constitution Act, 1867*, 30 & 31 Vict. c 3, s 91 (15), (18).

[55] Ibid., s 91 (2).

[56] See (n 53).

even in the more recent era that saw the break-up of Ontario Hydro and moves toward distribution privatization.

Alberta on the other hand began with governments being content to avoid major electricity system investments and leave development to the private sector. A critical point was the 1948 referendum when public pressure for government RE was strong. However, the result confirmed the private utility preference that continues today.

Leadership was important. The best example is Ontario's Adam Beck whose commitment to public power and dogged pursuit of extensive RE became legendary. He sold the 'power at cost' idea that was significant in embedding public acceptance of the different forms of subsidies required for aggressive RE.

III. Lessons Learned

The first lesson is that context matters, particularly geography, relative economic development, and political choices. These choices may determine allocation of benefits and burdens. Thus, access to electricity has explicit distributive justice outcomes. Leadership also matters at both the political and regulatory levels.

In all periods, the state of provincial and national economies is significant. Thus, there was little RE activity during the 1930s Great Depression. However, depression recovery conditions, as well as post-Second World War development contexts favoured RE initiatives.

Policy lock-in (e.g. public vs private RE institutional preferences) may occur early in the development of RE systems. The result can be long and strongly held preferences. Further, these preferences may be very different and may even seem inconsistent with regional and provincial economic and social contexts. Ontario's public power approach, developed in the early twentieth century with the HEPC and continued with Ontario Hydro, remains an embedded value even though partial privatization began in the 1990s. Agrarian, sparsely populated Alberta on the other hand steadfastly approached RE as a matter for private power.

Legal instruments, processes, and structures can be important. Legal innovation, such as development of the REA mechanism in Alberta can solve legal and policy constraints. REAs developed to the point of sometimes aggressive expansion under local agrarian leadership.[57] Earlier, Ontario's technique of extending municipal grids to serve rural residents relied on locally empowered municipal corporations. Decisions could be removed from the provincial political arena and brought down to local levels.

Comparing the Ontario public power and Alberta private power experiences suggests that where public governance is strong, whether power systems are public or private may make little difference for successful RE and for achieving distributive justice and social equity goals.

[57] For local empowerment on community energy, see Savaresi, Chapter 5 in this book.

IV. Conclusion

Distributive justice can be seen as underpinning the citizen push for RE in Canada. Aspirations of farmers and rural dwellers for material improvement that would increase the available time for and facilitate family, and community activities that can be seen as matters of social justice, lay behind the early twentieth-century push for RE.

Rural electricity service in most, but not all regions of developed countries is now taken for granted. Yet Canada's experience shows that, this public service developed unevenly in different provinces and territories. Political and social leadership and attention to distributional justice and social justice implications of economic and political choices, was critical for RE, as were local, national, and global economic and human development factors. Legal approaches and instruments used varied considerably. All of this suggests that this history may be useful for countries that are today in development stages in which at least some of the conditions discussed in this chapter can be seen.

15

Energy Poverty in the Middle East and North African (MENA) Region

Divergent Tales and Future Prospects

Damilola S. Olawuyi

I. Introduction

This chapter examines the dimensions of energy poverty in the Middle East and North Africa (MENA) region. It discusses law and governance innovations for promoting the availability, affordability, and accessibility of sustainable energy, especially electricity and modern fuels, across the region.

The MENA region provides a classic illustration of how energy injustice cannot be separated from other social ills, such as conflicts, political instability, social exclusions, and extreme vulnerability to climate change. The MENA region, especially the Gulf countries—Kuwait, Iran, Bahrain, Oman, Qatar, Saudi Arabia, and the United Arab Emirates (UAE)—is home to some of the world's highest exporters of oil and natural gas.[1] The MENA region holds the world's largest proven oil reserves (approximately 57 per cent),[2] and approximately 45 per cent of the world's proven natural gas reserves.[3] In 2018, Gulf countries accounted for about 32 per cent of the world's total crude oil production, with Saudi Arabia alone producing about twelve million barrels per day.[4] Also, for many years, the oil sector has accounted for over 80 per cent of export earnings in North African countries such as Egypt, Libya, and Algeria.[5] Furthermore, with the exceptions of Djibouti and Yemen, almost all MENA countries currently have electrification rates of close to 100 per cent.[6] Similarly, with a strong sunshine intensity, an

[1] Twenty countries are typically included as part of the MENA region: Algeria, Bahrain, Djibouti, Egypt, Iran, Iraq, Israel, Jordan, Kuwait, Lebanon, Libya, Malta, Morocco, Oman, Qatar, Saudi Arabia, Syria, Tunisia, United Arab Emirates, and Yemen. Similarly, the State of Palestine, a de jure sovereign state is also part of the MENA region. These countries have historical similarities in culture, language (Arabic), religion (Islam), and geography (most of the MENA region comprises arid desert countries characterized by little or no rainfall). See World Bank, Middle East and North Africa, https://data.worldbank.org/region/middle-east-and-north-africa accessed 27 June 2019.

[2] BP Statistical Review of World Energy (67th Edition, BP, June 2018), 12, https://www.bp.com/content/dam/bp/business-sites/en/global/corporate/pdfs/energy-economics/statistical-review/bp-stats-review-2018-full-report.pdf accessed 27 June 2019 (hereafter BP, 'Statistical Review of World Energy').

[3] Ibid., 12–16.

[4] Ibid., 12–16.

[5] Organization of Petroleum Exporting Countries, *Annual Statistical Bulletin 2017* (OPEC, 2017), 30.

[6] World Bank's Access to Electricity Database https://data.worldbank.org/indicator/eg.elc.accs.zs accessed 27 June 2019.

Damilola S. Olawuyi, Energy Poverty in the Middle East and North African (MENA) Region In: *Energy Justice and Energy Law.* Edited by Íñigo Del Guayo, Lee Godden, Donald N. Zillman, Milton Fernando Montoya, and José Juan González, Oxford University Press (2020). © The Several Contributors. DOI: 10.1093/oso/9780198860754.003.0015

estimated average annual insolation of about 6 kilowatt-hours per square meter per day, and approximately 3,000 hours of sunshine per year, the MENA region has significant solar energy potential.[7] Consequently, energy poverty is hardly discussed in the context of the MENA region.

However, despite the vast energy resources of the MENA region, the region is home to a significant portion of the world's energy-poorest people.[8] About 30 per cent of the people living in the MENA region still lack access to electricity, while an additional 30 per cent suffer from prolonged power outages and undersupply.[9] For example in Yemen, one of the poorest countries in the region, 13.8 million of the country's 24.9 million people lack access to electricity and modern fuels, mostly those in rural and conflict-affected communities.[10] Similarly, almost one-fifth of the population in the MENA region, particularly in countries such as Algeria, Comoros, Egypt, Djibouti, Morocco, Syria, and Yemen still rely on non-commercial fuels like coal dust, wood, animal dung, and crop residues for cooking, lighting, heating, and commercial activities.[11] In these countries, expanding access to modern forms of energy, such as electricity and modern fuels, remains a key priority. On the other hand, for energy-exporting countries in the Gulf, such as, Kuwait, Bahrain, Iran, Oman, Qatar, Saudi Arabia, and the UAE, achieving energy efficiency and low carbon energy transition, reforming energy subsidies to address unsustainable consumption patterns, and addressing climate change risks to energy infrastructure remain critical challenges.[12] The divergent dimensions of energy poverty in the region, coupled with increased political fragmentations in the region, have not provided adequate opportunities for harmonized and coordinated regional solutions.

While much of the literature on energy poverty has focused on sub-Saharan Africa and South Asia, little has been written about energy poverty in the MENA region. This chapter fills a gap in existing literature by examining the causes of, and legal framework for addressing, the different manifestations of energy poverty in the MENA region. It examines law and governance innovations for promoting sustainable energy generation and consumption in the region.

After this introduction, section II outlines the drivers and manifestations of energy poverty in the MENA region. While there are considerable differences in the energy

[7] Emirates Solar Industry Association (ESIA), *Sunrise in the Desert. Solar Becomes Commercially Viable in the MENA* (ESIA, 2012), 5–10.

[8] D. Camos, R.W. Bacon, A. Estach, and M.M. Hami, *Shedding Light on Electricity Utilities in the Middle East and North Africa: Insights from a Performance Diagnostic* (World Bank Group, 2017), 2–5 describing the paradox of energy poverty in the MENA region (hereafter Camos, et al., *Shedding Light on Electricity Utilities*).

[9] In North Africa, about one out of ten people do not have access to electricity. See T. Lindeman, '1.3 Billion are Living in the Dark' (*Washington Post*) https://www.washingtonpost.com/graphics/world/world-without-power/ accessed 27 June 2019.

[10] Ibid. See also L. El-Katiri and B. Fattouh, *Energy Poverty in the Arab World: The Case of Yemen* (Oxford Institute for Energy Studies, 2011), 1–5 (hereafter El-Katiri and Fattouh, *Energy Poverty in the Arab World*).

[11] El-Katiri and Fattouh, *Energy Poverty in the Arab World* (n 10).

[12] D. Olawuyi, 'Advancing Innovations in Renewable Energy Technologies as Alternatives to Fossil Fuel Use in the Middle East: Trends, Limitations, and Ways Forward', in D. Zillman, M. Roggenkamp, L. Paddock, and L. Godden, (eds) *Innovation in Energy Law and Technology: Dynamic Solutions for Energy Transitions* (Oxford University Press, 2018), 354–70 (hereafter, Olawuyi, 'Advancing Innovations in Renewable Energy Technologies').

situations in the region, there are a number of cross-cutting issues. The high intensity in energy demand and use, high susceptibility of energy infrastructure to climate change impacts, inadequate opportunities for private sector participation in the energy sector, and lack of regional and cross-border energy integration are common and multi-scalar threats to energy justice in the region. Section III assesses the main legal barriers to energy justice in the MENA region. It develops a profile of legal and regulatory questions that must be addressed in order to address energy poverty in the region. Section IV discusses the guiding principles of an energy justice-based approach to energy governance in the region. Section V is the conclusion.

II. Drivers and Manifestations of Energy Poverty in the MENA Region

Generally, there are four key drivers of increasing energy poverty levels across the MENA region. First is an unprecedented rise in domestic energy demand, due to a geometric rise in population and energy consumption across the region. Many countries in the region have witnessed a geometric rise in population and energy consumption at a median rate of 5–10 per cent per year.[13] According to World Bank estimates, primary energy demand in the region is projected to continue to rise at an annual rate of 1.9 per cent through to 2035, which will require a significant increase in generating capacity in order to meet peak energy demands.[14] Peak energy demand in the region, especially during daytime in summer months when air conditioning use is the highest, is currently close to, and in some countries, slightly above installed capacity.[15] For example, it is projected that peak time electricity demand will almost double across the Middle East by 2040.[16]

According to World Bank data, with the exceptions of Djibouti and Yemen, almost all MENA countries currently have electricity access rates of close to 100 per cent, which often obscures discussions on energy poverty in the region.[17] However, all MENA countries face long-term threats to electricity access, as well as access to modern fuels. Due to a rapidly growing population and high levels of urban migration, critical infrastructure investments will be needed over the next few years for MENA countries to be in a position to cater to the future energy needs of their fast-growing population, especially those living in rural and conflict-affected communities.[18] According to World Bank estimates, an annual electricity investment of about 3 per cent of the region's

[13] Since 2000, primary energy consumption in MENA has risen on average by 5.2 per cent a year. See BP, 'Statistical Review of World Energy' (n 2), 8.

[14] Camos, et al., *Shedding Light on Electricity Utilities* (n 8), 8–12.

[15] US Energy Information Administration, *International Energy Outlook 2016* (May 2016) https://www.eia.gov/outlooks/ieo/pdf/0484(2016).pdf accessed 10 July 2019.

[16] P. John, 'Middle Eastern Electricity Demand Will More Than Double to 2,419TWh by 2040: GECF' (25 December 2017) *Gulf Times*.

[17] World Bank, 'Access to Electricity' https://data.worldbank.org/indicator/eg.elc.accs.zs accessed 27 June 2019.

[18] Camos, et al., *Shedding Light on Electricity Utilities* (n 8), 2–5.

projected gross domestic product (GDP) will be required over the next thirty years to keep up with growing energy demand (this is three times higher than the world's average energy infrastructure requirement).[19] However, due to fiscal deficits and economic constraints, especially the economic downturn triggered by the sharp fall in oil prices in 2014, only few MENA countries are currently able to meet and sustain the required threshold of energy infrastructure investments.[20] The slow pace of investment in energy infrastructure expansion projects raises significant long term concerns of energy poverty in the MENA region.

Furthermore, many countries in the region import significant shares of their energy requirements to meet domestic demands.[21] Consequently, as energy-exporting countries of the region revisit their export capacities in the future, in order to meet increasing domestic energy demands, this could significantly alter the energy situations of net energy importing countries in the region. Given these realities, and in order to address the impacts of population growth and rapid urbanization on existing energy infrastructure, especially in vulnerable rural areas, many MENA countries will over the next thirty years need to: (i) increase installed electricity capacity to meet the increasing peak demand load; (ii) reduce the current electricity demand rate by promoting energy efficiency and eliminating waste; and (iii) ensure fair and equitable allocation of energy resources, especially in rural and vulnerable communities.[22]

A second driver of energy poverty in the MENA region is the political instability and conflict that has swept across many countries in the region over the last decade, especially in the aftermath of the Arab Spring.[23] Virtually all MENA countries have adequate energy resources that, if efficiently generated and distributed, could address the energy needs of their people. For example, even Yemen has significant oil and gas resources, as well as a high solar energy potential, which is generally sufficient to meet the needs of the people of Yemen.[24] However, many years of armed conflict and political instability, sabotage and destruction of energy infrastructure, and lack of sustained

[19] Ibid., 3–4, see also E. Ianchovichina, A. Estache, R. Foucart, G. Garsous, and T. Yepes, 'Job Creation through Infrastructure Investment in the Middle East and North Africa', (Policy Research Working Paper No. 6164) (World Bank, 2012), 8–12.

[20] Due to low oil prices, prolonged conflict, and political instability in some countries, and the slow pace of reforms, the MENA region faces a fiscal deficit of an average of 9.3 per cent of the gross domestic product (GDP). See World Bank, MENA Economic Monitor http://www.worldbank.org/en/region/mena/publication/mena-economic-monitor accessed 21 June 2019.

[21] With the exception of Algeria, Egypt, and Libya, all southern and eastern Mediterranean MENA countries are currently energy importers. Furthermore, all of the Gulf countries, as well as Algeria, Libya, Egypt, and Iraq, are energy exporting countries. For example, in countries such as Jordan, Lebanon, and Morocco the dependence rate on energy import is more than 90 per cent. See OME/Observatoire Méditerranéen de l'Energie, *Mediterranean Energy Perspectives 2015* (OME, 2015).

[22] I.A. Gelil, M. El Ashry, and N. Saab, 'Energy Demand Profile AFED Arab Environment: Sustainable Consumption', in I.A. Gelil and N. Saab (eds), *Annual Report of the Arab Forum for Environment and Development* (Arab Forum for Environment and Development, 2015), 84–91.

[23] The Arab Spring refers to a series of anti-government protests, uprisings, armed conflicts, and insurgencies that spread across the MENA Region in 2010 especially in Algeria, Djibouti, Tunisia, Lebanon, Jordan, Morocco, Syria, Yemen, Libya, Egypt, and Bahrain. See C. Merlini and O. Roy, *Arab Society in Revolt: The West's Mediterranean Challenge* (Brookings Institution Press, 2012).

[24] Yemen has more than three billion barrels of proven crude oil reserves as of 2012. See World Energy Council, World Energy Resources: 2013 Survey, p. 2.43 https://www.worldenergy.org/assets/images/imported/2013/09/Complete_WER_2013_Survey.pdf accessed 12 December 2019.

investment in energy infrastructure have negatively impacted the production and distribution of energy resources in the region.[25] For example, due to many years of war and military action in Yemen, critical energy infrastructure have been destroyed, therefore reducing the availability, accessibility, and affordability of modern forms of energy such as liquid fuels and electricity.[26] More than half of Yemen's population, especially those in rural areas, have no access to electricity needed for mundane activities such as cooking, heating, food refrigeration, and essential lighting. Similarly in Algeria, Libya, Egypt, Syria, Iraq, Lebanon, and Palestine, there have been high incidents of sabotage of energy infrastructure and disruptions of energy supply as a result of political uprisings, protests, and terrorism.[27] Furthermore, estimates suggest that over 18.5 per cent of electricity generated in Iran is wasted before it reaches consumers due to sabotage and infrastructure deficits.[28] The unstable political climate in many parts of the MENA region, has and may continue to, stifle the development and maintenance of the necessary infrastructure needed to produce and distribute energy.

A third and related threat to energy security in the MENA region is the deep and growing division between countries in the region, which has continued to stifle and decelerate regional cooperation on energy.[29] Over the last decade, the rise of a robust regional governance approach on energy security in the region, especially amongst Gulf Cooperation Council (GCC) countries, has provided a shared and progressive framework for addressing energy poverty in the region.[30] For example, in order to provide an integrated platform for addressing energy poverty in the region, the GCC Interconnection Authority (GCCIA) was established in 2001 to interlink the national power grids of all six GCC countries.[31] The GCC has played a major role in deepening regional cooperation and multilateralism on energy pricing and supply, by promoting common and coordinated positions for GCC members in multilateral negotiations within the Organization of Petroleum Exporting Countries (OPEC), as well as in the Gas Exporting Countries Forum (GECF).[32] Similarly, Qatar's long-term natural gas supply contracts, signed most notably with the UAE as well as Egypt, Kuwait, and

[25] L. El-Katiri, B. Fattouh, and R. Mallinson, *The Arab Uprisings and MENA Political Instability: Implications for Oil and Gas Markets* (Oxford Institute for Energy Studies, 2014)(hereafter El-Katiri, et al., *The Arab Uprisings and MENA Political Instability*).

[26] Congressional Research Service (CRS), *Yemen: Civil War and Regional Intervention* (CRS, 2019), 12–15; also, El-Katiri and Fattouh, *Energy Poverty in the Arab World* (n 10).

[27] El-Katiri, et al., *The Arab Uprisings and MENA Political Instability* (n 25), 1–5. For example, in Egypt, over sixteen pipeline attacks were recorded between 2011–2013. See 'Blast Shuts Egypt–Jordan Pipeline' (2013) 56 *Middle East Economic Survey*.

[28] International Business Publications, *Iran: Foreign Policy and Government Guide* (International Business Publications, 2011), 239.

[29] H. Verhoeven, 'The Other Gulf Cold War: GCC Rivalries in Africa', in R. Miller (ed.), *The Gulf Crisis: The View from Qatar* (HBKU Press, 2018), 136–44.

[30] King Abdullah Petroleum Studies and Research Center (KAPSARC), *Electricity Market Integration in the GCC and MENA: Imperatives and Challenges* (KAPSARC, 2018).

[31] GCC Interconnection Authority, 'Al-Taqrir al-Sanawy 2009' (2009) http://www.gccia.com.sa/Data/Downloads/Reports/FILE_13.pdf accessed 21 May 2019.

[32] A good example is the highly important 2016 agreement reached by OPEC members to limit oil production to 1.2 million barrels per day in response to oil price volatility.

Jordan, have allowed those countries to receive natural gas from Qatar to meet their domestic electricity demands.[33]

However, the Gulf crisis, triggered by the ongoing blockade of Qatar by several MENA countries, casts great doubt on the structural functioning, existence, and effectiveness of the GCCIA, OPEC, GCC, and GECF as well as other key regional institutions for energy cooperation.[34] For example, with Qatar already deciding to exit OPEC, any future decision by Qatar to alter its natural gas supply arrangements with some or all of the blockading countries could significantly affect electricity availability and impact energy security in those countries and in the region as a whole.[35] Similarly, such a development could have a much bigger impact on the potential utility and profitability of regional pipeline projects such as the Dolphin pipeline.[36] The Gulf crisis could upend future regional cooperation in the vital areas of energy supply and governance and may further exacerbate energy poverty in the region.[37]

A fourth threat to energy security in the MENA region is the high susceptibility of critical energy infrastructure to climate change risks.[38] Climate change poses complex economic, social, and environmental threats to the MENA region—arguably, more so than to any other region in the world.[39] Apart from climate-induced fatal heat waves and debilitating sea level rise, climate change could have wide-ranging effects on extant and future energy infrastructure in the region.[40] This could include potential failure of facilities, reduced life expectancy of buildings, and increased operational and maintenance expenditure of electricity, water, and aviation infrastructure, amongst others.[41] For example, even without climate change, MENA countries are currently subjected to tough arid conditions and extreme heat, which typically affect the structural integrity, operation, and life span of water, energy, coastal, and transportation infrastructure.[42] The MENA region is home to fourteen of the world's

[33] See J. Dargin, 'Qatar's Gas Revolution', in B. Fattouh and J. Stern, *Natural Gas Markets in the Middle East and North Africa* (Oxford University Press, 2011), 317–20 (hereafter Dargin, 'Qatar's Gas Revolution').

[34] B. Fattouh and B. Farren-Price, *Feud between Brothers: The GCC Rift and Implications for Oil and Gas Markets* (Oxford Institute for Energy Studies, 2017), 2–3.

[35] D. Olawuyi, 'International Energy Law and the Gulf Crisis', in R. Miller (ed.), *The Gulf Crisis: The View from Qatar* (HBKU Press, 2018), 127–35.

[36] The Dolphin Pipeline links Qatar's North Field with markets in the UAE and Oman via a subsea pipeline which supplies around two billion cubic feet a day of gas. See Dargin, 'Qatar's Gas Revolution' (n 33), 317–20.

[37] P. Mollet, I. Al-Mubarak, B. Efird, S. Al Muhanna, and O. Al-Ubaydli, *Assessment of the Political Feasibility of Developing a GCC Power Market* (King Abdullah Petroleum Studies and Research Center, 2018).

[38] Intergovernmental Panel on Climate Change (IPCC), *Working Group I Contribution to The IPCC Fifth Assessment Report. Climate Change 2013: The Physical Science Basis. Summary for Policymakers* (Intergovernmental Panel on Climate Change, 2013) (hereafter IPCC, *Fifth Assessment Report*).

[39] United Nations Development Programme (UNDP), *Climate Change Adaptation in the Arab States: Best Practices and Lessons Learned* (2019) http://www.undp.org/content/dam/undp/library/Climate%20and%20Disaster%20Resilience/Climate%20Change/Arab-States-CCA.pdf accessed 12 June 2019.

[40] H. Assaf, 'Impact of Climate Change: Vulnerability and Adaptation Infrastructure', 114–119 http://www.afedonline.org/afedreport09/english/char9.pdf (hereafter Assaf, 'Impact of Climate Change').

[41] R. Schaeffer, et al., 'Energy Sector Vulnerability to Climate Change' (2012) 38 *Energy*, 1–12.

[42] For example, the World Bank classifies Qatar as the most vulnerable Arab country to climate risks and the third most vulnerable developing country to climate-induced sea level rise, with projections ranging between 3 per cent and 13 per cent sea level rise. Other small Arab countries that are particularly at risk to climate-induced sea level rise include Bahrain, Comoros, and Kuwait. See World Bank, *Adaptation to A Changing Climate in the Arab Countries: A Case for Adaptation Governance and Leadership in Building Climate Resilience* (World Bank, 2012), 197 (hereafter, World Bank, *Adaptation to a Changing Climate in the Arab Countries*).

twenty most water-stressed countries.[43] Furthermore, the higher intensity and frequency of hot days in many MENA countries already affect the reliability of transportation networks, and energy supply systems.[44] Climate change would only escalate these pre-existing conditions.[45]

The projected increase in intensity and prolongation of very hot days can result in increased pressure and consequent damage to energy infrastructure.[46] For example, excessive heat could geometrically increase demand for cooling, placing additional demand and pressure on electricity infrastructure.[47] Furthermore, given that a significant percentage of greenhouse gases (GHGs) that cause dangerous climate change come from high emission buildings and structures, failure to build infrastructure that reduce GHG emissions, and that are resilient to the risks posed by climate change, could increase the vulnerability of MENA countries to climate change.[48] To effectively address the impacts of climate change on critical energy infrastructure in the MENA region, there is a need for increased investment in climate-smart infrastructure, that is, buildings, structures, and systems that reduce GHG emissions, and improve society's ability to adapt to, and cope with, the risks posed by climate change.[49] It is essential for MENA countries to enhance their domestic capacities to absorb future climate-related shocks and stresses to energy systems and infrastructures.

Given these challenges and drivers, several MENA countries are increasingly revisiting their energy policies and frameworks in order to effectively address energy deficits and achieve fair, equitable, and efficient distribution of the benefits and burdens of energy resources, especially to those living in rural and vulnerable communities. In addition to adopting some demand-side management measures, especially increased focus on renewable energy generation to diversify energy mixes, several MENA countries are also outlining ambitious plans to increase investments in energy infrastructure projects over the next twenty years in order to boost energy generation capacity.[50] However, despite increased commitment across the MENA region to enhance climate resilience and finance structural energy expansion projects, more work needs to be done to provide corresponding law and governance systems that can address non-structural challenges to energy access.

Section III develops a profile of key legal issues and non-structural gaps that must be addressed in order to promote sustainable energy generation and consumption in the region.

[43] United Nations Development Programme (UNDP)-Regional Bureau for Arab States (RBAS), *Water Governance in the Arab Region: Managing Scarcity and Securing the Future* (UNDP-RBAS, 2013), 1–10.

[44] Assaf, 'Impact of Climate Change' (n 40).

[45] IPCC, *Fifth Assessment Report* (n 38).

[46] Assaf, 'Impact of Climate Change' (n 40), 1–5.

[47] Ibid.

[48] World Bank, *Adaptation to a Changing Climate in the Arab Countries* (n 42), 361–3.

[49] J.G. Carter, G. Cavan, A. Connelly, S. Guy, J. Handley, and A. Kazmierczak, 'Climate Change and the City: Building Capacity for Urban Adaptation' (2015) 95 *Progress in Planning*, 1–66.

[50] For example, Government of Qatar, General Secretariat for Development Planning, *Qatar National Vision 2030* (General Secretariat for Development Planning, 2008) (hereafter Government of Qatar, *Qatar National Vision 2030*).

III. Addressing Energy Poverty in the MENA Region: Survey of Legal Barriers and Limitations

In order to address increasing levels of energy poverty in the MENA region, it is essential for national authorities in the region to adopt an energy justice approach to governance. An energy justice approach aims to build an efficient, inclusive, transparent, and sustainable energy system that balances the needs of all segments of the society, especially vulnerable groups.[51] This will be through the expansion of complementary structural and non-structural measures aimed at expanding energy access.[52] Structural measures include the design, construction, and upgrade of physical and associated energy infrastructure systems to meet the increasing peak demand for energy, especially electricity.[53] Non-structural measures on the other hand include putting in place adequate laws, policies, and rules that support broad-based participation and investments in energy expansion projects and activities, especially by private sector actors.

Despite the increasing commitment by national authorities across the MENA region to increase investment in structural measures and energy expansion projects, a number of non-structural barriers will need to be addressed to promote broad-based participation in energy access projects and investments across the region. This section examines legal barriers and non-structural gaps that must be addressed in order to advance the energy expansion goals set by MENA countries.

A. Weak Conceptualization of Energy Poverty and Absence of Comprehensive Energy Justice Strategy or Road Map

The conceptualization of energy justice, as well as energy poverty, is an emerging development across the MENA region. For much of the last two decades, only a few studies and institutions have measured, monitored, and reported on patterns of energy poverty in the region, and the specific landscape of vulnerability at country levels.[54] For example, the extent of rural electrification across the MENA region, especially in conflict zones, remains difficult to measure and assess.[55] The result is that while several MENA countries have developed national communications on improving energy access, as

[51] D. Olawuyi, 'Energy (and Human Rights) for All: Addressing Human Rights Risks in Energy Access Projects', in R. Salter, C.G. Gonzalez, and E. Kronk Warner, *Energy Justice: US and International Perspectives* (Edward Elgar, 2018).

[52] United Nations Development Programme, *Paving the Way for Climate-Resilient Infrastructure: Guidance for Practitioners and Planners* (United Nations Development Programme, 2011) (hereafter UNDP, *Paving the Way for Climate-Resilient Infrastructure*).

[53] Ibid.

[54] None of the few existing studies have provided legal analyses, see, e.g., L. El-Katri, 'The Energy Poverty Nexus in the Middle East and North Africa' (2014) 38 *OPEC Energy Review*, 296–322; also Camos, et al., *Shedding Light on Electricity Utilities* (n 8).

[55] Camos, et al., *Shedding Light on Electricity Utilities* (n 8), 9–26.

well as climate adaptation, only a few countries have put in place comprehensive national strategies to detect, measure, monitor, and transparently report on patterns of energy poverty at the country level. Furthermore, procedural barriers such as insufficient access to governmental records and information; and lack of adequate opportunities for non-state actors to measure, evaluate, and detect energy poverty levels, patterns of social exclusions, and environmental impacts in the design and implementation of energy projects, continue to stifle the development of an energy justice approach to energy governance across the region.[56]

Country-specific definition and measurement of energy poor, vulnerable households, and patterns of vulnerability of critical energy infrastructure to disasters, is critical for developing appropriate response and policies.[57] Furthermore, a comprehensive, inclusive, and transparent assessment of political, climate change, and other vulnerabilities is essential to guide a holistic and integrated domestic-level response to energy risks. It will also enable coherence and systemic integration in the formulation, design, financing, and implementation of energy management programmes.[58]

A national strategy on energy justice will clearly identify and outline national plans to enhance the fair and equitable distribution of energy resources, especially electricity and modern fuels, in urban and rural areas alike. It will also provide clarity on a country's energy access objectives, priority areas and the opportunities and requirements for stakeholder participation in identified areas. A comprehensive energy justice policy can also allow countries to identify opportunities for multi-sectoral, multi-stakeholder, multi-level implementation of energy expansion objectives, as well as roles of different stakeholders in public and private spheres. Also, such strategy could include targeted measures that can help improve energy situations of specific vulnerable groups, such as those in rural conflict-affected communities, low-income workers that are unable to access or afford energy needs.

To effectively address energy poverty in the MENA region, it is important to evolve coherent and transparent national strategy and action plans on energy access. Contextualizing the unique threats to energy systems at the domestic level, within a broader energy expansion strategy, will not only help to reduce the loss of buildings, physical damages and interruptions in critical energy infrastructure, but could also yield additional benefits that can promote the full realization of extant national visions on energy diversification, energy efficiency, and climate resilience.

[56] For example, R. Cervigni and H. Naber, *Achieving Sustainable Development in Jordan: Country Environmental Analysis* (World Bank, 2010), 215–219, discussing procedural barriers to environmental protection in Jordan.

[57] Government of Qatar, *State of Qatar Second Voluntary National Review 2018 Submitted to the High Level Political Forum* (2018) 42–3 https://www.psa.gov.qa/en/knowledge/Doc/QNV/Report%20of%20the%20National%20Voluntary%20review%202018.pdf accessed 13 December 2019, identifying the absence of a national public awareness strategy on disaster risk reduction as an ongoing challenge.

[58] S. Bouzarovski, 'Energy Poverty in the European Union: Landscapes of Vulnerability' (2014) 3 *Wiley Interdisciplinary Reviews: Energy and Environment*, 276–89.

B. Absence or Inadequacy of Legal Framework on Climate Resilience

One of the most significant barriers to advancing the resilience of energy infrastructure to the effects of climate change in the MENA region is the absence or inadequacy of domestic climate change laws. While climate awareness and action are increasing across the region, a comprehensive review of global climate change laws reveals that many of the countries in the region do not have specific legislation on climate change.[59] For example, while the Qatar National Vision 2030 expressly identifies climate change mitigation and adaptation as a national priority, a clear, specific, and comprehensive legislation on climate change is still in the works.[60] It is essential for MENA countries to support existing national strategies and programs on climate change with clear and comprehensive climate legislation.

The importance of developing specific domestic legislation to advance climate resilience planning cannot be overemphasized.[61] Climate proofing has emerged in the literature as a framework for integrating climate considerations into the design, operation, and management of public infrastructure.[62] For example, Article 7 (5) of the Paris Agreement specifically encourages countries to integrate climate adaptation into relevant socioeconomic and environmental policies and actions, where appropriate. This will include climate proofing extant energy infrastructure and buildings to enhance their resilience and adaptive capacity; upgrading infrastructure operating and maintenance practices to enhance climate resilience; upgrading building technologies to incorporate low-carbon and energy efficient materials; and investing in new climate-smart infrastructure to replace ageing and inefficient ones.[63] Enhancing the adaptive capacity of extant and emerging energy infrastructure to climate risks in MENA countries will require clear regulatory frameworks and strategic commitment to climate proof the design, approval, finance, and implementation of infrastructure projects.[64] There is need for significant investment in climate-smart energy infrastructure.[65]

[59] Sabin Center for Climate Change (2016) http://columbiaclimatelaw.com/resources/climate-change-laws-of-the-world-2/ accessed 23 June 2019.

[60] Government of Qatar, *Qatar National Vision 2030* (n 50), 33; also Government of Qatar, *State of Qatar Second Voluntary National Review 2018 Submitted to the High Level Political Forum* (n. 57) 42–3 identifying the need to review current legislation on climate change risk management and disaster risk reduction in Qatar. See also Algeria's Law No. 04-20 relative to the Prevention of Major Risks and the Management of Catastrophes in the Framework of Sustainable Development.

[61] Australian Government, Department of Climate Change and Energy Efficiency, *The Role of Regulation in Facilitating or Constraining Adaptation to Climate Change for Australian Infrastructure* (Department of Climate Change and Energy Efficiency, 2011), stating that the resilience of infrastructure to the effects of climate change will depend upon the applicable regulatory framework that eliminates and responds to climate risks. See also United Nations, *Sendai Framework for Limiting the Risks of Disasters 2015–2030* (2015), para 4.

[62] Climate proofing refers to the process of integrating climate change risks and opportunities into the design, operation, and management of infrastructure. See UNDP, *Paving the Way for Climate-Resilient Infrastructure* (n 52).

[63] Ibid., also Asian Development Bank (ADB), *Climate Proofing: A Risk-Based Approach to Adaptation* (ADB, 2005), 1–5 https://www.adb.org/sites/default/files/publication/28796/climate-proofing.pdf accessed 23 June 2019.

[64] Article 9 (e) Paris Agreement. See also World Bank, *Adaptation to a Changing Climate in the Arab Countries* (n 42), 361–3.

[65] Assaf, 'Impact of Climate Change: Vulnerability and Adaptation Infrastructure' (n 45).

A clear legal framework on climate resilience can provide legal basis and obligation for project planners and stakeholders to integrate climate resilience into the design, operation, and maintenance of energy infrastructure. Under this model, climate change planning would not be considered in a reactionary manner or when there is a disaster. Rather, actions to reduce climate-related risks can become an integral part of, and harmonized with, overall national planning and development processes, as well as disaster and emergency response planning.[66] A climate legislation can also provide project developers and planners clarity on the key design standards and measures that planners can comply with at the project design and approval stage. Furthermore, financing bodies and other participants and investors will want to have a clear knowledge of a country's climate proofing processes, impact assessments, efficiency standards, project approval process, eligible renewable technologies, registration and certification of projects; verification, validation, reporting, and monitoring. These are methodological questions that must be carefully laid out in legal frameworks designed to clarify and govern climate change mitigation and adaptation. A well-designed climate legislation can provide a framework for coordinated, systematic, and effective climate response by a wide range of policy makers and decision makers in different sectors of the economy and society.[67]

Given the urgency and need to address climate change, a clear and specific climate legislation could streamline or create exemptions for climate resiliency projects and provide incentives for private sector participation especially in priority climate and sustainable development projects.[68]

C. Lack of Legal Framework for Private Sector Participation

Expanding energy access, as well as developing climate-smart infrastructure, is a capital-intensive commitment. For example, about US$90 trillion in infrastructure investment is needed globally by 2030 to achieve climate-smart infrastructure.[69] Considering the high level of capital required to design, construct, and upgrade extant and future energy infrastructures to meet growing energy demand, as well as become climate resilient; government, with its many responsibilities in other sectors of the economy, cannot fund energy infrastructure projects alone. Mobilizing

[66] L. Ryan-Collins, K. Ellis, and A. Lemma, *Climate Compatible Development in the Infrastructure Sector: An Overview of the Opportunities and Challenges at the Nexus of Climate Change, Infrastructure and Development* (Overseas Development Institute, 2011), 16–25.

[67] B. Barton and J. Campion, 'Climate Change Legislation: Law for Sound Climate Policy Making', in D. Zillman, M. Roggenkamp, L. Paddock, and L. Godden (eds), *Innovation in Energy Law and Technology: Dynamic Solutions for Energy Transitions* (Oxford University Press, 2018), 24.

[68] Barton and Campion have identified five important elements of a comprehensive climate legislation. Ibid., 23–37.

[69] J. Rydge, M. Jacobs, and I. Granoff, 'Ensuring New Infrastructure is Climate-Smart' (Overseas Development Institute, Working and discussion papers) (October 2015) *New Climate Economy*; also J.P. Meltzer, 'Financing Sustainable Infrastructure', (2016), 1–5 https://www.brookings.edu/wp-content/uploads/2016/08/global_20160818_financing_sustainable_infrastructure.pdf accessed 21 May 2019 (hereafter, Meltzer, 'Financing Sustainable Infrastructure').

adequate finance to build and maintain energy infrastructure will require leveraging both public and private sector capital. There is therefore a need for governments in the MENA region to provide law and policy incentives for private sector participation and investment in energy infrastructure development.[70] According to analysis by Brooking Institute, about half of the additional $3 trillion per annum that will be needed for sustainable energy infrastructure over the next fifteen years must come from private investment, while other financing will come from public sources such as governments, development agencies, and multilateral, regional, and national development banks.[71] Secondly, private sector participation will be required to provide the technical and technological know-how required to drive low-carbon energy transition in the MENA region.[72]

However, despite these realizations, many MENA countries are yet to enact public–private partnership (P3) laws that will set out the requirements and process for developing, financing, and implementing P3 projects. Only a few MENA countries, such as Kuwait and Dubai in the UAE, have put in place P3 laws that set out legal frameworks for private sector participation in energy infrastructure projects.[73] The absence of P3 laws in MENA countries creates legal uncertainty for investors who would generally be wary of investing in a country where there is no legal protection for their investments. For example, in the United States alone, more than thirty P3 laws have been enacted across state and federal levels to incentivize private sector participation in large scale infrastructure projects.[74]

P3 laws can also be helpful to address legal frameworks that may hinder the broad-based private sector participation in energy infrastructure projects. For example, many MENA countries already have commercial and procurement laws that grant national authorities higher participation and ownership rights in business ventures.[75] This could range from local laws that stipulate that more than 50 per cent of a business venture must be owned by a government entity or laws that stipulate that public infrastructure can only be managed and maintained by the national authority. While such laws may work in traditional procurement models, they do not provide adequate legal basis for the effective implementation of P3 projects. For example, Qatar in recognition of the need to expand private participation recently enacted a new investment law that allows foreign companies and private individuals to directly invest in almost all of the key economic sectors in Qatar without the need for a local partner.[76]

[70] MENA-OECD Business Council Task Force on Energy and Infrastructure, *Spurring Growth of Renewable Energies in MENA through Private-Sector Investment* (OECD, 2010), 1–5.

[71] Meltzer, 'Financing Sustainable Infrastructure' (n 69).

[72] D. Olawuyi, 'Financing Low-Emission and Climate-Resilient Infrastructure in the Arab Region: Potentials and Limitations of Public-Private Partnership Contracts', in W.L. Filho and A.A. Meguid, *Climate Change Adaptation in the Arab Region: Case Studies and Best Practice* (Springer, 2017) , 533–47 (hereafter, Olawuyi, 'Financing Low-Emission and Climate-Resilient Infrastructure in the Arab Region').

[73] Ibid.

[74] D. McNichol, 'The United States: The World's Largest Emerging P3 Market: Rebuilding America's Infrastructure' (2013), 1–15. https://www.aig.com/content/dam/aig/america-canada/us/documents/insights/final-p3-aig-whitepaper-brochure.pdf accessed 21 May 2019.

[75] Olawuyi, 'Financing Low-Emission and Climate-Resilient Infrastructure in the Arab Region' (n 72), 533–40.

[76] *Qatar Law n. 1 of 2019 Regulating the Investment of non-Qatari Capital in Economic Activity.*

Such positive reforms, as well as the adoption of clear and specific P3 laws, could open up private sector participation in energy infrastructure projects in line with the P3 methodology. Enacting P3 laws will also send a positive signal to investors about a country's recognition, interest, and commitment to accelerating infrastructure development and growth through P3.

Considering the importance of private sector participation in financing and providing technical expertise and support for energy infrastructure projects, it is important for governments across the MENA region to provide robust legislative foundation for the recognition, financing, and implementation of P3 projects. Fast-tracking the adoption of legal frameworks on P3 could open up private sector participation and investment across the MENA region.

D. Limited Potential for Regional Cooperation and Cross-border Energy Trade

Regional cooperation and knowledge sharing on energy issues are currently at the lowest ebb in the MENA region. The Gulf crisis, as well as geo-political fragmentations in the region, has upended, and could further stifle, a regional-level coordinated approach to addressing the unique threats of, and vulnerabilities to, energy poverty in the region.[77] Apart from casting great uncertainty on the future of long-term energy supply agreements in the region, the Gulf crisis has also upended plans to enhance regional stability and security of electricity supply through cross border electricity linkages and trade.[78]

Several of the energy security challenges facing the MENA region are interconnected and cannot be addressed in isolation. International energy law, therefore, emphasizes the continued importance of, and need for, political cooperation to advance regional, as well as global, energy security.[79] Furthermore, the need for enhanced regional cooperation in addressing climate change in the MENA region cannot be overemphasized. The Paris Agreement encourages countries to uphold and promote regional cooperation in order to mobilize stronger and more ambitious action on climate change mitigation and adaptation by all parties.[80] Regional interaction and knowledge sharing could help generate greater awareness and political action on energy poverty and climate resilience in a region that is one of the most vulnerable to the impact of climate change on energy infrastructure.

[77] S. Wright, 'The Gulf Crisis and the Gulf Gas Markets', in R. Miller (ed.), *The Gulf Crisis: The View from Qatar* (HBKU Press, 2018), 119–126.

[78] Ibid., 119–122.

[79] See R.J Heffron, A. Rønne, J.P Tomain, A. Bradbrook, and K. Talus, 'A Treatise for Energy Law' (2018) 11 *Journal of World Energy Law and Business*, 45–7.

[80] Conference of the Parties to the United Nations Framework Convention on Climate Change, Paris Agreement, Twenty-first session Paris, 30 November to 11 December 2015. https://unfccc.int/resource/docs/2015/cop21/eng/l09.pdf accessed 21 June 2019.

Region centres and platforms can also enhance the exchange of ideas, best practices, and knowledge on measuring, monitoring, and developing responses to energy poverty. A good example is the European Union Energy Poverty Observatory (EPOV), an initiative financed by the European Commission to help Member States in their efforts to combat energy poverty.[81] Its aim is to help EU countries to improve the early detection, measuring, monitoring, and sharing of knowledge and best practice on energy poverty across the EU.

MENA countries can greatly benefit from such a regional knowledge sharing platform on energy poverty. A regional knowledge hub could help capture the common threats to energy security in the region, and guide the design and implementation of energy expansion infrastructure projects within the region. It could also help monitor and disseminate best practices on energy efficiency, climate resilience, energy diversification as well as energy technology absorption across the region. Despite the uncertain outlook on multilateral regional cooperation in the region, there are opportunities for countries to explore bilateral cooperation, cross-border energy trade, and mutually beneficial knowledge exchange. Greater emphasis should be placed on pursuing cooperation and trade that avoids competitive and conflictive geopolitics, but instead focuses on improving the availability, affordability, and accessibility of energy resources for the people of the region.

The foregoing legal and institutional barriers to broad-based participation in energy access projects and investments across the region can be addressed through an energy justice approach to governance. Section IV provides the guiding principles of an energy justice approach to governance as a framework for improving energy access in the region.

IV. Improving Law and Governance Frameworks on Energy Access in the MENA Region

While structural measures and investments are ongoing to increase investments in energy infrastructure project across the MENA region, the next step would be for national authorities across the MENA region to develop comprehensive and holistic legal frameworks to address non-structural barriers to energy expansion and access. In the absence of a comprehensive, transparent, and inclusive legal and institutional framework on energy justice; effectively detecting, measuring, and reporting on patterns of exclusions, energy poverty, and environmental risks, will be very difficult. Furthermore, without an energy-justice perspective, projects and actions designed to expand energy access risk exacerbating social exclusions, environmental impacts, and conflicts in already vulnerable communities.[82]

[81] European Union Energy Poverty Observatory (EPOV) https://www.energypoverty.eu/ accessed 21 June 2019.
[82] R. Salter, C.G. Gonzalez, and E. Kronk Warner, *Energy Justice: US and International Perspectives* (Edward Elgar, 2018), 1–10.

To advance the comprehensive implementation of an energy justice approach to energy governance, a number of action points (outlined in sections A, B, C, and D) should be considered.

A. Develop National Action Plans and Database on Energy Poverty

To effectively map and address increasing patterns of energy poverty across the region, a starting point is for national authorities to develop clear, comprehensive, and transparent national master plans and strategies that identify and outline energy access objectives, specific landscape of vulnerability, and the opportunities and requirements for private sector participation in identified areas. To develop comprehensive national strategies on energy access, there is a need for conceptual and country-specific analyses of the various social, environmental, economic, and political threats to energy security and how response measure programmes can be implemented, monitored, and supervised. A national strategy on energy poverty can also help to detect and address conflicting or overlapping programmes, strategies, and rules across the different sectors and institutions such as water, energy, food, sustainable development, and national planning. It can also allow for the development of consistent and coherent programmes that eliminate overlap and inconsistencies. Such an operational framework will also make it possible to evaluate the practical efficiency of energy justice programmes and measure and monitor progress based on predetermined timelines.

B. Establish Comprehensive Climate Laws and Policies

To achieve energy security, climate resilience planning must be a crucial component of energy infrastructure development. There is a need for a clear and comprehensive legal framework on climate change mitigation and adaptation. Domestic climate change legislation can provide the legal basis and obligation for project planners and stakeholders to integrate climate considerations into the design, operation, and maintenance of public infrastructure projects. By clarifying key design standards and measures that planners have to comply with at the project design and approval stage, a comprehensive legal framework could also address questions relating to permitting, licensing, efficiency standards, and climate financing instruments and opportunities amongst others.

C. Establish Comprehensive P3 Laws and Policies

The importance of leveraging private sector investment and expertise to meet energy infrastructure needs in the region cannot be overemphasized. To promote and simplify private sector participation in energy infrastructure, and as well as climate infrastructure development projects, it is essential for countries to establish comprehensive laws on P3 investments that can provide clear guidelines on energy projects. [83] The law should among other things remove barriers to private sector participation, and provide fiscal and tax incentives for investments in the energy sectors. Most importantly, the P3 legislation should establish a designated institution or focal point as a one-stop shop for P3 investments. This would help simplify the processes and procedures for obtaining regulatory permits and investment approvals. It would also serve as a rallying point that could foster intergovernmental coordination and linkages among the many institutions that currently play important roles in the approval and execution of public infrastructure projects.[84]

D. Promote Intra-regional Cross-border Energy Trade and Cooperation

Regional energy integration and trade between countries in the MENA region can help address increasing energy demand in the region. For example, interlinking cross-border electricity networks, as well as scaling up cooperative investments in natural gas supply networks, can help simplify cross-border energy trade. While current geopolitical conflicts in the region stifle the prospects of region-wide policy and linkage of energy systems, there are nonetheless opportunities for MENA countries to explore bilateral energy cooperation to promote cross-border energy trade.

Similarly, promoting knowledge sharing on energy poverty across the region can help improve measuring, monitoring, and decision-making on energy poverty in the region. A regional knowledge sharing platform could help capture the common challenges, opportunities, and best practices in the design and implementation of energy access projects in the MENA region. For example, the EU's EPOV portal has helped to provide a comprehensive range of information, resources, and knowledge material on energy poverty issues in the EU.[85] Establishing such regional platforms in the MENA region can simplify the exchange of ideas and best practices on energy poverty in the region.

V. Conclusion

The MENA region faces a wide range of structural and non-structural challenges that threaten the long-term availability, affordability, and accessibility of energy, especially electricity and modern fuels. While several ambitious energy diversification projects are being set up by MENA countries to meet increasing energy demand, legal

[83] Olawuyi, 'Advancing Innovations in Renewable Energy Technologies' (n 12).
[84] Ibid.
[85] The European Union Energy Poverty Observatory, https://www.energypoverty.eu/ accessed 21 June 2019.

and governance barriers that stifle broad-based participation in energy access projects, climate resilience planning, and energy infrastructure investments will need to be addressed across the region. Lack of clear and comprehensive conceptualization, assessment, and reporting of the energy poverty levels is exacerbated by absence of national-level master plans and strategies to advance investments in energy infrastructure and disaster response projects. Furthermore, geopolitical fragmentation and conflicts in the region have not provided adequate opportunities for harmonized and coordinated regional solutions on energy poverty.

Without an energy justice perspective, effectively detecting, measuring, and reporting on patterns of exclusions, energy poverty, and environmental risks, will be very difficult. The regional sharing of expertise, knowledge, and best practices on energy poverty could also provide an effective platform for MENA countries to improve decision-making on energy poverty. The implications of the Gulf crisis for energy cooperation can be mitigated through increased domestic action, and the scaling up of strategic bilateral trade linkages. Greater emphasis should also be placed on pursuing an energy policy and agenda that avoids competitive and conflictive geopolitics, but instead focuses on addressing domestic barriers to private sector participation in energy infrastructure investments and projects.

PART VI

ENERGY AT THE CENTRE OF SOCIAL (OR RECOGNITION) JUSTICE

16

Trump's America and its Impact on Energy Justice

Don C. Smith and Donald N. Zillman

I. Introduction: From the Paris Agreement to Populism

The Introduction and individual chapters explore the multiple meanings of energy justice and the importance of law in implementing its concepts. Law has an important role in advancing energy justice. Some aspects of law are aspirational (i.e. 'Here is what actions of governments and private actors *should be*'). Other aspects of law set binding standards (i.e. 'Here is what standards of energy justice *are* and how they are enforced').

Energy justice can be divided into two broad categories. The first involves those nations and regions in which large geographic areas (primarily rural ones) do not offer citizens essential modern energy services such as electricity, modern cooking and heating fuels, and vehicular transportation. These shortages define the lives of between one and three billion of the world's citizens. Today, most of these energy deprived regions are found in sub-Saharan Africa and South Asia. Their national governments probably need international assistance stimulated by law to improve those citizens' lives.

The second set of energy justice seekers are disadvantaged individuals and groups in nations that do offer modern energy access to most or all their citizens. Here the responsibilities to secure energy justice reside directly on the citizens' national governments. How much energy service should be provided to all citizens and at what cost? Does the provision of modern energy services unfairly disadvantage other citizens?

Our exploration of energy justice and law comes in the wake of events of the last four years that have given rise to nationalist and populist responses to a wide variety of matters of international concern. Our January 2019 article, 'The brave new world of energy and natural resources development', [1] examined those changes starting with the adoption of the Paris Climate Agreement in December 2015 and ending with the United States' mid-term congressional elections of November 2018.

[1] D.N. Zillman and D.C Smith, 'The Brave New World of Energy and Natural Resources Development' (2019) 37 *Journal of Energy & Natural Resources Law*, 3–46.

Don C. Smith and Donald N. Zillman, Trump's America and its Impact on Energy Justice In: *Energy Justice and Energy Law*. Edited by Íñigo Del Guayo, Lee Godden, Donald N. Zillman, Milton Fernando Montoya, and José Juan González, Oxford University Press (2020).
 DOI: 10.1093/oso/9780198860754.003.0016

The popular perception immediately following the Paris Agreement was that agreement on climate control goals marked a major gain for international agreements on climate change and for international agreements in general. The support of both the United States and China to the Paris Agreement appeared to indicate a growing worldwide consensus that would also apply to energy justice precepts.

By the end of 2016, however, that confidence had been shaken by the United Kingdom's vote to 'Brexit' from the European Union and the election of Donald Trump as President and a Republican-controlled Congress in the United States. Nationalist, populist, anti-elitist movements, and increasingly autocratic governments filled global headlines including developments in Brazil, China, Hungary, Italy, the Philippines, Poland, Russia, and Saudi Arabia. Common themes of these populist trends included opposition to immigration, aversion to international agreements, objection to governance by 'elites', and a perceived rejection of traditional national values. Put simply, these populist trends now call into question how energy justice legal objectives can advance in the world of the 2020s and beyond.

Scholars of energy justice cite several factors needed to provide modern energy services to all citizens of the world without seriously damaging the ecosystem. These factors then need to be implemented into international, national, and local laws. Among the factors are:

1. Support for international legal and policy directives recognizing the world-wide benefit of providing all citizens with access to reliable electricity service, access to clean fuels for cooking and heating, and access to necessary transportation to allow economically and socially beneficial human development.
2. Respect for human rights that support access to energy without discrimination based on race, religion, or gender.
3. Appreciation of the importance of national sovereignty combined with recognition that individual and group rights to energy may need to limit that sovereignty.
4. Recognition of the reality of climate change and an understanding that need for energy justice must co-exist with the need to control climate change and other environmental values.
5. Recognition of the rights of disadvantaged groups in society to have the right of fair participation in decision-making on energy justice matters.

This chapter involves the United States, with attention focused on President Donald Trump's administration. What changes has it made in America's approach to the energy justice precepts described above? What future changes may impact energy justice?

The chapter begins with an assessment of President Trump. The following section describes the likely position of the Republican Party on issues of energy justice. That is followed by a more detailed examination of the Trump-Republican Party actions involving matters of energy justice. Finally, the conclusion considers where governmental policies may be heading.

II. President Donald Trump

'The brave new world' article described Donald Trump's unusual path to the White House and the expectations for his presidency. However, a deeper understanding of Donald Trump requires a reference to *The Art of the Deal*, which he co-authored with Tony Schwartz.[2] Published in 1987, the book reflects Trump's thinking through his early forties.

As a young man, Trump had expanded on his father's successes as a real estate developer in New York City. That required work with both government offices and with numerous private sector businesses.

Most of the book centres on specific real estate 'deals' in Manhattan (the most visible New York City borough) that Trump had done and how the Trump 'art' evolved. While no admirer of government, particularly in New York City, Trump is shrewd about the need for working with government to advance his business objectives.

Trump described his approach to deal-making as such: 'My style of deal-making is quite simple and straightforward. I aim very high, and then I just keep pushing and pushing and pushing to get what I'm after.'[3]

To Trump, deal-making 'is an ability you're born with. It's not about being brilliant ... mostly it's about instincts'.[4] He is dismissive of 'number-crunchers', and 'fancy marketing surveys'.[5] He has learned more 'from conducting my own random surveys than I could ever have learned from the greatest of consulting firms'.[6] He praises his father Fred, who did not have a college degree but nevertheless 'could run circles around most academics'.[7] Donald Trump's time at the Wharton Business School at the University of Pennsylvania convinced him to 'not ... be overly impressed by academic credentials'.[8] He summarizes: 'When it comes to making a smart decision, the most distinguished planning committee working with the highest-paid consultants doesn't hold a candle to a group of guys with a reasonable amount of common sense and their own money on the line.'[9]

One of Trump's most visible deals involved the renovation of an ice-skating rink in New York City's iconic Central Park. Ample dollars spent and extensive work by government officers and consultants had accomplished nothing. Trump put his reputation on the line with his observation: 'If it took me [only] two and a half years to put up a major skyscraper, surely it was possible to build a $2 million ice-skating rink in a matter of months.' The city accepted Trump's challenge and gave him the go-ahead to undertake the project. Trump delivered.[10]

[2] D.J Trump with T. Schwartz, *Trump: The Art of the Deal* (Random House, 1987).
[3] Ibid., 45.
[4] Ibid.
[5] Ibid., 51.
[6] Ibid., 52.
[7] Ibid., 69.
[8] Ibid., 77.
[9] Ibid., 283.
[10] Ibid., 302–5.

III. The Republican Party

Donald Trump is a unique American president. He is the only one with no pre-presidential experience as a member of national, state, or local government or as a member of the US military. A political outsider, Trump won over the Republican Party in a little over one year's time in 2015–16 against a large field of mostly Republican office holders. This was, however, a Republican Party supportive of much of the Trump agenda and a Donald Trump ready to endorse or adopt many Republican initiatives.

A useful document to understand Republican Party policies is the Republican Platform of 2016—a campaign declaration officially reflecting Republican Party input from every state. Its Preamble begins: 'We believe in American exceptionalism. We believe the United States of America is unlike any other nation on earth.'[11]

The fifty-eight-page platform intensely criticizes two-term Democratic President Barack Obama, who won solid majorities of both individual votes and the Electoral College in 2008 and 2012, was the first racial minority president in American history, and received the Nobel Peace Prize. The platform preamble, however, summarizes Obama's tenure as such: 'For the past 8 years America has been led in the wrong direction.'[12]

Platform themes include:

a. 'Our standing in world affairs has declined significantly—our enemies no longer fear us, and our friends no longer trust us.'[13]
b. The national government and unelected national bureaucrats have taken power away from the states and the people in violation of the Constitution.[14]
c. The American military whose 'men and women ... remain the world's best' were harmed by President Obama who treated 'the Armed Forces and our veterans as a necessary inconvenience'.[15]
d. International trade policies should stem from 'better negotiated trade agreements that put America first'.[16]
e. Congress should reclaim its power over international agreements 'that would weaken or encroach upon American sovereignty ... '.[17]
f. Federal 'regulatory overreach', particularly from the Environmental Protection Agency (EPA), has harmed energy industries that are prepared to make America the world's leader in energy production.

[11] 2016 Republican Party Platform, <https://prod-cdn-static.gop.com/media/documents/DRAFT_12_FINAL[1]-ben_1468872234.pdf> accessed 6 January 2020.
[12] Ibid., i.
[13] Ibid.
[14] Ibid.
[15] Ibid., 1.
[16] Ibid., 2.
[17] Ibid., 10.

g. 'Climate change is far from this nation's most pressing national security issue. [It] is the triumph of extremism over common sense and Congress must stop it.'[18]
h. The Clean Air Act, the Clean Water Act, and the Endangered Species Act have been interpreted to support irrational environmental values at the expense of the American economy and the rights of citizens. 'The United Nations' Intergovernmental Panel on Climate Change is a political mechanism, not an unbiased scientific institution.'[19]
i. Uncontrolled immigration requires 'building a wall along our southern border'.[20]
j. The United States is required 'to retake its natural position as leader of the free world'. The Republican Party 'is committed to rebuilding the U.S. military into the strongest on earth, with vast superiority over any other nation or group of nations in the world'.[21]
k. 'Precisely because we take our country's treaty obligations seriously, we oppose ratification of international agreements whose long-range implications are ominous or unclear.' Among examples of such agreements are the Convention on Human Rights, the Convention on the Rights of the Child, various conventions from the U.N. Conference on Environment and Development, and the Law of the Sea Treaty.[22]

IV. Trump-Republican Actions

In January 2017, the Republican Party took control of the presidency and both the US Senate and House of Representatives. By the November 2018 mid-term congressional election, President Trump could—in some respects—claim a considerable set of accomplishments. Many corresponded to his campaign promises related to energy–environmental issues and nationalist and populist themes.

Despite having control of both houses of Congress, however, the Trump record was not defined by legislation. Much of it, as explained below, was the result of regulatory changes taken by executive level agencies such as the US EPA.[23] The single major piece

[18] Ibid., 20.
[19] Ibid., 22.
[20] Ibid., 25.
[21] Ibid., 41.
[22] Ibid., 51.
[23] The US EPA was established in 1970 as an independent executive-level agency reporting to the president. See Reorganization Plan No. 3 of 1970, https://uscode.house.gov/view.xhtml?req=granuleid:USC-prelim-title5a-node84-leaf178&num=0&edition=prelim accessed 12 September 2019. 'As an independent executive agency, the EPA has the authority to promulgate rules, enforce regulations, and adjudicate disputes. This authority, however, has many limitations derived from constitutional and administrative law. As a unit of the executive branch, the EPA's agenda is influenced by the agenda of the particular presidential administration in control ... '. F. Fonte, 'The Threat of Global Warming and the Roles of the EPA: EPA as an Independent Agency and as Advocate for the Environment and the Public?' (2007) 11 *Albany Environmental Outlook Journal*, 366–7. That said, the most important federal agency policy maker is the US president. 'Because [the US president] has the power to remove most agency heads, [the president's] opinion on regulatory questions is a matter of the utmost interest to subordinate decision makers. Obviously, his input can be outcome determinative, even if it does not come in the form of a command.' T.O McGarity, 'Presidential Control of Regulatory Agency Decision Making', (1987) 36 *American*

of Trump-driven legislation was a major taxation bill that provided considerable relief to high income taxpayers, modest relief to middle-income citizens, and a major increase in national debt.[24] The following discussion assesses major developments during 2019.

A. Trump Administration Actions on Major Energy/Environment Issues 2019

In July 2019 Trump delivered a major address focused on 'America's environmental leadership'.[25] Trump lauded his efforts to protect the environment while growing the energy sector. 'For years, politicians told Americans that a strong economy and a vibrant energy sector were incompatible with a healthy environment,' he said, adding, '[T]hat's wrong because we're proving the exact opposite'.[26] He said the goal of his environmental policy was to 'provide the highest quality of life to all Americans'.[27]

In many respects, however, the address was as notable for what the president did not say. For example, the word 'justice'—much less 'energy justice'—was never used. The dangerous increase of carbon emissions was never mentioned. And when he did speak about the Paris Climate Accords, he did so pejoratively. The headlines in two major US publications summed up much of the coverage of the president's remarks. *The Washington Post* stated, 'Trump defends environmental record that critics call disastrous',[28] while *Bloomberg Law* said, 'Trump touts environmental record after rolling back protections'.[29]

As reported by *E&E News*, a US-based energy publication, Trump attempted 'to flip the script of critics . . . , casting himself as an environmental advocate. But he also provided more ammunition to opponents who say his record doesn't support those assertions and stirred up debate about whether [the] speech was an energy playbook for 2020'.[30] Presidential historian Douglas Brinkley was even more pointed: 'It is an utter

University Law Review, 443, 459–60. Thus, the word 'independent' to describe the actions of the EPA is somewhat of a misnomer.

[24] 2017 Tax Act, Public Law 115-97 (22 December 2017), see https://www.congress.gov/115/plaws/publ97/PLAW-115publ97.pdf accessed 12 September 2019.

[25] See https://www.whitehouse.gov/briefings-statements/remarks-president-trump-americas-environmental-leadership/ accessed 12 September 2019.

[26] Ibid.

[27] Ibid.

[28] J. Eilperin and S.M Kim, 'Trump Defends Environment Record that Critics Call Disastrous' (8 July 2019) *The Washington Post* https://www.washingtonpost.com/climate-environment/trump-defends-environmental-record-that-critics-call-disastrous/2019/07/08/e46d390e-a193-11e9-bd56-eac6bb02d01d_story.html?utm_term=.8e4db8ea8f5e accessed 12 September 2019.

[29] J.A. Dlouhy, 'Trump Touts Environmental Record After Rolling Back Protections (1)' (8 July 2019) *Bloomberg Environment & Energy Law*,https://news.bloombergenvironment.com/environment-and-energy/trump-to-tout-green-record-after-rolling-back-climate-rules?utm_source=rss&utm_medium=NEVE&utm_campaign=0000016b-d2a4-d252-a96f-feac51990000 accessed 12 September 2019.

[30] K. Brugger, 'Trump's Energy Talk: Here's What it Means' (9 July 2019) *E&E News* https://www.eenews.net/energywire/stories/1060714483 accessed 12 September 2019.

farce for the president to talk about America's environmental leadership, when he has been a champion of the polluters.'[31]

Assessing the president's July 2019 speech more broadly, the remarks were one of the few times during 2019 when the administration's energy policies were linked to its environmental policies.[32]

Following is a brief look at the Trump administration's positions vis-à-vis major environmental and energy issues:

- Climate change: along with his ongoing dismissive attitude towards climate change, Trump administration 'agencies and departments are fearful of even mentioning the term climate change or referring to carbon pollution', former Republican US Congressman Carlos Curbelo from Florida has said.[33] Additionally, the president differed again with many world leaders by refusing to acknowledge the threat of climate change at the June 2019 meeting of G-20 colleagues[34] as well as simply not participating in a subsequent August 2019 G7 meeting where climate change was discussed.[35]
- Clean Air Act New Source Review (NSR) permitting: the administration intends soon to reduce the requirements for NSR permitting.[36]
- Renewable energy: since the beginning of his administration, Trump has 'slapped tariffs on solar cells and modules and has repeatedly proposed cutting the budget of the Energy Department's solar office'.[37]
- Arctic National Wildlife Refuge: the administration has finished reviews necessary before publishing a rule that will allow drilling in the refuge.[38]
- Clean automobile standards: the administration is close to publishing a final rule that will roll back standards for cars to consume an average of 54.5 miles per gallon, an Obama-era rule, to 37 miles per gallon by 2025. The administration also wants to repeal California's authority to establish stronger tailpipe pollution standards than those set federally.[39] The latter rule is particularly noteworthy in that it would appear to directly conflict with the administration's concept of 'cooperative

[31] K. Rogers and C. Davenport, 'Trump Saw Opportunity in Speech on Environment. Critics Saw a "1984" Moment' (8 July 2019) *The New York Times* https://www.nytimes.com/2019/07/08/us/politics/trump-environment-climate-change.html?searchResultPosition=1 accessed 12 September 2019.

[32] See Brugger (n 30).

[33] See Eilperin and Kim (n 28).

[34] I. Arkhipov and G. Viscusi, 'Trump Splits With Rest of G-20 Again on Climate Change Action' (1 July 2019) *Bloomberg Law* https://www.bloomberg.com/news/articles/2019-06-29/trump-splits-with-rest-of-g-20-again-on-climate-change-action accessed 12 September 2019.

[35] A. Chrisafis, 'G-7: Trump Skips Talks on Climate Crisis and Amazon Fires' (26 August 2019) *The Guardian* https://www.theguardian.com/us-news/2019/aug/26/donald-trump-skips-g7-talks-on-climate-crisis-and-amazon-fires accessed 12 September 2019.

[36] S. Reilly, 'EPA Works to Ease Industry's New Source Review "Burden"' (3 July 2019) *Greenwire* https://www.eenews.net/greenwire/stories/1060690947/search?keyword=new+source+review accessed 12 September 2019.

[37] See Brugger (n 30).

[38] H. Fountain, 'Interior Dept. Moves Toward Selling Oil Leases in Arctic Refuge' (20 December 2018) *The New York Times* https://www.nytimes.com/2018/12/20/climate/alaska-anwr-oil-drilling-proposal.htmlaccessed 12 September 2019.

[39] M. Joselow, 'EPA Adviser Says Final Rule Coming Soon' (9 July 2019) *E&E News PM* https://www.eenews.net/eenewspm/stories/1060712829/search?keyword=california+pollution+rules accessed 12 September 2019.

federalism', which rejects the idea of federally-based one-size-fits all measures.[40] Interestingly Trump has reportedly been 'enraged' by an agreement California reached with major auto makers in August 2019 to oppose the administration's vehicle missions rollbacks[41] and the Justice Department has purportedly opened an antitrust investigation into the agreement.[42]

- Leasing on federal lands: Trump has ordered the resumption of selling coal leases on federal land, thus reversing an Obama-era moratorium.[43]
- Methane emissions from gas and oil operations on federal lands: the EPA has proposed to end regulating some oil and gas sector methane emissions.[44] In defending the proposal EPA Administrator Andrew Wheeler said it 'removes unnecessary and duplicative regulatory burdens from the oil and gas sector'.[45]

An analysis by *The New York Times*, published in June 2019, reported that the Trump administration had, at that time, either rolled back or was in the process of rolling back eighty-three environmental regulations.[46]

B. Energy Justice and Climate Justice: President Trump's Perspective, Particularly on Coal

Trump has a long history of denying the existence of climate change. In a June 2019 TV interview he said again, 'I believe that there's a change in weather, and I think it goes both ways'.[47] As evidence he continued, 'Don't forget it used to be called global warming. That wasn't working. Then it was called climate change. Now it's actually called extreme weather, because with extreme weather, you can't miss'.[48] As a private citizen, Trump's ideas were of relatively little importance. However, as president, his actions have a great impact on the issue and particularly ways of addressing—or not—climate change.

[40] 'The great divide', *The Economist*, 29 June 2019, 21, 22.

[41] C. Davenport and H. Tabuchi, 'Trump's Rollback of Auto Pollution Rules Shows Signs of Disarray' (28 August 2019) *The New York Times*.

[42] R. Beene, D. McLaughlin, and J.A Dlouhy, 'Trump Ups the Ante in Feud With California Over Car Emissions' (6 September 2019) *Bloomberg Law*.

[43] J.A. Dlouhy, 'Trump Touts Environmental Record After Rolling Back Protections (1)' (8 July 2019) *Bloomberg Environment & Energy Law*https://news.bloombergenvironment.com/environment-and-energy/trump-to-tout-green-record-after-rolling-back-climate-rules?utm_source=rss&utm_medium=NEVE&utm_campaign=0000016b-d2a4-d252-a96f-feac51990000 accessed 12 September 2019.

[44] N.H Farah, 'EPA Unveils Plans to Scrap Obama-era Methane Rules' (29 August 2019) *Greenwire*.

[45] J.A. Dlouhy, 'In Latest Climate Retreat, Trump Proposes Ending Methane Curbs (1)' (29 August 2019) *Bloomberg Law*.

[46] N. Popovich, L. Albeck-Ripka, and K. Pierre-Louis, '83 Environmental Rules Being Rolled Back Under Trump' (7 June 2019) https://www.nytimes.com/interactive/2019/climate/trump-environment-rollbacks.html?smid=nytcore-ios-share accessed 12 September 2019.

[47] I. Stanley-Becker, 'Trump, Pressed on the Environment in U.K. Visit, Says Climate Change Goes "Both Ways"' (5 June 2019) *The Washington Post*https://www.washingtonpost.com/world/europe/trump-pressed-on-the-environment-in-uk-visit-says-climate-change-goes-both-ways/2019/06/05/77c8750c-8717-11e9-9d73-e2ba6bbf1b9b_story.html?utm_term=.cce7767dc81a accessed 12 September 2019.

[48] Ibid.

From a global perspective, Trump's assertion that the Paris Agreement was unfair to the US and his denial of any US responsibility to act has been characterized as 'problematic'.[49] As University of Washington professor Stephen M Gardiner has written, Trump's denial 'appears to presuppose that national leaders have no duties to other nations, even in cases where their behavior poses severe threats to very many (perhaps billions) of noncitizens'.[50]

In the context of considering the Trump administration's key decisions to deemphasize carbon reductions, the term energy justice focuses on the role the increase in carbon emissions is contributing to climate change, and, in particular saddling a 'disproportionate distribution of the cost or negative impact associated with building, operating, and maintaining electric power generation'[51] associated with burning fossil fuel on individuals who cannot avoid the impacts. There is also the matter of 'energy injustice' in 'the over-reliance of today's global societies on the historically embedded production system of fossil fuels to satisfy growing energy demands'.[52] Looked at from a broader perspective, 'A just global energy system is one that is safe, reliable, fair, affordable, and also sustainable for current and future generations and the natural world'.[53] Thus the background of tremendous investments in new energy infrastructure along with climate change 'calls for a moral examination of energy systems from an energy law perspective'.[54] Finally, it has been recognized that 'the link between climate change, energy, and environmental justice is unmistakable: the energy sector contributes to climate change more than any other industry; climate change is predicted to affect environmental justice communities most; and the energy sector has a long history with environmental injustice'.[55]

Bearing this context in mind, the Trump administration's lack of concern about climate change was demonstrated again in the US EPA's June 2019 decision to roll back one of the 'signature'[56] Obama-era climate change laws, the Clean Power Plan (CPP) regulation,[57] and replace it with the Affordable Clean Energy (ACE) regulation.[58] ACE

[49] S.M Gardiner, 'Trump and Climate Justice: The "Pittsburgh not Paris" Smokescreen' (27 July 2017) *Philosophersmag.com* https://www.philosophersmag.com/essays/168-trump-and-climate-justice accessed 12 September 2019.

[50] Ibid.

[51] A. Joroff, 'Energy Justice: What it Means and How to Integrate it Into State Regulation of Electricity Markets' (November 2017) 47 *Environmental Law Reporter*https://elr.info/news-analysis/47/10927/energy-justice-what-it-means-and-how-integrate-it-state-regulation-electricity-markets accessed 12 September 2019.

[52] D. McCauley and R. Heffron, 'Just Transition: Integrating Climate, Energy and Environmental Justice' (2018) *Energy Policy*, 1–7 https://research-repository.st-andrews.ac.uk/bitstream/handle/10023/17583/McCauley_2018_EP_JustTransition_AAM.pdf?sequence=1&isAllowed=y accessed 12 September 2019.

[53] R. Salter, C.G. Gonzalez, and E.A. Kronk Warner, 'Energy Justice: Frameworks for Energy Law and Policy', in R. Salter, C.G. Gonzalez, and E. A. Kronk Warner (eds), *Energy Justice: US and International Perspectives* (Edward Elgar Publishing Inc., 2018), 5 https://www.academia.edu/37660588/Energy_Justice_US_and_International_Perspectives_--_Introduction accessed 12 September 2019.

[54] Ibid., 4.

[55] Ibid., 6.

[56] J.A. Dlouhy, 'Why Trump's EPA Rollback to End "War on Coal" Won't Rescue the Industry' (19 June 2019) *Fortune Magazine* http://fortune.com/2019/06/19/epa-rollback-trump-coal-2/ accessed 12 September 2019.

[57] See https://archive.epa.gov/epa/cleanpowerplan/fact-sheet-overview-clean-power-plan.html accessed 12 September 2019.

[58] EPA Administrator A.R. Wheeler signed this notice on 19 June 2019, and EPA submitted it for publication in the Federal Register: Repeal of Clean Power Plan; Emission Guidelines for Greenhouse Gas Emissions from Existing Electric Utility Generating Units; Revisions to Emission Guidelines Implementing Regulations, final

was described as 'scaling back sweeping Obama-era curbs on greenhouse gas emission from power plants burning coal, [Trump's] biggest step yet to fulfill his campaign promise to stop a "war" on the fossil fuel'[59] and 'significantly less ambitious' than the CPP.[60]

ACE aims 'to try to revive the coal-power industry... [including] adopting rules that could allow older [coal-fired] power plants to continue operating'.[61] Andrew Wheeler, EPA Administrator, said ACE delivers 'on one of President Trump's core priorities: ensuring the American public has access to affordable, reliable energy in a manner that continues our nation's environmental progress'.[62] He also said the CCP would have resulted in lower- and middle-income Americans paying more for electricity.[63] Wheeler also indicated ACE might result in new coal-fired plants and said, 'I don't know who is going to invest in a new coal-fired power plant, but we're leveling the playing field to allow that investment to occur'.[64]

Announcement of the ACE regulation came after Trump administration efforts to support 'the coal industry and after years of lobbying by industry groups and conservatives to pare back the scope' of the Obama-era regulations.[65] In assessing the new rule, Nick Loris of the Heritage Foundation said the ACE rule was 'a sensible alternative to the Obama administration's climate alarmist agenda'.[66] By contrast, the CPP would have mandated 'a shift away from coal to cleaner sources of power, including natural gas, wind, and solar'.[67]

The regulatory rollback associated with ACE comes at a particularly perilous time for US electricity-based carbon emissions. Carbon emissions from the power sector grew by 1.1 per cent in 2018, a figure that 'amounted to a setback for US climate efforts' because in recent years the power sector had consistently experienced decreases

rule, 6560-50-P, https://www.epa.gov/sites/production/files/2019-06/documents/frn_ace_2060-at67_final_rule_20190618disc.pdf accessed 12 September 2019.

[59] J.A. Dlouhy, 'Trump Makes Move to End "War on Coal" But It Won't Save Industry' (19 June 2019) *Bloomberg Law* https://news.bloombergenvironment.com/environment-and-energy/trumps-biggest-move-to-end-war-on-coal-wont-rescue-industry accessed 12 September 2019.

[60] J.A. Dlouhy, 'Trump to Swap Obama's "Clean Power Plan" for Modest Upgrades' (18 June 2019) *Bloomberg Law* https://www.bloomberg.com/news/articles/2019-06-18/trump-to-swap-obama-s-clean-power-plan-for-modest-upgrades accessed 12 September 2019.

[61] T. Puko, 'EPA Overturns Obama-Era Clean Air Rules for Power Plants' (19 June 2019) *The Wall Street Journal*https://www.wsj.com/articles/epa-overturns-obama-era-clean-air-rules-for-power-plants-11560963259 accessed 12 September 2019.

[62] US EPA, 'EPA Finalizes Affordable Clean Energy Rule, Ensuring Reliable, Diversified Energy Resources While Protecting the Environment' (19 June 2019) https://www.epa.gov/newsreleases/epa-finalizes-affordable-clean-energy-rule-ensuring-reliable-diversified-energy accessed 12 September 2019.

[63] J. Eilperin and B. Dennis, 'Trump EPA Finalizes Rollback of Key Obama Climate Rules that Targeted Coal Plants' (19 June 2019) *The Washington Post*https://www.washingtonpost.com/climate-environment/trump-epa-finalizes-rollback-of-key-obama-climate-rule-that-targeted-coal-plants/2019/06/19/b8ff1702-8eeb-11e9-8f69-a2795fca3343_story.html?utm_term=.4a5f309cf7b7 accessed 12 September 2019.

[64] L. Friedman, 'E.P.A. Finalizes Its Plan to Replace Obama-Era Climate Rules' (19 June 2019) *The New York Times* https://www.nytimes.com/2019/06/19/climate/epa-coal-emissions.html accessed 12 September 2019.

[65] N.H. Farah, J. Chemnick, and M. Sobczyk, 'Wheeler Rolls Out Carbon Rule, Girds for Lawsuits' (19 June 2019) *Greenwire* https://www.eenews.net/greenwire/stories/1060632821/feed accessed 12 September 2019.

[66] N. Sobczyk, 'EPA Carbon Rule Draws Democrats' Scorn, GOP Praises' (19 June 2019) *E&E News* https://www.eenews.net/eenewspm/stories/1060634073 accessed 12 September 2019

[67] See Puko (n 61).

in carbon emissions.[68] During 2018, coal-fired electricity generated 28.5 per cent of the nation's electricity, natural gas increased from 31 to 34.1 per cent, and nuclear and renewable's shares were nearly flat.[69]

Despite the Trump administration and the coal sector's enthusiasm for the ACE, the new law's impact on public health and welfare has drawn considerable scrutiny—essentially all of it negative. For example, a study released in March 2019 that compared the then proposed ACE with the CPP concluded that annually there would be '1,630 more incidences of premature death, 120,000 additional asthma attacks, and 140,000 missed school days and 48,000 lost work days' as a consequence of the increased emissions allowed under the ACE.[70]

Several environmental non-governmental organizations (NGOs) expressed their unhappiness with ACE. For instance, Director of Regulatory Policy at the Environmental Defense Fund Tomas Carbonell said, 'It is telling—and outrageous —that neither the proposed version of the rule nor the [final rule] contain any substantive discussion of the severe and growing impacts of climate change. This rule is an appalling abandonment of EPA's legal and moral responsibility to protect the public from the harmful pollution that is driving destructive climate change'.[71] Similarly, Rhea Suh, President of the National Resources Defense Council, said the 'Trump administration's latest move to dismantle the landmark Clean Power Plan is a betrayal to our children, our nation, and our planet,' adding, '[H]e's trying to shut down one of the most effective laws we've brought to the fight to leave our children a livable world'.[72] And the Sierra Club was no less blistering in its assessment of ACE. 'Trump and Wheeler's decision to move forward with [ACE], despite significant public and scientific opposition, fits with a pattern of anti-climate, anti-public health policy', the Sierra Club asserted.[73] In describing the Trump administration's regulatory rollbacks on a series of issues, Joanne Spalding, a Sierra Club attorney, said, 'The Trump Administration is doing everything it can to eviscerate protections for the public. EPA in particular has issued rule after rule rolling back public health protections'.[74]

In addition to concern voiced by environmental groups, US medical and public health organizations expressed extreme displeasure with ACE. A group of fifteen

[68] B. Storrow, '2019 Power-Sector Trends Point to a Continued Rise in U.S. Emissions' (3 June 2019) *Scientific American/E&E News* https://www.scientificamerican.com/article/2019-power-sector-trends-point-to-a-continued-rise-in-u-s-emissions/ accessed 12 September 2019.

[69] T. Houser, H. Pitts, and H. Hess, 'Final US Emissions Estimates for 2018' (31 May 2019) *Rhodium Group* https://rhg.com/research/final-us-emissions-estimates-for-2018/ accessed 12 September 2019.

[70] The State Energy & Environmental Impact Center NYU School of Law, 'Climate & Health Showdown in the Courts' (March 2019), 5 https://www.law.nyu.edu/sites/default/files/climate-and-health-showdown-in-the-courts.pdf accessed 12 September 2019.

[71] E. Nawaguna, 'As EPA Finalizes New Carbon Emissions Rule, Blue States Gear Up for Legal Battle' (21 June 2019) *Governing: The State and Localities* https://www.governing.com/topics/transportation-infrastructure/tns-trump-carbon-emissions-rule-legal-battle.html accessed 12 September 2019.

[72] R. Suh, 'Trump's EPA Casts Asides Critical Climate Plan' (19 June 2019) *NRDC Expert Blog* https://www.nrdc.org/experts/rhea-suh/trumps-epa-casts-aside-critical-climate-plan accessed 12 September 2019.

[73] 'Sierra Club Vows to Continue Fight Against Coal and for Clean Energy,' (19 June 2019) *Sierra Club* https://www.sierraclub.org/press-releases/2019/06/trumps-dirty-power-plan-jeopardizes-jobs-health-and-environment accessed 12 September 2019.

[74] P. King and J. Hijazi, 'Trump Admin's Carbon Rule Faces Legal War' (20 June 2019) *E&E News* https://www.eenews.net/stories/1060635721 accessed 12 September 2019.

organizations,[75] led by the American Public Health Association[76] said, 'EPA's decision to finalize the ACE rule means that more Americans will experience illness and early death—plain and simple' adding, 'The ACE rule is wholly inadequate for reducing carbon pollution to address the urgent health crisis of climate change'.[77] Likewise, the American Academy of Pediatrics, representing 67,000 primary care physicians, said the ACE 'undermines policies to address climate change, which disproportionately harm children. The American Academy of Pediatrics opposes the rule, as it will worsen air quality, exacerbate the effects of a changing climate and increase unique health risks for children'.[78] Referring to a World Health Organization report, the APP noted that 'More than 80% of the current health burden resulting from the changing climate occurs in children younger than 5 years old, such as health-related illness and infectious disease. Children's lungs are still developing; they spend more time outside and breathe faster than adults, meaning environmental changes will more significantly impact them'.[79]

Irrespective of the differing views on ACE, the next step for the new law will be a federal court review. 'The regulatory battle over the Obama Administration's Clean Power Plan and the Trump Administration's Affordable Clean Energy rule is destined for months or years of litigation that may achieve a final resolution only in the Supreme Court', said Thaddeus Lightfoot, a former attorney with the US Department of Justice.[80]

C. Negative Attitudes Towards Multi-National Agreements

Numerous actions from the beginning of the Trump administration have demonstrated the president's distrust of multi-national legal agreements that include basic United Nations' agreements relevant to energy justice. In this context, the withdrawal from the Paris Climate Agreement is the most noteworthy.

[75] American Public Health Association, the American Lung Association, Allergy & Asthma Network, Alliance of Nurses for Healthy Environments, American Heart Association, American Thoracic Society, Association of Schools and Programs of Public Health, Asthma and Allergy Foundation of America, Center for Climate Change and Health, Children's Environmental Health Network, Climate for Health, Health Care Without Harm, Medical Society Consortium on Climate and Health, National Medical Association, and Physicians for Social Responsibility. See https://www.apha.org/news-and-media/news-releases/apha-news-releases/2019/epa-ace-rule accessed 12 September 2019.

[76] It is worth noting that the APHA has said that 'Climate change is public health's greatest challenge. While all of us will experience the health impacts of climate change, certain groups, like children, the elderly, the underserved and minority communities, are less climate-resilient, and, as a result, are more vulnerable to negative health effects of climate change'. APHA, 'Climate Changes Health: Climate Justice', https://www.apha.org/topics-and-issues/climate-change/climate-justice accessed 12 September 2019.

[77] APHA, '15 Health and Medical Organizations Decry U.S. EPA's Finalization of ACE Rule', 19 June 2019, https://www.apha.org/news-and-media/news-releases/apha-news-releases/2019/epa-ace-rule accessed 12 September 2019.

[78] K. Yasuda, 'AAP Statement Opposing EPA Rollback of Critical Carbon Pollution Rule' (19 June 2019) *American Academy of Pediatrics* https://www.aap.org/en-us/about-the-aap/aap-press-room/Pages/AAP-Statement-Opposing-EPA-Rollback-of-Critical-Carbon-Pollution-Rule-.aspx accessed 12 September 2019.

[79] Ibid.

[80] See King and Hijazi (n 74).

An editorial in *Climate Policy* likely explains the president's logic in withdrawing from the agreement: 'This stance apparently is rooted in his administration's electoral populism and economic nationalism, a particular interpretation of individual liberty and a conviction that humanity has a right to exploit nature. Such convictions ... are also echoed in deep traditions of US isolationism and rejection of multilateral institutions that could influence or constrain US actions, especially on economically important issues such as climate change.'[81]

This is a particularly troubling stance to many observers since, '[M]ulti-national approaches that motivate, coordinate, and implement an effective fight against climate change are essential.'[82]

D. The Preference for Bilateral Agreements

Historically, the US has 'supported a rule-based approach to global relations and strengthening of global and regional institutions.'[83] However, the Trump administration is dismissive of multilateral agreements, as noted above, and prefers—if not insists upon—bilateral agreements.

The *Art of the Deal* emphasized Trump's preference for negotiations involving only two or a few parties in which American benefits could be clearly advocated and insisted upon.[84] For example, Trump's preference for two-party deals appeared in his enthusiasm for separate two-party 'summit meetings' with the leaders of Russia and North Korea in Summer 2018 and beyond. In both cases Trump oddly praised the foreign leaders and appeared to agree with their positions on crucial international issues.[85]

Even though in the context of a global challenge such as climate change, bilateral approaches are obviously ineffective, Trump nevertheless sees no benefit to the US in partnering with a large group of countries. As he said in withdrawing from the Paris Agreement, 'This agreement is less about climate and more about other countries gaining a financial advantage' over America.[86] Calling his decision to withdraw a 'reassertion of our sovereignty,' Trump continued, 'I was elected to represent the citizens of Pittsburgh, not Paris.'[87]

[81] F. Jotzo, J. Depledge, and H. Winkler, US and International Climate Policy Under President Trump' (2018) 18 *Climate Policy*, 813–17, 813.
[82] J. Linn, 'Recent Threats to Multilateralism' (2018) 9 *Global Journal of Emerging Market Economies*, 86–113, 101.
[83] Ibid., 87.
[84] See Trump (n 2), 335.
[85] *The Economist*, 21 July 2018, 37.
[86] E. Stokols, 'Donald Trump Withdraws From Paris Climate Deal Despite Allies' Opposition' (2 June 2017) *The Wall Street Journal* https://www.wsj.com/articles/donald-trump-to-exit-paris-climate-deal-officials-say-1496343854 accessed 12 September 2019.
[87] Ibid.

E. Federalism

A crucial factor in American legal response to energy justice issues is the United States' position as a federalist state. The United States Constitution[88] spells out aspects of this dual sovereignty of the national (federal) government and the separate sovereignty of the fifty states (e.g. California, New York, Texas) of the Union.

The US Constitution identifies the powers granted to the US Congress (i.e. the Senate and the House of Representatives). Article I section 8 specifies powers granted to the Congress in eighteen subsections. Among the crucial powers granted are 'to lay and collect taxes ... to pay the debts and provide for the common defense and general welfare of the United States' (subsection 1); 'to borrow money on the credit of the United States' (subsection 2); 'to regulate Commerce with foreign Nations, and among the several States ... ' (subsection 3); 'to make rules for the Government and Regulation of the land and naval forces' (subsection 13); and 'to make all Law which shall be necessary and proper for carrying into execution the foregoing Powers ... ' (subsection 18).

Article II sets out the powers of the president. Section 2 specifies the 'President shall be commander in Chief of the Army and Navy (subsection 1); to make treaties' with the consent of the Senate and to appoint (again with Senatorial consent) ambassadors, federal judges and 'other officers of the United States' (subsection 3); and to 'take care that the Laws be faithfully executed' (section 3).

Article IV, section 3, subsection 2 gives Congress the power to 'make all needful rules and regulations respecting the Territory ... belonging to the United States'.

Article VI subsection 2 provides for the 'Supremacy of the National Government' where the federal action is authorized by the national Constitution and the 'laws of the United States which shall be made in pursuance thereof'. State judicial decisions or legislation shall yield to the 'supreme law of the land'.

The Tenth Amendment to the Constitution, approved shortly after the Constitution took effect, validated the separate powers of the individual states. 'The powers not delegated to the United States by the Constitution, nor prohibited by it to the States, are reserved to the States respectively, or to the people.'

The states are governed by their own Constitutions that establish the powers of their executive branch (headed by a governor), their legislatures, and their court systems. Lesser units of state government (cities, towns, counties, school districts, etc.) have powers but subject to the control of the state government (or the national government). The state governments, however, have independent powers and provisions of the federal Constitution that protect that sovereignty. While the federal government powers need to be based in a specific grant of Constitutional authority (e.g. in one of the seventeen specific grants of power to the national Congress), the state powers are typically more open ended. State legislatures generally exercise a 'police power' that is open-ended in scope.

[88] See https://www.archives.gov/founding-docs/constitution-transcript accessed 12 September 2019.

A substantial portion of American energy law has involved drawing lines between state and federal powers.[89] A federal government decision not to advance energy justice objectives does not preclude states from pursuing their own policies that would support those objectives unless the federal decision specifically precludes the state action. In states having the population, geographic area, and wealth of a California, Texas, or New York those state powers may be considerable.

As section IV A indicated, the Trump administration has vigorously opposed broad assertions of federal power over many, but not all, environmental matters. As a legal matter this often involves an assertion that state governments should have control over the development of energy resources within the state or the extent of protection of the environment in the state. But this does not mean that the Trump administration does not object to state assertion of authority in every instance. For example, the administration has vociferously opposed California's efforts to reduce vehicle carbon emissions.[90]

V. Conclusion

The dire impacts of climate change, particularly in the context of increased heat across the US, are rapidly becoming a reality. According to a 2019 study, 'For much of the contiguous United States, the frequency of extreme heat events has been increasing since the mid-1960s and the number of high temperature records has outpaced the number of low temperature records, particularly since the mid-1980s.'[91] Over the last sixty years, US cities 'have experienced not only more frequent extreme heat ... but also more intense and longer-lasting heat waves.'[92] This trend is of special concern because extreme heat is 'among the deadliest weather hazards society faces.'[93]

The health hazards associated with extreme heat are reflected in heat-related deaths and illnesses and hospital admissions increased for these maladies 'especially among people experiencing poverty elderly adults, and other vulnerable groups.'[94] Looked at another way, uneven economic opportunities as well as social discrimination extending back centuries 'have forced part of [the US] population—disproportionately minorities and people experiencing poverty—into a state of heightened exposure and vulnerability to climate-related threats.'[95]

[89] S.J. Humes, 'Supreme Court Walks Energy Policy Tightrope as it Addresses Federalism and States' Rights' (1 March 2016) *ABA Environment, Energy, & Resources* https://www.americanbar.org/groups/environment_energy_resources/publications/trends/2015-2016/march-april-2016/supreme_court_walks_energy_policy_tightrope_as_it_addresses_federalism_and_states_rights/ accessed 12 September 2019.

[90] N.H. Farah and S. Reilly, 'Keep an Eye Out for 7 Highly Anticipated Rules' (11 September 2019) *Greenwire*.

[91] K. Dahl, R. Licker, J.T. Abatzoglou, and J. Declet-Barreto, 'Increased Frequency of and Population Exposure to Extreme Heat Index Days in the United States During the 21st Century' (2019) 1 *Environmental Research Communications* https://iopscience.iop.org/article/10.1088/2515-7620/ab27cf accessed 12 September 2019.

[92] Ibid.

[93] K. Dahl, et al., 'Killer Heat in the United States: Climate Choices and the Future of Dangerously Hot Days' (July 2019) Union of Concerned Scientists, 1 https://www.ucsusa.org/sites/default/files/attach/2019/07/killer-heat-analysis-full-report.pdf accessed 12 September 2019.

[94] Ibid.

[95] Ibid.

As a result of the growing trend towards hotter US temperatures, there is a need 'to employ our most ambitious actions to prevent the rise of extreme heat—to save lives and safeguard the quality of life for today's children, who will live out their days in the future we're currently creating', according to a study by the Union of Concerned Scientists (UCS).[96] In particular, the UCS report notes that 'making swift and deep cuts in global carbon emissions will significantly constrain the amount of future warming with which we will need to contend'.[97] One of the study's authors, climate scientist Kristina Dahl, puts the forecast future in stark terms: 'Our analysis shows a hotter future that's hard to imagine today. Nearly everywhere, people will experience more days of dangerous heat even in the next few decades.'[98]

And yet the president's assertions of American environmental leadership, notwithstanding, one commentator has observed 'His claims [of leadership] are Orwellian in scope and mendacity'.[99] Despite 'overwhelming scientific evidence' to the contrary, 'Trump refuses to acknowledge the reality of climate change. He has derided the connection between human activities and the growing climate crisis as a "hoax," dismantled a number of well-functioning government climate change programs, reassigned or fired respected scientists, and appointed climate deniers with ties to polluting industry to key positions in the EPA and other federal agencies'.[100]

Moreover, the Trump administration has not only rolled back many 'Obama-era policies that aimed to curb climate change and limit environmental pollutions', it has also taken action 'to limit funding for science and the environment'.[101]

The unfortunate, but entirely foreseeable, result is that many of the most vulnerable Americans will suffer as a result of Trump's failure to treat climate change as the threat it is. The concept of energy justice for these Americans is ephemeral if not entirely non-existent.

On the other hand, many state and local governments are moving forward under the model of federalism to address climate change. An increasing number of 'blue', or Democratically leaning states, 'are adopting sweeping new climate laws … that aim to reorient their entire economies around clean energy, transforming the way people get their electricity, heat their homes and commute to work'.[102] For example, New York state adopted legislation in July 2019 that 'sets the nation's most aggressive targets for reducing carbon emissions and is intended to drive dramatic changes over the next

[96] Ibid.

[97] Ibid., 25.

[98] N. Sobczyk, 'Number of High Heat Days Could Go "Off the Charts"—Study' (16 July 2019) *GreenWire* https://www.eenews.net/greenwire/2019/07/16/stories/1060747831 accessed 12 September 2019.

[99] J.A. Mintz, 'Trump Trashes the Natural World and Calls it "Environmental Leadership"' (17 July 2019) *The Hill* https://thehill.com/opinion/energy-environment/453453-trump-trashes-the-natural-world-and-calls-it-environmental accessed 12 September 2019.

[100] Ibid.

[101] M. Greshko, et al., 'A Running List of How President Trump is Changing Environmental Policy' (3 May 2019) *National Geographic* https://news.nationalgeographic.com/2017/03/how-trump-is-changing-science-environment/ accessed 12 September 2019.

[102] B. Plummer, 'Blue States Roll Out Aggressive Climate Strategies. Red States Keep to the Sidelines' (21 June 2019) *The New York Times* https://www.nytimes.com/2019/06/21/climate/states-climate-change.html accessed 12 September 2019.

30 years'.[103] Moreover, Democratic-led states like California, Colorado, Maine, Nevada, New Mexico, and Washington have recently approved legislation 'aimed at getting 100% of their state's electricity from carbon-free sources ... while enacting a raft of measures to install more electric-vehicle charging stations and ratchet up efficiency codes for buildings'.[104] On the other hand, Democratic US Senator Martin Heinrich of New Mexico, has said, 'You have hundreds of cities out there working on [addressing climate change] now, figuring out what works really well, what doesn't work so well, and you should learn from that so that when you're trying to lean in in 2021, you're moving the needle as quickly as you can'.[105]

In summary, the Trump administration has been an enthusiast for further fossil fuel development and a reluctant supporter of renewable energy projects. These attitudes have been implemented in a wealth of executive orders and new regulations supporting those priorities. Often, an aspect of those Trump priorities has been a roll-back of environmental regulations and goals that slow, prohibit, or make more expensive the energy development goals. In contrast, energy justice goals can be served by efforts to reduce producing more energy from the fossil fuels and nuclear power.

The Trump view of international relations also threatens progress on energy justice. The goals of sustainability, equality of service, control of climate change need some degree of world-wide support of both aspirational goals and of binding legal implementation of those goals. Reliance on only two-party agreements will likely allow only limited progress on world-wide goals.

What is surprising is that the Trump administration's approach to climate change, as well as its often isolationist-focused policies, may not be supported by most Americans according to one recent report. A mid-2019 survey conducted by the Chicago Council on Global Affairs indicated that for the first time since the question was posed in 2008 'an overall majority of Americans (54%) consider climate change a critical threat'.[106] Moreover, 51 per cent said the US 'should begin taking steps now even if this involves significant costs'.[107] On the other hand, 69 per cent said it would be best if the US participated actively in world affairs.[108]

As discouraging as the forecast may be for American support of energy justice, there are modest signs of 'green shoots' ahead with respect to achieving the objectives enshrined in the concept of energy justice. First, the US remains a nation with recognized sovereignty in its fifty states. Clearly, energy justice goals would be better achieved by agreement between national and state leaders on how to achieve those goals. But, in the absence of that, dual sovereignty allows interested states to move in

[103] M. Esch, 'New York's Climate Plan Will Drive Big Changes, If It Works' (18 July 2019) *AP News* https://apnews.com/12d3074b7ca04233a0dec17b6344bbd0 accessed 12 September 2019.

[104] See Plummer (n 102).

[105] N. Sobczyk, 'When it Comes to Climate, Democrats Love Federalism' (18 July 2019) *E&E News* https://www.eenews.net/stories/1060754011 accessed 12 September 2019.

[106] D. Smeltz, et al., 'Rejecting Retreat: Americans Support US Engagement in Global Affairs' (2019) *The Chicago Council on Global Affairs*, 27 https://www.thechicagocouncil.org/sites/default/files/report_ccs19_rejecting-retreat_20190909.pdf accessed 12 September 2019.

[107] Ibid., 28.

[108] Ibid, 3.

the direction of promoting energy justice. Moreover, in September 2019, Democrats in the US Congress introduced measures aimed at improving low-income households' access to solar-generated electricity.[109] One of the sponsors, Illinois US Senator Tammy Duckworth, said, 'I'm proud to be introducing this legislation ... that would make it easier for low-income Americans to use solar energy and lower their utility bills, which will help our nation reduce our dependence on fossil fuels, combat climate change and decrease air pollution'.[110]

[109] P. Athey, 'Environmental Justice Caucus Introduces First Bill' (12 September 2019) *E&E News*.

[110] 'Duckworth, Booker introduce bill to make solar energy more affordable for low income families', https://www.duckworth.senate.gov/news/press-releases/duckworth-booker-introduce-bill-to-make-solar-energy-more-affordable-for-low-income-families accessed 12 September 2019.

17

Energy Justice, Law, and Poverty in the Context of Mesoamerican Countries

José Juan González

Introduction

Energy justice, energy poverty and connections between these two paradigms are still new and undertheorized issues for Mesoamerican energy law and jurisprudence.[1] The complicated task of dealing with energy justice and energy poverty from the arena of legal science demands that we first delimit the scope of these two paradigms and then identify the legal instruments that need to be adopted by national regimes in order to reach those aspirations set forth by the Sustainable Development Goals (SDGs) agreed by the international community in 2015.[2]

When the concept of energy poverty was first defined in the 1990s, scholars associated it with people's ability to afford the cost of energy.[3] For instance, according to Boardman, a family is in poverty condition when it spends more than 10 per cent of its income on energy.[4] In the same vein, in 2012, Tirado defined this concept as a situation in which a family is unable to pay for a sufficient quantity of energy to satisfy its domestic necessities and/or when it is obliged to spend an excessive part of its income to pay the energy bill of its home.[5] Finally, in 2013 the European Economic and Social Council described energy poverty as 'the difficulty or inability of sustaining a home in adequate conditions of temperature, as well as of having availability of other essential energy services to a rational price'.[6]

However, in line with the principles postulated by the SDGs, it is necessary to appraise energy poverty from a different point of view including, beyond affordability,

[1] The term jurisprudence is used in its general sense to refer legal doctrine elaborated by scholars. See P. Wahlgren, 'The Purpose and Usefulness of Jurisprudence' (2005) 48 *Scandinavian Studies in Law Stockholm Institute for Scandinavian Law*, 505, 516. Available at http://www.scandinavianlaw.se/pdf/48-30.pdf accessed 23 December 2019.

[2] D. French and L.J. Kotzé (eds), *Sustainable Development Goals. Law, Theory and Implementation* (Edward Elgar Publishing, 2018).

[3] D. Gerbery and R. Filčák, 'Exploring Multidimensional Nature of Poverty in Slovakia: Accesses to Energy and the Concept of Energy Poverty' (2014) 62 *Ekonomický casopis*, 579, 597. Available at: https://www.researchgate.net/publication/264541680_Access_to_Energy_and_Concept_of_Energy_Poverty accessed 23 December 2019.

[4] B. Boardman, *Fuel Poverty: From Cold Homes to Affordable Warmth* (Belhaven Press,1991).

[5] S. Tirado Herrero, et al., *Pobreza energética en España, Potencial de generación de empleo directo de la pobreza derivado de la rehabilitación energética de viviendas* (Asociación de Ciencias Ambientales, 2012), 21.

[6] Consejo Económico Social Europeo. *Por una acción europea coordinada para prevenir y combatir la pobreza energética*, Dictamen TEN/516, (18 September 2013).

José Juan González, Energy Justice, Law, and Poverty in the Context of Mesoamerican Countries In: *Energy Justice and Energy Law*. Edited by Íñigo Del Guayo, Lee Godden, Donald N. Zillman, Milton Fernando Montoya, and José Juan González, Oxford University Press (2020). © The Several Contributors. DOI: 10.1093/oso/9780198860754.003.0017

other elements of analysis. Indeed, some authors consider that in the context of developing countries, energy poverty **cannot be measured in the same way that this indicator is weighted in developed countries.**[7] In harmony with this argument, in Mesoamerican countries the concept of energy poverty needs to be adapted to take into account, besides the cost of energy, other technical, cultural, social, and environmental considerations.[8] In this way, energy poverty is not just a question of affordable access to energy, but of access to affordable, reliable, and sustainable modern energy in the region. Even for those sectors of population who have access to electricity and can afford it, energy poverty condition could be associated with an inefficient, unsustainable, and unreliable service.

On the other side of the coin, in this analysis, is energy justice. Energy justice remains also an undertheorized issue in Mesoamerican legal doctrine.[9] In the third chapter of this book, Íñigo del Guayo points out that from a social perspective energy injustice cannot be separated from other social ills, such as poverty and subordination based on caste, race, gender, or indigeneity.[10] All the same, energy poverty and energy justice are different but convergent ideas. In concordance with this thesis, it is possible to hold that the poorer the people are, the more reduced their access to energy justice is. Thus, lack of affordable, reliable, and sustainable electricity access exacerbates the poverty condition of the people, and *vice versa*, people's access to affordable, reliable, clean energy could contribute to alleviate poverty.[11]

This link between energy justice and energy poverty is rooted specifically on SDG 1[12] that proposes to eradicate extreme poverty for all people every where and SDG 7[13], which centres on achieving access to affordable, reliable, and sustainable modern energy for all by 2030. [14]

Based on what these two goals postulate and trying to hypothesize on the connections between energy poverty and energy justice, it is possible to assert that lack of access to energy is an indicator of people's poverty condition whereas lack of access to energy, in the sense defined by the United Nations' SDGs, that is to say, lack of access

[7] In southern Chile, where the winters are cold, the lack of indoor heating would be a much more important indicator of energy poverty than in a place with a more moderate climate. Social and cultural factors also come into play, García Ochoa said; for example, in some places people may cook with firewood by choice or custom, not because they cannot afford a stove. See: Energy and Climate Partnership of the Americas, 'Addressing Energy Poverty: More than Flipping a Switch' (26 January 2018) http://ecpamericas.org/News/Default.aspx?id=1469 accessed 5 July 2019.

[8] Mesoamerica is a region where many beyond the poorest households face stress, and where many economies face energy cost.

[9] See in this regard R. Salter, et al., 'Energy Justice: Framework for Energy Law and Policy', in R. Salter, et al., (eds), *Energy Justice, US and International Perspectives* (Edward Elgar, 2018), 4.

[10] See Chapter 3, by del Guayo, in this book.

[11] United Nations Development Programme (UNDP) and University of Bergen, 'Accelerating SDG 7 Achievement, Policy Brief #8 Interlinkages Among Energy, Poverty and Inequalities' (2018), 3–4, https://sustainabledevelopment.un.org/content/documents/17480PB8.pdf accessed 27 August 2019

[12] SDG 1: end poverty in all its forms everywhere.

[13] SDG 7: ensure access to affordable, reliable, sustainable, and modern energy for all.

[14] According to Garcia and Graizbord, access to energy is a key indicator of well-being and in this respect it is important how many families lack of this service. R. García-Ochoa and B. Graizbord, 'Caracterización espacial de la pobreza energética en México. Un análisis a escala subnacional' (2016) *Economía, Sociedad y Territorio*.

to affordable, reliable, and sustainable modern energy, illustrates the level of energy justice that prevails in a country. [15]

Therefore, moving from an energy poverty condition towards an energy justice scenario, signatory parties have to define a series of legal mechanisms aimed at reaching the principles established by SDGs.

This chapter has the aim of evaluating the connections between law and energy justice in the context of Mesoamerican legal regimes. From the perspective of the social justice dimension of distributional justice, it surveys the way legislation addresses the main drivers of energy poverty and how the law deals with them. The chapter analyses the objectives of affordability, reliability, and sustainability postulated by SDG 7 to elucidate the role of law in poverty alleviation as well.

To achieve its aim, this chapter surveys the way Mesoamerican's energy legal regimes pretend to make effective access to affordable, reliable, and sustainable modern energy for the population and, from the perspective of the social justice dimension of distributive justice it also evaluates the way legislation addresses the main drivers of energy poverty and how the law deals with it.

The study is divided into five parts. The first part introduces the problem of energy poverty in the region. In the second, a brief analysis of the Mesoamerican energy sector is conducted. The third describes the recent progress of Mesoamerican energy law. The fourth section discusses the way SDG 7 has been adopted by national laws, and finally, the last section points out some conclusions resulting from the analysis conducted in this chapter.

II. Light and Shadow of Access to Energy in Mesoamerica

In recent years, Mesoamerican countries have made great strides to increase population access to electricity.[16] For example, Nicaragua moved from coverage of just 54 per cent in 2006 to coverage of about **95.6 per cent.**[17] However, most of the countries in the region are below the Latin American average of access to electricity, which, according to the Inter-American Development Bank, is 96% per cent.[18] The only exceptions are

[15] The indicator that measures the Lack of Basic Services in Housing considers the population that resides in houses that present at least one of the following characteristics: (a) water is obtained from a well, river, lake, stream, pipe; or, piped water is obtained by carrying from another house, or from the public key or hydrant; (b) they do not have a drainage service, or the drain has a connection to a pipe that leads to a river, lake, sea, ravine, or crack; (c) they do not have electricity; and (d) the fuel used to cook or heat food is wood or charcoal without a chimney. J. Ortiz Galindo, H. Ríos Bolívar 'La Pobreza en México, un análisis con enfoque multidimensional. Análisis Económico' (2013) XXVIII *Análisis Económico*. Available at :http://www.redalyc.org/articulo.oa?id=41331033010 accessed 5 July 2019.

[16] F. Lecaros, J.M. Cayo, and M. Dussan, *Estudio programático regional para el sector energético de américa central* (ESMAP, 2010), 30 http://documents.worldbank.org/curated/en/937851468216597311/pdf/554180ESW0P1100a0Overview00Spanish0.pdf accessed 27 August 2019.

[17] Empresa Nacional de Transmisión Eléctrica, '90% de Nicaragua ya está electrificada' http://www.enatrel.gob.ni/90-de-nicaragua-ya-esta-electrificada/ accessed 3 July 2019.

[18] D.P. Damasco, 'Acceso a la Electricidad en Centroamérica: Desigualdad y Costo Ambiental'(Distintas Latitudes, información para entender y sobrevivir América Latina, 23 February 2017) https://distintaslatitudes.net/acceso-la-electricidad-centroamerica accessed 3 July 2019 (hereafter, Pérez, *Acceso a la Electricidad en Centroamérica*).

Costa Rica that has coverage of 99.4 per cent[19] and Mexico with coverage of 98 per cent.[20]

On the other hand, according to the Latin American Energy Association, most of the Mesoamerican countries generate electricity in a cleaner manner than the average of Latin American Countries.[21] For instance, in Guatemala renewables represent 59 per cent of the energy mix and in Costa Rica 98.9 per cent.[22] Conversely, this is not the case in Mexico where by 2017 renewables contributed with just 21.08 per cent of electricity generation (69,396.16 GWh)[23] and this percentage could fall below in the following years because the new government has cancelled important projects of clean energies generation and plans to increase fossil fuels production and consumption.[24]

Despite the above, due to different factors, access for the population to affordable, reliable, and sustainable modern energy is still an aspiration in the Mesoamerican region.[25] Indeed achieving the principles of SDG 7 in the region demands a series of legal changes.[26]

Energy poverty afflicts millions of homes in Mesoamerica not only because many householders are unable to afford the cost of energy but also because, even for those who can afford it, access to energy is neither reliable nor sustainable. As a result, many of those homes have difficulties in satisfying their needs of energy for cooking, lighting, heating, and entertainment.[27]

Among the indicators of energy poverty in Mesoamerica it is possible to identify: (a) inability to afford electricity; (b) lack of access to any kind of energy in certain areas; (c) poor quality of energy services and energy inefficiency; (d) lack of access to clean and modern forms of energy; (e) social opposition to new energy projects; and

[19] Instituto Costarricense de Electricidad, *Planificación y Desarrollo Eléctrico, Expansion del Sistema* (October 2017) https://www.grupoice.com/wps/wcm/connect/10261169-f251-465d-9b95-0b17c7baa49e/Cobertura+2013.pdf?MOD=AJPERES&attachment=false&id=1453148700496 accessed 5 July 2019.

[20] Comisión Nacional para el Uso Eficiente de la Energía, 'Cobertura de Energía Eléctrica – agua y energía-Bombeo de agua estados y municipios' (9 July 2014) https://www.gob.mx/conuee/acciones-y-programas/cobertura-de-energia-electrica-agua-y-energia-bombeo-de-agua-estados-y-municipios?state=published accessed 5 July 2019.

[21] M.J. Lippmann, 'Electricity Generation in Central America: Some Relevant Comments on the Importance of Renewables, Including Geothermal' (2017) 46 *Geothermal Resource Council, Bullet.* https://geothermal.org/PDFs/Articles/17MayJune_Electricity_generation_in_Central_America.pdf accessed 27 August 2019.

[22] Pérez, *Acceso a la Electricidad en Centroamérica* (n 18).

[23] Secretaría de Energía, 'Reporte de Avance de Energías Limpias 2017' (2017) https://www.gob.mx/cms/uploads/attachment/file/340121/Informe_Renovables_2017_cierre.pdf accessed 5 July 2019.

[24] The new government of the Mexican Republic has stopped both long-term auctions to generate electricity from renewable sources and the bidding of the direct current transmission line that would run from south of Oaxaca to the centre of the country, which puts at risk the installation of thirteen wind farms that would generate two thousand MW of electricity in the Isthmus of Tehuantepec.

[25] Supply of electricity in Central America is affected by the known blackouts or rationing of energy, which have come to cause major impacts on the production chain of coffee, in the case of Honduras.

[26] An author holds that 'The agenda is not, then, something to be taken wholesale and applied in every country context. Though the agenda is universal, it is clearly differentiated: that is, it permits countries to respond with their own level of ambition, tailored to their national circumstances. If the agenda is indeed meaningfully "accepted by all", it has been accepted in full awareness of the scope for national-level discretion in how to approach distant, non-specific targets'. G. Long, 'Underpinning Commitments of the Sustainable Development Goals: Indivisibility, Universality, Leaving No One Behind', in D. French and L.J. Kotzé (eds), *Sustainable Development Goals. Law, Theory and Implementation* (Edward Elgar Publishing, 2018), 100.

[27] E. Godoy, 'Millions of Homes in Mexico Suffer from "Energy Poverty"' (2017) *Inter Press Service News Agency*. http://www.ipsnews.net/2017/05/millions-of-homes-in-mexico-suffer-from-energy-poverty/ accessed 5 July 2019.

(f) natural disasters such as earthquakes and hurricanes, which generate a need for resilient systems. The following sections analyse all these issues.

A. Affordable Access to Energy

Regarding the principle of affordability, a report by the Economic Commission for Latin America and the Caribbean (ECLAC) indicates that in 2016, the average cost per kilowatt/hour (kWh) in Mesoamerica was US$0.1348[28] —while this cost in Costa Rica was US$0.1847, in El Salvador and Guatemala it was US$0.1103 and US$0.1154 respectively, and in Panama US$0.1092; in Mexico the cost was of kWh ranked from US$0.04 to US$0.15.[29] This data suggests that the cost of electricity in the region is like the cost in other regions of the world, but economic conditions of Mesoamerican populations are quite different from most developed societies. In consequence, in the region, electricity fees could be unaffordable for important sectors of the population. To deal with this issue some governments have adopted electricity subsidy regimens to provide low cost energy to targeted users.[30]

B. Lack of Access to Energy

Available data illustrates that several communities still lack access to energy in the Mesoamerican region. For instance, in Guatemala, the departments[31] of Alta Verapaz and Petén—both located in the northeast of the country—have limited access to electricity. In Alta Verapaz (one of the departments with the largest indigenous population in Guatemala), 66 per cent of the population lacks electricity access, and in Petén (where the famous archaeological site of Tikal is located), this percentage is 43.4 per cent of the population.[32]

In the same vein, in rural areas of El Salvador, just 74.3 per cent of households have access to electricity compared to 93.4 per cent in the metropolitan area of the country.

In contrast, in the case of Costa Rica, only 0.5 per cent of the population (22,653 inhabitants) does not have access to electricity. In this country, the most populated regions without access to electricity are Huetar Caribe (1.5 per cent of the population without access: 6,460 inhabitants) and Huetar Norte (1.5 per cent of the population

[28] M.E.R. Navarrete, *Estadísticas del Subsector Eléctrico de los Países del Sistema de la Integración Centroamericana (SICA) 2016* (Comisión Económica para América Latina y el Caribe, 2017) https://repositorio.cepal.org/bitstream/handle/11362/42720/1/S1701275_es.pdf.

[29] Comisión Federal de Electricidad, 'Tarifas' (2018) *Comisión Federal de Electricidad* https://app.cfe.mx/Aplicaciones/CCFE/Tarifas/Tarifas/Tarifas_casa.asp?Tarifa=DACTAR1&anio=2018 accessed 5 July 2019.

[30] G. Di Bella, et al., *Energy Subsidies in Latin America and the Caribbean: Stocktaking and Policy Challenges* (International Monetary Fund, 2015), 5.

[31] Guatemala's territorial division is comprised of twenty-two departments and 340 municipalities, which are organized into eight administrative regions.

[32] Pérez, *Acceso a la Electricidad en Centroamérica* (n 18).

without access: 5,859 inhabitants).[33] It is important to note that these are also the two poorest regions of the country and largest indigenous population.[34]

Similarly, in Mexico where there is a total of 24,006,357 households, only 588,864 of them do not have access to electricity. In this country, the states with the highest percentage of population lacking access to electricity services are Veracruz, with 13.9 per cent; Oaxaca with 9.7 per cent; Chiapas with 8.4 per cent; Guerrero, with 6.85 per cent; San Luis Potosi with 5.24 per cent; Chihuahua with 5.14 per cent, and the State of Mexico with 4.99 per cent of the total households without electricity.[35] Again, poverty condition drives up energy poverty, five of these states are considered among the ten poorest states of the Mexican republic.[36]

In consequence, in spite of the great progress in this field, universal access to electricity is still a concern for most of the countries in the Mesoamerican region. Small generation and distributed generation systems adopted by national legislations in a few countries could contribute to alleviate this ill and to make reality the principle of universal access.[37]

C. Poor Quality of Energy Services and Energy Efficiency

Supply of electricity in Mesoamerica is frequently affected by poor quality of energy services and energy inefficiency, voltage variations, blackouts, or rationing of energy. For instance, in 2019 due to a failure in the regional integrated electricity system a massive blackout left Panama and some regions of Nicaragua, Costa Rica, and Guatemala without electricity. As a result, in Panama the subway interrupted its operations and the Panama Canal and the airport needed to use electricity generators. [38]

These malfunctions of the electricity systems could cause damage to electronic equipment in both companies and homes. In Mexico, in 2014, voltage variations and blackouts caused loses of US$2.262 billion in just six months.[39] In this country, the frequent damages caused to people´s electronic equipment due to voltage variations have resulted in a series of civil actions against the Federal Commission of Electricity. In this regard, the Mexican Supreme Court of Justice has consistently ruled that the state is responsible for those damages resulting from the inefficient service of electricity and has

[33] Pérez, *Acceso a la Electricidad en Centroamérica* (n 18).

[34] R.R. Alfaro and Á.J.P. Solís, 'Población, empleo y pobreza en los territorios rurales de Costa Rica' (2018) 8 *Revista Rupturas*, 59–76.

[35] M.Z. Machado, et al., 'Recurso Eólico en Baja California' (1 February 2010) 11 *Revista Digital Universitaria* http://www.revista.unam.mx/vol.11/num2/art24/int24.htm accessed 5 July 2019.

[36] Forbes Staff, 'Los 10 estados con más pobres en México' (30 December 2017) *Forbes Mexico* https://www.forbes.com.mx/los-10-estados-con-mas-pobres-en-mexico/ accessed 5 July 2017.

[37] W.V. Herrera, 'Generación distribuida para autoconsumo en Costa Rica: Desafios regulatorios', in L. Ferney (coord) *Anuario Iberoamericano de Derecho de la Energía* (ASIDE-Universidad Externado de Colombia, 2019), 479–97.

[38] BBC News Mundo, 'Un apagón deja sin electricidad a Panamá y a partes de Nicaragua, Costa Rica y Guatemala' (20 January 2019) https://www.bbc.com/mundo/noticias-america-latina-46936504 accessed 5 July 2019.

[39] Forbes Staff, ' Las variaciones de voltaje ponen en riesgo a tu empresa' (7 October 2015) *Forbes Mexico* https://www.forbes.com.mx/las-variaciones-de-voltaje-pone-en-riesgo-a-tu-empresa/ accessed 5 July 2019.

obliged the public corporation Federal Commission of Electricity to pay an economic compensation to affected users.[40] However, poor people that cannot afford the energy fees are also unable to support the expenses associated with a trial and so it could also contribute to exacerbate energy poverty.

D. Lack of Access to Clean and Modern Energy

Despite the great efforts of the region to transit towards cleaner energy sectors, some countries still depend on fossil fuels to satisfy electricity demand.[41] A study holds that, while the energy matrix is transitioning to a greater use of renewables, electricity generation still depends on fossil fuels.[42] The same study sustains that, despite the region's natural wealth and strong potential for producing its own clean energy, generation and consumption is based on polluting sources, particularly petroleum products and carbon.[43]

For instance, in Mexico, electricity generation by thermoelectric power plants is one of the main sources of greenhouse gas emissions.[44] In fact, in Mesoamerica for decades electricity generation has been an example of the tensions between availability and unsustainable use of natural resources.[45] In this regard, the Fourth State of the Region Report (2016) holds that Mesoamerica has the double challenge of ensuring the provision of the necessary energy for its development and, at the same time, reducing the social, economic, and environmental impacts associated with the use of natural resources.[46] In consequence, providing clean and modern energy for all people in Mesoamerica is still a pending issue. Energy transition is a concern recently adopted by Mesoamerican energy law; for example, it was only 2014 when Mexico passed the Law of Energy Transition.

[40] See for instance: Mario Alberto Hernández de la Rosa v Comisión Federal de Electricidad. Amparo en revisión, Segunda Sala, Décima época.

[41] As the study says 'Central America has seen promising new investments in renewable energy—both in large-scale and grid tied technologies such as geothermal, biomass, wind, and solar energy, as well as in household-scale and off-grid technologies. But most countries in the region also have plans for increasing oil imports, and some are exploring greater use of coal and natural gas in their energy mix'. A. Dolezal, A.M. Majano, A. Ochs, and R. Palencia, *The Way Forward for Renewable Energy in Central America. Status Assessment | Best Practices | Gap Analysis* (World Watch Institute, 2013), 9.

[42] Fifth State of the Region Report on Sustainable Human Development Summary—Electronic data (1 file: 1.9 MB)—San José, C.R.: PEN, 2017 (Report no. 5), http://repositorio.conare.ac.cr/bitstream/handle/20.500.12337/731/Fifth%20State%20of%20the%20Region%20Report%20on%20Susteinable%20Human%20Development%20 2016_libro.pdf?sequence=1&isAllowed=yaccessed 24 December 2019 (hereafter, Fifth State of the Region Report).

[43] Ibid.

[44] Thermoelectric plants represent 55.60 per cent of generation, while hydroelectric power plants represent 30.4 per cent, followed by the coal-fired power plants that generate 7.2 per cent of the total electricity in the country, while the nucleoelectric plants contribute with 3.8 per cent and with lower capacity are the geothermal power plants with 2.6 per cent of total generation and the wind power plants with only 0.2 per cent. See Explorando México, 'Princiales plantas de Energía en México', http://www.explorandomexico.com.mx/about-mexico/6/106 accessed 5 July 2019.

[45] 2.5 per cent of water available for human consumption, 70 per cent is used for agricultural irrigation, 10 per cent for industry, and 20 per cent to produce electricity.

[46] Fifth State of the Region Report (n 42).

E. Social Opposition to New Energy Projects

Social opposition to new energy projects frequently negatively affects access to affordable, reliable, and sustainable modern energy. For instance, in Mexico, social conflicts have stopped the investment of US$7.37 billion in gas pipelines. An example is the gas pipeline 'Samalayuca-Sásabe' built by the company Carso Energy, which represents an investment of US$570 million and cannot operate because inhabitants of the area obstruct the project. This construction has been significantly interrupted in sixteen segments totalling 86 kilometres and delaying by more than a year the completion of the project.[47] This stoppage affects the supply of natural gas to power plants in the south of Mexico and has provoked prolonged blackouts.

Frequently, social conflicts also result in obstacles for developing new renewable energy projects. For example, in Guatemala since 2000, sixteen projects of hydroelectric plants have been suspended because of social conflicts with the host communities.[48]

In Honduras, in 2018, nine renewable energy generation projects were forcibly stopped. Attacks by affected communities and environmental NGOs were reported on hydroelectric technology generation projects.[49] The above described negative aspects sometimes eclipse the virtues of social participation.

F. Natural Disasters

Due to its geographical position, Mesoamerica is the scene of a number of meteorological and geological natural disasters that could affect energy infrastructure. For instance, in 1998 the hurricane 'Mich' left Honduras without electricity service for months and caused serious damages to the electricity system in Nicaragua.[50] In 2017 Costa Rica faced three earthquakes in less than ten minutes that interrupted the electricity service in Alajuela and Orotina,[51] and in 2018 hurricanes in Mexico caused damages of US$131,145,625 to the Federal Commission of Electricity and provoked interruptions of electricity service.[52] Therefore, natural disasters have also contributed to energy poverty in Mesoamerica, and so legislation has to focus on resilience of energy infrastructures.

[47] A. Sánchez, 'Conflictos sociales frenan inversión de 7,370 mdd en gasoductos' (18 February 2019) *El Financiero* https://www.elfinanciero.com.mx/empresas/conflictos-sociales-frenan-inversion-de-7-370-mdd-en-gasoductos accessed 5 July 2019.

[48] R.M. Bolaños, 'Hidroeléctricas: Los 16 proyectos suspendidos por conflictividad' (26 September 2018) *Prensa Libre, Periódico Líder de Guatemala* https://www.prensalibre.com/economia/q11-mil-millones-ha-perdido-el-pais-por-conflictividad/ accessed 5 July 2019.

[49] N. Singh, 'Empresarios Denuncian Atentados a Proyectos de Energía Renovable en Honduras y Solicitan Nueva Legislación' (, 14 September 2018) *Energía Estratégica*http://www.energiaestrategica.com/empresarios-denuncian-atentados-a-proyectos-de-energia-renovable-en-honduras-y-solicitan-nueva-legislacion/ accessed 5 July 2019.

[50] B. M. Lugo, 'Huracanes y Ciclones en Centroamerica' (May 2011) *ResearchGate* https://www.researchgate.net/publication/236626694_Huracanes_y_Ciclones_en_Centroamerica_Hurricanes_and_Tropical_Storms_in_Central_America_Compilation_by_Bernardo_Mendez_Lugo_Mexican_Diplomat accessed 23 December 2019.

[51] BBC News Mundo, 'Costa Rica registra tres fuertes sismos de hasta 6,4 en menos de 10 minutos' (13 November 2017) https://www.bbc.com/mundo/noticias-america-latina-41959054 accessed 5 July 2019.

[52] A. Solís, 'CFE se alista para enfrentar 5 huracanes intensos durante 2019' (8 May 2019) *Forbes Mexico* https://www.forbes.com.mx/cfe-se-alista-para-enfrentar-5-huracanes-intensos-durante-2019/ accessed 5 July 2019.

III. Mesoamerican Energy Law

A brief survey of the Mesoamerican legal regimens reveals that during the last three decades all the countries in the region modified their electricity industry legal frames by passing new pieces of legislation. Before the 1990s, the countries of Mesoamerica had electricity markets operated by state-owned companies, mostly vertically integrated, operating in a context of legal monopolies. Currently, most countries have carried out different reforms that have resulted in legal frameworks to regulate the activities of the electrical subsector but each country has implemented the changes differently and the development of the markets are at different stages of progress.[53]

The following table illustrates these legal changes.

Table 17.1 New Energy Laws of Mesoamerican Countries

Country	Law	Year
Guatemala	General Electricity Law	2000
	Law of Social Tariff for Electricity Supply	2000
El Salvador	General Electricity Law	1996
Nicaragua	Law of Electricity Industry	2011
Costa Rica	Energy Efficiency Law, Ley 7447	1994
	Law that Authorizes the Autonomous or Parallel Electrical Generation	1990
	Energy Subsector Organization Regulation No. 35991	2010
Panama	Law Number 6 by which the Regulatory and Institutional Framework for the provision of the public electricity service is dictated	1997
Honduras	General Law of Electricity Industry	2014
Mexico	Law of Electricity Industry	2014
Belize	Electricity Act	2000

Most of the mentioned laws were passed with the aim of opening the electricity sector to private investment. For example, Article 1 of the general electricity law of Guatemala states that electricity generation is free and no prior authorization or condition by the state is required. In El Salvador, the General Electricity Law contemplates in its Article 2 the objective of developing a competitive market in the activities of generation, transmission, distribution, and supply of electricity.

In Nicaragua the intervention of private investment is not as free as in Guatemala, the Law of Electricity Industry of Nicaragua states that qualified economic agents, whether national or foreign, that can carry out activities of the electricity industry, require a concession or license duly granted by the state. In Panama's Article 6 of Law Number 6 by which the

[53] C.U. Hernández, *La ruta hacia la integración de los mercados eléctricos de centroamerica y México* (Alianza para Centroamérica in collaboration with Fundación Friedrich Naumann para la Libertad Proyecto Centroamérica, 2017), 16. https://fnst.org/sites/default/files/uploads/2017/08/31/mercadoselectricoscentroamericamexicoweb.pdf accessed 27 August 2019.

Regulatory and Institutional Framework for the provision of the public electricity service is dictated (hereinafter Law Number 6) considers promoting competition and the participation of the private sector, as basic instruments to increase efficiency in providing services.

In Honduras, Article 4 of the General Law of Electricity Industry also contemplates the participation of private companies in the sector establishing that the activities of the electricity sector may be carried out by private, public, or mixed companies that comply with the requirements established in the law.

In the same context, Belize's Electricity Act establishes in Article 14 (1) that the Public Utilities Commission may grant a license authorizing any person to generate electricity for the purpose of giving a supply to any premises or enabling a supply to be so given; to transmit electricity for that purpose in that person's authorized area; or to supply electricity to any premises in that person's authorized area.

Finally, Mexico's Law of Electricity Industry states that even though planning and control of the National Electric System, as well as the public service of transmission and distribution of electricity, are strategic areas reserved to the state (Article 2); generation and commercialization of electricity are services that are provided under a regime of free competition (Article 4).

Conversely, in Costa Rica the state-owned company, the Costa Rican Electricity Institute, is still the country's largest generator and functions as the sole buyer of the energy generated, since according to its founding law[54] it is responsible for satisfying the national demand for electricity.

In addition to this trend of energy sector privatization, Mesoamerican countries have also passed new laws addressed to promoting the use of cleaner sources of energy, as the following table demonstrates.

Table 17.2 Laws on Renewable Sources of Energy in Mesoamerica

Country	Legislation	Year
Guatemala	Law of Incentives for Renewable Energy Projects and its Regulation (2003)	2003
El Salvador	Law of the Electricity and Telephony National Investment Fund	1998
	Law of Tax Incentives for Promotion of Renewable Energies in Electricity Generation	2007
Nicaragua	Law for Promotion of Renewables Sources of Electricity Generation (2005)	2005
Honduras	Law for the Promotion of Electricity Generation with Renewable Resources	2007
Costa Rica	Amendment of Article 38 of Law No. 7447 Regulating the Rational Use of Energy, of 03/11/1994 and its amendments, Law to Encourage the Development and Use of Renewable Sources of Energy	2010
Mexico	Law for Energy Transition	2014
Panama	Law 45 Establishing a Regime of Incentives for the Promotion of Hydroelectric Generation Systems and Other New, Renewable and Clean Sources, and Issuing Other Provisions (2004)	2004

[54] Law No. 7593 of the Public Services Regulatory Authority [2015].

Notwithstanding the above-described legal changes, Mesoamerican legislations must be reviewed again in light of the commitments assumed by national governments under SDGs. Currently, only a few of the objectives of SDG 7 have been partially recognized by the new legislation, others are totally absent from it.

IV. Energy Justice in Mesoamerican Energy Law

According to SDG 7, the principle of access to affordable and clean energy involves five requirements to be accomplished by 2030:

1) ensure universal access to affordable, reliable, and modern energy services;
2) increase substantially the share of renewable energy in the global energy mix;
3) double the global rate of improvement in energy efficiency;
4) enhance international cooperation to facilitate access to clean energy research and technology, including renewable energy, energy efficiency and advanced and cleaner fossil-fuel technology, and promote investment in energy infrastructure and clean energy technology; and
5) expand infrastructure and to upgrade technology for supplying modern and sustainable energy services for all in developing countries, in particular least developed countries, small island developing States, and land-locked developing countries, in accordance with their respective programmes of support.

All these requirements involve substantial adaptations of energy law in the Mesoamerican region.

It is relevant to note that when the SDGs were adopted, Mesoamerican energy legislation had already introduced a series of mechanisms addressed to deal with affordable access to clean energies.[55] However, as analysed in this chapter, some of the other objectives grouped in SDG 7 are still absent from Mesoamerican national energy regimes.

A. General Access to Energy

The analysis of the national energy legislation of Mesoamerican countries allows the assertion that universal access to electricity has been a government's long-standing concern. For instance, in El Salvador, Article 2 of the General Law of Energy (1996) establishes that one of its objectives is to promote access to electricity supply for all sectors of the population. In the same vein, the General Electricity Law of Guatemala

[55] United Nations Development Programme, 'Goal 7 Affordable and Clean Energy' https://www.undp.org/content/undp/en/home/sustainable-development-goals/goal-7-affordable-and-clean-energy.html#targets accessed 5 July 2019.

(1996) states in Article 51 that all users have the right of requesting the supply of good quality electricity services. In Nicaragua, the Law on the Electricity Industry (2011) holds in its Article 29 section II, that the public electricity service concessionaires are obliged to supply the public service of electricity to any person. In Mexico, the Law of the Electricity Industry (2014) obliges public and private suppliers to provide electricity to all individuals who request it. In fact, in Mexico, this access is considered as an obligation of universal and public service (Article 4).

However, in some cases the law conditions this right to electricity access on the technical feasibility of providing it. For example, in Mexico the Law of the Electric Industry states in its Article 4 that 'it is considered an obligation of the public and universal electricity service to offer and provide electricity supply to any individual who requests it, when technically feasible, in conditions of efficiency, quality, reliability, continuity, security and sustainability'. In the case of Panama, the Law Number 6 asserts in its Article 4 that the state has to intervene in public electricity services to ensure the efficient, continuous, and uninterrupted provision of the service, except when there are reasons of force majeure or unforeseeable circumstances of a technical or economic nature.

Thus, even though energy laws in Mesoamerica already recognize the right of access to energy for all, this right can be conditioned by technical factors and it does not necessarily mean that in all cases such access is aimed to alleviate energy poverty and contribute to energy justice.

B. Affordable Electricity

Access to affordable electricity has been a relevant issue for Mesoamerican national energy legislation for a long time. For instance, in Belize the Electricity Act (2000) sets up the principle of universal access to basic electricity services at an affordable price. In some cases, legislation has established subsidy-based schemes addressed to make more accessible electricity service to certain sectors of population. For example, in Nicaragua Article 12 of the Law of Electricity Industry states that it is an obligation of the National Energy Commission to prepare, review, and evaluate the strategic plan of the energy sector, especially the aspects of price policies and subsidies on electricity service, including those consumers of less than 50 kWh per month. Similarly, the Law Number 6 of Panama, in its Article 5 establishes that the granting of direct subsidies to people of lower income constitutes an instrument for state intervention in the public services of electricity. In other cases, as in Mexico, energy legislation empowers regulators to establish official rates for small consumers. For example, Article 139 of the Law of Electricity Industry states:

> The Regulatory Commission of Electricity will apply the methodologies to define the calculation and adjustment of regulated tariffs, the maximum tariffs of the last

resource suppliers and the final tariffs of basic supply. The Regulatory Commission of Electricity will publish the calculation reports used to determine these rates and prices.

In addition, the analysis conducted in this chapter reveals that Guatemala's legislation recognizes more specifically than other legislation in the region the principle of affordable access to energy. In 2001 the Congress of this country passed the Law on the Social Fees for Electricity Supply. This law states in Article 1 that, with the aim of benefitting the most affected users of the increasing costs of electricity,[56] a special fee with social character is created.

Accordingly, subsidy schemes and special fees are the main legal instruments for Mesoamerican energy law for making energy more affordable to poor people.[57]

C. Access to Clean Energies

As mentioned, El Salvador,[58] Guatemala,[59] Honduras,[60] Mexico,[61] Nicaragua,[62] and Panama[63] have passed laws aimed at promoting access to clean energies. In most of the cases, the Mesoamerican legislation strategy is based on the use of economic instruments such as tax incentives and subsidies to promote clean energies.[64] For instance, in El Salvador, the Law of Tax Incentives for Promotion of Renewable Energies in Electricity Generation and in Guatemala the Law on Incentives for the Development of Renewable Energy Projects, grant a series of tax incentives to those individuals or corporations that invest in new projects of electricity generation from renewable sources. In the case of El Salvador such incentives include exemption from the payment of the following taxes: import–export taxes, income tax, and taxes on trade of certified reduction emissions; whereas in the case of Guatemala, besides income tax and import–export taxes exemption, the law establishes the exemption from the payment of the tax on mercantile and agricultural business.

[56] The benefit is limited to those users who consume no more than 300 kWh.

[57] C. Pantanali and J. Benavides, *Subsidios eléctricos en América Latina y el Caribe: Análisis comparativo y recomendaciones de política* (Publicaciones IFM, Parada W-0508 Banco Interamericano de Desarrollo, 2006).

[58] Law on Tax Incentives for the Promotion of Renewable Energies in Electricity Generation [2007].

[59] Law on Incentives for the Development of Renewable Energy Projects [2003].

[60] Law for the Promotion of Electricity Generation with Renewable Resources [2007].

[61] Energy Transition Law [2015].

[62] Law for Promotion of Electricity Generation with Renewable Sources [2005].

[63] Law 45 Establishing a Regime of Incentives for the Promotion of Hydroelectric Generation Systems and Other New, Renewable, and Clean Sources, and Issuing Other Provisions [2004].

[64] In Central America programmes on energy efficiency have started. Regarding illumination, the strategy has been to substitute incandescent light bulbs with compact fluorescent lamps with low consumption (LFC), by the free distribution of LFC or, in the case of Costa Rica, throughout a sales programme. Within the framework of the Regional Strategy for Efficient Lighting in Central America various projects were presented, for example, the 'en. lighten' initiative from the United Nations Environment Programme (UNEP) and the Mesoamerica Project, proposed a series of actions that had to be fulfilled by 2018 and that may achieve an annual reduction of 2.578 million of kW/h in energy consumption.

In the same vein, in Nicaragua, the Law for Promotion of Electricity Generation with Renewable Sources of 2005, as amended in 2015, includes as incentives for promoting renewable sources of energy: exemptions from the import tax, value added tax, income tax, municipal taxes, taxes on natural resource exploitation, and stamp tax. In Honduras, the Law for Promotion of Electricity Generation with Renewable Resources includes the exemption from tax on sales, income tax, and imports tax.

In the case of Mexico, the Law for Energy Transition committed the country to generate 35 per cent of electricity from clean energy by 2025. In order to achieve this goal, Mexican legislation created the 'Clean Energy Certificates'. These certificates are titles issued by Mexican energy authorities that certify the production of a determined amount of electricity from clean sources. The obligation of acquiring Clean Energy Certificates is stated in Article 68 of the Law for Energy Transition, which states:

> With the purpose of promoting the growth of Clean Energies referred to in the present Law and in the terms established in the Electric Industry Law, the Ministry of Energy shall establish obligations to acquire Clean Energy Certificates. In order to maintain equal competition, these obligations shall apply to those assets consumed in the national territory whose production process is energy-intensive.

However, unlike what happens with other legislations in the region, in Mexico the Law for Energy Transition does not grant any tax incentive as mechanisms to promote renewable energies.

The analysis of comparative legislation makes evident the interest of Mesoamerica in energy transition and consequently in contributing to realizing the SGD 7 postulates.

D. Poverty and Access to Energy

Costa Rica, Mexico, Guatemala, and Panama are the only countries in the region where legislation links access to energy with poverty alleviation. Costa Rica's Energy Subsector Organization Regulation No. 35991 does not directly refer to that connection but in its Article 5 this regulation states that:

> The objectives of the energy subsector are to improve the living conditions of Costa Ricans and contribute to improve the national economy, seeking a balance between the conservation and protection of the environment and the sustainable development of natural resources.

In Mexico, Article 113 of the Law of Electricity Industry holds that the Federal Government shall promote the electrification of rural communities and marginalized urban areas. In order to achieve this aim, it creates the Fund for Universal Electricity Service.[65] The fund has the purpose of funding electrification actions in rural communities and marginalized urban areas.

In Panama an amendment in 2016 to the Law Number 6 also created the Fund for Rural Electrification. According to this amendment, those corporations investing in rural areas' electrification are allowed to deduct the invested amount from their obligatory contributions to the fund. In addition, Article 4 of this law points out that the state is empowered to intervene in the public service supply of electricity with the aim of guaranteeing the service quality and availability in order to ensure the improvement of people's living conditions; to ensure the efficient, continued, and uninterrupted availability of the service and to protect the environment.

As mentioned before, in the case of Guatemala, the Law of Social Tariff for Electricity Supply created the so-called *social tariff* with the objective of benefitting those users most affected by increasing energy costs.

Another strategy to make electricity accessible for poor people is the idea of distributed generation, introduced by both Mexican and Costa Rican energy law. The idea of distributed generation is to generate clean energy on a small scale and close to the points where it will be consumed in order to satisfy the local demand of poorest populations.[66]

In consequence, some Mesoamerican legislation tries to alleviate energy poverty through providing access to energy, adopting special fees and subsidies, as well as by offering the possibility of deciding between clean or carbon-based energies.

E. Incorporation of Goal 7 into National Legislation

Despite the references to some of the principles contained in SDG 7 by Mesoamerican legislation, it is possible to assert that this international instrument has not yet really strongly influenced the energy policy in the region. The analysis conducted in this chapter shows that only two of the analysed national legal regimes clearly refer to the principles postulated by SDG 7. In this regard, since 1997 in Panama, the Law Number 6[67] recognized energy security as one of the objectives of electricity power services under criteria of economic efficiency, financial viability, quality and reliability

[65] In accordance with Article 114 of the Law of Electricity Industry, the Universal Electric Service Fund will be integrated by the surplus of income resulting from the management of technical losses in the Wholesale Electricity Market, under the terms of the Market Rules, until the national objectives of electrification are met.

[66] According to official data, in Mexico 112,660 contracts for distributed generation have been signed. Comisión Reguladora de Energía, 'Evolucion de Contratos de Pequeña y Mediana Escala / Generación Distribuida' (2019) *Comisión Federal de Electricidad* https://www.gob.mx/cms/uploads/attachment/file/483322/Estadisticas_GD_2019-1.pdf accessed 27 August 2019.

[67] By which the Regulatory and Institutional Framework for the provision of the public electricity service is dictated.

of services, within a framework of rational and efficient use of the various energy resources of the country.[68]

In Mexico, according with Article 1 of the Law of Electricity Industry this legal body has the objectives of:

a) Promoting sustainable development of the electricity industry.
b) Guaranteeing reliability, efficiency, and security of the electricity industry to benefit the final users.
c) Complying with obligations with regard to public and universal access to clean energies and pollutant emission reduction.

In harmony with Article 4 of the mentioned law, obligations regarding public and universal access include the goal of providing electricity service to all people who request it under conditions of efficiency, quality, reliability, continuity, security, and sustainability.

However, the incorporation of SDG 7 into national legislations has not been followed yet by the incorporation of the necessary legal instruments to make them reality.

F. Energy Access and Affordability as a Human Right in the Mexican Political Constitution

Even when access to energy postulated by SGD 7 has not been recognized yet as a human right in any jurisdiction, as an author says, 'the 2030 Agenda repeatedly references the importance of human rights, and claims to be grounded in a human rights approach'.[69] In that direction, in Mexico recently, Senator Mayuli Latifa Martínez Simón submitted to the Federal Congress an initiative to modify the Federal Constitution with the triple aim of: (i) recognizing the principle of access to electricity as a human right; (ii) eliminating the high cost of the service; and (iii) guaranteeing the universal access to electricity. [70]

The initiative proposes to modify Articles 4, 25, and 73 of the Mexican Federal Constitution. According to the initiative, Article 4 is added with a new paragraph to recognize the right of universal access to sufficient, reliable, secure, acceptable, and affordable electricity. In consonance with such an amendment, the initiative points out in Article 25 that the right of universal access will be guaranteed by the state and that secondary laws will define the basis, subsidies, and modalities for equitable and sustainable access and use of clean energies.

[68] Article 2 of Panama's Law Number 6.

[69] L.M. Collins, 'Sustainable Development Goals and Human Rights: Challenges and Opportunities', in D. French and L.J. Kotzé (eds), *Sustainable Development Goals. Law, Theory and Implementation* (Edward Elgar Publishing, 2018), 68.

[70] This initiative is available at: <www.senado.gob.mx/64/gaceta_del_senado/documento/88938> accessed 5 July 2019.

Finally, the initiative introduces a section X Bis in Article 73 with the aim of empowering the Federal Congress to pass general laws on electricity and nuclear power that shall define the basis, subsidies, and modalities for access to clean energies and its equitable and sustainable use. The proposed amendment of Article 73 also repeals the power of Federal Congress to impose taxes on electricity, which could contribute to electricity cost reduction.

The approval of this initiative by the Federal Congress, could provide enough basis for implementation of SDG 1 and 7 of the SDGs, that is to say for using access to electricity as a strategy to both mitigating poverty and making energy justice a reality.

V. Conclusions

Even though Mesoamerican energy laws had incorporated the concerns about universal access to energy, affordability, and clean energies, long before the adoption of SDGs; there is still a long way to go for the laws to realize the principles of affordable, reliable, and sustainable modern energy for all, postulated by the mentioned international instrument.

To date, energy poverty, energy justice, and relations between these two paradigms are issues that are still undertheorized by Mesoamerican energy legal doctrine and practically absent from national legislation in this region as well.

Although during the last decades, important changes have been introduced in Mesoamerican national energy legal regimens, energy justice and distributional justice paradigms are not yet relevant concerns for Mesoamerican energy law. References to these issues in legislation are tangential and incomplete even in the most developed economies of the region (Costa Rica and Mexico).

Based on the idea that lack of access to affordable, reliable, and clean energy is an indicator of people's poverty condition, whereas, universal access to energy is usually an indicator of well-being, one of the strategies in the region to reduce poverty has been to expand the coverage of distribution networks and to guarantee universal access to energy as postulated by SDG 7. This strategy has been complemented in some national energy legal regimes with the adoption of special rates for targeted users and subsidies-based schemes. In other cases, distributed generation schemes are emerging as an option to bring electricity services to the poorest populations of the region.

Nevertheless, on one hand universal access to energy could be limited by a series of social, technical, and economic factors and on the other, it is not always affordable, efficient, sustainable, and reliable.

In spite of the above, adoption in 2015 of the SDGs by most of the members of the international community could motivate a future transformation of the national energy law and policy in the region. Such transformation must recognize access to energy as a human right, and under such basis must define those instruments and procedures to implement the principles defined by SDG 7.

This new energy legal reform has to be aimed at contributing to energy poverty alleviation and in general to mitigate people's poverty. Modernization of Mesoamerican energy law has to take into account the drivers of energy poverty: (a) inability to afford electricity cost; (b) lack of access to any kind of energy in certain areas; (c) poor quality of energy services and energy inefficiency; (d) lack of access to clean and modern forms of energy; (e) social opposition to new energy projects; and (f) natural disasters such as earthquakes and hurricanes.

The better the legislation responds to these challenges, the closer the countries in the region will be to achieving the SGD 7 principles and objectives.

18

Reflection on China's Energy Justice During a Transitional Period

Wang Mingyuan and Yang Xue

I. Introduction

Aristotle studied the issue of justice a long time ago.[1] After the mid-twentieth century, famous scholars studying the theory of justice have emerged in western countries, such as John Rawls,[2] Robert Nozick,[3] Ronald Dworkin,[4] and Amartya Sen.[5]

In Rawls' opinion, the main issue of justice is the basic structure of society, which should distribute the basic rights and obligations of all citizens and allocate the interests and burdens generated from social cooperation.[6] In Rawls' theory of 'justice as fairness', the distribution of basic items received great attention, emphasizing the equality.[7]

Amartya Sen elaborated on the relationship between freedom, justice, and development in 'Development as Freedom'.[8] He believes that social arrangements are decisive for ensuring and expanding individual freedom.[9]

The most important meaning of justice is to identify obvious injustice. For example, a society that allows the occurrence of famines when it can prevent these famines, shows in a remarkable way that it is an unjust society.[10] Today in the twenty-first century, different values exist in the process of unified social development, and a civilized society should be able to coordinate the relationship between different values. Benign theories of justice imply the coordination of different values. Therefore, there should be different dimensions, such as economic and social.

[1] Aristotle, *The Nicomachean Ethics*(The Commercial Press, 2003). Aristotle discussed justice in Volume V of *The Nicomachean Ethics*.

[2] J. Rawls, *Theory of Justice* (China Social Sciences Press, 1998) (hereafter Rawls, *Theory of Justice*). John Rawls conducted a complete discussion of justice and put forward two principles of justice.

[3] R. Nozick , Anarchy, State and Utopia(China Social Sciences Press, 2008). Robert Nozick refuted John Rawls' Theory of Justice from a liberal point of view.

[4] R. Dworkin, *Taking Rights Seriously* (Shanghai Sanlian Bookstore, 2008). Ronald Dworkin discussed justice and rights in Chapter VI of *Taking Rights Seriously*, and questioned John Rawls' *Theory of Justice*.

[5] A. Sen, *Development as Freedom* (China Renmin University Press, 2013) (hereafter Sen, *Development as Freedom*). Amartya Sen discussed the relationship between freedom, justice, and development.

[6] Rawls, *Theory of Justice* (n 2), 5.

[7] Ibid., 56, 95.

[8] Sen, *Development as Freedom* (n 5), 34.

[9] Ibid., 24–25.

[10] Ibid., 287.

Wang Mingyuan and Yang Xue, Reflection on China's Energy Justice During a Transitional Period In: *Energy Justice and Energy Law*. Edited by Íñigo Del Guayo, Lee Godden, Donald N. Zillman, Milton Fernando Montoya, and José Juan González, Oxford University Press (2020). DOI: 10.1093/oso/9780198860754.003.0018

Under the framework of justice, scholars have proposed subordinate concepts such as distributive justice, corrective justice, and intergenerational justice. Among these subordinate concepts, distributive justice and intergenerational justice are fundamental and thus determine the existence of other types of justice. Aristotle believed that justice is manifested in the distribution of honour, property, and every other thing that a citizen has the right to receive.[11] The principle of justice distribution should be based on the value of each individual.[12] The distributional justice advocated by Rawls is more inclined to regarding equality as the primary principle.[13]

Rawls believes that the issue of intergenerational justice 'is a way of treating all generations fairly in the entire historical process of a society'.[14] Scholars have defined the meaning of intergenerational justice as 'the same fair distribution of various social and natural resources and the enjoyment and inheritance of human civilization achievements'.[15] The views of various scholars on intergenerational justice are similar, mainly being that social resources and natural resources should be distributed between the present generations and the future generations. In this broader sense, distributive justice includes intergenerational justice or, intergenerational justice is part of distributive justice.

Energy justice also needs to consider how to balance the values of freedom and equality in economic and social dimensions. Energy-related distributive justice and intergenerational justice are just the application and development of distributive justice and intergenerational justice in the specific field of energy social relations. It's been seventy years since the founding of the new China. The development of China's energy exploitation, utilization,distribution, and justice in the energy sector have gone through distinct stages. A scholar divided the early evolution of China's energy policy, before the reform, into three stages: (i) the early years of new China (1949–1957); (ii) the Great Leap Forward period (1958–1964); and (iii) the Cultural Revolution period (1966–1976). [16]

During the early years of new China (1949–1957), its energy policy was devoted to the recovery and initial development of the energy industry. In 1949, new China established the Ministry of Fuel Industry, which was responsible for formulating energy production plans, specific production and operation issues.[17] Through the setting up of the Ministry of Fuel Industry and its various bureaus and departments, new China established a central management system for the energy industry, under which various industrial and mining enterprises were mainly subject to the direct leadership of each major administrative region,[18]

[11] M. Litian (ed.), *The Complete Works of Aristotle: Volume VIII* (China Renmin University Press, 1994), 99.

[12] Ibid., 100–01.

[13] In regard to justice, Rawls proposed the principle of equality and freedom, the principle of fair and equal opportunity, and the principle of difference.

[14] Rawls, *Theory of Justice* (n 2), 229.

[15] L. Xuebin, 'Justice, Inheritance of Civilization and Future Generations: Probable and Limited Intergenerational Justice' (2007) 6 *Law and Social Development*, 120

[16] X. Zhiguo, *Research on Energy Policy in New China—An Investigation and Analysis of the Development Process of New China's Energy Policy* (Doctoral dissertation), (University of Science and Technology of China, 2006).

[17] The first plenary session of the Chinese people's Political Consultative Conference (1949), Organic Law of the Central People's Government of PRC, http://www.npc.gov.cn/wxzl/wxzl/2000-12/10/content_4237.htm, accessed 22 December 2019.

[18] New China set up six administrative regions based on provinces during the early years. http://www.gov.cn/test/2007-03/23/content_558770.htm accessed 27 August 2019.

and the principles of centralized leadership and level-to-level administration were applied.[19] During the early years of new China, the energy sector featured planned economy.

During the 'Great Leap Forward' period, the energy production and administration authority were highly concentrated in the central government and local governments through the principle of making production plans 'taking steel as the key link'.[20] The Great Leap Forward not only caused a serious imbalance between heavy industry and light industry, a serious imbalance between processing industry and mining industry within the heavy industry, but also resulted in a variety of imbalances within the energy industry.[21]

During the Cultural Revolution period, for the needs of national economic development and national defence, China's energy policy vigorously developed various local industries, including small coal mines, coal mine enterprises under 'Small Third Front', [22] and large state-owned coal mines. As oilfields such as Daqing Oilfield came on stream, the steady rise in crude output also changed the structure of energy production and consumption in China. The development of energy resources in the 'Third Front'[23] areas created the conditions for energy exploitation and utilization in the southwest and northwest of China. However, due to the influence of bad atmosphere such as the left-leaning thoughts and the tendency toward boasting and exaggeration, the energy exploitation and utilization was of limited benefit during the Cultural Revolution period, and some development activities even directly damaged the normal production and operation of energy industry and destroyed energy resources.[24]

During the transitions from one stage to another, before the reform and opening up, China's energy sector also made some initiatives such as the reform of the management

[19] The first plenary session of the Chinese people's Political Consultative Conference (1949), Organic Law of the Central People's Government of PRC, http://www.npc.gov.cn/wxzl/wxzl/2000-12/10/content_4237.htm, accessed 22 December 2019.

[20] In August 1958, the enlarged meeting of the Political Bureau of the CPC Central Committee at Beidaihe adopted the 2nd Five-Year Plan, in which it was clearly stated that 'in terms of heavy industry, steel is the key link in the arrangement'. After the structural policy of 'taking steel as the key link' was determined, the amount of energy produced was determined by the planned steel production. See The Selected Important Documents since the Founding of New China (Volume 11, Central Party Literature Press 1995).

[21] See X. Zhiguo, (n 16).

[22] The ;Small Third Front; refers to the war readiness areas planned by various provinces and cities themselves, with the requirements of 'factories entering mountains', 'scattered concealment', and 'guarantee of military industry'.

[23] In the mid-1960s, the international situation around China was tense and China was faced with major hidden dangers to its national defence. On 19 May 1964, Li Fuchun, Bo Yibo, and Luo Ruiqing jointly wrote a report to the Central Committee of the Communist Party of China and Mao Zedong to put forward suggestions on how to guard against sudden attacks by enemies in the national economic construction. All new projects should not be located on the first front area; existing old enterprises on the first front area, especially those in the military and machinery industries, should be moved to the third and second front areas as much as possible, and the ones that could be split in two should be partially moved to the third and second front areas; the national key universities and research and design institutions on the first front area should be moved to the third and second front areas as much as possible, and the ones that could not be moved should be split in two. In the future, all new projects should implement the principle of entering the mountains for scattered concealment. See The Selected Important Documents since the Founding of New China, Volume 19 (Central Party Literature Press, 1998).

[24] See X. Zhiguo, (n 16).

system, the restructuring of production organization, and the exploration of marketization. However, the lack of energy resources, the hidden dangers to national defence security, and backward social management determined the absolute dominance of the State in energy exploitation and utilization, and the participation of the main body of market economy was extremely limited.

In 1981, the Sixth Plenary Session of the Eleventh Central Committee adopted the 'Resolution on Several Historical Issues of the Party since the Founding of the People's Republic of China',[25] after which China's work priorities gradually shifted to socialist modernization. With the increasing supply of domestic energy resources and the guarantee of national defence security, China's energy sector changed from merely pursuing 'security' to pursuing more diversified values and concepts such as 'efficiency' and 'justice'. In 1992, the Fourteenth National Congress of the Communist Party of China released the 'Report on Accelerating the Steps of Reform and Opening up and Modernization, and Winning the Great Success of Socialism with Chinese Characteristics',[26] stating that the goal of China's economic system reform was to establish a socialist market economy, correspondingly, China began to gradually shift to a market-oriented system. The energy sector is one of the last bastions in China's socialist market economic system reform. In the process of transitionng from the planned economic system to the socialist market economic system, energy development has shown some new trends. With the deepening of economic, social, and political reforms, the issue of justice has also become an important problem that China has to face. In this chapter, with reference to the basic theories of energy justice, especially distributive justice and intergenerational justice, we will summarize the new trends in China's energy sector policies, laws, and reform practices during the transitional period, and analyse whether these new trends are consistent with energy justice.

II. New Trend in China's Energy Sector

Since the reform and opening up in 1978 of China's energy sector, the laws, policies, and reform practices have increasingly shown a market-oriented, human-oriented, and eco-friendly development.

[25] The Sixth Plenary Session of the Eleventh CPC Central Committee, Resolutions on Certain Historical Issues of the Party Since the Founding of the People's Republic of China (1981), Party Documents Research Office of the CPC Central Committee (ed.), Selected Reading of Important Documents since the Third Plenary Session of the Eleventh Central Committee(1st People's Publishing House, 1987).

[26] The Fourteenth National Congress of the Communist Party of China, Accelerate the Reform and Opening Up and Modernization and Win a Bigger Victory for the Cause of Socialism with Chinese Characteristics (1992), Administration Department of the Party School of the Central Committee of the Communist Party of China (ed.), Selected Reading of Important Documents of the Party and the State since the Third Plenary Session of the Eleventh Central Committee (December 1978–October 2007) (Party School Press of the CPC Central Committee 2008).

A. Outstanding Situation of Marketization

Through the implementation of the '1st Five-Year Plan', China basically formed a planned economic system in 1956.[27] In 1993, the Communist Party of China adopted the 'Decision on Several Issues Concerning the Establishment of a Socialist Market Economic System',[28] proposing that 'the goal of China's economic system reform is to establish a socialist market economic system'. From 1992 until the end of the last century, China's economic system was in a transitional period, and the energy sector was still characterized by the planned economy, lacking the institutional design and competition mechanism in the energy market. During this period, the separation of enterprises from the government, corporate restructuring, and commercialization of energy enterprises were main areas for institutional reform of the energy sector.[29] During the '10th Five-Year Plan' period, with the promulgation of the 'Special Plan for Energy Development in the 10th Five-Year Plan for National Economic and Social Development',[30] it was defined that the policies and measures for energy development were mainly 'establishing and improving macro-control system for energy development, with economic and legal means and supplemented by necessary administrative measures'. Since the beginning of this century, China's socialist market economic system has been established, and the role of the market in allocating domestic energy resources has been continuously enhanced.

Since the implementation of the policy of 'multiple-player power operation' in 1985, the power system reform has experienced major changes such as the separation of enterprises from the government,[31] and the separation of power plants from the grid.[32] In March 2015, the State Council issued the 'Several Opinions on Further Deepening the Reform of the Power System',[33] initiating a new round of power system reform, including the following six core objectives: power market construction, establishment and standardized operation of trading institutions, orderly liberalization of power generation and consumption plans, reform of transmission–distribution prices, sales-side power reform, and regulation of self-supply power plants. Acceleration of the

[27] Z. Yougui (ed.), *Economic History of the People's Republic of China (1949–2012)* (Contemporary China Publishing House, 2016), 30–9.

[28] The Third Plenary Session of the Fourteenth Central Committee of the Communist Party of China, Decision of the Central Committee of the Communist Party of China on the Establishment of a Socialist Market Economic System (1993), Educational Administration Department of the Party School of the Central Committee of the Communist Party of China (ed.), Selected Reading of Important Documents of the Party and the State since the Third Plenary Session of the Eleventh Central Committee (December 1978–October 2007) (Party School Press of the CPC Central Committee 2008).

[29] X. Guoxing and Y. Rongsi (eds), *China Energy Law Research Report* (Law Press China, 2008), 12.

[30] State Planning Commission of the PRC, Special Plan for Energy Development in the 10th Five-Year Plan for National Economic and Social Development (Ji Gui Hua [2001], 711) http://www.nea.gov.cn/2011-08/19/c_131059805.htm accessed 5 July 2019.

[31] State Economic and Trade Commission of the PRC (1999), Opinions on Doing a Good Job in the Reform of Separating the Power Industry and Enterprises from the Government (Guo Jing Mao Dian Li [1999], 445).

[32] State Council of the PRC (2002), 'Power System Reform Plan'. Beijing, (Guo Fa [2002], 5). http://www.gov.cn/zhengce/content/2017-09/13/content_5223177.htm, accessed 22 December 2019.

[33] CPC Central Committee & State Council (2015), Several Opinions on Further Deepening the Reform of the Power System (Zhong Fa [2015], 9).

construction of effective competition-oriented market structure and system was proposed. In October 2015, the Communist Party of China (CPC) Central Committee and the State Council promulgated the 'Several Opinions on Promoting the Reform of the Price Mechanism',[34] in which it was proposed that price reform in the sectors of oil and natural gas should be promoted to liberalize the competitive prices, thus giving full play to the role of the market in determining prices.

The marketization process in the coal sector has been pushing forward. From 1978 to 1992, coal production and sales were uniformly deployed by the State.[35] In 1992, China conducted pilot projects to release the control of coal prices in the two mining bureaus of the cities Xuzhou and Zaozhuang,[36] and the market-oriented reform of coal prices kicked off. In 1994, the State announced the abolition of the national unified and planned coal price, but the sales of thermal coal still needed to implement the indicative price.[37] In 2002, China cancelled the government indicative price for sales of thermal coal and started to implement the market price.[38] As of 2009, China has been focusing on promoting the return of thermal coal contract prices to market prices. In 2012, the State Council issued the 'Guiding Opinions on Deepening the Reform of Thermal Coal Marketization',[39] according to which the major thermal coal contracts should be cancelled to realize the integration of thermal coal prices, and a coal trading market system that is compatible with the market economic system should be established with the National Coal Trading Center as the main body and supplemented by regional coal markets; in 2013, coking coal and thermal coal futures were successfully listed, and the national system of coal trade fairs, in which all parties involved in production, transportation, and purchasing, was gradually established. In 2017, the Coal Industry Association promoted the establishment of a pricing system for medium- and long-term coal contracts, that is, the 'base price + floating price' system.[40]

The particularity of natural gas supply sources and channels determines its natural monopoly. Comparatively speaking, the natural gas market reform has been slow. However, the process of marketization has been ongoing.[41] In 1994, the State Council

[34] CPC Central Committee & State Council (2015), Several Opinions on Promoting the Reform of the Price Mechanism, the Research Institute of Party History and Documentation of the CPC Central Committee (ed.). Important Documents since the Eighteenth National Congress of the Communist Party of China. Volume Two (Central Party Literature Press, 2018).

[35] State Council of the People's Republic of China (1978), Notice of the State Planning Commission and Other Ministries on Quantitative Supply of Certificated Fuel and Electricity State Council (1994), Decision on the Abolition of Some Administrative Regulations Promulgated Prior to the End of 1993 (Order No. 154 of the State Council of the People's Republic of China).

[36] State Council of the PRC (1992), Notice on Raising the Prices of Railway Freight, Coal and Natural Gas (Guo Fa [1992], 37) http://www.gov.cn/zhengce/content/2016-09/01/content_5103490.htm accessed 5 July 2019.

[37] State Planning Commission of the PRC (1994), Notice on Issues Related to Coal Prices (Ji Jia Ge [1994], 566).

[38] National Development and Reform Commission of the PRC (2012), Notice on the Abolition of Intervention Measures on Temporary Prices of Thermal Coal (Fa Gai Jia Ge [2012], 3956) http://www.gov.cn/gzdt/2012-12/23/content_2296735.htm accessed 5 July 2019.

[39] State Council General Office of the PRC (2012), Guidance on Deepening the Reform of Thermal Coal Marketization (Guo Ban Fa [2012], 57) http://www.gov.cn/zwgk/2012-12/25/content_2298187.htm accessed 5 July 2019.

[40] National Development and Reform Commission of the PRC (2017), Notice on Promoting the Implementation of the Medium- and Long-Term Coal Contract Signing in 2018 (Fa Gai Ban Yun Xing [2017], 1843) http://www.ndrc.gov.cn/fzgggz/jjyx/zhdt/201711/t20171129_868364.html accessed 5 July 2019.

[41] W. Wenju and C. Zhenling, 'Phase Characteristics and Strategic Choices for the Development of the Energy Industry in the 40 Years of Reform and Opening Up' (2018) 9 *China Reform*, 64.

released the 'Notice on Reforming the Circulation System of Crude Oil and Refined Oils',[42] stipulating that all crude oil and refined oil products shall be subject to national pricing; the import of crude oil and refined oil products shall be integrated into the national planned quota management, that is, unified deployment among all regions. The marketization of China's petroleum sector didn't start until the promulgation of the 'Plan for Crude Oil and Refined Oil Price Reform',[43] stipulating that the retail prices of gasoline and diesel shall implement the government indicative prices instead of government planned prices, so as to integrate with the international market for gasoline and diesel import.

There are more companies in energy market. In 1999, China issued the 'Opinions on Clearing and Reorganizing Small Refineries and Regulating the Circulation Order of Crude Oil and Refined Oils',[44] stipulating that a small proportion of domestically produced crude oil shall be deployed to a number of small refineries with annual processing capacity lower than 1 million tons/year, other than PetroChina and Sinopec, and all of the refined oil products shall be put into the market. More and more entities started to engage in the diversified energy market. In 2006, the Ministry of Commerce promulgated the 'Measures for the Management of Crude Oil Markets'[45] and 'Administrative Measures for Refined Oil Markets',[46] stipulating that the State implement a licensing system for crude oil and refined oil operation. The licensing system is conducive to standardizing the operation of the energy market. However, due to the restricted access to licensing, only a few large state-owned enterprises were qualified, with little effect in stimulating market competition. In 2014, the National Development and Reform Commission issued the 'Guiding Opinions on Accelerating the Construction of Gas Storage Facilities'[47] to encourage diversified businesses to participate in the construction and operation of gas storage facilities. In August 2015, China further liberalized the oil import market. Any legal entities engaged in the wholesale of oil products shall be qualified to import crude oil independently without engaging a state-owned unit.[48] In March 2019, the Central Comprehensively Deepening Reforms Commission adopted the 'Opinions on the Implementation of the Reform of the Operation Mechanism of

[42] State Council of the PRC (1994), Opinions on Reforming Crude Oil and Refined Oil Circulation System (Guo Fa [1994], 21) http://www.gov.cn/zhengce/content/2015-12/22/content_10492.htm accessed 5 July 2019.

[43] State Planning Commission of the PRC (1998), Plan for Crude Oil and Refined Oil Price Reform (Ji Dian [1998], 52).

[44] State Economic and Trade Commission, Ministry of Foreign Trade and Economic Cooperation, State Administration for Industry and Commerce, State Administration of Taxation & State Bureau of Quality and Technical Supervision of the PRC (1999), Opinions on Closing and Rectifying Small Refineries and Regulating the Circulation Order of Crude Oil and Oil Products (Guo Ban Fa [1999], 38) http://www.gov.cn/gongbao/content/2000/content_60202.htm accessed 5 July 2019.

[45] Ministry of Commerce of the PRC (2006), Measures for the Management of Crude Oil Markets (Order of the Ministry of Commerce of the PRC [2006], 24). (Revised in 2015.)

[46] Ministry of Commerce of the PRC (2006), Measures for the Management of Crude Oil Markets (Order of the Ministry of Commerce of the PRC [2006], 23). (Revised in 2015.) http://www.nanyue.gov.cn/swj/xxgk/zcfg/201807/t20180726_2394331.html accessed 5 July 2019.

[47] National Development and Reform Commission of the PRC (2014), Guidance on Accelerating the Construction of Gas Storage Facilities (Fa Gai Yun Xing [2014], 603) http://www.ndrc.gov.cn/zcfb/zcfbtz/201404/t20140429_609361.html accessed 5 July 2019.

[48] The Seventh Session of the Central Committee for Comprehensive Deepening Reform of the PRC (2019), Opinions on Implementing the Reform of the Operational Mechanism of Oil and Gas Pipelines Network.

Oil and Gas Pipelines Network'[49] to promote the formation of an oil and gas market with a multi-channel supply of upstream oil and gas resources, efficient and unified collection and transportation through midstream pipes, and full competition in the downstream sales market.

The market's mechanism for determining energy prices has been expanding. According to the 'Notice of the State Planning Commission on Improving the Integration of Petroleum Prices and Adjusting the Refined Oil Prices'[50] issued in 2001, China's domestic crude oil prices were integrated into the international system of crude oil prices for further marketization of the energy price mechanism. In 2008, domestic onshore crude oil prices were directly linked to the international market, while domestic refined oil prices were indirectly linked with the prices of refined oil products on the international market.[51] In November 2015, China officially proposed to push forward price reforms in oil and natural gas sectors and liberalize the prices in competitive links, so as to promote the role of the market in determining prices.[52] At the end of May 2019, the National Development and Reform Commission and three other ministries jointly issued the 'Measures for the Administration of Fair Opening of Oil and Gas Pipelines Network'[53] to promote a more fair opening of the oil and gas pipelines network and facilitate diversified competition in the oil and gas market. In March 2019, the China National Offshore Oil Corporation (CNOOC) and the Shanghai Oil and Gas Trading Center jointly launched the 'Import LNG One-stop Window' for the import of medium- and short-term agreement products, signifying the scaling up and normalization of fair and orderly opening of the liquefied natural gas (LNG) infrastructure in China.[54]

During the process of continuous reform of energy marketization, the law will, on the one hand, legally define the mature reform practices, and on the other hand, provide a direction for market-oriented reforms. The promulgation of the 'Renewable Energy Law',[55] the 'Regulations on Civil Buildings Energy Conservation,'[56] the 'Safety

[49] Ministry of Commerce of the PRC (2015), Notice on the Work Related to the Application for Non-State Import Certificates by Crude Oil Processing Enterprises (Shang Mao Han [2015], 407) http://www.mofcom.gov.cn/article/b/e/201507/20150701056066.shtml accessed 5 July 2019.

[50] State Planning Commission of the PRC (2001), Notice on Improving the Integration of Petroleum Prices and Adjusting the Refined Oil Prices, Beijing. (Ji Dian [2001], 96) http://www.nea.gov.cn/2011-08/16/c_131052067.htm accessed 5 July 2019.

[51] State Council of the PRC (2008), Notice on Implementing the Reform of Refined Oil Prices and Taxes (Guo Fa [2008], 37) http://www.gov.cn/zwgk/2008-12/19/content_1182128.htm accessed 5 July 2019.

[52] CPC Central Committee & State Council (2015), Several Opinions on Promoting the Reform of the Price Mechanism, the Research Institute of Party History and Documentation of the CPC Central Committee (ed.).) Important Documents since the Eighteenth National Congress of the Communist Party of China. Volume Two (Central Party Literature Press, 2018).

[53] National Development and Reform Commission, National Energy Administration, Ministry of Housing and Urban-Rural Development & General Administration of Market Supervision of the PRC (2019), 'Measures for the Administration of Fair Opening of Oil and Gas Pipelines Network', Beijing. (Fa Gai Neng Yuan Gui [2019], 916) http://www.gov.cn/xinwen/2019-06/02/content_5396824.htm accessed 5 July 2019.

[54] Shanghai Petroleum and Natural Gas Exchange Center: 'Announcement of Medium- and Short-Term Agreement Products for "Import LNG One-stop Window"', Shanghai: China National Offshore Oil and Gas Group Co., Ltd. Trade Branch, Shanghai Petroleum and Natural Gas Exchange Center Co., Ltd. (Exchange Center [2019], 2).

[55] The Fourteenth Session of the Standing Committee of the Tenth National People's Congress of the PRC (2005), Renewable Energy Law of the People's Republic of China (Presidential Decree No. 33 of the People's Republic of China) http://www.nea.gov.cn/2017-11/02/c_136722869.htm accessed 5 July 2019.

[56] State Council of the PRC (2008), Regulations on Civil Building Energy Conservation (Beijing. Order No. 530 of the State Council) http://www.gov.cn/flfg/2008-08/07/content_1067062.htm accessed 5 July 2019.

Production Law',[57] and the 'Cleaner Production Promotion Law'[58] provided stipulations on the government roles, incentive policies, and the cultivation of energy markets, so as to adapt to the new development of the energy market. In October 2016, with the promulgation of the 'Measures for the Administration of Access and Exit of Power Distribution Companies' and the 'Management Measures for the Orderly Release of Distribution Network Businesses',[59] the access and exit mechanisms of the energy market was further improved.

In addition to the development of the domestic energy market, China's energy sector adheres to reform and opening up. First is the implementation of the 'introduction' strategy to optimize the foreign investment environment and ensure the legitimate rights and interests of investors. In order to provide legal guidance for foreign nations to participate in the Chinese energy market, China has successively issued laws and regulations such as the 'Law on Sino-Foreign Equity Joint Ventures'[60] and policy documents such as the 'Catalogue of Industries for Guiding Foreign Investment'.[61] The 'Special Administrative Measures (Negative List) for the Access of Foreign Investment (2018)—Amendment Notes'[62] issued in 2018 required a 'lift of the Chinese holding's restriction on special and scarce coal exploration and mining' and to 'abolish the Chinese control of the grid construction and operation', so as to provide space for foreign-funded enterprises to enter the Chinese energy market. The 'Foreign Investment Law'[63] promulgated in 2019 further provides legal protection for increasing the energy market participants.

Second is the implementation of the 'going global' strategy to actively integrate into the global market. China's accession to the World Trade Organization in 2001 accelerated the opening up of China's energy market. As of 2013, as a new starting point for opening up China's energy market, China started the 'Belt and Road' construction, the

[57] The Twenty-eighth Session of the Standing Committee of the Ninth National People's Congress of the PRC (2002), Safety Production Law http://xxgk.ganzhou.gov.cn/c100475ks/2018-03/07/content_08423e54260b46bb91e6e626a0e9d5ef.shtml accessed 5 July 2019.

[58] The Twenty-fifth Session of the Standing Committee of the Eleventh National People's Congress of the PRC (2012), Cleaner Production Promotion Law of the People's Republic of China http://www.gov.cn/flfg/2012-03/01/content_2079732.htm accessed 5 July 2019.

[59] National Development and Reform Commission & National Energy Administration of the PRC (2016), Notice on Printing and Distributing the 'Measures for the Administration of Access and Exit of Power Distribution Companies' and 'Management Measures for the Orderly Release of Distribution Network Businesses' (Fa Gai Jing Ti [2016], 2120) http://www.ndrc.gov.cn/zcfb/zcfbtz/201610/t20161011_822225.html accessed 5 July 2019.

[60] The Forth Session of the Ninth National People's Congress of the PRC (2001), Law of Sino-Foreign Equity Joint Ventures (Presidential Decree No. 48 of the People's Republic of China) http://www.gov.cn/banshi/2005-08/31/content_69775.htm accessed 5 July 2019.

[61] State Council General Office of the PRC (2002), Catalogue of Industries for Guiding Foreign Investment (Guo Ban Han [2002], 17).

[62] National Development and Reform Commission & Ministry of Commerce of the PRC, Special Administrative Measures (Negative List) for the Access of Foreign Investment (2018)—Amendment Notes (Order of the National Development and Reform Commission and the Ministry of Commerce [2018], 18) http://www.mofcom.gov.cn/article/b/f/201806/20180602760432.shtml accessed 5 July 2019.

[63] The Second Session of the Thirteenth National People's Congress of the PRC (2019), Foreign Investment Law (Presidential Decree No. 26 of the People's Republic of China).

setting up of free trade pilot zones, and the planning of free trade ports with Chinese characteristics.

Thirdly, China has become an active participant in international energy cooperation. In terms of bilateral cooperation, China has established energy dialogues and cooperation mechanisms with the U.S, the EU, Japan, and other countries and regions; so as to strengthen dialogues, exchanges, and cooperation in the field of oil, gas, coal and energy policies. In terms of multilateral cooperation, China is a full member and an important participant in various organizations and mechanisms such as the Asia-Pacific Economic Cooperation Energy Working Group, the G20, the Shanghai Cooperation Organization, the World Energy Council, and the International Energy Forum. In addition, as an observer of the Energy Charter, China maintains close ties with the International Energy Agency and the Organization of Petroleum Exporting Countries.

Since the reform and opening up, China has been committed to promoting energy market reforms. The marketization effects are mainly reflected in three aspects: the increase in market participants, the increasingly equal status of market participants, and the increasingly effective role of the market in deploying resources. First, in China's transition from a planned economic system to a socialist market economic system, more and more market participants are involved in energy development and utilization, and their needs are reflected and satisfied through the market. Second, the marketization of the energy sector is also manifested in the increasingly equal status of market participants: (i) market participants enjoy equal rights such as property ownership and independent operation rights; and (ii) market participants abide equally by laws and regulations and fulfil their obligations.[64] And third, the government has been restraining its intervention in energy resource allocation. Especially in recent years, it has been emphasized that the government must expand the reform of its 'delegating, regulating and servicing' role for the energy sector and regulate the operation of power.[65] As an important means of deploying energy resources, the market mechanism respects and gives play to the role of market participants for diversified and independent operation, so as to meet the market demand and realize rational allocation of resources.

[64] In the process of transformation, China promulgated a number of laws such as the 'Electricity Law', the 'Water Law', the 'Coal Law' and the 'Renewable Energy Law'. In 2019, China issued the 'Opinions on Deepening and Pushing Forward Legal Governance in the Energy Industry', requiring specific progress of legal construction in the energy sector in seven aspects, including legislation, law enforcement, law popularization, and institutional reforms.

[65] National Energy Administration of the PRC (2019), Opinions on Deepening and Pushing Forward Legal Governance in the Energy Industry (Guo Neng Fa Fa Gai [2019], 5). Certain achievements have been made in marketization reforms in various sectors such as electricity, coal, natural gas, and petroleum. From 2013 to 2014, the Chinese government issued the 'Decision of the State Council on the Cancellation and Decentralization of a Batch of Administrative Approval Items' (Guo Fa [2013], 44); 'Decision of the State Council on the Cancellation and Decentralization of a Batch of Administrative Approval Items' (Guo Fa [2014], 5); and 'Notice on Cancellation, Suspension and Exemption of a Batch of Administrative Fees' (Cai Shui [2014], 101), including the cancellation of the approval and issuance of coal production licenses, the cancellation of the administrative examination and approval such as the advanced review of the applications for sino-foreign cooperative exploration and mining of mineral resources, the suspension of oil (natural gas) exploration and mining registration fees, the suspension of mineral resources exploration registration fees, and so on. The decentralization measures and reduction of taxes and fees are incentives to the role of market mechanisms in the energy sector.

With the overall marketization of the energy sector, there is the phenomenon of partial marketization in some regions. In addition, oil and power sectors are experiencing limited marketization. For example, the petroleum industry's downstream circulation has been continuously liberalized and the competitiveness has been significantly enhanced. However, the mid- and-upstream operating mechanisms still reflect the national planning and the monopoly by large state-owned enterprises.

B. Deepening Trend of Humanization

In China's transition from a planned economic system to a socialist market economic system, the energy sector has been increasingly focusing on 'people-oriented' development, with an increasing stress on providing fair opportunities and rights for vulnerable groups.

In 2010, China's total energy consumption was 3,606.48 million tons of standard coal, in which the total energy consumption by agriculture, forestry, animal husbandry, fishery, and water conservancy was 64.773 million tons (standard coal),[66] accounting for less than 2 per cent. In the winter season, cities in northern China only provide central heating services in urban areas; while in rural areas, households burn coal and firewood for heating. According to the 2008 and 2012 survey results, rural energy consumption is still based on straw and firewood burning, accounting for more than 60 per cent of household energy consumption.[67] Rural populations' access to energy use in agriculture-related industries and rural areas is relatively underdeveloped.[68] The objective situation of China's natural environment and social history determines that the eastern region is able to give priority to the development of the secondary and tertiary industries, and make quick investments in modernization; while the vast western region is dominated by the primary industry 'agriculture', with relatively primitive industrial development, which means that in China's modernization process, agriculture, rural areas (concentrated in the western region), and farmers are lagging behind. In the historical 'urban–rural dual system', agriculture, rural areas (concentrated in the western region), and farmers in China's energy sector have always been a vulnerable industry, region, and group. According to Article 8 of the 'Electricity Law' promulgated in 1995, 'the State helps and supports the development of electric power in ethnic minority areas, remote areas and poverty-stricken areas', and pays attention to the fair distribution of electric power development among different regions and different ethnic groups. China has launched 'The Grand Western Development Program' focusing

[66] See National Bureau of Statistics of the PRC http://data.stats.gov.cn/easyquery.htm?cn=C01 accessed 5 July 2019.

[67] Q. Huan'guang, Y. Jianbiao, L. Dengwang, et al., 'Analysis of the Status Quo, Development Trend and Determinants of Rural Energy Consumption in China—Based on Empirical Study in 4 Provinces in 2 Phases' (2015) 11 *China Soft Science*.

[68] Z. Zhongmin and X. Xiaoqing, 'Legal Realization of Rural Energy Justice in China' (2016) 12 *China Population · Resources and Environment*, 127.

on macro regions and the 'precise poverty elimination campaign' focusing on micro individuals.

'The Grand Western Development Program',[69] adopted by the Central Economic Work Conference in 1999, is dedicated to promoting the coordinated development of both eastern and western regions. The tasks include strengthening the construction of infrastructure such as natural gas pipelines and power grids. In the energy sector, important projects such as 'West-to-East Power Transmission' and 'West-to-East Natural Gas Transmission' have been carried out. In March 2001, China's '10th Five-Year Plan' included the 'West-to-East Power Transmission' project with China's medium- and long-term development strategy. Based on the 'West-to-East Power Transmission' project, a number of large-scale hydropower stations and high-efficiency thermal power bases have been built in the western region, which has promoted the optimization of energy structure. The implementation of the 'West-to-East Natural Gas Transmission' project has resulted in the longest and largest gas transmission pipelines in China, serving more than 400 million residents and more than 3,000 enterprises in more than 120 large and medium-sized cities.[70] China has also proposed systematic projects such as the 'Village-to-Village Project', involving the construction of electricity, communications, and highway infrastructure. For example, in order to implement the 'Three-Year Action Plan for Comprehensive Electricity Supply for the Population in Shortage of Electricity (2013–2015)',[71] the Chinese government allocated a total investment of 24.78 billion yuan, including 14.55 billion yuan from the central government fund, to be used for the construction of power grid extension projects and renewable energy power supply projects. As a result, 2.73 million people lacking electricity, obtained access to electricity.[72] The implementation of multiple energy projects in 'The Grand Western Development Program' has transformed the western advantage of energy resources into an economic advantage, which has promoted and accelerated the economic development in the western region, increased local fiscal revenues and employment opportunities, and produced good social benefits.

In addition to macro-regional policy programmes such as 'The Grand Western Development Program', China has launched the 'precise poverty elimination campaign'[73] to provide assistance to vulnerable groups and vulnerable regions. In 2015 and

[69] 'The Grand Western Development Program' is a systematic project involving infrastructure construction, eco-environmental protection, consolidation of agriculture's basic status, industrial restructuring, science and technology education, and development of cultural and health undertakings. See in State Council of the PRC (2000), Notice on Implementing Several Policy Measures for Western Development (Guo Fa [2000], 33) http://www.gov.cn/gongbao/content/2001/content_60854.htm accessed 5 July 2019.

[70] Song Yan: 'The main gas source of the West-to-East Natural Gas Pipeline supplies more than 230 billion cubic meters of gas to the downstream' http://www.gov.cn/xinwen/2019-06/02/content_5396897.htm?_zbs_baidu_bk accessed 5 July 2019.

[71] National Energy Administration of the PRC (2013), Three-Year Action Plan for Comprehensive Electricity Supply for the Population in Shortage of Electricity (2013–2015) http://www.xjdrc.gov.cn/info/11805/7703.htm accessed 5 July 2019.

[72] Announcement of the National Energy Administration of the PRC http://www.nea.gov.cn/2015-12/24/c_134948340.htm accessed 5 July 2019.

[73] On 18 October 2017, the report of the Nineteenth National Congress of the Communist Party of China proposed that it is necessary to make resolute efforts to address major risks, to realize precise poverty elimination, and to achieve pollution prevention and control. Precise poverty elimination has become one of the main tasks for the Chinese government.

2018, China issued the 'Decision on Winning the War of Eliminating Poverty'[74] and 'Guiding Opinions on the Three-Year Action Plan for Winning the War of Eliminating Poverty'.[75] According to these two documents, China will help relieve poverty in various aspects, including the goal of improving major public service indicators, such as electricity service indicators, to a level close to the national average. Correspondingly, various ministries have adopted a series of policy measures to promote poverty alleviation work in the energy sector, stating that China will improve energy use infrastructure, accurately implement energy poverty alleviation projects, and effectively improve the general energy service level, as well as other tasks and objectives. These ministries also proposes that in economically feasible situations, major projects for energy development and utilization, major trans-regional energy transmission projects, and new energy projects, shall be deployed in poverty-stricken areas first.[76]

In view of the long-term vulnerable position of rural areas, agriculture-related industries, and rural populations, the Chinese government has decided to adopt the 'government-led, grid implementation' approach to provide universal services for vulnerable regions, industries, and groups, and provide equal opportunities of economic development through energy infrastructure construction, so as to protect the basic 'human' dignity and freedom of the socially disadvantaged groups in China.

C. Continuous Trend of Ecologicalization

Ecologicalization of the energy sector is mainly reflected in direct ecologicalized regulations and work requirements in laws, policies, and reforms, as well as indirect guidance for the ecologicalized development of the entire energy industry through market mechanisms.

First, there are more specific provisions in laws, policies, and reforms for promoting energy conservation and development of renewable energy. In terms of energy conservation, China enacted the 'Energy Conservation Law'[77] in 1998, with two amendments and one revision made by 2018, to promote all-society energy conservation, improve energy efficiency, and protect and improve the environment. In 2006, the Chinese government issued the 'Decision on Strengthening Energy Conservation'.[78] In 2007, the

[74] CPC Central Committee & State Council (2015), Decision on Winning the War of Eliminating Poverty http://www.gov.cn/zhengce/2015-12/07/content_5020963.htm accessed 5 July 2019.

[75] CPC Central Committee, State Council (2018), Guiding Opinions on the Three-Year Action Plan for Winning the War of Eliminating Poverty http://www.gov.cn/zhengce/2018-08/19/content_5314959.htm accessed 5 July 2019.

[76] The National Development and Reform Commission, the National Energy Administration and other ministries have successively issued the '13th Five-Year Plan for Energy Development' (Fa Gai Neng Yuan [2016], 2744); 'Notice on the Action Plan for Further Supporting the Energy Development in Poverty-stricken Areas to Help Eliminate Poverty (2018–2020)' (Guo Neng Fa Gui Hua [2018], 42); 'Opinions on Implementing Poverty Alleviation Work for Photovoltaic Power Generation' (Fa Gai Neng Yuan [2016], 621); and 'Management Measures for Photovoltaic Power Stations for Poverty Alleviation' (Guo Neng Fa Xin Neng [2018], 29); and so on. http://www.ndrc.gov.cn/zcfb/zcfbtz/201701/t20170117_835278.html accessed 5 July 2019.

[77] The Thirtieth Session of the Standing Committee of the Tenth National People's Congress (1998), Energy Conservation Law (Presidential Decree No. 16 of the People's Republic of China) http://www.gov.cn/ziliao/flfg/2007-10/28/content_788493.htm accessed 5 July 2019.

[78] State Council of the PRC (2006), Decision on Strengthening Energy Conservation (Guo Fa [2006], 28) http://www.gov.cn/zwgk/2006-08/23/content_368136.htm accessed 5 July 2019.

Chinese government issued the 'Comprehensive Work Plan for Energy Conservation and Emission Reduction',[79] including the 'top ten energy conservation projects' to be deployed in key sectors such as industry, construction, and transportation. During the '11th Five-Year Plan' period, the level of energy consumption per unit GDP fell by 19.1per cent.[80] In 2011, China issued the '12th Five-Year Plan for Comprehensive Energy Conservation and Emission Reduction',[81] which specified the main energy saving and emission reduction targets and tasks for the '12th Five-Year Plan' period. It can be seen that China has been promoting energy conservation and emission reduction since the 1990s.

In the development of renewable energy, China enacted the 'Renewable Energy Law'[82] in 2005 and revised it in 2009 in light of social realities. The 'Renewable Energy Law' provides clear regulations on renewable energy-related resource survey and development planning, industrial guidance and technical support, as well as renewable energy promotion and application, price management and cost compensation, economic incentives, and supervision measures. In 2012, the National Development and Reform Commission issued the '12th Five-Year Plan for Renewable Energy Development',[83] which includes guiding principles and basic principles, development goals, key tasks, industrial layout, safeguard measures and implementation mechanisms for the development of hydro, wind, solar, biomass, geothermal, and ocean energy. Correspondingly, relevant ministries provided policy support in terms of new energy industry planning, new energy subsidies, operational mechanisms, and investment incentives.[84]

Second, is the use of market transmission mechanism for guiding ecologicalized transformation of the energy market. In July 2007, the former State Environmental Protection Administration, the People's Bank of China, and the China Banking Regulatory Commission jointly issued the 'Opinions on Implementing Environmental Protection Policies and Regulations to Prevent Credit Risks',[85] requiring credit control for enterprises and projects not complying with industrial policies and committing environmental violations, that is, using 'green credit' to control the blind expansion

[79] State Council of the PRC (2007), Comprehensive Work Plan for Energy Conservation and Emission Reduction (Guo Fa [2007], 15) http://www.gov.cn/zwgk/2007-06/03/content_634545.htm accessed 5 July 2019.

[80] State Council of the PRC (2011), Government Work Report.

[81] State Council of the PRC (2011), Comprehensive Work Plan for Energy Conservation and Emission Reduction (Guo Fa [2011], 26) http://www.gov.cn/zwgk/2011-09/07/content_1941731.htm accessed 5 July 2019.

[82] The Fourteenth Session of the Standing Committee of the Tenth National People's Congress of the PRC (2005), 'Renewable Energy Law'. Presidential Decree No. 33 of the People's Republic of China http://www.gov.cn/ziliao/flfg/2005-06/21/content_8275.htm accessed 5 July 2019.

[83] National Energy Administration of the PRC (2012), The 12th Five-Year Plan for Renewable Energy Development http://www.nea.gov.cn/2012-08/08/c_131767651.htm accessed 5 July 2019.

[84] National Development and Reform Commission of the PRC (2013), Notice on Matters Related to the Adjustment of Renewable Energy Electricity Price Additional Standards and Environmental Protection Electricity Prices (Fa Gai Jia Ge [2013], 1651). National Energy Administration (2014), Notice on Requirements Related to the Regulation of Wind Power Equipment Market Order (Guo Neng Xin Neng [2014], 412). National Energy Administration (2014), Notice on Further Implementing Relevant Policies on Distributed Photovoltaic Power Generation (Guo Neng Xin Neng [2014], 406).

[85] State Environmental Protection Administration, People's Bank of China & China Banking Regulatory Commission (2007), Opinions on Implementing Environmental Protection Policies and Regulations for Prevention of Credit Risks.

of high-consumption, high-pollution industries. The China Banking Regulatory Commission has successively issued the 'Guiding Opinions on Credit Granted for Energy Saving and Emission Reduction',[86] 'Guidelines for Green Credit',[87] and 'Guidelines for Credit Granted for Energy Efficiency'.[88] In 2016, the People's Bank of China, the Ministry of Finance, the China Banking Regulatory Commission, and four other ministries jointly issued the 'Guiding Opinions on Building a Green Financial System',[89] which provided clear definitions of green finance and green financial systems and proposed to vigorously develop green credit. Various commercial banks have successively adopted green credit mechanisms to use economic levers for guiding energy companies to conduct eco-friendly business operations.[90] China has initially established the institutional framework of green credit.[91]

The adoption of legal, policy, and reform measures for the ecologicalization of the energy sector, as well as the addressing of climate change, aim to achieve the ultimate goal of sustainable development. China signed on 11 June 1992 and ratified on 7 May 1993 the United Nations Framework Convention on Climate Change. As an important obligation in implementing the Convention, the Chinese government has formulated the 'China National Plan for Coping with Climate Change',[92] including specific targets, basic principles, key areas, and policy measures for addressing climate change by 2010. In 2011, China issued a report on 'China's Policies and Actions for Coping with Climate Change'[93] as a contribution to the global actions for addressing climate change and for joint promotion of green and low-carbon development.

China's goals of, and the progress made in, promoting energy conservation, developing new and renewable energy sources, promoting the clean development of fossil energy and coping with climate change, reflect the importance attached to sustainable economic and social development. In China's transition from a planned economic system to a socialist market economic system, with the continuous expanding of the concept of sustainable development, the ecologicalization trend in the energy sector has become more outstanding.

[86] China Banking Regulatory Commission of the PRC (2007), 'Guiding Opinions on Credit Granted for Energy Saving and Emission Reduction' (Yin Jian Fa [2007], 83) http://www.cbrc.gov.cn/chinese/newIndex.html accessed 5 July 2019.

[87] China Banking Regulatory Commission (2012), 'Guidelines for Green Credit' (Yin Jian Fa [2012], 4) http://www.cbrc.gov.cn/chinese/newIndex.html accessed 5 July 2019.

[88] China Banking Regulatory Commission (2015), Guidelines for Credit Granted for Energy Efficiency (Yin Jian Fa [2015], 2) http://www.cbrc.gov.cn/chinese/newIndex.html accessed 5 July 2019.

[89] People's Bank of China, Ministry of Finance & National Development and Reform Commission (2016), Guiding Opinions on Building a Green Financial System.

[90] See in the 'Announcement of Industrial and Commercial Bank of China Co., Ltd. on Completing the 2017 Self-evaluation of Green Credit Implementation'. The board meeting of China Construction Bank Co., Ltd, held on 16 June 2016, adopted the 'Proposal on the Green Credit Development Strategy of China Construction Bank Co., Ltd.'.

[91] Q. Lihua, 'China Banking Industry's Green Credit System' (2016) 22 *China Finance*, 70–1.

[92] State Council of the PRC (2007), China National Plan for Coping with Climate Change (Guo Fa [2007], 17) http://www.gov.cn/zhengce/content/2008-03/28/content_5743.htm accessed 5 July 2019.

[93] The State Council Information Office of the PRC (2011), China's Policies and Actions for Coping with Climate Change http://www.gov.cn/jrzg/2011-11/22/content_2000047.htm accessed 5 July 2019.

III. Analysis of the Consistency between the New Trend of Energy Development and Energy Justice

For the time being, China is in a new stage of social transformation, China's social productivity has been greatly improved. Meanwhile, the pattern of social interests is going through overall restructuring, from the pattern of all people benefitting during the initial stage of reforms, to the polarization between the rich class and the general public with the loss of relative or absolute interests.[94] This kind of polarization has widened the gap between the rich and the poor, and the contradictions of interests have become increasingly prominent. How to achieve social justice has become a matter of great concern. As the basic material for human survival and development, energy distributive justice between various contemporary groups and between contemporary and future generations is an important part of realizing social justice. In China's transition from the planned economic system to the socialist market economic system, the promulgated energy policies, laws, and reform measures have shown a trend of market orientation, humanization, and ecologicalization, which generally support the promotion of the concept of energy justice and the realization of goals. The theory of energy justice is gradually being integrated into China's local practice during the transitional period, mainly through marketization, humanization, and ecologicalization.

A. Marketization and Energy Justice in the Energy Sector

To change the injustice caused by market failures, western developed countries have increased the level of redistribution through administrative means, which is a 'market-to-regulation' model. In contrast, China's energy justice is realized in the transition from the planned economic system to the socialist market economic system, which is a 'regulation-to-market' model. In general, China's energy sector's marketization is in line with the realization of energy justice concepts and principles.

Marketization has three important characteristics. First, sufficient and diversified market participants; second, equal participation in market activities by all participants; and third, resource allocation through market mechanisms instead of administrative measures.[95] In the energy market, full competition by equal market participants is conducive to optimized allocation of energy resources and higher production efficiency and quality. Therefore providing the supply of various energy commodities in larger quantity and better quality as well as better energy services. While in a monopolistic energy market, intentional elimination of domestic or foreign competition will result in inefficiency and huge losses to the society.[96]

[94] L. Peilin, et al., *Social Stratification in China* (China Social Sciences Press, 2004).

[95] N.G. Mankiw, *Principles of Economics* (Peking University Press, 6th edn, 2012), Chapter IV(hereafter Mankiw, *Principles of Economics*).

[96] Sen, *Development as Freedom* (n 5), 119.

The connotation of justice should contain the value of freedom. Energy justice in the economic dimension requires a more sufficient supply of energy and expanded freedom of energy use. Amartya Sen believes that development may be seen as a process of expanding people's enjoyment of true freedom, and gross national product and personal income growth is the means for expanding the freedom of members of society.[97] The form of non-freedom includes the lack of economic security.[98] If the social system prevents members of society from expanding their freedom and hinders the growth of gross national product and personal income, obviously it is not in line with the human pursuit of a higher standard of living in a better state, which is contrary to the concept of justice. The market-oriented reform in the energy sector, through improving market access and exit mechanisms, creating a fair competitive market environment and reducing administrative intervention, provides more freedom for more participants to share in energy production and consumption. Therefore, the supply of more and better products and services for society is acheived. A pure energy plan management system will lead to inefficient energy development and insufficient supply of energy products for people to pursue a better life, which is not in line with the concept of justice. This is one of the important reasons for China's energy sector to embark on the path of socialist marketization.

B. Humanization and Energy Justice in the Energy Sector

Freedom, in form and in substance, relies on economic arrangements, but also relies on social arrangements as well as political and civil rights.[99] Market logic pursues efficiency and, in the economic dimension, marketization is a way of expanding the freedom of people in their use of energy resources, which is in line with the theory of justice. However, the 'invisible hand' does not guarantee enough food, decent clothes, and adequate medical care for everyone.[100] A completely competitive market does not exist. Due to information asymmetry and other reasons, market failures always exist. For capable market participants, marketization will help them make fuller use of public resources and energy. However, for the vulnerable groups, without access to energy resource development and utilization and corresponding benefits, they are trapped in energy poverty. In addition, energy marketization will lead to rapid reduction of energy resources preserved in nature and unfair distribution of energy resources, which is a deviation from energy justice.

In China's transition from the planned economic system to the socialist market economic system, social wealth has been increasing and people's living standards have been improving significantly; meanwhile, the gap between the rich and the poor in society has been

97 Sen, *Development as Freedom* (n 5), 1.
98 Sen, *Development as Freedom* (n 5), 11.
99 Sen, *Development as Freedom* (n 5), 1.
100 Mankiw, *Principles of Economics* (n 95), Chapter I.

widening,[101] and the level of energy resource utilization varies between different groups, regions, and sectors. Energy is elementary, social, and ecological. In the social dimension, 'distributive justice' requires redistribution of certain resources throughout the society through national mandatory measures, so as to provide certain levels of material treatment to each member of society.[102] In order to promote the coordinated development of society, China's energy sector is increasingly aware of the interests of disadvantaged industries, regions, and groups. Redistribution of interests through national-level policies and applicable laws and regulations such as 'The Grand Western Development Program' and 'Poverty Alleviation Campaign', provides basic guarantees for meeting the energy interest demand of disadvantaged industries, regions, and groups, reflecting the value and dignity of 'people as the purpose'.[103]

C. Ecologicalization and Energy Justice in the Energy Sector

Energy ecologicalization is an important way to achieve intergenerational justice in the energy sector, and sustainable development is the link between the two. On the one hand, intergenerational justice in the energy sector must be based on sustainable development and utilization of energy, requires for fair distribution of energy resources between contemporary and future generations, that is, contemporary generation's exploitation and utilization of energy shall not affect future generations' ability to exploit and utilize energy. If future generations lose this ability, it's not consistent with intergenerational justice. On the other hand, ecologicalized exploitation and utilization is an important means for achieving sustainable development and utilization in the energy sector, which requires an ecologicalized approach—'broadening the sources and regulating the flow'. 'Broadening the sources' mainly refers to the development of renewable energy; 'regulating the flow' mainly refers to the saving of energy, especially non-renewable energy. Ecologicalized exploitation and utilization, through improving energy efficiency and exploring alternative energy sources with no harm to the environment, is conducive to extended periods of energy exploitation and utilization and sustainable development. In China's transition from the planned economic system to the socialist market economic system, China needs to adopt a more ecologicalized exploitation and utilization approach in the energy sector, to meet the energy demand of the contemporary generation without affecting the ability of future generations to meet their energy demands, so as to effectively promote the fair distribution of energy resources between contemporary and future generations and realize intergenerational justice.

[101] L. Yifu, C. Rifang, and L. Zhou, 'Analysis of Regional Disparities in China's Economic Transition Period' (1998) 6 *Economic Research*, 4–5.

[102] T. Jianbo, 'Three Preconditions for Distributive Justice: The Enlightenment of Rawls, Hayek and Nozick' (2011), 3 *Philosophical Trends*, 66.

[103] Kant, 'Critique of Practical Reason' (The Commercial Press, 2003), 95.

IV. Conclusions

After more than two thousand years of development, the theory of justice has been endowed with rich meanings, and energy justice has the universal characteristics of justice theory. The coexistence of multiple values in the energy sector requires both economic dimension and social dimension, based on which the relationship between freedom and equality shall be coordinated. Distributive justice requires respect for the differences between individuals. In the energy sector, the freedom of energy production and consumption shall be expandable. Meanwhile, fair use of energy resources by disadvantaged groups, industries, and regions shall be guaranteed as a bottom line; intergenerational justice requires for fair distribution of the use of energy resources between contemporary and future generations.

In the past forty years of reform and opening up, China is transforming from a traditional planned economy to a modern market economy, in which energy is one of the last bastions for institutional transformation. The energy sector is characterized by marketization, humanization, and ecologicalization, which is generally consistent with the theory of energy justice. In this process, the Chinese government has been adopting market-oriented, humanized, and ecologicalized energy policies, laws, and reform measures to broaden the participation in the energy sector, protect the interests of vulnerable groups, and reserve necessary space for the development and utilization of energy by future generations. These measures have made positive progress in achieving energy justice. However, China's energy sector has shown a new trend in the transitional period; more efforts need to be made in promoting energy justice, such as addressing the insufficient level of marketization in the petroleum and power sectors, the lack of careful management of ecologicalization measures, and so on. China's energy justice still has a long way to go.

19

Legal Dimensions of Access to Modern Energy Services in Africa

Lessons from Nigeria, Ghana, and Rwanda

Yinka Omorogbe

I. Introduction

For the better part of this century the absence of modern energy services has been recognized as an essential factor for sustainable development and modern living as we know it. This has led to the establishment of Sustainable Energy for All, from an initiative in 2011. This was followed by the designation of 2012 as the International Year of Sustainable Energy for All and then the creation of Sustainable Energy for All as an international organization in 2016.[1] Its aim is to help actualize the goal of achieving universal access to modern energy services by 2030, as contained in SDG 7 of the Sustainable Development Goals (SDGs), which were adopted on 25 September 2015, and which call for universal access to modern energy services for all by 2030.[2] However, while appreciable progress has been made in many countries, in many others, the problems of access to modern energy services remain acute. On the one hand, there have been some significant successes. China achieved full electrification in 2015, and Indonesia and India are on track to also achieve this objective.[3] On the other hand, over 1 billion people on Earth currently live without electricity, and 95 per cent of these are in Sub-Saharan Africa (SSA).[4] For clean cooking, the figures are even worse. In 2017, according to the International Energy Agency (IEA), 2.8 billion lacked access to clean

[1] See generally *Sustainable Energy for All* http://www.seforall.org accessed 16 September 2019 (hereafter *Sustainable Energy for All*).

[2] SDG 7 is also concerned with the reduction of greenhouse gas emissions so as to limit climate change warning. However, the focus of this chapter is on universal access to modern energy services. See generally Y. Omorogbe and A.O. Ordor, *Ending Africa's Energy Deficit and the Law: Achieving Sustainable Energy for All in Africa* (OUP, 1st edn, 2018) (hereafter Omorogbe and Ordor, *Ending Africa's Energy Deficit and the Law*).

[3] See H. Daly and M.A. Walton, 'Energy Access Outlook 2017: From Poverty to Prosperity' (2017) *International Energy Agency*, 11 http://www.iea.org/publications/freepublications/publication/WEO2017SpecialReport_EnergyAccessOutlook.pdf accessed 16 September 2019 (hereafter Daly, 'Energy Access Outlook 2017'). In 1949, when the People's Republic of China was founded more than 90 per cent of the Chinese rural households were estimated to be unconnected to the national grid. A century later, the story is very different. See Z. Bie and Y. Lin, 'An Overview of Rural Electrification in China: History, Technology and Emerging Trends' (2015) 3 *IEEE Electrification Magazine*, 36.

[4] See 'Energy Access Database' (2019) *International Energy Agency* http://www.iea.org/energyaccess/database/ accessed 15 September 2019.

Yinka Omorogbe, Legal Dimensions of Access to Modern Energy Services in Africa In: *Energy Justice and Energy Law*. Edited by Íñigo Del Guayo, Lee Godden, Donald N. Zillman, Milton Fernando Montoya, and José Juan González, Oxford University Press (2020).
 DOI: 10.1093/oso/9780198860754.003.0019

cooking fuels, using inefficient stoves or open fires in poorly ventilating spaces, with the majority of affected persons being in SSA and South Asia.[5] These depressing figures are symptomatic of the huge problems of poverty and underdevelopment that remain prevalent in certain sectors within countries in these regions.[6] In SSA, the story is mixed. While some countries such as Ethiopia, Gabon, Ghana, and Kenya are also expected to achieve universal electricity access, the number gaining access is failing to keep pace with population growth, and it is therefore expected that, without significant changes in policy and implementation, over 600 of the estimated 674 million people that will still be without energy access in 2030 will be in SSA.[7] Presently, lack of access to electricity is endemic, regardless of income as an Agence Française de Développement/ World Bank report states.[8]

This chapter examines strategies to achieve access to electricity, premised against the necessity for legal solutions and structures that will stimulate or encourage effective implementation of necessary objectives, and primarily focuses on three sub-Saharan African countries, Nigeria, Ghana, and Rwanda, while drawing examples as necessary from other countries in Africa. Nigeria has been selected because it is the most populous African state, with an estimated 200 million people,[9] and therefore successes or failures in energy access will impact on regional statistics. Currently Nigeria's electricity access rates are 45 per cent.[10] As this chapter will show, in the absence of a deviation from present practices that are clearly not yielding results, there will be no appreciable change. Like Nigeria, Ghana, is in West Africa. Unlike Nigeria, with constantly improving energy access rates and development indicators, it has recorded appreciable success in this area. The third country, Rwanda, is a small land-locked country in central Africa, which achieved worldwide prominence through a ferocious war about three decades ago that resulted in the genocide of millions of citizens of a particular ethnic group; but which has over the last few years, received positive attention because of upwardly mobile development indicators which include increased access to modern energy. The marked gains in Rwanda and Ghana cannot be explained away only by the vast differences in population between Nigeria and the other two countries. The premise of this chapter is that the root of these discrepancies appears to lie in how energy is governed and regulated. Therefore, this chapter examines the role that the domestic legal and regulatory regimes in these countries have encouraged or impeded energy access, particularly electricity access, in rural and urban areas.

[5] Ibid.

[6] *Transforming Our World: the 2030 Agenda for Sustainable Development*, UNGA Res 70/1 (25 September 2015) UN Doc A/RES/70/1 https://sustainabledevelopment.un.org/post2015/transformingourworld.

[7] Daly, 'Energy Access Outlook 2017' (n 3), 11.

[8] M.P. Blimpo and M. Cosgrove-Davies, *Electricity Access in Sub-Saharan Africa: Uptake, Reliability, and Complementary Factors for Economic Impact* (World Bank Group, 2019), 12 https://openknowledge.worldbank.org/bitstream/handle/10986/31333/9781464813610.pdf accessed 16 September 2019.

[9] For information on Nigeria see the official Nigerian website, *Federal Republic of Nigeria* <www.nigeriastat.gov.ng> accessed 15 September 2019. See also *National Bureau of Statistic*, http://www.nigeriastat.gov.ng. and 'Nigeria' (*The World Bank*, 2019) https://data.worldbank.org/country/nigeria accessed 15 September 2019.

[10] 'Nigeria: Power Africa Fact Sheet' (*USAID*, 2019) http://www.usaid.gov/powerafrica/nigeria accessed 15 September 2019.

II. Access to Modern Energy Services as a Means for the Realization of Energy Justice

A consideration of the legal dimensions of the realization of access to modern energy services has to be premised against the concepts of energy justice, and sustainable energy for all, according to SDG 7 which is to ensure access to affordable, reliable, sustainable, and modern energy for all.[11]

SDG 7 has been seen as an expression of the right to energy justice, because it honours the ideal of the universal provision of safe, affordable, and reliable energy for all, all of which are contained within the phrase 'sustainable energy'.[12] Energy Justice, the central theme of this book, is discussed in several chapters. It has been analysed within the context of access to modern energy services, and this section leans heavily on that earlier scholarly work.[13] Very briefly, energy justice incorporates the themes of distributive, procedural, restorative, and social justice. Distributive justice, within the context of energy justice, would imply the equitable distribution of the benefits and burdens of energy activities to the people, which in the view of this writer is problematic. Procedural (or participation) justice refers to the right of all communities to participate in decision-making regarding energy projects and policies that affect them. This dimension of energy justice often includes procedural rights to information and access to courts. Reparation or restorative justice is concerned with access to remedies when legal rights are violated. Social justice is the recognition that energy injustice cannot be separated from other social ills, such as poverty and subordination based on caste, race, gender, or indigeneity.

Energy justice provides a justification for and lies at the heart of the move towards access to modern energy services for all. It could be said that SDG 7 is premised on the ideal of distributive justice, which provides for access to all, irrespective of class or income. This is quite novel, when one takes a historical look at the growth of modern energy services, and what factors were considered in extending access to other segments of the population.

A. A Historical Look at the Growth of Energy Access

The evolution of modern energy is tied up with the industrialization of the West. Until the eighteenth century, the energy used by humankind was totally organic or renewable, consisting of the sun and basic biomass such as leaves, firewood, and dung,

[11] See the 'Sustainable Development Goals Knowledge Platform' (*United Nations*) https://sustainabledevelopment.un.org/sdg7 accessed 15 September 2019.

[12] H. Mostert and H. van Nierkerk, 'Disadvantage, Fairness and Power Crises in Africa: A Focussed Look at Energy Justice' in Y. Omorogbe and A. Ordor (eds), *Ending Africa's Energy Deficit and the Law: Achieving Sustainable Energy for All in Africa* (OUP, 1st edn, 2018), 45, 50 (hereafter Mostert and van Nierkerk, 'Disadvantage, Fairness and Power Crisis').

[13] Mostert and van Nierkerk, 'Disadvantage, Fairness and Power Crisis' (n 12).

and energy uses were primarily connected to cooking, heating, light, and protection from wild animals at night. Until the twentieth century, the combusted gases and changes resulting from the expenditure of energy were within the capacity of nature to sustain and handle any possible effects. All this changed with the discovery of how to harness modern fossil-fuel energy—initially coal—as a fuel for engines, and therefore as a tool for removing drudgery out of life and allowing for greater productivity. This led to what is now known as the Industrial Revolution in the eighteenth century, which occurred in Europe and later spread to the United States. It is the name given to the movement in which engines used to power various machines changed people's ways of life, and exponentially increased productivity in manufacturing processes. As stated below:

> It is impossible to imagine what the world would be like if the effects of the Industrial Revolution were swept away. Electric lights would go out. Automobiles and airplanes would vanish. Telephones, radios, and television would disappear. Most of the abundant stocks on the shelves of department stores would be gone. The children of the poor would have little or no schooling and would work from dawn to dark on the farm or in the home.[14]

Production increased exponentially, leading to the rise of manufacturing and industry, particularly in Great Britain, France, the Netherlands, and a little later in the United States. Whilst it was initially powered by coal, at the beginning of the twentieth century, crude oil commenced its rise, gradually overtaking coal as the superior fuel for powering engines, and as the force behind industrialization and modern living. This revolution was accompanied by access to modern energy services in all communities and areas in cities where the industrial revolution occurred. Societal stratification in, for instance, Great Britain, meant that first line beneficiaries of energy access were the mercantile class and those directly involved in production and manufacturing, as opposed to the gentry. The spread of modern energy services therefore spread across lines of class and income.

In the developing world, modern energy services came via colonialism. Unlike in the West, its spread was strategic and elitist, with electricity use concentrated in colonial offices and residential areas, and industry. South Africa provides an interesting example of how electricity access furthered the interests of the state during apartheid.[15] A study of the interplay between the minerals industry and energy shows that

[14] 'Industrial Revolution' <www.history.com>. See also J.R. Ward, 'The Industrial Revolution and British Imperialism, 1750–1850' (1994) 47 *The Economic History Review*, 44. For a perspective on electrification in India, see S. Sarkar, 'The Electrification of Colonial Calcutta: Role of the Innovators, Bureaucrats and Foreign Business Organization, 1880–1940' (2017) 34 *Studies in History*, 48 https://journals.sagepub.com/doi/pdf/10.1177/0257643017736194.

[15] J. Froestad, M. Nokleberg, C. Shearing, and H. Trollop, 'South Africa's Minerals-Energy Complex: Flows, Regulation Governance, and Policing', in Y. Omorogbe and A. Ordor (eds), *Ending Africa's Energy Deficit and the Law: Achieving Sustainable Energy for All in Africa* (OUP, 1st edn, 2018), 308 (hereafter Froestad, et al., 'South Africa's Mineral-Energy Complex').

electricity in South Africa evolved to serve the needs of heavy industry, and to build a 'modern industrial state'. In the interpretation of the time, it involved the use of state institutions which assisted poorer segments of society, such as Afrikaner farmers (who were white), to gain access to electricity. As the black population was not considered part of the nation-building project, they were not included in this expansion. Indeed, the need to keep black labour cheap led to continuous denial of modern energy to black settlements. According to the study:

> The rural black population was denied the advantages of electrical power out of fear that a more prosperous peasantry would be more able to resist the demands for labour at the mines and the power stations.[16]

In other African countries, access to modern energy was also denied to colonized people, as electricity was often produced for use in industry, and for the colonial population. This was the case in the three countries considered below, and in the absence of a clear and conscious policy change, it has continued post colonialization in many countries, so that the needs of the less advantaged are seen as secondary and not contributory to national development. This belief is now clearly recognized as a fallacy, which has to be countered by pro-poor policies that recognize the imperative of modern energy as an essential tool for development for all.

III. Nigeria, Ghana, and Rwanda

The three African countries under particular focus are in SSA. Ghana was the first country in SSA to gain independence, on 6 March 1957. Like Nigeria, it is located in West Africa. Nigeria is the most populous country in Africa, and it became independent on 1 October 1960. Rwanda is one of the smallest countries in area, but also one of the most densely populated, with a population of about twelve million people all occupying a land area of 26,798 square kilometres.[17] Rwanda is a former colony of Belgium and has been independent since 1962. In their journeys of nationhood, all have experienced traumas, with Nigeria and Rwanda respectively gaining some international attention and notoriety from the Biafran War of the 1960s, and the Rwandan genocides of the mid-1990s. However, their energy paths have evolved very differently.

This section gives a brief political and demographic overview of each country, against the background of their respective energy experiences.

[16] Froestad, et al., 'South Africa's Mineral-Energy Complex' (n 15), 317.

[17] 'The 10 Smallest Countries in Africa' (2019) *World Atlas* http://www.worldatlas.com/articles/which-are-the-10-smallest-countries-of-africa-by-size.html accessed 15 September 2019.

A. Nigeria

Electricity generation started in Nigeria in 1896 with the installation of the first plant in Ijora, Lagos.[18] The plant was managed by the Public Works Department of the colonial government. The first electric utility company, the Nigerian Electricity Supply Company, was established in 1929. In 1950 the colonial administration established the Electricity Commission of Nigeria (ECN) in a bid to distribute public electricity. After independence, in 1962, the government established the Niger Dam Authority (NDA) to optimize the huge hydro resources in the country to generate more electricity for a growing population and economy.[19] Later, in 1972, the ECN and the NDA were merged to create the National Electric Power Authority (NEPA) as a vertically integrated public utility that had monopoly power to generate, supply, and transmit electricity throughout the country. The NDA managed the hydro stations that generated much of Nigeria's electricity, especially the Kanji Dam and focused on optimizing the huge potential for hydro electricity generation in the north, while the ECN operated mainly as a distributor of electricity. The rationale for this merger was that it would 'result in a more effective utilization of the human, financial and other resources available in the electricity supply industry throughout the country'.[20] Years later, this business model was reversed after it failed to 'result in a more efficient utilization of human, financial and other resources' in the Nigerian electricity supply industry. It operated as a vertical, integrated utility company with a total generation capacity of about 6,200 MW from two hydro and four thermal power plants. This situation resulted in an unstable and unreliable electric power supply situation in the country with customers exposed to frequent power cuts and long periods of power outages, with an industry characterized by lack of maintenance of power infrastructure, outdated power plants, low revenues, high losses, power theft, and non-cost reflective tariffs.

In the 1970s and the 1980s, Nigerian National Development Plans had the primary objective of industrialization. However, they failed to take into account the importance of electricity, with the possible exception of Vision 2020 which had the very modest goal to generate and distribute 20,000 MW of electricity before 2020.[21] For a populous country like Nigeria, that target was inadequate. Unfortunately, not only is that goal not going to be realized, but present generating capacity falls far short of that target.

[18] This entire section leans heavily on S. Amadi, 'Improving Electricity Access through Policy Reform' in Y. Omorogbe and A. Ordor (eds), *Ending Africa's Energy Deficit and the Law: Achieving Sustainable Energy for All in Africa* (OUP, 1st edn, 2018), 344 (hereafter Amadi, 'Improving Electricity Access through Policy Reform'). See Y. Oke, *Nigerian Electricity Law and Regulation* (Lawlords Publications, 1st edn, 2013) , 2, cited in Amadi, 'Improving Electricity Access through Policy Reform' (n 18), 345.

[19] The latest census figures estimate that Nigeria has a population of about 170 million. From 2000–2010 Nigeria grew by about 6 per cent annually. See 'GDP by Country 1960–2015' (*The World Bank*, 2017) http://data.worldbank.org/indicator/NY.GDP.MKTP.CD accessed 6 June 2017.

[20] See I. I. Ukpong, 'A Case Study of the Power Corporation of Nigeria', in M.J. Balogun (ed.), *Managerial Efficiency in the Public Sector: Patterns and Problems in Nigeria* (University of Ife Press, 1980).

[21] National Planning Commission, *Nigeria: Vision 20:2020: Economic Transformation Blueprint* (2009) http://www.nationalplanningcycles.org/sites/default/files/planning_cycle_repository/nigeria/nigeria-vision-20-20-20.pdf accessed 18 September 2019.

The reform of the electricity industry in Nigeria commenced in 2000, during the administration of President Olusegun Obasanjo, under the auspices of the National Council of Privatisation and its secretariat, the Bureau of Public Enterprise (BPE). The blueprint was contained in the National Electric Power Policy which was adopted in 2000, and the Electricity Power Sector Reform Act (EPSRA), which came into being in 2005. The eleven business units of NEPA were unbundled into eleven distribution companies. The six generation plants became the six generation companies of the new electricity market. Whilst the transmission network remained in public ownership under a new successor company, the Transmission Company of Nigeria, as the monopoly provider of transmission services. The next stage was the establishment of the eighteen successor companies followed by the establishment of the Nigerian Electricity Regulatory Commission (NERC) as an independent technical and commercial regulator of the entire electricity supply industry. The sector was liberalized to allow for private sector participation through a prescribed licensing regime contained in the EPSRA. In 2010, the Nigerian Bulk Electricity Trading PLC (NBET) was established as a credible off-taker of electric power from generation companies. By November 2013, the privatization of all generation and ten distribution companies was completed with the Federal Government retaining the ownership of the transmission company. The privatization of the eleventh distribution company was completed in November 2014.[22]

The chosen path was liberalization and commercialization, but this was not accompanied by tariff liberalization or a cash-backed subsidy system which would have provided comfort for investors and allowed the derelict transmission system to be repaired and expanded as needed. In addition, whilst the power sector in Nigeria has been predicated on gas pricing and availability, both have proved problematic. In a nutshell, what Nigeria has is an impracticable and unworkable electricity system that is unattractive to investors, compounded by an extremely elaborate regulatory structure.

Rural electrification is run through the Rural Electrification Agency of Nigeria (REA). Established under the EPSRA, the REA shall administer the fund for the purpose of promoting rural electrification in Nigeria and coordinate rural electrification programmes. The mission of the REA is:

> To provide access to reliable electric power supply for rural dwellers irrespective of where they live and what they do, in a way that would allow for reasonable return on investment through appropriate tariff that is economically responsive and supportive of the average rural customer. [23]

Renewables are negligible in Nigeria and are not part of the energy mix for the electrivity grid, although there are some promising private sector projects, including some being spearheaded by the REA. Notwithstanding this, there are some encouraging signs,

[22] See Amadi, 'Improving Electricity Access through Policy Reform' (n 18). See also the *Nigerian Electricity Regulatory Commission* http://www.nerc.gov.ng accessed 15 September 2019.

[23] 'About us' (*Rural Electrification Agency*, 2017–2019) https://rea.gov.ng/theagency accessed 15 September 2019.

such as the commissioning of a 7.1 MW solar hybrid power plant in Kano, Nigeria, in September 2019, by the REA, under the Energizing Education Programme. According to the REA, this is the largest of such plants in Africa.[24]

The Energy Commission of Nigeria (ECN) does not play a pivotal role in energy planning in Nigeria. It is a statutory body which has been in existence for about thirty years, as the body to be responsible for coordinating and supervising energy functions within Nigeria. Its Vision Statement is, '[t]o ensure adequate, reliable, cost-effective and sustainable energy supply for the nation's economic and socio-political development'.[25]

For reasons that are unclear, the ECN was situated as a parastatal[26] of the Federal Ministry of Science and Technology. However, as petroleum is under the Ministry of Petroleum, and electricity is under the Ministry of Power, the ECN has never been able to coordinate or effectively plan for Nigerian energy. This lack of synergy has definitely contributed to the continuous sectoral problems. The result is that presently, every Nigerian who can buy a generator buys the one with the largest capacity that they can afford; as no one wants to rely on the present electricity framework. The infrequent power obtained through the national grid still only covers half the population—concentrated in urban areas. Rural areas are largely underserved, and off-grid and renewable solutions are still a rarity. Most rural communities have no electricity at all or rely on private generation from affluent community members. This explains why electricity in Nigeria has been at a standstill for the past twenty years, notwithstanding privatization, commercialization, and billions of dollars expended.[27]

B. Ghana

Ghana's electricity sector commenced in the early nineteenth century, with supply from diesel generators owned by various industrial establishments.[28] In 1914, the Gold Coast Railway Administration was the first to supply electricity for the operations of the railway sector in Sekondi. This was extended to Takoradi in 1928. By 1955, electricity had been extended to some major cities in Ghana including Kumasi, Tema, Accra,

[24] 'Energizing Education Programme Press Release' (*Rural Electrification Agency*, 2017–2019) https://rea.gov.ng/press-release-federal-government-nigeria-commissions-largest-off-grid-solar-hybrid-power-plant-africa-bayero-university-kano-energizing-education-programme-september-3-20/ accessed 15 September 2019.

[25] See *Energy Commission of Nigeria* (2019) http://www.energy.gov.ng accessed 16 September 2019.

[26] The word 'parastatal' is commonly used in African countries to describe State organizations that are separate from State ministries or departments, but which advance or serve State interests.

[27] See *Power Sector Report: Nigerian Power Sector Review 2018* (*Stakeholder Democracy Network*, 2019) https://www.stakeholderdemocracy.org/power-sector-review/ accessed 15 September 2019. See also B. Nnaji, 'Power Sector Outlook in Nigeria' (2011) https://sec.gov.ng/files/Prof%20Nnaji%20Presentation.pdf accessed 16 September 2019 (Prof. Nnaji is a former Minister of Power); Banwo & Ighodalo, 'The Nigerian Power Sector Reforms: Overcoming Post-Priviatisation Challenges', http://www.banwo-ighodalo.com/assets/grey-matter/1c9335c3bfcc05ceff009c17beed5f7d.pdf accessed 16 September 2019; 'Five Years of Power Privatisation: Still a Litany of Woes' (10 December 2018) *Punch* https://punchng.com/five-years-of-power-privatisation-still-a-litany-of-woes accessed 16 September 2019.

[28] E. N. Kumi, 'The Electricity Situation in Ghana: Challenges and Opportunities' (Center for Global Development2017) http://www.cgdev.org/sites/default/files/electricity-situation-ghana-challenges-and-opportunities.pdf accessed 16 September 2019 (hereafter Kumi, 'Electricity Situation in Ghana').

Nsawam, Tamale, and Bolgatanga under the auspices of the Public Works Department. However, in 1947, an Electricity Department was established within the Ministry of Works and Housing to take over electricity supplies from the Public Works Department and the Railways Administration. Electricity remained generated from diesel generator plants.

The completion of the Akosombo Dam Project over the Volta River in 1972 provided a total installed capacity of 912 MW for electricity generation. Although the primary aim of the project was to provide electricity for the aluminium industry, it made it possible for most of the major electricity consumed to be switched from diesel generators to hydroelectricity. The major consumers of electricity during this period were the Volta Aluminium Company and the National Electricity Distribution Company.[29] The completion of the Akosombo Dam also saw the Volta River Authority (VRA), managers of the Akosombo Hydroelectric Power Station, commence supply of electricity to neighbouring Togo and Benin. In 1982, the Kpong Hydroelectric Power Station was commissioned, increasing the installed generation capacity by 160 MW.

Notwithstanding the increase in generation capacity, Ghana started to experience problems of supply in 1984, as the result of a severe drought between 1982 and 1984, during which the total inflow into the Akosombo Dam was less than 15 per cent of the long term expected total.[30] This led to a diversification in the energy mix, with the construction of thermal power plants, the first of which was a 550 MW facility (Tapco and Tico) at the Takoradi Thermal Plant managed by the VRA. As at the end of 2018, the total installed capacity of thermal plants in Ghana was 2,796 MW, out of a total installed capacity of 4,399 MW. Hydroelectricity was 1,580 MW, with renewables at 22.5 MW. Current figures however put it at 4,420 MW composed of 36 per cent hydro, 64 per cent thermal, and less than 1 per cent solar.[31]

The Ministry of Energy is responsible for formulating, monitoring, and evaluating policies, programmes, and projects for the power sector in Ghana with financial support from the Ministry of Finance and Economic Planning (MOFEP). The Ministry is also directly responsible for the implementation of the National Electrification Scheme in various parts of the country.

The Energy Commission (EC)[32] and the Public Utilities Regulatory Commission (PURC)[33] are responsible for regulating the activities of the power sector. The EC is responsible for technical regulation of the power sector, including licensing of operators and also advising the Minister of Energy on matters relating to energy policy and planning. The PURC, on the other hand, is an independent regulatory agency responsible for economic regulation of the power sector, specifically approving rates for electricity

[29] Ibid., 5.

[30] Ibid.

[31] 'Ghana: Power Africa Fact Sheet' (*USAID*, 2018) http://www.usaid.gov/powerafrica/ghana accessed 16 September 2019. See also *Ghana Investment Promotion Centre* (2019) http://www.gipcghana.com accessed 16 September 2019, which gives slightly lesser figures for 2015.

[32] The Energy Commission was set up by the Energy Commission Act, 1997. See *Energy Commission* (2019) http://www.energycom.gov.gh accessed 15 September 2019.

[33] Ibid.

sold by distribution utilities to the public. PURC is also responsible for monitoring the quality of electricity services delivered to consumers.

Ghana has a current electricity access rate of 83 per cent, with 50 per cent in the rural areas, and 91 per cent in urban areas.[34] It was recently plagued by supply challenges resulting from factors such as high-level losses in the distribution system, non-payment by customers, and a poor tariff structure.[35] This led to shortages and rationing which the government endeavoured to remedy through aggressively stimulating the emergence of new power plants with take-or-pay clauses. The government is said to have contracted three emergency power producers through a selective bidding process and signed forty-three power purchase agreements to cover anticipated demand which never materialized because of tariff increases and slow economic growth (also as a result of the impact of the shortages, considering the nexus between electricity and development). Ghana has ended up with plants that are producing excess capacity, above peak demand of 2,700 MW and the government is said to be paying $500 million annually for this excess capacity.[36] As the power is primarily thermal, due to take-or-pay gas provisions, the government could end up paying between $550 and $850 million for annual excess gas capacity.[37]

C. Rwanda

Rwanda is a small, densely packed, central African landlocked country of 26,338 km^2 with a population of 12,374,397 million people.[38] Since the genocidal war in 1994, it has made remarkable achievements, including having one of the most inclusive parliaments in the world, with women filling 64 per cent of the seats.[39] Until 2004, the country was dependent on hydropower. Later that year the government made a significant policy decision, driven by its 2004 Energy Policy. It decided that energy was of critical importance and that access to energy was a priority.[40] As a result, Rwanda has recorded impressive growth over the last decade, and last year, its GDP growth was 8.6 per cent, the highest on the continent.[41] It aspires to be a middle-income country by

[34] 'Ghana: Power Africa Fact Sheet' (USAID, 2018) http://www.usaid.gov/powerafrica/ghana accessed 15 September 2019.

[35] Kumi, 'Electricity Situation in Ghana' (n 28).

[36] S. A. Sarkodie, 'Lessons to be Learnt From Ghana's Excess Electricity Shambles' (6 August 2019) *The Conversation* http://www.theconversation.com accessed 15 September 2019.

[37] Ibid.

[38] See 'Geography' (Republic of Rwanda, 2017) http://www.gov.rw/home/geography accessed 15 September 2019.

[39] 'The World Bank in Rwanda: Overview' (The World Bank, 2019) http://www.worldbank.org/en/country/rwanda/overview accessed 16 September 2019.

[40] Generally, Rwanda's energy aspirations are stated in strong passionate language that emphasizes the centrality of energy. For instance, the Foreword to the 2015 Energy Policy commences with a statement that energy is pivotal to most of the challenges and opportunities the world faces today. See *Rwanda Energy Policy* (17 March 2015) http://www.mininfra.gov.rw/fileadmin/user_upload/new_tender/Energy_Policy.pdf accessed 15 September 2019 (hereafter *Rwanda Energy Policy*).

[41] *Rwanda Economic Update: Lighting Rwanda* (June 2019, Edition No. 14) http://documents.worldbank.org/curated/en/593831561388957701/pdf/Rwanda-Economic-Update-Lighting-Rwanda.pdf accessed 15 September 2019 (hereafter *Lighting Rwanda*).

2035, and high income by 2050. Not surprisingly, it has an aggressive stance towards modern energy access for its citizens. It states in its 2015 Energy Policy that, 'Energy is the life-blood of development'.[42] The result is that the Rwanda power sector is now one of the best in the region in terms of quality of electricity, and the country is aiming to have 100 per cent energy access by 2024.[43] The 2015 Energy Policy clearly states that 'the lack of a modern, long-term approved energy policy is widely recognized by stakeholders as contributing to coordination failures'.[44]

Rwanda's energy sector is driven by the Rwanda Energy Group (REG), which is a publicly owned company, with the private sector as a strategic partner. As the approach of the government is people-centred, Rwanda's electrification programme has put emphasis on electrifying facilities that are critical for social and rural development. Under the Energy Sector Strategic Plan, street lighting is expected to be expanded to cover 100 per cent of national and district roads, and 100 per cent of productive users are expected to have access to electricity, up from the current level of 69 per cent.[45]

In the words of a World Bank report:

> Rwanda's power sector has grown rapidly in the past decade and outpaced many of its peers in Sub-Saharan Africa. More than half of Rwandans have access to electricity in their home, compared to 10 percent in 2009, generation capacity has more than tripled in the same period, and outages have become shorter and much less frequent. These impressive achievements are the result of large investments in the sector but also substantial institutional reforms to improve governance of the publicly-owned electricity company, the Rwanda Energy Group (REG). The private sector has become a strategic partner for Rwanda's power sector. The governance framework in the power sector in Rwanda can become a model for sector governance if the Government continues the path towards making REG financially independent and the new Public Private Partnership (PPP) Law is implemented as planned.[46]

Rwanda has set very ambitious targets for itself. In a bid to position it as a services hub for east and central Africa, the Rwandan government committed itself to a large number of power purchase agreements with independent power producers to increase generation capacity. With a projected surplus of power set to exceed demand by approximately 200 MW in 2024, the Rwandan Government is shifting its focus to increasing access, stimulating demand, and strengthening the transmission network.[47] By 2024, Rwanda plans to supply electricity to 100 per cent of the population, 52 per cent through the grid expansion and 48 per cent through off-grid technologies. It also targets improvements in

[42] *Rwanda Energy Policy* (n 40), 6.

[43] 'Rwanda: Power Africa Fact Sheet' (*USAID*, 2018) http://www.usaid.gov/powerafrica/rwanda accessed 15 September 2019.

[44] *Rwanda Energy Policy* (n 40), 8.

[45] Ibid., 28. See also *Energy Sector Strategic Plan 2013/14–2017/18* (17 March 2015) http://www.mininfra.gov.rw/fileadmin/user_upload/new_tender/Energy_Sector_Strategic_Plan.pdf accessed 18 September 2019.

[46] *Lighting Rwanda* (n 41), iv.

[47] *Rwanda Energy Policy* (n 40), 8.

the grid network, including reducing system losses and improving reliability, as well as connecting with neighbouring countries and importing and exporting power across borders.[48] As a result Rwanda is seen as a land of opportunity for power investors, and there are several private ongoing developments in that sector.

There are downsides to Rwanda's rapid energy expansion however, and these centre on affordability. As mentioned earlier, the policy of expansion placed cost considerations as secondary to the imperative of power acquisition. Most contracts for power were procured through bilateral negotiations rather that competitive procurement. As a result, the cost of electricity is one of the highest in Africa. Even though tariffs are subsidized, it is unaffordable to more than three-quarters of the unelectrified population, comparable only to Burkina Faso and Madagascar. To mitigate this situation, the government is being forced to increase its subsidies to the power sector, up to 10 per cent of its annual budget. Again, the report raises possible problems as a result of contingent liabilities that may arise as a result of various sovereign guarantees for power purchase agreements. These issues are being addressed by the government under an overarching vision to deliver clean and reliable power and phasing out subsidies. This means further diversifying its energy mix, incentivizing off-grid private sector solutions in areas where grid expansion is not viable, in the short term, and improving household access to affordable finance. In a nutshell, a study of the Rwanda energy sector shows a nation in transition, flexible in its policy approach, focused on bridging its energy deficit and ensuring 100 per cent access to its people.

IV. Planning for Power: Policy and the Law

The three countries of focus have had very different experiences in achieving modern access to electricity services, notwithstanding its importance as a catalyst for development. In trying to discern reasons for discrepancies, one discovers a reduced level of synergy in the country which has recorded the least success—Nigeria. Synergy is an essential component in energy planning cooperation, as various government agencies have roles to play, and need to be moving in the same direction, in harmony. As identified, Nigeria's energy sector is not being driven by an energy plan, and therefore the activities of the various essential ministries and government agencies are neither guided nor impacted by the energy policy and other documents of the ECN. This can be contrasted with Ghana which has an inter-ministerial and inter-departmental approach to energy planning and policy. It has a Ministry of Energy with a minister and three deputy ministers for petroleum, power and finance, and infrastructure. It also has an active synergy and cooperation with the National Development Planning Commission, the Environmental Protection Agency, and the Energy Commission. In Rwanda, energy is clearly a priority; it is treated as an essential component of the development

[48] 'Rwanda Country Commercial Guide' (*Export.gov*, 2019) http://www.export.gov/ccg accessed 15 September 2019.

process. It has been covered by the framework development document for Rwanda, Vision 2020, which was launched in 2000, when Rwanda had an energy access rate of six per cent as stated in the original document.[49] Vision 2020 sets out the various goals necessary for Rwanda to transform into a middle-income country, and it was revised in 2012. Within that document, three indicators relate specifically to energy; annual electricity consumption, access to electric energy, and wood energy in the national energy consumption.[50] More recently, Rwanda has fully keyed in to the Sustainable Energy for All Initiative,[51] with the target of achieving both 100 per cent electricity access, and universal access to improved cooking stoves, by 2030.

The Rwandan energy sector is clearly driven by the Ministry of Infrastructure, and its Energy Policy which unequivocally states:

> This Energy Policy has been elaborated to guide and influence decisions on the extraction, development and use of Rwanda's energy resources in a transparent and sustainable manner. The policy framework outlined herein comprises a set of governing laws and regulations, strategic directions and guiding principles that Rwandan institutions and partners shall adopt and adhere to, in subsequent implementation of actions. The vision of the energy sector is to become one of Rwanda's most dynamic sectors and investment destinations. [52]

Within the policy, ensuring availability of efficient, reliable, and affordable energy supplies for all Rwandans is clearly stated.[53] Energy is dealt with in strategic documents such as those mentioned above, and there is strong cooperation between the several key stakeholders, which the *Rwanda Energy Policy* identifies as:

> The Ministry of Infrastructure; the Ministry of Trade and Industry, the Ministry of Finance and Economic Planning, the Ministry of Natural Resources, the Ministry of Education (for building competency and human resource development), the Ministry of Local Government and the Ministry of East African Community. It also mentions the Rwanda Energy Group Ltd, (formerly the Power and Energy Holding Company), the Rwanda Development Board, the Rwanda Utilities Regulatory Authority, the National Industrial Research Development Authority, the Rwanda Environment Management Authority, the Rwanda Standards Board, and the National Commission of Science and Technology.[54] These are many entities, but all operate within their given mandate, and in alignment with country objectives.

[49] *Rwanda Vision 2020* (July 2000), 20 http://www.sida.se/globalassets/global/countries-and-regions/africa/rwanda/d402331a.pdf accessed 18 September 2019.

[50] ENRICH and SUCCEED Network projects, 'Blueprint for Cooperation in Energy Access and Efficiency in East Africa' (International Conference on Fostering Cooperation in Energy Efficiency and Accessibility in East Africa, Zanzibar, March 2017), 28 http://www.enrich-project.eu/sites/default/files/BLUEPRINT%20ENRICH%20-%20SUCCEED%20final.pdf accessed 28 April 2019.

[51] See I. Introduction of this chapter and *Sustainable Energy for All* (n 1).

[52] *Rwanda Energy Policy* 5 (n 40).

[53] Ibid.,14, 20.

[54] *Rwanda Energy Policy* (n 40), 34–6.

Conversely, a perusal of Nigeria's energy sector shows that it is regulated by the ministries of Power, Works and Housing, Petroleum and Solid Minerals. Energy planning is done by the ECN, which is under the Ministry of Science and Technology. Unlike Rwanda, there is no unifying factor and no obvious synergy. The SE4ALL in Africa page for Nigeria is futuristic, and it refers to the Sustainable Energy for All Action Agenda (SE4ALL-AA) for Nigeria, adopted by the Inter-Ministerial Committee on Renewable Energy and Energy Efficiency (ICREEE) in 2016. That document recommends the establishment of an inter-ministerial steering committee to be headed by the Minister of Power, which will also include funding partners, and other stakeholders.[55] At the time of writing, there are no indications that this has yet been done. Neither the ministries of Petroleum nor Science and Technology will be part of this Steering Committee, and the ECN gets a peripheral mention.[56] This means that the Energy Policy will never be able to provide needed guidance to the sector. It also means that the production and regulation of natural gas, which is the primary feedstock of electricity generation and regulated by the Ministry of Petroleum, will not be impacted by the activities of this committee.

V. Energy Access in Africa

This section examines the roles of policy and law,[57] against an examination of energy access on the African continent, as pictorially shown on the map below.

Figure 19.1 graphically shows the number of persons who live without access to modern energy services in Africa in 2012. The first striking point is that SSA is the most affected. The North African countries of Morocco, Tunisia, Algeria, Libya, and Egypt all have 99 per cent access rates. Clearly, geography plays no part, as the access rates of Mauritania[58] and the Sudan show. Similarly Lesotho and Swaziland would have the

[55] 'Africa Hub: Nigeria' (*Sustainable Energy for All*, 2019) http://www.se4all-africa.org/seforall-in-africa/country-data/nigeria/ accessed 28 April 2019. Members of the Steering Committee will include the Inter-Ministerial Committee on Renewable Energy and Energy Efficiency (ICREEE) team, Federal Ministry of Finance (FMF), Federal Ministry of Education (FMEdu), Central Bank of Nigeria (CBN), Transmission (TSP/SO/OM), State and Local Governments, DisCos, and GenCos. International Partners EU, GIZ, ECREEE, UNDP, JICA, USAID, AfDB, Civil Society Representatives, National Banks, Private Sector, SME Reps etc. will serve as Donors Executive Committee. See *Sustainable Energy for All Action Agenda (SE4ALL-AA)* (1st edition, July 2016), 15 http://www.se4all-africa.org/fileadmin/uploads/se4all/Documents/Country_AAs/NIGERIA_SE4ALL_ACTION_AGENDA_FINAL.pdf accessed 18 September 2019 (hereafter *Sustainable Energy for All Action Agenda*).

[56] See *Sustainable Energy for All Action Agenda* (n 55), 24, 95.

[57] Whilst the terms 'policy' and 'law' are often used interchangeably, the former belongs in the realm of public administration, while law is a function of the legislative arm of government. While policies are statements of direction and intent, laws are the instruments that render these statements into mandatory provisions that must be complied with, and which provide the parameters within which activities in furtherance of stated policy objectives will be carried out. Both are essential components for good planning, and successful execution is dependent on the extent to which both are in harmony. Invariably, a country that is not measuring up to supposed parameters has a problem with articulated policy. Again, articulated policy aids in the fulfilment of state objectives, once it is complied with. Often the compliance is accomplished through legislated provisions.

[58] In Mauritania, 57 per cent of the population makes traditional use of biomass, while the national electrification rate is 28 per cent. In South Sudan and Sudan, electrification rates are 1 per cent and 35 per cent respectively. The percentages of people traditionally cooking with biomass are 98 per cent and 70 per cent for South Sudan and Sudan. See tables on traditional use of biomass for cooking in Africa (2012), and Electricity Access in Africa (2013), both available within the WEO 2015 Electricity Access Database and the WEO 2015 Biomass

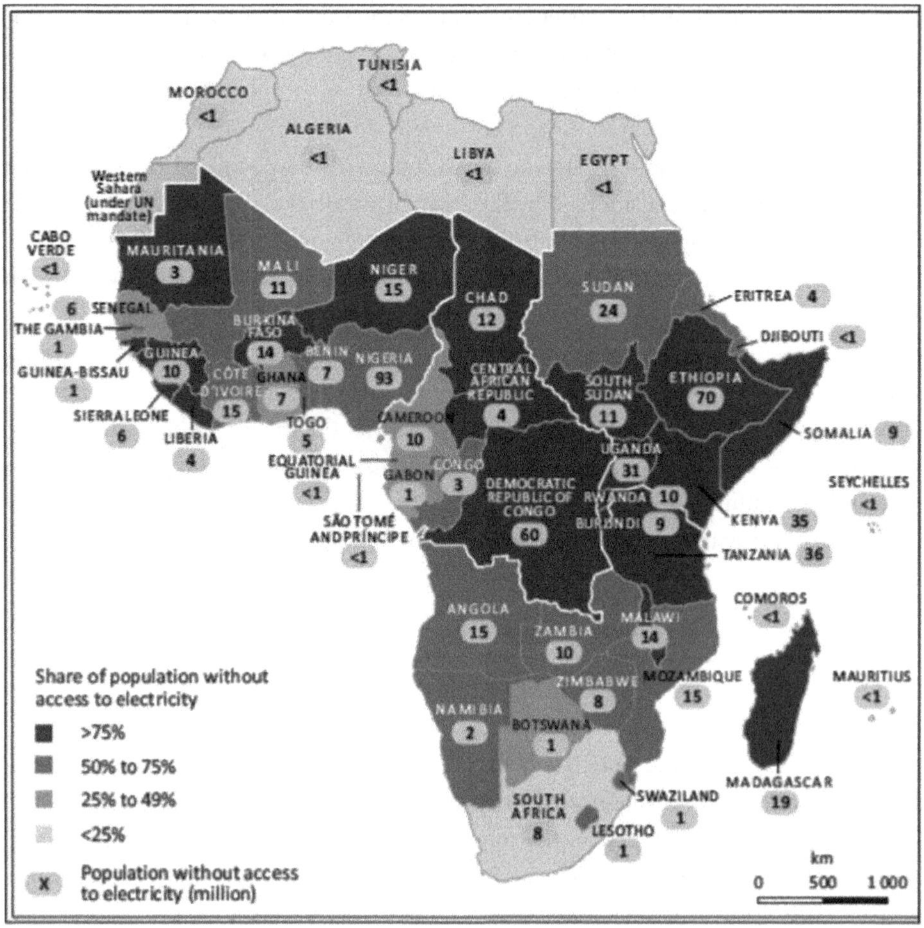

Figure 19.1 Number and share of people without access to electricity by country 2012

same high access rate as South Africa, the country that surrounds them, if that were the case. Race also plays no part, as Namibian access rates are the polar opposite of South Africa's, even though both have significant white minority populations.[59] Considering the example of energy access in South Africa under apartheid, it might be tempting to ascribe Namibia's poor access rates to the dominance of the white minority, and South Africa's far better rates to the emergence of a black government, particularly when one finds that the Namibian national electrification rate of 32 per cent consists of a 50 per cent urban percentage of access against the rural rate of 17 per cent.[60] However, a

Database. See 'World Energy Outlook' (*International Energy Agency*, 2019) http://www.iea.org/weo/ accessed 18 September 2019.

[59] While white populations are a negligible minority in most African countries, whites are 6 per cent of the population in Namibia, and 8.4 per cent in South Africa. See Namibia Demographic Profile <www.indexmundi.com> accessed 19 January 2016; and http://www.statssa.org accessed 19 January 2016.

[60] See *World Energy Outlook 2016—Electricity Access Database* (2016) http://www.iea.org/media/weowebsite/2015/WEO2016Electricity.xlsx accessed 18 September 2019.

further look shows that not only is this disparity between urban and rural electrification not unusual in Africa, but it is much better than the situation found in the mono-racial black African countries of Burkina Faso (56 per cent and 1 per cent), Cameroon (88 per cent and 17 per cent), Gambia (60 per cent and 2 per cent) and Niger (62 per cent and 4 per cent). It is therefore not merely a disparity resulting from possible racial discrimination.

A. Access to Energy for All

A deeper look at South Africa, and the North African countries, shows that in all these countries priority has been given to electrification of the entire country, and to access to energy for all, including those in rural areas. In the words of the then minister of Energy in South Africa:

> When the newly-elected government of South Africa assumed office in 1994, it was faced with a myriad of infrastructure and service delivery backlogs. Prior to 1994 the minority white population were the main beneficiaries of the government's energy investments in the residential sector. Since democracy however, access to electricity by urban and rural households across class and racial categories has become a core priority of the state.[61]

The success of this change in policy is evident in the progress made in achieving access to modern energy services from 1994 to 2012, as the government successfully increased the proportion of households that have access to energy from 30 per cent to 87 per cent. The example of South Africa—which has since remained in the forefront of energy access in SSA— highlights the fact that successful implementation is the product of intent articulated by policy and backed by complementary laws and regulations. The same can be said of Egypt,[62] Tunisia, Morocco, Libya,[63] and Algeria, which owe their respective comparative successes to the implementation of effective policies backed by law.[64] South Africa's Energy White Paper gave policy direction for the National Electrification Programme, and the Integrated National Electrification Programme, with the latter providing for non-grid electrification and increased use of renewables. From its actions it is clear that post-apartheid South Africa sees energy access as a necessity, if not as a right, and as being essential to the sustainable

[61] *A survey of energy-related behaviour and perceptions in South Africa: The Residential Sector* (2012) 1 http://www.energy.gov.za/files/media/Pub/Survey%20of%20Energy%20related%20behaviour%20and%20perception%20in%20SA%20-%20Residential%20Sector%20-%202012.pdf accessed 15 September 2019 (hereafter *A survey of energy-related behaviour and perceptions in South Africa*).

[62] See African Development Bank Group, *Annual Report* (2010) http://www.afdb.org/fileadmin/uploads/afdb/Documents/Publications/Annual%20Report%202010%20EN.pdf, accessed 4 January 2020.

[63] Libya's domestic energy is primarily from petroleum. It has Africa's largest reserves. See EIA (2015), https://www.eia.gov/beta/international/analysis.php?iso=LBY accessed 4 January 2020.

[64] See *United Nations Economic Report on Africa* (2012) http://www.uneca.org/sites/default/files/PublicationFiles/era2012_eng_fin.pdf accessed 18 September 2019.

development of its people. It is therefore willing to promote expansion through the use of incentives that recognize the lower purchasing power of the targeted communities. Between 1991 and 2001 Eskom, the electricity public utility, financed energy access through a cross-subsidy of industrial users and bulk sales to local authorities.[65] When it became obvious that electrification of these communities could not be self-funding, a South African Electrification Programme commenced under which part of the electricity costs are borne by the government and the connection fee is nominal. Under Free Basic Electricity, introduced in 2004, poor households get the first 50 kWh free. Furthermore, renewable energy electrification is subsidized at both investor and consumer levels.[66]

Countries that have achieved near universal access, such as North African countries; and those that are well on the way, such as Ghana and Rwanda, owe their successes to policies that emphasize the need for energy as a critical factor in development, accompanied by the enactment of supporting laws and the will to both implement the laws and policies, and create the required institutional frameworks. Morocco and Tunisia are both positive examples which show the primacy of good policy for success in energy access. Both countries are dependent on imported energy.[67]

A premise of this chapter is that a primary factor mitigating against access to energy services is the failure to place less advantaged persons, particularly those in rural areas, at the centre of energy policy and development, to accept that the provision of energy services to them is essential for their sustainable development, and to realize that the development of any nation is dependent on the sustainable development of all its people, not just the urban or more advantaged people. A denial of access to energy services to less advantaged persons amounts to the perpetuation of an environment within which their basic human rights to life, dignity, health, and education cannot be realized.[68] In the same way as people have to be at the centre of development, rural dwellers and poor communities have to be at the centre of policies, laws, and actions to promote energy access.

[65] 'South African Electrification Programme' (*GNESD*, 2019) http://energy-access.gnesd.org/cases/22-south-african-electrification-programme.html accessed 25 January 2015. See also *A survey of energy-related behaviour and perceptions in South Africa* (n 61). For a comprehensive view, see R. Pashke and J. Glazewski, 'Ex Post Facto Authorisation in South African Environmental Assessment Legislation: A Critical Review' (2006) 9 *Potchefstroom Electronic Law Journal*, 1; K. Odeku, 'An Analysis of Renewable Energy Policy and Law Promoting Socio-economic and Sustainable Development in Rural South Africa' (2012) 40 *Journal of Human Ecology*, 53; H. Winkler, *Energy Policies for Sustainable Development in South Africa: Options for the Future* (University of Cape Town, 2006).

[66] But see Mostert and Naude (n 12), where it is stated that Eskom is facing problems that include finance and aging infrastructure.

[67] Although Tunisia is also a crude oil producer its domestic supply is predominantly from imports. With regard to Morocco, see *Morocco 2014: Energy Policies Beyond EIA Countries Executive Summary* (2014) http://www.iea.org/Textbase/npsum/morocco2014sum.pdf accessed 18 September 2019 and 'Morocco' (*International Energy Agency*, 2019) http://www.iea.org/countries/non-membercountries/morocco/ accessed 25 January 2016.

[68] This fact underpins the need for the Sustainable Energy for All organization, and why goal 7 of the SDG goals is about achieving access to modern energy services for all. It is the central theme of Omorogbe and Ordor, *Ending Africa's Energy Deficit and the Law* (n 2).

B. Success in Achieving Energy Access for All

For energy access to be successful, the objective of increasing the number of persons who now have electricity access cannot be said to have been achieved only in terms of an increase in percentages or in the numbers of people who now have access. It has to include means of assessing the extent to which there has been penetration into previously unreached areas of the country. To do this successfully the focus cannot be on an increase in the amount of people who now have electricity, or who are now cooking with clean fuels. It has to be on ensuring that any percentage increments include the provision of modern energy to the least advantaged populations in rural and inaccessible places. Disadvantaged rural persons have to be the ultimate beneficiaries.

If electricity access in Africa (and in any developing country) is to be successful, implementation has to be driven by the right stated policies that incorporate the objective of access for all, preferably by a specified date and incorporating targets that include both urban and rural populations such as:

- The use of renewable technology as an essential component of achieving connectivity for off-grid communities.
- The use of appropriate and renewable technologies for clean energy fuels.

Good policies in this area must recognize at the outset that the poor cannot pay economically viable prices for electricity, and therefore the state should acknowledge the need for state-funded access programmes from its own revenues, or from other avenues. In practice, financing energy access for the poor, and stimulating growth in renewables, comes from three main sources: from financing by the energy investor, from revenue allocated for the purpose by the state, and from banks or equity markets.[69] Once access to modern energy services is seen as a state development goal, this should create the required mindset that encourages innovative solutions such as has been done in South Africa under the Electrification Programme.

In addition, a premise of this chapter is that successful access to sustainable energy requires the realisation of a concept that was not a part of energy planning at inception in colonized countries, the absence of which has affected the growth of electricity access in, and has amounted to a fundamental limitation to successful energy planning in countries such as Nigeria. This is that modern energy matters to all, and that the energy rights of poor disadvantaged persons must also be addressed, in the interests of all. A mindset shift by energy planners and decision makers is essential if success is to be achieved.

[69] See http://www.worldenergyoutlook.org/resources/energydevelopment/energyforallfinancingaccessforthepoor/ accessed 25 January 2016.

VI. Conclusion

Amartya Sen sees development as freedom. He defines poverty as the deprivation of opportunity, and the lack of economic development as the deprivation of five distinct freedoms: political freedoms, economic facilities, social opportunities, transparency guarantees, and protective security. Freedom, he says, is a principal determinant of individual initiative and social effectiveness; it is useful primarily because it enhances the ability of individuals to help themselves, a property that Sen describes as the 'agency aspect'[70] of the individual. Thus, his definition of poverty is individual: it is the deprivation of basic capabilities, always defined as individual capabilities.

In words that are reminiscent of Amartya Sen's concept of development as freedom, energy poverty can be seen as the deprivation of the many freedoms that accrue when persons are released from the grind of daily lives devoid of engine power and electricity. Energy lies at the heart of life and impacts on practically every sector. It is critical to development, particularly for the poor and vulnerable, and its absence can cause severe deprivations that amount to a denial of basic human rights, including the right to life. Examples that could lead to such final outcomes easily come to mind. For instance, if a pregnant women in an impoverished rural area falls into labour in the middle of the night and she has to walk to the nearest dispensary in the dark; or if she is delivered at night, using light from an oil or kerosene lamp, in a clinic that is necessarily devoid of modern implements because of the absence of electricity, her child may not survive, and in such an instance that child will be suffering deprivations that have occurred as the result of lack of access to modern electricity services. If she does survive, the presence or absence of electricity will often impact on whether she goes to school, as her presence may be necessary for the energy and basic needs of her family to be met (she may have to scavenge for biomass and fetch water for the family). Ultimately, the type and amount of energy she has at her disposal will decide whether she will ever be able to arise from the drudgery of life as a rural female in an energy-poor community. Therefore, energy access is about giving power to the people, so that they can make choices, and live life sustainably.

This chapter has primarily analysed the legal frameworks and activities of the sovereign states of Ghana, Nigeria, and Rwanda, and examined the state of their various efforts to increase electricity access. The results reveal mixed successes, with sub-optimal signs from Nigeria, and very promising signals from Ghana and Rwanda. This is ominous, as the population of Nigeria is around 200 million—several multiples of the other two countries combined, and about one sixth of Africa's estimated 1.2 billion people. Nigeria's statistics therefore strongly impact on Africa's electricity access rates, and even on global figures. Sooner rather than later, Nigeria should borrow a few leaves from these countries, approach energy planning and development in a coordinated and synergistic way, and truly put people at the heart of its energy industry.

[70] A. Sen, *Development as Freedom* (Oxford University Press, 1999), 19.

PART VII
CONCLUSION

20

Conclusion

Energy Law and Justice for a Better World

Íñigo del Guayo, Lee Godden, Donald N. Zillman, Milton F. Montoya, and José Juan González

I. The Law of Energy Justice

This collection of chapters has surveyed the evolving scope, theory, and practice of energy justice and energy law. A starting hypothesis for the research in this book was the view that energy justice was a distinctive topic of inquiry. Our analyses based in law could both further develop this scholarship and inform the policy and practical platform for the implementation of energy justice—in all its diverse attributes. Second, given the potential scope of the concept of energy justice, we identified four aspects of energy justice: distributive justice, procedural justice, restorative or reparation justice, and social justice. We recognized, however, that those four dimensions are usually inextricably linked in real life—and in the ethical dilemmas faced.[1]

Noting these interlinkages, our survey of energy justice, and its articulation with law and legal measures, has comprised a rich canvass of case studies from jurisdictions in Africa, Asia, Meso-America, South America, Europe, North America, and Australasia. Our objective in energy justice and energy law therefore has been to explore how the goals of energy justice are being implemented in the laws of nations and international organizations. It is this 'law in action' that will decide whether objectives can be realized. The law is often the realm in which compromises between conflicting interests must take place. Thus, in many jurisdictions, energy justice while a pressing matter is part of a wide matrix of issues confronting energy law and regulation. Many issues, such as climate change, environmental protection, human health, and poverty eradication need to be considered alongside and/or as an integral component of achieving energy justice—a phenomenon crystallized in the concept of the Sustainable Development Goals (SDGs).

Our authors frequently cite the United Nations' SDGs which envision a world in which all citizens will have access to modern energy 'essentials'. Policy makers, practitioners, and scholars from many disciplines have contributed to defining and setting those 'energy justice' goals. Increasingly, those goals take on aspects of a 'human right'.[2] In some jurisdictions we see the nascent emergence of a 'right to energy'.[3]

[1] See Chapter 2 by Aileen McHarg, in this book.
[2] See Chapter 4 by Catherine Redgwell and Lavanya Rajamani.
[3] See Chapter 9 by Hanri Mostert and Tjakie Naude; and Chapter 8 by Anatole Boute, in this book.

Íñigo del Guayo, Lee Godden, Donald N. Zillman, Milton F. Montoya, José Juan González, Conclusion In: *Energy Justice and Energy Law*. Edited by Íñigo Del Guayo, Lee Godden, Donald N. Zillman, Milton F. Montoya, and José Juan González, Oxford University Press (2020). DOI: 10.1093/oso/9780198860754.003.0020

Moreover, clearly there are linkages between concepts of environmental justice and energy justice, but our analyses have entailed a specific legal focus on energy justice and law; including identifying intersections with energy poverty. This emphasis is apparent also in the thematic chapters that explore energy justice dimensions, such as consumer protection or energy investment strategies to extend or maintain energy access, across jurisdictions and legal systems.

Our chapters have identified the breadth and diversity of the concept of energy justice today. Phrases like 'energy poverty', 'distributive justice', 'energy efficiency', and 'social justice', occur frequently in the chapters. The terms may mean different things to different parties and nations. Our case studies from around the world illustrate this spectrum but also bring a means of identifying coherent attributes to the various terms through a comparative lens.

II. Energy Justice Contexts

This conclusion now turns to consider four contexts in which 'energy justice' issues pertain.

People suffer energy injustice when they are not given a voice in the adoption of the decisions which affect the way their energy needs must be satisfied. Often those who will suffer the worst consequences of energy decisions, in terms of environmental sustainability and/or energy access have the least input into those procedures.

We conclude that laws are needed worldwide to ensure that energy decisions are subject to a procedure in which all stakeholders 'have a say'. This may satisfy the consultative requirements of procedural justice. Likewise, we advocate better participation of communities in the decision-making procedure.[4] Indeed, as Redgwell and Rajamani note, in an analysis that identifies links between human rights and energy justice; '[p]rocedural human rights are also of increasing relevance in securing, inter alia, access to information, participation in decision-making, and access to energy justice'.[5]

Since energy activities create potential or actual damage to people and the environment, several chapters have shown ways to promote restorative justice from a dual perspective: geographical (compensating people suffering an intense, harmful consequence of energy supply and/or production) and temporal (satisfying our duties towards future generations).[6]

In a decarbonized energy paradigm, we envisage a greater role for consumers, whose multi-faceted needs are dealt with in several regional and national jurisdictions.[7] Energy poverty and energy access are two key components of energy justice, and that is why the roots of poverty (and lack of access to energy), as well as the legal means to fight

[4] See, e.g., Annalisa Savaresi, Chapter 5 in this book.
[5] See Catherine Redgwell and Lavanya Rajamani, Chapter 4 in this book.
[6] See, e.g., Barry Barton and Jennifer Campion, Chapter 12 in this book.
[7] For an examination of energy justice in the context of decarbonization and energy transition see Wang Mingyuang and Yang Xue, Chapter 18 in this book.

against it, are addressed in many of the chapters. Where there is energy poverty, aspects of a deficiency of social justice are present.[8]

Another contextual factor reminds us that energy poverty can apply to many regions and to rural portions of otherwise wealthy nations today.

The third context then moves from geographic energy poverty to individual or small group energy poverty; often evident in cities where modern energy is readily available but may not be affordable for portions of the population.[9]

The fourth context centres on the negative consequences of energy availability on the human and natural environment and how energy justice should address those concerns in the underdeveloped and the developed world.[10]

A. Energy-poor Nations

Studies of sub-Saharan Africa,[11] parts of south and central America,[12] and Central and South Asia often reveal entire nations in which considerable portions of the population lack basic modern energy. These regions while designated as energy poor, may have significant energy resources but there is not the infrastructure—physical, institutional, and financial—to provide effective access to energy or to ensure existing infrastructure is maintained and functioning.[13]

Overall, in widespread national poverty, energy is only one of the essentials that many citizens lack. Where is energy poverty to rank with scarcity of food, clean water, adequate housing, basic education, and health care? The intersections between energy goals, sustainable development, and poverty alleviation are clearly what the SDGs are seeking to highlight, as did the previous Millennium Development Goals.

The challenges of national impoverishment, including energy impoverishment, can be blamed on or exacerbated by autocratic, corrupt, or ineffective national and local governments.[14] The situations may also reflect conscious discrimination against minority races, tribes, or religions in the nation. For example, some 'wealthy' democracies are also distinguished by significant disparities of energy access and utilization on a racial and ethnic basis. In this regard, see for example, Australia, Canada, USA, and New Zealand in respect of indigenous levels of energy poverty. South Africa historically also was characterized by severe inequalities, and despite contemporary efforts, many of those disparities remain. Further discrimination, intentional or not, against women m

[8] See, e.g., Chapter 3 by Íñigo del Guayo; Chapter 13 by Milton Fernando Montoya and others; and Chapter 15 by Damilola S. Olawuyi in this book.

[9] See Chapter 7 by Lee Paddock and Achinthi Vithanage, in this book.

[10] See Chapter 16 by Don Zillman and Don Smith; Chapter 10 by Martha Roggenkamp and Lea Diestelmeier; and contrast for example, Chapter 13 by Milton Fernando Montoya and others.

[11] See, e.g., Chapter 19 by Yinka Omorogobe, in this book.

[12] See, e.g., Chapter 17 by Jose Jaun Gonzáles and Chapter 13 by Milton Feernando Montoya and others, in this book.

[13] See Chapter 15 by Damilola S Olawuyi, in this book.

[14] See Chapter 8 by Anatole Boute, in this book.

ay increase injustice as they disproportionately bear the burden of a lack of sustainable and affordable energy.

In many of these impoverished nations, assistance from international organizations such as the World Bank, wealthier national governments, the private business sector, and non-governmental organizations will be essential to energy access improvements.[15] However, failing national governments may make it less likely that international help will be offered, or if offered, will be successful. In extreme cases international intervention may be needed to support human rights including access to basic energy services in order to ensure the survival of vulnerable populations—although any such 'intervention' needs to be qualified and alert to national sensitivities. Through the international law and human rights paradigm, however, we can perceive how national sovereignty may need to yield in certain respects to individual and community rights including 'energy rights'.[16]

Innovations in recent years offer options to small communities and individuals who live outside existing electric power grids.[17] Solar and wind power and other renewables can provide both local electricity and heating without the need for anLavanya extensive and expensive power grid. Here again, a combination of national government, international support, and customer funding can provide clean energy services that both benefit the individual user and stimulate business opportunities for rural and urban areas.[18]

B. Rural Impoverishment in Developed Nations

The energy justice challenges just discussed occur even in some rural and remote regions of developed nations and societies. Several chapters examine examples of distributive justice inequities that have specific geographic expression. Governments (national, state, or local) will need to make the energy justice decisions about their underserved communities through their political processes. These decisions then will be embodied in statutes and regulations that seek to correct the energy injustices for rural citizens.[19] 'Who pays?' becomes a crucial question. Does the government subsidize the disadvantaged community through general government revenues? Do the private energy businesses that provide the new service initially cover the cost and seek reimbursement from all their ratepayers or customer base? How great a contribution should the rural beneficiaries of the new energy services make? Alternatively, should traditional grid arrangements be foregone, and local generation models be used? The studies of the Middle East and North Africa, Central Asia, China, South and Central

[15] While loan 'conditionality' is no longer as apparent, many organizations such as the World Bank have principles that seek to ensure equity and energy access as a consideration when financing energy projects.
[16] See Chapter 4 by Catherine Redgwell and Lavanaya Rajamani, in this book.
[17] See Chapter 11 by Lee Godden, in this book.
[18] See, e.g., Chapter 5 by Annalisa Savaresi, in this book.
[19] See, e.g., Chapter 14 by Alastair Lucas, in this book.

America, New Zealand, Canada, and Australia all provide examples and possible solutions.

C. The Vulnerable Urban Citizens

Beyond the rural geographic challenges are the concerns of any citizens who are unable to afford what are deemed minimum necessary quantities of energy.[20] Numerous chapters consider the challenges facing these 'vulnerable' customers as they seek access to necessary amounts of energy be it electricity, clean heating and cooking fuels, or efficient and affordable transportation. Alternatively, the vulnerable consumer may be identified in relative terms of capacity to pay rather than governments prescribing necessary amounts of energy.[21] Vulnerable consumers can occur in public-owned energy systems as well as in liberalized, private energy markets. What defines a 'vulnerable' customer? What amount of energy provides 'justice' for them?[22] Should demands be made of the 'vulnerable' customer to avoid 'waste' of the energy resource?

The chapters caution about financial subsidy programmes.[23] These may worsen energy injustice. Wealthy users of the subsidy for electric vehicles or solar panels may not need them. Financially 'vulnerable' customers may not be able to afford the innovation or renovations to make it usable. The vulnerable customer may pay so little tax as to make a government tax rebate meaningless.

Several chapters also expressly consider the various roles of government and the private sector in energy provision, access, and pricing. Government is certainly capable of playing all the roles of energy producer, transmitter, and distributor. There the state has decided that energy, like national defence or protection from crime, should be the responsibility of the state. Often the energy is provided to its citizens at well below the actual cost of its production and distribution.[24] Alternatively, production, transmission, and distribution may be left to the private sector and the workings of the free market.[25] The early years of electricity and natural gas use in some nations exposed the risks of the 'natural monopoly' in which one for-profit private business would produce, transmit, and distribute the electricity or natural gas to the end-consumers. The high cost of the infrastructure would discourage more than a single supplier. The first, or most efficient, business to enter the market would drive out later or less efficient competitors. The remaining monopolist would then be free to charge any prices and set any conditions of service. That prompted government intervention and the 'regulated public utility' was

[20] See, e.g., Chapter 11 by Lee Godden. See also in respect of energy poverty, Chapter 3 by Íñigo del Guayo, in this book.

[21] For example, the vulnerable consumer definition in some jurisdictions is designed to act as a safety net on prices, thus it may not set a free amount of electricity but have hardship payment provisions. This is more common in the liberalized energy markets than a guaranteed right to a certain amount of energy. For discussion see Chapter 9 by Hanri Mostert and Tjakie Naude, in this book.

[22] See, e.g., Chapter 12 by Barry Barton and Jennifer Campion, in this book.

[23] See, e.g., Chapter 3 by Íñigo del Guayo, in this book.

[24] See, e.g., Chapter 19 by Yinka Omorogobe, in this book.

[25] See Chapter 8 by Anatole Boute, and Chapter 6 by Catherine Banet.

born.[26] Typically, government would give a for-profit private business a monopoly over a geographic area to run its business. Government however, would mandate that only 'just and reasonable' rates (prices) could be charged to customers and that all customers in the geographic region would need to be served in a non-discriminatory fashion. We also see hybrid models emerging, such as in the EU where retention of competition laws is maintained but increasingly augmented by government intervention around consumer protection, and to encourage community participation.[27]

The public utility model served the United States and other democracies for much of the twentieth century. Then in the 1980s rising costs and government inefficiencies encouraged a closer look at 'free market' treatment of some aspects of energy. Most significantly, this applied to the generation of electricity where a variety of plausible potential competitors promised a lower priced and more efficient generation of power from the use of fossil or renewable fuels.

The chapters also explore different public and private partnerships that can advance energy justice goals. The private sector is often the best source of entrepreneurial innovation and energy transition. Many chapters consider energy transition an integral component of the context for achieving energy justice.[28] Government may provide initial financial assistance to encourage research into that new development. Alternatively, government may wait for free market competition to identify the potentially successful new technologies and then offer financial subsidies such as outright grants or tax benefits to the development of that technology.

The studies worldwide also emphasize varied national approaches to issues of energy justice. The programme to benefit the vulnerable customer in the EU may not work in Nigeria or Canada and vice versa. Reliance on single worldwide standards may not be effective. It is fascinating, but not surprising to lawyers and students of the political process that approaches to energy justice issues can vary widely even amongst close geographic neighbours.

D. Environmental and Social Energy Injustices

The chapters also emphasize the social and environmental consequences of energy production or use, and the conjoined implications for energy justice. All energy development decisions impose environmental and social costs. The energy justice challenge is to carefully examine the costs and benefits of the energy that is provided, to assure that all parties who are impacted have a role in the decision-making, and to reach decisions about the new technologies that can be modified as circumstances change. Easier said than done!

[26] See for discussion Chapter 14 by Alastair Lucas .

[27] See for discussion Chapter 5 by Annalisa Savaresi,and Chapter 2 by Aileen McHarg, in this book.

[28] See, e.g., Chapter 6 by Catherine Banet ; Chapter 5 by Annalisa Savaresi; Chapter 7 by Lee Paddock and Achinthi Vithanage; and Chapter 18 by Wang Mingyuang and Yang Xue, in this book.

Earlier energy justice decisions focused on energy access gave limited attention to what we now call environmental matters. The goal then was to provide modern energy to people without it. Attention to environmental and social harms of energy development began with attention to air and water pollution, species preservation, land preservation, and other environmental matters. Scientists and health professionals began to trace the negative impacts of energy technologies. Their findings then inspired laws.

Prior to the 1970s, environmental consequences were primarily matters for local law as the location in which the pollution took place and where the human impact would be felt. Scientific research then began to recognize that water pollution could flow many miles downstream. Air pollution could be carried by the wind many hundreds of miles, crossing state and national boundaries. The elimination of a species could have wide ranging consequences. National legislation and international law grounded in the 'no harm' principle sought to address transboundary effects to control the wide-ranging harms that gave rise to energy injustice.

The recognition of dangerous anthropogenic climate change or global warming under the United Nations Framework Convention on Climate Change 1992 and the efforts to mitigate emissions under later instruments such as the Paris Agreement are detailed in Chapter 4 'And Justice for All? Energy Justice in International Law'. That chapter also examines the growing 'regime convergence' between sustainability and human rights; and climate change mitigation and adaptation. A stark reminder of the energy justice implications of a failure to reduce emissions is the recent devastating fires in the Amazon Basin in 2019.

The chapters reflect the variety of environmental matters that have an impact on energy justice. Carbon releases to the atmosphere are often the product of fossil fuel extraction and use—which includes many activities seen as central to energy access—the use of fossil fuels for heating and cooking and the use of coal, petroleum, and natural gas for electricity generation. Large scale fossil fuel activities may also have disproportionate impacts on energy-vulnerable populations. Few citizens choose to live next to major pollution-generating facilities or energy waste dumps. Even renewable energy activity, wind turbines, for example, can have community impacts; and the energy justice implications of these situations are explored in several chapters.[29] These chapters canvas vexed issues such as who should participate in community energy projects?

III. The Future of Energy Justice Law

This project on 'Energy Justice and Energy Law' was conceived after the 2015 Paris Agreement on Climate Change. The Agreement which requires Nationally Determined Contributions to reduce emissions to below two degrees of warming was a path-breaking international agreement that reinvigorated international action. Different nations have different concerns about how to advance climate mitigation, and still

[29] See Chapter 5 by Annalisa Savaresi, and Chapter 7 by Lee Paddock and Achinthi Vithanage, in this book.

advance their national development goals, including their goals in the emerging field of energy justice.

Since our work on the book began in 2018, the world has changed rapidly. World events such as the United Kingdom vote to 'Brexit' from the European Union and the American election of Donald Trump as President of the United States continue to reverberate into the energy law space with implications for energy justice. The Brexit saga continues with the UK Prime Minister, Boris Johnson, advancing a 'hard Brexit' position. Trump campaigned on his scepticism of environmental protection generally and climate change specifically. His presidency has doubled down on those positions. The strong nationalist positions of Johnson and Trump have mirrored or encouraged nationalist positions in Brazil, India, Poland, and Hungary among other nations.

Trade disputes have led economic news around the world. In future, the intersections of nationalism and trade are likely to be important factors that will impinge on matters of energy justice and energy law; and upon whether the nations of the world will be able to agree to and implement a pathway forward to achieve Goal 7 of the SDGs—sustainable energy for all! Our long-time colleague, Anita Rønne, would have welcomed that future, and indeed she has helped to shape it as her insights have informed many of the analyses in individual chapters.

In summary, ideal energy justice concepts can provide a strong frame of reference for building a better world for all citizens, and could provide clean, efficient, and sustainable electricity, heating and cooking fuels, and transportation for citizens of every nation. The law will be essential in shaping and implementing those developments.

Index

Note: *For the benefit of digital users, indexed terms that span two pages (e.g., 52–53) may, on occasion, appear on only one of those pages.*